D0209633

IMPRESARIO

IMPRESARIO
The Life and Times of Ed Sullivan

James Maguire

BILLBOARD BOOKS
an imprint of Watson-Guptill Publications
New York

For Corinne, of course

ON THE COVER: Sullivan in 1954, shortly after he signed his first
lucrative contract with CBS. (Globe Photos)

Quotations from *Prime Time* by Marlo Lewis and Mina Bess Lewis
copyright © 1979 by Marlo Lewis and Mina Bess Lewis. Used by permission
of Jeremy P. Tarcher, an imprint of Penguin Group (USA) Inc.

Quotations from *A Thousand Sundays: The Story of the Ed Sullivan Show* by Jerry
Bowles copyright © 1980 by Jerry Bowles. Used by permission of G.P. Putnam's
Sons, a division of Penguin Group (USA) Inc.

First published in the United States in 2006 by Billboard Books
an imprint of Watson-Guptill Publications
a division of VNU Business Media, Inc.
770 Broadway, New York, New York 10003
www.watsonguptill.com

Executive Editor: Bob Nirkind
Editor: Meryl Greenblatt
Design: Jay Anning/Thumb Print
Senior Production Manager: Ellen Greene

Library of Congress Control Number: 2005933953

ISBN: 0-8230-7962-7
   978-0-8230-7962-9

Printed in the United States of America

First printing, 2006

1 2 3 4 5 6 7 8 9 / 14 13 12 11 10 09 08 07 06

Contents

Acknowledgments

This book would hardly have been possible without the generous assistance of many talented people.

A number of individuals at research and cultural institutions deserve special mention. In particular, Mike Mashon, a curator at the Library of Congress, not only allowed me access to the Sullivan show library before it was opened to the public, but provided invaluable research aid. Felicia Reilly at the Museum of Broadcast Communications in Chicago went above and beyond the call of duty in assisting my research. Thank you, also, to Tara Olivera at the Center for American History in San Antonio, Texas, and to Jane Klain at the Museum of Television and Radio in New York.

Jacqueline Willoughby, at the New York Public Library, understands the Byzantine politics of interlibrary loan better than anyone, and Warren Platt is one of the NYPL's most helpful librarians; Dorinda Hartmann provided critical assistance as I explored Sullivan's personal papers at the Wisconsin Center for Film and Theater Research; Judith Caplan's aid with genealogical research helped greatly.

I am indebted to Walter Podrazik, a leading television historian, for his expertise and his enthusiastic research help, and to Bruce Spizer, one of the foremost Beatles historians, for his helpful feedback.

Andrew Solt, who owns the Sullivan library, was unfailingly helpful and kind, as was Greg Vine of Solt Productions.

Thank you with a cherry on top to Mr. John Frain and Ms. Sydney Jones, for their wise words about my manuscripts, including this one.

Very special thanks to this book's executive editor, Bob Nirkind, for his remarkable insight into the inner workings of a manuscript; and to its editor, Meryl Greenblatt, for her sense of style and attention to detail. Special thanks, too, to my agent, Agnes Birnbaum, for her support—I will *always* owe her lunch.

Among the many other individuals who lent guidance, a helpful hand, or general moral support, a big thanks to: Bill Gallo and Angela Troisi, at the *Daily News*, for their generosity and their memories, as well as Lenore Schlossberg at the *Daily News* for her advice; Deborah Kelman, Jerry Hamza, and Richard Grant for help with interviews; David Margolick, for lending an ear and for interview assistance; Scott Omelianuk, for his writing advice; Florence Eichin at the Penguin Group for her unfailing good cheer; Eric Fettmann at the *New York Post* for his encyclopedic knowledge of the New York newspaper business; Christopher Saunders, Devin Comiskey, and, most especially, Dan Muse, for being my patron saints; and Mr. Vincent Favale at CBS, for being a dude, and for believing in this project.

And the biggest thanks of all goes to Corinne, for keeping my heart running, a particularly important thing when one faces a blank page.

"Ah, who can tell how hard it is to climb the steep where Fame's proud temple shines afar?"

– JAMES BEATTIE (1735–1803)

Prologue

O N AN OVERCAST SUNDAY MORNING he sat in his robe and hurriedly typed his column. Next to the typewriter sat his usual breakfast—a lamb chop ordered from room service, an artificially sweetened pear, and iced tea—and he ate while he worked. Sundays were the longest days. He cranked out his New York *Daily News* column late morning, his driver picked him up early afternoon, then it was dress rehearsal—in which he pummeled the show into shape—followed by a lengthy production meeting, numerous last minute details, and finally, at eight o'clock . . . the cameras blinked on and he walked into fifteen million living rooms. So this morning, his poodle Bojangles (named after storied tap dancer Bill "Bojangles" Robinson) went neglected. And he could not so much as glance at his clutter of office mementoes: the caricature of him drawn by Walt Disney, a framed copy of *Time* magazine with his face on the cover, and, by the typewriter, a photo of his wife, Sylvia, inscribed *To Ed with love—till the winds stop blowing*.

Sylvia. When he and Sylvia Weinstein began dating in 1926, she told her parents she was seeing a boy named Ed Solomon, who worked as a sports reporter for the *New York Evening Graphic*. "Oh," her brother said, "you mean Ed Sullivan." The possibility of a Jewish–Catholic marriage made both families apprehensive—Ed's much more so—and the romance was on-again, off-again for three years. Now, however, Sylvia and Ed formed a unit. Yes, there had been rumors of Ed and other women, but they never derailed the marriage. The couple went out to eat five nights a week, rotating through their favorite Manhattan nightspots—trendy places like Danny's Hideaway or Jimmy Kelly's. Like the show he produced, the marriage was a union of supposedly dissimilar elements that was larger than the sum of its parts. Ed called Sylvia every Sunday night immediately after the show—she watched at home—wanting to know how it had gone, but she understood he wanted only reassurance. Sylvia was a cheerleader, a supporter, tolerant of his moods, a safe harbor in a world filled with critics.

And, on that day in late 1969, she was the wife of the greatest impresario television had ever known. On that evening's program would be the Rolling Stones, whose lead singer, Mick Jagger, was four years old when Sullivan debuted his program. Throughout all those years Sullivan had beaten the odds, the critics, the network executives, the talent agents, the well-financed competition. That so many people across boundaries of age and class were captured for so many years by one individual's idea of entertainment was a cultural first, and perhaps a last. He created a strange alembic of highbrow and corn pone, Borsht Belt and middle America, shaping it week after week down to the last punch line. And the folks at home, regardless of the critical carping, loved it.

1

Later that day, as part of his Sunday ritual, he took a walk prior to showtime. A little night air on Broadway, invariably running into fans, some pressing of the flesh to get the juices flowing for live TV. Ed walking up Broadway was like a creature in its most natural habitat. It was some seventy blocks uptown, in a Jewish and Irish neighborhood in Harlem, that he had been born. And it was in this very neighborhood, the heart of the theater district, that he had earned his stripes as a gossip columnist, making side money by producing countless vaudeville shows. Over on 48th, in his early twenties he lived above a tavern, driving a new Durant roadster and dating flappers. It was on 53rd at the Stork Club that he had, according to Broadway lore, dunked the head of gossip king Walter Winchell into a toilet. With a few exceptions—childhood years in rural Port Chester, a three-year stint in Hollywood—he had lived his entire life within a hundred-block area of Manhattan. When he made big money in the mid 1950s, he and Sylvia bought a 180-acre estate in Connecticut, but later sold it because, as he put it, he was "temperamentally unsuited to country life." Clearly, the street he was walking down was where he was meant to be. As he finished his walk and neared the theater, he saw his name up in lights; CBS had renamed Studio 50 the Ed Sullivan Theater. It was everything that he had ever dreamed of.

Yet he remained oddly insecure. He pretended to laugh off the critics but they bothered him terribly. He wrote long harangues back at any reviewer who took sport with him, explaining that it was unfair to suggest a man be put out of a job, that they did not understand the first thing about show business, that the very job *they* had was almost immoral. Sylvia pleaded with him to merely write the letters then throw them away, but he would send them. He was furious at the critics, for whom acerbic pokes at this famously monochromatic emcee were a given. Like reviewer Harriet Van Horne, to whom he wrote an uncharacteristically short missive: "Dear Miss Van Horne. You Bitch. Sincerely, Ed Sullivan."

Early on, in an act of creative defensiveness, he hired a Yiddish comic from vaudeville to heckle him—to yell comments like "Come on Solomon, for God's sake, smile, it makes you look sexy"—hoping the resulting exchange would make him appear more natural. Later, he booked a succession of impressionists who skewered his stiff onstage persona. Will Jordan built a career on this, coming on the show and replicating the Sullivan trademark arms-crossed gesture, contorting his face as if he had just sucked a lemon: "Tonight on our rilly big show we have seven hundred and two Polish dentists who will be out here in a few moments doing their marvelous extractions. . . ." The audience roared and Ed laughed along, although in truth he had never used the phrase "really big show" in quite that way. Attempting to imitate Jordan's imitation of himself, he kept mangling the words, only growing comfortable with the phrase later.

His persona as the maladroit master of ceremonies prompted *Time* magazine in 1955 to call him "about the longest shot ever to have paid off in show business." That may have been true if he was merely the stone-faced host the impressionists lampooned. What many observers missed was his real role: the man behind the curtain, the show producer, the shaper, the impresario who assumed dictatorial control. His talent lay not in being a charismatic emcee—which he certainly was not—but in his ability to understand a changing audience. "Public opinion," he explained, "is the voice of God." In the end he had understood that voice so well and so long that *The Ed Sullivan Show* was not just a success but an institution. All of his original competitors, Milton Berle, Bob Hope, Eddie Cantor, Jerry and Dino—the list goes on—saw their shows canceled. But Sullivan ran nonstop from 1948 to 1971, from Harry Truman to Jim Morrison, from the arrival of television to man on the moon. In human terms that's a generation, but in TV years it's closer to an epoch.

The story of Ed Sullivan's life is one of the core stories of the birth of mass communications in the twentieth century. His unlikely tale—where he came from, what forces molded him, how he in turn influenced his audience—is the story of the education and fulfillment of a pioneering showman who largely invented the rules of a new medium as he went along.

Television, of course, has been a force of oceanic power and influence in American culture, and he, in the small screen's frontier days, proved remarkably adept at harnessing this power. That a mass audience would follow one man's vision of cultural life for nearly a quarter of a century was testament to his odd, almost unconscious genius at sensing and gratifying his audience's desires. It was as if he possessed some hypersensitive awareness that allowed him to feel an audience's every fidget and thrill, what transported them, what might offend them. In the early years of his variety show, which was always broadcast live, he sometimes changed the running order *during the broadcast*, sending stagehands scrambling, because he sensed the audience might be drifting away.

More accurately, he didn't need to rely on sensing the audience's desire—he *knew* its desire. He was the audience itself, a middle American Everyman, needing no focus group because his sense of what worked and what didn't—honed through producing countless vaudeville shows in Depression-era New York—fell in lockstep with the larger public taste. This experience, and his intuition (and a constant scan of the hit charts) kept him in perfect harmony with what viewers wanted, making the twenty-three seasons of his show a perfect cultural mirror of his time.

A central paradox of his life was that he was simultaneously the ultimate establishmentarian and an agent of social change. As the great guardian of the status quo, he ran his national showcase with a puritan's nose for what might offend, using his total control over the program to bar the slightest suggestion of a blue joke, keeping fabric backstage to cover up female cleavage. The audience, which in his earliest days was allowing a large noisy box into the sanctum of the family living room for the first time, quickly grew to trust him. They understood that he would guard their sensibilities with all of his being. This audience trust granted him a major power. Any performer invited on the show had earned a sort of Good Housekeeping seal of approval. As comedienne Joan Rivers said, "If he put his arm around you, you knew you had made it. The power he had was enormous."

And yet this guardian of middle America, this Minister of Culture, exerted a subtle—and sometimes not so subtle—disruptive force on the American living room. *The Ed Sullivan Show* was based on Ed's belief in the "Big Tent," the variety show as all-inclusive three-ring circus, with elephants and movie stars and jazz singers and football heroes all sharing the same bill. In his view, America was one big family every Sunday night at 8 P.M. He offered something for everyone, all blended together with his signature formula that, in theory, kept the divergent voices from being too discordant. Central to this formula was that Ed always wanted to stay one step—but only one step—ahead of where the audience was willing to go. As the longtime newsman that he was, he had a reporter's hunger for the hot scoop, the act whose appeal was as fresh as that day's headlines. Therein lay the destabilizing influence of his supposedly staid Sunday night variety show.

In the course of his push and pull with his beloved audience he presented sights and sounds that helped cause a crack in the cultural dam. In the 1950s, when black faces were invisible on television, they were a constant on the Sullivan stage, and he enraged his sponsor by hugging jazz chanteuse Sarah Vaughn. Ed's urban sensibilities meant that his trove of Manhattan nightclub discoveries, most notably the rich vein of Jewish comedy, was exported to small towns across the country. In the largest sense, his program demonstrated that everything could be integrated; his appreciation for high art, learned as a boy from his music-loving mother, pushed him to offer a highbrow's cornucopia of ballet, opera, and legitimate theater on the same stage with slapstick and pop crooners. And finally, and most revolutionary, he used his trusted national showcase to allow into the American living room the great flaying id itself—rock 'n' roll—that unwashed legion of guitar twangers, the Pied Pipers of sex and antiestablishmentarianism, which, by the mid 1960s, appeared ready to fell the walls of Jericho. This became a bedrock element of the Sullivan offering. As one reviewer noted, the showman was "one of the fathers of rock 'n' roll."

The viability of Sullivan's Big Tent philosophy faded toward the end of his career. His "everyone's invited" formula, the variety show producer as curator of national culture—combining old, young, black, white, Jewish, gentile—was supplanted by a niche approach, a strategy of creating television shows (or magazines, or most anything) to appeal to narrow demographics, like young affluent suburbanites, or urban blacks in the eighteen to thiry-four age group. Whether this is good or bad is an open question, though it certainly separates us into distinct, mutually exclusive camps.

Yet while his Big Tent ethos fell into disrepute, one of the concepts he was an original embodiment of would not only live on, but perhaps be the central legacy of the small screen: the television producer as image maker.

He was a supreme imagist. As television is the home of the manufactured world, Sullivan proved to be one of the most talented wizards of this odd alchemy. He knew how to create the special brand of living room magic known as TV, how to produce a really big show, how to weave an hour of fantasy and escape. Using his signature formula, his combination of high and low, he created the bright and shiny bauble known as *The Ed Sullivan Show*, entrancing a weekly audience for more than two decades. He changed the elements as the national mood changed, but his image of the well-wrapped package of All-American entertainment would spin on, week after week, year after year.

His own image would be the most manufactured of all. Within the confines of the television screen he appeared as a wooden but sincere emcee, everyone's Uncle Ed, a believer in the Boy Scouts and the American Way, who probably went home to a big wood-paneled den after the show to spend time with the youngsters, as he called anyone under age thirty-five. In the late 1950s he published a book called *Christmas with Ed Sullivan*, a collection of reminiscences by his "friends"—from Walter Cronkite to Lucy and Desi Arnaz—suggesting he lived in a world of big warm holidays where everyone gathered 'round the hearth. In reality he was a loner and a driven careerist who was typically too busy to bother with a Christmas tree until 9 P.M. Christmas Eve. In his view, family life was greatly overrated, as were close personal friendships, and he took precious little time for either. He had elbowed his way into television based on the power of his gossip column, which could be surprisingly salacious, and he was every bit as profane as the column's yellowest tidbit—possessing a sailor's salty vocabulary, a volcano's sense of decorum, and a pugilist's belief in diplomacy. These qualities, however, were kept far offstage (most of the time). And since he presented himself as Uncle Ed on television, so he was seen in the public's eye. He carved his own image with as much skill as he built every Sunday's show.

This would create considerable confusion as to who Ed Sullivan really was. His public face as a stiff but earnest host was actually the far smaller of his two roles on the show. The early critics, new to the sport of television reviewing, mistakenly assumed that his emcee duties were his central role—and panned him accordingly. When Sullivan debuted in 1948, New York *Herald-Tribune* critic John Crosby wrote, "One of the small but vexing questions confronting anyone in this area with a television set is: Why is Ed Sullivan on it every Sunday night?" That perception would change over the years. In 1965, *New York Times* critic Jack Gould, who once had wholeheartedly agreed with Crosby, opined that Sullivan "is unquestionably one of the medium's great intuitive showmen."

The Ed Sullivan Show was very much his show, his to shape and color as he saw fit. As its producer he not only chose the performers, creating balance and mood by determining their running order, he also took enormous control over their performances. Comedians found their routines reshaped, singers saw their repertoire—or, famously, their lyrics—changed. He told actors which section of a play to reprise, and he overruled his Yale-educated set designer. Even animal trainers, whose chimps and big cats knew their routines by rote, bent to the Sullivan edict. This was not a democracy, nor even a particularly benevolent dictatorship. When opera star Maria Callas refused to sing her famed interpretation of *Tosca*, Sullivan made it clear: you'll sing what I tell you to sing or your performance is canceled. The diva had met a bigger diva.

On Sunday afternoons he ran the entire show as a dress rehearsal in front of a full house, standing just offstage, watching both the acts and the studio audience, getting a feel for the relationship between the two. He made notes on his yellow legal pad, and after rehearsal those notes dramatically reshaped what the audience would see and hear that evening. No detail was too small to be controlled. He could compromise, and in fact often did. But he was also known for sending performers to "the wailing wall"—an area outside the theater where they kvetched to their agents after Sullivan had reworked or canceled their acts (and many performers saw their appearance canceled the day of the show). When the cameras began broadcasting live that evening, much in that hour had been molded by the pucker-lipped host who mangled his lines in the spotlight's glare.

The show was very personal to him—it *was* him. Said comedian Alan King, a Sullivan favorite who had the temerity to appear on a rival show: "Ed literally came close to slapping me in the face at Danny's Hideaway. He called me a traitor . . . for five years Ed didn't talk to me." The showman's visceral attachment to his program gave him something of a Dr. Jekyll and Mr. Hyde quality. In the theater, shaping an evening's show to conform to his vision, Sullivan the raging tyrant could erupt; outside the television studio, the glad-handing newsman chatted amiably. "He was a whole different man offstage," recalled his friend Jack Carter. "He was very charming."

Because the show so closely reflected the man himself, the story of his early life and education is an essential part of the Sullivan narrative. The way he produced his odd weekly circus reflected everything he had done and everywhere he had been, from the Victorian parlors of his youth to the decidedly non-Victorian celebrity gossip column he penned for decades. Although early television critics skewered him as an unskilled amateur, in reality no more grizzled veteran of a show-man existed in 1948. He had skipped college but earned a rough-and-tumble Ivy League education in American show business, from the speakeasy cabarets of his twenties, to his abortive radio and film career, to—especially—his years spent pro-ducing sawdust-and-sweat vaudeville shows. And his influential syndicated column made him as much a show business player as a chronicler. In fact, his New York *Daily News* column, with its rapid-fire pastiche of items covering many quarters, was his model for *The Ed Sullivan Show*. Like a daily journalist, the showman opened big and kept a brisk pace. Quipped one comedian: "You wanna know the day Christ died? It was on the Sullivan show, and Ed gave him three minutes."

The story of his life, like the television show he produced, formed a perfect mir-ror of his time. Born with the century's birth in 1901, the seasons of his life flowed in tandem with the seasons of American life: running away to join World War I, com-ing of age in the giddy 1920s, finding his voice as a popular Depression-era colum-nist, pitching in during World War II, pioneering in the dawn of television, grappling with McCarthyism, becoming an unofficial Minister of Culture in the conformist 1950s, ushering in the rock 'n' roll era—including its seminal moment, the Beatles' 1964 U.S. debut—and, finally, seeing changes in television that presaged the medi-um's defining ethic on into the twenty-first century. If the century itself had written a diary from an American perspective, he could well have been its protagonist.

As his show combined dissimilar elements—jazz with rock 'n' roll, boxers with ballerinas—so he himself carried a mass of contradictions. He was, at one time or another, a melancholic introvert, a frustrated performer who craved a mass audience, a columnist for a socialist newspaper, a Red baiter, a peacenik who led a tour of the Soviet Union, a small-town boy, an urban sophisticate, a street fighter who played by his own rules, a Puritanical moralist, a racetrack habitué, an opera promoter, a sin-gle-minded bully, a tender sentimentalist, and a self-contained egoist whose greatest joy came from pleasing others, that is, his tens of millions of viewers.

Fame and his long-frustrated hunger for it was a central theme of his life, as this man who could neither sing, dance, nor tell jokes strove tirelessly to thrust himself center stage, in newspapers, vaudeville, film, radio, and finally, television. This hunger, his own gut-devouring desire to put his name atop the marquee, was his pri-mary psychic gasoline. Yet while he became hugely famous, he remained—again, the contradictions—a regular Joe, transporting his own wardrobe, speaking as an equal to doormen and network executives alike. He carried his fame, as one associ-ate described it, "like it was built-in," never indulging in the smallest moment of pretentiousness. He eschewed an entourage or the requisite limousine, instead tak-ing cabs, invariably quizzing the driver, "What did you think of the show?"

Approaching the stage door after his preshow walk, Sullivan stamped out his cigarette and was immediately surrounded by autograph seekers. These admirers would be in tonight's studio audience, a mix of young couples in their Sunday best, some older folks, a few servicemen in uniform, and teenage rock fans. The Sullivan show was one midtown Manhattan event that never attracted the tuxedo and evening dress crowd. It was only a couple of hours before showtime yet he took the time to sign several autographs, as he would again after the show. He never stopped being willing—happy—to sign autographs. During a tour with Frank Sinatra, while the singer avoided the crowds, Sullivan stood for lengthy periods not just signing but asking fans how they wanted them inscribed. When it came to his audience, his energy appeared boundless.

In truth, the sixty-eight-year-old producer was feeling his years. In the old days he never would have taken a nap after dress rehearsal, as he now did. Privately, his family saw signs of senility; the forgetfulness had become frequent. So tonight after the show, dinner at Danny's Hideaway, a short Courvoisier at the Colony, then home.

As the guard let him into the theater, there it was. The nerves. He still felt the butterflies after all these years. But there was no time to worry. On to room 21, his dressing room, where the makeup artist worked her magic, during which the celebrities he would introduce from the stage stopped by. Then, several last-minute changes with show staffers and a flurry of details; tonight he would perform a humorous sketch with the Italian hand puppet Topo Gigio—were his lines ready? As always, he touched up his introductions; he would rewrite many of them four to five times the day of the show, sending his assistant scurrying to the copy machine to remake the master script.

Then, at 7:50 P.M., backstage went dark. The telephone bell was turned off. He stood in the wings, where he could hear the studio audience. He was in his own world at this point, focused on his introduction and the myriad aspects of the show, unaware of the last-minute movements of stagehands. All across America, people were expecting to see him: tens of millions of people, sitting in their living rooms with the TV tuned to CBS—the teenagers, the parents, the little ones. And then it was eight o'clock sharp.

"Tonight, from the Ed Sullivan Theater on Broadway . . . The Ed Sullivan *Show . . . and now, live from New York . . . Ed Sullivan! . . ."*

PART ONE

A SHOWMAN'S EDUCATION

"*I have no spur to prick the sides of my intent, but only Vaulting ambition, which o'erleaps itself.*"

— WILLIAM SHAKESPEARE,
from *Macbeth*

CHAPTER ONE

Twins

East Harlem in 1901 was a volatile mix of Irish, Jews, Italians, and blacks, many of them living with multiple generations squeezed into cold-water tenements. The Irish weren't fond of the Italians, neither group liked the Jews, and all three looked down on the blacks. Yet for most of them it was a step up from where they had come from, and they managed to coexist, if not always peacefully. The streets of Harlem had begun to see their first few motor cars, like the puttering steam-powered Locomobile, but much of the traffic still cantered forth on horse-drawn wagons and carriages. Throngs of bicycles competed with pushcarts selling hot potatoes or sweet cakes for 2 cents, weaving among pedestrians who spoke a polyglot of tongues. Despite the neighborhood's collection of sweatshops and sulfurous iron factories, it was not a ghetto. It took pride in being solidly working class, however slight the distinction.

For Peter Sullivan, guiding his horse-drawn milk wagon through the Harlem streets in the predawn darkness, the great city of New York had become a dream deferred. A proud man who felt cheated by the roll of life's dice, he spent most of his days in a moody funk. Peter broke his taciturn reserve usually only for a fit of temper or a snort of disappointment. He had come to the city hoping for a better life for himself and his family, but he had fallen short.

The plan had been a simple one. In the late 1890s, he and his wife Elizabeth left their hardscrabble farm life in upstate New York when Peter landed a patronage job as a city clerk. New York's Tammany Hall political machine ran the city with a wink and a nod, a few bucks here and a little grease there, and the city's Irish ward heelers consolidated their political influence by doling out patronage jobs to members of their own tribe. For Peter, taking a low-level clerkship was an opportunity to vault into the middle class. Farming in the small upstate town of Amsterdam had been hand to mouth, a season-by-season gamble at avoiding the creditor's knock. Working in the U.S. Customs House in lower Manhattan provided a steady salary.

Had Peter been another sort of man, the job might have been his first step up the bureaucratic ladder. But he lost his reappointment to the Customs House. The patronage system required him to write a thank-you note to the ward heeler who secured him the job, a kind of loyalty oath. Peter refused. He was smarter than the party hack and he knew it. Guided by his inflexible moral absolutes, he felt it was wrong to write the petty bit of fawning. That proud decision would be the beginning of downward mobility for him. Out of work, he managed to find one of the better jobs open to an unskilled Irishman, saloon manager. But that, too, proved short-lived. Being a saloon keeper required a rough-and-ready bonhomerie, a good cheer, and an easy word that Peter lacked. Casting around for a post that would suit him, he became a milkman. Guiding a slow-moving delivery wagon through the streets of Harlem required him to get along with no one, save his horses.

Central to his resentment was that, unlike his brothers, he hadn't been able to complete his education. Peter's parents, Florence and Margaret O'Sullivan, had emigrated from County Cork, Ireland, fleeing the ravaging famine of the mid 1800s in which more than a million souls starved. Florence and his brother John and their families made the journey together. Stopping in London on their way to the New World, the O'Sullivan brothers decided to Americanize their surname; they would now sign their name as Sullivan. Despite this effort at assimilation, Florence and Margaret's circumstances were only marginally better in their new home. They settled in the fertile valley around Amsterdam, New York, but the family farm took years to rise above subsistence level. Peter, as the oldest son in a family of eight, was forced to leave school and go to work to help support his family.

As the family's fortunes improved, Florence was able to send his younger sons to college. Two of Peter's younger brothers, Charles and Daniel, were honor students in college, and another, Florence Jr., became a noted attorney in New York City. Peter possessed the intelligence to have joined them had he been allowed to finish school. He was a gifted mathematician and—when he deigned to speak—a passionate debater about the issues of the day; he ardently supported workers' rights and railed against industrialists like J.P. Morgan and John D. Rockefeller. More than anything, though, as his son Ed recalled, Peter felt frustrated by not having achieved more. He was a failure in his own eyes.

If Peter was darkness and clouds, then his wife Elizabeth, called Lizzy, was sunshine and warmth. While Peter, ten years her senior, was an iron-willed believer in corporal punishment, viewing compromise as weakness, Lizzy was gentle and encouraging, and usually handled her children with a soft touch. Years later Ed wrote, "My father was, in every sense, the head of the family, but my mother was its heart." The difference was clear simply by looking at them: Peter had a solid frame and a square, firm jaw; Lizzy was slender, with flowing brunette tresses surrounding her comely face. With Lizzy, Peter had married above his station. Although her mother had been a poor Irish squatter's daughter, her father, Edward Smith, was a man of means, a landholder in upstate New York. Lizzy's family imbued her with a genteel Victorian sensibility, and she was educated in the arts. She loved music, especially the light operas of the late 1890s, and was an amateur painter.

In the early fall of 1901, Peter and Lizzy were expecting a new arrival in their Harlem flat on East 127th Street. The baby would join Helen, born in 1897, and Charles, born in 1899. When Lizzy gave birth on September 28, she and Peter were met with a surprise: twin boys. Edward, husky and healthy, and Daniel, small and sickly. The lucky one, christened Edward Vincent, was a robust, squalling infant, crying at the top of his lungs to be fed. Young Danny, however, was a worry; he seemed hardly to have made it into this world.

As the months wore on, nothing that Lizzy did succeeded in helping the child gain weight. She tried feeding him a mixture of light barley, water, and milk, yet he only grew sicklier. The family's tenement apartment wasn't the best place to nurse a sick infant, and though his weight kept falling, he apparently was never admitted to a hospital. In the middle of the night on July 19, Danny died at home. The cause was listed as infant marasmus, emaciation due to malnutrition, possibly caused by problems in the child's digestive tract. Two days later the family made a mournful trip up to the town of Amsterdam to bury their ten-month-old son in the family plot.

The death of his twin brother would haunt Ed throughout his childhood. Later, he recounted that when he was "whaled" by his father—a common occurrence—or given the switch by nuns at parochial school, he would imagine that his life would have been different "if only Danny were here." Much later in life, Sullivan attributed his high energy level to Danny's premature death, as if the surviving brother had been supernaturally granted the energy of his deceased twin. One Sunday evening, while hosting his show in front of a television audience of some thirty-five million people, Ed noted a location in New York from which one of his guests hailed. For a moment, he seemed to lose himself in thought, then confided, "That's where my brother Danny is buried." (And if Danny's problem had been a gastrointestinal defect, it was surely shared by his brother, who was plagued by such problems throughout his adult life.)

The Sullivans soon had another child. Lizzy greeted the girl with a renewed maternal instinct, naming her new daughter after herself. But young Elizabeth, like Danny, was also colicky and cranky. Again, Lizzy was up nights trying to comfort her, but, like Danny, nothing seemed to help. On the morning of August 1, 1905, the twenty-month-old girl died in the Sullivans' apartment. The cause, similar to Danny's, was listed as gastroenteritis. The family was forced to make another gray journey to upstate New York to bury Elizabeth. Lizzy, having lost two children in three years, was in a panic of grief. Normally good-natured, she now made a non-negotiable demand.

She blamed the conditions in Harlem for the deaths of her children. Indeed, in the first few years of the 1900s the area was changing rapidly. Throughout the 1890s, real estate developers had quickly bought and sold property in well-to-do West Harlem, making a fast profit with each sale and pushing prices ever higher. In 1904 the bubble burst and speculators were left with too many properties and too few occupants who could afford them. By 1905 banks stopped making loans to these developers. When the market went bust, landlords were forced to slash rents severely to lure tenants. An enterprising black real estate entrepreneur named Philip Payton devised a plan to fill these empty buildings. He guaranteed their owners the rent, then subcontracted the dwellings to black tenants, charging them a small premium above the depressed rent levels. Large numbers of poor blacks moved into Harlem and the area's neighborhoods became ever more crowded.

Lizzie, already disenchanted with the neighborhood, demanded that her family move from the area. Because Peter's income didn't allow a move to one of the city's better neighborhoods, she told him to find a job outside the city. They had come to New York to build a better life, but that hadn't worked. She now wanted to leave as soon as possible.

Peter, apparently without much argument, agreed. In 1906 the Sullivan family bundled up their few belongings and boarded the New Haven line of the New York Central Railroad. They moved to the working class burg of Port Chester, New York, where Peter found employment in a hardware factory. Although only twenty-six miles north of the city, Port Chester lived in a world of a few decades earlier. Its quiet streets were lined with watering troughs for horses, and its town doctor still made house calls in his buckboard wagon. As they had since the 1800s, traveling medicine shows stopped and sold quack elixirs and mystery tonics like "Dr. Pink's Pale Pills" and "Thayer's Slippery Elm Lozenges." But the town's proximity to New York City meant this otherwise drowsy outpost of Americana was a confluence of unadulterated Old World influences. There had been a time in the 1800s when local Protestants had pulled down their curtains to avoid watching a Catholic church being built. But with the waves of immigrants flowing into and out of New York City, the town became an ethnically mixed alembic of Italians, Irish, Germans, Poles, Jews, and other recent arrivals.

Most importantly for Lizzy, she found what she wanted: a quiet, clean place to raise her family. And a place, of course, to have more children, which the Sullivans soon did.

Decades later, social commentators would point to Ed Sullivan as the apotheosis of square, a prude, a man who ran his great national showcase by tight moralistic strictures. Certainly Sullivan himself, the showman behind the curtain, was in reality far from this. But to the extent that the man projected this quality, the boy learned this prim and pious worldview on the leafy streets of Port Chester.

The Sullivans found modest lodging in the top floor of a two-family house. Though the family never seemed to have enough money, Lizzy decorated the parlor in typical Victorian style, with velveteen upholstered furniture and gilt frame engravings. Her and Peter's brass double bed was topped with crocheted lace pillow covers over a blue sateen lining. An avid and talented gardener, Lizzy grew vegetables and flowers in the house's garden; she constantly clipped the roses and gladiolas and arrayed them in vases around the living room. Within a few years Ed, Helen, and Charles were joined by two sisters, Mercedes and Frances, who were born healthy.

Radio had yet to arrive, but music was plentiful in the Sullivan house. Lizzy scrimped to ensure that all her children took music lessons, and an old upright piano dominated the parlor. Someone was always plinking out a waltz or warbling a sentimental ballad. Ed's older sister Helen was an accomplished pianist, and his older brother Charles, a violinist who sang in the choir, joined her in duets. Lizzy often led the family in group sing-alongs of hit musicals like "O, Promise Me," or

From left: Ed's older brother Charles, his older sister Helen, and Ed, circa 1905. (Globe Photos)

gay '90s stalwarts like "She's Only a Bird in a Gilded Cage." She particularly enjoyed the syrupy operettas of Victor Herbert.

Knowing their mother's passion for music, the children broke open their piggy banks and (with help from an uncle) bought her an Aeolian music box for Christmas one year. When she saw it, Lizzy gasped and gave out an "Oh, children!"—her response whenever she was deeply touched. Even Peter, never one for expressing his feelings, managed a wide smile. Later the family purchased a gramophone and gathered around to relish the recordings of opera singers like Enrico Caruso and Nellie Melba. (And five decades later, *The Ed Sullivan Show* presented more opera bookings than its Nielsen ratings indicated was a good idea.)

For all her love of music, Lizzy's hopes of turning Ed into a musician came to naught. The coins she gave him for piano lessons were diverted to the local movie house, where he spent many afternoons immersed in the chiaroscuro fantasy of that week's silent two-reeler. He worshipped William S. Hart, who played a rugged stand-alone cowboy hero, mowing down rows of Indians in melodramas like *Hell's Hinges* and *The Return of Draw Egan*. Or, Ed bought a nickel ticket to the traveling vaudeville shows that visited Port Chester, spending Saturday afternoons "marveling at the people who had the nerve to stand in a little white spotlight and dance, or sing, or make jokes." If no nickel was available, Ed and his cohorts perched on a hill outside town and gawked at the lines of Packards and Pierce-Arrows roaring past en route to collegiate football games.

Although Ed's mother was gentle, she wasn't permissive. Right and wrong were clearly defined in the Sullivan home. In one formative episode—which, like most of Ed's own stories of his boyhood, comes straight from a Norman Rockwell painting—he and some neighborhood boys pilfered a handful of candy from Mr. Genovese's grocery store. When Ed offered some to his mother and she realized it came from petty theft, she dragged her son back to the store and made him confess to the grocer, after which she paid for the candy.

While the story may be true, its most revealing point is that it was his mother that he offered the candy to. He certainly would not have made the same mistake with his father, whose moral sense had a darker quality. The Sullivans raised chickens to stretch their overstretched budget, and one day a neighbor stole a rooster from their yard. When Ed and his older brother Charles told their father, he glowered at them for not handling the offense themselves—then he jumped the fence into the neighbor's yard, stormed into their kitchen, took back the rooster, and threatened the family with a thrashing if they laid hand on his property again.

One activity interested Ed above all else: sports. The school day was merely tedium to be endured until he was released to the nirvana of Port Chester's open fields. Day after day he played anything with a ball—basketball, football, and especially baseball—throwing himself into athletic combat. A naturally strong boy, with tough, sinewy muscles, he was a hard-nosed player. He gave no quarter in the heat of battle. Adding fuel to his competitive spirit, like his father he was prone to storms of temper. "He could be very kind and gentle but he was quick to anger sometimes," his sister Helen recalled. The ball field warrior often came back from skirmishes with a split chin or a bloodied nose, and at one point, a four-stitch gash over his left eye. Yet he was right back out the next day.

"As an athlete Ed always came back the hero. A bit battered but always the fighter," Helen said. It was indicative of things to come. He ran, jumped, and rushed on sports teams year round, playing catcher for the baseball squad, running sprints on the track team, elbowing through the opposition on the basketball court. On the football field his rough tackling earned him a broken nose, which he later claimed diminished his sense of smell.

The young athlete contributed to the meager family budget by caddying at the local golf course. At age ten he and his brother Charles walked three miles from working-class Port Chester to affluent Rye, New York, to make 35 cents a round at the Apawanis Club. Ed once caddied for Columbia University president Nicholas Butler, whom he found to be a "real stinker." Ed told his father, who explained the situation with his usual dour outlook. "You'll find that all through your life," Peter said.

Jumping at any chance to play baseball, Ed played in games against teams throughout Westchester County and beyond. Though this was decades before blacks broke the color line in professional baseball, he played against integrated amateur teams. Sharing the field with integrated squads taught him a lesson, he recalled: "When we went up into Connecticut we ran into teams that had Negro players. In those days this was accepted as commonplace, and so my instinctive antagonism years later to any theory that a Negro wasn't a worthy opponent or was an inferior person."

His passion for sports didn't carry over into the classroom. An indifferent student, he suffered by comparison to his straight-A older sister Helen. Ed's teachers at St. Mary's Parochial School and later at Port Chester High constantly asked him why he didn't earn grades like hers. He resorted to some well-timed cheating to pass his Latin class, as one of his teachers recalled: "Luckily, he sat near Bill Cigliano, who apparently took Caesar and Sullivan through Gaul."

The sole academic subject that captured his attention was English. He read hungrily, submerging himself in tales of knights and jousting, fanciful stories of medieval chivalry and heroic battles between good and evil. He was especially fond of the Scottish historical novelist Sir Walter Scott, who in the early 1800s churned out torrid tales of conquest like *The Pirate*, *Ivanhoe*, and *Rob Roy*. His mother and Helen encouraged his love of reading, and innumerable hours were spent sprawled in the backyard devouring adventure tales.

Early in Ed's teenage years, Europe was heading inexorably toward war. In the summer of 1914, Serbian nationalist Gavrilo Princip assassinated Archduke Franz Ferdinand, heir to the Austro-Hungarian empire, sparking the bloodbath of World War I. Port Chester, with its many European immigrants, was full of talk about the growing conflagration. When President Woodrow Wilson declared war in April 1917, emotions ran high as the draft called Port Chester's young men to serve. The *Port Chester Daily Item* ran ads for French and British flags, which townspeople flew to show their heartfelt support for U.S. allies. Ed, caught up in the spirit of the conflict, began to dream of going off to fight in the Great War. Although he was too young, he had friends who were ambulance drivers and he hungered to be part of the action. Ed decided to join the Marines—a decision he didn't share with his parents.

In the fall of 1917, the sixteen-year-old high school junior dropped out of school to work in a defense factory. Ed's plan was to save the money for a trip to Chicago, where he would enlist. He could have tried to enlist in New York, but chose Chicago because "the farther I got from home, the safer I was from my father's anger." In the late fall, after he earned train fare, he left home without telling his family where he was going.

Once in Chicago, he found a Navy recruiting office, making it through part of the enlistment process using a false name and fictitious Chicago address. He seemed close to attaining his dream of joining the Great War until a military doctor requested his birth certificate. He had no such document with him, and if he had, it would have proven he was too young. Ed left the recruiting center and never went back.

His dream dashed, he found himself at loose ends in Chicago. Developing a backup plan hadn't crossed his mind, so caught up had he been in hopes for military adventure. Chicago's winter winds blew fierce and biting, and all Ed had was a light jacket. Completely on his own and almost totally broke—the train fare took most of his money—the sixteen-year-old wandered the frigid big city streets, not sure what to do and feeling like a failure. Briefly, he considered wiring his family for a return ticket, but fear of his father's wrath kept him from making the request.

He found a room at the YMCA for 25 cents a night. As he walked the streets he enviously viewed the sailors from the Great Lakes Naval Training Station in their heavy Navy coats and thick knitted caps. At the Y he heard of a job at the Illinois Central freight yards, so a few days before Christmas he traveled out to the yards, but could find no one to take his application. Out of money and now homeless, he searched for a place to sleep, finding a small area behind some crates of geese next to a radiator. In the middle of the night a workman loading freight onto the train dis-

With classmates at St. Mary's junior high school, 1914. Sullivan is the fourth from the left. (Globe Photos)

covered the runaway. The yard bull kicked him awake, but to Ed's relief—and amazement—instead of forcing him to leave gave him a job.

Ed pushed hand trucks full of train cargo through the frozen freight yard, working the night shift and sleeping days at the Y. He took the Christmas day shift, relieved to have somewhere to be but feeling deeply sorry for himself. On Christmas morning his mood sunk still further. He walked into the refrigerator compartment and discovered, to his horror, that someone had inadvertently placed in there a crate with two puppies, and they had frozen to death. At the sight of them Ed broke down and bawled in torrents.

Yet he still didn't want to go home. He left his freight yard job and found employment as a busboy at Thompson's Cafeteria, still sleeping on a cot at the Y. Finally, wearied and exhausted by his hand-to-mouth existence, he wrote to his brother Charles and told him where he was—the first the family had heard from Ed—and asked for the money to travel home. As he arrived back at the Sullivan house, Ed expected his father to "beat the hell out of me." But Peter was overcome with joy and relief at seeing his son again, sobbing and throwing his arms around him. "It was the first time I'd ever seen my father cry," Ed said.

Whether Ed understood it or not, it's likely that his time in Chicago was largely about running away from his father. Despite the warm welcome home, father and son remained deeply estranged throughout their lives. Years later, Ed's daughter Betty remembered, "My father was not close to his father—there was some bad blood between them." At the time of Peter's death in 1949, Ed had never once brought his only child, then nineteen, home to meet her grandfather.

It's speculation, of course, but it's probable that his father's domineering anger led to the development of Ed's stiff, overly guarded persona, as if the constant threat from this font of rage necessitated donning a permanent protective armor. His wooden quality, in the view of many who knew him, was much less so offstage; he was much warmer in person. But in the tension of the possibly critical eye of an audience he never escaped it. "Old Stoneface," as he became known as a show host, may have been a response to or a reflection of Peter's malcontent. One thing does seem clear: from his father he inherited the burden of a raging temper, which might explode at any time, for slights real or imagined. At times his erupting Vesuvius actually aided Ed, helping him in the heat of competition. But in most instances it weighed him down, especially when it took charge, as was often the case.

Ed seemed to feel completely different about his mother, who acted as his cheerleader and his guiding light. Years later he mentioned Lizzy as he described his philosophy for producing each week's show. He assembled each program with an eye to how it would play for the four women he most admired: his mother, his wife, his daughter, and his sister. His mother would be foremost in his mind at the arrival of Ed's only child, whom he named after her. And when he returned to school after running away to Chicago, Lizzy's guidance played a particularly important role.

Considering his absence, Ed resumed his junior year of high school with little problem, though his grades and his interest in his studies remained marginal. Despite Ed's academic diffidence, his mother and Helen continued encouraging his interest in reading, and often urged him to work on his writing, which they recognized was one of his natural talents.

In his senior year, Ed combined his writing skills with his love of sports. He approached Tom Blain, the irascible, highly opinionated publisher of the *Port Chester Daily Item*, and asked to cover high school sports for the newspaper. The publisher agreed, paying Sullivan $1 per article. Ed began writing regularly for the paper. Blain liked the high school student, appreciating that sports seemed to be his greatest inspiration, and began teaching him the newspaper trade. The Sullivan boy began spending many of his afternoons around the offices of the *Item*.

In Ed's senior year he glimpsed something else that inspired him: New York City. That fall he went on a date with a Port Chester girl named Alma Burnes, with whom he would be on-again, off-again for a couple of years. They took the train to Manhattan to see a Broadway show, the hit comedy *Lightnin'*, which ran for over twelve hundred performances. Ed wanted to impress Alma into thinking he knew his way around the city, so he asked Helen to draw him a map. He used it to navigate from Grand Central Station to the show at the Gaiety Theater on 46th Street and Broadway, surreptitiously glancing at the map then proceeding as if he were a native. Though his relationship with Alma came to a natural end, Ed found something permanently enchanting about the city. He began to dream of moving there.

"He didn't think of Port Chester fondly," his daughter recalled. "It was a small town and my Dad had visions of a big bustling city." Ed, in one of his *Item* articles, wrote, "It is not yet decided if the Saxers' annual dinner will be in Port Chester or New York City." It's unlikely that the baseball team traveled en masse to the city for their annual dinner, but it was apparently Ed's wish. If the team wouldn't go there

The young athlete: with the Port Chester basketball team, circa 1916. Sullivan is the
second from the right. (Globe Photos)

he himself certainly wanted to. He wasn't ready to make the leap, yet the city's magnetic pull would soon have an effect on him.

By the spring of 1919, Ed wore two hats—athlete and reporter—and the two
roles became one and the same. With his hard-charging competitive spirit he was
voted captain of the baseball team, one of his proudest achievements; as a freelance
reporter for the *Item*, he reported on the very games in which he himself played. It
was a conflict of interest, to be sure, but one the paper freely admitted on May 20:

> "To maintain a position of strict neutrality in the Port Chester–Green-
> wich athletic engagements is a tough proposition, for it is only human
> and natural that the contentions of the Port Chester teams should be up-
> held by our correspondent. The following article is from the pen of our
> High School writer, who is a member of the team, and therefore hardly
> in a position to give an unbiased view on the merits of Port Chester's
> grievances. It is published as Port Chester's side of the story."

The young reporter's coverage of his own teams was as spirited as it was partisan. "Port Chester High sure came back with a vengeance yesterday afternoon, when they defeated the crack Mount Vernon team to the tune of an 8-2 score," Ed wrote. Furthermore, he enthused, "Port Chester displayed the same punch and aggressiveness that they showed in the recent Mount Vernon game and outclassed the New Rochelle High School team at every stage of play." Typical of the sports headlines that spring was "High School Plays Excellent Ball."

Ed's own role in these contests was always fully reported. "Sullivan drove in both runners ahead of him with a circuit-clout [home run] into deep center field," he wrote that summer. "The slugging of Walker of the visitors and Sullivan of the Saxers were added features of the game."

Covering local baseball for the *Item* was a taste of celebrity, and Ed loved it. He attracted far more attention as a reporter than he had as an athlete. He clearly relished his reporting, writing lengthy blow-by-blows of the day's athletic skirmishes, spotlighting his opinions even more prominently than his bat and glove work. In an age before television, before radio became commonplace, the newspaper was the only way for townsfolk to get the full story. And in Port Chester the only source of a complete postgame report was Ed's animated coverage. The *Item*, with a daily circulation of thirty-six hundred, spread the name Ed Sullivan to barbershops and taverns and informal bull sessions all over the area.

The young sports reporter became a minor hero in town, finding himself center stage for the first time in his life. It was a feeling he enjoyed, perhaps even craved, immensely.

CHAPTER TWO

Two Loves

THE PORT CHESTER HIGH GRADUATION CEREMONY in June 1919 paid homage to the sacrifices of the Great War. Many of the forty-one seniors presented a pageant entitled "The Torch," in which students played The Captive Nations and The Allied Nations. As the Three Fates swirled and danced, Mother Earth fought Strife and Greed. In the end, Democracy defeated the Forces of Evil.

Ed played the role of Strife, which was as close as he was to get to his dream of taking part in the war. Armistice had been signed eight months earlier. Instead of facing the trenches of Europe, as had the boys who graduated a year earlier, he received varsity letters for basketball and baseball. In the final class assembly he led the school choir in a rousing rendition of "Onward Christian Soldiers," and in the graduation ceremony he gave a speech about the importance of continuing to conserve even after the war.

The *Port Chester Daily Item* reported, "He delivered his address with a natural ease that served to make his words all the more impressive and called for extended applause when he had finished." It would be the only printed account of Sullivan onstage that described him as having "natural ease."

And he may have written the article himself. The piece had no byline, and on June 24 the paper had added a new name to its masthead: Edward V. Sullivan. Two days before graduation, the seventeen-year-old was hired full-time for $10 a week. One of his father's brothers, most likely Florence the New York attorney, had offered to put Ed through college. But Ed turned him down. School had never interested him, and besides, the high school graduate already had his dream job, sports reporter.

The *Item* proudly displayed its rock-ribbed Republicanism. "Splendid Record of Republican Town Administration" was a characteristic headline. Denouncing what it called the misguided leadership of President Woodrow Wilson, a Democrat, was a routine exercise on its editorial page. The paper reflected the Victorian morality of 1919, with a raft of stories like "Commission to Force Women Bathers to Wear

Stockings." ("Young women bathers at Oakland Beach who have been in the habit of showing off their physical charms by parading stockingless through the park . . . may be deprived of that privilege.") In addition to covering local events, the *Item* reported the personal, with a steady stream of articles like "Wife Won't See Hubby" ("says the sight of him nauseates her"), "Wifey Acted As Her Own Detective" (because her husband was "mushing it up" with another lady), and "Wife Confesses to Kissing Another."

Item publisher Tom Blain got his money's worth from Ed, turning him into a newspaper jack-of-all-trades. Aside from his sports beat, the cub reporter covered weddings, fires, courts, social events, and funerals, and also handled layout and other production chores. "I never worked so hard before or since," Sullivan recalled.

The paper didn't give its three staff reporters bylines, so it's not known who covered what, but the sports section was clearly Ed's. A month after he went full-time, a burst of energy infused the *Item*'s sports section. He launched a new column, *In the Realm of Sport*, and expanded coverage of boxing and tennis. In some of Ed's pieces he adopted an approach that was like nothing else in the *Item*. Instead of blocks of text he wrote short clips of pithy opinion, a layout style then fashionable in the New York papers:

> "Slim" Kelly played a fine game for the Electrics at the hot corner. "Slim" is rapidly developing in to a crack third-sacker.
>
> _____
>
> The Abendroth–P.R. Mallory game was a fine exhibition of baseball as it ain't.
>
> _____
>
> Of course we realize the teams had an off day. They always have.
>
> _____
>
> If you stand on your head while reading the league standings, the Abendroth team is leading the league.
>
> _____
>
> Well, so long!

When readers disagreed with Ed's firmly opinionated reports, the young reporter always stood ready for a fight. He ignited a major fracas with his coverage of an exhibition game between the Philadelphia Athletics, a professional team, and a Port Chester semipro squad. He opined that the Athletics made "a laughingstock" out of the Port Chester team by using their third-string catcher. It may have been true, but the editor soon got a phone call from an irate reader demanding an apology. Sullivan was biased, the caller claimed, because he played catcher for a competing local team, a Catholic squad called the Saxers.

Ed refused to apologize. He told his editor that his opinion came from his baseball expertise, not his team affiliation. Blain, exasperated with his young reporter, snorted, "Oh, you Irish!" Complicating the situation, the caller was W.L. Ward, a local hardware store owner and prominent Republican booster—not a man Blain wanted to offend. Reluctantly, the editor called back Ward and told him no apology was forthcoming. "Good for him," said Ward. "Tell him always to stick to his guns if he's right." Ed was impressed with what he saw as Ward's largesse. As he put it, "Even to a young Democrat, Mr. Ward's support of my position was impressive proof of his genuine bigness." Sullivan arranged a match between the two local teams as a way of settling the dispute.

Although Ed was on his way up at the *Item*, garnering a raise to $12 a week, a larger world beckoned. In the fall of 1920 he learned of an opening for a sports reporter at the Hartford *Post*. Without hesitation he made the trip to Connecticut to apply and was hired that day—at $50 a week. He was overjoyed at the job offer. The Sullivan family, however, had a heated discussion as to whether he should take the position. His mother and Helen saw it as a great opportunity but Ed's father said he should remain in Port Chester. Yet Ed himself felt no doubt about taking the job. Before he left, the town of Port Chester threw its departing celebrity a grand going-away party, presenting him with an engraved watch. The *Item*, in reporting his departure, boasted that he had "built up its sports page from a humble beginning to a place where it was on a par with the best in the country."

Sullivan never wrote a single story for the *Post*. He arrived in Hartford the week before Christmas, and two days later the employees learned the bad news: the paper had been sold and everyone was losing their jobs. Ed had two weeks severance pay in his pocket and no idea what to do. Embarrassed at what he saw as his failure, he devised a plan to keep the paper's closing a secret from his family. He rented a cheap room in a Hartford boarding house and found a stock boy's job in the basement of a department store. When he went home on the weekends he used his severance pay to be a big man about town, as if he were still the *Post*'s sports reporter. Underneath the façade he was terrified and kept hoping something would turn up.

Luck shined on him. A former colleague at the *Item*, Jack Lawrence, had found work at the New York *Evening Mail*. He wrote Ed a reference letter, which Ed sent to the *Mail*'s management. Just a few weeks after the *Post* folded he received a letter from Sam Murphy, one of the *Mail*'s sports editors. The New York paper hired Sullivan to cover high school and college sports. If the job offer in Hartford had been a major opportunity, landing the big city post was a minor miracle. Ed went home to Port Chester to trumpet his accomplishment.

Just before he began working in New York, his mother said to him, "I read about the Hartford paper failing, Edward. Since Christmas I've been praying for you."

Ed was nineteen years old when he reported for duty at the *Evening Mail*'s offices in lower Manhattan in early 1921. New York City, a far different burg than the one his family had fled years earlier, now cantered at a markedly faster clip. In 1917 the city had boasted of an important benchmark: for the first time, its streets were crowded with more motor vehicles (one hundred fourteen thousand) than horses (one hundred eight thousand). As the financial hub of the country that had turned the tide in the Great War, the city strode with a pronounced spring in its step; New York now stood shoulder to shoulder with world capitols like London and Paris. And it was an easy town in which to be naughty; after Prohibition went into effect in January 1920, the city's drinking establishments more than doubled in number. Gentlemen—and now even ladies—could quench their thirst almost anywhere. Speakeasies were illegal, of course, and the Ladies Temperance Union warned of the demon rum, but that merely added an extra thrill to hoisting a cocktail.

Ed's reporting work in Port Chester had hardly prepared him for what he was about to attempt. While the *Port Chester Daily Item* still considered a carriage crash front-page news, the *Evening Mail*'s front page was a riot of national and international news, with more than twenty headlines crowding page one: Wall Street, Broadway, American and European politics, crime and corruption, the arts, women aviators— all the world, or so it seemed, was contained in its pages. In January, Ed's first month, Paramount Pictures founder Adolph Zukor contributed a piece to the *Mail*'s entertainment section: "I predict a year's run for pictures on Broadway, so confident am I of the character and drawing power of the picture of the future." That same month the paper opined, with more optimism than accuracy, that "No Occupation Bars Women Now" ("Girls Today May Be Steamboat Captain, Bank Director, Steel 'Man'—and No One Will Say Her Nay"). American mores were changing, and the *Mail* was keeping track. "Ban on Petting Parties? No! Chorus Columbia Men" ("Petting parties are only successful if played with a '20th-Century girl,' a Columbia man declared").

Ed was overwhelmed. At the *Item* he had turned in handwritten articles, but the composing room at the *Mail* quickly let him know this wouldn't pass muster. One of Sullivan's editors, Jack Jackowitz, demanded that the new hire learn how to type. So Ed found an unused typewriter and spent hours copying editorials from *The New York Times*, hunting and pecking with two fingers.

Typing was the least of what he had to learn. His writing at the *Item* had been plucky, often tongue-in-cheek and flavored with unabashed hometown vinegar. But for the *Mail* Ed attempted to write in what he thought was a more sophisticated style, resulting in some frozen prose. On January 13, his column, *College Sports, Notes and Gossip*, displayed his unease:

> "The Columbia *Spectator* directs attention to the fact that although the army athletic authorities are correct in stating that although no monetary advantages accrue to the athletes who enroll at the academy, that very fact that football stars are allowed to play another four seasons of varsity ball after entering West Point is sufficient inducement for a great number of collegiate luminaries."

As Ed struggled through January it was unclear as to whether he would succeed at the *Mail*. An editor suggested that reporting might not be the career for him. When he was assigned to cover the annual Westminster dog show at Madison Square Garden in early February, he immediately assumed it was an effort by one of his editors to embarrass him. The assignment could be his last, he worried—he knew nothing about dog breeds.

At the show, he overheard a little girl ask her mother, "How do they wash their faces with all those wrinkles?" Inspired by this simplistic question, Sullivan decided to drop his attempt at big city sophistication—which clearly wasn't working— and have fun with the piece. He wrote:

> "The truth of the matter is that the harassed dogs have been patted and petted to death, and now, tired and exhausted, big dogs and little dogs alike are not above grabbing off a surreptitious nap at each and every opportunity. . . . The fond caresses of the visiting proletariat have undermined the morale of the defenseless bologna-questers."

A theme emerged in this piece that would run throughout Ed's newspaper work for years to come: he resented the affluent. He saw himself as distinctly apart from them, and took every opportunity to poke fun at the moneyed classes. There were two groups of people at the Madison Square Garden event, he explained, and it was easy to tell them apart.

> "The former class converse knowingly of the days when Hector was a pup, assume Rolls Royce grins, and park their patrician selves within the sacred precincts of the rings. The latter class gets nailed for life memberships in every dog society in the world and buys cartons of dog biscuits at the behest of total strangers."

As he went home that night after turning in the piece, he began to worry. "I became more and more terrified as I imagined what the sophisticated New York sportswriters would think when they picked up this piece of whimsy," he said.

On the way to work the next morning he bought the *Mail*, and, reading the paper on the train, was amazed to see that the story had been given prominent play. It was spread across two columns—a first for him. The nineteen-year-old reporter was mesmerized by the success of his article. Rather than complete his trip downtown, he kept riding the train uptown and downtown, repeatedly reading his piece as he traveled in a circuit. He felt an almost overwhelming urge to point out the story to a fellow train rider. If there was a single moment when he felt he had "made it" in the big city, this was it.

The lesson he learned, he later explained, was that he would fail if he tried to be sophisticated. The only approach that would work for him was the one that came naturally. Ed had to be Ed; any other strategy was bound for failure. In truth his writing style would soon adopt every bit of the 25-cent sophistication of his fellow New York sports reporters. But he recounted this anecdote in the 1950s, when his decidedly unsophisticated television persona was under fire from critics, and anecdotes like this seemed to justify his unadorned stage manner.

That May he wrote his first front-page story, covering a collegiate boat race between Princeton, Columbia, and Penn State on the Harlem River: "The challenge was met with a quick acceleration of the Columbia stroke, and from that [*sic*] on the two boats fought it out stroke for stoke, while the crowds went wild." Throughout 1921 Ed inched his way up the *Mail*'s masthead, getting promoted to cover professional golf and tennis in addition to college sports. By the end of the year his writing had regained the cheeky humor of his Port Chester reports. Covering swimmer Helen Wainwright, who had just broken four world records in the 500-yard freestyle, he observed her at lunch. His goal, he wrote, was to discover what makes a champion. "Miss Wainwright ordered a club sandwich, a piece of watermelon, a large slice of lemon meringue pie, ice cream and a glass of milk, and after stowing that away the youngster started on a box of chocolates. Of such stuff are champions made."

With his promotion Sullivan earned $75 a week, a handsome salary in the early 1920s when a furnished room in Manhattan rented for well under $50 a month. He had lived at home in his early *Mail* days, but with his raise he rented an apartment in midtown, on West 48th Street, over a bar called Duffy's Tavern. Equipped with a place of his own, he dipped a tentative toe into the swirling waters of Manhattan nightlife. At first, the Port Chester boy was ill at ease, yet he soon found a tour guide. The *Mail*'s boxing editor managed a fighter named Johnny Dundee, then a top featherweight contender, and he introduced him to Ed. The twenty-seven-year-old boxer, born Giuseppe Carrora in Sicily, had fought professionally since age seventeen. He won the junior lightweight title in 1921 and the featherweight title in 1923. He would later be inducted into the Boxing Hall of Fame and become such a revered ring hero that Angelo Mirena, Muhammad Ali's lead trainer, legally changed his surname to Dundee in Johnny's honor.

Ed and Johnny became fast friends. As a celebrity athlete, Dundee had entrée to the city's most exclusive haunts. The boxer took Ed under his wing, introducing him to major figures in many walks of life. In the late 1930s Sullivan recalled how Dundee had shown him around, and how Ed "died a thousand deaths every time he met a celebrity, but didn't want to let on."

Now that Ed was a New York fellow he wanted to look like one, and he spent every penny of his *Mail* salary to do so. He outfitted himself in high-quality hand-tailored suits and shirts; photos from the period show him to be nattily attired, with his hair slicked back, often sporting a fedora. One of the *Mail*'s advertisers was the Durant motorcar company, which must have caught Ed's eye; he was soon motoring around town in his own Durant roadster. As a young man he was ruddily handsome, with wavy auburn hair and strong blue eyes, his masculine mien reflecting the glow of his Port Chester athleticism.

On weekends he drove home to date his Port Chester sweetheart, Alma Burnes, but during the week he pursued the young women he met in New York's nightclubs. The *Mail* referred to these female speakeasy habitués as "flappers"; in the 1890s the term referred to a young prostitute, but by the 1920s it had come to mean any girl with a thin, boyish figure and an informal manner. The flappers lived up to their reputation for flouting convention. The practice of young women frequenting drinking establishments by themselves was new, and frowned upon by many. Worse, many of the flappers wore dresses with hemlines a full twelve inches above the ground and visibly used cosmetics, and some even smoked in public.

Ed's favorite nightspot was the Silver Slipper, on West 48th Street, a roaring upscale speakeasy not far from his apartment. He was there almost every night, cigarette and drink in hand. His Port Chester shyness long gone, he was now an avid socializer, a natural glad-hander who conversed with anyone and everyone. One of those he became friends with was Joe Moore, a top speed skater who would compete in the 1924 Olympics, and later become a press agent who worked with Ed.

More than lighting up his nights, the Slipper and other Broadway speakeasies introduced Ed to show business. He sat in jam-packed audiences as dozens of New York's biggest acts strutted and twirled, like dancer Ruby Keeler, who later high-stepped in a raft of Busby Berkeley musicals, and Van and Schenk, a vaudeville comedy-music duo who crooned "All She'd Say Was 'Umh Hum.'" Ed described the Slipper as the "hottest of the 'hot' spots when the heat was turned on . . . [full of] sporty, informal rendezvous with semi-nude chorines nodding to big shots, half-hidden by pitchers of fizzing champagne. . . . Where Ruby Keeler, with a gold chain . . . did a tap dance that was later to intrigue Al Jolson."

Ed spent many late evenings enjoying the comedy-music-dance act of Clayton, Jackson, and Durante. The trio didn't limit their antics to the stage; instead, they hurled themselves around the club in rough, exuberantly riotous routines. Ed became good friends with one of the trio, tap dancer Lou Clayton, who by one account was a "soft shoe man, tough guy, gambler, and with the ladies, a gentleman." Sullivan and Clayton sometimes stayed out all night, completing their nocturnal revelries with a round of golf as the sun came up.

The *Evening Mail* continued to assign the young reporter an ever-widening area of coverage. During 1921 and 1922 Ed churned out four or five articles a week, and by 1923 he earned sports reporter-at-large status, writing tartly trenchant accounts of horse races, swim meets, and tennis matches—he dubbed court ace Helen Wills "little poker face" for her ability to baffle opponents. He also garnered sought-after professional boxing and baseball assignments. He brought the immediacy of the ring into his pieces, as in his report of the Pal Moore–Frankie Jerome bout at Madison Square Garden:

> "Moore, who is reported to be a Klu [*sic*] Klux, was in rare form last night, and his laughable antics redeemed the show from being an utter failure. Pal slapped at Jerome from every angle of the landscape, and when he wasn't slapping the Bronx youngster all over the ring he kept the crowd roaring by jigging. The combination was too much for Jerome and, although he did his best to land a damaging punch, Moore made him look ridiculous.
>
> "Jerome, time and again, swung viciously at the dancing, tantalizing figure in front of him, only to miss and zigzag around in a semicircle, when Moore deftly stepped out of range. Every time Jerome missed— and he missed plenty—Moore would cuff him dizzy with an open-glove slap that for all their lightness enabled the southerner to pile up an enormous advantage."

Ed often used a sly humor in his pieces, as in his explanation of "the razzberry," the characteristic form of booing used in New York sporting events:

> "Slipping the gentle razzberry is America's most expressive indoor sport. The razzberry, one of this country's best beloved vegetables, conveys a distinct thought to the razzberr-ee and the value of this thought is measured by the tone, displacement, and volume of the gentle razz. . . . [One evening at Madison Square Garden] all was silent as the announcement cut its way through the smoke clouds hanging over the ring and mounted into the galleries, but ere the echoes of Joe's voice had died away the gentle razz began to pervade the summer air. Louder and louder it grew until the whole Garden was rocking to its tune."

In the spring of 1923 the *Mail* paid Sullivan a career-boosting compliment, placing his photo above his column on a weekly basis. His headshot portrayed him as dapper in a coat and tie, gazing out with a determined mug into the middle distance. Ed Sullivan was now a known personality, a sports expert, a wise guy whose dictums were agreed with or disparaged in barroom banter. The twenty-one-year-old reporter's coverage kept growing in color and humor, as in his profile of boxing promoter Jimmy Johnston:

> "Down and out a hundred times, busted at one time or other in every State in the Union, wealthy beyond the wildest dreams at intervals, but

always game, the Boy Bandit's fantastic career has ceased to startle the crowd who have been sunburned under the bulge of the great White Way.

"Daniel Webster would have liked Jimmy a lot had he known him. For James Joy breathes, sleeps, and eats most of the glowing adjectives that the elder Webster corralled for our convenience.

"Words are Jimmy's pet diet. All advertising men, believers in publicity, like to dabble with 'em; in fact, they have to. Johnston, greatest publicity man the modern world has ever produced, not only dabbles with syllables. He makes them sit up and beg, and his finished products are evidence complete that Jimmy learned more than a little of human nature in his nomadic tours of the world.

"King Tut received a lot of publicity when they trumped his coffin with a spade, but if the Bronx word juggler had been on the job we'd have learned more about Tut in one story than we gleaned from a batch of star correspondence in a month of overtime labor. In fact, Jimmy could have written better stuff sitting behind a 'mill' in his publicity bureau in the West Forties than was cabled by the writers on the spot."

During Ed's many long nights spent watching cabaret acts at the Silver Slipper, he became friendly with the club's owners, a trio of syndicate crime figures named Owney Madden, Frankie Marlow, and Bill Duffy. The syndicate plowed some of its enormous profits from illegal liquor sales into business interests in horse racing and boxing. Marlow owned ponies and oversaw the management of two fighters, and Duffy had an interest in boxer Primo Carnera, a lumbering mountain of a man who would briefly hold the heavyweight title. According to Broadway scuttlebutt, these syndicate figures saw benefit in socializing with sports reporters, expecting it to improve coverage of their investments in pugilists and racehorses.

The trio of mobsters welcomed the *Mail*'s young sports reporter. "At the club, we used to sit at Frankie Marlow's own table," Ed said. "Bill Duffy would join us." One evening as Ed chatted with Duffy and Marlow at the Slipper, they were joined by Larry Fay, a racketeer and taxi fleet operator who wanted to enter the burgeoning speakeasy business. "Fay had just bought the Rendezvous from Marlow and Duffy and apparently he hadn't paid up," Sullivan said. "I heard Marlow call him over—remember, this guy Fay was pretty tough himself—and Marlow said to him, 'Just a reminder, Larry, I gotta get the dough by Monday or you'll find your ears lopped off.'

"That's how friendly I was with those guys. I got to overhear a conversation like that. I remember that line about lopping off the ears. . . ."

Ed's friendship with vaudeville dancer Lou Clayton often brought him to Club Durant, a speakeasy on West 58th Street. Soon after Jimmy Durante opened the club in early 1923, it became one of the city's most notorious nightspots. Because Durante and Clayton were close friends, the soft-shoe man was present most nights. With his tough demeanor, Clayton was given the task of checking the patrons' guns, storing them on ice (he considered it a good hiding spot) until they left. The intimate club, seating one hundred thirty-five and decked out with black velvet walls, stayed open until 7 A.M., and was a popular hangout for mobsters, whose business was flourishing with Prohibition. One small-time hood told Durante that he had "brought some sunshine into the lives of the mob."

Club Durant catered to big spenders: the entrance fee was a hefty $4 and a gallon of illegal wine fetched $25. Its orchestra played until dawn, and, noted one patron, "There are winsome girlies, too, who run true to cabaret type in conformation, appointment and program." The club's star was Durante himself, especially when he performed his wildly physical routine called "Wood." As the band vamped brassy honky-tonk music, Durante mugged through a song and dance routine that entailed smashing every wooden item on stage. At the act's climax, with the band screaming full bore, he tore apart a piano piece by piece and threw it into the orchestra (the musicians ducked artfully). The audience roared and laughed and demanded more as Durante dismembered the instrument. Ed, sitting in the audience sometime around 3 A.M. drinking illegal spirits, was so impressed he would book the act decades later.

The high point of the reporter's career in 1923 was his September interview with heavyweight champion Jack Dempsey, then in New York for a title bout. The pugilist was America's idol that fall. Boxing was an ascendant sport in the 1920s and "The Manassas Mauler" led the way. His 1921 match against George Carpentier had boasted the first $1-million gate, and Dempsey was now the country's highest paid athlete. His fabled "long count" match against Gene Tunney in 1927 would be one of the decade's signature events. Having knocked down Tunney, Dempsey stood over him instead of returning to his corner, delaying the referee's count; those few extra seconds allowed Tunney to recover, after which he went on to win. Whether Dempsey would have won had he quickly returned to his corner was debated endlessly in barrooms across the country.

For Sullivan, who idolized sports figures (an idolization that continued throughout his life), meeting the champion was like being ushered into the presence of a Greek god. Even more heart-fluttering, Dempsey greeted the young reporter in his room at the Alamac Hotel, and invited Ed to join him for breakfast. "When I knocked at Dempsey's door, he opened it himself—and I remember how big he looked," Ed recalled. "He seemed to fill the doorway. He was wearing a loud striped bathrobe and he was smiling." As they sat eating breakfast, the two men found common ground apart from the reporter–athlete interview. Sullivan, noticing a grapefruit packed in a bowl of ice, noted that he had never seen it served that way—he had never eaten in a restaurant in his youth. Dempsey one-upped him in terms of a humble background. The boxer said he had never seen grapefruit at all as a kid.

Simpatico established, Sullivan and Dempsey would consider themselves friends from then on, staying in touch through the years. Toward the end of their lives they often had lunch together on Saturdays at Dempsey's Broadway restaurant, talking about old times.

In October 1923, Ed's reporting career took a hard turn to the left. The *New York Call*, the city's socialist newspaper, was revamping its format. Its new name was the *New York Leader*, and its self-proclaimed goal was to be "more than a propaganda organ. To be a REAL newspaper." Its meager sports section, limited to desultory coverage of baseball and boxing, was being expanded to cover all major sports. It needed an editor to oversee its new sports staff of six contributors. Ed, at age twenty-two, saw the job as a chance for advancement.

If moving from the *Port Chester Daily Item* to the New York *Evening Mail* had been a journey to a different world, Ed's jump to the *Leader* required a still more fantastic voyage. The paper had so vigorously opposed U.S. involvement in World War I that it was prosecuted under the Espionage Act. Its offices were raided and wrecked during the "Red Scare" of 1919, a government campaign to harass suspected communists prompted by the recent Bolshevik overthrow of Russia. Later, the *Leader* published articles supportive of Sacco and Venzetti, the Italian radicals whose politically charged trial and subsequent conviction stirred controversy throughout the 1920s.

Although the paper's leftist sympathies were wide in scope—it published a sex education column by Margaret Sanger that included her writings about birth control—its chief focus was the burgeoning organized labor movement. The *Leader* provided detailed coverage of labor–management battles, with headlines like "Printers Win 44-Hour Week" and "Alabama National Guard Set Serious Precedent in Suppressing Miners." Its hero was socialist labor organizer Eugene V. Debs ("Eugene V. Debs, former political prisoner of the United States government, would not leave San Francisco until he had visited Tom Mooney in his prison cell in San Quentin."). The paper published a weekly listing of all the socialist meetings in New York, and also espoused brotherhood with its communist compatriots overseas, with stories like "Russian Workmen Made Sharers in Prosperity." The *Leader*'s publisher, Norman Thomas, would be the Socialist Party presidential candidate from 1928 to 1948, and would help launch the American Civil Liberties Union (ACLU).

Ed, as the *Leader*'s sports editor, was also its top sports columnist. His column, *East Side—West Side, All Around the Town*, covered any sports topic he found interesting. For his debut piece on October 1 he wrote his own version of a workers' solidarity piece, skewering racetracks and baseball stadiums for overcharging the common man. Baseball teams, he pointed out, haul in great sums from their fans—up to $1 million in the recent season, by his count—yet the best seats for the upcoming World Series tickets were set at the unconscionably high price of $6 a seat. "Instead of acknowledging the fans' support throughout the season by a reduction in current baseball admission prices the judge boosted them, evidently using reverse English to arrive at his decision," Ed opined. "It's a great old world."

A few days later he wrote about how the Ku Klux Klan had influenced a southern sporting event, the Klan being a favorite target of the *Leader*. He began his piece with a reference to a black boxer named Battling Siki, who was originally from Senegal, Africa:

> "Battling Siki, the Senegalese dark horse, can't speak English fluently, but if he could, he probably would express himself somewhat after this fashion: 'Any Irishman who risks a world's title down below the Mason–Dixon line of Kukluxland is about as crazy as any colored boy who risks one against an Irishman in Dublin on St. Patrick's Day.' Yesterday's near-riot in Columbus, Ga., precipitated by the Mike McTigue–Young Stribling championship go, can be traced directly to the Ku Klux clan [*sic*]. McTigue, an Irish Catholic, managed by Joe Jacobs, a Jew, has as much chance of getting an even break in Georgia as the well-known snowball has of enduring the scorching blasts of Dante's Inferno."

After his first week, though, Ed's *Leader* writing turned largely apolitical, however much the newsprint around him trumpeted the international proletariat. His move to the *Leader* seemed less a reflection of his politics than a desire to step up a career rung, less about the working class than about one individual worker. Although he advanced from reporter to editor, he covered sports much as he had at the *Mail*, offering sharply opinionated reports of everything from horse racing to the upcoming Olympics. He touted Illinois sophomore Red Grange as one of the great football halfbacks, lauded Notre Dame coach Knute Rockne's competitive spirit— "Army never got over the shock of Notre Dame's cocksuredness"—and plugged his friends, speed skater Joe Moore, on his way to the Olympics, and boxer Johnny Dundee, now featherweight champion. When he was wrong, which was not infrequent, he poked fun at himself. Covering the 1923 World Series, he forecast a Giants victory over the Yankees by four games to two; instead it was the Yankees, propelled by Babe Ruth, who won by that very score. Ed acknowledged his strikeout by adding a drawing to his column showing a group of men looking quizzically at a newspaper, with the caption, "Yes, We Picked the Giants!"

But Ed's newfound editorial status proved ill-starred. On November 13, less than six weeks after launching with its new name, the *Leader* suspended publication. Organized labor and socialist groups had pooled $100,000 to revamp the newspaper but increased costs quickly devoured the investment. "It seemed in every way right to suspend the *Leader* while it is solvent rather than try to continue at a financial hazard a paper of greatly reduced size," announced one of its worker-managers. That may have made sound business sense but it didn't change the fact that its entire staff, including its sports editor, was now unemployed.

His newspaper contacts came in handy. The *Evening Mail*, which Ed had left to work for the *Leader*, threw him a lifeline, hiring him to cover winter sports in Florida. It was a plum job. He had canvassed the New York area covering sporting events but this was his first travel assignment. And covering baseball's spring training was an added perk. Sullivan headed south sometime after the first of the year, 1924.

This door, however, closed even faster than the *Leader*. On January 25, publishing mogul F.A. Munsey bought the *Evening Mail* for a price rumored to be in excess of $2 million, planning to incorporate the paper into one of his existing dailies. In the shuffle, Ed lost his assignment and found himself stranded in Florida.

He was not only unemployed but nearly broke. Living the high life in Manhattan hadn't entailed a savings plan. A golf pro named Tommy Armour loaned him $50 and referred him to famed sportswriter Grantland Rice (who wrote the oft-quoted aphorism "It's not whether you win or lose, it's how you play the game"). Rice helped Ed get a job as a publicist for a golf course at Ormond Beach, Florida, a career detour that taught him a skill he often used later in life, event organizing. He gained his first experience as an event producer by putting together exhibition golf tournaments, which he promoted with minor publicity stunts.

He supplemented his salary by writing freelance sports stories for the Associated Press and United Press International, and that winter Ed spotted a potential big scoop. Leading financier George F. Baker was traveling south in a private railcar to play golf with industrialist John D. Rockefeller, who owned a mansion in Ormond Beach. Ed checked with some New York dailies: Would they buy a story about the famous tycoons playing golf? That Ed had just finished a stint on a socialist newspaper didn't deter him from covering Rockefeller, the very embodiment of capitalism. Finding interest, he gathered details about Baker and Rockefeller's golf game and wrote his story. But he ran into an obstacle when his employer, the manager of the Hotel Ormond, refused to allow him to send it, fearing the piece might offend the two men. Ed began maneuvering to get his piece published. "When you are broke you become inventive," he said.

He suggested to his boss that the Hotel Ormond offer its services to the train car that Baker had traveled on. The manager liked the idea, and Ed volunteered to present the offer himself. Once there, he convinced the railroad manager to read his story, having him initial it to show his agreement that it contained nothing offensive. Ed's employer, seeing the initials, agreed to let him send his story, which became a major sale for the reporter. The story was presumably the one in *The New York Times* on March 28, 1924 detailing a Rockefeller golf game in Ormond Beach. The glowing three-paragraph piece carried no byline and didn't mention the businessman's partner that day, yet one day earlier the paper had reported that George Baker was headed south for business meetings. As Ed later told it, Rockefeller himself sent the reporter "a very human note," shortly after the article ran, explaining that Baker had won hole by hole, yet the industrialist was victorious in the final score. The letter may have been Ed's embellishment of the story—he claimed he didn't keep it—yet it's true that after decades of distrusting the press, late in life Rockefeller actively courted reporters, especially adoring ones.

At any rate, Florida held little appeal for Sullivan. After a few months in the sun he eagerly sought another sports-reporting berth. Between April 1924 and early 1925, he worked at three newspapers, hopping from one to the next, searching for what he had at the *Mail* and the *Leader*: a high-profile job covering a smorgasbord of sports. In April he took a job at the Philadelphia *Public Ledger*, a staid daily that mixed national news with voluminous coverage of local debutantes. But as at each of his three short-lived posts, the *Ledger* gave him no byline. In May, publisher Frederick Enright launched a new evening paper, the *New York Bulletin*, a Democratic broadsheet. Ed jumped at the chance to move back to New York, yet before he was established at the *Bulletin* he found an opening at the *New York World*.

Established by Joseph Pulitzer in 1883, the *World* was a big, prosperous daily with offices throughout the United States and Europe—just the sort of publication an ambitious newsman would desire. *World* sports editor George Daley, however, proved to be a minor tyrant and Ed chafed under his supervision, calling him a perfectionist. Even worse, Daley covered all the choice events himself. The reporter kept looking for an ideal position.

Sometime in the fall of 1924 he took a sportswriting job at the New York *Morning Telegraph*, a racing sheet that whispered insider's tips about that afternoon's track action, and whose front page covered the careers of hot ponies. For a reporter fluent in all the major sports, the *Telegraph* offered a much smaller world. The paper, as described by famed New York chronicler O.O. McIntyre, was "a barney refuge for the journalistically forlorn," which "harbored a dozen white-hair paragraphers." Still, it did deliver Sullivan from George Daley's clutches. From his tenure at the tip sheet he developed a passion for horse racing, and throughout his life spent many afternoons at the tracks; when he became wealthy later in life he bought his own racehorse. But the *Telegraph* didn't provide enough to hold him.

Finally, in early 1925 he ran into a casual friend, Will Gould, a sports cartoonist for the *New York Evening Graphic*, who told him of the paper's plans for a Saturday sports magazine. Gould recommended Sullivan write articles for the new insert. Ed jumped at the opportunity. At age twenty-three he was, astonishingly, starting his eighth newspaper job—and the most unusual. Launched in September 1924, the *Graphic* was a screaming two-fisted tabloid, dispensing with all journalistic rules except the inviolable precept that tawdry sensationalism draws readers. Yellow journalism had never been quite so yellow. The *Graphic* influenced Ed in numerous ways, the first of these being that it allowed him to meet someone who moved him profoundly.

When Ed met Olympic swimming star Sybil Bauer while covering a meet in 1925, it was love at first sight. Perhaps it was her winsome smile, or the sight of her in a swimsuit, but whatever the case, suddenly, even the fact that she lived half a country away didn't matter.

By the mid 1920s Bauer was something of a national celebrity. In 1921 she won her first Amateur Athletic Union backstroke championship, a title she claimed every year until 1926. In 1922 she became the first woman to break a men's record, besting Stubby Kruger's 440-yard backstroke record by four seconds. (The meet in Bermuda was not officially sanctioned so her performance was never formally recognized.) By the time she qualified for the 1924 Olympics, Bauer held world records at every backstroke distance. That year in Paris she won Olympic gold with ease, flashing through the 100-meter backstroke four full seconds faster than the silver medalist. She would eventually set twenty-three world records in swimming.

For all her competitive prowess, Sybil was easygoing, gentle, and upbeat. She wasn't classically pretty—her features were blunt—yet she possessed a swimmer's svelte form. When Ed and the twenty-one-year-old swimmer met, he wasn't the only one to swoon: the young Olympic star also found the sports reporter quite charming. Because the two lived in different parts of the country it was an unlikely romance; Sybil was a student at Northwestern University in Chicago, where she had grown up, and Ed lived in New York. But that proved no obstacle for Sullivan, and he pursued Sybil with a passion.

The romance blossomed. Sybil's swimming career brought her to the East Coast at times, and Ed made the trip to Chicago when he could. Several months after meeting, the two were quite serious about each other. In an unusual gesture, Ed even brought Sybil home to Port Chester to meet his family. Once established in New York he had rarely gone back, preferring to keep his distance from his father, if not from Port Chester itself. However, the trip home with Sybil proved a major success. Everyone in the Sullivan family liked her enormously.

The romance, while growing, remained a long-distance relationship, with Sybil attending college in Chicago and pursuing her swimming career while Ed remained immersed in his life as a New York sports reporter. He continued burning the candle at both ends, covering athletics during the day and nightclubbing virtually every night of the week.

Sybil appeared to have everything—athletic prowess, renown, winning charm—yet her life took an unexpected turn in early 1926. While being honored in a parade in St. Augustine, Florida, after winning an AAU swimming championship in February, Sybil suffered a momentary dizziness and fell from a slow-moving touring car. Though she suffered no major injuries, it soon became evident that her dizziness was symptomatic of a very real health problem. One newspaper attributed her fall to a nervous breakdown caused by the strain of her vigorous athletic training—the idea of a prominent female athlete was resisted by many. The real cause, however, was far more serious, and Sybil's health began to deteriorate, precipitously. Sometime in the next several months her family was told that she had cancer. The champion swimmer, in peak physical shape just months before, was now gravely ill.

In New York, Ed stayed in touch with Sybil while maintaining both his vigorous work and night lives. One of his favorite Manhattan nightclubs was the Casa Lopez, an upscale speakeasy owned by famed bandleader Vincent Lopez. Socializing at the club one evening in early October, Sullivan spotted a young woman at the next table he described as a "very stunning brunette youngster." He asked the Casa Lopez's publicity man, Joe Russell, to arrange an introduction.

Her name was Sylvia Weinstein. Elegantly dressed, the twenty-two-year-old possessed almost movie star good looks, with a trim figure, high cheekbones, and dark hair that complemented her pretty dark eyes. Her family was distinctly upper crust; her father, Julius Weinstein, a first-generation émigré from Lithuania, had made a considerable fortune in New York real estate.

When Ed sat down at her table the attraction soon became mutual. Their conversation turned, naturally, to sports, and Ed asked Sylvia if she liked tennis. "Of course I said I loved it. Ed was very attractive," she recalled. Ed brought up boxing and it turned out that, yes, Sylvia was also enthusiastic about attending boxing matches. Over the course of the evening's animated chat, Ed asked Sylvia for not one but two dates. The answer to both was yes. They made a date to attend tennis star Suzanne Lenglen's match at Madison Square Garden on Saturday, October 9, and they also planned to see the Harry Wills–Jack Sharkey prizefight at Ebbets Field in Brooklyn on Tuesday, October 12.

Both events had an element of glamour. French tennis star Suzanne Lenglen, a dazzling player and star of the 1920 Olympics, was the first female tennis pro to wear an outfit that afforded a generous view of her calf—stirring a mild scandal. Her Madison Square Garden match that Saturday, attended by thirteen thousand fans, was the start of her first tour as a professional. Upon arriving in New York to launch the tour, she had hiked up her skirt for reporters and announced she had come to America to make a whole lot of money.

The prizefight between Harry Wills, known as the "Brown Panther," and Jack Sharkey was a precursor to a title bout, with the winner earning a shot at champion Gene Tunney. (Wills, a black man, had signed a contract in the early 1920s to face then-champion Jack Dempsey, but New York's governor canceled the bout, fearing a race riot after the fight.) Ebbets Field was crammed with forty thousand fans, and in the high-octane economy of New York in the 1920s plenty of high rollers were sprinkled among the crowd. The evening was Sylvia's first at a boxing match, and she did her best to enjoy it.

Although pugilism held little interest for her, she felt quite intrigued by her date. At age twenty-five, he was in his element at events like these. As a well-known

Sullivan's first love, Sybil
Bauer, an Olympic gold
medalist in the 1924
games. (International
Swimming Hall of Fame)

sports reporter he was part of the party, a major fellow who knew the inside scoop.
He likely had good seats, and plenty of opportunities for glad-handing with important personages—which he never failed to do. With his tailored suit and easy fa-
miliarity with everybody who was a somebody, he cut an attractive figure. If his goal
was to impress his date, the two events were the perfect venue.

In Chicago, Sybil's health showed no sign of improvement. At the end of October her
condition took a turn for the worse and she entered the hospital. In November, Ed
made a trip to see her, after which the couple made a major announcement. Ed had
proposed, Sybil had accepted, and the two were now engaged. The wedding was set
for June. Due to Sybil's celebrity status the engagement was a minor national news
item, reported in papers across the country. Ed, perennially short on money, borrowed enough from his older sister Helen to buy a diamond engagement ring at
Black, Starr and Frost, an elegant high-end jeweler.

Or, Helen may have insisted that Ed take the money. Given Sybil's ill health, his
proposal may have been as much a gesture of sympathy as love. Decades later, Ed's
daughter Betty recalled that his sisters Mercedes and Helen urged Ed to propose

because they knew Sybil was dying. The sisters were fond of her and apparently saw the proposal as fulfilling her last wish. "From what I understand he was sort of pushed into that by Helen and Mercedes," Betty said.

After proposing, Ed returned to New York as Sybil's condition continued to worsen. In late January, he again made the trip to Chicago, likely knowing that this was his last visit. As his fiancée died on January 31 he was sitting by her bedside, along with her two brothers, her sister, and her parents. The Bauer family gave Ed back his ring, and he returned to New York. Sybil Bauer's untimely death was a far bigger news story than had been her engagement, and was splashed on the front page of many newspapers, with Ed mentioned as her bridegroom-to-be. Her pall-bearers were six well-known swimmers, including 1924 Olympic gold medalist Johnny Weissmuller (who later played Tarzan in a string of B movies). Some editorialists pointed to Sybil's illness as proof that women shouldn't be allowed to compete in athletics, but, noted one swimming organization in its obituary, "her life had contradicted those claims."

In 1967, Sybil was inducted into the International Swimming Hall of Fame. The organization asked Ed, then famous, to record a voiceover to accompany Sybil's photo in its museum. In the recording, he summarized her athletic achievements, adding, "Sybil, a girl from Chicago, was a very attractive girl. Most of us sportscasters had a crush on her. I know I did. Sybil really belongs in the Swimming Hall of Fame." Claiming he had a crush on her like all the boys was quite an understatement for the fiancé who held Sybil's hand on her deathbed. Ed seemed to have a need to exorcise her from his history, and after her death he never again made reference to her. In the early 1950s, after he became a major television star, he was interviewed constantly about his life history, yet never once mentioned his former fiancée. Even when he detailed his life story in a multipart series for the *New York Post* he included not one word of Sybil. Perhaps the episode was too grief inducing, or perhaps he simply preferred to keep it to himself. Like his father, he was a man who rarely spoke of his inner feelings, even to those closest to him.

Back in New York, Ed was not alone in his loss. Sylvia had become his steady date. Not that there was anything steady about the stormy sea of the Ed–Sylvia romance. The two were together as often as they decided to break things off. They would meet for a dinner date, or go out to a nightclub, only to call it quits by the end of the evening. But Ed couldn't stay away, and a few days later he would call and say, "I can't stand it anymore." The farewell dinners became a routine element of their relationship. "Afterward we would say 'Meet you for another good-bye party in two weeks,'" Sylvia recalled.

The chief problem, or so it seemed, was their religious backgrounds. For Sylvia, it was one thing to accept a date with an attractive Catholic boy she had met in the intoxicating atmosphere of the Casa Lopez; it was another to tell her family she was dating a gentile. "I guess Ed was the first Christian boy I ever really knew," Sylvia said. When some months later she informed her family that she had a steady boyfriend, she told them his name was Ed Solomon. After her brother heard he wrote for the *Graphic*, he said, "Oh, you mean Ed Sullivan, not Solomon."

Sylvia described herself as coming from a "regular Marjorie Morningstar world," a reference to the Herman Wouk novel about an affluent Jewish girl in the 1930s who disobeys her family's wishes to pursue her own desires and date a gentile. Her family, however, was not particularly observant, going to temple only on High Holy days, and despite her reluctance to acknowledge dating Ed, they seemed to have no serious objection. Sylvia later contradicted her reference to Marjorie Morningstar, saying, "I can honestly say that there was very little opposition from my family." And according to Ed's grandson, Rob Precht, the Weinsteins were happy to see Sylvia date Ed. "Her family was thrilled," he said. "He was a man about town, a go-getter, attractive, an all-American sports guy. They liked him."

However accepting Sylvia's family felt about Ed, their attitude met its equal and opposite reaction in Ed's family. The Sullivans were unequivocally opposed to him dating a Jewish girl. That he would marry Sylvia was not in the realm of possibility, in their view. Ed, bowing to the supposed immovable obstacle of their different religious backgrounds, kept insisting to Sylvia that their relationship could never work out. Then he would once again tell her he couldn't see her anymore.

Still, nothing could keep them apart. Their chemistry worked. Sylvia, warm and easygoing, understanding, a good conversationalist; Ed, ambitious, moody, sometimes hot-tempered, yet exceptionally fond of her. Sylvia knew how to let Ed be Ed, how to take his moods with a grain of salt. She was also, like his mother, encouraging. She believed in him. He was always on the lookout, for the next job, the next hand to shake, the next opportunity. She knew he was headed somewhere, and she allowed him to take the lead. Ed was very much in charge, and Sylvia was happy to go along.

And they both loved to go out. For the two of them, the New York nightclub was like a second living room. Ed made the rounds practically every evening and Sylvia often accompanied him. She took pleasure in dressing with great style, and Ed himself was invariably nattily attired. Sylvia favored elegant dresses and her date usually wore a double-breasted jacket topped with a fedora; so dashing a figure did he cut that in the early 1930s Adam Hats ask him to pose for a newspaper ad. They made an attractive couple, Sylvia with her dark good looks and Ed still ruddily handsome from his days as a Port Chester athlete. The two sat and socialized in various expensive speakeasies on most nights, Ed with his cigarette and drink, Sylvia sipping a cocktail. Throughout the evening they greeted passersby and chatted with Ed's many acquaintances and friends; after years of knocking around newspapers and nightclubs, he seemed to know most of the city.

So, as soon as they called the whole thing off, it was back on again. The romance between Ed and Sylvia—intermittent and mercurial at one level—was as steady and predictable as the train schedule at Grand Central Station.

CHAPTER THREE

The Porno Graphic

THE *NEW YORK EVENING GRAPHIC* knew how to elbow its way through the clutter of New York dailies. The paper's frothy mix of scandal, sleaze, sex, and sensation provoked howls of protest. Many claimed the *Graphic* was moral corruption in print. "Negress Bares Rich Man's Love Notes" blared a typical headline, or "Doctor's Death Bares Exotic Sex Orgies." Each day the paper found a fresh way to assault the respectable, with shockers like "Dating Bureaus for Lonely Co-eds to Solve Undergraduate Sex Problem" and "Beauty and Married Man Take Poison in Love Pact." The city's other leading tabloids, the *Daily News* and the *Daily Mirror*, were paragons of thoughtful, in-depth journalism by comparison to the Porno Graphic, as it was called. But if few respected the *Graphic*, quite a few read it. The paper's circulation was near three hundred thousand in the mid 1920s.

Graphic publisher Bernarr Macfadden was a notorious eccentric. A physical fitness buff who often walked barefoot through the newsroom, he hosted a radio show that guided listeners through rigorous morning calisthenics. The *Graphic* espoused his lusty appreciation of the human body and sex. The newspaper's daily article about exercise featured photos of two scantily clad showgirls demonstrating moves, with captions: "Does your boyfriend's driving get on your nerves?" asked one. "Yes," answered her companion, "sometimes it seems as if he'll never get out to the parking place!"

Like Macfadden's other publications, *True Story* and *Physical Culture* magazines, the *Graphic* relied heavily on photographs. And if the *Graphic* lacked an exclusive photo, it invented one. When the tabloid wanted a revealing shot of a debauched Broadway party or a celebrity divorce trial, it fabricated one using an unorthodox technique called the composograph. Staffers re-created scenes from news events by dressing up actors (sometimes reporters), photographing the tableau, then using scissors and glue to create a single "photograph." Including as many seminude models as possible was imperative.

For Ed, moving to the *Graphic* wasn't a step up the ladder as much as a step toward greater notoriety. The paper screamed from the newsstand, and a *Graphic* byline gave a newsman a pronounced notoriety, if not respectability. Unlike some of the papers Ed worked for, at which he labored in anonymity, the *Graphic* moved him center stage.

He landed his own daily column, *Ed Sullivan's Sport Whirl*, with his photo gracing the top. In his headshot he was squarely handsome, the young athlete with his hair slicked back and parted in the middle, looking out with a firm gaze. As a columnist he no longer had to chase down stories but instead offered his opinions, with a generous dose of gossip and barroom philosophizing. *Sport Whirl* was a freeflowing insider's notebook of tidbits and factoids, sometimes with an actual story thrown in. His column roamed freely through the world of professional athletics, from the personal to the political to the trivial, as if the *Graphic* had said to him: *Here's a typewriter, we'll publish anything you want to write.*

Ed's column pondered whether Babe Ruth and Lou Gehrig, the godlike stars of the New York Yankees, would continue their home run streaks. He reported that Pittsburgh Pirate captain Pie Traynor gave up cigars when the season started to aid his batting eye. Readers learned that tennis star Bill Tilden had every phonograph record made by opera star Mary Garden, and that William Wrigley (the chewing gum magnate and Chicago Cubs owner) operated an aviary on Catalina Island, but quit after a $1,500 bird died.

Sullivan had a special fondness for boxing, which in the 1920s vied with baseball as the nation's leading sport. In his column the give and take of the ring could be analogous to almost anything. In a 1928 piece he compared the battle for the Republican and Democratic presidential nominations, led by Herbert Hoover and Al Smith, respectively, to the battle between fighters to determine who got a shot at heavyweight champion Gene Tunney. Boxing also allowed Sullivan to write about race, a visceral issue in the sport at the time.

Although Jack Johnson's 1908 victory made him the first black pugilist to win the heavyweight title, after he lost in 1915 the boxing industry closed ranks to prevent another black champion. Ed addressed the issue in his 1928 column about George Godfrey, a fighter who he opined had a good chance of winning the title: "after peering at the two hundred twenty-five pound negro [*sic*], one can readily imagine him telling even Dempsey to go get a reputation." But after a conversation with top promoter Tex Rickard, Ed reported Godfrey would be denied a title bout against reigning (white) champion Gene Tunney due to his race:

> "Why does Tex shy from another mixed heavyweight scrap? I asked that question in his office one afternoon. 'I saw pictures of colored men strung to lampposts after the Johnson–Jeffries fight. . . . I resolved that I'd never try that again,' Rickard replied. Tex believes that the country has grown more tolerant, but he refuses to believe that our present degree of tolerance can prevail against passions which are a great deal older than any of the present generation. So Godfrey can be counted out definitely."

Sullivan's *Graphic* writing about race and sports was as much advocacy as reporting. He continued to cover a cause he had touched on at the *Leader*: civil rights. Ed claimed he had gotten access to a contract for a football game between New York University and the University of Georgia. In the document, according to Sullivan, New York University agreed to a demand by the southern university to bench one of its players because he was black. "For the next week, I castigated New York University's immorality and suggested that their Hall of Fame be torn down and transferred to some other university with a higher regard for a boy's dignity."

In advocating for the rights of black athletes, Ed took a stand that there was little public demand for, and likely not what the *Graphic*'s sports readers paid their 2 cents to read about (though the paper itself relished controversy in all its forms). His vocal and unstinting support of equal rights would be one of the few facets of his career he pursued regardless of how the audience felt about it.

In one of Sullivan's columns about boxing and ethnicity, he wrote that the results of three recent Madison Square Garden boxing matches "erased any immediate possibility that the Jewish race would break what amounts to an exclusing [sic] Irish–Italian monopoly on the world's pugilistic titles." He observed that titles once capably held by Battling Levinsky, Louis "Kid" Kaplan, and Charlie Rosenberg were now taken by Irish and Italian pugilists.

His own Irish–Jewish matchup continued apace, as he and Sylvia Weinstein maintained their tempestuous romance. The couple continued to be on-again, off-again, but remained steady despite the turbulence. She grew ever adept at handling his moods, knowing when to let him be and avoid the subject. And he began taking her to events other than sporting matches. As a *Graphic* staffer, he received tickets to events of many kinds, and one evening he took Sylvia to opening night of an Eddie Cantor movie, *Kid Boots*—a special thrill for his date. In a major step, the couple even made the trip to Ed's home in Port Chester, though it did nothing to change the Sullivan family's attitudes toward a potential marriage. And as always, Ed and Sylvia spent many evenings hopping between Manhattan speakeasies.

For Ed, nights on the town were a way to engage in his favorite sport: glad-handing. He was an incurable socializer whose crowd of acquaintances became a stepping-stone to a still larger crowd. The sports columnist socialized around the *Graphic* office as much as he worked, perhaps more so, never missing a chance to shoot the bull or trade the latest gossip. "While his associates sped hither and thither in a rush of activity, Sullivan just lounged around and talked to people," wrote *Graphic* editor Frank Mallen. "He got more use out of a chair than anyone connected with the place. . . . He was a friendly person whose attribute of easily making acquaintances gradually spread his personality around New York." Ed called everyone at the office by his or her first name, except for Macfadden. He became such a popular figure at the *Graphic* that the other sportswriters elected him sports editor.

But the social butterfly wasn't neglecting his work, in Mallen's view. "Those who mistook his easy-going [sic] gait as an indication of languor, however, were wrong. It was purely a matter of mathematics. It would take him half the time to write his stories than others needed. The reason was that he never had to stop to find the right word, an angle, a good start, or to look things up. They cascaded freely right into his typewriter, attesting to an uncanny gift of expression and memory."

The columnist was continually looking for his next venture. He began organizing and promoting "Strong Man" tournaments, in which great hulking slabs of men performed unlikely feats of strength. Contestants bent and lifted a plethora of iron and steel contraptions, grunting while attempting to outdo the competition. He held the carnival-like events in New York's Webster Hall, emceeing the contests himself, introducing the men onstage and enthusiastically directing audience applause. He also judged the tournaments, deciding—presumably based on audience reaction—which of the bulked-up behemoths won top honors. On occasion, some of the strongmen disputed Sullivan's rulings. One giant demanded that Ed follow him to the freight yards and watch him move a train car using his head.

Ed also began organizing and acting as master of ceremonies for the celebrity-studded *Graphic* sports dinners, held at swank locations like the Hotel Astor. With Macfadden's backing, Ed assembled rosters of star athletes, like Gene Tunney, Jack Dempsey, Babe Ruth, Red Grange, and golf star Gene Sarazen; the charismatic Mayor Jimmy Walker made cameos as well. On certain evenings Sullivan assembled and hosted *Graphic* dinners with marquee stage performers, like Rudy Vallee, the popular crooner who sometimes sang through a megaphone, and Sophie Tucker, the risqué comedienne who warbled double entendre chestnuts like "Nobody Loves a Fat Girl, But Oh How a Fat Girl Can Love." At one *Graphic* soiree Sullivan presented Al Jolson, the vaudeville singer whose blackface performance in the first talkie, 1927's *The Jazz Singer*, helped introduce a new Hollywood era.

Being a master of ceremonies was a job that Ed found that he liked immensely. It put the young columnist right were he wanted to be, in the spotlight.

The *Graphic* employee that Sullivan would have the most longstanding relationship with was Walter Winchell, the paper's gossip columnist and its biggest star. An egoistic workaholic whose column commanded the attention of Manhattan's "in crowd" as well as those with their nose pressed against the window, Winchell is considered the original show business gossip columnist. Other publications covered Broadway, and gossip was a staple of newspapers long before Winchell, but he combined the two with a go-for-the-jugular ethic and streetwise verbal wit like no one before him. *Graphic* readers could hardly wait to read *Your Broadway and Mine*, his irreverent daily peephole into the lives of the rich and famous.

In an age when it was viewed as improper to report even a pregnancy, the *Graphic* allowed Winchell to chronicle the glamorous classes in intimate detail, including divorces, affairs, courtships, and illnesses. With a sprawling network of sources and a rat-a-tat-tat machine gun style, he exposed the peccadilloes of the well known seemingly without censor. That he was widely read didn't mean he was widely loved. In fact he was loathed by many, by those who felt his skewering of the status quo was immoral, and by those whose secrets he exposed. But Winchell didn't care. He was driven by his column. The public felt profoundly ambiguous about him—as it did about the *Graphic* itself—with some calling him a corrupting influence, but he sold newspapers.

And Winchell was powerful. Broadway shows sold more or less tickets and starlets gained or lost bookings based on his pronouncements, which were repeated up and down the Main Stem, as Broadway was known. Over time he would become a one-man media empire. At his height in the late 1930s and 1940s, Winchell's column was syndicated in more than two thousand newspapers, and his hit radio show was talked about across the country. It's estimated that more than half the adult population either read his column or heard his broadcast. As his influence grew, so did the scope of his subject matter. In addition to Broadway and Hollywood celebrities, he dispensed pithy opinions on novels, records, radio programs, and even national affairs, on which he editorialized with a populist bent. His seat-of-the-pants take on current affairs was so well regarded that government officials established a liaison to court his influence, and he was called to the White House on a number of occasions.

Over decades, Sullivan and Winchell would have a complicated relationship. It was often described as a feud, and it was that; the two squabbled bitterly. But at times they had something of a friendship and could be warm and almost brotherly. Each had reason to dislike the other. Ed felt deeply envious of Walter, whose column made him more famous than many of the stars he wrote about. Walter, for his part, was highly insecure, and disliked even his minor competitors, like a popular sports columnist with his photo atop his column. A loner with few, if any, real friends, Winchell was not susceptible to Sullivan's easygoing glad-handing, and tended to be unimpressed with "Eddie Sullivan," as he sometimes called him.

The feud–friendship began as soon as the two met. One of their early skirmishes involved Emile Gauvreau, the *Graphic*'s tough, shrewd editor. Gauvreau came to the paper from the Hartford *Courant*, a respected small paper, and he retained some memory of journalistic ethics. Paradoxically, Gauvreau supervised the *Graphic*'s fabricated news stories but tried to rein in Winchell as the columnist pushed the prim boundaries of 1920s propriety. After Winchell included a column tidbit about a married couple expecting a child, Gauvreau bellowed at him: "This is a family newspaper! You cannot say people are having babies!" Winchell changed the reference to a "blessed event," but the battle between Winchell and Gauvreau raged constantly.

According to Sullivan, Winchell at one point asked Ed to intervene on his behalf, to get Gauvreau to go easier on him. The idea was that Sullivan, having plenty of friends at the paper—unlike Winchell—would have influence where the gossip columnist did not.

Sullivan went on a fishing trip with a *Graphic* executive, O.J. Elder, and put in a good word for Winchell. When Gauvreau learned about Sullivan's attempt to influence senior management, he bawled him out for going over his head. After the editor vented his rage, he explained that it had been Winchell himself who had informed him of Ed's attempt to go over his head. Sullivan felt he had been double-crossed.

At that point, Gauvreau called Winchell to his office. The gossip columnist admitted that, yes, he was the one who had told the editor—but he claimed Gauvreau had forced him. Sullivan, himself now enraged, said, "Walter, what can I do with a cringing coward like you? If I hit you, you might get hurt. If I spit in your eye, it will be coming down to your level."

Winchell claimed this story was a Sullivan fabrication. And it may well be a case of the Sullivan Story. It's not likely that Winchell would have asked Sullivan to intervene on his behalf. The Broadway gossip had considerable clout due to his immense popularity with readers; he wouldn't have needed the sports editor to plead his case. According to Winchell, he himself lobbied management to stop cutting items from his column.

But the anecdote, if it was an exaggeration by Ed, says something about his envy of Walter, which he admitted only decades later. The story portrays Sullivan as having influence where Winchell did not—and it was exactly Winchell's power and influence that Ed so admired. And it shows Ed as clearly the dominant victor, one-upping the star gossip columnist. That would always be Ed's hope, and he would struggle to do so for quite some time. From this rocky beginning the two men would stay oddly intertwined throughout their lives, and would still be playing out their rivalry–brotherhood in their seventies. Ed had lost his twin brother Danny in infancy, but in Walter he found something of a replacement.

Over the course of his many nights at the Silver Slipper, Ed's friendship with the mobsters who owned the speakeasy grew stronger. After racketeer Frank Marlow was shot to death near Flushing Cemetery in 1929, Ed wrote a fond remembrance of the syndicate figure:

> "Along Broadway they are selling extras telling of Frank Marlow's death, and yet some of us expect to see his fine eyes crinkle in a pleased smile and to hear his cheery 'Hello pardner,' a salutation that was not paralleled along Broadway for pure warmth of feeling. . . . To sit in a night club, to watch his eyes sparkle with pleasure, to hear him gently teasing the little blonde-haired girl with whom he was head-over-heels in love with. . . . To some, Frank Marlow was a racketeer . . . to us, who rejoiced in his friendship, he was an eager, impulsive, loyal friend."

In the view of Dan Parker, a sportswriter for competing tabloid the *Daily Mirror*, Sullivan's unabashed friendship with the mobsters who managed boxer Primo Carnera had led to journalistic fraud. Although Carnera, "the Ambling Alp," would briefly take the heavyweight title in 1933, accounts of his career invariably mention rumors that he was aided by strong-arm tactics other than his own. Parker claimed that Ed's *Graphic* column was part of the fix, that Ed was helping the mob groom Carnera for an eventual title shot—a claim that Ed disputed. Sullivan was indeed the boxer's cheerleader, writing plugs for the mountainous pugilist on a regular basis. But he claimed that his belief in Carnera was sincere: "I really thought a lot of Carnera, and praised him all the way up," Ed said.

Parker and Sullivan became embroiled in a fisticuffs of their own. Parker wrote, "Speaking for the Duffy interests which he seems to represent, Mr. Sullivan, the columnist, and, as he confesses, 'the original booster of the big man from the South of Italy,' offers to take 'any odds such a scoffer as Danyell Parker will offer and back Carnera to beat such as Godfrey, Jim Maloney, K.O. Christner.' . . . Now look here, Eddie, you old sheik . . . do you think I'd be foolish enough to bet on a fight in which Primo Carnera participated—assuming, of course, that he will ever participate in a real fight? . . . And, oh, what I know about Eddie Sullivan!"

Ed quickly counterpunched. He filed a $200,000 lawsuit against the *Daily Mirror* and Dan Parker, charging them with libel and defamation of character. For Parker, that was more fuel for the fire. "Eddie picked the argument and then ran off sniveling to his lawyer and threatened to sue me! Hot cha cha! What a powerful writer! I mean Eddie's lawyer. . . . A nice kid but he can't take it . . . that is, he can't

Sullivan's arch nemesis, Walter Winchell, who in the 1930s and 1940s commanded a vast radio and newspaper audience. (Globe Photos)

take a bit of rough joshing . . . otherwise he can—and does—take it. . . . Now hop back into Primo's left shoe, Eduardo, until I need you again."

Those words made Ed even more determined to fight back, but his court case suffered a setback. A State Supreme Court judge ruled that Sullivan had mistaken "facetious twitting for malicious libel." Ed, however, didn't give up. His honor had been impugned and he would, as always, keep slugging until he got what he wanted. He appealed the case to a higher court, where he won a reversal. The court case went forward and this time the judge ruled in his favor. But it wasn't the money he was after. "I considered the reversal vindication enough," Ed said. "I settled with the Hearst lawyers for my lawyers fees, about $850, I think. They were astonished when I said I didn't want any money for myself." As Ed reiterated after his court victory, he was indeed a friend of Bill Duffy's, but his many plugs for Primo Carnera had been genuine. As such, "I was willing to call the whole thing off after I succeeded in defending my reputation."

(In 1956 Carnera sued the movie studio that produced *The Harder They Fall*, based on the Budd Schulberg novel about a fighter whose fights are fixed; many felt it was based on Carnera. The boxer lost his suit. In the film, a sportswriter named Eddie Willis is hired by the mob to promote a fighter until he can win a title bout with a champion named Gus Dundee.)

On the morning of October 29, 1929, Wall Street brokers began the trading day under a cloud. Soon after the gong was struck to begin business, their worst fears were realized. The great bull market, after weeks of hiccupping, and a handful of very bad days, was now heading dizzily, devastatingly, downward. The day's collapse was the worst carnage in the history of American markets. As stocks had climbed in the late 1920s, they lured legions of small investors—teachers, seamstresses, railroad men. Every cabbie, it seemed, had a hot stock tip. Their nest egg was now gone. With the breathtaking declines of Black Tuesday, even large institutions cashed in their chips. Herbert Hoover assured the country that fundamental conditions remained sound, but the crash reverberated throughout the economy. Businesses failed and commodity prices tumbled. Within six months, unemployment soared. One of the sectors hit hardest was newspaper advertising, affecting the *Graphic* as much as any New York daily. The paper had always been a hard sell to advertisers. Its impressive circulation was offset by its questionable reputation; many businesses were reluctant to be associated with the lurid tabloid. Now, as advertising budgets grew tight, the paper's fortunes began to slide.

The Depression, of course, was a change of mood as much as a change in business fortunes. The world that Ed inhabited, the nightspots and cabarets of Broadway, felt a sobering chill. It could hardly have been otherwise: by March 1930 the breadlines in New York snaked block after block, and the city's YMCA fed twelve thousand unemployed workers daily. The mad spirit of the 1920s—the rouged flappers, the insouciant evenings at gin joints—was slipping away. The carefree effervescence was replaced by a deepening shadow. Even romances, once content to be casual, now faced a make-or-break point.

Ed and Sylvia's relationship had grown ever stronger since its beginning in the fall of 1926, despite their steady-as-a-clock pattern of breakups and reconciliations. Although by the spring of 1930 it was clearly a longstanding romance, Ed appeared to be moving no closer to marriage. Sylvia, however, needed to move things along. "Ed had no intention of getting married," she recalled much later in life, "but finally I trapped him into eloping."

In April, Sylvia told Ed that she was pregnant. Hurried discussions ensued. Ed agreed to get married, but the two decided to keep the wedding a secret from their families until after a short honeymoon. Ed planned a City Hall ceremony, witnessed by close friends, to be followed the next evening by a short Catholic ceremony. (Ed wanted any children raised as Catholics, which Sylvia agreed to.) Then the couple planned on honeymooning for the weekend in Atlantic City, after which they would break the news to their parents.

Ed and Sylvia went to City Hall on April 28. The witnesses were Sylvia's close friend Ruth Sanburg, and Ed's friends Jim Kahn, a sportswriter from his *Evening Mail* days, and Johnny Dundee, the boxer who had shown him around New York when he first arrived. A quick wedding ceremony was performed, and the couple went to dinner at the Roosevelt Hotel with Dundee.

Everyone understood it was to be kept secret until Ed gave the okay, but apparently someone at City Hall hadn't agreed to the plan. As soon as the newlyweds got back to Ed's apartment the phone started to ring. Reporters quizzed them about the details; a photographer was on the way. This put Ed and Sylvia in a quandary—their families would soon read about their wedding in the newspapers. They realized they had no choice. The two of them placed hurried calls to their parents to let them know they had gotten married.

Sylvia's family took the surprising news with relative equanimity. "At that point I was so emotionally involved with Ed that they wanted me to have anything that would have made me happy," she said. But the Sullivans were aghast. As Sylvia described it, Ed's family was "all devout Catholics—who were opposed to the marriage." It would take several years—and diplomatic efforts on Sylvia's part—before Ed's family would speak to him.

Ed and Sylvia moved into an apartment on 154 West 48th, not far from where Ed had lived when he first moved to New York. They lived over Billy LaHiff's tavern, a Broadway watering hole frequented by show business types, celebrity athletes, and politicians. (The apartment, owned by LaHiff, had once been rented by Jack Dempsey and, later, by Broadway chronicler Damon Runyon.) The couple's only child, Elizabeth, named after Ed's mother, was born on December 22.

In June 1931 the *Graphic* needed a new Broadway gossip columnist. Walter Winchell had gone to Hearst's *Daily Mirror* in 1929, lured by a hefty salary increase and a signing bonus. Winchell's high-profile post at the *Graphic* had been filled by Louis Sobol. As written by the mild-mannered Sobol, the *Graphic*'s gossip column was never as talked about as it had been under Winchell, yet Sobol still parleyed it into a career boost. In mid June, he too landed a column in a Hearst publication, the *New York Journal-American*. With Sobol's departure imminent, the *Graphic* needed a new Broadway scribe to keep tabs on the glitterati.

The job was offered to Ed. Or, as he later claimed, he was forced into it. The *Graphic*, he said, gave him an ultimatum: "I didn't want the job, but it was either take it or be fired." He did agree to take the Broadway gossip column, yet in truth it may not have required the arm-twisting he later recounted.

Management changes at the paper were casting doubt on Ed's job security. Lee Ellmaker, who co-owned a tabloid in Philadelphia with publisher Bernarr Macfadden, had joined the *Graphic*'s senior management. Ellmaker brought with him the Philadelphia tabloid's sports editor, Ted von Ziekursch, to be the *Graphic*'s managing editor. But von Ziekursch had little interest in being managing editor; he wanted to cover sports. Hence, he looked enviously at Ed's column.

As recalled by Walter Winchell, the new managing editor began encroaching on Sullivan's turf. Ed ran into Walter one evening as he was buying a newspaper on 47th Street, and as they stood chatting, Ed told Walter of his troubles. "He takes my ringside seats to the fights and World Series. He covers them himself. My column doesn't run. It's humiliating." Walter recommended that Ed live up to his contract regardless. "Keep turning in your column. If you don't, he'll use that as a reason to say you broke it. Give me some time to think. I'll call you."

However, the *Graphic*, despite von Ziekursch's intrusion on Sullivan's beat, wasn't going to force out Ed to allow its managing editor to cover sports. When Ed finally began the Broadway column, his sports column was given to new hire Sam Taub—not von Ziekursch. Moreover, when Ellmaker offered Ed the Broadway beat, it wasn't accompanied with a take-it-or-you're-fired ultimatum, recalled editor Frank Mallen: "Ellmaker . . . called him to his office and asked him to make the switch saying he believed that Sullivan understood the Broadway setup better than anyone else."

In fact, Ed even felt in a strong enough position to negotiate a raise, remembered Mallen. Sullivan told Ellmaker he would take the new assignment "on [the] condition that $50 a week be added to his pay for night club expenses. Ellmaker agreed." Ed's new pay was $375 a week.

Although he had agreed to write the Broadway column, Ed would never have admitted an interest in being a gossip columnist. He had always had a streak of the puritanical. That is, he presented a moralist's face in his writings and later on television, though in reality he was far from this. And in 1931 being the *Graphic*'s gossip columnist was only a step away from being a pornographer, to some observers not even a step.

Underneath his reluctance to switch columns—clearly genuine—was likely some desire for the gossip beat. The last two men to have filled it went on to lucrative high-profile positions at better newspapers. For someone who had always enjoyed the attention that came with being a prominent columnist, the Broadway column surely held appeal.

As Ellmaker had said, the reason the *Graphic* wanted Ed to take the Broadway beat was that they knew he was well qualified. Like any good gossip, he was an inveterate socializer. He rubbed elbows with all and sundry up and down Broadway, from mobsters to flappers to barkeeps to shoe shine boys. His army of sources was already in place. And it was no secret he possessed the foremost job qualification for the Broadway reporter: he was a confirmed nightclub habitué. He had seen all the cabaret routines and musical revues for the last few years, the very acts he would cover. He had organized and emceed the *Graphic*'s celebrity dinners, with stars like Al Jolson and Sophie Tucker. His name and face were familiar to readers, and his sports column was already as much a gossip's diary as straight sports coverage.

Still, this was a life-altering shift. In moving to the Broadway column, Ed was making more than a career change; he was making an identity change. A sports columnist was a man's man, discussing Tunney's uppercut and the Yankees' pennant chances; a Broadway columnist was an odd creature, both sought after and shunned by society, living among musicians and comics and actors. Ed was not new to the milieu he was about to enter, but his new post would entail an unpredictable journey away from familiar terrain.

When Louis Sobol wrote his farewell column for the *Graphic*, he gently jibed the columnist-to-be: "I understand Eddie's going to use his picture in this column. It's a grand idea, because this Sullivan fellow is one of the good-looking, he-man type of fellows. When he turns his firm-chinned pan at a certain angle, he's a dead ringer for Gary Cooper. Running his picture should help him a lot in the matter of mail from gal readers, and mail's mighty important to a columnist."

Sullivan was "not a newcomer to Broadway . . . his daily routine has brought him constantly into contact with Broadway," Sobol noted. But he had some things to learn: "It's only fair to warn Eddie, of course, that his home life is a thing of the past.

He'll be coming home anywhere from 5 to 8 in the morning. He'll be coming home worn out, tired, grouchy and resentful at the world in general. He'll toss around in bed wondering what in the world he'll use for a column the next day." Sobol went on to reassure Mrs. Sullivan: "They'll only mean that Eddie is a good Broadway columnist. Only good Broadway columnists act that way."

In the last week of June, the *Graphic* began running ads touting Ed's debut as a Broadway columnist. On the Friday before his first week, it ran a half-page ad with Sullivan posed in a movie poster countenance, fedora at an even set, gazing out with an insider's knowing look. The ad read:

> "He's a curiosity! He actually was born and brought up along the main stem of the big town. He's the pal of Jimmy Walker, Jack Dempsey, Marilyn Miller, Buddy Rogers, Bernarr Gimbel, George White, Earle Sande, Nancy Carroll, Gene Tunney, Paul Whiteman, Flo Ziegfeld, Babe Ruth—of Mrs. O'Grady and Officer 666—and he will tell you all about them as you've never been told before. He's been famous as a reporter and sports reporter these many years. Maybe you know Ed Sullivan, but, if you don't, be sure to meet him Monday in the *New York Evening Graphic*."

Ready or not, Ed was about to make his Broadway debut.

CHAPTER FOUR

Broadway

E D'S COLUMN, *ED SULLIVAN SEES BROADWAY*, debuted on Monday, July 1, 1931. For someone who professed to not want the job, he jumped in headfirst. He began by taking a broad swipe at his colleagues in the gossip trade, a strategy guaranteed to maximize his profile—they were duty bound to swipe back.

"So many have asked me my sensations in turning from sports to Broadway that I will answer them in this introductory column. I feel, frankly, that I have entered a field of writing which offers scant competition, a field of writing which ranks so low that it is difficult to distinguish any one columnist from his road companies. . . . *I charge the Broadway columnists with defaming the street.*"

He proclaimed that his column would not indulge Broadway's undesirable elements, as his competitors' did.

"The uppermost stratum of Broadway, as revealed in the writings of its contemporary historians, the columnists, is peopled with mobsters, cheap little racketeers and a vast army of phonies. . . . As I sat at the gala opening of Hollywood Gardens on Friday night, I marveled to myself. . . . I marveled at the phonies who were there for no better reason than they had a mad desire to be seen. . . . They will betray themselves by rushing up to Mayor Jimmy Walker and shaking his hand as an endless stream of pests did on Friday night . . . they will gape at racketeers and mobsters who are tough killers and can prove it by the list of victims they have shot—always through the back. . . . *I pledge you this huge army of phonies will receive no comfort in this space. To get into this particular column will be a badge of merit and a citation.*"

Breaking from the practice of other Main Stem reporters, he announced, his column would not promote the prurient.

"Divorces will not be propagated in this column. . . . I will always experience greater pleasure in seeing Gus Edwards roadhousing with his wife than in seeing a celebrity flaunting his mistress. . . . So with high resolve and no fears, I enter upon my career as a Broadway columnist. . . . I confess that the prospect of competing against the present field leaves me quite cold. . . . It looks like a breeze and, as Mike Casale would say, 'Weather clear, fast track.'

P.S. No apprentice allowance claimed."

When the paper hit the stands the Broadway community was agog. Ed's debut was the talk of the town. *Graphic* publisher Bernarr Macfadden wondered if Sullivan could be serious: a clean Broadway column? The publisher of *Variety*, Sime Silverman, reprinted the column in full, with commentary: "Sullivan is well known, if not famous, as a sports reporter. He will become equally so as a Broadway writer if continuing the way he started. The tabloids have been called the trade papers of the racketeers. Sullivan is on a tab [an apparent reference to the *Daily Mirror* claim that he was on the mob's payroll]. His initial outburst sounds as if he intends to disprove the allegation. It's a great opening." Many thought the column's claim of propriety merely funny, like a Burlesque dancer lecturing on grammar. Some speculated it was the columnist's standard ploy: to gain readers by starting a feud. Winchell and Sobol, understanding that the jabs were aimed directly at them, were incensed.

The evening after his column's debut, Sullivan ran into Winchell at the Reuben Delicatessen. According to Sullivan, he himself was talkative and Winchell was quiet, until Winchell asked, "Did you mean what you wrote today?" The freshman columnist soft-pedaled his attack, explaining that he had merely wanted to make a dramatic entrance. Winchell said he accepted this as an apology, at which point it was Ed who took offense. The Sullivan hair-trigger temper leaped out of the bag. "I got so mad I grabbed him by the knot in his necktie and pulled him over the table, right on top of the cheesecake. 'Apologize to you?' I said, 'You son of a bitch, I did mean you and if you say one more word about it I'll take you downstairs and stick your head in the toilet bowl.'" In Sullivan's telling of the story, Winchell then fled the Reuben.

Sobol, in the *Journal-American*, parried Sullivan's opening salvo by writing a column entitled "The Ennui of His Contempt-oraries." Referring to Ed, he archly noted, "Empty vessels make the most sound."

Sobol's riposte was standard stuff by the rules of the Broadway gossips; throwing barbs back and forth was part of their stock-in-trade. They were as much performers as the nightclub acts they covered. But for Ed, hypersensitive and in a new situation, it was too much. Sobol's column enraged him. One evening shortly after it ran, Sullivan ran into Sobol outside a Broadway performance. Ed grabbed his rival columnist and, according to Sobol, bellowed, "I'll rip your cock off, you little bastard." Sobol, all of one hundred twenty-five pounds, ducked out of Sullivan's reach while bystanders held him back.

As if Ed hadn't vented enough, he also took Sobol to task in his column, writing:

"To my former associates in the field of sports writing, I must report that THIS is a soft touch in an unusually responsive arena. . . . While all my columning contemporaries are fuming and fretting at my invasion, one of them has even carried his personal alarm into the two-column measure of his daily piece. This particular fellow has never had much competition. He's got it now. I have not decided whether to chase him over the right field fence or the left field fence. This, however, is purely a matter of route, and immaterial."

That would be easier said than done. In claiming he would write a Broadway column free of gossip, Ed faced a gaping void. He had to churn out six columns a week, Monday through Saturday, each about fifteen hundred words—an enormous amount of space to fill without the usual patter of petty scandal.

His claim of journalistic piety lasted as long as two bits in a Broadway speakeasy. On Tuesday, one day after his opening roundhouse punch, he wrote a padded piece of treacle mourning vaudevillian Joe Schenck, who had died prematurely. On Wednesday he went back on the attack, decrying the "velvet hammer" of the Broadway drama critics, how they "hem and haw, they beat about the reviewing bush and extract from it critical thorns with which to puncture the hide of agonized producers. Primarily, they seek arty phrases in which to couch their barbs. These, they hope, are destined for mouthing in salon and drawing room." In contrast, Ed promised, "If I like a show, I will say so without any ambiguity of phrasing which might protect my *Variety* box score."

In that same Wednesday column—just forty-eight hours after proclaiming, "divorces would not be propagated in this column"—he included an item about Jack Dempsey's divorce. Its expense was placing the boxer in "desperate need for ready cash," Ed wrote. "The ex-champion is seriously considering a fight at Reno against a guaranteed tanker. Dempsey would promote it, and would not have to cut Estelle in on the net." In one fell swoop he had abandoned his promise and publicized the personal troubles of a friend. It was as if he hadn't realized how deep the waters would be, and now, not sure if he could swim, was grasping at anything to keep himself afloat. He would print another item about Dempsey in a few months, claiming that the boxer had ducked in and out of New York quickly because of rumored kidnap threats. That column item prompted an angry telegram from Dempsey, which Ed printed: ALWAYS CONSIDERED YOU A FRIEND STOP DIDN'T EXPECT YOU TO WRITE AND PRINT A STORY YOU KNOW IS RIDICULOUS AND WITHOUT FOUNDATION STOP ONE NEVER KNOWS WHAT TO EXPECT THESE DAYS, HOWEVER. JACK DEMPSEY.

By Friday of his first week, it seemed, he was out of material, reduced to a windy paean lauding the glories of opening night. In lieu of actual news, he provided a dollop of pandering to the hometown crowd (and a florid description of the world the twenty-nine-year-old columnist was entering):

> "A First-night supplies all these things to all men of Broadway. Gorgeous women flicking red-tipped cigarettes, suave gentlemen suavely tailored, and the whole against a background of curious crowds at the theater entrances, their gaping delight occasionally blotted out by the brawny shoulders of the cops holding them in restraint. . . . It has a glittering spread to it that reduces the rivalry of other cities to inconsequence. Depreciatingly, these other cities sneer, 'New York is a sucker town.' And then these other cities bend frantically to their work in order to get carfare to reach it. For they all want to gaze at the steel-ribbed frame of the 'sucker city.'"

By the end of the month, gossip flowed from the column in a steady trickle. He began regularly including items like "Grover Cleveland Alexander is back with his wife and off the booze." In mid July he informed readers, "Everyone who played a lead in *The Marriage Circle*, including Lubitsch, the director, has been divorced." In August he reported, "Abe Lyman's sister is returning from the coast . . . without her hubby." And shortly thereafter, "Jean Malin belted a heckler last night in one of the clubs. . . . All that twitters isn't pansy . . ."

Walter Winchell described a scene at LaHiff's Tavern shortly after Sullivan started including gossip. Ed stopped by the bar and joined Winchell and an assortment of Broadway types who were drinking and talking shop. Walter couldn't resist needling Ed about his journalistic change of heart:

"Eddie," I cooed, "what happened? Did your editor tell you to get interesting or get out?"

"No," he sighed. "My wife did."

Initially, Ed's job as a Broadway columnist included drama criticism. If dealing with gossip meant swimming in uncharted waters, writing serious theater criticism put him in over his head. Just weeks earlier he had been reporting blow-by-blows from the bouts at Madison Square Garden. Now, having never read a single play, he found himself at the opening night of a production of August Strindberg's *The Father*, an intense psychological drama. Sullivan didn't like the play and made that clear in his review. In his best imitation of a drama critic, he recommended that the playwright rewrite the entire second act. Not until the following day did Ed realize that Strindberg was long dead.

But *Graphic* readers didn't pay 2 cents to read in-depth reviews of Strindberg productions, and Ed quickly navigated away from serious theater criticism. Henceforth he would go no closer to legitimate theater than comments like, "those cocktails at Alice Brady's party would have jolted Eugene O'Neil [*sic*] into writing a musical comedy." Instead, Sullivan's column provided readers with his tell-it-like-it-is descriptions of lighthearted Broadway fare, the broad comedies and showy musicals that lit up the Main Stem.

More than covering light theater, though, Ed's column created a kind of parallel universe. As the Depression cast deep shadows, even the *Graphic*'s headlines turned serious: "6,000 Hunger Marchers Set Out for Washington" and "Mid-West Farmer Pays Taxes with Nuts in Lieu of Money." Ed's column was a respite from the grimness. He mentioned the Depression, to be sure—it was unavoidable at this point. But more often he wove a pixie-dust fairy tale of Broadway glamour, peopled with big spenders, shapely chorines, and talented showbizzers. This beautiful set had the luxury of falling in and out of love with dizzying frequency, usually at high-class speakeasies where the headwaiter understood the importance of seating stars around the room at a discreet distance.

He didn't have to invent this world; some vestige of it still existed from before the Crash, and he was quickly invited in. For a columnist who could provide publicity, the invitations were numerous. Ed visited Fred Astaire's dressing room at the New Amsterdam Theater. The thirty-one-year-old dancer was then appearing in the original Broadway production of *The Band Wagon*, having yet to make his first trip to Hollywood:

"If you find [vaudeville star] Joe Schenck at Richman's dressing room, you are more apt to find a Vanderbilt or a Whitney in Astaire's place. The youthful dancing star claims most of the social set as his bosom pals, or, perhaps I should twist that around and point out that they claim him.

"Fred's droll colored dresser provides a lighter note for the guests here, providing he knows them. If he likes them, he will even go out of the theater and get them a glass of Fred's favorite after-performance beverage, milk. Bob Benchley is a member in good standing of the Astaire Dressing Room and Milk-Drinking Benevolent Association."

Musical theater producers buttonholed the new columnist to hobnob with their stars. "Before Larry Hart and Dick Rodgers left for the Pacific Coast to write songs for Maurice Chevalier's next picture, I had lunch with them and George Gershwin on Broadway," Ed reported, as if he dined with Main Stem superstars on a regular basis. It was impossible to say which of that day's lunch companions was more famous; Gershwin had debuted the groundbreaking *Rhapsody in Blue* in 1924, and Rodgers and Hart's bubbly musicals continuously delighted Broadway. "The conversation switched to aviation. We all agreed that we were safer on the ground. Rodgers, who doesn't like flying, suddenly remembered something. 'I shouldn't be opposed to flying,' he said, 'for an airplane trip gave me an idea for one of our best songs.'" Rodgers, Sullivan wrote, explained that he composed "With a Song in My Heart" after listening to the roar of an airplane engine.

Ed seemed to become fast friends with Florenz Ziegfeld, whose leggy *Ziegfeld Follies* comedy-dance revue was one of the signature acts of the 1920s. "In a speakeasy the other night, before the 'Follies' left for Philadelphia, Flo Ziegfeld chided me for writing that he was sixty-seven years old," Ed wrote. "'It's sixty-three,' protested Ziggie, forgetting that two weeks previous, at the Peacock Ball, he had given me sixty-seven as his correct age." (Ziegfeld in fact was sixty-three in 1931.)

Sullivan sat in the lobby of the Hotel Warwick with Jack Benny and Eddie Cantor and debated the effect of various theaters on the success of a show. "Jack Benny felt that the Manhattan Theater, the former Hammerstein Theater, contributed to the poor reception of *Free for All*. Cantor disagreed volubly," Ed noted. (The Manhattan Theater would later be renamed the Ed Sullivan Theater.)

The columnist sometimes journeyed uptown, to Harlem, to investigate the newest jazz orchestras. He preferred bandleader Cab Calloway to Duke Ellington, a position he conceded was controversial: "I said he would overhaul Ellington . . . the town giggled at the thought. . . . But I ask you now . . . who's bigger, Ellington or Calloway?"

By the early 1930s, Broadway faced an upstart rival in the business of fame, Hollywood, and this new world was often feted in Ed's column.

"Every time one of the West Coast picture stars arrives in New York the playboys go into action on all fronts, for it is a particular badge of merit to have wooed and won, even for a fortnight, a movie star . . .

"You can imagine the commotion that was raised by the Men About Town when the petite Raquel Torres, one of the smarter-looking coasters, detrained in the local trainshed. I don't blame the local Men About Town for the haste in placing orders at the greenhouses; Raquel is an unusually pretty girl and, in addition, seems to know what time it is without looking at the Paramount Building clock."

Ed was thoroughly thrilled by his new status as a Broadway chronicler. He had, he admitted, no desire to go back to sports, the field in which he had labored so long to establish himself. "So many have asked my reaction to the new field of work that I will tell them now that Broadway columning is more varied and more interesting than sports columning," he wrote in September 1931, having launched his column two months prior. "I believe that the people you meet in theater and its wings are, in the aggregate, smarter and more interesting." If he had been coerced into this job, as he later claimed, he took to it like an actor to the stage.

New York had been a good place to cover sports, but it was *the* place to report on the breathless business of glamour. "They say that Broadway and 42nd Street is the junction of the universe and it's about right, at that," he rhapsodized. "Not many nights ago, I sat in one of the more elaborate speakeasies in the Fifties and marveled at the diversity of life gathered together in one spot.

"There, by the wall, with a blue sailor hat pulled down over her eyes, sat Greta Garbo with Berthold Viertel . . . on the left side of the room was Harry Richman, matinee idol, and with him was Bert Lahr, comedian of screen and stage [later to play the Cowardly Lion in *The Wizard of Oz*] . . . two tables to the right . . . was Jim Turner, vice-president of huge R.K.O.

"Where else but on Broadway would you find all these various types all in the same room, and nobody paying any attention to them."

For all of Ed's outwardly jaunty tone, all was not well. He had always been moody, prone to fits of melancholia and sudden anger. But now an event plunged him into a dismal funk. On September 28, 1931, his thirtieth birthday arrived. As he saw it, the day dawned like a late edition headline proclaiming his personal failure. He fell into a gray mood, a cloudy depression as dark as that on the streets of New York. In essence, he felt deeply frustrated at not having achieved more. By external measure he was in splendid shape; not only was he employed, no small achievement in 1931, but at $375 a week he could easily afford to travel in the circles of those he covered. He had just landed a high-profile job that opened doors all over the city. Yet by his self-evaluation he was nowhere.

Years later his daughter recalled, "I remember my mother saying my father was lying on the bed, and it was his thirtieth birthday, and he felt he should have accomplished more than he had. . . . He was a moody person, he might have even been depressed. In those days we didn't pay attention to that."

His wife described that blue mood as "one of the unhappiest days of Ed's life. I'll never forget that day as long as I live. There he was looking as if the end of the world had come. Ed felt he was getting old and not getting where he wanted to be."

As fortunate as his life had been, he hadn't gained the one thing he so hungered for. "He didn't have national prominence—and that's what he wanted," Sylvia said. "I was perfectly happy with him the way he was but he was born with a desire to be a big success." This frustrated desire for greater recognition made him "terribly tense," she said.

What Ed wanted, in short, was to be a star like those he wrote about. He had always idolized athletic heroes—Jack Dempsey, Gene Tunney, Babe Ruth, even perhaps his former fiancée, Olympic gold medalist Sybil Bauer. Now he lived in an even brighter solar system, meeting the likes of Rodgers and Hart, Fred Astaire, Eddie Cantor, and George Gershwin. These were the mythic figures whose names were known coast to coast, who traveled on the gossamer wings of fame and renown. This is what *he* wanted, but the calendar said he was thirty and it still hadn't happened. He wasn't going to give up, of course—the desire, the hunger, burned too fiercely. He wanted to be famous. He was going to have to work on that.

Having violated his vow against gossip early on, after a few months Ed let it fall away altogether, reporting a constant stream of divorces and romantic intrigues. As he wrote about Broadway closets he used a new journalistic convention created by Walter Winchell: a series of phrases connected by ellipses. The effect was freeing, as if journalism, having loosened the moorings of propriety, would now dispense with the tired sentence-period-sentence format. "I linked Thelma Todd to Ronald Colman . . . That's wrong . . . the real romance is with a married man, and it looks like a house wrecking," he reported. "Claire Windsor, on tour with Jolson's 'Wunderbar' . . . is taking iron injections . . . She's still bothered by injuries suffered in the Phil Plant yacht crash . . . Reid, her coast honey, will join her as soon as he recovers from scars inflicted in an airplane wreck . . . But I'll tell you confidentially that there will be no marriage." In Ed's column the giddy merry-go-round of love never paused: "The Ginger Rogers–Mervyn Le Roy romance is still blazing, and Ralph Ince is going places with Mervyn's wife while she awaits the divorce decree."

The blind items, with no specific names attached, could go that extra step: "conspicuous on the [dance] floor was that well-known widow . . . with her gigolo." But even with the names attached the gossip sometimes took a darker turn. "Mrs. Violet Swanstrom plans a doctor's examination to disprove those drug charges." The gambling losses of the elite were steady diet. "Al Jolson has sworn off the gee-gees [horse races] for the balance of the season," Ed reported. And the uncle of CBS radio network head Bill Paley "wound up by blowing $27,000" in an Atlantic City casino, he wrote.

The freshman columnist freely admitted that he was a scandalmonger. In early January Ed described the ethic of the Broadway columnist—now that he was very much one of them:

> "The idea is that we go along, in our own humble way, trying to spread seeds of dissatisfaction where orchids grew before . . . Harmony is our ruin and our downfall . . . We seek discord, divorce, lawsuits, and you will pardon the smug chuckle as I say: We got them! . . . We are the vultures winging above the Empire State Building . . . Eyeing you hungrily . . . You think at night you are hearing airplanes . . . not so . . . that's us.
>
> "Scandal, gossip, rumor . . . Founded or unfounded . . . to us, they're a wagonload of hors d'oeuvre . . . Life to us is a bowl of cherries . . . with the razzes for you . . . You only offend me when you say, for instance, that I'm constructive . . . Constructive? . . . You wound me to the soul . . . You mean that I don't hurt your feelings . . . My gracious, I'm a floperoo . . . What? Oh, I do belt now and then . . . Well now, that's bet-

ter ... I wouldn't want to think I was smothering to death in a pot of honey ... Eh, what? ... You have an exclusive story for me ... Don't be crazy ... I printed that two weeks ago."

Paradoxically, as much gossip as Ed shoveled, he presumed to maintain his own sense of the puritanical. He did not, for example, approve of women who told dirty stories: "It puts them in the same catalogue with birds who carry filthy pictures in their pockets ... It is an unhealthy lewdness that adds nothing to a girl's charm ... Just as it is an ugly practice for such a talented lyricist as Harold Arlen to write double-entendre lyrics for Leitha Hill."

Although he was now a Broadway fellow, Ed made it clear he was no dandy. He was, as rival columnist Louis Sobol had described him, "a he-man type fellow." Perhaps to keep the score clear, Ed wrote regularly of the "pansies." "Bert Savoy ... Effeminate in the days when pansies wore skirts ... Today they wear swallow-tails ... Fashions change, and the pansies with them." Yet Ed readily acknowledged that not everyone shared his standoffish attitude. If big money stopped investing in speakeasies, "the late spots will be patterned after the crude loft building which houses the pansy cabaret in the 1200s on 6th Avenue," he opined. "The pansies, under the leadership of one of their veterans, have rigged out a spot that represents an investment of perhaps $50. Instead of a cash register, they use a butter tub to hold the receipts. Daubs of paint furnish the coloring. Yet Greta Garbo and other celebs storm the place to watch the effeminate men serve hard liquor."

As Ed mined the gold of celebrity news through the fall and winter of 1931–32, he also reported what he saw as the hidden truth behind its luster: the talented and the famous were not really happy. Underlying the façade of celebrity was a foundation of worry and concern. "Not long ago we had dinner with the Babe Ruths ... here must be a happy soul ... an orphan boy ... greatest idol of the country ... at a fabulous salary ... playing better than he had ever played, in his thirty seventh year ... he had every reason to be happy and content." But he wasn't happy, Ed wrote. "He was fretting over his income tax ... over the choice of a school for his daughter, Julia."

No matter who you are, his column explained, happiness is a mere chimera. "I watched Maurice Chevalier ... and Walter Donaldson ... at Abe Lyman's opening at Hollywood Gardens ... One is the matinee idol of the continent ... and the other is one of the great songwriters of all time ... These two have the world by the throat ... And Lyman is leader of one of the great bands of the country ...

"Yet Chevalier was moody ... Donaldson was inattentive ... Lyman was nervous and upset ... What is this thing called happiness?" he asked, rephrasing the lyric to the recent Cole Porter hit, "What Is This Thing Called Love?"

Part of the problem was Broadway itself. As he saw it, the street was chock full of phonies. It was a theme he returned to again and again. The phonies. He hated them.

"In case you don't know ... a phoney is a pretender ... a sham and a larcenous fraud ... and what a magnificent collection of phonies on your dear old Broadway ... They could call this stretch of pavement Phoney Boulevard ... Kept women and kept men ... Roues and men-about-town ... half-pint racketeers ... all in the parade of Boulevard de Phoney ... Insincerity marks all of them ... the moral paupers of this fastest of all centuries . . . their ambitions condensed into a single line . . . 'Mention me in your column' . . . What a magnificent ambition . . . To crash a Broadway column . . . They can't conceive of any decoration to match this one . . . The poor phonies!"

In January 1932, Ed's newfound celebrity status afforded him a sought-after opportunity: radio. The medium had arrived by the early 1930s. Although newspaper advertising was eviscerated by the Depression, radio advertising jumped ninety percent in the years following the Crash. Many Americans didn't have enough money to cover basic necessities, yet radios kept flying off storeroom shelves. Between 1928 and 1932 the number of receivers catapulted from eight million to eighteen million. Part of radio's attraction was its intimacy. Fans idolized film stars, but radio personalities visited their living rooms. The warmth and immediacy of the medium created a sea change in news and entertainment, and electronic broadcast created a new class of stars. Performers previously limited to a single theater now sang, joked, and told stories to a national audience with the flick of a switch. Many of vaudeville and legitimate theater's biggest names now angled for a chance in a medium they had at first ignored.

Walter Winchell's success in radio, through a series of twists and turns, led to the beginning of Sullivan's broadcast career. Winchell began his radio career in 1929, hired by CBS for a weekly gossip show sponsored by La Gerardine, a woman's hair tonic. As popular as Winchell was in newspapers, he was born for radio, with an intense, confidential tone that invited listeners into his fantastic milieu of celebrity. The gossip's stream of wry chatter about the personal and romantic fortunes of Hollywood and Broadway stars entranced the public.

Winchell's show caught the attention of George Washington Hill, the head of American Tobacco Company. Hill called his ad agency and told them to hire the fast-pattering gossip maven for a show sponsored by Lucky Strike cigarettes broadcast on NBC. The Lucky Strike program offered Winchell a major step up. The CBS program had paid $1,000 a week; the NBC program offered $3,500 a week and was accompanied by top-flight dance orchestras.

But the sponsor of the CBS program, La Gerardine, wouldn't let Winchell out of his contract unless he found a replacement. The new hire would need a proper radio voice and good delivery, and was required to bring celebrity guests. Winchell first asked Mark Hellinger, another Broadway reporter. Hellinger turned him down, telling Walter, "I wouldn't be known as a Winchell imitator for ten thousand a week." Walter then recommended Sidney Skolsky, a gossip columnist for the *Daily News*. Skolsky's audition served up plenty of show business tidbits but the ad agency found his voice thin and squeaky.

Walter then phoned Ed and recommended he go after the job. Ed's audition lacked Winchell's fluid patter, but he had done some emceeing and his column enabled him to deliver well-known guests. La Gerardine gave him the job. His fifteen-minute show on CBS, *Broadway's Greatest Thrills*, debuted on January 12, 1932, broadcasting Tuesday nights at 8:45. This was the opportunity he had so greatly desired—radio was an open doorway to fame—and he threw himself into it. To promote the program he took the unusual step of buying his own ad in *Variety* every week to tout that week's star.

Using an interview format, he conversed with celebrities about their lives and careers. For his debut show he pulled out all the stops, landing legendary tunesmith George M. Cohan, who, remarkably, had opened a new show on Broadway every year since 1903. The composer-producer told the story of the first performance of his patriotic crowd-rouser "Over There," during a World War I rally in which Woodrow Wilson was scheduled to attend. Adding a touch of drama, Cohan recalled that when the stage lights went out unexpectedly the audience feared it was sabotage by German spies, until a performer spontaneously broke into "Over There" to inspire the anxious crowd.

Ed only briefly mentioned his radio debut in his column, in a bit of underplayed promotion not characteristic of him. Three weeks later, in an item buried deep in his column, he wrote: "The greatest thrill I got from that first radio broadcast was the very sweet wire from the charming Delores Hutchins, at Loomis Sanitorium." With time he played up *Broadway's Greatest Thrills* much more in his column. After hosting Broadway star Jack Haley (who later played the Tin Man in *The Wizard of Oz*), he wrote, "The mail from St. Louis was unusually heavy," and reprinted part of a Haley fan letter. He worked in a mention of his radio interview of Broadway promoter Earl Carroll, whose greatest thrill was owning his own theater, by reporting that Carroll was now losing it due to the Depression's downturn.

Ed's guests that winter included his friend from the Silver Slipper, Jimmy Durante; Broadway actress Helen Morgan, whose career was launched by her version of "Can't Help Lovin' Dat Man" in the 1927 debut of *Show Boat*; the songwriting team of Lew Brown and Ray Henderson, who wrote the music for the current Broadway hit, *George White's Scandals*; Buddy Rogers, a screen idol known as "America's Boyfriend"; and Ruth Etting, a wildly popular vocalist who would have more than sixty hit records by the end of the 1930s.

On March 29, Sullivan hosted Jack Benny, in the laconic comic's radio debut. Benny would soon become one of radio's leading voices, remaining so until the mid 1950s, yet that evening he was only modestly well known, having appeared on Broadway and been a top vaudeville emcee. He began his routine on Sullivan's show by saying "Good evening, folks. This is Jack Benny. There will be a slight pause for everyone to say 'Who cares?'" That night's program was a huge hit and Ed recapped their exchange in his column. (Benny reprised the evening on his own show ten years later.)

But *Broadway's Greatest Thrills* suffered from a glaring flaw. Ed himself was not making the translation from the printed page to the radio wave. The jocular humor of his column, the sense of a flesh-and-blood Broadway wise guy who provides a peephole to the fantastic, was lost. Radio was an intimate medium, its personalities just a few feet from living room listeners, and Ed was too stiff to create this connection. In its review, *Variety* made reference to this: "In announcing Sullivan doesn't go in for gossip such as he partially columnizes each day. Rather, it is straightforward announcing, and in that style. Perhaps this is through the limited time or that Sullivan believes it is sufficient."

La Gerardine had wanted a replacement for Winchell's staccato gossip, but Ed was being straight. Too straight, based on the ratings. The broadcast industry's first rating service, Cooperative Analysis of Broadcasting, or C.A.B. (started in 1929), revealed that not many listeners tuned in to *Broadway's Greatest Thrills*. Radio's most popular show, Pepsodent's *Amos 'n' Andy*, earned a 38.1 C.A.B. rating; plenty of programs earned respectable second-tier ratings, like the *Eddie Cantor Show* (28.9), *Eno Crime Club* (22.8), and *Paul Whiteman's Orchestra* (19.1). Walter Winchell's *Lucky Strike Orchestra* earned a 19.6. Sullivan's show received an abysmal 1.5. There were dozens of programs that earned no rating at all, but among those that were assigned ratings, Ed's was in absolute last place. The management at La Gerardine wasn't happy.

In the spring of 1932, Ed juggled his radio program and daily *Graphic* column. To keep his column current he relied on what he called his "new friends," a network of Broadway denizens who fed him tips. These sources—bartenders, doormen, and theater staff who were close to the social pipeline—required cash, a generous tip, or a well-greased palm, and Ed kept the dollars flowing. "My operatives never sleep," he noted.

In one column he wrote a humorous bit about a young source who failed to get him a story.

> "At the premiere of *Jewelry Robbery* he crept up on me and pulled at my coat to attract my attention. 'Boy, oh boy,' he gasped. "I had a wonderful story for your column, Mr. Sullivan. I always try to get stories for you Mr. Sullivan!'
>
> "'What is it?' I asked. 'I'm sorry,' he said, 'but when I didn't see you I gave it to Skolsky.' With a great show of indignation, your reporter snapped: 'Well you're certainly a fine pal. Why didn't you call Winchell or Hoffman and give it to them, too?' The youngster smiled with relief: 'I've been waiting for you so I could borrow two nickels to call them.'"

But even his myriad operatives couldn't always keep up with the insatiable appetite of his column, which devoured gossip and celebrity news six days a week. When the pace became too much, Ed was adept at riffing, filling column space with nothing but his impressionistic visions of the Broadway scene, as when he spent a half column describing a gypsy girl waiting for a traffic light to change. Or he provided a touch of sardonic human interest, as when he wrote about a homeless man who was helping fight a fire, only to get roughed up by police when they arrived.

If nothing else turned up he could ruminate on the city's news. In 1932 gangster Vincent "Mad Dog" Coll was the victim of a mob hit, which put Ed in a philosophical mood:

> "The rubbing out of Vincent Coll . . . as he stood in a telephone booth . . . Putting the finger on a dial phone . . . While others were putting the finger on him . . . Makes you wonder to yourself what were his last thoughts . . . Only an insane man could be brave when Death cuts in on a busy wire . . . So if Coll choked up . . . if his heart struggled to pound out of his casing . . . And if sickening terror gripped him . . . He was entitled to that recession in courage . . . Your last bow belongs to you alone.
>
> "What a dreadful feeling must come over a Coll . . . As the evil snout of an sub-machine gun adjusts its evil leer . . . No time to cry out 'Wait just a minute please' . . . No time for explanations . . . Death has arrived . . . And the shortest path between two points . . . Is the path traveled by a leaden bullet."

Although these unstructured tone poems might have disappointed readers looking for show business news, some of Ed's riffs provided the clearest glimpse of
Broadway—and his life—as he saw it. His days and nights had changed radically
since launching his new persona as a gossip maven. As Louis Sobol had predicted,
satisfying the demands of his column was all consuming. In February, seven months
after it debuted, he acknowledged, "Like Broadway, those of us who traverse it night
after night . . . Are haggard and worn . . . We, too, slumber with one eye open . . .
Keyed to an unnatural pace. . . . Restless because of the city's restlessness . . . And
if our skin is pasty . . . it is because . . . Columnists like me . . . are awake at hours
like this . . . to write columns like this . . . for you."

By June, a year after beginning the Broadway beat, the pace of the column had
begun to not just exhaust him but to consume him.

> "Success on Broadway . . . that is, considerable success . . . Is attained
> at a terrific physical and mental expenditure . . . Family, friends, partic-
> ularly the family . . . Must be subordinated to intense concentration on
> the angles of a many-angled street . . . Probably that's why so many ro-
> mances crack up here . . .
>
> "I don't believe it's a street for happiness . . . it's a street of opportu-
> nity . . . Opportunity for work that yields cash dividends . . . So, if the peo-
> ple of Broadway expect to be happy they must first slave along the Stem for
> the dough that will later take them out of the grind . . . so long as they re-
> main on Broadway, they must expect the nervous tension of ambition."

The nervous tension of ambition. The pressure of it all was very much on Ed's
mind as the summer of 1932 arrived. He had made it on Broadway, but now events
were taking it all away from him. The hook was pulling him offstage.

The *Graphic* was sinking. The tabloid had long been hemorrhaging money; it was
as much as $7.5 million in debt by publisher Bernarr Macfadden's estimate, though
tallies of the paper's debt varied widely. In a desperate effort to save it Macfadden
had tried making the *Graphic* resemble a legitimate newspaper, publishing only stories that were, roughly speaking, factually corroborated. But it was too little too late.
The tabloid that provided Ed his Broadway column—from which all other things
flowed—wouldn't survive the summer. It was common knowledge among employees
that they would soon be out of a job.

Making matters worse, he was being replaced on his radio show. As *Variety* reported on July 5, the La Gerardine company had hired *Daily News* columnist Sidney
Skolsky to host the show. Apparently the sponsor had gotten tired of Ed's stiff announcing and poor ratings. The show had been his opening, his chance to rise above,
to gain recognition and renown. Now his broadcast career was being cut short.

Which meant that Ed was on the verge of unemployment. He had faced jobless-
ness before, on several occasions, but now he had a wife and child at home. And
now it was 1932, commonly known as the Depression's nadir. There were no more
jobs to be had, just long lines of hollow-eyed men and women waiting for their daily
soup kitchen dole. The nervous tension of ambition, indeed.

CHAPTER FIVE

Café Society

THE *GRAPHIC*, TO THE RELIEF OF RESPECTABLE NEW YORKERS, published its last issue on July 7, 1932. The following day, the city's daily dose of 2-cent scandal mongering suspended publication. The paper had filed for bankruptcy on July 2, by one account collapsing under $3.1 million of liabilities. Part of this astronomical sum was a string of unpaid libel judgments, two for $500,000 a piece, and at least two more for lesser amounts. Controversial to the end, the paper's demise provoked street demonstrations as unpaid printers and tradesman paraded up Varick Street with an effigy of Bernarr Macfadden, shouting what a reporter described as "uncomplimentary ballyhoo." The cops had to be called to contain the crowd.

For weeks afterward there was talk of bringing the *Graphic* back—optimistic scuttlebutt about investors who might be interested—but nothing came of it. In truth, the mood had passed. Those oversized headlines about suicide pacts between flappers and married men were titillating when the paper's readers had an extra nickel in their pocket. But the deepening gloom accompanying the long breadlines at Broadway and 47th Street had caught up with the *Graphic*. The paper was from a different era. Other scandal sheets, like *The Tatler* and *Town Topics*, were also felled by the Depression.

One week before the paper closed, Ed received a call from someone identifying himself as Captain Joe Patterson, the publisher of the New York *Daily News*. Would Ed like to be a Broadway columnist for the *News*? The caller invited Sullivan over to discuss the terms of his new employment. Ed could hardly believe his good fortune—in fact he didn't believe it. As soon as he put down the phone he was consumed with doubt. Could the call have been a prank? Perhaps someone he had offended in his column was exacting revenge with a cruel practical joke. Or so Ed thought; fortune this good couldn't be trusted. He immediately phoned the *Daily News* and asked: had Joseph Patterson just called him? Yes, it was verified, it had been Patterson. Amazing—Ed had just been offered a job. Relief competed with euphoria.

Getting a call from the *Daily News* publisher was like being called up to the big leagues. Patterson's father had published the Chicago *Tribune*, and Patterson had been the *Tribune*'s editor. During his army stint in World War I the flashy British tabloids had caught his eye, and he guessed the formula would succeed in America. Soon after Patterson launched the *Daily News* in 1919 it became a rousing success.

Originally called the *Illustrated Daily News* because of its emphasis on photos, this first modern American tabloid also proved to be one of the hardiest. It would survive through the decades as the majority of newspapers from that period were swallowed by larger papers or ceased publication. The *Daily News* continues to be one of New York's leading papers.

The *News* spawned a legion of competitors. The *Graphic* had been inspired by the *News*, and its booming circulation also impressed William Randolph Hearst. Soon after the tabloid's initial vaulting success, the newspaper magnate tried to buy it rather than compete with it. When Patterson refused to sell or stop publishing, Hearst launched a competing tabloid, the *Daily Mirror*. (Hearst's strategy was to hire journalistic superstars, hence Winchell's post as a *Daily Mirror* columnist.)

Patterson, an ardent socialist in his youth (though later highly conservative), wanted to publish a paper for the working man. Its style would be straightforward, and it would eschew lofty analysis. But if the *Daily News* lacked pretension, no one could say it wasn't entertaining. The paper thumbed its nose at staid journalistic tradition: its headlines blared, its front page was often exclusively photos, and its stories emphasized emotional appeal over objective observation. Like the British tabloids it copied, the *News* was half the size of traditional papers, yet its circulation quickly grew far larger. By the mid 1920s the *News* had the largest daily circulation of any paper in New York City, at seven hundred fifty thousand; in fact, its circulation would be the largest in the country until the late 1940s.

Where the *Graphic* had dismissed any concern for journalistic propriety, the *Daily News* walked to the edge without jumping off. Its coverage could be sensational, even lurid, but it could not be fabricated. Patterson's guideline was "no private scandal or private love affairs," though if they became public through divorce proceedings they were fair game. Patterson understood the power of celebrity news and so nurtured a stable of gossip reporters. As Ed joined the paper, it already had two established show business columnists, John Chapman and Sidney Skolsky.

Although Sullivan had blasted his competitors as he launched his *Graphic* column, decrying the moral turpitude of the veteran gossips, he launched his *Daily News* column as an incumbent. As he began his *News* column in mid July—just two weeks after the *Graphic* folded—he made no grand proclamations, he simply went back to work chronicling Broadway life. His salary was $200 a week, a sharp step down from the *Graphic*'s $375 but a highly desirable paycheck nonetheless. He began with three columns a week, which put him in a kind of probation status; many Broadway scribes turned out a daily column as he had at the *Graphic*.

While his debut featured no grand announcements, his new column displayed a markedly different attitude. Ed's new approach would not be as colorful or as free as it had been at the *Graphic*; there would be no more half-page descriptions of gypsy girls at stoplights and no philosophic meanderings about mob slayings. He was now a coolheaded, evenhanded veteran, like his colleagues Skolsky and Chapman.

More significantly, he was now an unabashed populist. At the *Graphic* he had written only periodically about the Depression and the struggles of the common folk; primarily his column had been a window into the lives of the swank set, even as his theme of their essential unhappiness pulled away the curtain. At the *News* he would still cover this half-mythic world. His column was full of stories about people like actress Peggy Hopkins Joyce, whose "only drink was champagne" and who went out on the town in a $3,000 ermine coverlet. As he churned out tidbits about actors, singers, cabaret stars, and well-to-do socialites—their dizzying round-robin of romance rotating faster than their nightclub of choice—the portrait could transport the average reader to a fabulous world.

But getting much more weight were the average people themselves. His writing now focused on and celebrated—empathized with—the life of the common man. As a freshman Broadway columnist he had been a fabulist with a touch of populism; now the populism came first. The shift was in keeping with the times, and with his new employer. The *Graphic* had embraced the giddy, no-tomorrow 1920s; the *Daily News*, sometimes called a newspaper that wore overalls, was an archetypical representative of the populism of the 1930s.

Soon after beginning his *News* column, Ed wrote about the phrase "You can't do that to me," and how often it expresses desperation. "All the ache and hurt that can be summoned is compressed into these six words," he wrote. "The labor and work of a lifetime is about to be swept away as a veteran employee is dismissed from a business office. He wants to cry out that he has children at home to be fed and clothed . . . But his heart has stopped beating its normal tempo . . . and he can utter only six words: 'You can't do that to me.'" Ed incorporated this vox populi theme in his gossip blurbs by reporting the romances of people like Artie Cohen, a Broadway tailor who eloped with his bride to Rye, New York.

And Sullivan seemingly never passed up the chance to include items like those that chastised the "nationally-known comic [who] chiseled $2.50 from the pay of $7.50-a-day extras on the local Warner lot." He tweaked actor Charlie Winniger, then starring on Broadway, because "his refusal to cut his "Show Boat" salary from $1,000 a week to $750 a week may throw 230 people out of work."

His anecdotes were now more often about life outside the world of affluence:

> "Overhead the L trains rattled and jolted along, between grimy buildings . . . On the street surface, cars honked impatiently and tense-faced traffic cops, nearing the end of a wearying tour, signaled curtly . . . In front of a restaurant, two derelicts feasted their eyes on the day's menu, as if unable to tear their eyes from it. I thought to myself, 'Here is the very essence of this huge city of ours' and turned to go, almost colliding with a tall mendicant, his face coarsened by a two-day stubble of beard . . . 'Cowboy songs, Mister?' he said . . . 'Get the songs of the open range, 5 cents' . . . Overhead the L trains rattled as I paid him his modest fee . . . 'Songs of the Open Range' . . . On Third Ave. and 42nd Street."

It's likely that Ed's populism came to him naturally, but it was also an effective competitive strategy for a columnist in a crowded field. It set him apart from many of his competitors, like the *News*' Sidney Skolsky, who would no sooner report the elopement of a tailor than print a Sunday school prayer. By playing to his audience, mingling mentions of the hoi polloi with the illuminati, Ed curried favor with those readers who could never hope to sip a champagne cocktail, which was most of them. He was an anti-elitist covering the elite.

But hard-pressed average readers also wanted release from the daily grind, and Ed gave it to them. These readers turned to Broadway columns for the same reason they flipped on a radio: to be transported, to enter a fantasy world. Ed was their membership card to an exclusive club, a fantastic world sometimes referred to as "café society."

The milieu known loosely as café society was a glittering alloy of screen and stage performers, radio personalities, star athletes, debutantes, musicians, old money socialites, press agents, promoters, and producers: those who were talented and those who wanted to associate with the talented. Despite the Depression, café society rubbed elbows nightly in 1930s Manhattan. Its gathering places were nightclubs like the Colony, El Morocco, Dave's Blue Room, the Hollywood, and—foremost— the Stork Club, nightspots where entrance alone—if you could get past the doorman—would set you back $5 or even $10.

This gathering of the beautiful and the lucky was a living incarnation of what moviegoers paid two dimes to see on-screen in the 1930s: cool glamour, light conversation attended by chilled champagne, and romances begun while fox-trotting to elegant orchestra music. That right outside the door the unemployment rate was twenty-five percent made this privileged party seem closer to dreamscape than reality.

Being a star in this world meant getting noticed, being one of those that others mentioned when they talked about their evening at Lindy's or Jimmy Kelly's. One of the best ways to do this was to appear, as frequently as possible, in Broadway's leading gossip columns. In an era before television, these columns had inordinate power on the celebrity social scene. To rate a boldface tidbit in the pages of the *Daily News*, the *Post*, or the *Daily Mirror* meant you were a somebody, you existed, that others would turn their heads as you walked in. Ed, as a columnist for the *News*— far above the ever-shaky *Graphic*—was now the ultimate insider in this scene. His *News* berth made him a player, someone whose opinion was talked about and sought after, a leading social arbiter of café society.

The job allowed him to live in his natural habitat. Ed was a nightly sight at Broadway's openings and ritzy watering holes, dressed in a tailored double-breasted suit, cigarette in hand, hair slicked straight back, socializing with an ever-expanding network of performers, politicos, socialites, and athletes. A magazine profile from the mid 1930s described him: "He seldom gets home before five a.m., in the meanwhile having taken in, on a typical night, '21,' the Stork Club, the Hollywood, Dave's Blue Room, Lindy's, and Jimmy Kelly's. . . . Courvoisier brandy is his only but not single drink; then it's bed until one or two in the afternoon. The column is written—at home. That takes a couple of hours and Sullivan then drives down to the *Daily News*, reads his mail, and waits while the composing room gives him a proof."

Central to his column were the vagaries of love among the smart set, the intoxicating sexual merry-go-round of Broadway romance:

> "Take, for instance, slender and blonde June Knight . . . her affairs of the heart have kept my operatives working in double shifts since she arrived here to "hot cha" for Ziegfeld . . . First it was Elliot Myer . . . Then it was

> Elliot Sperber . . . Succeeded by Leo Friede . . . Who, in turn gave way to Sailing Baruch, Jr., . . . Neil Andrews stepped in when Baruch stepped out . . . Now it looks as though Tommy Manville, Jr., is the lucky guy."

Ed reported on a mythic group of people who had been liberated from the staid sexual mores of Victorian America. The 1920s had seen a revolution in morals and manners. Women, having picketed the White House and gotten hauled away in paddy wagons, had won the right to vote. Hemlines inched up and young ladies went out on the town by themselves. In 1926, Mae West premiered her play *Sex*, which scandalized the public with tunes like "Honey, Let Yo' Drawers Hang Low"—and scored a box office bonanza. And though hemlines had fallen with the crash, something had been loosened by that giddy decade, and Ed's column covered the results. He dished out a heady catalog of morsels like "Phil Baker, the only bird who can make love over the top of an accordion" and "Maurice Chevalier, who'd rather go places with his pal Primo Carnera, than make love to Jeanette MacDonald. . . ." Printing material like this would have been forbidden not that many years previously—and would seem merely quaint a few decades hence—but it sold newspapers in the 1930s.

Ed's reports of the rapid pace of modern love, which in his column seemed to twirl faster than ever, offered readers a vicarious thrill. "Romances fizzle and burn out in a hurry on the Queerialto that is tagged Broadway . . . the big heart affairs pass into the hands of receivers quicker than that," he reported. (Sullivan invented his own slang term for Broadway, "Queerialto," a combination of "queer"—he always found the Broadway world odd—and "Rialto," after the famous Broadway theater.) If he could fit in a bit of moralizing with his coverage of romance, all the better:

> "Funny, the reactions of the fellows who are involved in these affairs of the cardiac . . . Tommy Manville, Jr., heir to the asbestos millions . . . is typical of the wealthier playboys of the Main Stem . . . Interested in the lovelies of the stage, Manville, like his fellows, will go just so far . . . The breaking point arrives when a column like this reports that Manville is thinking of buying an engagement ring . . . The current romance is dead the following day . . . to the wealthy fellows, wedding bells make a noise like a police riot car."

The *News* gave Sullivan wide latitude in terms of what he covered, and, like his TV show in later years, his column offered something for many audiences: romantic travails, theater news, political predictions, show business gossip, odd quotes that celebrities gave him, and bits of shopworn wisdom. It was all jumbled together without any differentiation, a stream of consciousness Broadway diary, like the circuitous route taken by a cabbie trolling all of Manhattan. On a daily basis he veered from wedding news, denoted as "hunting for a license bureau," to announcing a starlet's pregnancy, referred to as "the arrival of Sir Stork," to alimony payments, all within the space of a single paragraph.

As at the *Graphic*, he rarely wrote detailed theater criticism, but he often passed pithy one-line judgment on new Broadway shows (which, if positive, were used in a show's advertisements). "By far the smartest premiere of the winter season . . . Was the inaugural performance of *Design for Living*, featuring Noël Coward, Alfred Lunt, and Lynn Fontanne," he opined. But even in these hit-and-run reviews he usually spent more ink on the evening's social scene than on the dramaturgy.

In the Coward opening, he went on to list many of the well-heeled theater patrons in the audience. "Coward's play delights this audience of the elite . . . it is as light as champagne bubbles, and produces the same gayety . . . You leave the theatre and mounted cops are holding back the curious sidewalk onlookers . . . There is a double line of cars in West 47th street, waiting for their mesdames and messieurs . . . Most of them are Rolls Royces . . . it was that kind of opening," Ed observed, displaying, as he often did, his sense of being a reporter looking at the privileged from afar.

One of his column's constants were bite-sized descriptions of famous people, opinionated portraits of those with whom he rubbed elbows. He would string together a number of these, as if bringing the reader to an exclusive Broadway party.

> "Jack Benny, stage, radio, and movie comedian . . . Sleepiest of all Broadway personalities . . . He invites 20 people to 55 Central Park West, and then curls up on the living room couch and goes to sleep . . . On the level . . . If he could learn to sleep standing up, he'd make a fine cop . . . Estelle Taylor, ex-frau of ex-champ Dempsey . . . one of the keenest wits I've ever encountered . . . With a marvelous sense of humor that bewilders plenty of Coast dumbbells . . . [actress] Lupe Velez, madcap of movieland . . . Whose 70 coats, 230 dresses, and 126 pairs of shoes don't mean a thing because she bought them only for ONE man . . . And then Gary Cooper wasn't the fellow she thought he was."

When he couldn't actually be present he relied, as always, on his citywide network of sources developed while at the *Graphic*. They allowed him to report that Jimmy Cagney was in town and "secretly registered" at the Wellington Hotel, or that the Hollywood party thrown for George Burns and Gracie Allen featured some odd sights: "On the way to the dining room, a naked fellow, sitting in a tub of water, hailed the guests as they passed the door, and advised them not to eat, as the food was terrible."

Sullivan was quick to trumpet any tidbits he scooped his competitors on, however reliable the scoop might be. "Months before Wild Bill Donovan forced his recognition as a gubernatorial candidate, the news was printed in this column . . . A week before Jimmy Walker resigned, my Monday column predicted it." (In truth, predicting the forced resignation of the embattled mayor, known as the "Night Mayor" for his fondness for the high life, was hardly prescient; at any rate, a few months earlier Ed had predicted Walker would be cleared.)

"The information I got late last night . . . is loaded with political dynamite," he wrote in October 1932, three weeks before the election that sent Franklin Roosevelt to the White House. "One who is in the know named for me the cabinet which he says Franklin D. Roosevelt plans to install at Washington . . . and it is SOME combination." Ed listed eight members of the potential FDR cabinet, only one of whom became an actual cabinet member. In the early days of the Roosevelt administration, Ed was boundless in his support of the new president, as was the *Daily News* itself. In April 1933, he enthused: "Hugest individual hit of the season, Franklin Delano Roosevelt!!!"

True to the ethic of the Broadway columnist, Ed's scoops were sometimes more timely than accurate. But that was the nature of this new brand of journalism. (The *New York Post* would later print page after page of Walter Winchell's mistakes, his so-called "wrongoes.") The Broadway column was less about authoritative news than it was the diary of a community, an ephemeral compilation of what the Manhattan tribe was chattering and whispering about. The writings of the Broadway columnists from this period were riddled with factual inaccuracies, half-truths, conjecture, and the alcohol-fueled imaginings born of typing against a 5:30 A.M. deadline. But while these columnists, Sullivan among them, provoked a public outcry from those who called them a moral corruption, their readers didn't seem to care. The world that Ed was writing about was hungry for coverage, and those on the outside looking in were even hungrier for the details.

Sullivan's unstinting dedication to his column left little time for home life. Replacing the domestic scene was a blur of Manhattan nightspots. Several months after landing his *Daily News* post he wrote about his recent nocturnal jaunt with Freeman Gosden and Charlie Correll, stars of the *Amos 'n' Andy* radio show, then listened to by tens of millions of fans weekly. "I left them at 5 A.M., and I was pale and haggard," he wrote. "Dave Marks, the toy millionaire, was in equally bad condition . . . 'You're not going home, Ed?' Gosden queried reproachfully . . . I assured him that I was going home . . . 'That's too bad,' said Correll, 'we thought that as it's only 5 A.M., we could go to Place Pigalle and then taper off with a cup of coffee.'" Being out all night was an occupational hazard for the columnist.

But Ed never missed home life. He seemed to take little interest in it. As recalled by his grandson Rob Precht, Ed found the concept of family life to be greatly overrated. He did, however, continue to take Sylvia out to dinner almost every night, as when they were courting. Sylvia was invariably elegantly dressed—she loved to go out—and the two made the rounds of New York's fashionable restaurants; this also allowed Ed to continue his society reporting. Sylvia never learned to cook and never had the slightest desire to do so. Eventually the couple would move into an apartment with hardly any kitchen at all. As their daughter Betty recalled, "My parents never ate at home. My father liked to be able to choose what he wanted to eat. I don't think he was that thrilled about eating."

Betty herself was cared for by a paid companion during Ed and Sylvia's evenings out. "When I was about two years old, my parents took me to Saratoga [in New York] to see the races. I was a very little girl, and I banged with my feet on the bottom of the table," she remembered. "And my father was so distressed, embarrassed, that I really don't think I went out with them until I was twelve. Until I could act like a young adult." Her companion took her to eat at a succession of Manhattan restaurants, though Betty chose less formal places than those frequented by her parents.

As Ed took little time for home life, he also found little time for close friendships. In his twenties he had sought the companionship of boxer Johnny Dundee and soft-shoe dancer Lou Clayton, both largely as mentors. But while he now traveled a social circle as large as the Manhattan phone book, he was close with virtually no one. The sole exception was Joe Moore, the former speed skating star who was now a press agent, and whose friendship with Ed made him a conduit to Sullivan's column. But even this was as much professional as personal. Having close friends "wasn't in his nature," recalled his daughter.

Covering the famous only whetted Ed's appetite to be famous himself. His *Daily News* column greatly increased his profile but didn't satisfy this core desire. That he was now a Broadway somebody only made the question more urgent: how could he turn himself from a reporter into somebody who was reported on? His first attempt at radio had been canceled, but in 1933 he found a far more intriguing opportunity: the movies. Or rather, he didn't find the opportunity, he created it. Sullivan conceived of and wrote a film script, featuring himself as the star, called *Mr. Broadway*. He convinced a film laboratory and a large New York optical house to back the movie. To help him, Ed hired Edgar G. Ulmer, who later became a leading B movie director, and actor Johnnie Walker, who had starred in scores of silent movies.

Mr. Broadway was a two-part film, with the first part a cinematic portrayal of the columnist's life as he made his rounds every night, and the second part a short melodrama. At the opening of the fifty-nine-minute movie, Ed introduces himself, then tours three of Manhattan's busiest nightspots, the Hollywood, the Casino, and the Paradise. Along the way he talks with, or watches the performances of, a glittering galaxy of celebrities: Jack Benny and Mary Livingston, actor Bert Lahr, vocalist Ruth Etting, dancer Hal LeRoy, vaudevillians Benny Fields and Blossom Seeley, bandleaders Eddie Duchin and Abe Lyman, and boxers Jack Dempsey, Maxie Rosenbloom, and Primo Carnera.

At about the film's forty-five-minute mark, Ed confides that there's a broken heart for every broken light on Broadway, reprising the theme of "unhappiness despite stardom" that ran throughout his *Graphic* column. At this point the film turns into an overheated melodrama about a young woman, her two suitors, and a stolen necklace. The director, Ulmer, later said he "didn't like it at all, because Sullivan forced

On the town, 1935: As a gossip columnist with a daily column to fill, Sullivan circulated through Manhattan's Café Society nearly every night of the week. Here he is at the Versailles Club with, from right, his wife Sylvia, Ziegfeld Follies performer Mary Alice Rice, and silent screen star Conrad Nagel. (New York *Daily News*)

it into one of these moonlight-and-pretzel things. It was a nightmare, a mixture of all kinds of styles."

Reviewers agreed. "There is nothing particularly new or entertaining in all this unless one happens to be the type that enjoys glimpsing the near greats at play," sniffed *The New York Times*, which pronounced the story element "unintentional burlesque." *Variety* found the nightclub tour interesting but judged the movie unsatisfactory overall: "As entertainment, it fails to measure up." The low-budget production was "many leagues behind the average as to story, action, direction, photography." As for Ed's soap opera at the film's end, "The meller [melodrama] sequence to which [the] film cuts in telling the story is very amateurishly carried out. . . . It shows how a man murders his best friend to please a girl whom he later learns is a prostie."

Although the movie was roundly panned, Ed tried again in 1934 with *Ed Sullivan's Headliners*. This twenty-minute short was directed by Milton Schwarzwald, who directed dozens of 1930s musical-comedy shorts; the film's music was supervised by Sylvia Fine, a composer who later wrote some sharp material for singer-actor Danny Kaye, her husband. The short, again, was a collection of appearances by Broadway's leading lights, with Sullivan as tour guide. But despite its celebrity sightings and directorial and musical talent, *Headliners*, like *Mr. Broadway*, disappeared without a trace. Because both films were made without the help of a studio, it's likely they received limited distribution. Whatever minimal success they might have had, they failed in their primary goal: to launch Ed in a film career. Nevertheless, he wasn't giving up.

After being hired by the *Daily News* in 1932 to write three columns a week, by early 1933 the paper promoted Sullivan to full status, with five Broadway columns weekly. He had made it on the Main Stem. As if to prove he was a force to be reckoned with, he began the year by picking a fight with no less a star than Eddie Cantor.

Having grown up in Yiddish theater, Cantor sang and joked his way to vaudeville's pinnacle, topping it off by winning a role in Ziegfeld's *Midnight Frolics* revue in 1916. His physical comedy fueled a passel of wildly popular silent films through the 1920s. Soon after the advent of talkies in 1927, Samuel Goldwyn hired him to croon, mug, and dance in a string of lavishly produced musical comedies. By 1933 Cantor was one the country's most admired celebrities.

Sullivan, in a column segment called "Cantor Goes to Dogs," claimed that the performer had stolen the comic dog routine of vaudevillian Bert Lahr. Worse, he compared Cantor to Milton Berle, an up-and-coming comedian well-known for lifting material from other comics. "I can't give Cantor a great deal of credit in lifting Lahr's act," Ed wrote. "If Broadway has been intolerant of Milton Berle, a youngster, it should be doubly of Cantor for establishing a nasty precedent."

Cantor, enraged, phoned Sullivan and cursed at him vehemently. In a follow-up column, Ed made sport of the conflict, recounting Cantor's anger as a source of amusement. He described the performer's verbal tongue lashing with typographical discretion:

> 1:04 A.M.—"Hello, Ed, this is Eddie Cantor. I just read that story and I want to tell you something. . . . I never had anything to do with those *!*"!* dogs! . . ."

1:05 A.M. (Sullivan) "Now wait a min-"

1:05¼ A.M. Cantor—"No, let me finish. . . . In the first place I'm not doing the dog act, Jessel's doing it. . . . I don't need those *!*"! dogs in my act . . . ."

It turned out that Sullivan's claims of plagiarism were inaccurate. But Ed, characteristically, admitted no mistake. Instead he obfuscated, conceding that another producer had indeed been responsible, yet noting that the theatrical theft occurred in Cantor's revue. At the skirmish's end he threw one last column jab at the popular performer: "I suggest Cantor urge Jessel to drop Lahr's dog act. That would do more to discourage theatrical banditti than any preaching in this space."

The point Ed was making, really, was that he was now big enough to tweak a Broadway heavyweight. Just nineteen months before he had been a sports columnist, but now he was scolding one of the Main Stem's top names, a star with an adoring national following. He had arrived.

Furthermore, his minor tussle with Cantor was Ed at his most natural: in conflict. As in the athletic fields of Port Chester, he always dove in headfirst, never backing down and never fearing the resultant split lip. For him conflict was as comfortable as breathing. And, it was good for the column. In tweaking Cantor, Ed was doing what Broadway columnists did. They engaged in arguments; they fought, bickered, and had spats with whomever was at hand, regardless of the merits of the case. It was a reliable way to keep their column a topic of conversation, and to ensure people turned to it shortly after glancing at the front page.

Toward the end of 1934, Ed combined his taste for journalistic fisticuffs with his populist instincts. As Christmas approached he used his column to write an open letter to Barbara Hutton, heiress to the massive Woolworth fortune. In the popular imagination Hutton was a cipher for easy wealth and the high life. At age four her mother had committed suicide, leading the tabloids to dub Hutton the "Poor Little Rich Girl." In 1933, at age twenty-one, she inherited the $50 million Woolworth estate. She was then married to her first of seven husbands, Russian-born Prince Mdivani, commonly thought of as a society playboy.

Ed wrote Hutton a holiday request. "How about establishing an annual Princess Barbara Christmas Dinner for some of the poor of New York City?" he asked, suggesting she donate one thousand Christmas baskets to charity.

The item was characteristic of Ed's writing, which played to his Depression-worn readers while reporting on the glittering set. But Ed didn't stop with his request. He went on to give Hutton, and especially her husband, a journalistic thrashing:

> "The unreality of your existence must be boring, Princess. You have a husband who has little or no relation to everyday life . . . I have heard grim and resolute men say some nasty things about your husband . . . I have heard underworld chieftains speak about him and his apparently callous disregard for human suffering, and I would not want them to speak that way about me."

The article's arm-twisting request for money was decried by, among others, a writer in *The New Yorker* magazine's "Talk of the Town" section, who opined, "We think the time has come for someone to do something about the Broadway columnists who write open letters to people for money." Hutton, seeking defense from the full-bore fusillade—she called it blackmail—sought the help of Walter Winchell. Winchell eagerly took up battle against his *News* counterpart, firing a return volley in his *Daily Mirror* column:

> "We endorse anybody who helps the poor, but that's beside the argument . . . The open-letter sender took pains to point out that her husband wasn't popular with the gang chiefs 'who would like to meet him on some waterfront.' A remark, incidentally that some of the 'boys' resented . . . we subscribe to the sentiment of many who considered the article in the ugliest taste . . . and we pledge them all, that every time anybody uses (or abuses) a newspaper in that manner, we'll fight it and protest against it at the top of our lungs and typewriter . . . That means YOU!"

But Sullivan's strong-arm tactic prevailed. One week before Christmas a $5,000 check arrived from Hutton. And Ed, in his manner, thanked her. He wrote an open letter to New York's children, describing the many letters he had received from needy parents:

> "There's one letter from one of your mothers, and it is typical . . . She says that the three of you had chopped meat for Thanksgiving, and the older boy said: 'Mamma, why aren't you and papa eating?' . . . She told you that she and your dad had eaten earlier and that they weren't hungry, but listen, you three little kids . . . Your mother and father were fibbing . . . When you grow up, I want you to be pretty swell to them. [These parents don't ask for much,] just enough to stuff small stomachs on Christmas Day . . . it seems to me that in the richest city in the world, that is a reasonable request. A very lovely lady, who doesn't want her name used, thinks that it is a reasonable request, too . . . she's the kind of lady you read about in story books . . . She sent me a check for $5,000."

Although Ed had achieved his goal, the incident marked a new season in his relationship with Walter Winchell. They would now be archrivals.

It hadn't always been so. There was a period after Sullivan took over Winchell's former spot at the *Graphic* that it looked as if the two, while professional rivals, might have something of a friendship. Walter had called Ed about the CBS radio opening, and Ed had sent Walter a series of affectionate notes. "Your Monday column still fills me with respectful amazement," he wrote in one missive to Walter. "It's gorgeous great. Where you get it, I don't know but as I pay better dough, I believe your operatives, with the possible exception of Dorothy Parker, will see the error of their ways and get on the Sullivan bandwagon."

After Winchell got into a contretemps at the Casino Park Hotel, in which stage producer Earl Carroll told him he wasn't "fit to be with decent people" because of his brand of gossip, and Winchell had stood his ground—the incident became the talk of Broadway—Ed dashed him off a lighthearted memo: "If you let me know who's fighting at the Casino next week I would like to make my reservations in advance." Even after Ed moved to the *Daily News*, establishing himself in a secure post, he sent Walter a note combining flattery with affectionate chiding. A recent Winchell radio show, Sullivan opined in his letter, hadn't lived up to the quality of

Walter's column; however, Ed confided, "you are the only one for whom I hold a sincere personal and professional respect." When Walter's nine-year-old daughter Gloria died on Christmas Eve of 1932, Ed and Sylvia sent a condolence note. But by 1934 their relationship had changed. Ed was no longer a freshman columnist, and any need to curry favor with an upperclassman was gone. They would henceforth only snarl at one another.

An element in Ed's column that was as constant as conflict was his appreciation of female pulchritude. An attractive woman was "an eyeful," and he used the phrase frequently. The avenues of Manhattan were chock-full of such creatures, by Sullivan's account. In a typical column, he wrote about spending the evening at a Greenwich Village nightclub owned by Barney Gallant. "The other night, sitting in the half-gloom of the place . . . I asked him the one question he has always avoided . . . I asked him who, in his opinion, was the most gorgeous woman he'd ever seen."

To further investigate New York beauty, he assembled an "All-American, All-Gal Eleven," a mock all-star football team of female performers:

> "Picking the first team, my All-American, All-Gal Eleven, was no part of a cinch . . . I spent a small fortune taking out each of the candidates, feeding 'em, and noting their reactions.
>
> "In the course of my selections, I had to drop at least twenty girls for one reason or another. I had Peggy Joyce lined up for quarterback, but when she insisted on magnums of champagne for the training table I had to let her go. Claire Carter was ideal for tackle and she would have added blonde charm to the forward wall, but she wouldn't leave Jay C. Flippen for practice."

Not all of the women were picked because they were an eyeful. Gracie Allen, who played a ditzy counterpart to George Burns' straight man, was chosen as quarterback for her ability to confuse the defense. Aunt Jemima, a heavyset vaudeville singer later memorialized as the advertising icon for a pancake syrup, was selected for her heft.

A few weeks later, Ed assembled a corresponding men's Broadway all-star team, but he gave it short shrift by comparison, and apparently felt it unnecessary to take each man to dinner.

In the fall of 1933, Ed's high profile as a *Daily News* columnist led to a series of invitations to produce and host charity shows. In November he organized and emceed an all-black show for the Urban League benefit at Manhattan's Town Hall, presenting tap dancer Bill "Bojangles" Robinson, singing quartet the Southernaires, and the Nicholas Brothers, a two-brother vaudeville tap dance team. The following evening he emceed a revue he produced for the Jewish Philanthropic Societies, held at the Waldorf-Astoria hotel, featuring a raft of radio and stage stars.

At the end of November he walked onstage for an event that would mark the beginning of a life-long career: his first variety show.

The manager of Manhattan's Paramount Theatre, Boris Morros, invited him to produce and host the show. The phone call from Morros became a favorite anecdote

Broadway tough guy: although he would later present himself as the staid guardian of the American living room, Sullivan came of age in the rough-and-tumble of the 1920s New York newspaper business. This 1954 photo reveals the streetwise side of the showman. (Globe Photos)

of Ed's, though it appears to be an exaggeration. Morros called Sullivan to offer him $1,000 for a one-week run; for this fee, Ed would choose and pay the performers, taking the remaining money for himself. Ed—overjoyed by the lucrative offer— said, "You must be crazy." In Sullivan's telling, Morros thought the columnist was negotiating and so quickly raised the offer to $1,500. They went back and forth like this, and by the end of the day Morros agreed to pay him $3,750, according to Sullivan. It's highly unlikely that a theater manager in the depth of the Depression would almost quadruple his offer based on a simple misunderstanding. But the anecdote portrays Ed as highly sought after, and he loved to repeat it. Whatever the actual negotiation process, he readily agreed.

To organize the show, he relied on a format with a rich tradition: vaudeville. By the early 1930s classic vaudeville was on its last legs. The Depression meant there were fewer people with an extra dime, and movies and radio were offering overwhelming competition. After the first talkie in 1927 the allure of moving pictures had proven irresistible, and radio brought theater into listeners' homes for free. As Ed had written in 1932, "No longer does an actor boast of playing ten weeks at the Palace . . . Now they're interested only in how many stations they're on." Vaudeville had grown stale and dated as many veteran acts offered the same routine year after year. Yet the American taste for the new and different had continued apace, the Depression notwithstanding. Forward-looking social commentators in the early 1930s were writing nostalgic eulogies for vaudeville.

Although vaudeville circuits were closing, the form's guiding principles would live on; its roots ran too deep to disappear. Borne of the English music hall, Yiddish theater, and the traveling minstrel show, vaudeville had come into its own in America in the 1880s and had flourished for decades. Several generations of American performers grew up on its stage, including Bob Hope, Jack Benny, Al Jolson, Bill "Bojangles" Robinson, W.C. Fields, Mae West, Will Rogers, Ethel Waters, Jimmy Cagney, Bessie Smith, Burns and Allen, Fred Astaire, Gene Kelly, Sammy Davis, Jr., and the Marx Brothers.

Ethnic distinctions were very pronounced in vaudeville. Irish, Italian, and Jewish performers played their routines according to the broad stereotypes associated with these groups. Present in almost all shows was a blackface act, typically a white performer whose face was blackened with burned cork, affecting a dialect and playing the role of a happy-go-lucky shiftless black man for laughs. The crude caricature of blackface routines was a facet of vaudeville that appeared most dated by the 1930s.

A vaudeville show moved at a relentless tempo, with a blink-and-you-miss-it succession of one-legged tap dancers, comics, ventriloquists, blackface song and dance acts, legitimate musical theater, jugglers, acrobats, and one-liner artists, all pushed along by a master of ceremonies who kept things moving—briskly, at all times. If you didn't like a routine there was no time to get bored; you'd soon see a new one.

If people enjoyed watching it, an act usually found its way to vaudeville. The Mayo Brothers did a two-man dance-acrobatics routine on a small tabletop. One popular performer was a skilled regurgitator who swallowed live fish and brought them back up at will. Jack Spoons lifted chairs with his teeth while he played the spoons, and Joe Frisco smoked a cigar while doing soft-shoe. Lady Alice balanced trained rats on both arms, with a rodent on top of her head that was trained to blow into a kazoo. Fuzzy Night and his Little Piano featured a man who danced with his piano.

The audience felt that their 10-cent ticket gave them the right to participate as much as the performers. The hecklers and "gallery gods," as vocal audience members were known, voiced their opinion with full-throated freedom, letting fly with a thin shower of coins or last week's leftover produce. If the jeers of the gallery gods pronounced an act unworthy, a large hook pulled the performer offstage.

Vaudeville's core principle was offering something for everyone. The businessmen who ran the major circuits, most notably Benjamin Keith and Edward Albee, knew that an all-inclusive philosophy drew the biggest audience. A single show might offer the likes of Mae West making the men roar with pleasure at her risqué "shimmy" dances; a well-muscled and shirtless Man of Steel providing male pulchritude for the ladies; for recent émigrés, Benny Rubin telling funny stories in Yiddish dialect and Maggie Cline, the "Irish Queen," belting out *Throw Him Down, McCloskey*; the Nicholas Brothers, two young black boys in elegant suits, dancing a dazzling tap routine; and Poodles Hanneford playing the slapstick clown. Vaudeville was the great wellspring of American entertainment, the heterogeneous offering of every voice. All of its acts existed side by side in a show business melting pot, exposing all the audience members to the dissimilar tastes of their seatmates. The performers, too, experienced cross-cultural pollination, as acts reached across ethnic divisions to steal the comic or musical inventions of their competitors.

Something for everyone, and everyone was invited: the credo of the Keith–Albee circuit was family entertainment. Vaudeville houses had been bawdy places, but under Keith and Albee's iron-fisted control the shows were cleaned up. It was good for business. The use of vulgarity onstage was strictly prohibited under threat of instant dismissal. Benjamin Keith once advertised that he employed a Sunday school teacher at rehearsals to ensure propriety—though vaudeville shows were earthier than that suggests. But certainly the whole family could attend, kids and all.

Part of vaudeville's "something for everyone" formula was appealing to the local tastes of the city the show found itself in. Local jokes were inserted into stock skits and a burg's major ethnic groups were played to. Nowhere was this big tent approach as complex and cacophonous as in New York City. With its divergent immigrant population, satisfying New York audiences compelled producers to cater to a discordant quilt of attitudes and backgrounds. Fortunately for the city's showmen, every performer they needed for this unlikely task was locally available. New York was vaudeville's heart, its mecca that all vaudevillians dreamed of.

The Olympian pinnacle of New York vaudeville was the Palace, at Broadway and 47th Street. Just thinking about the Palace brought a faraway gleam to a performer's eye. In 1919 its brightest stars were commanding the heavenly salary of $2,500 a week. In the late 1920s, Eddie Cantor made $7,700 a week. However, by the early 1930s even the Palace was fading. Despite some glorious 1931 shows by Kate Smith, Sophie Tucker, and Burns and Allen, by the early 1930s it was largely a movie house.

The Paramount, where Ed produced his first show in November 1933, was also in transition. The theater was hedging its bet between film and vaudeville. For one ticket price, patrons saw both a live stage show and a Hollywood film, one following the other. This practice would become standard in New York theaters throughout the 1930s and 1940s. Sullivan's Paramount revue, called *Gems of the Town*, shared the bill with the recently released musical comedy *Take a Chance*, starring James Dunn and June Knight. (Ed had reported on Knight's love life in his column.)

Sullivan's variety show at the Paramount was not classic vaudeville, though it was close. The program featured a similar up-tempo parade of fast-paced acts with an emcee as a central ringmaster. But Sullivan left out some of vaudeville's most characteristic routines, like blackface minstrel singing and broadly ethnic acts. To headline the show he booked clown-comic Jimmy Savo, a top vaudeville star who had played the Palace in its prime; Charlie Chaplin had called him "the best pantomimist in the world." That night at the Paramount he bounced and bounded all over the stage. The show's reviewer, who enjoyed the show, wrote that Savo, "knows when to strike; when to efface himself; when to leave the stage altogether; and how to get the maximum effect out of a sudden, unheralded return." Sharing the bill with Savo were two tap dancing acts, Betty Jane Cooper and the Lathrop Brothers, and an acrobatic troupe, the Uierios. Based on his other shows from this period, it's likely that Ed added a contemporary touch to his revue: introducing celebrity athletes or performers from the audience, whom he had invited to be on hand.

In essence, Sullivan's Paramount stint was what was then called a variety show. It was updated vaudeville, a quick-stepping stage show offering something for everyone—comedy, music, acrobatics—without the most dated acts. (The terms "variety" and "vaudeville" had been used interchangeably to describe stage shows for many years, and "vaudeville," though the genre was declared dead, would still be used for years to come.)

Vaudeville's near-death state probably contributed to Paramount Theatre manager Boris Morros' decision to invite Ed to produce a show. As vaudeville withered, theater managers started using tricks like hiring columnists to produce revues. The advantage was twofold: a columnist could advertise his own show, and he could also cajole performers to appear for less by offering them publicity (or threatening to pan them). As *Time* magazine observed years later, "Though at war with Winchell, Ed, like a good general, learned a great deal from his enemy. Winchell emceed a stage show at Manhattan's Paramount, using the pressure of his column to line up good acts at a nominal cost. Ed did the same and earned $3,750 for a week's stand."

Sullivan's first attempt at radio had been short-lived, but in March 1934 he found another opportunity. NBC was launching *Musical Airship*, a half hour of dance music and show business gossip, and he leaped at the chance to be its host. In the mid 1930s radio broadcasts of dance bands held America in a semihypnotic trance. Dozens of swing orchestras like those of Paul Whiteman and Eddie Duchin played live as tens of millions of listeners fox-trotted, tangoed, and waltzed. As one reporter noted, "During a single evening twenty or thirty nationally recognized batoners hold sway." Combining dance music with humor and witty banter was a winning format. A top radio show that season was CBS's pairing of the Guy Lombardo Orchestra with the George Burns–Gracie Allen comedy team.

When *Musical Airship* debuted on March 7, it featured the Vincent Lopez Orchestra, one of the country's leading swing outfits. Sometimes called "The Tango Terror," Lopez had been a successful bandleader for more than a decade; over the years his bands were a way station for the likes of Glenn Miller and Tommy and Jimmy Dorsey. Sullivan had been friends with Lopez for years; it was at the bandleader's nightclub that Ed had met Sylvia in 1926.

The show was a joint effort: Ed was master of ceremonies, introducing Lopez's band. He interspersed the music with show business news and chatted with a celebrity guest he brought along each week. On many weeks the Lopez band was fronted by vocalist Frances Langford, an elegant chanteuse whose star soared the following year in the Hollywood film *Every Night at Eight* with George Raft. Also on the show was a three-man vocal group called the Three Scamps. *Musical Airship* was broadcast live every Wednesday at 10 P.M. from New York's elegant St. Regis Hotel. Sponsored by Gem Razor, the show paid Ed $1,000 a week.

The program got off to an auspicious start. *Radio Guide* immediately made the show its "high spot selection"—its favored choice—for the 10 P.M. hour. In April it was reported that Ed's presence on the show "has been renewed for some time to come." In May, a *Radio Guide* reviewer praised Ed, though he quibbled with one of his opinions: "Ed Sullivan, who writes a mean column, and master-of-ceremonies the Wednesday evening *Musical Airship* (NBC) quite well, passed a counterfeit when he intimated it was odd that radio had never yet contributed to the stage—only taken away from it."

Despite the favorable coverage, *Musical Airship* had trouble finding its audience. That spring it earned a C.A.B. rating of 7.3, far better than Ed's first show, but far behind leaders like the *Jack Benny Program* (25.3) and the *Fred Allen Program* (18.5). One month after its debut Sullivan's show was moved from 10 P.M. to 9 P.M.— a better timeslot, but directly opposite the popular *Old Gold* program, hosted by charismatic tenor Dick Powell. In the middle of May it was moved again, to 8 P.M., and in early June it was back at 9 P.M. Then on June 20, with little notice, *Musical Airship* was canceled.

Based on the results of *Radio Guide*'s mail-in popularity contest, the show was hardly noticed, or at least Ed's portion never was. Vincent Lopez garnered some modest attention; among bandleaders, readers voted him toward the bottom half. That was far better than Ed. Among the one hundred twenty-two stars ranked, with Bing Crosby and Eddie Cantor at the top, and Walter Winchell in about the middle, Sullivan wasn't rated at all. Apparently no one sent in an entry listing him as their favorite performer. Radio wasn't turning out to be the elevator to fame that Ed had hoped for. His first show in 1932 had lasted a little more than four months; this year's program barely made it past three.

———

With his broadcast career appearing fruitless, Ed turned to the stage. Churning out a column five days a week, which many Broadway scribes viewed as more than enough, left him wanting more. In May, toward the end of *Musical Airship*, he had produced a single vaudeville program at Brooklyn's RKO Albee Theatre. On July 7, just two weeks after his radio cancellation, he launched his vaudeville career in earnest.

He called his revue *Ed Sullivan's Dawn Patrol*. Like his first show at the Paramount the previous November, *Dawn Patrol* was an up-tempo vaudeville revue with a mixed bag of comedy, dance, and music. But the new show was more elaborate and showcased a more contemporary lineup. Opening at Manhattan's Loew's State Theatre, on the bill were ballroom dancers Mr. and Mrs. Paul Mears, vocalist Joan Abbott, tap dancer Georgie Tapps, singer-hoofer Delores Farris, acrobatic dancer Barbara Blane, and banjo player Ken Harvey. Unlike his one-week stand at the Paramount, his revues would now run regularly, with a fresh lineup of performers for every new revue. Sullivan's stage shows jumped from theater to theater, but his chief venue was Loew's State, whose marquee headlined the name Ed Sullivan in oversized letters on a routine basis.

His revue's title, *Dawn Patrol*, was a double entendre. It referred to the popular 1930 Howard Hawks talkie, *The Dawn Patrol*, about daring and chivalrous World War I flying aces; it also referred to Sullivan's own practice of club crawling until the sun came up. He often subtitled his column "Dawn Patrol" because it reported on his nocturnal wanderings, and because the phrase helped advertise his vaudeville shows.

Sullivan wore two hats in his *Dawn Patrol* revue, as he would throughout his career: producer and emcee. As producer, he was the show's business manager, taking a fee from the theater then dividing it among the performers and himself as he saw fit. More important, he made *Dawn Patrol*'s creative choices, building the show from the ground up, deciding which acts to book, placing them in order, determining the balance between comedy and music and dance, and giving the show its pacing. He refreshed the show constantly, mixing and matching performers as he spotted new talent in nightclubs. At some point, probably not as early as 1933, he took his control of the shows a step further: he decided which material performers would present, choosing their songs, making decisions about dance numbers, and editing the comics' jokes. Standing right offstage as the show ran, he was its chief critic. He monitored each revue act by act, making changes based on his sense of the crowd's response. Innumerable hours spent watching his stage shows and gauging audience response would be an invaluable education.

In contrast to his role as producer, his role as emcee—while much more visible to the public—was relatively insignificant. He simply ushered acts on and off the stage, building up the act beforehand and leading the audience in applause afterward. In fact, in his earliest shows he chose not to be master of ceremonies. Instead he hired Harry Rose, known as the "Broadway Jester," to keep the show moving. After Rose began as emcee, there appears to be a period in which they shared hosting duties. Only after about a year of producing *Dawn Patrol*, when it was highly successful, did Ed make himself its master of ceremonies.

Ed's career as a vaudeville producer-emcee demanded a grueling pace. Like many theaters, Loew's State offered patrons a stage show and a movie for a single ticket. The double bill started in late morning and repeated itself, back to back, until after midnight, sometimes until 3 A.M. The greasepaint and sweat stayed on all day long. It was no wonder that many vaudeville performers brought their children into their act; the family lived at the theater. But as demanding as it was for performers, for the audience it was joy. As in traditional vaudeville theaters, some audience members bought a ticket in early afternoon and stayed all day—the Depression meant they could afford little else. (Some vaudeville producers placed a heinously bad act at the show's end in an attempt to clear the theater.)

The vaudeville audience of the 1930s was a tough crowd. While more restrained than their recent forebears, who hurled rotten produce, people heckled mercilessly, and they wouldn't clap or laugh out of polite protocol. Nor would they return to a revue if they weren't getting their hard-earned 10 cents' worth. A few years later Ed wrote about an attempt at humor in one of his shows. Eleanor Powell, a tap dancer, stood in front of the stage curtain and announced that she would reveal what happened when famed card manipulator Cardini played poker with the cast. The curtain opened to show Cardini losing everything but his dress shirt to a group of poker players. The audience "sat in complete silence . . . not even a murmur," Ed wrote. It was a rigorous education for a showman. Pleasing this audience was like running a race carrying a forty-pound weight; if you could survive in these conditions you would likely be in good shape anywhere. And competition was fierce. Within a few blocks of Loew's State in midtown Manhattan there was a plethora of such shows competing for their customers' limited pocket change.

Ed's motivation for mounting variety shows was partially money. His $200 a week *Daily News* salary was more than comfortable, yet his notoriety from his column made being a stage producer a lucrative second job. As a variety show producer with a well-known name he could command a large sum; anything left over after paying performers was his. And singers and dancers, with the incentive of his column mentions, could be cajoled to appear in *Dawn Patrol* revues at a competitive rate. As the shows became ever more successful, it's likely that Sullivan made still more.

In addition to the money was the magnetic draw of being star of the show, center stage, with his name up in lights. Even after his television career made him wealthy, he found a way to get onstage or in front of a camera again and again. In the mid 1950s, then the producer of a hugely successful TV program, he acted in a summer stock production for fun. And in that same period he launched a live vaudeville tour of the country. He would not—could not—stay away from the spotlight. Once he debuted his *Dawn Patrol* revue in 1934 he was onstage constantly until almost the very end of his life.

Although he called the shows vaudeville, they owed as much to the New York nightclub as to the Keith–Albee circuit. As a denizen of Manhattan's nightspots, that was where Ed found his talent and earned his show business education. He played up the nightclub element in his shows, dubbing some versions the "All-Star All-American Nightclub Revue." A reviewer in 1934 noted that Sullivan offered "a variety of singers, dancers, and comics from the night clubs," and three years later, another observed, "In customary fashion, the production has a nightclub setting, is brilliantly lighted and well-staged." That the shows drew talent from the city's cabarets and nightclubs meant that they were more contemporary and more urban than traditional vaudeville. (Though, of course, the worlds of nightclub and vaudeville performers overlapped.)

He also broke with vaudeville tradition in the way he ordered the show. Vaudeville custom called for the biggest act to be saved for near the end—to keep the audience waiting. The opening act might be a greenhorn tap dancer who was likely to be booed offstage. But Ed, as a newsman, was guided by the journalistic practice of starting with a hot lead, an arresting opening sentence to lure the reader into reading the entire article. He brought this reporter's ethic to his stage shows, beginning each revue with a bang. Years later, when he competed in a medium in which audiences changed programs with the flip of a channel, his strategy of grabbing viewers upfront proved crucial to his success.

Sullivan's players were a constantly revolving cast, though he had a few favorites. On any given night his show might include vocalist Josephine Huston, who appeared in Gershwin's 1933 musical *Pardon My English*; the Three Berry Brothers, a troupe that sang and danced "in the true Harlem manner," as one reviewer wrote; Gali-Gali, a Turkish magician who told jokes; Gloria Gilbert, a soft-shoe artist who starred in Broadway revues throughout the 1930s; and Frances Faye, a hard-driving jazz singer who originated a syncopated vocal style known as the Zaz-Zu-Zaz. Providing musical accompaniment was usually the house band, Ruby Zwerling and his Loew's State Senators. A favorite performer of Ed's was Yiddish dialect comic Patsy Flick, an old-time vaudevillian with whom he occasionally did a comedy sketch. Sullivan himself, in addition to hosting, narrated clips of silent movies, providing stories and humorous quips about the on-screen action.

One typical 1935 *Dawn Patrol* opened with Rita Rio, a jazz singer who would become a well-known big band vocalist; she sang that evening "in the accepted hot-cha fashion," noted a reviewer. Lending a more traditional feel, Babs Ryan and Her Brothers sang vocal harmonies, and song stylists Gross and Dunn crooned updated versions of vaudeville duo Van and Schenk's hits. Providing laughs was Dave Vine, a Jewish dialect comic, and Peg Leg Bates, "a one-legged Negro tap and acrobatic dancer, proved a sensation at yesterday's matinee with his amazingly facile routines," wrote a reviewer. (Bates would appear on Sullivan's television show three times.)

Sullivan's stage shows were uniformly well reviewed; in a small mountain of vaudeville notices there wasn't a single sour note. Typical of the reviews was the *New York Journal-American*'s description of the show as "swift, funny . . . once again he has assembled an ingratiating lot of performers who trot out their talents in an admirable fashion." Audiences agreed. Theater owners knew that Sullivan could be counted on to sell tickets, and between 1934 and 1937 his revues grew progressively more successful at the box office. (The city's tepid emergence from the Depression surely helped this.)

In 1936, fellow Broadway columnist Louis Sobol reported, "Some weeks ago, columnist Ed Sullivan established a new record at Loew's State when something like $41,000 rolled into the box office." (Sobol, however, tweaked Sullivan by pointing out that his record was broken the following week by a George Burns–Gracie Allen show at Loew's.) The following year, the *Journal-American* noted, "Ed Sullivan's *Dawn Patrol* revue, at Loew's State Theatre has broken all attendance records and will be retained for a consecutive week's engagement. . . . This marks the second time in the vaudeville history of the State that a show had been held for a consecutive week's engagement."

As for Ed as emcee, reports were mixed. Most positively, one *Dawn Patrol* reviewer wrote, "In his third appearance here, Mr. Sullivan is much more at ease than he was in his debut, doing a commendable job as master of ceremonies." Modest praise, to be sure, and contradicted by other sources. Based on eyewitness accounts of his vaudeville shows, Sullivan's persona was much like it was in his television show, that is, stiff. As canny and skillful as he was as a producer, he was never a natural onstage. A *Variety* reviewer noted this after an early Sullivan vaudeville production, when Ed still shared emcee duties with Harry Rose: "Harry Rose with his aggressive style of emceeing is working hard this week and looks responsible for keeping the show together. . . . His sustained clicking makes it easier for the rest of the troupe, especially for Sullivan, who found Rose's help quite handy in the microphone moments. . . ."

It was a central irony of his life: despite his countless hours onstage, as much as he hungered to be in front of an audience, he was never comfortable in its eye. Part of it was simple stage fright. As numerous staffers from his television show recalled, he suffered from stage nerves. This avid socializer, one of Broadway's leading gladhanders, lost his natural charm when facing a full theater.

Adding still more gravity to Sullivan's stage presence may have been his feelings about what he called "phonies"—those people, as he wrote in his column, who put on a false front, who pretended. He despised the fakers. Although he himself could be disingenuous, the act of adopting a suave show business persona was not in his nature. Perhaps he was too rigid, or perhaps putting on a happy face was simply distasteful to him. Either way, Ed, unequivocally, had to be Ed.

Another person, realizing he was essentially uneasy onstage, might have found an alternative. Sullivan could have been the show's producer without acting as emcee, as in his first few shows at Loew's State. He had the option of continuing to hire Harry Rose or another performer as master of ceremonies. Certainly the kings of vaudeville, Benjamin Keith and Edward Albee, weren't known as onstage personalities. But something powerful drew Ed to a live audience, regardless of what small agonies this required of him. He needed to be in the spotlight. So when the

Brooklyn RKO Albee, the Capitol, or Loew's State ran ads, it was always: "In Person—Ed Sullivan—and his All New Dawn Patrol Revue."

In 1936 Sullivan began emceeing the Harvest Moon Ball, the annual whirling-blur finale to the city's amateur dance competition. Sponsored by the *Daily News*, and promoted by the paper heavily, Harvest Moon had an almost religious following. When the first unofficial contest was held in Central Park Mall in 1927, 75,000 people showed up to watch or compete, forcing city officials to cancel later contests for fear of public safety. The *News* relaunched the annual event at Madison Square Garden in 1935, and it grew bigger every year through the 1930s and 1940s. The Harvest Moon Ball became the country's top amateur dance contest.

Thousands of energetic dancers competed in preliminary contests at nightclubs like the Savoy and Roseland to earn a spot in the finals, where top swing orchestras vamped as couples swirled and swung their best Lindy hop, collegiate shag, fox-trot, tango, or rhumba. The *News* promoted the contest as a chance at fame. "Booking agents will grab up any dance teams whose routines have the stuff upon which stardom is built," tempted the paper. In the second year that Sullivan emceed Harvest Moon, two hundred thousand people bought tickets in the first fourteen days of the competition.

While Ed didn't produce these yearly events, hosting them greatly boosted his profile. He parlayed their popularity to his advantage by booking the winners in his vaudeville shows. And because Harvest Moon was a dazzling visual spectacle, it was filmed for newsreels, a fact that later would profoundly influence his career.

Between writing five columns a week and producing a steady stream of vaudeville shows, Ed ran a continuous circuit between several nightclubs, that week's vaudeville house, the *Daily News* office, and whatever charity event he was hosting. Meeting the incessant demands of a daily column meant trawling nightspots until near dawn and sifting through piles of tips from press agents and publicity flacks. The lineup for upcoming stage shows had to be selected and booked, and the shows themselves often played all day long. He worked the phone constantly. The pace of it all meant he sometimes banged out his column while backstage at his variety revue. One evening, theater promoter A.C. Blumenthal brought author H.G. Wells, famous for *War of the Worlds*, to Loew's State to introduce him to Sullivan. Ed, typing away backstage, was so distracted that when he heard the name, he hardly looked up from his typewriter. Instead, he absented-mindedly said, "Oh, just like the English writer," at which point Blumenthal had to tell Ed it *was* the English writer.

To help with his errands, Ed hired Carmine Santullo, a Bronx-born shoe-shine boy, a shy, skinny teenager with big dark eyes. He became Ed's tireless factotum. Carmine worshipped Ed, always calling him Mr. Sullivan, and he was happy to do virtually anything for his employer: deliver Ed's column to the *Daily News* office, filter and respond to mail, and help with the unending stream of phone calls. He could shrug off Ed's sudden bursts of temper with hardly a care and anticipate his boss's answer to any question. Carmine would remain with Ed throughout his life, becoming more of a family member than an employee. In the late 1960s, Carmine arranged for a passel of state governors to declare that February 9 would be Ed Sullivan Day.

Hollywood. By the mid 1930s the word had a whisper all its own, a come-hither suggestion of glamour and money and sex and, most of all, boundless fame. In the

1920s, Broadway and Hollywood had been close rivals in the public imagination. Broadway's glorious *Ziegfeld Follies* and many touring stage shows were held in a regard similar to that of the silent pictures of Valentino. But by the 1930s the fame machine was shifting inexorably westward. Since Jolson's first talkie in 1927, show business had never been the same.

The Broadway columnists took notice, including ever more Hollywood tidbits in their coverage. The columnists' affection for Hollywood was far from unrequited. The studios understood the value of romancing New York's entertainment columnists. Some columnists were even hired to appear or star in movies. If the picture made a profit—more likely with the columnist's clout—it was an added benefit. But at the very least the studios considered the money well spent on the care and feeding of publicity sources.

Walter Winchell authored the story for 1933's *Broadway Thru a Keyhole*, and it had propelled his already considerable profile still higher. And the film's studio, 20th Century Pictures (later 20th Century Fox) was requesting more from Winchell. Sidney Skolsky, Ed's gossip colleague at the *Daily News*, wrote the screenplay to the 1935 Hollywood production *Daring Young Man*.

Paramount in 1935 invited Ed to make a cameo appearance in *Paramount Headliner: Broadway Highlights No. 2*. The first *Broadway Highlights* film, made earlier in the year, had featured appearances by stars like Jack Benny, Al Jolson, and Sophie Tucker, emceed by Paramount studio head Adolph Zukor. Like its predecessor, *Highlights No. 2* was a showcase for brief celebrity appearances, spotlighting personalities like comedian Milton Berle, crooner Rudy Vallee, screen star Norma Talmadge (whom Ed called "my favorite actress"), and boxer Benny Leonard. The short film was shown before full-length features as a studio promotion, and so was given wide release. But Ed's minor role in this star vehicle was dwarfed by the success enjoyed by Winchell and Skolsky—and he was aware of that.

In April 1936, Fox Movietone News hired Ed to narrate a biweekly newsreel, to be shown in nine thousand theaters across the country. This was the same series of newsreels narrated by famed newsman Lowell Thomas in his march-tempo gravitas cadence. The acclaim that Ed had wanted, the national exposure, now seemed so close—but still wasn't there. Ed's Paramount cameo and his newsreel narration only increased his appetite for more.

By the mid 1930s, Ed began to turn his eyes westward, drawn by the allure of Hollywood. Growing up, he had dreamed of New York, and he had succeeded there, as a Broadway columnist and stage show producer. But now a far more compelling siren song called, trilling from a place that offered stardust far surpassing that found in New York. He was well known in the city, arguably famous as a local celebrity, but he hungered for something bigger. He hobnobbed day and night with the truly famous, luminaries who were admired from coast to coast, and that's what he wanted for himself.

He devised a plan. He had already accomplished one unlikely metamorphosis, from sports reporter to Broadway potentate. Now, in 1937, he dreamed of a far grander change: moving to Hollywood, which would catapult his star to where he had always wanted it to be. He could be a Hollywood columnist, attaching his fortunes to the ever-growing notoriety of the film capital. But the most compelling possibility was doing what Winchell and Skolsky had done. If those two typewriter-bangers could make it onto the silver screen, then surely Ed could also. He hadn't had any success with his own attempt at film, 1933's *Mr. Broadway*, but if he were a Hollywood columnist, romanced by the studios as the Coast columnists were, he could parley his status into a film career. He could be a screenwriter, maybe try his hand at acting—with the nascent film industry growing so quickly, there was no telling where it might lead.

Many had a similar plan. With the pace at which the film industry churned out pictures, its appetite for scripts was insatiable. In the summer of 1937, F. Scott Fitzgerald moved to Hollywood, enticed by visions of scriptwriting riches. At around this time or in the next few years a small crowd made a similar pilgrimage, including Robert Benchley, Dorothy Parker, Aldous Huxley, and Nathaniel West. They were undeterred by studio head Jack Warner's description of screenwriters as "schmucks with Underwoods"—or perhaps that made the task seem all the easier.

One person stood in Ed's way. Sidney Skolsky already covered the *Daily News'* Hollywood beat and showed no signs of wanting to give it up. The paper had sent Skolsky to the Coast in 1933 to write a gossip column from inside the film colony. He had stretched his one-year assignment into four; Skolsky enjoyed the beat, with its lavish perks and access to what he thought of as the real action. Although Skolsky's Hollywood column was printed side by side with Ed's Broadway column—or maybe because of it—Skolsky sang the praises of the Coast over the Stem constantly. The very week that Ed's Broadway column debuted in July 1932, Skolsky archly noted, "Notice how all the Broadway columns these days are dotted with Hollywood items. That's because there's nothing doing on Main Street."

By 1936, Ed was writing of the "decline and fall of the legitimate Broadway theater" in the face of Hollywood's advance. The problem, he explained, lay in the twelve cans of film delivered to New York's Ziegfeld Theater. Where once the great Ziegfeld had produced his *Show Boat* gala live, now it was delivered to this same theater in twelve cans of film. "This is the new show business . . . twelve cans of film . . . Three hundred copies are made in the Coast laboratories . . . Each copy will play perhaps thirty theatres. . . ." Live theater, Ed reported, was "romantic, stimulating, exciting . . . but the new way is more profitable." (And it was no secret that the Depression had dimmed Broadway's lights considerably, and that the public's hunger for Hollywood fantasy was only increased by the downturn.) Ed's column in 1936 became a kind of de facto Hollywood–Broadway column, as he liberally sprinkled tidbits about film personalities into his Broadway coverage.

Skolsky, in what must have been agonizingly attractive to Ed, kept dropping bon bons about the joys of the Hollywood columnist. "When Gary Cooper and Madeline Carroll were announced for the cast of the flicker *The General Died at Dawn*, Paramount didn't know that John O'Hara, Clifford Odets, and Sidney Skolsky would also be in the cast," he wrote in 1936. His reporting suggested that with enough proximity, even a newshound was invited into the hallowed set, as when he went to the movies with child film star Shirley Temple. "When I arrived at the theatre Shirley was already there, seated. She didn't say, 'You're late, you kept me waiting.' She merely said, 'Good evening, Sidney,' and shook hands with me."

Ed began to lobby *Daily News* editor Frank Hause to replace Skolsky. Exactly when he began his extended effort is unknown, but by 1937 the *News* management relented.

They agreed to recall Skolsky to write the Broadway column and send Sullivan to Hollywood. But there was a problem: Skolsky didn't like the idea and refused to come back to New York. "I pleaded with him by wire and phone to return but no dice," Hause later wrote. "I guess the competition on the Broadway beat was too much for the Little Mouse, and he liked the easier tempo and climate of Hollywood."

The *News* kept pushing Skolsky to return. And he kept pushing back. Finally, he chose to resign rather than return to New York. He aired his feelings publicly in *Variety*. "Broadway columns are as passé as Broadway," he wrote. His column's tagline had been "Don't get me wrong—I love Hollywood," but in *Variety* he altered it: "They got me wrong—I love Hollywood." He took a job as the Hollywood columnist for the *Daily Mirror*. With Skolsky out of the way, the *News* assigned Ed to the Hollywood beat for one year, as they had Skolsky.

As Sullivan sat down to write his farewell Broadway column in September, he certainly had reason to feel fondly toward his New York position. The perks had been numerous. That summer the columnist had sailed to Europe aboard the SS *Normandie* with a group of show business stars that included Jack Benny and his wife (and comedy partner) Mary Livingston. Cole Porter was onboard to serenade the guests; one night he played the Gershwin tune "Lady Be Good" as a tribute to the composer, who had died a week earlier. Ed had plenty of free time in between filling columns with breathless tidbits like "the Cole Porters are Marlene Dietrich's favorite shipboard companions." While crossing the Atlantic he watched movies (appropriately, the 1937 Preston Sturges comedy *Easy Living* was shown). He also practiced his dance steps in preparation for hosting that fall's Harvest Moon dance competition, and polished his Ping-Pong skills. "Your athletic reporter worked out on the desk tennis tables and thought himself pretty good," he wrote. "Then a boy of twelve came along . . . he gave me a terrible shellacking, and I slunk away to the library."

Ed's good-bye column on September 10 was a sentimental recap of his New York years, from his beginnings at the *Evening Mail* in 1921 through his joy at landing his *Daily News* position in 1932. He veritably shoveled praise onto the *News*—not surprising, considering the paper had just granted him the assignment he so coveted.

Ed had begun to say farewell to Broadway in his column the day before, letting his readers know that the good-bye letters and telegrams were pouring in (and reminding them of his popularity): "You get a funny feeling reading them . . . After you've written for a long time, the readers accept you as one of their own immediate family, and the letters from them are penned in that style." A mother in New Jersey warned him to be careful of drafts on the trains, and another wrote to say she lit a candle for him at her church. "There is a letter from Sing Sing, saying that the boys up there wish me luck . . . 'We'd all like to be going with you, Sully.'"

In that same column was one of Ed's most unusual qualities as a Broadway scribe. He devoted half his column—and the entire column the day before—to giving tourist advice to the Legionnaires, then in New York for a convention. He wrote as if he were taking these American Legion members under his wing, providing detailed advice for their New York visit. To the average Broadway columnist, a Winchell or a Skolsky, American Legion members were visiting rubes, hometown squares who were best ignored. These columnists—the very embodiment of the urbane—would merely shudder as they hurried past a nametag-wearing American Legion member from Hoboken or Poughkeepsie.

The columnist and his wife preparing to sail to Europe aboard the SS *Normandie,* in the summer of 1937, as part of a group that included Cole Porter and Jack Benny. (New York *Daily News*)

But not Ed. He was the kind of Broadway columnist who gave the Legionnaires a step-by-step rundown on how to enjoy the city. That contradiction, if it was one, defined him. Here he was, going off to Hollywood in search of something bigger and better, in effect saying that New York was no longer the center of the world. He dreamed of something grander, some larger fame or status he might acquire. He was a Broadway columnist who had outgrown Broadway. On the face of it that put him in a very different world than the Legionnaires who were looking forward to a 10-cent ride on the Staten Island ferry. But to Ed, catering to the Legionnaires was every bit as important as reaching the Broadway sophisticates, perhaps more so.

So on the way out the door to chronicle the lives of Clark Gable and Myrna Loy, this Courvoisier-sipping Stork Club habitué gave the American Legion tourists some advice about Broadway:

> "Patronize the standard clubs and restaurants; avoid the down-at-the-heels clip joints . . . Avoid the jackals who will offer to guide you to disreputable joints, where they will drug your drinks and swipe your bankroll and perhaps hit you on the head . . . it's a great street, and we want you to enjoy it."

The Legionnaires would be well tended to. As for Ed, he was off to Hollywood.

CHAPTER SIX

Hollywood

EVERYTHING SEEMED BRIGHT THAT SATURDAY in September as Ed, Sylvia, and six-year-old Betty left New York to begin their new life in Hollywood. Ed was going out to cover the kingdom of glamour for the paper with the largest circulation in America; it was a plum assignment and at age thirty-five he was at the top of his game. The three of them boarded the deluxe 20th Century Line in Manhattan's Grand Central Station, carrying only the essentials for the three-day trip. Their belongings had been sent along to the house Ed had rented in Beverly Hills. The three-bedroom Spanish-style bungalow at 621 North Alta was modest by comparison to many in the elite neighborhood, but it allowed Ed proximity to the stars he would cover, not to mention the status of a Beverly Hills address.

Ed filed columns during the trip out, wiring them back to New York from cities along the way. As closely as he scoured the passengers for a scoop, he found nothing more substantial than a tidbit about Pandro Berman, a young RKO film producer in the next compartment who had just delivered the first print of Katharine Hepburn's *Stage Door* to New York.

By the second day of the trip the inactivity was weighing on Ed, who was used to a nonstop schedule. He sat in the dining car and chatted with the chef, J.A. Day, whose trout and turkey dishes Ed raved about, but the banter didn't stem the brooding: "As I devoured them, I recalled the time in 1918 when I ran away to Chicago to join the Marines and worked in Thompson's Cafeteria in the daytime and the Illinois Central freight yards at night . . . Pass me another trout, please, Mr. Day, I'm feeling morbid."

As Ed's beat on Broadway had been the nightclubs and theaters of the Main Stem, on the Coast he would haunt the movie sets and celebrity nightspots of the film colony. The studios, of course, were eager to give him access, knowing his column anecdotes would stimulate interest in upcoming pictures.

On his first few days on the job he received a whirlwind tour of the movie lots. On the 20th Century Fox lot, he met nine-year-old Shirley Temple, then in her second of three years as the country's top box office draw, having charmed audiences with 1935's *The Littlest Rebel* and 1936's *Poor Little Rich Girl*. Ed reported that the "curly-haired youngster" took breaks from filming *Rebecca of Sunnybrook Farm* to satisfy the California state law requiring four hours of school a day. He said hello to composer Irving Berlin having lunch in the Fox commissary while working on *Alexander's Ragtime Band*, and on the MGM lot he watched a Christmas scene being filmed for *Navy Blue and Gold*, starring Jimmy Stewart and Lionel Barrymore.

On the RKO lot he visited the set of *Bringing Up Baby*, the Cary Grant–Katharine Hepburn comedy that featured a one hundred sixty-five pound leopard. Ed reported that one of the bit players had been on a drinking binge, so director Howard Hawks decided to play a practical joke, summoning the actor to the office, placing the sleeping leopard on a chair, then leaving the partially inebriated fellow alone with the big cat. The incident may or may not have happened (it sounds suspiciously prepackaged for visiting reporters), but it's exactly the kind of thing RKO hoped Ed would write about; by giving him access and feeding him morsels they were generating free publicity.

By the end of his first week he had set up a Sunday golf date with Fred Astaire. The outings with Astaire at the Bel-Air Country Club would become a constant, with Ed and Fred typically joined for a foursome by other film colony members, like Douglas Fairbanks or David Niven. Ed often wrote about his matches with Astaire, as when he described the dancer's golf technique: "'I am not envious generally,' says Astaire, 'but I do envy anyone who plays good golf.' Later, on the course, he shows us how he hit those golf balls during his dance in 'Carefree,' and after his preparatory dance he whaled a drive two hundred fifty yards straight down the middle. Can you imagine how nutty he'd drive an opponent if before every shot he did a jig?" And, after a later outing: "Fred Astaire and your correspondent are feeling very happy this bright February morning, incidentally . . . we teamed up at Bel-Air against Randy Scott and Tyrone Power, and beat them in a harrowing match that will go down in golf history (at least our golf history). . . ."

Also in his first week he visited the MGM lot to chat with Joan Crawford and director Frank Borzage, who stopped work on *Mannequin* for the publicity effort. Sullivan and Crawford had tangled in New York a few years earlier, when Ed tried to enlist her to appear in a charity event he was hosting and she refused. He had taken journalistic revenge, writing in his column, "One wonders how Joan Crawford has gotten this far in show business with so little talent." Crawford had hit back, sending an open letter to a fan magazine decrying Sullivan's efforts as "cheap, tawdry, and gangster journalism." But on the set of *Mannequin*, all was apparently well between the screen goddess and the new Hollywood columnist. Crawford, according to Ed, greeted him warmly: "'The night we had dinner at 21 in New York I said you belong in Hollywood,' remembers La Crawford, 'And here you are. . . .'" For Ed, who had so often attacked "phonies" in his column, his report of an affectionate meeting with Crawford was a remarkable about-face.

But life was different on the Coast, and Ed knew it. Although he came to Hollywood as an established columnist for a major newspaper, he was a guest in a world owned by the film colony's reigning gossips, Louella Parsons and her new archrival Hedda

Hopper. Parsons, syndicated by Hearst, and Hopper, syndicated by the Chicago *Tribune* and published in the *Los Angeles Times*, ruthlessly dominated Hollywood stars, exacting homage and wielding the power of their huge readership with an iron hand. There were other gossips in Hollywood, including Jimmy Fidler, the actor turned radio host, and legions of scribes for movie pulps, but none had the studio access that Parsons and Hopper did. The manner in which these two enthroned columnists plied their trade defined the gossip business in Hollywood, and Ed was bound to live in the system they perpetuated.

The two women had taken very different paths to their lofty perch. Hopper, born Elda Furry in rural Pennsylvania, had been pretty and slender as a young woman and enjoyed modest success in theater and film through the 1920s and early 1930s; by 1936 she was a middle-aged single mother with a child to support. She launched a gossipy radio show on a Hollywood station, mining her network of film and stage connections (and employing creative guesswork) to provide a scintillating dose of celebrity stardust. As the show grew in popularity she parleyed it into newspaper syndication. Hopper was known for her passion for large hats and her ability to hold long, bitter grudges.

Parsons, born Louella Oettinger in rural Illinois, dreamed of being a reporter from a very young age; in her teens she covered social events for the Dixon, Illinois, *Star*. Heavyset and ungainly, she married a well-to-do real estate agent, moved with him to Iowa, had a child, and promptly divorced. Parsons relocated to Chicago, remarried, and worked her way up through the newspaper business, shifting to New York as her career took off, eventually landing a job as the motion picture editor for Hearst's *New York American*. There she became friends with actress Marion Davies, the romantic partner of William Randolph Hearst. After socializing with Davies and Hearst in Hollywood, the newspaper magnate syndicated Parsons' column. By the mid 1920s, just as silent movies were set to give way to talkies, Parsons was established as the top Hollywood gossip.

While Parsons was there first, Hopper, with her network of contacts, quickly grew to challenge her gossip supremacy. It was even rumored that the studios had created Hopper, feeding her choice tidbits, to counterbalance Parsons' overweening influence. But regardless of the competition between them—and they loathed each other—they were essentially mirror images of one another. Both women had a symbiotic relationship with the studios, relying on a regular dole of access and timely news and in turn helping promote films and stars. And both women held as sacrosanct the studios' unwritten rule: don't damage our property, that is, our stars.

MGM, Universal, and other star factories spent huge sums building mere actors and actresses into semimythic screen idols. To report that any of these investments were tarnished with an undue fondness for alcohol or a questionable sexual proclivity would have been an unpardonable act of corporate vandalism. Doors would have shut and phone calls would have gone unreturned. So Louella and Hedda lived within carefully prescribed boundaries. Romances, studio news, and benign glimpses of personal lives were promoted; even the whirlwind of divorce, as stars changed partners as casually as ballroom dancers, helped create a glow of ardent sexual energy that pushed ticket sales. And certainly each tilled her own trademark brand of cattiness. But reporting actual scandal was strictly prohibited (unless, of course, the studios gave tacit approval).

Both Louella and Hedda needed to be treated with ultimate care by those in their fiefdom. Sidney Skolsky learned this the hard way. Leaving the *Daily News* for Hearst's *Daily Mirror* placed him in direct competition with Louella. After one of Skolsky's early columns contradicted a Parsons scoop, she intimated to Hearst that Skolsky was a communist; he was let go after his contract expired and was unemployed for most of a year. (Skolsky called Hearst shortly after Parsons' claim, attempting to reclaim his job, asking the newspaper magnate, "Are you sure she didn't say 'columnist'? You know, she has a difficult time pronouncing words. 'I know what she said,' Hearst snapped. 'You'll work out your contract, and when we're through with you you'll be nothing.'")

Ed understood the tender treatment the queen bees required. In the rare instances he mentioned Louella or Hedda—all the papers frowned on acknowledging rival columnists—he tossed them peace bouquets, much as a visiting explorer paid homage to a local potentate. In a typical chummy aside, he wrote, "Dr. Harry Martin, who is Louella Parsons' hubby, seriously ill from pleurisy (he is a swell guy, this 'Doc' Martin, and the whole town is pulling for him)."

On Broadway, Ed had played by the rough-and-tumble rules of the Main Stem. Broadway columnists were fevered fellows, up all night, working a typewriter and a shot glass with equal fervor, always leading with their elbows. They picked fights, with performers, with each other, or with anyone else, as part of doing business. They weren't happy if they weren't in the middle of a minor or major skirmish. This quotidian jousting was a perfect fit with Ed's personality. But the Hollywood columnists, under the Parsons–Hopper system, were well-oiled and well-feted adjuncts to the studio machinery. The emphasis was less on conflict and more on promoting studio product.

The charge that Ed had leveled against Eddie Cantor back in New York, accusing him of stealing material from another performer, was good for boosting readership on Broadway. But that kind of ad hominem attack could damage a performer, and thus was not allowed by the studios. In fact, a month after arriving in Hollywood, Ed wrote a column in homage to Cantor, who had matched his legendary vaudeville success with Hollywood stardom. "I know of no performer more deserving than Cantor, and I say that although he and I have severe differences of opinion," Ed purred. Likewise, his assertion in his Broadway column that Joan Crawford lacked talent. As a Broadway wise guy he could be a cur to Crawford and no matter. If he did that in Hollywood he never would have gotten near her; her studio would have frozen him out—a death knell for someone on the movie beat. "There are certain things you shouldn't do in Hollywood," he wrote in a column about actors offending studio heads and being thrown out of work. He clearly understood the same rules applied to columnists.

In their first few weeks away from New York, Ed and Sylvia didn't like California. They were homesick, and in addition to missing their friends they missed the city's tempo. By comparison, Hollywood moved at a pastoral gait, and the two felt out of place. Their young daughter, however, loved it. This was the first time she had lived in a house, and she relished the freedom to play outside whenever she wanted, taking great pleasure in the bungalow's nice yard and garden.

As they had in New York, Ed and Sylvia hired a live-in babysitter to take care of Betty as they dined out, which they did almost every evening. This post was first filled by a woman Betty remembered as a dominant German governess, who was nice to Ed and Betty but not to Sylvia, and so was summarily dismissed. She was replaced by a succession of paid companions; one was a student at the University of California, Los Angeles.

After Ed and Sylvia gained a circle of friends, they began to enjoy California. They entertained at their house frequently, inviting stars Ed had become friends with for dinner, drinks, and frivolity. To help, they hired a live-in cook and butler, a couple named Jack and Melissa. (Jack, after working for the Sullivans for a while, confided to Ed that he had spent time in prison for a minor offense, but Ed said he didn't care, he wanted him anyway.)

The Sullivan get-togethers were spirited affairs, and Betty remembered her parents acting silly and young. Groucho Marx, whose huge success in vaudeville turned into even greater fame in Hollywood, became a personal friend. He and his wife Ruth came over for dancing lessons with Ed and Sylvia, and the foursome clowned around the house as they went through their dancing paces.

Virtually all of Sullivan's Hollywood social circle, like Ed himself, had worked in vaudeville in New York, and most were duplicating that success on the Coast. Bob Hope had toured the Keith–Albee circuit and starred on Broadway before coming to Hollywood in 1937; he played golf with Sullivan and asked him to be the godfather of his daughter Linda. Jack Benny, a popular vaudeville emcee-comedian who starred in a raft of 1930s romantic comedies, was a regular Sullivan houseguest. (Mrs. Hope, Mrs. Benny, and actor Hal LeRoy's wife came over to give Sylvia decorating suggestions when the Sullivans moved in.) Barbara Stanwyck had been a Ziegfeld chorus girl before launching a Hollywood career that earned her four Academy Award nominations. Likewise frequent houseguests Dick Powell and his wife Joan Blondell: Powell enjoyed great success as a musician and emcee in New York before Warner Bros. hired him for string of "nice guy" roles; Blondell played vaudeville for more than ten years before landing a contract with Warner Bros., which cast her as a bubble-headed blonde (or gold-digger) throughout the 1930s.

Over drinks and laughter, the Sullivan partygoers played whimsical games. Sometimes they cavorted through hide-and-seek around the house and in the yard. On one occasion the group devised a ploy with Barbara Stanwyck's wedding ring, a gold band, hiding it in various rooms and attaching a tiny electric current to it so that anyone picking it up would get shocked.

The line between Ed's personal socializing and his professional duties was blurry, since his beat included a full schedule of Hollywood gatherings. Dinner parties at the Marx's, for instance, were a regular social event for Ed, which he also reported on: "Midnight—the guests have departed. Chico [Marx] and I are at the piano singing 'I Wonder Who's Kissing Her Now' when there's an interruption. Mrs. Marx suggests that we shut up. We did, but it cost her two Scotch and sodas." As a teen in Port Chester he had reported on the baseball games that he himself played in, and now he was mixing his reportage and his life in a similar way. His social circle fed him news tips and in turn benefited professionally from his friendship; Joan Blondell was one of a handful of screen stars who got far more column exposure than they otherwise would have.

His job, as it had been on Broadway, was to allow his readers a glimpse into a fabulous world they would never enter. "I wish you could attend some of these Hollywood parties with me," Ed confided, explaining how ruthlessly fame-driven the film colony's social scene was. "The hostess often doesn't know more than ten percent of her guests . . . Ninety percent of them have been invited solely because they have won success in their last picture, or because their husbands are powerful at some studio."

At a typical see-and-be-seen soiree hosted by Countess Dorothy Di Frasso, a wealthy Italian socialite, Ed's listing of the guests surely gave his readers a vicarious thrill. On the dance floor, fox-trotting to a seven-piece swing band, were Claudette Colbert, Bette Davis, Cary Grant, Irene Dunne, and a handful of similar screen luminaries. Late in the evening, Groucho Marx corralled Ed and a few others and challenged them to come up with more than three words with the suffix "dous." The revelers quickly named three ("tremendous," "stupendous," and "horrendous") and Ed asked his readers to help by sending him some more. His mailbox was soon so deluged he had to cancel the request.

He became a connoisseur of the Hollywood party, to the point that he quibbled with the local experts:

> "Cornelius Vanderbilt, Jr., in listing the best hostesses in Hollywood, rates Doris Warner LeRoy, No. 1; Carmen Considine, No. 2; and Mrs. Harry Lachman, No. 3 . . . Throw his selections out and rate them this way: No. 1, Joe Schenck; No. 2, Dorothy Di Frasso; No. 3, Mrs. Hal Roach; No. 4, Mrs. Jack Warner; No. 5, Edward Everett Horton, and you'll have a truer picture of what goes on out here . . ."

As Ed had haunted nightspots like Jimmy Kelly's and Dave's Blue Room in New York, his home away from home in Hollywood was the city's trendiest gathering places, like the Clover Club, the Brown Derby, and the House of Murphy. Hollywood's equivalent of Manhattan's Stork Club was the Trocadero, owned by the publisher of the *Hollywood Reporter*, Billy Wilkerson. A troop of autograph seekers stood vigil outside this Sunset Boulevard club, besieging any screen star heading to a celebrity appearance in its oak and red-cushioned bar. The famed paparazzo Hymie Fink was often on hand to snap glossies for *Photoplay* and other fan magazines (the stars reportedly loved him because he would rip up a bad photo). Ed fed his column's voracious hunger for celebrity gossip by table-hopping among terraces full of star-laden get-togethers at the Troc.

Ever the show organizer, Sullivan also used the Trocadero as a venue for an All-Broadway revue he produced to benefit the film actors' relief fund; he organized this show just a month after arriving in Hollywood. Whatever other altruistic aims he had, the benefit show helped introduce and ingratiate him within the film community. (But he would not, of course, produce vaudeville shows in Hollywood; the idea of a live stage show was merely quaint in the movie colony.)

If Broadway had served up plenty of grist for the gossip mill, Hollywood offered all the more. Based on Ed's column, the sexual merry-go-round of partner hopping was even more rapid on the Coast than on the Main Stem:

> "Don't be startled if Robert Taylor and Barbara Stanwyck get married the same week that Clark Gable and Carole Lombard take the leap . . .

That should be about St. Patrick's Day, as Mrs. Gable gets her divorce March 6."

"Greta Garbo really told off Leopold Stokowski when her name was dragged into his wife's Reno [divorce] action. 'It's a disgrace—you are trying to ruin me,' she burned over the long distance phone. Incidentally, Garbo and Boyer in *Conquest* make all other screen lovers look sophomoric . . . Jimmy Stewart is helping Virginia Bruce forget her stock losses . . . Joan Bennett's most persistent honey is that New York attorney, but he's married."

"Howard Hughes making passes at Arleen Whelan, but the red-haired eyeful is true to her Richard Greene."

Especially titillating was the love triangle between contract players Tyrone Power, Sonja Henie, and Janet Gaynor, which Ed chronicled as if he were privy to their diaries. In one episode he informed readers, "Tyrone Power and Sonja Henie started spooning as soon as Janet Gaynor stepped on the eastbound train." In his reporting, starring in a picture together seemed to produce a combustible form of romance: "The Ross girl and Eddie are a real life combination . . . Gloria Blondell and Ronald Regan [*sic*] are an item . . . Rochelle Hudson, the Oklahoma ouchamagoucha, and Norman Krasna are a four-alarm blaze. . . ."

As in his Broadway column, his blind items allowed him to include truly salacious items without fear of a libel suit. "A Filipino manservant will be named by a famous star as a housewrecker," he wrote, going several steps further with, "One of the local writers, always panning movie stars for deserting their wives and taking up with younger girls, has deserted his for a sixteen year old." If his readers wanted still more, he willingly obliged: "Hollywood dance director who invaded that girl's apartment and tore her face apart in a sadistic orgy was saved because the girl refused to tell the police . . . she feared the publicity."

His chronicles of the personal peccadilloes of the famous frequently involved interviews of the stars themselves, as when he spoke with Joan Crawford a year after moving to Hollywood. His kind column treatment of the actress had won him extensive access. When he interviewed her in August 1938, Crawford was at the tail end of her third of five marriages.

> "I asked Joan Crawford yesterday if she'd ever try Love again. She shook her head emphatically: 'I don't believe there's a man in the world who has the capacity for taking love seriously for more than a few months. Girls can and do, but not men.' I suggested that perhaps her own driving ambition for a career had overpowered Daniel Cupid. She said: 'I was most ambitious to make a success of marriage.'"

After speaking with her, he wrote an extended analysis of Crawford's troubled relationship with Franchot Tone, a serious dramatic actor on the New York stage. "Undoubtedly he must have resented (as any young husband would) the fact that his wife was a star." Perhaps, he theorized, it was alcohol—Tone liked vodka and Crawford reportedly didn't drink (though she later drank heavily), or perhaps it was something as simple as "the noise he made brushing his teeth . . . on such trifles was [divorce capitol] Reno constructed," Ed noted.

He concluded his analysis—doubtless devoured by his readers, for Crawford was now blazingly popular—by describing the actress as she rehearsed for 1938's *The Shining Hour*. Despite being on his best behavior, Ed found a way to tweak the screen star. When she and co-star Tony De Marco practiced a ballroom dance on a deserted soundstage, Ed wrote that Crawford was dressed in "a black evening dress, cut low in the back [which] revealed her shapely and tanned shoulders and back . . . Solemnly sitting on the blue chair was a tan daschund who persisted in hopping down to the dance floor and following his mistress as she whirled and pivoted. 'He chewed through his leash,' explained Joan. 'He's Franchot's dog.' There was no connection between the thoughts."

Sullivan also gave his readers behind-the-scenes peeks at the wheeling and dealing that took place just off the movie lots. "Business perked up all over the country last week, and the movie moguls have rehired the yes-men they fired during the slump," he reported in the summer of 1938. Adding glitter to his coverage were details about Hollywood's astronomical pay scale, like reports that Douglas Fairbanks, Jr., received $100,000 to appear in *The Rage of Paris*, and Rouben Mammoulian made $178,000 for directing *High, Wide, and Handsome* (a major flop). He noted that Universal's *Mad About Music* was heading toward an impressive $3 million gross.

Ed frequently recounted anecdotes about films in progress, tidbits gathered by visiting the set. "[Jack] Haley had the afternoon off from [*The*] *Wizard of Oz*. He's playing the Tin Man, and he's supposed to be a rusty tin man. The prop man suddenly observed that there was no rust on the tin, so Haley had to take off his costume while they rusted it." Ed saw "four midgets on the MGM lot for [*The*] *Wizard of Oz* . . . You grow accustomed to all sorts of sights in this town, but your correspondent can be pardoned a start of surprise when he rounded a corner and found the passageway jammed with the little men. . . ."

No film of the late 1930s reached the mania of pre-release publicity of *Gone with the Wind*. Ed followed every twist and turn of the production's progress, as the studio dribbled out news bites like breadcrumbs in an effort to mesmerize the public. The suspense over who would land the coveted role of tempestuous Scarlett O'Hara became as much a soap opera as the film itself, with dozens of actresses considered for the part. "I spoke with blonde Miriam Hopkins this afternoon and asked if she had won the role of Scarlett O'Hara," Ed wrote in September 1937, reporting an inconclusive answer. His detective work was ongoing; at the end of 1938, he confided: "Carole Lombard still has the inside track on Scarlett O'Hara." Finally, in January 1939, he informed his readers that the odds were "1,000 to 1" that Vivien Leigh would win the role.

The next day he received a letter from David Selznick, the film's producer. "Dear Ed, in reference to your paragraph yesterday, Vivien Leigh is by no means cast as Scarlett. There are three other possibilities." But Selznick's note was coy. He detailed the many reasons Leigh would be superb for the role (and in fact just four days later he announced Leigh would play Scarlett) and he asked Ed for his support: "If she gets the role, I'd like to think that you'll be in there rooting for her." Ed would indeed root for the picture, exhaustively covering the tidal wave of audience interest that led up to its release. He reported, for instance, that months before its release a Hollywood nightclub hosted parody script readings, and had renamed its mens' and ladies' rooms as Rhett and Scarlett. After premiering for capacity houses, the film won eight Oscars, including Best Picture, a record that stood for sixteen years.

Ed saw virtually every film churned out by the studios. His viewing ranged from Jimmy Cagney gangster movies like *Angels with Dirty Faces* to the lighthearted musicals of Ginger Rogers and Fred Astaire, from westerns starring taciturn strongman Gary Cooper such as *Cowboy and the Lady* to big-budget star vehicles like Katharine Hepburn and Cary Grant's *Holiday*. While he wasn't a film critic per se, he sprinkled his reactions to recent releases through his column and doubtless sold tickets to the films he praised.

For those he didn't like, he could have fun with a pan, as in his reaction to 1938's *Rich Man, Poor Girl*: "Answer this question: In the boating party in this comedy, what falls overboard and is lost? Answer: The plot and the MGM stockholders." He was contrary enough to describe Luise Rainer's performance in *The Great Ziegfeld*, for which she won an Oscar, as "hammy." Sometimes he simply dismissed a picture altogether, opining that the soon-to-be-forgotten *Pacific Liner* "hardly qualified as palatable entertainment." If a film did poorly at the box office he dubbed it a "floperoo."

More often, Ed employed his one-line reviews to cast kudos on his favorites, as in his yearly wrap-up prior to the 1938 Oscars. Among the dozens of film performances he praised were "Edward G. Robinson's college professor in *I Am the Law*," "The charge of the Scots in *The Bucaneer* that sent chills up your spine as the thin line advanced," and "Leslie Howard, Wendy Hiller, and her pa in *Pygmalion*, although they should have eliminated her cockney father's last scene . . . His first scene was dynamite, when he came to Howard's house to blackmail him for dough."

The studios invited all the leading columnists to pre-release screenings, and Ed's reaction to a round of screenings in May 1938 prompted some members of the film colony to question his judgment. He saw eleven films that month, soon-to-be released pictures from MGM, 20th Century Fox, Warner Bros., Paramount, and Columbia. Of all of them, his favorite was *Alexander's Ragtime Band*, a bubbly musical about the early days of jazz, in which Tyrone Power and Alice Faye hoofed and warbled their way through dozens of sunny Irving Berlin tunes. "Reel for reel, this had more solid, down-to-earth entertainment value than any of the others, and the cavalcade of Irving Berlin hit tunes gives this picture an added nostalgic value that raises it to the classification of GREAT flicker," he wrote.

His opinion that this straight-laced ice cream sundae of a musical was the best of the eleven caused guffaws among the film colony intelligentsia. He listed only a few of the other contenders, including *Toy Wife*, starring Luise Rainer; *Kidnapped*, starring Arleen Whelan; and *Holiday* (which he also liked), so the full list is not known. But when *Ragtime*'s premiere that summer proved a box office bonanza, Ed confronted his critics. "When this reporter, after the local premiere of *Alexander's Ragtime Band*, declared that it was the greatest entertainment ever produced in Hollywood, you should have heard the derisive hoots at the Beverly Brown Derby," he wrote in August. "The picture, of course, is cracking records all over the country. One master mind from MGM . . . declared that the picture would end the Zanuck legend by costing his studio a fortune . . . Uh-Huh!"

He had been vindicated by the box office response—his taste, as it so often would, coincided with that of the mass audience. But he couldn't let the issue go. Having been mocked, he would bring up the movie again and again, reminding his readers of the accuracy of his opinion. (Indeed, over time the film would become a minor classic.) That September Ed was back in New York for a month to emcee the annual Harvest Moon dance competition, and after he spoke with Berlin he quoted the songwriter at length:

> "Listen Ed, don't think that Zanuck and Joe Schenck and I will ever for- get that you were the first writer to say *Alexander's Ragtime Band* would be a smash hit. After the picture started clicking, the rest of them climbed on the bandwagon, but you said so the night of the preview, and you didn't hedge on the prediction. Hollywood thought it was a flop; you were right and I'm as pleased for your sake as for mine."

A few nights later he was at Billy Rose's Casa Manana nightclub to see a live per- formance from the *Ragtime* musical, and reported that, "the house comes down" in response to the music. Back in Hollywood in January, he overviewed the year's best film moments, including "Alice Faye and John Carradine in the taxicab scene in *Alexander's Ragtime Band*."

Ed hadn't moved out to Hollywood merely to report on movies—he wanted to make them. He had come to transform himself from a reporter into a player, perhaps even a movie star, and he started work as soon as he arrived.

He crafted the story line for a romantic comedy called *There Goes My Heart*, and by March 1938, six months after moving to the Coast, he had found financial back- ing and signed contracts with the film's lead actors. He partnered with Hal Roach, a powerful independent producer who had written and directed films since 1915. Roach's successes included the *Our Gang* series of humorous shorts and the highly popular Laurel and Hardy comedies; toward the end of his life he would receive an honorary Oscar for his countless film productions. (And on Roach's ninety-fifth birthday an Ed Sullivan impersonator was hired to attend.) Films with Roach's back- ing got wide national release. In 1938 Hal Roach Studios switched its distributor from MGM to United Artists; *There Goes My Heart* would be his first film to be re- leased by UA.

Roach hired bankable stars, Frederic March and Virginia Bruce, to play the ro- mantic leads. The rakishly handsome March received a Best Actor nomination for 1930's *The Royal Family of Broadway*, won Best Actor for 1931's *Dr. Jekyll and Mr. Hyde*, and garnered an Oscar nomination for Best Actor for 1937's *A Star Is Born*. Bruce, whose striking good looks earned her a spot as an original "Goldwyn Girl," played a supporting role in the 1936 box office smash *The Great Ziegfeld*. Filmgo- ers knew her as the vampish society blond in the Jimmy Cagney vehicle *Winner Take All*; after a volcanic kiss with Cagney she had seductively inquired: "You could stand a cold drink after that one, couldn't you?" The director of Sullivan's film was Norman McLeod, who had directed the 1931 Marx Brothers romp *Monkey Business*, among other successes. Roach hired two veteran screenwriters, Eddie Moran and Jack Jevne, to punch up Ed's story line.

When *There Goes My Heart* opened on October 13, 1938, it enjoyed modest box office success. Unfortunately for Ed, its greatest weakness was its story line. The film's plot was widely criticized for being too close to that of *It Happened One Night*, the 1934 Frank Capra classic starring Clark Gable and Claudette Colbert (a rare winner of all five major Academy Awards: Best Picture, Actor, Actress, Director, and Screenplay). Some called Ed's story the work of a plagiarist, and certainly his tale was close to that of the 1934 hit.

Both plots center on an unlikely pairing between a worldly reporter and a rich heiress, thrown together by unlikely circumstances. In the original, after the requisite bickering and misadventures, they realize they're hopelessly in love, though she needs a nudge from her father to complete their union. In Ed's story, the young lovers end up shipwrecked on a small island, and continue skirmishing until a wise minister appears out of nowhere to convince them they're destined for one another. Recycling plots with minor variations is, of course, a standard Hollywood practice; if that were outlawed, studios would quickly cease production. (Dorothy Parker once observed that the only "ism" that Hollywood believes in is plagiarism.) But Ed had taken a well-loved storyline and made it maudlin and semipious, even by the standards of romantic comedy.

That didn't bother the critic from his own paper, the *Daily News*' Kate Cameron, who described the film as "a hilarious and dexterous game of tossing a fast quip and pulling a smart gag," opining that "the picture achieves its purpose beautifully." But *The New York Times*' Frank Nugent, voicing an opinion echoed elsewhere, took a different view. Dismissing it in a review titled "The Original Sin of Hollywood Is Unoriginality," he described *There Goes My Heart* as "virtually a play-by-play repetition of *It Happened One Night*." He observed archly that the movie "seems to be based on an Ed Sullivan yarn—and not, as we supposed, on the [*It Happened One Night* author] Samuel Adams Hopkins story." Worse, the shameless remake was hardly funny, he wrote.

It's likely that Capra's *It Happened One Night* had resonated deeply with Ed; its story is not dissimilar to his own life. When he met Sylvia he was something of a worldly newspaperman, and Sylvia was the heiress of a well-to-do real estate entrepreneur. Their unlikely pairing, after extended squabbling, became a love story. But regardless of how honestly Ed may have come to the story for *There Goes My Heart*, its apparent unabashed borrowing prompted plenty of chuckling in the film colony.

The critical barbs didn't stop Sullivan from diving right back into another film project. In fact, his second movie embodied his hopes for still greater acclaim: he included a major on-screen role for himself. On May 11, 1939, just seven months after the debut of *There Goes My Heart*, Universal released *Big Town Czar*, based on a story by Ed. The tagline of the gangster melodrama screamed from its movie poster: "DICTATOR . . . Of the Sinister Empire Behind the Big City's Bright Lights!"

The cast and crew, a step down from Hal Roach's, were characteristic of the production staffs churning out B movies. Director Arthur Lubin had supervised a handful of undistinguished crime dramas for Universal in the 1930s, and scriptwriter

Edmund Hartmann had just finished the Lucille Ball drama-comedy *Beauty for the Asking* (Ball was a little-known contract player at the time). Lead actor Barton MacLane, with his bulky torso and doughy face, had been typecast as a tough guy gangster or cop; his greatest successes wouldn't come until the 1940s, when he appeared in the Humphrey Bogart classics *The Maltese Falcon* and *The Treasure of the Sierra Madre*. The love interest, Eve Arden, was also still on her way up in 1939. Her first career break had been two years before, when she landed a minor role in the drama *Stage Door*, starring Katharine Hepburn and Ginger Rogers. Her wisecracking portrayal worked so well in rehearsal that her part was rewritten to make her a friend of the lead. She brought this same tough-girl quality to *Big Town Czar*.

If *There Goes My Heart*'s story had come from Ed's life, *Big Town Czar* seemed to mine even deeper ground from his personal history. Ambitious gangster Phil Daley knocks off his chieftain to take control of the mob, only to realize he lacks what he really wants: the respect of his working-class Irish parents and his sweetheart; Ed was estranged from his father and his mother had died. Phil, as Ed had in real life, has a brother named Danny. Phil takes a paternal approach toward Danny, wanting to protect him, but to no avail. As the real-life Danny had died in infancy, so the film Danny dies, in this case in a hail of dum-dums after he fixes a prizefight for Phil. When a rival gangster loses big money on the fight, he sends his henchmen to kill Phil, but they kill Danny instead. Phil feels guilt that the death meant for him befell Danny; thoughts of the infant death of real-life Danny would stay with Ed throughout his life. In the end, Phil faces the electric chair, and on his way to the death chamber realizes crime doesn't pay. Ed plays himself in the picture, the knowing columnist as a one-man Greek Chorus, noting the unchanging nature of moral certitude as he pens his memoirs at the end.

One other element of the film relates closely to Ed's life. Echoing the theme of racial equality he had espoused in his sports columns, the film featured gang warfare by both white and black gangsters, with both outfits equally competent—a highly unusual twist in a 1930s movie.

A few months before the film's release, one of Ed's rivals back in New York, a columnist for the *New York Journal-American*, imagined the consequences of bad reviews with a barely disguised schadenfreude. Sullivan, the writer noted, will play himself in the upcoming release. "Now watch all the film writers he panned get even. He wrote the opera himself, and it better be good or he'll be a two-time loser."

And so he was, given the blistering reviews and tepid box office. The notices for *Big Town Czar* were even more damning than those for Ed's previous picture. "Story has many weak moments and slow spots," observed *Variety*, calling the film suitable for "lower-bracketed action houses where patrons like their melodrama spread rather thick." *The New York Times*' Frank Nugent called it "a bustling little melodrama, all puffed up with its own unimportance. . . . It was written by Ed Sullivan in his best water-under-the-bridge style, which, as you know, is extremely first-personal, quite sentimental, and edifyingly moralistic." As for the performances, most of them were passable in Nugent's view. However, "The only word for Ed Sullivan's portrayal of Ed Sullivan is 'unconvincing.'" It was a humiliating blow for someone thinking of branching into acting—a critic had pronounced him unable to play even himself. He was not, apparently, destined for a career in front of the camera.

Christmas was always a last-minute affair in the Sullivan household. Ed's daughter Betty remembered that the tree was never bought until late on December 24, and the final mad scramble was usually accompanied by irritated arguments and something verging on domestic panic. But in one of their Christmases in Hollywood, Ed endeavored to change this. On the morning of December 24, he told Sylvia and Betty he had already bought the tree—breaking all previous family records for advance preparation. However, when mother and daughter went into the living room to see his purchase, they found a short, shapeless, near-death evergreen. It might have passed muster back in their small New York apartment, but in their three-bedroom Californian home it resembled an underfed waif.

Betty's heart sank at the sight of the scrawny pine. Sylvia, wanting domestic peace, recommended that Ed and Betty drive down to Wilshire Boulevard and choose a better tree, which they did. Wilshire that week was full of big tree lots, so father and daughter quickly found a healthy replacement. Betty, thrilled, could hardly wait to have it in their living room. But before they brought it home, Ed decided to have it sprayed white, a new trend in Christmas trees that year. The tree seller told them to come back at 7 P.M. for the sprayed evergreen.

When Ed and Betty went to pick it up, however, Ed realized he had neglected to jot down the lot's address. He told her not to worry—they would easily spot a white tree among all the green. But when they parked on Wilshire and started searching the lots, they walked among a forest of white trees. Everyone wanted a sprayed evergreen that year.

They searched and searched, to no avail. Betty, tearful, felt they would never find their tree, and had visions of a giftless Christmas; with no tree, where would the presents go? "We went down Wilshire and we *finally* found the tree, but it was hard," she recalled. After all the worry, there it stood—and to Betty's eyes it was gorgeous. They hurried home with it. As was family custom, Ed decorated the tree very late in the evening, then woke up Betty around three in the morning to see his handiwork. She remembered the tree that year as beautifully and extravagantly decorated, her clearest memory of any of the Christmas trees they had.

Although Ed's nascent film career was sputtering, his newspaper career had never been better. Covering Hollywood gave him a far higher profile than he had ever enjoyed on Broadway. He met virtually every major film star, and interviewed many of them.

In late 1937, he drove forty miles outside Hollywood to Malibu Lake for a long one-on-one with Katharine Hepburn. Then 30 years old, Hepburn's career was at low ebb; after her first Academy Award for 1933's *Morning Glory*, she developed a reputation as difficult and distant. Some fans complained that she wore slacks all the time and refused to put on makeup; some reporters claimed she wouldn't pose for photographers or give interviews. Her audience began drifting away and her box office value dwindled.

Her interview with Ed was an attempt to warm up her image, and she spoke at length about her many struggles on stage and screen. She recalled that when she first worked on Broadway she felt so painfully shy that she wouldn't eat in restaurants.

Ed asked her about her image as a "spoiled brat," and she claimed that she had never refused to pose for photos or give interviews, but that she objected to the fabricated romantic gossip. After their afternoon together the columnist summed up his thoughts:

> "Let this be entered in the records. The people who work with her are nuts about this girl. She's generous, breezy, a good two-fisted curser, informal. She won't take any shoving around, and if she thinks she's being imposed upon, she'll let it be known quickly. She is a bit affected, but no more so than any other star in this colony, and considerably less affected than most. The sensitive, aristocratic features are just as compelling off screen as on, the blue eyes just as alert. I'd say that she was a thoroughly nice person, suffering from no malady more serious than youth."

About a year later, Ed interviewed Walt Disney over a two-hour lunch at Hollywood's Tam O'Shanter Inn. The two men would have oddly parallel lives. Like Sullivan, Disney was born in 1901 and lied about his age to take part in World War I (but Disney's lie succeeded and he joined the American Red Cross). Decades later, Disney's television show was a direct competitor with Sullivan's for the Sunday night audience. Unlike Ed, on that August afternoon in 1938, the film producer was awash in success; the previous year's release of *Snow White and the Seven Dwarfs* had been wildly successful. "We ate out on the porch, and ladies and children clambered out of cars with Canada, New York, and Illinois license plates, and asked him for his autograph, grinning happily and appearing a trifle dazed by their good luck in having Disney drop out of the skies," Ed wrote. "'We've traveled six thousand miles,' bubbled one nice-looking lady, 'and this is the nicest single thing that has happened to us.'"

Disney spoke about his struggles in the Depression, about having to show a preview of *Snow White* to save a shaky bank loan, and about needing to ask employees to return part of their bonus during the bank panic. He explained his policy of barring visitors to his studio, claiming that people didn't seem interested enough when touring the facility. The exception was writer H.G. Wells, who was thrilled by the carpentry shop, and Charlie Chaplin, who spent the day entertaining the animators.

"I asked him what he learned from the industry-shaking success of *Snow White*," Ed wrote. "His brown eyes twinkled. 'I'll tell you what it has taught me, Ed—a deep respect for the juvenile audience. I never had it before. You see, I figured it was idiotic to make pieces for children, because a 10-cent or 15-cent audience is unimportant to this business. So all of our work was slanted principally at an adult audience. *Snow White*, road-showed at prices ranging from 85 cents up, proved that parents would pay even those prices for their children's attendance." Disney's comments that day marked still another thing the two men would have in common; like Disney, Ed learned a profound respect for the juvenile audience.

The day that Ed drove out to interview W.C. Fields at the actor's mansion became a favorite memory of his, so much so that decades later he recounted it to Peter Prichard, a young talent agent he spent time with in his older years. Ed arrived at Fields' house at about 11 in the morning. The butler ushered him into the foyer, told him Mr. Fields would be with him shortly, and offered him a cocktail. Ed demurred, noting the early hour, but the manservant insisted. "Mr. Fields would prefer that you have a drink." Ed complied, finishing his drink, and over the next forty-five minutes servants brought him to two more locations in the mansion; at each spot he was arm-twisted into downing another cocktail. Finally he was brought out to the pool, where Fields was holding court. The comic offered him yet another tipple. "I've been waiting forty-five minutes and I've already had three drinks," Ed protested. "Yes, my dear boy, let me tell you one thing," replied the heavy-drinking Fields, explaining why he had plied Ed with alcohol, "Always meet a man on a level playing field."

Ed, as a onetime sports writer, brought the conversation to boxing, but Fields turned it back to the virtues of Bacchus. The actor explained that boxer Max Schmeling's storied loss to Joe Louis was due to his abstemious habits:

> "After the Louis Massacre of Schmeling, Fields held forth long and earnestly on the conclusion to be drawn from Schmeling's explanation that the first blow to the kidney paralyzed him. 'It simply bears out what I've always contended,' said Fields, 'A kidney needs a good alcoholic lining to stand up under wear and tear. Schmeling was the victim of clean living. I dare say that if Louis or any other professional slasher dealt me such a blow that their hands would crumple from the impact.'"

As Ed began work on his third film in the fall of 1939, he wrote a long column about critics, detailing how scathing they could be and how wrong they often were. He gave myriad examples of their blunders and overly acid commentary:

> "An Indianapolis poison-penner scored this direct hit on Tyrone Power in *Jesse James*: 'Young Tyrone played his role as if Zanuck had been undecided to cast him or Shirley Temple in the part . . .' A Kansas City assassin, with a grudge against Don Ameche, wrote: 'Ameche, through eight reels, laughed and laughed while his audience endeavored with some difficulty to locate the reason for his merriment. This reviewer concludes Mr. Ameche's laugh stems from sadism.'"

Ed himself was a critic of sorts, and he charitably included a Sullivan fumble.

> "When *Tobacco Road* opened on Broadway, I remarked smugly that it would be fortunate to last out the week. It is still running."

The point, of course, and one he wanted to convince himself of, was that past pans don't prevent future success. After the dismal reviews of his first two films he certainly hoped that this was true as he started production on *Ma, He's Making Eyes at Me*, his new romantic comedy. Universal, for its part, appeared to have no great hopes. The studio funded the project but kept its investment to a minimum. Co-stars Tom Brown and Constance Moore were undistinguished contract players. Brown, who had been acting since his first silent film at age ten, had been typecast as the boy next door; he played fresh-faced Danny in *Big Town Czar*. Moore, previously a big band singer, recently scored a career high point in W.C. Fields' 1939 comedy *You Can't Cheat an Honest Man*; she would play lead in a string of B movies in the 1940s. Director Harold Schuster had been a film editor for most of his career, becoming a director just three years earlier. Scriptwriter Edmund Hartmann had churned out sixteen scripts in his four years as a screenwriter, one of which was *Big Town Czar*.

In Ed's story, a fast-talking press agent schemes with an out-of-work chorus girl to publicize a clothing line. He dubs her "Miss Manhattan" and hires a young man to play "Mr. Manhattan," staging a fake wedding for publicity. After a series of nutty stunts, the press agent realizes that he loves "Miss Manhattan" and he eventually proposes to her. All the while the young lady is equally fond of her press agent, as the movie's tagline trumpeted: "When she saw him wink, her head said 'NO'... but her heart didn't stop to think!" Interspersed with the general zaniness were musical numbers, most notably the title song.

When the movie opened on April 26, 1940, it was a clear flop. It's likely that the daily headlines screaming of war in Europe dampened the reception to this frothy piece of cinematic cotton candy. But it might not have done well at any point. "This is the season for fashion shows, and that is about all you get with *Ma, He's Making Eyes at Me*," pronounced *The New York Times*' B.R. Crisler, calling it a "cut-rate, bargain-basement story" and "a limp and foolish little picture, inexcusable on any other grounds than as a chaser to follow the main picture." *Variety* felt likewise, dismissing it as a "picture that's deficient in every department, except implausibilities." Worse yet, there was no box office success to offset the critical fusillade.

As the movie's notice faded, so did Ed's hopes for a film career. As he knew from his days on Port Chester's baseball fields, three swings meant the batter was out. He felt his failure in movies deeply. Winchell had received huge offers from Hollywood for his story lines, Skolsky had appeared in a handful of pictures (and later produced *The Eddie Cantor Story* and *The Jolson Story*). Ed had produced nothing but a string of flops. His dream of moving to California to become a star had come to nothing. In truth, his Hollywood reporting had pushed his star far higher, yet that didn't seem to matter to him. Fame was what he had come for, but as he had neared it, it had scurried from his grasp.

In the late spring of 1940 his sisters Helen and Mercedes took a train trip to Hollywood to visit Ed. The sisters were looking forward to a family reunion, but Ed was in a sour temper and in no mood to be the jovial host. His mind seemed elsewhere. After less than a week, Helen and Mercedes left for Yosemite. Ed was hurt by their departure, but the sisters wanted to enjoy their vacation.

His ulcer was acting up; he had developed an irritated stomach several years back that had grown steadily worse since moving to Hollywood. He made light of it in his column—reporting that a piece of baked halibut from the MGM commissary "swims upstream"—but it was a serious concern. At times he was completely incapacitated by intestinal pain, forced to spend a half day in bed at his doctor's orders.

Although discouraged, he hadn't completely given up on a film career. With his track record at Universal he knew he would find no interest there, but in June 1940 he sold a short to Warner Bros., *Ed Sullivan's Hollywood Revue*. In November the studio released another short with a Sullivan story line, *Alice in Movieland*. But selling two preview pictures was a major step down from creating the story line for full-length features.

In his *Daily News* column, he had made no mention of any of his three features, not even as United Artists' and Universal's publicity machines were promoting the films with quarter-page newspapers ads in the *News*. (He did, however, toss positive column tidbits to their stars, writing a glowing laud for Frederic March.) Ed presumably didn't want to further impress the *News* management that he was pursuing a second career while working for them.

But they noticed. By the premiere of his third film, the *News* management had grown restive with Sullivan's Hollywood tenure. It became a replay of Sidney Skolsky three years earlier. Like Skolsky, Ed had used his column as an entree into a film career. And, as Ed had lobbied to replace Skolsky, now John Chapman, another *News* columnist, began lobbying to replace Sullivan. The *News* agreed. It was time for Ed to come home.

Sullivan and the *News* got into a tussle. He didn't want to return to New York. Failing in films was bad enough; having to return to the Broadway beat after covering Hollywood was a big step backward. He had come to enjoy life on the Coast, particularly those almost-daily trips out to the Santa Anita racetrack, where he sometimes wrote his column. Several months earlier he had written a column entitled "The Typical Hollywood Male," which described the many qualities of this mythic creature—and the portrait was close to a self-portrait. He is, wrote Ed, between thirty and forty years old, he is liberal, his wife likes Chinese or French food, he himself like an Eastern cut steak. He tends to lose when he bets on horses. Furthermore:

> "Having come to Hollywood with a sense of superiority to the movies, he is alarmed deeply when he finds himself becoming convinced that the movies are a greater and more important medium than the stage which spawned him . . . Having come to California with a sneering attitude toward California's climate, he finds himself perturbed by the fact that the state has exercised its mellifluous charms . . . he never quite shakes off these reproaches; never is quite happy when he should be most happy . . . So he compromises; he squares his ambition and his reproaches by agreeing that he isn't going back East because the California climate is better for his children."

Ed dug in his heels in the summer of 1940. After being summoned back East, he fired off a wire to *Daily News* publisher Joseph Medill Patterson: he would not be returning to New York. Managing editor Frank Hause visited Sullivan in Hollywood in an effort to coax him back to Broadway. "I pointed out to the great Port Chester athlete the advantages of the Broadway beat, and the *Daily News* growth and prestige," Hause later wrote. Whatever else he said, it must have been convincing. Hause soon sent a wire back to Patterson with Sullivan's words: "I acted hastilly [*sic*]. Please ignore earlier telegram. Am returning New York."

The decision made, Sullivan moved quickly. In early July, Ed, Sylvia, and Betty boarded the Chief—the same train they had traveled out on—to move back to New York. Nine-year-old Betty was truly disconsolate at leaving. It wasn't Hollywood she missed; Ed had introduced her to Shirley Temple and she found the experience less than thrilling. It was having her own house and yard she so loved, and the freedom to play outside whenever she wanted, unlike being cooped up in a New York apartment. "I was heartbroken," she said. "I remember pulling out of Union Station, and saying to my parents, 'Are we coming back, when are we coming back?'" Ed, clearly, was no happier than his young daughter at having to return to New York.

He had written a column in late 1938 about winning and losing, and how losing had to be kept in perspective. It was part of a series he called "Listen, Kids," in which he gave advice about life to "youngsters," as he called them. (That he sometimes addressed his Hollywood gossip column to children was an oddity, but he saw his audience as all-inclusive.)

"Don't place too great an emphasis on defeat, and don't yield to the American habit of overemphasizing victory, because one is no more important than the other," he advised, noting that Warner Bros. had fired Clark Gable and Universal had fired Bette Davis. Considering his funk at having failed at films, he probably needed his own advice during the trip east. The scores from victories and defeats, he noted, are not written in indelible ink. "Through life, you'll encounter your share of both of them, and you'll find that defeats are really the prep school of victories."

CHAPTER SEVEN

The War Years

N ew York was miserable in July of 1940. As Ed returned to the Broadway beat late that month, a four-day heat wave hit the city, engulfing the canyons of Manhattan in an oppressive blanket of humidity. So many overheated people thronged to Jones Beach that authorities had to close roads leading to the shoreline. Although America was not yet at war, the headlines made it feel that way. In June the Nazis had overrun France, and each day's newspaper blared the grim developments in bold, oversized type. Dark times lay ahead. Furthermore, the economic hardship of the Depression, though only a wan shadow of its former self, meant New Yorkers were still far from flush.

Ed's mood mirrored the city's funk. In the debut of his relaunched Broadway column, now dubbed *Little Old New York*, he portrayed his move back to the city as his fondest wish. "When I asked the boss to transfer me to New York, he wanted to know the reason and I told him that after all, this was my city, where I'd been born and lived . . . No city ever has been so kind to me," he claimed, disingenuously. Having no news, he riffed through his twelve-hundred-word column, explaining that this time around his beat would be bigger than Broadway, it would encompass the city in its entirety. "No one will be too big or too small to get entree to this column . . . through these portals will pass the most beautiful and the least lovely characters of Baghdad-on-the-Subway: the only ticket of admission they'll need to this daily vaudeville show, two columns wide, will be a common denominator of interest to all of us."

But his frustration that summer spoke large between the lines. Because he wrote five pieces a week his column had always been a diary of sorts, no matter how happy a face he attempted. In early August, Ed's replacement on the Hollywood beat, John Chapman, was writing about the joys of Beverly Hills and the hot news from Hal Roach Studios (where Ed, had his collaboration with Roach not been a failure, might now be a hitmaker). Seemingly in response, Ed devoted a column to fallen stars of all kinds, individuals who had risen high only to see their dreams dashed.

Joe Helbock, onetime owner of the Onyx Club, was now a bartender at Ben Marden's Riviera. Rube Marquard, once a pitcher for the Giants, was now a pari-mutuel ticket seller. However, Ed reported, these frustrated dreamers were gamely coping. "Instead of sitting in the corner and moping about the injustice of the current setup, they've adapted themselves to the changed conditions and altered circumstances and are working it out the hard way."

Indeed he would not sit in the corner. If he could not be a film star, then he would throw himself into emceeing and stage producing with more passion than ever before. He moved his family into the Hotel Astor in midtown Manhattan so he could be across the street from Loew's State Theatre, on Broadway and 45th Street. He seemed unaware that the unsavory center of New York's theater district was no place to raise a child. The Depression had stripped the luster from the city's once-glorious core, and a cadre of sleazy burlesque houses was taking over the neighborhood. The Times Square area was on a downward slide that, by the 1950s, would make it a haven for drug dealing and prostitution. The neighborhood was full of seedy types, and ten-year-old Betty sometimes had to step around drunks to get to school. "It was a terrible place for a young kid to be," she recalled.

But Ed felt compelled to be close to the theater. His *Daily News* salary was more than sufficient to live in a nicer neighborhood, but Loew's State drew him like a moth to a flame. It was where he wanted to spend most of his days and nights. Not that this seemed to afford him any great joy. His ulcer was giving him hell; the family's small suite had no refrigerator so he kept a carton of milk on the windowsill for his frequent nocturnal battles with stomach pain.

By the end of August, Ed mounted a new variety revue at Loew's State. As before, his stage show was updated vaudeville. Providing a contemporary feel were the recent Harvest Moon Ball winners, swing dancers who juked and jived to Big Band music; harking back to vaudeville's roots was Dave Vine, a Jewish dialect comic. Also on the bill were vocalist Luba Malina, singing Spanish tunes (the fashion that year favored all things South American), and the Paul Remos acrobats, tumbling and twirling. As always, Ed was both emcee and producer. He "headlined" the show as its emcee, with his name in block letters on the marquee, yet his more important role was shaping the program. He chose the acts and determined their order, creating the pace and feel of the show, standing just offstage to gauge audience response, making adjustments based on his instinct. Judging from ticket sales, he had a knack for this; his first show was held over into September and Loew's State management gave him an open invitation to produce more.

But he didn't want to be there. He couldn't get over his desire to live on the West Coast, and Hollywood kept calling to him like a song he couldn't get out of his mind. In mid November, Ed made a surprise announcement: He was leaving the *Daily News* to take a job as the editor for the *Hollywood Reporter*, a film industry trade paper. In addition to being its editor he would write some of its movie reviews, making him a Hollywood tastemaker. He had also arranged with his current syndicator, the Chicago Tribune–New York News Syndicate, to write a feature every Sunday about screen stars. He gave his two-week notice to the *News*; his last day at the paper would be December 2, after which he would move back to Hollywood.

News publisher Joseph Medill Patterson was on a Florida fishing trip with his wife that week. But on November 16 he interrupted his vacation to telegram a paternal appeal to his star columnist: "If you can better yourself permanently, I would not wish to stand in your way. Mary [Patterson] suggests your health might be involved and that, of course, is a matter you know best. But I want to make it clear I consider you one of our best men and that, *rebus sic stantibus* [as matters stand], you can stay with us as long as you want."

That was a seductive offer. Ed had navigated the choppy seas of newspaper job-hopping in his twenties; reporter-editor posts tended to come and go, but his *Daily News* column had the feeling of permanency. Patterson made it clear: if you stay with us you have job security. So he made his decision: he would forego his dreams of Hollywood for the stability of the *News*. Ed explained his change of heart to reporters by saying that he was staying at the *News* "because of his high regard for Captain Patterson." The telegram from Patterson, in fact, became a prize possession he dug out when the slings and arrows of his columnist's life became too much.

Like it or not, he was now a New Yorker again. He was home for good.

Crazy with the Heat appeared to be a doomed Broadway show when it opened in January 1941. The two-act revue rambled through an ill-fitting medley of comedy and dance routines, guided by a mere wisp of a story line. In theory, the show had been improved by revisions in smaller cities before opening in New York, but its Broadway premiere still presented a work in progress. Produced and directed by Kurt Kasznar, a twenty-seven-year-old Viennese actor, the production survived a scant seven performances before closing. A phalanx of uniformly negative reviews turned it into an instant money pit for its investors.

For Ed, the failed show offered an opportunity to become a Broadway producer. He decided to take over the show, revamp it, and then relaunch it. Entering into negotiations with the show's various parties, he convinced the theater owner to host it with no additional rent payments, and won concessions from the Actors Equity Association and Musicians Local 802. After raising $20,000, he reshaped the production, pruning and adding based on critics' reviews and his own stage sense. He added a pair of ballroom dancers, Mary Raye and Naldi, who were considered the city's finest; vocalist Carlos Ramirez parodied an excerpt from the opera *Figaro*; comedian-pianist Victor Borge goofed through a comic turn; a black tap-dance team, Tip, Tap & Toe, soft-shoed in both acts; Betty Kean tap-danced and told jokes; original stars Willie Howard and Louella Gear provided the show's thin continuity in a series of comic sketches; and songwriter Lew Brown helped with the music direction. As Ed described it, "We are taking the constructive criticism offered by the critics . . . and are going ahead with a $3.30 top." Although the show had just closed on January 18, he had it ready for its second debut on January 30.

The critical response, though still not enthusiastic, was markedly better. "Being a person of unusual compassion, Ed Sullivan, the celebrated columnist, hated to see all the good things go to waste in *Crazy with the Heat*, which succumbed to prostration nearly a fortnight ago," wrote *The New York Times*' Brooks Atkinson. "With the assistance of Lew Brown, songwriter and beer jongleur, he revived it last evening at the Forty-forth Street Theatre in an improved condition." Atkinson noted, however, that the show still lacked the material for a first-rate revue, and audiences agreed. *Crazy with the Heat* ran just ninety-two performances. Still, after it closed on Broadway, Ed revised it again, booking a pared-down version into Loew's State, where he gave it a lengthy run. With its odd melange of fast-moving acts the show was better fit for vaudeville than Broadway.

As the show was running, so was the rumor mill. Ed, or so some said, was having an affair with one of its actresses. Who the actress was remains unclear because Ed maintained discretion, whatever the extent of the dalliance. Yet knowledge of the affair seemed widespread. In 1941, Walter Winchell began a very public romance with Mary Lou Bentley, a leggy twenty-year-old showgirl. All Broadway columnists followed an unwritten rule that prohibited the reporting of affairs involving anyone who was married, as was Winchell, unless they were clearly separated from their spouse. A blind item was permissible but naming the participants was forbidden (and the *Daily News'* editorial policy also forbade it). But Ed, always envious of Walter, tried to include an item about Winchell and Bentley. After *News* editor Dick Clark deleted it, Ed ran into his office screaming, wanting it put back in before publication. Clark calmly explained to the columnist that if the item ran, Winchell would take revenge by printing bits about Sullivan's own affairs. Ed decided it was best to let the matter drop.

Whatever romance Ed may have been having during *Crazy with the Heat*'s run on Broadway, it must have been on-again, off-again; he flew down to Miami Beach that winter for his first of many annual two-week press junkets. Perks for columnists were numerous but this all-expense-paid trip was one of the dearest. Ed stayed in a lavish penthouse suite and the staff feted him like royalty. "By day a columnist surveys the trimly proportioned misses lounging around the beach or around the pools; by night he sits at ringside tables of Florida clubs and is entertained by the cream of the performers," he reported. In exchange he wrote glowing reports about the joys of Miami tourism, though he noted that the city suffered a severe crime problem. He could be influenced, but, his caveat seemed to say, he could not be bought.

Soon after the Eastern Airlines Douglas airliner returned him to New York, he began laying the groundwork for another radio program. Producing stage shows was lucrative, but true fame required getting inside the living room radio; the most successful stage performers resembled mere understudies next to broadcast stars. Debuting on April 27 on WABC, the new program was a weekly talk show, every Sunday night at 6 P.M. As the headliner, Ed alternated between interviewing guests and sprinkling celebrity pixie dust, offering an insider's glimpse into Broadway and Hollywood by reprising his column.

Accompanying him were drummer-comedian Ray McKinley and vocalist Terry Allen, with Will Bradley's orchestra vamping swing music. Sponsored by the International Silver Company, the show was titled *Summer Silver Theater*. The network clearly viewed the thirty-minute program as a seasonal replacement for its serial radio drama, but with luck—in the form of high ratings—the show would earn its own time slot when fall arrived. To boost ratings, Ed used his column's influence to cajole appearances by some big names, like Eddie Cantor and bandleader Tommy Dorsey, though most of the guests were only modestly known.

Throughout the summer, Ed's radio program, vaudeville shows at Loew's State, and daily column became a circular path for performers. Once the showman-columnist invited them in he could circulate them between the three. That a singer had performed at Loew's State gave him reason to tout him or her in his column; once the singer appeared on his radio show, he or she could be introduced at Loew's State as having just been on the air. In the early summer, Gertrude Niesen, a popular big band chanteuse, performed in his Loew's State show, sang on his radio program, and enjoyed plugs in his column. It was his own one-man show business circuit, a revolving platform for singers and comics, a cross-venue promotional device placing the name Ed Sullivan front and center in print, on marquees, and over the airwaves.

For a short time, that is. On September 28 the radio show saw its last broadcast. True to the original schedule, Sullivan's program proved to be simply a summer replacement. Huge listener interest, of course, would have won it another spot, but that hadn't materialized. Ed's latest attempt to launch a broadcast career lasted slightly longer than five months.

Toward the end of the year it finally happened. After long and rancorous national debate about whether to intervene, and years of anxious anticipation, events forced a decision. On December 8, 1941, the *Daily News* reported the previous day's carnage in type so large that only three words fit on the front page: JAPS BOMB HAWAII.

Although Ed, a forty-year-old family man, wasn't going to don a uniform, he threw himself into the war effort as if he had. As his age had kept him from the first war it also kept him from this one, yet he was as eager to take part now as when he ran away to join the Marines at age sixteen. The *News* had been isolationist, and Ed had nominally echoed this. As late as February 1941 he dashed off column asides like, "At any continental dinner party Uncle Sam always gets stuck with the check." But with the attack he was ready. That June, six months before Pearl Harbor, he volunteered to be an air-raid warden, part of the city's new civil defense plan; in the event of German attack each district's air-raid warden would coordinate its response. Ed signed up the first day the program was announced. (And he wasn't alone in his enthusiasm. "Chinese, Italians, Germans, Jews, and Irish all appeared to respond," reported *The New York Times*.) And in May he had joined Irving Berlin, the Jimmy Dorsey Orchestra, and others at the Greek Festival for Freedom, a fund-raiser for the Greek war-relief effort.

Suddenly, life moved faster. Slapped awake by Pearl Harbor, New York no longer slogged along in its late Depression funk. One month after the attack, Mayor Fiorello La Guardia declared a six-day work week for city employees, and the city's nightlife, as if responding in kind, also sprang to life. "Nightclubs did a terrific business starting Friday night . . . All joints jammed," Ed reported in January. The Copacabana started including table maps showing all fire exits, and the Stork's receipts soon leaped by more than thirty percent. But as fast as the city would spin, Ed would spin still faster.

His primary battle had always been his career, his indefatigable effort to push his star higher. The war, and indeed nothing, would ever interrupt this. But the war required him to redouble himself, because he would also be needed—and would answer the call eagerly—for war benefit drives, hospital shows, and a plethora of fund-raising personal appearances.

In the few short months before war rallies became a steady drumbeat, Ed launched his second Broadway show, this one an all-black production in partnership with Noble Sissle. A fifty-one-year-old composer and bandleader, Sissle cowrote the hit "It's Your Fault" with pianist Eubie Blake, and would win a posthumous Tony Award for Best Original Score in 1979 for the Broadway musical *Eubie*. When Ed began their collaboration, Sissle's orchestra was the house band for Billy Rose's Diamond Horseshoe club, a fashionable Manhattan nightspot.

Sullivan, as producer and codirector, and Sissle, as codirector and performer, conceived of a rollicking, high-energy revue. They recruited the stars of black vaudeville: Moke and Poke, the 5 Crackerjacks, the Harlemaniacs, Pops and Louie, and several others, with Sissle himself performing two numbers. In a nod to the headlines, some of the vocalists dressed as air-raid wardens, and a sketch portrayed a young man grappling with a draft questionnaire. Opening at Broadway's Ritz Theater in May 1942, *Harlem Cavalcade* offered a fresh twist on Ed's variety shows. The production presented vaudeville as practiced above 125th Street, in the neighborhood to which the show paid homage.

As *The New York Times* described it, "*Harlem Cavalcade* goes in for dancing, swing, stomp, for the blare of the trumpet and the shuffle of feet, for the golden tooth widely shown, for eagerness and cheer. . . . On the stage of the Ritz they are hopping and bouncing, they are dancing tap and tumble, they are singing swing spirituals and popular songs. . . . No doubt about vaudeville's coming back."

For all its kinetic high spirit, an all-black vaudeville show was not well-suited for Broadway. The only black-themed Broadway production to have done passably well had been George Gershwin's classic *Porgy and Bess* in 1935, and even that was a financial loss in its first run, playing only one hundred thirty-five shows. *Harlem Cavalcade* saw just forty-nine performances. However, like Ed's first Broadway show, *Harlem Cavalcade* enjoyed its greatest success in its post-Broadway run. Sullivan and Sissle booked it into Harlem's Apollo Theater, where it played a long run of four shows daily at prices ranging from 20 to 55 cents. Despite the show's short Broadway run, it displayed a key aspect of Ed's success as a producer: the ability to work with and appreciate black performers, which benefited him greatly in the years ahead.

While *Harlem Cavalcade* was showing uptown, Ed helped organize war benefits in midtown and downtown. The first, in June, by The Yiddish Theatre Division for Army and Navy Relief at the National Downtown Theater, featured skits by Menasche Skilnick and Aaron Lebedeff and a chorus of a hundred. The second, in July on the steps of the huge public library at 42nd Street and Fifth Avenue, was a massive war bond rally. A crowd of twenty thousand gathered to see Mayor Fiorello La Guardia and a cast of Broadway stars, along with a swing orchestra, with Ed as emcee. The makeshift stage was festooned with red, white, and blue bunting, a coast guard lifeboat, and a seventeen-hundred-horsepower airplane engine. Rain interrupted the event; the audience screamed and laughed as thunderclaps competed with the swing band. As the storm cleared, the crowd, drenched but undeterred, kept raising its bids and buying more stamps and bonds from the volunteers walking among the throng. "Triumphantly at the end, the master of ceremonies, Ed Sullivan, newspaper writer and columnist, announced the total of $1,405,000 in bonds and $30,000 in stamps as 'an American record,'" a reporter wrote.

As soon as the war bond rally ended, Ed began organizing an even bigger extravaganza, a benefit for Army Emergency Relief at Madison Square Garden on September 30. As chairman of the entertainment committee, he worked the phones to enlist a glittering crowd of his Hollywood and Broadway contacts: Bob Hope, Bing Crosby, Fred Astaire, Barbara Stanwyck, and many others. Working double-time, he simultaneously produced and emceed a Loew's State vaudeville show, hosting his usual hodgepodge of singers, jugglers, and comics. After opening in August, the Loew's State show's brisk ticket sales kept it running into September, ending just in time for Sullivan to emcee the war benefit at Madison Square Garden, which raised $203,000.

In November, he helped with a United Jewish Appeal benefit attended by twenty thousand people, sharing master of ceremonies duties with Milton Berle and Henny Youngman. In December, he headed the entertainment committee for a Police Athletic League event seen by eighteen thousand, featuring Hollywood and Broadway actors. In January, he took part in a United Service Organizations (USO) show at the Waldorf Astoria, and in February, he led the entertainment committee for the annual Israel Orphan Asylum benefit. While working on these events—and continuing to write his daily column—he launched a winter version of his Loew's State revue, starring the Louis Jordan swing orchestra, impressionist Neal Stanley, and harmonica player John Sebastian. As this closed he began putting together the largest single war benefit to date, for the American Red Cross at Madison Square Garden. It featured a mock striptease by a group of male movie stars; appearances by Helen Hayes, Ray Milland, and Ozzie Nelson; and a three-hundred-seventy-five-member chorus singing "The Star Spangled Banner." To increase contributions, Sullivan named the box seats after recent war heroes and charged $5,000 apiece; front row seats were $100. The April benefit raised $249,000.

In addition to his whirlwind of war benefits, Ed organized a constant stream of celebrity-filled shows at New York–area hospitals filled with wounded soldiers. He often recounted moments from these shows in his column, always in highly emotional terms. Typical of his anecdotes was one from a variety revue he put together at Staten Island's Halloran Hospital, starring comedienne Beatrice Lilly, Jimmy Durante, and Peg Leg Bates. In the show, Durante reprised his wildly physical 1920s act from Club Durant in which he tore apart a piano, hurling the pieces pell-mell through the hall. After his act, standing offstage with Ed as Peg Leg Bates performed, Durante pointed out two soldiers. "Then I noticed the tears on his face," Ed wrote. "'Ed,' he said, in that hoarse whisper, 'take a look at those two kids out there.' He indicated two youngsters, one a lieutenant and the other a G.I., each of whom had lost an arm . . . They were applauding Peg Leg Bates. With great spirit and not the slightest self-consciousness, they were clapping their hands—the lieutenant's left against the G.I.'s right."

Ed's story of the one-armed soldiers clapping was, to some, quite maudlin, though few would have carped about such a thing at the time. But his constant reports of his own exploits in aiding the war effort—myriad items like "Editorialists throughout the land are praising this column for suggesting the idea of the Carole Lombard Bond Memorial"—did earn him critical flak. Harriet Van Horne, a *World Telegram & Sun* reporter whose trenchant wit resembled Dorothy Parker's, wrote a parody of a Sullivan column and tacked it up on the newsroom bulletin board. Her editor liked it so much he printed it in the paper. Sullivan, livid, dashed her off a furious letter.

The trivia of Broadway romance still played a major role in his column, but this ephemera was now heavily overweighted by war chronicles. Almost every column reported tales of soldiers on the front, war rally schedules, Ed's comments on a battle's progress, or the effect of government rationing: "Erasers on pencils out for the duration!" he reported, and, "The wolves no longer offer etchings . . . The switch: 'Come up and see my nylon stockings.'" Even upcoming birth announcements, formerly reported as "a visit from Sir Stork" were now written as "The Lieut. Douglas Fairbanks Jrs. expecting a little ensign."

He frequently printed letters from soldiers that pointed to his own connection with the troops: "Dear Ed: From us fellows in the 340th Bombardment Group, whom you mentioned in a column in mid June . . . Most of the gang who read your article got so swell-headed that we've been going around hatless."

And: "Dear Ed: Over here in England, some of us got to thinking about songs that were popular when we were back home. The one we all remembered was Joe E. Lewis' 'Sam, You Made the Pants Too Long.' Can you get the words of it from Joe for us, and in return we'll send you lyrics of our marching song, 'Dirty Gertie from Bizerte.' If you run this letter with our names, please send us a copy so we can be G.I. hotshots."

The most notable of his war-related columns told the story of Arthur Ford, a critically wounded soldier from Midgeville, Georgia, in a ward at New York's Halloran Hospital. In his telling, Ed had sort of adopted the soldier, working to cheer him as he struggled to live: "'Would you like to meet Jack Benny?' I asked him, and then he grinned and whispered: 'Stop your kidding.' . . . so I got Jack from another ward, and so strong is training that the badly wounded boy asked me if his hair was combed right . . . 'Want to look my best when Mister Benny comes in,' he explained weakly."

The Benny visit buoyed the soldier and Ed told him that he would soon return with more celebrity visitors. "'Maybe I won't be here,' he whispered. 'I don't feel too hot, Mister. They got me right through the stomach' . . . So I pretended to bawl him out, and told him he'd BETTER be there when we came back to the ward in two weeks, figuring that if he had some definite date to look forward to, it would keep him holding onto life . . . we shook hands on it." Ed kept calling the hospital and "Each succeeding telephone call confirmed the optimistic news . . . Ford was holding his own." The soldier's condition, in fact, seemed to be improving while waiting for Ed's visit with a celebrity. However, "After keeping that date, the worn boy died that night, very peacefully."

Ed's column about Arthur Ford concluded with a statement addressed to his family:

> "In his last struggle, they should know that their son, or brother, was not a small-town Georgia boy alone in a big city of Yankees . . . He was with people who considered him one of their own, and when he died, in the North, of wounds received while landing on a faraway shore, we regretted it bitterly, while acknowledging that the wearied and wounded boy finally had found the one opiate to ease his pain."

The column displayed the two sides of Ed simultaneously. Certainly it showed him to be the egoist whom Harriet Van Horne had skewered, the reporter who relentlessly detailed his own good work, with a dollop of saccharine rivaling that in any of the war movies now flooding theaters. Yet coming when it did, during some of the war's darkest days, his homespun elegy resonated deeply with his readers.

The piece was Ed at his most empathetic, a touch of the blue-collar poet, and it was read on the radio and reprinted by organizations promoting war bond drives.

But it wasn't enough for him. All of it—the personal appearances, the syndicated column, the long-running vaudeville shows, being a well-known New Yorker—only left him wanting more. The things he had achieved only served to point out the one thing he hadn't achieved: fame. And nothing made that disparity more galling than comparing himself with Walter Winchell.

Winchell had been on the radio nonstop since he and Ed were at the *Graphic*, and now Winchell's show, a half hour of incantatory gossip delivered in a transcendental manic staccato, was followed ritually by nearly a quarter of all Americans. In contrast, Sullivan had never succeeded in getting a show past the six-month point. Winchell was wealthy; Sullivan lived in the Hotel Astor, a residential hotel in a seedy neighborhood. Winchell was courted by Hollywood; Sullivan had been a flop in Hollywood. Winchell was nationally known; Sullivan was a New York celebrity. They both stood on the same pedestal—newspaper columns—but Walter had reached so much higher. In short, Walter was famous, and Ed, clearly, was not.

In Ed's moodier moments—and he had many of them—he felt this difference acutely. At some point, there's no record of exactly when, he began to shave a year off his age, as if he was born in 1902 rather than 1901. (He stuck to this so consistently that even the Webster's Dictionary entry about him lists his birth date as 1902.) He felt he had not accomplished enough for his age. As his father had before him, Ed felt frustrated by his status in life. Something essential was lacking.

Radio was the vehicle that propelled Winchell from mere notoriety to true stardom. Outside of film it was the only medium that pushed a performer, not his words on paper, into the lives of his fans. No amount of vaudeville appearances could compete with the fame-creating magic of the airwaves. Ed, in 1943, saw that now was his time to make a major effort in radio. Regardless of how busy he was, how breakneck his schedule, the time was now. With his war-related columns and his constant high-profile event hosting, his star shone its brightest, his name on more lips and marquees than ever before. It was the time to parley his notoriety into a successful radio show, and finally achieve the fame he had so long desired.

He told his readers the big news on September 11, 1943, in a column entitled "My Secretary, Africa, Speaks." (The "secretary" format was an imitation of a Winchell trope in which he wrote his column as if it was a note from his personal secretary.) His "secretary" that day wrote her boss an excited note: "Your CBS radio program tees off Monday night at 7:15 o'clock! Nervous?"

Unlike Ed's earlier radio shows, mostly straightforward productions, his new program was high concept. Entitled *Ed Sullivan Entertains*, it broadcast from the swank Club 21 nightclub, with the background chatter of the Manhattan nightspot lending urban cachet; as Winchell seemed to allow listeners into the mystique of celebrity lives, so Sullivan would present the ambiance of the smart set. The show more overtly copied Winchell in its signature sound: Walter opened with an urgent telegraph effect; Ed opened with the clickety-clack of a Remington typewriter.

Winchell, of course, never had guests; they would have broken the runic trance of his manic delivery. Ed, with a budget provided by sponsor Mennen Shave Cream, booked the biggest stars available, including Humphrey Bogart, Orson Welles, George Raft, Marlene Dietrich, and Ethel Merman. Along with stage and screen stars he invited little-known personalities from various walks of life, much as he mixed the famous and the hoi polloi in his column.

The show played as if it were capturing Ed in his nightly club hopping, with many of the guests just "dropping in" to say hello to the well-known columnist. (In reality, the show originated from a roped-off area upstairs, so no one just happened by.) A fifteen-minute program, with a commercial break and a newsflash from the *Daily News* "newsroom," *Ed Sullivan Entertains* moved at an urban pace; no one took the microphone for very long.

In the show's debut evening, Ed chatted with Irving Berlin about composing "White Christmas," which won the 1942 Academy Award for Best Song and topped the charts for eleven weeks, no doubt partially spurred by wartime family separation. For all the tune's popularity, Berlin that night said his favorite of his own songs was "Alexander's Ragtime Band," the theme to the movie Ed had touted during his Hollywood stint. Also chitchatting with Ed were Marine private Dana Babcock, and the wife of actor Gilbert Roland, then in the military. The guest who "happened by" was actor Melville Cooper, who recently played a supporting role in the Henry Fonda–Maureen O'Hara tearjerker *Immortal Sergeant*.

Reviews were generally positive, about the show itself if not its host. One critic apparently struggled to find something positive to say about its headliner: "Although Sullivan's voice did not have the weight and authority for this kind of work, it's no drawback. Different type pipes are welcome." *Variety* observed that the Marine seemed more comfortable at the microphone than anyone, but that the show was "a bright quarter hour, having more substance than the usual celebrity interview session in that a name emcee, Sullivan, himself no slouch as a conferencier, is at the helm."

Because he was so determined to succeed, Ed took the unorthodox step of scripting the entire show—including many of the guests' responses. The resulting exchanges were highly unnatural, as when Sullivan invited new crooning sensation Frank Sinatra on a show with aging vaudevillian Bert Wheeler. Ed suggested that the veteran Wheeler give young Sinatra some singing advice. Wheeler hesitated, after which Sinatra—in surely the most unlikely request the singer ever made— eagerly implored him to provide vocal coaching. Finally, Wheeler relented:

Wheeler: Well, Frank, it seems to me that you stand too close to the mike.
Sinatra: Well, that's easily corrected. How far away from the mike should I stand?
Wheeler: If the mike's here, I'd say you ought to stand around Fort Wayne, Indiana.
Sinatra: Uh-huh. Any other suggestions?
Wheeler: Get a collar that fits you. Your collar always looks as though it's crawling up to whisper in your ear.
Sinatra: Check—anything else?
Wheeler: Yes, comb your hair. Just once, comb your hair, and get out of mine.

Not surprisingly, listeners found the canned exchanges far from enchanting; three months into its run the show earned a mediocre 6.4 Hooper rating. That wasn't all the way at the back of the pack, but it was far from the *Bob Hope Program* at 31.6, *Walter Winchell* at 22.4, or Fred Allen's *Texaco Star Theater* at 19.8. The sponsor,

Mennen, didn't see enough interest to justify the expense, and *Ed Sullivan Entertains* was canceled in June 1944. The only consolation for its host, if any, was that its nine-month run was almost twice as long as any other Sullivan show.

———

Despite the doldrums of his broadcast career, Ed's lifestyle improved markedly in 1944. A friend of his, Jerry Brady, sat down with him and Sylvia for an earnest conversation. Brady, as Betty recalled, "didn't think it was appropriate for us to be living at the Astor Hotel with a young girl." The couple agreed—the threadbare Astor was no place to raise a child—and the family moved into a suite at the Delmonico, at Park Avenue and 59th Street. Their apartment in this deluxe residential hotel bore little resemblance to their home at the Astor. Located in one of Manhattan's most desirable neighborhoods, the luxurious three-bedroom suite on the eleventh floor came complete with maids and room service. Its kitchen facilities were almost nonexistent, but Ed and Sylvia had no desire to eat at home; as always they dined out nearly every evening.

Moving to the Delmonico was a happy day for Betty. Even getting to class at Marymount, an all-girls Catholic school on the Upper East Side, was easier. "I couldn't believe I was going to live on Park Avenue and didn't have to walk blocks across Broadway to get the bus to go to school." At the Astor, Betty had eaten many of her dinners with a paid companion, a woman named Paula, often going to a restaurant across the street from the hotel called Child's. After moving to the Delmonico she still ate most of her meals with Paula, but on certain evenings the young teenager accompanied her parents to dinner. They made the rounds of tony restaurants like the Colony or Pavillion. On Wednesdays, the family typically went to Toots Shor's, one of the city's best-known celebrity haunts. Their dinners were lengthy, with Ed and Sylvia talking about events of the day and Ed chatting with passersby.

As a father, Ed's expressions of affection came in small, restrained doses. An occasional brief hug was "overdoing it," as Betty remembered. This same sense of being removed, of distance, defined his relationship with most of the people around him. "He was sort of a loner," his daughter said. Betty saw her father as single-mindedly determined to succeed, and in this drive leaving behind some of life's small rituals of friendship and family recreation. Her view was echoed by Ed's grandson, Rob Precht, who spent considerable time with his grandfather, and who described Ed as "an intimate stranger."

Certainly he inspired great affection on a personal level. Bill Gallo was a young cartoonist with the *Daily News* in the 1940s who knew Sullivan well, and sometimes went to lunch with him. "He was one of my heroes," recalled Gallo. "He was the newspaperman that all the kids wanted to be." Being out every night, socializing with the famous, having a huge readership—it all looked good to Gallo. "He was the personification of a star. He carried that aura about him like it was built in," he remembered. "He was a regular guy, there was nothing uppity about him, no pomposity. And he didn't just try to be a nice guy—he *was* a nice guy." Gallo's comments concurred with those of many who knew Sullivan personally. Despite the stiff personality he projected on television years later, on a one-on-one basis he had great social ease, even charm, and spoke to anyone as an equal, whether the person was a cab driver or a major film producer.

Yet the social ease extended only so far. The wall remained. Ed's inner reserve, the sense of apartness right underneath his man-about-town affability, stayed firmly in place. For all his limitless list of friends and contacts, his life was essentially a solo voyage.

Although the war's end brought a halt to the steady stream of bond rallies Ed organized, his career as an emcee and event producer stayed just as busy. He had become the first person almost any organization called, producing and hosting events for an unlikely quilt of entities, from B'nai B'rith to the League of Catholic Charities. Down in Miami for his yearly press junket, he hosted a hospital dedication show with comedian Jack Carter, the Ames Brothers, and singer Theresa Brewer. He traveled to Philadelphia and put together an event for the Poor Richard Society with vocalist Patti Page, comic Victor Borge, and ventriloquist Senor Wences. He took singer Vic Damone and vaudevillian Sophie Tucker up to the Catskills to emcee a birthday bash for Jenny Grossinger, owner of the famed Borsht Belt resort. He traveled to Boston to put on a show for the Maris Nuns, and drove to his hometown of Port Chester to emcee for the Marching and Chowder Society.

In March 1946, the White House Correspondents Association invited Ed to be master of ceremonies at an event honoring President Harry Truman. After the eight hundred guests tried the new wheat-saving dark bread, professional and amateur entertainers performed comedy skits and sang a humorously rewritten version of the 1920s Eubie Blake tune "I'm Just Wild About Harry." The song, featured in Sullivan's *Harlem Cavalcade* a few years earlier, now sported new lyrics: "I go swimming with Harry / That's one thing Harry enjoys / 'Cause there's no women / To spoil the swimmin' / He just invites the boys."

The war and its immediate aftermath created a minor conundrum for the Broadway columnists. For them, controversy was like oxygen; they could live on less, but without an occasional inhale they withered and died. With a world war raging, however, the petty internecine squabbles they had indulged in throughout the 1930s were kept to a minimum. Skirmishing with each other would have been unseemly with real battles being fought overseas. Nonetheless, Ed had permitted himself a small jab at Walter Winchell in 1942—though only a token dig given the enmity between the two. Winchell had begged the military to allow him to enlist, so the government, wanting to placate him but concerned for his safety, sent him to Brazil for a month on a fact-finding mission. The columnist, bubbling with excitement at the chance to wear a uniform—and, of course, to trumpet his wartime achievement when he returned—tried to keep it quiet as he left. But Ed popped his bubble, writing, "The town is chuckling at Winchell's 'secret mission . . .'"

Ed had ferreted out only a few minor targets to attack in the war years. Notably included were those "phonies" who pretended to have war medals they didn't earn, and those elected officials in the same league: "Tip to Washington, D.C.: Nothing has hurt New Deal prestige in N.Y. so much as the sight of capital czars, married, flaunting their girlfriends in Broadway nightclubs and supper clubs one weekend after another . . . can't that be rationed?"

But these subjects didn't create the splash a Broadway columnist craved. In June 1946, Ed found a fresh source of controversy, one that had headlines blaring. The

New York City police, he wrote, were involved in "the most cynical grafting spree in New York history." Reporting what he called the widespread practice of "Broadway grabbing," he claimed that "detectives' rake-offs range from $1,700-per-book-maker–phone per month in a Manhattan division to $3,000 per month in the Bronx," and that the city was suffering from a "complete breakdown in police control."

Certainly Ed knew the world of the Broadway bookie. On occasion in his column he guffawed about the widespread practice of illegal gambling, including tidbits like, "When 666 came up on Friday, policy bankers went to the cleaners for fresh dough." And his friend Joe Moore, an Olympic speed skater when they met in the 1920s, turned to bookmaking after his athletic career ended. (Moore, because of his friendship with Sullivan, was then hired by a press agent named Ed Weiner, who had close ties to Walter Winchell. Between the two of them, Weiner and Moore had access to the city's leading gossip columnists.)

As soon as Ed's column hit newsstands, city government experienced convulsions. That same day, Mayor William O'Dwyer ordered an investigation, prompting a fierce round of bureaucratic infighting. The mayor wanted the investigation headed by the Commissioner of Investigation; the police commissioner, however, "pleaded with the Mayor" to allow the police department to investigate itself first. After hurried discussion the mayor announced he had reversed himself: the police department would investigate itself without the Commissioner. Reporters asked O'Dwyer if Sullivan would be summoned, and the mayor said no. "I always respect the confidential sources of newspapermen," he said.

After the initial splash, Ed's allegations slid quietly off the front page. In July, the police staged a crackdown on bookies, arresting five hundred sixty-two in one month. Following this purported clean up, Mayor O'Dwyer announced in late August that the police department's investigation of itself had produced no evidence of graft. With the hundreds of bookies arrested and the police department apparently clean, the matter was closed. But while Ed's muckraking had only token effect on the city's police, it did point to a new direction in his column. The war had taught him that *Little Old New York* could address weightier issues than Broadway romances and celebrity effluvia. In the late 1940s, his daily column grazed across most any topic that suited him. Although at its heart it remained a show business gossip column, it now traveled far afield, touching upon—always briefly—foreign affairs, domestic politics, sports, books, odd news items, or whatever interested Ed that day.

After he penned an extended homage to the loving nature of dogs—"Dogs have the capacity for grief, and they have the capacity for love, with no string attached"—he received an appreciative letter from Federal Bureau of Investigation (FBI) director J. Edgar Hoover. "I couldn't refrain from writing this personal note to tell you how much pleasure I gained from reading your column," Hoover confided. "Your understanding affection for what some ill-informed individuals call 'dumb' animals touched my heart." The two men communicated regularly through the years. Sullivan used his column to toss kudos to the FBI director, which Hoover relished. After Ed included a column tidbit about his fifty-third birthday, Hoover sent him an affectionate thank-you: "It does warm one's heart to be remembered by friends on his birthday. . . . Sincerely, Edgar."

Yet the column, as far and wide as Ed stretched it, was always just the foundation from which he tried to reach higher, to grab some greater notoriety. In the spring of 1946, he once again heard the siren song he couldn't resist. That his first four attempts to launch a radio show, spread over the last fourteen years, had been short-lived failures—the longest lasting just nine months—did not tempt him to concede defeat. So, as if bound by some kind of seasonal migration, he was back knocking at radio's door.

On April 2, he debuted *Ed Sullivan's Pipeline* on New York's WJZ. Broadcasting every Tuesday at 9 P.M., the show offered a quarter hour of Ed solo, intoning the daily scuttlebutt from New York, Washington, and Hollywood. Lending an urban dash to his delivery was the sound effect of rapid-tempo typing, punctuated by a typewriter bell—this gossip was hot off a newsman's Underwood, the percolating sound effects suggested.

The pages of the show's scripts reveal that Ed was attempting to add extra urgency to his performance. For those who had panned his radio persona as too straight and stiff, he had an answer. To jazz up his vocal rhythm he included plenty of dashes in his script, and he handwrote in extra exclamation points:

> "New York—Vindication has finally come to the bobby socks!! Sinatra is more than just The Voice!! Distinguished American sculptor Jo Davidson tells me that the bone structure and shape of Sinatra's long, lean face is amazingly similar to—hold your breath—Abraham Lincoln."

The show was a broadcast version of his column, but what worked in print didn't work over the air. Ed's attempt to match the hyped-up hypnosis of Walter Winchell proved ill-fated. On September 30, six months after its debut, *Ed Sullivan's Pipeline* saw its last broadcast. Inarguably, his talents were not suited to the airwaves.

In his Loew's State variety show in September 1946, Sullivan booked an exceptionally pretty twenty-two-year-old singer-comedienne named Jane Kean. For Ed, the irrepressible young performer—blonde, funny, and lively—was irresistible. Over the weeks they worked together he formed a romantic attraction for her, though it appears to have been largely unrequited.

Jane and her older sister Betty performed as a duo in New York's nightclubs, singing and telling jokes; the bubbly good humor of their sister act made them highly successful. Betty had performed a comic tap-dance routine in Ed's 1941 Broadway production, *Crazy with the Heat*. In later years, Jane appeared on Broadway and landed a raft of TV roles, most notably on the 1960s version of *The Honeymooners*, starring Jackie Gleason. She played Art Carney's wife Trixie, replacing original actress Joyce Randolph.

Kean remembered Sullivan as having real allure. "He was very attractive to women—and he was interested in them," she recalled. But Kean's initial attraction to Ed soon faded. "I did not have a big love affair with him—that was a man in pursuit." By her account, Ed sent her love letters, off and on, over the next year or so, including some he mailed from his yearly mid-winter stint in Florida. He penned her endearments like "I miss you," among others. "Yes, he was very fond of me," she remembered, with a chuckle.

Kean soon began a long-standing romance with Walter Winchell, whom she grew to love. Walter took a much different approach to her in his column. "Winchell, if he liked you, he would just promote you and praise you every time you opened someplace," she said. "Ed wasn't that much of a fan or press agent for people."

Ed booked Jane and her sister Betty on his television show in 1949, though Kean said by this point any romantic overtures were forgotten. Due to the exposure from their Sullivan show booking, the duo received a series of lucrative engagements in Chicago, Las Vegas, and New York.

In Kean's remembrance, it was not uncommon for Ed to have affairs. "He was not Simon Pure, let's put it that way," she said. Her recollection is backed up by Jack Carter, a comedian whom Ed booked in his postwar vaudeville shows, as well as some forty times on his television show. Over the years the two men frequently had drinks together at Danny's Hideaway, a popular New York bar-restaurant. Carter recalled that during one of his Loew's State shows with Sullivan, Ed had an affair with one of the performers, whose name Carter didn't remember. She was "an acrobatic dancer with a great body— he was jazzing her," he said. But Ed was careful to maintain discretion about his liaison. "It was his own private little trick—we knew about it," Carter said. "It was a quiet thing . . . if that would have ever gotten out, Winchell would have eaten him alive."

In the fall of 1947 Ed became chairman of the entertainment committee for the Heart Fund Drive, which presented him with a daunting task. He needed to organize an extensive radio ad campaign, which required writing scripts, lining up voice talent and musicians, and contacting a slew of radio stations—and convincing everyone to work gratis. Mentioning the mountainous workload to performers backstage at his Loew's State show, one of them, a young singer named Monica Lewis, suggested Ed call her brother, Marlo Lewis.

Lewis, an advertising executive at the Blaine Thompson agency, produced a daily radio show called *Luncheon at Sardi's*. The thirty-two-year-old adman possessed matinee idol good looks and a correspondingly outsized ego. He tended his appearance fastidiously, always sporting an impeccable coif and visiting the gym constantly; in later years he insisted all his employees visit the gym to stay fit. Lewis projected a natural charisma that some found overbearing; he was described as "egocentric—very much so" by one colleague. Yet he was grateful to Sullivan for booking his younger sister, and after a little cajoling by Ed agreed to help.

Working for free, Lewis and Sullivan put together a thirty-spot radio campaign. Ed corralled the talent: Bob Hope, Jack Benny, Jimmy Durante, Jerry Lewis and Dean Martin, Bing Crosby, and others voiced the spots; Marlo Lewis convinced the head of the musicians union, James Petrillo, to allow the striking musicians to record the music, and coordinated logistics such as contacting radio stations. After the spots ran in March 1948, Ed produced a standing room–only variety show with the celebrities at the Capitol Theatre, emceed by Milton Berle.

The partnership of Marlo Lewis and Ed Sullivan was highly successful—the Heart Fund Drive broke the charity's fund-raising record. To Ed, this suggested a greater possibility, one that stemmed from his perennial desire to break into broadcasting. Lewis, as an ad executive and radio producer, had contacts with CBS management. Sullivan, a veteran show producer and emcee as well as an influential columnist, had the phone number of every star in show business. Could they pool their talents for this new medium of television?

PART TWO

THE BIRTH OF TELEVISION

"It used to be that we in films were the lowest form of art. Now we have something to look down on."

— BILLY WILDER

CHAPTER EIGHT

A Temporary Job

THE WAR, HAVING AFFECTED VIRTUALLY EVERY ASPECT of American life, slowed the development of a force that would exert a still greater influence: television. After NBC technicians broadcast a sputtering image of Franklin Roosevelt's opening speech at the 1939 World's Fair, the nascent medium appeared to be just a step away from the living room. But the war's global conflagration sucked all the energy from television's development. Some suggested, darkly, that the war provided an excuse for those threatened by television—newspaper, radio, and film concerns—to suppress the new medium. An anonymous commentator in the *Saturday Evening Post* opined in 1942 that these powerful interests put TV "as far back on the shelf as they could because they saw it as a threat to the status quo."

If newspapers and film studios could have united to stop the upstart, they surely would have. But the genie was out of the bottle soon after the war ended. Dominant networks NBC and CBS, followed by ABC and Dumont, began competing to stake out a position in television, offering the first few crudely produced shows. Initially, the public took little notice. Television sets in the immediate postwar years were chiefly located in neighborhood bars; the sets were expensive and the programming so scant that few middle-class families were tempted to buy one.

In the fall of 1947, however, the small screen gave viewers a jolt of excitement: for the first time, the World Series was broadcast on television. An estimated audience of three million people gathered in bars and department stores to watch grainy images of the New York Yankees, led by the mythic Joe DiMaggio, defeat the Brooklyn Dodgers, whose lineup featured Jackie Robinson, who just that year broke baseball's color line. Advertisers, too, felt a quickening pulse as they contemplated television's power. Early in 1947, Kraft experimented with a television ad for its new McLaren's Brand Cheese, which was pricey and hadn't been selling well. In the ad, an attractive young woman was transported by the delicious taste of McLaren's. By the ad's third week on the air, New York stores couldn't keep the cheese in stock.

"When somebody got a TV set, they would invite the whole neighborhood in to watch—it became a social thing," recalled Paul Winchell, a ventriloquist who performed in Ed's shows at Loew's State. "They were so filled with awe that people would say, my God, the pictures are *moving*."

The big moment came the following summer. On June 8, 1948, NBC debuted the *Texaco Star Theatre*, starring Milton Berle. The comic's success had been limited on radio, but his humor—direct, immediate, and visual—played perfectly on the small screen. He joyfully took pies in the face, wore wigs, and fell flat on his face at every cymbal crash. His format was the one he grew up in, vaudeville, with a rapid-tempo parade of comics and singers and acrobats, many of whom Berle interacted with. He pretended to perform with the acrobats, mining his own maladroit moves for laughs, and he romped through skits with the comics as one of them. Although there were only five hundred thousand television sets in the country that summer, Berle became an instant phenomenon; within a year his grinning mug graced both *Time* and *Newsweek*. A handful of shows had preceded Berle's, but none so captured the public. For the first time, people began scheduling their Tuesday nights around a television program.

Berle's success threw down a challenge for CBS. The network ran a close second to NBC in radio. Now the popularity of *Texaco Star Theatre* suggested that NBC was on its way to dominating television as well, especially given that NBC's *Philco TV Playhouse* already held a grip on Sunday night, the evening with the largest home audience. To avoid being left at the starting gate, CBS needed to respond—and fast.

Ed and Marlo Lewis had proved to be an effective team. The success of their Heart Fund Drive demonstrated that their strengths were complementary. Ed, with his skill at producing stage shows, and Marlo, with his social ease and talent for handling logistics, formed a partnership that was greater than the sum of its parts. At Ed's urging, the two of them dedicated their partnership to launching a TV variety show. But the story of how that show came about would diverge into the Sullivan Version and the Lewis Version, with each giving himself primary credit for making the show possible.

Sullivan's version, which he repeated in countless interviews in later years, became accepted as TV lore, though it neglected Lewis's role altogether. In Ed's telling, CBS asked him to host a show after network executive Worthington Miner saw him host the Harvest Moon dance competition in the fall of 1947. On the evening of September 3, Miner was at Harvest Moon to oversee CBS's live broadcast of the event. Ed, unaware that he was being broadcast live, recalled feeling completely at home onstage; he thought the cameras were filming a newsreel for later use. "If I had dreamed I was on television, I wouldn't have been so relaxed," he said.

He had impressed the right person at the right time. Miner, who had been a highly successful Broadway director, was a plump, owl-faced man whose brainy demeanor belied a demanding nature. Fortunately for Ed, Miner was moving up the CBS corporate ladder that year. In the spring of 1948, he was assigned to create two shows, a dramatic series (the renowned *Studio One*, which debuted that fall) and a variety program. Remembering thinking that Sullivan seemed "likeable and relaxed" as host of Harvest Moon, Miner recruited him in May 1948 to produce and host a variety show. Remarkably, the very thing Ed had so wanted all these years, a broadcast berth, fell into his lap not through his own efforts, but because of his effortless onstage charm.

Or at least that's the way Ed recounted it. Marlo Lewis' telling of the story, in contrast, cast Sullivan not as a passive recipient of Miner's interest but as actively pursuing a TV show.

Inarguably, Ed was drawn to the nascent medium and hungered to be part of it. By his own account, he had conceived of a show about golf called *Pros and Cons*, featuring him interviewing pros about their technique. He pitched the concept to CBS (in one telling of the story Lewis did the actual pitching), but the network turned him down. It wasn't a bad idea; it tapped the visual nature of television, but viewership hadn't grown large enough to support programs aimed at niche audiences. Succeeding in these pioneering days required an all-inclusive approach.

According to Lewis, immediately after their Heart Fund collaboration, Ed began lobbying him, essentially berating him, to use his connections to sell a variety show to CBS. Lewis, inspired by Sullivan's enthusiasm, agreed. He worked his way through a series of pitch meetings with network executives, first with program director Jerry Danzig, then with network vice president Charles Underhill. Network interest was lukewarm. But, almost by default, they agreed to try the show, if only until better programming could be found. In Lewis' telling, the fact that Worthington Miner had seen Ed emcee Harvest Moon contributed to getting network approval.

But the network had no enthusiasm for Sullivan. No less an eye for talent than CBS head Bill Paley thought of him as merely a stopgap. The forty-six-year-old Paley (who coincidentally was born on the same day as Sullivan) was considered a genius at programming. Paley's Ukrainian-born father had earned a vast fortune in the cigar business and bought into a minor Philadelphia-based radio chain known as CBS. He made his son Bill the president at age twenty-seven. It was young Paley's knack for choosing the right shows and performers that enabled him to build CBS into a broadcasting leviathan. His list of successes began with 1929's hit *Amos 'n' Andy* and continued apace, and the list of talent he wooed to CBS went from Will Rogers to Bing Crosby. As CBS grew, so did Paley's reputation, and with time he was viewed as a sovereign master of broadcasting—a man whose opinion was the gold standard. When Bill Paley looked at Ed Sullivan, he saw someone who was ill-suited for television. Paley recalled: "Ed Sullivan was hired as a temporary master of ceremonies for a variety program I wanted in 1948 because the programming department could not find anyone like Milton Berle. . . . We planned to replace him as soon as we could afford a professional master of ceremonies."

While Sullivan and his partner Marlo Lewis told very different stories about the show's inception, they agreed about the contract that CBS offered. Its terms were almost feudal. While the networks understood television's awesome potential, they correctly assumed it would be a financial drain for the first few years. In 1949, television lost $25 million while radio made $56 million. The networks expected to finance their television groundwork with profits from their radio divisions, but wanted to use as little of these profits as possible. CBS's niggling offer to Sullivan and Lewis reflected a desire to shave up-front costs, even if that shortchanged the actual programming.

The three-year contract stipulated that the show could be canceled with two weeks' notice; the network owned the show completely, so Sullivan and Lewis would see no profit or residuals; although Ed would be the producer and emcee, the show would not bear his name, allowing the network to replace him easily at any point. As for pay, Sullivan and Lewis would have to produce the show essentially for free.

CBS would provide the studio and technical crew and a nominal talent budget; the rest was up to Marlo and Ed. The talent budget was $375 per show, which would cover Sullivan and Lewis' salary as well as fees for each week's performers. For this amount, Sullivan was obligated to provide six acts a week, two of which had to be nationally known. Projecting no great confidence in the years ahead, the contract called for an increase to $650 per show in the second year, and $900 per show in the third year. An additional $1,000 per show was allotted to pay a fourteen-piece orchestra, six dancers, and additional production staff.

In Lewis' account, he was the one who handled the contract negotiations, such as they were, then delivered the news to Sullivan. He expected Ed to have his doubts, especially about working for free, but Ed's reaction was enthusiastic—wildly so. "Screw 'em! Grab the deal! I don't care what they're offering us," Lewis claimed Ed said. "A contract with the network is not the Holy Gospel. When we're a hit, and we're gonna be a hit, they'll give us anything we want!"

Worthington Miner may have been impressed with Ed's emceeing at Harvest Moon, but CBS saw a quality in Sullivan far more attractive than his onstage persona. Ed was an influential columnist; if anyone could convince stars to work cheap, he could. In a notion that would soon seem quaint, a broadcast network was leveraging the power of a print journalist to deliver major stars. And Ed did just that. He went to work calling in his chits.

For his debut television show, he conceived of a variety program that traveled in uncharted territory. While it shared many qualities with his Loew's State vaudeville shows, the format he created for television was a profound break from his earlier work.

In booking acts for his first broadcast, he overspent his minimal talent budget, though not by much, offering more cajoling and column exposure than dollars. Headlining would be comedy duo Jerry Lewis and Dean Martin, then a white-hot nightclub act, currently at the Copacabana ($200); Broadway stars Richard Rodgers and Oscar Hammerstein would chitchat about their recent stage projects (gratis), and bring along a dancer from their show *Allegro*, ballerina Kathryn Lee ($75), to perform a ballet; classical pianist Eugene List, who had just performed for Truman, Churchill, and Stalin at the Potsdam Conference, would render a Chopin *Polonaise* ($100); Ed would interview Ruby Goldstein, who was about to referee the title bout between Joe Louis and Jersey Joe Wolcott ($75); Bronx fireman John Kokoman, winner of a local singing contest, would croon ($25), as would Marlo Lewis' sister, Monica ($50); comedy team Lee Goodman and Jim Kirkwood, a cerebral New York nightclub act, would counterbalance Martin and Lewis' comic antics (gratis).

The program's core formula was clearly vaudeville—briskly paced acts with high contrast between them. But the show itself would hardly have been recognized by the gallery gods of old. A boxing referee and a ballerina on the same bill? Rodgers and Hammerstein, who walked the Broadway stage like giants, sharing an evening with a singing fireman? The zany tang of Jerry Lewis and Dean Martin on a program with Chopin? Sullivan had never combined high and low art in this style, had never ventured so boldly beyond his updated vaudeville format.

For what audience was this intended? Certainly not his Loew's State audience, nor any local New York audience, who wouldn't have stood for a singing fireman and a classical pianist on the same program. Ed was imagining a vaudeville bill for that most catholic of halls, the national audience. But the national television audience was largely an unknown quantity. Little in the way of programming successes and failures yet existed to point to, to emulate, or to avoid the pitfalls of. What did the national audience want? No one really knew. Ed was aiming his show at a viewership he imagined, a fictional audience—not quite real because there were only five hundred thousand television sets in the nation, and most were still scattered in neighborhood taverns. The viewers themselves weren't sure what to expect from the little boxes. In certain hours, television networks were still broadcasting test patterns, stationary designs with no sound, and some viewers found even this intriguing, as if it heralded something momentous.

Years later, Worthington Miner claimed that Sullivan's debut lineup wasn't the first list the showman submitted to him. The initial list was full of tired recycled stage acts, Miner said, asserting that he told Sullivan he wanted "new" acts. If that's true, whatever Miner said must have crystallized something in Ed, for this debut lineup reflected the formula he would use throughout the show's twenty-three seasons, long after Miner was gone. As much as Sullivan's choice of performers would change as the culture changed, season by season, almost headline by headline, his signature formula evolved little in the decades ahead.

While Ed chose the talent, conceiving of the show's pace and feel, Marlo Lewis handled logistics, from getting the theater ready to working with technicians. Because CBS had never televised a variety show, Lewis had to organize the show's technical aspects from scratch. Complicating his task was the network's sluggishness; after signing the contract, CBS had done little to prepare—until the June 8 debut of NBC's Milton Berle show. Then CBS sprang into action. Suddenly, the Sullivan–Lewis show needed to go on the air posthaste. The debut evening was set for Sunday, June 20, at 9 P.M. Several names for the program were bandied about, with CBS issuing a press release calling it *You're the Top*, but sometime in early June it was changed to *Toast of the Town*.

Two weeks before the first broadcast, the network was hurriedly attempting to finish converting the Maxine Elliot Theater on West 39th Street and Broadway into a TV studio. When Lewis visited and spoke with the construction crew, he began to doubt whether the hall would be ready. Previously home to small stage plays, the theater was ill-equipped to handle the volume of gear needed to broadcast a television program. CBS had spent $12,000 to renovate the space, but the quickly re-laid stage tilted slightly to one side, with a grainy surface that made it hard to dolly cameras across. A small dressing room had been turned into the master control room, but it allowed no line of sight to the stage—essential for directing lighting changes and camera angles. For musical accompaniment, Ed contracted the Ray Bloch Orchestra, a top-flight radio ensemble, but they, too, would have to play with no view of the stage. The renovated theater no longer had an orchestra pit, so Bloch would have to conduct his band from a small room in the theater's back area, following the show using a jerry-rigged microphone setup. And since the show would be broadcast live, all this juggling would happen in front of the audience.

Lewis fervently hoped he and his crew would be allowed into the Maxine Elliot a few weeks ahead of time. But the foreman supervising renovation told him he would have no access to the space until the day of the show. There would be no time to rehearse in the theater, and no time to work out technical snafus. However, in what the foreman apparently meant as reassurance, he told Lewis that he and the show's crew "could come in early that Sunday morning and go to work."

When Marlo called Ed to give him a progress report, he found him distracted and uninterested in the technical details. Ed's wife and daughter also found him preoccupied in the days before the show's debut. "We would always leave notes for one another—that was our way of communicating during the day," Betty recalled, noting that Ed wrote her and her mother a note shortly before the show's debut. She didn't remember the exact words, yet in effect he wrote, "I'm sorry that I've been moody and uncommunicative, but I really want to make a go of the show. I know I've been nervous and not really agreeable."

And no wonder. At age forty-six, he had so long hungered for the national spotlight, for renown and fame, and now a freshly born medium and his own determination had given him another roll of the dice. By some accident of history, this new medium of television came into being just as he was supremely ready for it. He hadn't even known he had been waiting for this moment, but it had arrived. And with it had come probably his best opportunity yet, perhaps his last. Radio had been a bust, film no better. But television was a version of something he knew how to do—put on stage shows—as skillfully as anyone. This was his chance.

On June 18, the Friday before his Sunday debut, Ed wrote a column about television. It was ostensibly addressed to his readers, yet it read like his own diary:

> "This is the most fascinating thing that has happened in entertainment since the movies were succeeded by talkies and radio came a-burstin' on the scene . . . You thought to yourself that here was a medium of entertainment that would have challenged the imagination of a P.T. Barnum, a Charles Frohman, a Sam S. Shubert, a David Wark Griffith, a George M. Cohan, a Belasco, or any of the great creators of show business . . . Radio developed freak attractions, who could read from a script, but television demands more than that, and the experienced performer, with a stage background, will find that his or her experience will pay off . . .
>
> . . . Television is sight and sound, similar to the movies but dissimilar in that there are no retakes. What happens at any exact moment on a television stage is written in indelible ink, and not one tear can remove any part of it . . .
>
> . . . It is a medium which places a high valuation on pace, on speed. A singer may better eliminate the opening or throwaway number and sock with his or her strongest piece of material . . . The comic may find it advisable to trim a vaudeville monologue down to its bare comedy essentials and score quickly . . .
>
> . . . Quite by the accident of appearing at Madison Square Garden shows this writer sort of got in on the ground floor of television . . . In radio, I had the same opportunity but wasted it . . . But I'm not making the same mistake this time, brethren . . . This time, as a ground-floor tenant, I'm concentrating on a long-term lease from which the television landlords will have to evict me bodily."

CHAPTER NINE

"Really Big Show"

I

T WAS UNSEASONABLY WARM IN THE EARLY MORNING of June 20, 1948 as Marlo Lewis parked his car in the alley behind the Maxine Elliot Theater. Tonight was his and Ed's television debut, yet today was the first day he had access to the theater. There was a lot to do and not much time to do it. But when he opened the large iron backdoor, what he found was alarming.

The stage manager, looking exhausted, gave Lewis a progress report: "Marlo, you're going to have a shit-hemorrhage." Along with several stagehands and technicians, he had been up all night, hacking and sawing and installing equipment in a mad sprint to finish the renovation. It was unclear whether the theater could be readied for tonight's broadcast. And even if it were, it seemed doubtful the production would appear more professional than a high school play.

Lewis had worked with a CBS set designer to create a stage backdrop, a crudely painted wooden and canvas structure depicting the New York skyline topped with puffy white clouds. A network press release described it, with great imagination, as "a roof garden with the Manhattan skyline silhouetted against the starlit sky." Constructed in a CBS warehouse across town, the backdrop had been too big to get through the doors of the Maxine Elliot, forcing the carpenters to take it apart. Yet when they stitched it back together they realized it was too large for the stage. The stagehands and carpenters had worked into the early morning hours to remake and position the structure so that it curved enough to fit. But the resulting backdrop left gaps on both sides of the stage, revealing all the detritus piled backstage.

Three cameramen, attempting to station their equipment on the stage's edge, discovered that their cameras couldn't handle the theater's bright lights. The only solution was to turn off most of the stage lights and set up a dynabeam spotlight to direct light as needed. But this required scrambling to find both a dynabeam and someone who knew how to use it. Fortunately, the theater's head stagehand (who maintained a peephole between his office and the ladies' restroom) knew of a veteran spotlight operator, who rented a dynabeam and hurriedly hauled it to the theater.

Ray Bloch and his fourteen-piece orchestra arrived late morning, learning they were to be installed in a storage area backstage. With no line of sight to the stage, the conductor would need to listen to commands over his headphones. As Bloch began rehearsing, a fire department supervisor showed up to inspect the newly renovated facility, issuing the bandleader a $50 fine for smoking his pipe in the theater. After his inspection, the supervisor gave Lewis the bad news: the theater contained so many violations of the fire code that he couldn't allow it to host a performance. That evening's show would have to be canceled. Unsure of what to do, Lewis called Sullivan at home, where he was hastily finishing his column.

Ed didn't hesitate. "I've done plenty of benefits for those boys and the Chief's a good friend of mine," he told Marlo. Ed placed a quick call and worked out a compromise: the fire department would station men with extinguishers around the backstage area during the performance, and any foliage would be sprayed prior to broadcast. (When the foliage around the set was sprayed, the resultant chemical bath gave some of the performers headaches that afternoon.) Ed asked how everything else was, and Marlo, not wanting to spook him, told him everything was fine.

When Ed arrived that afternoon he made a bravura entrance, saying hello and shaking hands with everyone, the performers as well as the technicians and stagehands. The morale of the cast and crew seemed to brighten as he announced that tonight would be a "blockbuster of a show." Then, as he had for countless Loew's State shows, he took a seat on a stool near stage right and began working out details with a pad and pencil: who would appear when, how long they would be given, what material they would perform, and when to introduce the celebrities in the audience. He had the performers run through the program in its entirety, then directed a round of changes, making adjustments to timing and entrances. After watching the comedy duo Jim Kirkwood and Lee Goodman, Ed felt their cerebral routine didn't stand up next to the high-voltage vibrancy of Jerry Lewis and Dean Martin. He told them to edit their act down to three minutes; the duo felt they couldn't do that, so he cut them altogether.

When the rehearsal concluded, Sullivan and the performers gathered onstage for a photo, the performers along the back row and the June Taylor dancers—who would shimmy in a short nightclub number to introduce Ed—kneeling in plumed costumes up front. As the camera flashed, Jerry Lewis appeared bored, staring off to his left in mid yawn. Dean Martin, oblivious to the photographer's efforts, chatted with Marlo Lewis' younger sister, who would sing that night. Ed, looking dapper in a double-breasted jacket, stared down and to his right, unsmiling, intent, lost in thought.

The preparation done, there was nothing to do but wait; this was live television and the broadcast wasn't until 9:30 P.M. (The show soon moved to 8 P.M.) These hours of waiting were excruciating for Ed. He had wanted this for most of his adult life, craving this kind of an opportunity since he made his first film in New York in 1932. Yet his past gave him little encouragement. He was certainly a veteran showman, having produced his first variety revue some fifteen years back, and having lived and breathed show business since then. But each of his attempts on the airwaves had

failed, miserably so; five radio shows launched, five short-lived radio shows canceled. A critic had described his one major onscreen effort, in *Big Town Czar*, as
"unconvincing"—and he had been playing himself. The note that he wrote to Betty
and Sylvia described how he felt in the days before the show—"anxious and distracted"— yet now, waiting in his tiny dressing room upstairs at the Maxine Elliot,
that anxiety coalesced into a gut-churning terror.

A half hour before the broadcast, Marlo Lewis walked into Sullivan's dressing
room and was horrified by what he saw. Ed's face was a colorless white and his eyes
were glazed over. A plastic tube hung from his mouth, attached to a small rubber sy-
ringe he held in his hand; the apparatus was directed into the dressing room sink.
The two men's eyes met in the dressing room mirror, and Ed downplayed the unusual scene. "It's nothing," he said, his speech garbled, "I'm just pumping my stomach—acid's too high, ulcer's killing me." He motioned Marlo to take a seat while he
finished the procedure, which took a few minutes longer. Ed swallowed a large dose
of Belladonna, a commonly prescribed ulcer medication. (Belladonna can cause
blurry vision, which Lewis felt contributed to Ed's mangled introductions—he may
have had a hard time reading cue cards; the drug can also result in drowsiness and
mental confusion, possibly adding to the host's difficulties onstage; and in older
adults it can cause memory loss, which Ed suffered greatly from in his later years.)
Within a few minutes the emcee seemed to recover partially from his ulcer attack,
though his hands continued to shake in jittery tremors. Marlo, uneasy and wanting
to reassure Ed, said only that everything would be great, then informed him of the
camera cue before leaving him alone.

Precisely at 9:30 P.M., Ray Bloch struck up a drumroll, and deep-timbered announcer Art Hannes intoned: *"Ladies and gentlemen, the Columbia Broadcast System is proud to present its star-studded revue, the* Toast of the Town, *with the nationally known newspaper columnist . . . Ed Sullivan!"* No tape of that first show exists, but by all accounts it went well. A standing room–only audience crammed the
Maxine Elliot, clapping as six showgirls pranced onstage to introduce Ed. True to
his newsman's formula, he presented his splashiest attraction first: the studio audience screamed with laughter as Jerry Lewis played the antic high-energy clown
to Dean Martin's suave man-about-town. After Ed interviewed Rodgers and Hammerstein about their 1943 hit *Okalahoma!* and their upcoming production, *South
Pacific*, they received an affectionate ovation; then Kathryn Lee, a ballerina in the
duo's show *Allegro*, pirouetted and twirled around the onstage piano. Pianist Eugene List rendered Chopin, fireman John Kokoman crooned, and Monica Lewis
jazzed up a nightclub number, forgetting the microphone hidden in her bouquet
and sending it skidding across the stage with a hand gesture. Ed, in a set that
looked like a boxing ring's corner, chatted with fight referee Ruby Goldstein about
the Joe Louis–Jersey Joe Walcott title bout. As he introduced the acts and spoke
with some of them, he fidgeted uneasily, always looking away from the camera, his
hands visibly shaking. (He may have developed his signature arms-crossed pose—
unusual for an emcee—to hide his trembling hands.) CBS, in its haste to get the
show on the air, hadn't found a sponsor, so any commercial breaks were for the network itself.

The size of the television audience for this first broadcast is unknown. The television networks at that time were capable of broadcasting only to cities in the east-

ern part of the country, in an area running from Richmond to Boston. Not until January 1949 did a coaxial cable connect these cities with a Midwestern area that extended to Chicago, and coast-to-coast broadcasting didn't begin until September 1951. Before 1951, viewers in nonconnected cities watched *Toast of the Town* on kinescope, which was a grainy copy shot directly from the television screen, sent from station to station by mail. (As Mike Dann, an NBC programming executive in the 1950s, recalled: "When somebody asked 'How'd the show go last night?' you said, 'Just great, it came out clear—you could see it.'") At the time of the show's first broadcast in June 1948, there were some five hundred thousand televisions in the United States. Given that ratings reports soon showed Sullivan handily winning his time slot, most of the TVs on the east coast were likely tuned to CBS that evening; assuming three to four viewers per set, perhaps approximately a million viewers watched.

Three days after its debut, a review in *Variety* praised *Toast of the Town*, but said that it suffered by comparison to Berle's *Texaco Theater*, which had also just debuted. Berle "brought to his emcee role one of the best showmanship lifts yet given a television show," the trade publication opined, concluding that "Vaudeo—the adaptation of old-time vaudeville into the new video medium—came of age last Tuesday night in a performance that may well be remembered as a milestone in television." *Variety* reported that Berle's NBC show benefited from an enviable Tuesday night time slot and a budget of $10,000 per show. As for *Toast of the Town*, the reviewer wrote, "With a top talent array, the new CBS offering couldn't help but be entertaining. . . . It lacked [the] sparkle of the Texaco show, chiefly because Sullivan, as an emcee, is a good newspaper columnist. He's affable enough and certainly has enough showbiz knowhow to lend authority to his job, but he doesn't have the comedy touch of Milton Berle."

The second Sunday's *Toast of the Town* followed the formula of the first. To headline, Ed booked The Ink Spots, a black rhythm and blues vocal quartet who had just ended a long engagement at Harlem's Apollo Theater, and whose hit "If I Didn't Care" currently backed a Lucky Strike cigarettes radio ad. Also appearing were Irving Berlin, preceded by a song-and-dance routine featuring his songs; famed ballroom dance team Raye and Naldi (Mary Raye had danced with screen idol Rudolph Valentino in 1925's smoldering *Cobra*); singing policeman Peter Hayes; big band songstress Nan Wynn; and ventriloquist Paul Winchell with his hand-carved dummy Jerry Mahoney.

Like the debut evening, this program stretched the boundaries of a late 1940s variety show beyond recognition. On no local New York stage would the Ink Spots have appeared with Irving Berlin—presenting a black R&B group with the "White Christmas" composer was counterintuitive, even daring; pairing a big band vocalist like Nan Wynn with a singing cop would have confounded a local audience. On the other hand, Sullivan often booked dancers Raye and Naldi along with a ventriloquist at Loew's State, so the evening's bill presented comforting combinations even as it stretched the genre. His show was often called vaudeville, and it did resemble this venerable form, but the evening veered sharply from traditional vaudeville as Sullivan felt his way toward reaching a television audience.

Ventriloquist Paul Winchell recalled the technical difficulties of mounting that evening's show. During rehearsal, Ed, from the control room, told Winchell that his dummy's voice was too soft. To compensate, the ventriloquist spoke Jerry Mahoney's part louder, yet it still didn't project enough, so he tried it even louder. But, still, Ed told him the dummy's voice wasn't coming through in the control room. "I panicked," Winchell said. "I became convinced that my aspirations for this new medium were totally over." He began to suspect that for some reason ventriloquism couldn't be broadcast on television. Finally, Winchell looked up and saw that every time he spoke Jerry Mahoney's part, the boom operator moved the microphone toward the dummy—which of course moved the microphone away from the real sound source. In other words, the production crew was pretty green.

His panic about the microphone snafu was part of an almost debilitating stage fright. "What I remember most was how scared I was," Winchell said. Although he had played vaudeville and radio for years, making his television debut felt like jumping off the end of the earth. Ed, sensing the ventriloquist's nerves, attempted to reassure him. "Look, there's nothing different about it, don't pay attention to the cameras," Winchell recalled Ed saying. "You just do your routine and don't worry about it. This is not a big bugaboo, we'll do the shots—you won't even know it." Certainly there was an irony to the showman who was himself knock-kneed in front of the camera telling one of his performers to relax. As the ventriloquist recalled from working with Sullivan throughout the 1950s, Ed was as scared as he was.

Despite its terrors, Winchell soon found out that this new medium conquered all. As a result of his debut on *Toast of the Town*, ad agency Young & Rubicam approached him to launch his own television show on NBC, *The Bigelow Show*, which debuted that October. And a short time after that, Macy's department store began selling little Jerry Mahoney dolls.

After Ed's second night on the air, *New York Times* critic Jack Gould wrote a piece reviewing both Berle's and Sullivan's shows. Berle, he wrote, was proof that television had arrived. "Register Mr. B. as television's first real smash!" he effused. "The increasing maturity of Mr. Berle's art was, perhaps, best demonstrated in the likable accord which he established with the other acts on the bill. His wonderful bit of business with the incomparable Bert Wheeler and his blackface routine with Harry Richman brought back nostalgic memories which through the sheer force of personality of all three acquired a 1948 newness and pace."

Toast of the Town, however, was a weak competitor in Gould's view. "In terms of lavishness and expense, it is on a par with *Texaco Star Theatre* but suffers badly if the comparison is extended to such matters as routining and general professional know-how. . . . For a variety revue, where a dominant personality is so helpful in tying up the loose ends, the choice of Ed Sullivan as master of ceremonies seems ill-advised. . . . CBS has all the necessary ingredients for a successful program of variety. Once it appreciates more fully the need for knowing hands to guide the proceedings—both onstage and off—it, too, should have an enjoyable hit."

Ed, who rarely let a jab go by without jabbing back, immediately fired off a long rebuttal to the *Times*, which the paper printed the following week:

> "Your review of my CBS *Toast of the Town* television show, in last Sunday's issue, is in error on so many points that I must challenge it. . . .

"From every survey we have been able to make, the CBS *Toast of the Town* has the biggest audience in television and the most enthusiastic. . . . Oscar Hammerstein II, a rather experienced hand in show business, has expressed his delighted amazement at our progress in a completely new medium and specifically praised 'the professional polish, the pacing of the show, and high entertainment value.' Eddie Cantor, after seeing the show, on a television set, said that we were so far ahead of any program he's seen that he was dumbfounded at the potentialities of a medium he had disregarded. . . .

"Your conclusions are at such variance to the expressions of expert showmen, and so opposed to public reaction, that I feel very strongly you are in error. . . .

"So much for the overall show. As to your opinion of me as master of ceremonies, I won't challenge that, because difference of opinion makes horse racing. However, I do feel that when you compare me to Milton Berle, you misunderstand my position on the show. They wanted a working newspaperman, sufficiently versed in show business, to nominate acts that could live up to a *Toast of the Town* designation. As it is a Sunday show, they wanted a certain measure of dignity and restraint, rather than a vain attempt to work with acrobats, tumblers, etcetera, which Berle does brilliantly."

Despite his assiduous defense, as a series of reviews echoed Gould's and *Variety*'s, CBS began to grow embarrassed by its show host. The pans of Sullivan hampered efforts to find an advertiser, and the program remained unsponsored as the weeks went by. The lack of sponsorship money led to another problem: the talent budget, which the CBS contract stipulated at $375 per show, remained at this token level. Since this wasn't enough to mount the show, Sullivan and Lewis were chipping in to cover expenses. In effect, they were paying to work for CBS.

Three weeks after the debut, an actors' union, Associated Actors and Artists of America, launched an inquiry into *Toast of the Town*. The show paid performers so far below customary compensation that the union threatened to ban its members from appearing. Additionally, the union was concerned that Sullivan was using his column as a club, coercing performers to appear for low pay. As the headlines turned negative, a CBS spokesman disavowed all responsibility, explaining that the network "paid a flat fee to Mr. Sullivan and that he arranged for the appearance of the artists."

Sullivan agreed to sit down with the union. He defended the show by noting that television performance rates had not yet been set, and saying that he knew of other shows that paid less. "Apparently we're being made the whipping boy for the whole field," he said. Ed and Marlo opened their books, which placated union officials about the payment issue; Ed said that if his show were to find a sponsor the rates would increase. He denied using his column to twist the arms of performers, saying that he brought "no pressure, direct, indirect, inferential, or practical," to persuade entertainers to appear. The meeting seemed to settle the issue. Although the union made noises about establishing a separate rate for columnists-hosts, no action was taken. But the union left its options open, noting that it would advise Sullivan at "a later date" about its final decision.

Ed was, of course, using his column to get performers to appear—that was why CBS hired him—but it was more of a carrot than a stick. He wrote no rash of negative tidbits about entertainers likely to have spurned his show invitations. He did, however, trumpet the success reaped by artists who appeared on *Toast of the Town*, dangling a tantalizing offer of greater exposure. "Ventriloquist Paul Winchell landed a Columbia Pictures project, Jackie Miles a $1500 television spot because of *Toast of the Town* clicks!" he wrote in mid July. The following week, "As a result of his *Toast of the Town* click, Roxy Theatre wants band-poll sensation Illinois Jacquet for the Harvest Moon Show." (Since Ed headlined this Roxy bill it's probable that he himself was the reason the theater requested Jacquet.) He also explained in his column, by quoting someone else, why performers needed television exposure regardless of pay. "[MCA talent agency executive] Sonny Werblin defines MCA's policy on television: 'We want all our acts to get into television. The fact that there is little money in it at the moment is unimportant. Now is the time for them to learn all about it, and get in on the ground floor.'"

Meanwhile, Ed received a ray of sunlight amid the otherwise gray critical response to the show. *Variety* issued a softer follow-up review of *Toast of the Town* on July 21, less than a month after its initial critique. The paper may have been influenced by Ed's highly empathetic eulogy of a recently deceased *Variety* critic, one of two such lauds he wrote for the reviewer that week. At any rate, the trade publication observed that the show was making progress, and seemed to suggest that Sullivan himself had moved past the sheer terror of his debut. The emcee "kept the event moving smoothly and with a minimum of words. It was his most ingratiating job to date on this series, which seems to be taking on that quickening know-how complexion from week to week. The lighting could still stand improvement."

The critics, by focusing on Sullivan as host, were critiquing his most visible but least important role on the program. He was the show's producer, its creator and shaper, the one who molded it into something enjoyed by a mass audience. His talent was as an impresario, not as a show host.

On camera, he stood center stage and ushered acts on and off in a reserved monotone, pointing out celebrities in the crowd, prompting audience applause with his jerky arm movements. The critics were correct in noting he did this with surprising lack of ease. He had been in front of an audience since the early 1930s, yet tapes of the show reveal that the stage was still an alien atmosphere for him in 1948. At moments he smiled or even laughed, but, living up to his nickname Old Stoneface, he kept it to a minimum, as if this were a serious business that required a sober demeanor. In his view, his onstage persona wasn't what the audience came for; his work was mostly done by the time the cameras clicked on.

A big part of his job was being a talent scout. Within his first year on the air, he introduced Brooklyn-born Jackie Gleason to the television audience—four years before the comic made a major impact on TV with *The Jackie Gleason Show*. A master of the wordless grimace, Gleason was appearing in New York nightclubs when Ed booked him to perform a monologue about an unfortunate man who was love struck with a jukebox. In this same period, Sam Levenson, a former schoolteacher, launched his long career with a critically lauded *Toast of the Town* stand-up routine about life in New York City.

More important was taking this talent and mixing it into a concoction that enchanted the living room audience. Throughout 1948 Sullivan was testing his formula, his version of updated vaudeville: highbrow and lowbrow, something funny, something for the kids. The bookings could ever so slightly challenge the audience, but he always included material to soften any edge. In July he booked tap dancer Bill "Bojangles" Robinson, a vaudeville legend who had danced with Shirley Temple in numerous 1930s musicals, to perform with jazz vocalist Ella Fitzgerald, a virtuoso scat singer. As Fitzgerald scatted through what *Variety* described as "neo-modern jazz vocalistics," Robinson's feet flashed in a flurry of heel and toe. To keep the evening from overwhelming the folks at home, Sullivan balanced Fitzgerald–Robinson with lighter material: a novelty singer who warbled about a bearded lady, acrobatic team Toy and Wing, comedian Dick Buckley, and Baltimore city official Elmert Reinhart rendering "Home on the Range." (Spotlighting common folks was a key part of the Sullivan blueprint.) Ed's formula was square enough for a mass audience, but rarely bland; he offered the spice of the new—like a Fitzgerald–Robinson jazz-dance duet—then provided cotton candy comforts.

As the show's producer, he took dictatorial control over every aspect of its production. In contrast to his persona as the reserved and respectful host, as producer he didn't care who he offended, with the exception of a very few high-profile guests. He brought his formula to the stage with a single-minded intensity, and he was "very much in charge," recalled several Sullivan performers.

After conceiving of that week's show and choosing a group of acts that realized his conception, he often dictated the material the artists performed. Comics would have their material cut or reshaped; singers might be assigned a given song (it's likely that Ella Fitzgerald sang "Easter Parade," the current chart-topping Judy Garland movie theme, at Ed's directive). Then he developed the running order down to the minute, coordinating various technical aspects with Marlo Lewis.

On Sunday afternoons he ran the entire show without pause in front of a live studio audience—a full dress rehearsal. (Performers complained about the afternoon audience; it was let in for free and many of its members were Boy Scouts and the elderly, and hence greeted many comics' acts with polite silence. A new audience was invited in for the evening broadcast, so that response was fresh.) As the show played, Ed stood offstage, simultaneously watching the audience and each performer, making decisions about how to shape the show for broadcast. As he watched, he relied on his long education: the many speakeasy revues he saw in his twenties, the countless Loew's State vaudeville shows he produced, the innumerable productions he reviewed as a Broadway columnist, even his failed radio and film career. While his awkward stage demeanor made him appear a neophyte, he was a veteran long before his television debut.

After dress rehearsal he went to work. A comic's or singer's routine was, again, shortened or changed, as were those of the ventriloquists, the acrobats, the slight-of-hand artists, and the plate spinners—he reshaped even the animal acts, creating havoc with tigers or monkeys who knew their part by rote. And if Ed felt a performer didn't have the magic that Sunday afternoon, after rehearsal that performer was cut altogether, a common occurrence (Marlo Lewis had the unpleasant job of informing their agents). Everything, in short, had to jibe with his gut instinct of what would reach the home audience.

The producer at work: Sullivan in rehearsal with his original television staff. From left, director John Wray, Sullivan, coproducer Marlo Lewis, and talent coordinator Mark Leddy. The showman attempted to control every aspect of the program. (Globe Photos)

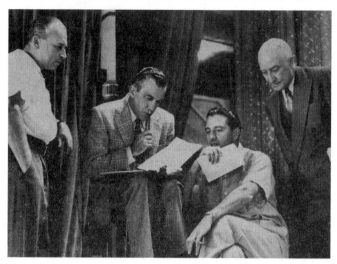

Since his most significant role on the show was producer, Ed could have hired someone else as emcee. It would have saved him myriad slings and arrows from critics and undoubtedly aggravated his ulcer much less. But that wouldn't have satisfied the core craving that had driven him to this point: his hunger for fame. No matter how stilted he was as the show's host, center stage was where he wanted to stand. The program was called *Toast of the Town*, but he imagined a time when it would be called *The Ed Sullivan Show*.

However, he had learned a painful lesson from his many failed radio shows, a mistake he took care not to repeat on television. In each of his short-lived shows he had been a performer; his chitchat with guests played a central role. But experience had taught him that an audience wouldn't respond to him as a performer. So on *Toast of the Town* he walked an awkward middle path. He refused to hire anyone else as emcee—he wanted this high-profile spot for himself. Yet, knowing the show would fail if he put too much of himself onstage, he acted as a transparent host, simply pointing at the talent and getting offstage. He offered a reserved hello, a few comments, then a quick setup: "Let's hear it for. . . ."

Critics didn't accept his withdrawn concept of hosting; it ran counter to the accepted notion of the master of ceremonies as a charismatic performer in his own right. But Ed, though the critics bothered him terribly, wasn't going to be deterred by them. If placing himself center stage meant he would be thrashed by reviewers on a regular basis, so be it. The spotlight was what he had come for, and he had no plans to leave it.

His decision to be the show's emcee put a major hurdle in his path. As the show's first summer wore on, the search for a sponsor bore no fruit. Certainly the cost was modest. Although CBS announced an advertising rate hike effective October 1, it would still cost just $1,000 per episode to sponsor an hour-long television show, up from $700 per hour that summer. Yet even with these rock-bottom rates the sales staff found no takers. Reviews of Sullivan's onstage persona made advertisers hesitate; his wooden delivery was becoming a running joke among industry observers. Finally, in mid September, the Emerson Radio and Television Corporation agreed to sponsor the show for a year. Emerson's sponsorship would not increase the show's

$375 weekly talent budget, but it did, in theory, put Sullivan and Lewis on safer footing with the network.

The first broadcast of *Toast of the Town* for which a tape exists was on November 28, 1948. The tape reveals that Sullivan had found his signature formula for mixing acts, but that his presentation of this formula was still far from ideal. With no budget and only the most rudimentary production facility, this was television at its most primitive.

The show opens with bandleader Ray Bloch's razzmatazz orchestra music, the curtain rising to reveal the June Taylor dancers—a troupe of six leggy, festively costumed nightclub dancers. They shimmy while singing the show's jingle in front of a painted backdrop depicting the Manhattan skyline. As they sashay offstage the audience applauds and Ed walks on briskly, looking ruddily handsome, his hair slicked back, wearing an elegant double-breasted jacket with wide lapels and a dark tie.

The showman addresses the studio audience yet never looks into the camera. His manner is upbeat but restrained, and his erect posture has a frozen quality, as if he's held tightly by an unseen straightjacket. He dedicates the evening's show to the city of Baltimore—part of Ed's effort to romance each city in his viewing audience—but throughout the broadcast he mispronounces the city's name as "Balt-ee-more." To open the show, he doesn't list who will appear (in fact he has no celebrity performers), but instead rambles through a stilted introduction:

"Good evening ladies and gentlemen, as you all know, in this particular *Toast of the Town* show for Emerson, this is Balt-ee-more night." The crowd cheers and he allows himself a smile, but he keeps his hands firmly clasped behind his back. "And Balt-ee-more is feeling mighty happy today; they feel the way Navy felt yesterday in reverse. Navy felt by tying, they won. Balt-ee-more Colts came up here today and knocked off Brooklyn, so let's have a nice hand from all of the Balt-ee-more crowd."

The crowd obliges and he urges them on. "C'mon, make some noise!" He gestures with his arms for more applause and flashes a brief smile. "Well, c'mon, let's hear it! I wanted to see if you could still cheer after that rooting today. . . . Now we're going to open up our show tonight, we're going to take you to the boulevards of Gay Paree. We're going to meet a little mademoiselle and the big, bad wolf. Raymond, take it away."

The orchestra jumps into a jazzy horn number as the camera cuts to a male–female dance duo named Olsen and Joy, the woman dressed in a trampy caricature of a French woman, the man dressed as an American sailor. They dance and strut in an elaborate mock courtship, swing dancing, leaping, mugging with big smiles, handstanding across the stage. They stop in the middle for a comedy routine that plays on his lust for her, then launch into ever more pyrotechnic flips, feet over head, seemingly gravity-free. In their final gesture, the sailor puts a cigarette in his mouth, lights a match, attaches the lit match to his shoe, then lifts his foot back over his head to light the cigarette; he waves his lit cigarette as the duo dances offstage.

Ed urges the audience to keep cheering for the duo, then stows his hands safely in his pockets to introduce the evening's celebrities in the audience. As he points out actor Jack LaRue, a Humphrey Bogart–style player of tough guys and mobsters, he attempts a momentary gangster dialect that gets a chuckle despite its labored quality. He then introduces Temple Texas, whose sole movie role was 1947's *Kiss of Death*, calling her "the prettiest girl in town." Both performers stand and take a bow to polite applause.

To set up a commercial, all of which are performed live onstage, Ed introduces Ray Morgan, the announcer-actor who voices the Emerson ads, explaining that he's been trying to get Ray interested in music. The camera cuts to Morgan, sitting at a desk, auditioning a young female singer. To prove her skills, she trills a love song to her Emerson radio. Morgan then dives into a hard sell as the camera cuts to a variety of Emerson radios, then he wraps it up: *"Better tone! Better performance! Better value!"* as the audience applauds heartily.

Ed takes only a single sentence to introduce the next act, Red and Van Loper, a male–female dance duo who prance through a routine with a mock Indian snake-charmer theme, accompanied by jazzy swing music. They have no set; the pair simply dances in front of the show's painted backdrop.

As the audience applauds the dancers' three-minute routine, Ed attempts a joke with a football theme: "When they were doing this here," he says, mimicking one of the dancer's moves, "that means Balt-ee-more 21, Buffalo 18." There's no time for audience response as the camera cuts to an operatic diva who belts out a Broadway show tune in front of the stage curtain. Suddenly, the curtain opens to reveal the evening's most elaborate set—a papier-mâché mock-up of an adobe wall. The June Taylor dancers sway in curvy unison through a Spanish-themed number, which the vocalist brings to a high point with a triumphant soprano note and a toothy smile.

While the audience cheers, the show appears to be interrupted by hecklers, who in reality are a husband-and-wife comedy team. They interact with Ed in a vaudeville routine whose vintage was circa 1915:

Ed: How did you get in?
Wife: On my sister's tickets.
Ed: Where's your sister?
Wife: Looking for her tickets! (audience laughs)
Ed: I trust your sister's smarter than you.
Wife: (laughing hysterically) My sister's dumber than me.
Ed: (correcting her grammar) You mean "dumber than I."
Wife: She's dumber than both of us! (audience laughs)
Ed: You're the one who lives in Washington, D.C.?
Wife: Yeah.
Ed: Do you know where the nation's capitol is?
Wife: All over Europe! (big audience laugh; the joke is a reference to the Marshall Plan, in which the United States made a huge postwar capital investment to rebuild Europe.)
Wife: (referring to Ed) He's some dope, I'll say.
Husband: Why do you call that master of ceremonies a dope?
Wife: Why do you call that dope a master of ceremonies? (audience laughs)

Ed introduces the evening's act for children, puppeteer Virginia Austin. A matronly woman in her fifties, Austin wheels on a small wagon with two puppets aboard. As she operates her two diminutive characters, she sings the falsetto voice of both male and female puppets; they warble romantically and tap dance to a snappy tune. To demonstrate how easy marionettes are to operate, she works the strings of an oversized puppet, which in turn appears to operate its own smaller puppet. The smaller character then picks up a still smaller hand puppet, creating a three-level marionette act, to great audience delight.

Ed claps largely and exhorts the audience to keep cheering, after which he sets up an Emerson Radio skit. Mom, Dad, sister, and brother, after some comic hijinks, realize they need a radio in every room. Announcer Ray Morgan explains the easiest solution—buy Emerson—then presents the evening's climactic sales offer. With a flourish, he reveals the top of the Emerson line: a television. It's an imposing piece of furniture in a mahogany case, with an eighteen-inch speaker, costing $349.50 "plus installation" (a month's salary for many workers). As the commercial ends the audience claps wholeheartedly.

Ed then introduces audience members Nicholas Joy, a Broadway performer, and—to wild applause—Baltimore Colts player Billy Hildebrand. The mention of the Colts sets up a dance number by the team's drum majorettes, six lithesome young women in short skirts and knee-high white boots, who twirl batons and march around the stage. They're joined by six June Taylor dancers, dressed in similarly short skirts, who perform a mock-football number, tossing a pigskin around as they strut and shake. The melding of the twelve dancers creates a blur of flashing female limbs on the small stage, a mélange of high stepping and waving. The group finishes in a tight formation with the Colts' pennant prominently displayed.

Ed, now appearing almost relaxed, concludes the show by introducing a Baltimore city official who solemnly presents him with a key to the city. Amid applause and cheers, Sullivan thanks viewers—"You've been the most wonderful audience in all the world"—and the orchestra breaks into the bouncy *Toast of the Town* jingle.

Whatever the show's charms, the critics weren't seeing them. In December, a piece by John Crosby of the New York *Herald-Tribune* seemed to encapsulate the year's reviews. "One of the small but vexing questions confronting anyone in this area with a television set is: 'Why is Ed Sullivan on it every Sunday night?' . . . in all respects it's a darn hard question, almost a jackpot question, and it seems to baffle Mr. Sullivan as much as anyone else. . . .

"After a few bars of music, Mr. Sullivan, who is introduced as a nationally syndicated columnist, wanders out onstage, his eyes fixed on the ceiling as if imploring the help of God. . . .

"One entertainer I know who gets from $1,500 to $2,000 a week in nightclubs was talked into doing his cherished routines—he only has three—on the show for $55. Mr. Sullivan is a persuasive fellow. If he has any other qualifications for the job, they're not visible on my small screen. Sullivan has been helplessly fascinated by show business for years. . . . He remains totally innocent of any of the tricks of stage presence, and it seems clear by now that his talents lie elsewhere."

Sullivan, livid, wrote Crosby an enraged rebuttal. "Public opinion, I'm certain, would agree that I've contributed more to television in its embryonic state than you have contributed with your reckless and uninformed backseat driving. You belt away at performers and producers as a means of earning a weekly salary. At least I give them a gracious introduction and a showmanly presentation that enhances their earning power. Your column acquires a tremendous importance. When it's employed to recommend that a man be thrown out of his job it becomes quite an evil instrument." And Ed went a step further in private. On a copy of a similar Crosby review a year later, he handwrote a comment: "I'd like to meet this fella some dark night when I'm learning to drive the largest Mack truck made!"

As vehemently as he disagreed with Crosby or any of the reviewers who criticized him or the show, when he was through firing back, Ed often took their words into account. He did this throughout the run of the show, making booking changes or altering the production in response to a critical barb. After critics roasted his wooden stage presence, he attempted to warm up his onstage persona by hiring Patsy Flick, an old Yiddish vaudeville comic, to heckle him. When Ed walked onstage to introduce an act, Flick would shout out "Come on, Solomon, for God's sake, smile. It makes you look sexy," or, "Did you look dat vay when you were alive?" Ed did a similar bit with Gertrude Berg, star of the popular television series *The Goldbergs*. Berg bantered from the audience in a heavy Yiddish accent, calling him Solomon; Ed got laughs by answering in his own attempt at a Yiddish inflection.

The critics, however, were unimpressed, and in truth Ed's back and forth with hired hecklers didn't fundamentally alter his stiff stage persona. The parade of negative reviews kept coming, as did the showman's acerbic letters written in rebuttal. Sylvia pleaded with Ed to simply write the letters and throw them away, but he was too angry for that. Especially blistering was his retort to Harriet Van Horne, New York *World Telegram & Sun* television and radio critic, who wrote, "He got where he is not by having a personality, but by having no personality; he is the commonest common denominator." In response, he wrote her an uncharacteristically short missive: "Dear Miss Horne. You Bitch. Sincerely, Ed Sullivan."

It was the audience, not the critics, who Sullivan set out to romance, and he succeeded at that in his debut year. As 1948 drew to a close, the Hopper ratings ranked *Toast of the Town* as television's third most popular program, ahead of approximately eighty other prime time shows. It was topped only by Berle's *Texaco Theater* and Arthur Godfrey's *Talent Scouts*, a televised version of the longtime hit radio show. Additionally, a Pulse survey, reporting on local preferences in various cities, placed *Toast of the Town* as the top-ranked program in New York and Philadelphia. Sullivan touted his success in his column, writing a note to himself, "Don't get swellheaded over the Hooper television rating, son." The show, unlike his many attempts at radio, was finding an audience.

And it was doing so on the cheap. At the end of 1948, CBS reported that it had paid Sullivan $53,500 that year; its reported salary for network president Frank Stanton was $109,000. That CBS would pay its fledgling show host about half the compensation of its president was certainly not true. What the network neglected to clarify was that the $53,500 it paid Sullivan had been the year's total talent budget for *Toast of the Town* (the $375 a week for performers, plus $1,000 a week for the orchestra, plus miscellaneous fees, for a half year). Sullivan and his partner Marlo Lewis, after expenses, worked for CBS for free that year.

Although *Toast of the Town* enjoyed healthy ratings, the critical fusillade directed at Sullivan became a problem. If NBC could hire the multitalented Milton Berle, why was CBS presenting this frozen-faced newspaperman who bumbled through his brief introductions? CBS knew the answer—Sullivan was delivering a ratings triumph at almost no cost—but the program's sole sponsor, Emerson Radio, saw it differently. Company executives felt embarrassed to be associated with an emcee who generated such critical vitriol.

In February 1949 Marlo Lewis got a call from Ben Abrams, Emerson's president; Lewis' ad agency handled the account. "Frankly Marlo—Sullivan stinks! Even from here, and holding my nose. He stinks!" Emerson was canceling its sponsorship, effective immediately. When Lewis reminded him he had agreed to a long-term commitment—the agreement had been oral, not written—Abrams retorted that CBS had taken advantage of Emerson by aligning his company with a show hosted by an amateur. The network made a tentative attempt to enforce the agreement, but to no avail. *Toast of the Town* had lost its sponsor.

Sylvia heard the news before Ed. She was home by herself the day the call came. Assuming that Emerson's cancellation portended the show's cancellation, the call was a major blow. "You can't imagine how sick I was," she said. For Ed, the loss of sponsorship called to mind his radio programs, none of which survived past nine months. Now his luck with television, with his show at the nine-month point, appeared all too familiar. He fell into a pitch-black mood. Of that evening, Sylvia recalled: "We were out having dinner, and some fans came over to compliment the program. We both felt so empty we just sat there with sinking hearts."

CBS was flummoxed. *Toast of the Town* had attracted an audience, but it had been a hard sell to advertisers, and was now looking like a money loser. The network felt pressed to rectify that. With the search for a sponsor now urgent, the word was put out, quietly, that CBS was soliciting advertisers for the show "with or without Ed Sullivan." The network had specifically kept Sullivan's name off the show for this possibility; according to his contract he could be replaced at any point.

When Ed heard about the "with or without Sullivan" offer, he erupted into a rage. He had produced a ratings win for the network while subsidizing the cost himself, and now they were about to jettison him? His daughter Betty recalled his response to this news as "making him more of a fighter," and indeed he sprang into full battle mode. He stormed the halls of CBS, entering the office of network president Frank Stanton, voice at full volume, demanding to know what was going on. Stanton and network chairman Bill Paley reassured him, claiming they hadn't agreed to sell the show without him. The offer, they said, had come only from one executive, Jack Van Volkenburg. The "with or without" proffer was rescinded and Sullivan was given an apology. Nonetheless, CBS retained the right to replace him at any time.

The show's high ratings meant it didn't have to wait long to find a new sponsor— and a far more prestigious one. Benson Ford, grandson of Henry Ford, enjoyed *Toast of the Town* immensely. Soon after Emerson Radio's cancellation, the Ford Motor Company's ad agency, Kenyon & Eckhardt, contacted CBS. Ford agreed to sponsor the show for thirteen weeks beginning March 27. For Ed the news was profound validation; the show had attracted one of the country's largest corporations. And, in addition to promoting its Lincoln Mercury line on the program, Ford would tout *Toast of the Town* in all its nationwide print advertising for the automobile line—reminding readers to tune in Sunday night at 8 P.M.

If that alone wasn't manna from Heaven, Ford was throwing its corporate weight behind not just the show but, remarkably, Sullivan himself. Due to Benson Ford's enthusiasm for Ed, Kenyon & Eckhardt developed plans to make him the spokesperson for Lincoln Mercury. Ford would pay him $25,000 per year to travel across the country, city by city, attending community events and giving speeches, promoting the automobile line. When he wasn't on press junkets he would hold press conferences by phone with groups of editors. In short, he was to be the face of Lincoln Mercury. He would become so associated with the boxy sedans that buyers called him about problems and concerns they had with their new Lincoln Mercurys.

(Over the next two years he would log so many miles for Ford that in February 1952 he wrote an exhausted letter to a Lincoln Mercury executive, claiming his physician had forbidden him to keep traveling: "As a result of this session with the doctor, who long has warned me against what he terms 'idiocy,' I have come to this firm conclusion—that a weekly TV show and a five-times-a-week column are as much as I can handle well. I do not want to be a promotion man in the field because it takes too damn much out of me, completely disrupts my home life, and certainly reduces the time I should devote to a big league TV show." Ford agreed to a lighter schedule.)

Ford's sponsorship prompted CBS to increase *Toast of the Town*'s talent budget to $2,000 per episode—still just a fraction of Milton Berle's budget but a quantum leap from $375. Marlo and Ed discussed how to spend the money, in particular, what share they themselves should take. Ed, according to Marlo, argued that all of it should be spent on the show. "My problem is that I can't keep squeezing the talent. We've got to pay them more. . . . I hate to say this, but you and I will still have to wait before we can take anything for ourselves." Lewis agreed. Later that year, the Ford sponsorship allowed Sullivan and Lewis to start taking home modest paychecks.

In addition to the vote of confidence from Ford, Ed received validation from an unusual source in this period. Sometime in late 1949 or early 1950, he took a rare trip home to Port Chester. All of his siblings had remained there; his mother had died in 1929 and his father was now eighty-nine. His older sister Helen, who worked as a factory foreman, had become the family conduit to Ed. When someone needed something, usually financial help, the request was funneled through Helen to Ed. His salary as a *Daily News* columnist and his success as a vaudeville producer made him the affluent sibling.

He may have made the trip home because he knew his father was dying, for Peter was seriously ill and would die in April 1950. This was likely the last time Ed saw his father, from whom he had remained estranged. Even at age eighty-nine, Peter had never once met Ed's daughter Betty, who was now nineteen years old.

Television had made it into the Sullivan home in Port Chester, and Ed's father, with great mental confusion, mentioned that he had seen Ed's show. "Ed, you were in that little box there!" he exclaimed. "How did you get in there?" He could not, even after considerable explanation, understand how his son's image had appeared in his living room.

———

By the late 1940s, Ed's *Daily News* column traveled far afield from its roots as a gossip chronicle. Nearly in his twentieth year of writing five columns a week, he turned

Little Old New York into a stream of consciousness compendium of his opinions and observations. Anything could now be commented upon, from the low price of whale steaks in Vancouver—good for housewives, he observed—to the fact that marijuana was sold openly on Seventh Avenue. He explained the code used by tugboats sailing off Manhattan ("one long blast is 'right your rudder'") and covered the glory days of Yankee demigod Joe DiMaggio. As always, his blind items took a darker turn; he included rumor of an unnamed producer who paid $5,000 to hush up a morals charge. Ed even dispensed advice to the underworld: "Tip to mobs: don't try to heist the shipment on the West Side docks. You've got to get hurt." Broadway and Hollywood remained leading players, as he reported that *A Streetcar Named Desire* was one of the few plays with a busy box office, and he whispered updates like "the Humphrey Bogart stork checks in January" and "Before she filed [for divorce], Jane Wyman and Ronald Reagan had a friendly hour's confab at Warner's."

He gave ample coverage to the funeral for Bill "Bojangles" Robinson, the storied black tap dancer who died in November 1949. Robinson and Sullivan had had a long friendship, and the dancer was one of the first performers Ed booked on his television show. The funeral for Robinson, a larger-than-life folk hero in New York City before earning Hollywood fame, was attended by scores of public figures, including Mayor O'Dwyer, Milton Berle, Danny Kaye, and Ethel Merman. According to *The New York Times*, approximately five hundred thousand people lined the streets as the flag-draped hearse drove slowly from the church service in Harlem to Times Square to the cemetery in Brooklyn. Robinson had made a small fortune as a performer, yet he died destitute. The pastor who eulogized him explained that he had but two vices, "ice cream and gambling." Ed, along with composer Noble Sissle (his partner in the Broadway show *Harlem Cavalcade*), took charge of the funeral arrangements, partially funding it and soliciting contributions for the rest. Adam Clayton Powell, New York's pioneering black Congressman, thanked Sullivan in his eulogy to Robinson, and Ed also delivered a eulogy at the service.

Aside from show business events like Robinson's funeral, or Broadway–Hollywood news, Ed's column now most often spotlighted politics. At times he covered the intersection of politics and show business, as when he reported in the summer of 1948 that Frank Sinatra and Jimmy Durante donated large sums to the new state of Israel, a favorite cause of Ed's. But more often now he put aside show business to write about politics itself. He analyzed the 1948 Dewey–Truman presidential race at length, clearly leaning toward the Republican Dewey, a shift from when the young columnist was a cheerleader for Franklin Roosevelt. Truman, he observed, appeared "grayer and plumper," and seemed "pretty grim over the coldblooded disinterest in his own party." Indeed, Truman faced an all-but-certain loss in the fall election. Which would be good for the country, Ed opined. "Can you imagine the cleanup job J. Edgar Hoover's FBI will do if former DA Tom Dewey gets in? Truman group has handcuffed Hoover, while the henchmen loaded the boodle."

The political development that most concerned Ed was the rise of the Soviet Union. He dissected the internal power struggles of the U.S.S.R. down to the minutiae: "The Russian conflict is between Stalin's group . . . versus forty-nine-year-old Andrei Zhdanov and Zhukov's Red army officer clique, arch foes of U.S. and England . . . They tell me that even in the Russian embassies in this country, the current bitter communist rift has split apart Russians, with each spying on the other."

As the Cold War settled in, he warned constantly of the threat Russia posed to the United States. He supported those who called for increased defensive measures, as he wrote in July 1948: "GOP leaders, burning at the call for a special session of Congress, first will ask President Truman why the Air Force hasn't a single assembled atom bomb? It would be two weeks for one to be assembled, if Russia pulled a Pearl Harbor in Europe."

Ed reported what he saw as the growing influence of communist subversives in the United States. "Commies in this area bolder now that all books of twelve Commie leaders destroyed," he wrote shortly after his show debuted. A few weeks later, "Commies in this area have labored overtime, through the years, to bag [boxer] Joe Louis. At one big political rally in Harlem, the Commie speaker suddenly pointed to Louis and screamed: 'Even the heavyweight champion of the world isn't permitted to play golf at white clubs. Isn't that so, Joe?' . . . Louis rose to his feet and said, 'No, you're wrong again. I play golf with Bob Hope, Hal LeRoy, Lou Clayton, Ed Sullivan, Bing Crosby, and I play at the top clubs in the country' . . . Only time on record that golf flogged communism . . . Have you noticed the sudden silence of local Commies? Not a pink peep out of them for weeks."

In late 1949, the anticommunist fervor Ed supported came into conflict with his role as a television producer. He booked Paul Draper, a dancer known as "The Aristocrat of Tap" for his ability to adapt his flashing feet to any genre, from samba to classical. Scheduled for January 1950, the Draper booking created controversy almost as soon as it was announced.

Mrs. Hester McCullough, a Connecticut housewife and anticommunist crusader, had declared that Draper and harmonica player Larry Adler were communist sympathizers. It appears her charge was based on nothing more substantial than Draper and Adler's high-profile support of third-party presidential candidate Henry Wallace, the 1948 nominee of the Progressive Party. (Wallace, a former vice president under Roosevelt, was a constant target of red-baiters in the late 1940s due to his left-of-center beliefs.) Prior to a 1949 performance by Draper and Adler in Greenwich, Connecticut, McCullough had launched a letter-writing campaign, aided by Hearst columnist Igor Cassini, who wrote as "Cholly Knickerbocker." With Knickerbocker's support, she demanded the concert be canceled, asserting that performers with communist sympathies were traitors. Draper and Adler denied her charges, issuing a statement picked up by the Associated Press that they were not and never had been communist sympathizers, and that their allegiance stood solely with the United States. The two performers filed suit against McCullough and played their concert as planned, which went well.

That Sullivan decided to book Draper after this much controversy was a clear risk. It's probable that he knew Draper had lost nightclub bookings after his support of Wallace's campaign—which Ed himself had vehemently opposed. Yet Ed knew Draper and had worked with him, booking him on numerous occasions for his local variety shows, and Draper and Adler played many USO shows during the war. Ed knew the dancer well enough to know that McCullough's claims were groundless. And Draper was a perfect performer for the modestly funded *Toast of the Town*: his tap brilliance played well on television, yet he wasn't well-known enough to command a large paycheck. At any rate, it appeared that Draper had successfully stood up to McCullough, having filed suit against her and performed as planned. Furthermore, any action by a Hearst columnist (a group that included Winchell) was likely to produce an equal and opposite reaction by Ed.

Soon after Draper's *Toast of the Town* appearance was announced, a full assault began. Cholly Knickerbocker, now aided by conservative Hearst columnists Westbrook Pegler and George Sokolsky, demanded that Ford Motor Company cancel the appearance. Ford, its ad agency Kenyon & Eckhardt, and Ed circled the wagons, holding tense meetings about how to handle the issue. One sticky problem: Draper had filed suit against McCullough; if Ford canceled Draper's television appearance, would they themselves be faced with legal action?

The decision was made to go ahead with the Draper booking, but Ed dressed it up beyond reproach. He directed the dancer to perform to "Yankee Doodle Dandy," and, right after Draper's performance, the camera cut to Benson Ford in the audience, no more wholesome representative of mainstream America, clapping with gusto. But the other side was not to be appeased. Hearst's *New York Journal-American* decried the show with banner headlines, and the Hearst columnists led a letter-writing campaign that sent nearly thirteen hundred angry letters to Ford. Some were duplicates, with large numbers coming from the same post office, but the meaning was clear: Ford had stepped into a public relations quagmire. Worried meetings were again convened between Ford, its agency, and Sullivan, after which Ed wrote a letter, supposedly to the head of Kenyon & Eckhardt, but in reality to be distributed as a press release:

"I am deeply distressed to find out that some people were distressed by the appearance . . . of a performer whose political beliefs are a matter of controversy . . . You know how bitterly opposed I am to communism and all it stands for . . . If anybody has taken offense, it is the last thing I wanted or anticipated, and I am sorry . . . Tell everybody to tune in again next Sunday night, and if I can get a plug in, it will be a great show—better than ever."

It was a strategic retreat—after the battle was done—but Ed had, in essence, learned his lesson. Booking a performer with even an imagined shadow over his credentials was profoundly hazardous. Never again would he do so. The show and its success were primary; nothing would ever challenge that as his guiding precept. While he had been a bellicose Cold Warrior before the Draper incident, he now redoubled his efforts. Soon after the controversial booking, he let it be known that he checked each show's lineup with Theodore Kirkpatrick, a former FBI agent and now coeditor of *Counterattack*, which billed itself as "a newsletter of facts on communism." If Sullivan thought a musician or comic might be considered a communist sympathizer, he invited Kirkpatrick, a self-appointed expert on such matters, to meet with the performer in Ed's suite at the Delmonico. Ed made it clear that *Toast of the Town* would be above even the suggestion of subversive taint. "Kirkpatrick has sat in my living room on several occasions and listened attentively to performers eager to secure a certification of loyalty," he wrote in June 1950. "On some occasions, after interviewing them, he has given them the green light; on other occasions, he has told them 'Veterans' organizations will insist on further proof.'"

Those evenings at the Delmonico reflected a larger national mood. In February 1950, Joseph McCarthy, a little known junior senator from Wisconsin, made a speech in Wheeling, West Virginia in which he alleged there were communists in the U.S. State Department. He had a list, he said, of two hundred five State Department personnel who were members of the Communist Party; furthermore, he claimed they continued to actively shape U.S. foreign policy. That the list was never actually produced was beside the point. McCarthy had placed a seed in fertile soil. It was a season of fear, and, given world events, not without reason. Communists had taken control of mainland China a year earlier, and the Soviets had detonated their first atomic bomb six months earlier. Just one month before McCarthy's speech, Alger Hiss, a low-ranking State Department employee, was convicted of perjury in a case involving his alleged membership in the Communist Party. Hiss continued to maintain his innocence, but that, too, was immaterial. His highly publicized congressional hearings—the first televised hearings, in 1948—suggested that something subversive and pervasive lurked just beyond sight.

Amid it all, in June 1950, Ed announced in his column that a "bombshell" was on its way, a publication to be distributed to all broadcast networks, sponsors, and ad agencies. Kirkpatrick had told Sullivan, and Ed, by giving advance warning in his column, let readers know he was on the inside track. The two-hundred-fifteen-page book lived up to its billing. Published by *Counterattack* and entitled *Red Channels: The Report of Communist Influence in Radio and Television*, the publication warned of a Soviet effort to infiltrate American culture using radio and television. It listed one-hundred fifty-one individuals with "citations" for communist sympathies. The list, shockingly, contained some of the leading lights of stage and screen: Zero Mostel, a comic actor whom Ed worked with on numerous benefits for United Jewish Relief; actor John Garfield, a Sullivan houseguest in Hollywood; playwright Arthur Miller, whose *Death of a Salesman* was a 1949 Broadway hit; composer Aaron Copland, whose paean to homespun Americana, *Appalachian Spring*, debuted in 1944; and Hollywood star Edward G. Robinson, whose florid portrayals of mobsters had inspired Ed's own *Big Town Czar*. Adding credence to the hysteria trumpeted by *Red Channels*, within a week of its release communist forces from North Korea invaded South Korea.

That the luminaries listed in *Red Channels* were part of a communist conspiracy was an absurd assertion; the most common denominator among the group was support for the New Deal. Even one of its publishers conceded that some performers shouldn't have been listed. Regardless, the list was read and in many cases treated as gospel by broadcasting executives. Though rarely spoken of in public, the list became a powerful force behind the scenes. And while the "transgressions" of those listed were usually imaginary or close to it, they had no redress once they were unemployed. One of *Red Channels'* chief backers was Laurence Johnson, a supermarket executive in Syracuse, New York, whose association with the publication gave him unquestioned power across the television and advertising industries. "If he put the word out on you, you were through," recalled Mike Dann, who then worked in NBC's programming department. Dann also remembered the wholehearted enthusiasm that Ed brought to his support of *Red Channels*. As he understood it, Ed "wasn't a reactionary, he was square—he was very square."

The irony of Ed's involvement with *Counterattack* is that he himself had written for a Socialist newspaper in his twenties. The *Leader*, for which he was sports editor and a columnist, regularly listed all the communist cell meetings in the New York area, and espoused kinship between American and Russian workers; these groups were all part of the international proletariat, as the *Leader* saw it. (One of the government raiders who ransacked *The Leader*'s offices in 1919 was a young agent who then went by the name of John Edgar Hoover.) Certainly his writing had been largely apolitical, but then many blacklisted performers had done nothing more serious. Yet Ed's youthful indiscretion went overlooked—helped, no doubt, by his silence on the topic. In interviews, he always glossed over this period, and in a 1956 article he wrote for *Collier's* magazine detailing his early newspaper career, he pointedly omitted *The Leader*.

At any rate, the host of *Toast of the Town* had now thrown himself into the pitched battle to protect America from the communist threat, real and perceived, which was joined by virtually all major American institutions. In December 1950, Ed was a member of an expert panel enlisted to judge an essay contest sponsored by the Veterans of Foreign Wars. The contestants wrote on the topic "What Strategy Should the V.F.W. Recommend to Our Government in Combating the Communist Threat to America?" The other judges on the panel included newspaper magnate William Randolph Hearst, *Counterattack* publisher Theodore Kirkpatrick, Westbrook Pegler— the columnist whom Ed defied in booking Paul Draper—and Julius Ochs Adler, an executive with *The New York Times*.

Despite the depth of his involvement, Ed maintained a level of critical judgment about some of the actions taken in the name of anticommunist fervor. In 1952, the *New York Post* launched a full-scale assault against Walter Winchell, running a series of articles attacking him from every angle; naturally they enlisted Ed for commentary. In the *Post* series, Ed remarked, "Long before Senator McCarthy came into the character-assassination racket, there was a guy by the name of Walter Winchell." The roundhouse punch against Winchell aside, the public denunciation of McCarthy was unusual for someone in Ed's position. Certainly the description was accurate—reckless character assassination was McCarthy's forte—but in 1952, the Republican senator was still very much a force to be reckoned with.

Even Dwight Eisenhower, then a popular war hero running a heavily favored campaign as the Republican presidential nominee, opted to cut a McCarthy rebuke from one of his speeches. Eisenhower's advisors convinced him to remain mute on the subject, "fearing McCarthy's retaliation against their candidate," according to historian David Halberstam. That Sullivan, producing a television program aimed at a mass audience, supported by a public relations–sensitive corporate sponsor, would so openly declaim McCarthy was just short of foolhardy. It was also typical of the contradictions that ran throughout his political attitudes. He cooperated with *Counterattack* but called McCarthy a character assassin; he was an avid blacklister but professed to voting for Adlai Stevenson, the Democratic presidential candidate in 1952 and 1956, who stood against the practice. Although he could pander, by telling Paul Draper to dance to "Yankee Doodle Dandy," his swipe at McCarthy demonstrated he remained a pugilist at heart.

And that quality would be an essential one in Sullivan's television career—especially in the early 1950s. Not long after launching his show, his pugilistic spirit would face its greatest test yet.

CHAPTER TEN

David vs. Goliath

B Y THE SPRING OF 1950, Ed and Marlo Lewis could point to *Toast of the Town* as a success. It had been on the air close to two years, and while Ed himself still drew negative reviews, the show was a clear hit. The previous August, *New York Times* critic Jack Gould had written a satirical piece about the difficulty of taking a vacation without television: "It was toward the end of the evening that one most missed Ed Sullivan . . . all in all it was pretty nerve racking, never getting the signal when to applaud, and meeting people who were not Ed's friends." While Gould meant that tongue in cheek, he also knew his readers would understand the reference. Television ratings for October 1949 published by *Variety* identified *Toast of the Town* as the number two show on television, second only to Berle's *Texaco Theater*. It even bested Arthur Godfrey's *Talent Scouts*, whose beloved host benefited from years of national radio exposure. To give the show an extra ratings boost, Ed produced fresh episodes of *Toast of the Town* year-round, with guest hosts filling in during his three-week vacation—there was no time to rest when an audience was being built.

Ed and Marlo had, finally, begun to make money from the show. With Ford's continued sponsorship, CBS knew it had to make a real investment in the program, and the show's weekly talent budget jumped to several thousand dollars. It was time for Ed and Marlo to start taking home more than token payment. But how much would it be?

The two, by Marlo's account, had signed an agreement before the show launched to split any profits equally. Since there had been precious little profit, the issue had been moot. But by early 1950 the success of *Toast of the Town* prompted a discussion. One day in April, Ed asked Marlo to have lunch with him in the Delmonico's dining room to talk about the show's future. When Marlo arrived he was surprised to find that Ed had also invited his lawyer, Fred Backer. Ed was talkative through lunch, regaling Backer with tales of how he and Marlo had run the show on a shoestring. As lunch ended, though, Ed's mood took a serious tone. He removed a piece of paper from his pocket, the original agreement between Marlo and him; he paused for a moment, not sure of how to handle the subject. "I don't want you to misunderstand, but the fact is—I've got star status now," Ed said, according to Marlo. "I've worked like a dog, paid my dues . . . and our deal is not equitable. Lord knows, you've done a great job, and we're a great team. But this old agreement of fifty-fifty doesn't make sense anymore."

At that point Ed's lawyer took over the conversation. "What Ed is getting at is that he wants to change the deal. It's no longer fair to him. We want it to read seventy-five percent for him, twenty-five percent for you. That's it in a nutshell." Lewis was dumbstruck. He conceded that Ed deserved more for his starring role, but he pointed out that he, like Ed, had worked for almost nothing since the show's debut. Complicating the issue was the fact that Lewis had quit his job at the Blaine Thompson agency to devote himself to the show. He asked for a few days to think over the matter. Backer agreed, but, he said, "that won't change our position."

While Marlo glared at Backer, Ed reached over and took hold of his arm. As Marlo recalled the meeting—Ed never made reference to this discussion—Ed said, "Come on, Marlo. You're gonna get rich on this show. Don't take it so big. I need you, you need me. You gotta remember, I'm a lot older than you, and without my muscle there never would've been a show in the first place." He told Marlo to have his own lawyer get together with Backer and rework the contract. "I'll see you Sunday, same time, same station."

Marlo left the Delmonico in a daze, feeling betrayed and unsure of what to do. Ed, of course, had a point: the show was his, from conception to choice of talent; he created the onscreen product down to the minute, shaping many of the comics' acts and selecting many of the vocalists' songs. And Sullivan's column enabled the show to attract talent long before Lincoln Mercury provided major backing. But Marlo couldn't shake the feeling that he was being taken advantage of, that the deal was changed only after he invested countless hours. Full of doubts about continuing on the show, he went to see Hubbell Robinson, CBS executive in charge of programming. Robinson, understanding that the Lewis–Sullivan conflict threatened the network's Sunday night flagship, went to CBS head Bill Paley, who decided to take control of the situation.

Paley called a meeting at his St. Regis apartment, inviting Sullivan and Lewis along with Robinson and network president Frank Stanton. He kept the meeting light, making no allusion to the contract conflict, instead complimenting Ed and Marlo on the job they had done. *Toast of the Town*, Paley said, might be just the beginning; he wanted both men to become integral parts of the network. To cement their relationship with CBS, he made each of them an offer. To Marlo, he offered a position as an executive producer for the network; Lewis would work on *Toast of the Town* and might also produce other shows. To Ed, he offered a five-year contract as the producer of *Toast of the Town*. Sullivan would not be a CBS staff member, but instead would work as an independent contractor. The answer from Ed and Marlo was unequivocal: we accept.

Ed's new contract set his pay at a minimum of $1,500 a week until September 1955. His compensation would increase if sponsorship revenue increased; that is, if the show's ratings allowed CBS to charge Lincoln Mercury more, then Sullivan would make more. If the program was still on the air in 1955, he would begin to receive a one-percent share of sponsorship revenue in addition to his weekly pay.

The talent budget was set at $10,000 per show for the first year, increasing to $12,000 over the following two years. The amount wasn't stated for the contract's last two years—apparently the network felt it wasn't reasonable to guess talent budgets more than three years out.

While the contract specified that both Ed and Marlo would work on *Toast of the Town*, it clearly placed Ed in charge. Oddly, in the document's language, Ed was referred to as "Producer," while Marlo was referred to by his own name. One clause specified that Marlo would be the show's coproducer, to which Ed insisted upon an amendment; this was handwritten in and initialed by all parties: "Any successor to Mr. Lewis shall be subject to Producer approval." In other words, *Toast of the Town* was Sullivan's show.

The terms agreed upon, CBS issued a press release, picked up by *The New York Times* in a terse one-paragraph news item. Reporting that the two had been hired as producers, the paper noted, "They will work as a team, creating new productions and working on existing programs." The news, for those watching, announced that Sullivan and Lewis weren't arrivistes anymore; they had earned the blessing of a major network. For Marlo, it was both a relief—a way around what he saw as Ed's arm-twisting—and a step up; the door was open for him to produce other shows. For Ed, it was a dream come true. He had won the support of CBS. He was no longer a mere columnist; he had achieved what he most hungered for: a solid foothold in broadcasting.

Rumors started sometime in the spring of 1950 about a monster being created in the NBC studios. It was to be one of the most lavish television shows, perhaps *the* most lavish show, to date—a jewel in the NBC lineup. It would be a weekly variety program, mixing comedy and music and celebrity, starring the brightest names in show business. The extravaganza would be backed by a budget large enough to fell Rocky Marciano in a single blow: $50,000 an episode by some accounts, still higher by other reports. To be called *The Colgate Comedy Hour*, it was scheduled to debut that fall. Its time slot was one that the television industry had learned was particularly desirable, when families were most likely to gather around the set: Sunday at 8 P.M.

In short, NBC decided to end Sullivan's dominance of Sunday evening. The network had seen *Toast of the Town* own Sunday night since its 1948 debut. In the 1949–50 season, Sullivan had easily bested NBC's Sunday evening program hosted by singer Perry Como. (ABC, perpetually third-ranked, wouldn't have a show in the Top 20 until 1955; a fourth network, Dumont, offered little competition and ceased broadcasting in 1954.) NBC apparently took a look at *Toast of the Town* and figured, if he can do it, we can do it better. *Comedy Hour*, by sheer weight of budget, was the network's move to grab the coveted Sunday 8 P.M. slot. If the public wants a variety show, NBC's strategy appeared to be, we'll give them the best variety show money can buy. Sullivan would be buried.

In a novel approach, *Comedy Hour* would rotate hosts, each starring for a week. Hosting week one was Eddie Cantor, who was not just wildly popular but almost an institution, having conquered Broadway, vaudeville, radio, and Hollywood as a singer, comedian, and actor; three years later Warner Bros. granted him the ultimate honor, producing *The Eddie Cantor Story*. Lined up for week two was comedy team Dean Martin and Jerry Lewis, the suave paesano and the overactive adolescent, whose fame had zoomed skyward since their television debut on *Toast of the Town* for $200; the duo were paid a breathtaking $100,000 for their first night, and $150,000 per show after that. Week three was hosted by Fred Allen, whose jaunty, cerebral wit had made him a top radio comic for more than a decade. He had, for example, invited boxer Joe Louis on his show to help him train for an imaginary bout with Jack Benny; the final Fred Allen–Jack Benny showdown had been a gargantuan ratings success, near that of the highest-rated Roosevelt fireside chat. The fourth week featured vaudeville–Hollywood comic Bobby Clark, the least famous of the crowd. However, he was scheduled to alternate with comedic powerhouse Bob Hope.

These celebrity hosts would emcee live variety revues—showcasing still more big names—that broadcast from a huge New York theater with flashy sets and first-rate orchestras. *Comedy Hour*, it seemed, planned not only to dominate Sunday night but to push television itself to a higher level.

CBS, seeing the freight train rushing toward it, told Sullivan there was more money if he needed it. As the network knew, the stakes in this competition were high. In the early days of television, many local stations were deciding which network to affiliate with; each of the networks knew it was vitally important to offer a successful lineup to attract long-term affiliates. Still, *Toast of the Town*'s budget, even with the infusion from CBS, would hover around $20,000 per program in the early 1950s, far smaller than *Comedy Hour*'s—which seemed to balloon markedly with every new report.

In fact, CBS appeared to be hedging its bet. The network, perhaps thinking it needed to work on securing a new night in the face of NBC's assault on Sunday, poured money into Saturday evening. Set to launch that fall on CBS on Saturday nights was *The Frank Sinatra Show*, a variety show that guaranteed its star $250,000 for the first thirteen weeks. (The show was canceled after thirteen weeks; Frank sang brilliantly but his ability to work with others proved negligible.)

When *The Colgate Comedy Hour* debuted on September 10, it sparkled with all the transporting brilliance its massive prepublicity had promised. Eddie Cantor was as charming as he had been in vaudeville in 1925 or Hollywood in 1935, weaving a story line between the show's variety acts, interacting with each as he sang, danced, and told jokes; the show culminated with Cantor in blackface singing one of his signature hits, "Ain't She Sweet." The following week, Jerry Lewis and Dean Martin turned the small screen into a spirited night at the Copacabana, mugging and cracking wise through a lighthearted romp of an hour. Suddenly television had a new hit, and critics labored to find enough superlatives to laud it.

In contrast, *Toast of the Town* experienced a ratings collapse. Ed had been sanguine that summer, telling Marlo not to worry. "For the most part, all they've got are the same old clowns doing the same old shtick. Eddie Cantor will clap his hands and sing 'Susie' and talk about Ida and the five daughters. Fred Allen will fall back on his old radio material. . . . Sure we'll take it on the chin a few times. Martin and Lewis and Hope will win their rounds the first time out. But I'm not worried one bit about the rest of 'em." However, his show's ratings tumble clearly required him to counterpunch if he expected to stay on the air.

The weakness in *Comedy Hour* was those weeks when its less-popular hosts emceed; when Fred Allen or Bobby Clark took the stage, *Toast of the Town* surged back in the ratings. Ed exploited this advantage to its fullest. In October, against a Bobby Clark *Comedy Hour*, he booked Margaret Truman, the president's daughter, who aspired to a career as a classical soprano. The twenty-six-year-old singer had performed only on local television, which to Ed presented an opportunity. He took her to lunch at the fashionable restaurant Sardi's and asked her: would you like to make your national TV debut? When she agreed, Ed paid her $2,000 and touted it as her professional debut. Headline writers obliged, providing waves of free publicity. For that evening's performance the backstage area was thick with secret service agents, who insisted that Sullivan (who was frisked by the agents) give his dressing room to Margaret for security reasons; several hours later they reversed themselves after deciding a nearby alley posed a risk, and the dressing rooms were switched back. The attendant publicity lifted Sullivan to an easy ratings win against that evening's *Comedy Hour*.

Two months later, Margaret Truman was again thrust into the news. After *Washington Post* music critic Paul Hume panned one of her recitals, President Truman dashed him off an angry letter that was reprinted in many national newspapers: "I've never met you, but if I do you'll need a new nose and plenty of beefsteak and perhaps a supporter below. Westbrook Pegler, a guttersnipe, is a gentlemen compared to you." Ed, sensing a ratings spike in the petty tempest, offered Margaret $3,000 for a return appearance, allowing him to trounce a Bobby Clark *Comedy Hour*. After her performance, the president called Sullivan to thank him for the gracious way he had presented his daughter.

In the late fall, Ed began to go after Eddie Cantor. He again used his newshound's instincts to exploit headlines. Roberta Peters, an understudy in a Metropolitan Opera production of *Don Giovanni*, stepped into the lead role and earned a full-throated standing ovation. The almost fairy-tale story of the young coloratura—from a modest home in the Bronx—triumphing at the Met made headlines across the country. Ed instantly booked her to reprise her *Don Giovanni* role opposite a Cantor *Comedy Hour* the following Sunday, riding the publicity for a ratings boost. Peters proved so popular that Ed booked the opera singer forty-one times over the years.

In another effort to dislodge Cantor, Ed booked Milton Berle against one of Cantor's *Comedy Hour* nights. CBS executives must have been flabbergasted to present NBC's biggest star, unless they laughed along with Sullivan as the Trendex ratings proved it worked. Showcasing the competition's heavyweight was not only counterintuitive, it sent a signal. Due to the gaping budget disparity between *Toast of the Town* and *Comedy Hour*, it didn't look like Sullivan could win the ratings battle—the NBC show could hire bigger names week after week. But the Berle booking revealed he was willing to try most anything.

Berle was electric that evening. As Sullivan introduced him, Berle bounded onstage and pumped Ed's hand. "Thank you, Ed Solomon," he said, as the emcee faded offstage. Without taking a breath, Berle whirled into a comedic tornado, interrupting himself, ad-libbing, inserting jokes within jokes, making fun of himself, and scolding the audience for not laughing enough—"these are the jokes, let's face it"—

although the laughter was almost continuous. As he bobbed and weaved, the camera had to swivel to keep him in the frame. His punch lines were like short jabs, with few of his setups longer than five or six words; as a boy named Milton Berlinger he had grown up in vaudeville, and his style was straight from the Keith–Albee circuit.

He took great pleasure in pointing out that his own hit show ran on a competing network. "You know what CBS means? Catch Berle's show"; "I only have two words to say to each Mercury Lincoln dealer—buy Texaco"; "Wait a second—What are these cameras here?—Is this show televised? Gee, I didn't know that Sullivan's show was televised"; "C'mon now, if you're going to applaud, applaud all together! . . . (looking skyward). . . . Oh Milton, you're *wonderful!*"

Berle brought onstage a young trumpet player named Leonard Souse, who acted as a straight man, and then he produced his own trumpet. "Don't laugh," he said, "I used to be with Dorsey." "Tommy or Jimmy?" asked Souse, to which Berle responded: "Fifi." Souse riffed through a showy version of "Blue Skies," after which Berle danced an impromptu classical ballet, mock-pirouetting around the stage and pulling up his pants legs to reveal tall black socks.

Ed came back onstage to join Berle, attempting to smile with limited success. "There's the camera, Eddie," Berle instructed, placing his body in front of Sullivan's to shield him from the painful sight. They horseplayed with each other, each jostling to monopolize the camera's eye, as the audience roared.

Bantering back and forth, Berle handily one-upped Sullivan, throwing a final barb as he exited the stage: "Eddie, you know we made a pact, I said I'd never become a columnist, and you said you'd never become an actor—well, you've kept your promise."

Following Berle's raucous act that evening was the ever-mellow Nat "King" Cole, in a booking that displayed Ed's audacity in pushing the era's racial boundaries. The showman gave the singer a big introduction: "And now let's hear it for the calypso blues and *Nat . . . King . . . Cole!—Let's hear it for Nat!*"

In a tropical set with palm trees and a painted island backdrop, the tall and dapper Cole rhythmically crooned a calypso tune, his silky voice as smooth as an ocean breeze. Four female dancers shook their hips in time to the music, their long skirts flowing with the Caribbean groove.

While highly pleasant for many audience members, Ed surely knew that the performance prompted dark stirrings in living rooms across the land. White women onstage with a black man—moving their hips in time to his voice, no less—was, at the very least, the height of exoticism in November 1950. And to some viewers it proved that America was becoming a modern-day Sodom and Gomorrah. Helping make this mixed-race performance palatable was Nat "King" Cole's milquetoast charisma and his ability to cover himself with a blanket of profound deference. The handsome singer never once glanced at his attractive stage mates. Even so, that Ed booked this number revealed an odd fearlessness in a man who was otherwise hypersensitive to his audience's comfort level. He was exporting a sight that hitherto had been seen chiefly in Manhattan nightclubs.

Not that Cole gave the slightest indication that what had just gone on was revolutionary. As he performed his own fade-out, doffing his hat and singing ever more softly while strolling offstage, his smile beamed large and genial. Ed led the applause and brought the singer back out to shake his hand.

In case Ed harbored any doubt about how some of his viewers regarded such performances, the show received regular waves of hate mail to this effect, which continued through the decades. The southern Lincoln Mercury dealers—and they were far from alone—furiously insisted he stop shaking hands with and hugging black performers, but he never gave in to their demands. "I'll never forget when Ed kissed a black girl" on the air, recalled Mike Dann, who worked in NBC's programming department in the 1950s. "Ed was certainly not a racist—particularly if [the performer] was good."

Sharing the bill with Cole that evening was vocalist Nanette Fabray, recreating a number from the recent Broadway show *High Button Shoes*. Clad in a full-length bathing gown, she sang the up-tempo tune on a beach set decorated with ocean-side dressing huts. In mid song, she and her four dancers shimmied out of their gowns to reveal summer jumpers, and a verse later they removed their jumpers to reveal 1919-era bathing suits. For all the outfits' modesty, there was a lot of well-turned gam on display as the dancers posed and strutted. Fabray wrapped it up with a coy smile amid great clapping and cheering.

Lest the evening get too racy, Sullivan booked the Boy's Town choir—forty boys dressed in angelic robes harmonizing a church hymn—after which Ed introduced Father Schmidt, a Catholic priest from Boy's Town. Next, Sullivan presented Buster Keaton, who with Charlie Chaplin had been a comic giant of silent film. His career had collapsed with the advent of talkies but he was making a comeback. Keaton performed a slapstick routine without speaking, in a set made up as a rural fishing hole, complete with a small swimming pool. Every time he attempted a fishing maneuver—*splash*—he fell face first into the water. Ed, offering high art after low comedy, followed Keaton with international ballet stars Andre Eglevsky and Rosella Hightower, who floated through a six-minute classical ballet.

No Sullivan broadcast was without something for the kids, which that evening was Spanish acrobatic duo Montez DeOcha. Midway through their routine, Ed walked onstage to pump up the excitement: "This trick here is a thirty-foot leap in the air by Lolita, and Montez, with his back turned, will catch her—I hope." The audience chuckled at his tag, but this was live television and there was no net so the chuckle was more anticipatory than humorous. Lolita climbed the ladder and Montez turned his back to her—he would have no way to compensate if she didn't leap just right. She jumped, bounced on a trampoline and sailed forth some thirty feet in the air, landing in a perfect headstand on top of his upraised arms. He twirled her over his head as Ed led the cheers—"That's really something, huh?"

Throughout the hour were Lincoln Mercury ads; Ford was *Toast of the Town*'s sole sponsor. As the auto line's spokesman, Ed always set up the commercials himself, with intros like, "You know, nostalgia has its place, but if you're thinking of buying a new car, don't settle for anything less than a great, new, 1951 Mercury." The Ford ads were ninety seconds long, with sunny images of bulbous sedans driving at moderate speed on clean, wide roads. As each spot concluded, the camera cut to the studio audience, which clapped with great enthusiasm.

———

By the end of the 1950 fall season, NBC canceled Fred Allen as host of *Comedy Hour*. His intimate, offbeat humor hadn't translated to television. Absurdly, his popular characters, which in radio he brought to life in the listener's imagination, were turned into hand puppets for television. Allen, bitter, quipped about his competitor: "What does Sullivan do? He points at people. Rub meat on actors and dogs will do the same." To this, Ed riposted: "Maybe Fred should rub some meat on a sponsor." Bobby Clark, too, was soon dropped from *Comedy Hour*. But the challenge to Sullivan remained intractable. *Comedy Hour*'s glittering pay scale ensured that a long list of stars—brighter stars—stood ready to replace Allen and Clark. Bob Hope, Abbot and Costello, Spike Jones, Jackie Gleason: each hosted *Comedy Hour* by the end of the 1950–51 season. Competing against the NBC program was like trying to win some mad carnival game; as soon as Sullivan shot down one target, several more appeared.

Attempting to find a creative alternative, he began presenting shows from remote locations, which strained television's primitive technical capabilities. In the 1950–51 season, he hosted shows from Philadelphia, Pittsburgh, Detroit, and Boston. The power went out during the Boston show, halting *Toast of the Town* in the middle of its live broadcast. In the darkened theater were two-hundred wounded veterans from the Korean War; Ed asked the audience to allow them to leave first. In each remote show, he catered to the city itself, spotlighting its native attractions as if he were a visiting politician courting the locals.

Seeking more ways to outpoint *Comedy Hour*, he began offering something beyond the purview of the NBC program: legitimate theater. Ed used the natural resources of Manhattan, culling from among the city's dozens of current stage productions to present excerpts geared for the television audience.

He chose a scene from Carson McCullers' *The Member of the Wedding*, which won the 1950 New York Drama Critics' prize for best American play. The scene was one in which Julie Harris sat on Ethel Waters' knee as Brandon De Wilde leaned tenderly against them. As Marlo Lewis recalled, this broadcast stirred controversy because it involved a black performer having physical contact with a white performer.

Ed mined Broadway throughout the season, presenting a who's who of stage stars, from Sarah Churchill and Charles Laughton to Jessica Tandy and Hume Cronin. Among the notable performances were James Barton in Erskine Caldwell's *Tobacco Road*, Flora Robson in Lesley Storm's *Black Chiffon*, Eva Le Gallienne in Anton Chekov's *The Cherry Orchard*, and Judith Anderson in Euripides' *Medea*. On the lighter side, Ed booked a medley of songs from Frank Loesser's *Guys and Dolls*, currently playing to full houses on Broadway. All these stage excerpts, of course, shared billing with contrasting performers on the Sullivan stage. So Anton Chekov was followed by acrobats, Euripides was preceded by a comic, and *Guys and Dolls* shared billing with an animal act.

But it wasn't enough. When the Nielsen ratings for the 1950–51 season were tallied, *Toast of the Town* was soundly bested by *Comedy Hour*. In its first season, *Comedy Hour* grabbed the number five ranking—impressive given that television now had a full schedule of competently produced programs. And since *Comedy Hour* ran directly opposite *Toast of the Town*, its high ranking necessarily meant fewer viewers were watching Sullivan. Having produced the number two–ranked show the previous season, Ed now tumbled to the fourteenth spot.

In a field of one hundred ten prime-time programs, *Toast of the Town* still sat near the top, but hadn't won the majority of Sunday evenings. Sullivan's ratings for the year were higher because he offered new shows throughout the summer, unlike *Comedy Hour*. But if he was to stay truly competitive, he needed a fresh strategy—some novel way to capture viewers.

While he was rolling out this new strategy, which debuted in the 1951–52 season, he encountered an old rival. The *Comedy Hour* wasn't the only thing he battled in 1951.

By the early 1950s, Ed began to be, in a sense, two men. On one hand, his immersion in the new world of television meant an entirely new audience knew him only from the small screen. The world he chronicled in his Broadway column existed in a universe far from that of most middle-class viewers. To them he was the avuncular host, the stiff-but-sincere purveyor of opera, comedy, and jugglers. He fully embraced this new world as he began to receive the national notoriety he had long craved. He stopped producing his Loew's State vaudeville shows. His daily column for the *Daily News* lost its spark as he handed off more of its legwork to his assistant Carmine Santullo. On the other hand, the old Ed still very much existed, the two-fisted gossip columnist, the acerbic New Yorker who was always at least a little dissatisfied. He hadn't given up membership in the local Broadway tribe. And, as an episode from the early 1950s revealed, he remained fueled by jealousies that had driven him since the 1930s.

In October 1951, famed stage performer Josephine Baker returned to the United States for a series of appearances. A star of black vaudeville as a child, and of Paris' La Revue Negre at age nineteen, Baker's buoyant charm and exotic eroticism—she once gyrated through the Charleston clad in only a girdle of bananas—made her a popular figure in France, where she took citizenship. Picasso, for whom she posed, described her as having a smile to end all smiles. Now age forty-four, she had become a symbol of black advancement after succeeding in integrating a whites-only nightclub in Miami, and the NAACP (National Association for the Advancement of Colored People) organized a party to celebrate her return to New York.

Baker and her entourage stopped at the Stork Club for a late-evening dinner, which didn't go as planned. For all its glamour, the Stork's attitude toward black patrons was decidedly backward. The service she received was, at best, slow, and by her description, contemptuous. The owner, Sherman Billingsley, refused to acknowledge her—unusual for a major star, but Billingsley's reputation as a racist was well established. Baker claimed Walter Winchell, who used the Stork as his office, "looked right through me." Baker ordered a steak, a crab salad, and a bottle of French wine; after waiting an hour she inquired about her food and was told the kitchen was out of both steak and crab salad. One of her fellow diners urged her to call the NAACP to complain. She went to the phone but the attendant claimed to be too busy to dial. Baker dialed the phone herself to report that the Stork had refused to serve her, though when she returned to her table "a pathetic little steak finally appeared," as she described it. Angry, she and her party stormed out of the Stork.

What exactly happened at the Stork was unclear; there were various conflicting accounts. Some claimed Baker had visited the club with intent to expose its racist door policy, and had deliberately created a scene—the Stork's service was always

slow, according to some. At any rate, in the ensuing controversy the NAACP picketed the nightspot and the mayor ordered an investigation. The Baker camp wanted
Winchell to denounce the Stork in his hugely influential radio show. But Walter, for
whom the Stork was his home away from home, and who was upset at being pulled
into the contretemps, instead broadcast a segment defending himself and his civil
rights record.

As the incident divided the city into warring factions, Winchell was forced to
choose between supporting Baker and his loyalty to the Stork. He not only chose the
Stork, he launched a broadside against Baker, printing a fifteen-year-old news item
about her offer to recruit a black army for Italian dictator Benito Mussolini. Worse,
he charged her with communist sympathies. Among the chattering classes, the conflict devolved into Winchell versus Baker, and, by extension, Winchell versus civil
rights. This was the irony of the conflict: the powerful columnist had a strong civil
rights record and often aided black causes.

In Ed's view, Winchell's entanglement in the Josephine Baker melee provided a
welcome chink in the gossip's armor. After Baker went on Barry Gray's radio show to
attack Winchell, Sullivan appeared on the program the following night to blast the
columnist. Gray's show broadcast from the front table of Chandler's restaurant, and a
standing room–only audience gathered to watch Sullivan denounce Winchell. "I thought
a shameful thing had been done," Ed said, claiming that Winchell had attempted to deny
Baker's fundamental right to protest. "I despise Walter Winchell because he symbolizes
to me evil and treacherous things in the American setup." Sullivan said that Winchell
had launched a journalistic attack against Baker "recklessly and with great abandon . . .
confident in his power and buoyed by the fact that no New York newspaper except one
had taken this thing up, because they didn't want to give him publicity on it. . . . I say
he's a megalomaniac and a dangerous one."

Not satisfied, Ed appeared on Gray's program a second time. "I don't think that
Winchell is a great American anymore," he declaimed. "I think that something has
happened to him. I don't know what it is, but I think the effects of it are evil." Some
of this was far afield from the issue of racism, particularly the charge of megaloma-
nia. But Ed, while indulging his own longstanding grudge, gained extra currency by
voicing a commonly held opinion of Winchell: his enormous power had no counterbalance. Most performers were afraid of him, as were an array of public figures in
several walks of life. These otherwise influential people felt they had no recourse
against the off-the-cuff judgments he rendered in his column and on his radio show.
Ed knew he tapped a wellspring of tacit approval as he attacked Walter.

After Sullivan's attack, Broadwayites waited for Winchell's counterpunch. One
Winchell associate urged the columnist to sue Sullivan for libel. But when a reporter
for *Time* asked Winchell for comment, the normally vindictive columnist feigned in-
difference. "I didn't hear what Sullivan said," he claimed. "I do not want to engage
in bouts with small-timers. I would rather hear what the president has to say about
me." In his column he remained curiously mum, going only so far as to print a poem
by sportswriter Grantland Rice that ended, "They rarely ever knock a guy / Who
doesn't matter much." This was a pulled punch by Winchell's standards.

The rumored reason for Winchell's quiet was that Sullivan held a weapon in reserve against his rival. According to Marlo Lewis, it was a document "so devastating that Winchell knew he could never tangle with Sullivan publicly and survive."

Ed never confided to Marlo what the item was, saying only, "I've got it—and Walter knows I've got it. He also knows that I'll never use it unless he tries to push me too far. That's all I'm ever gonna say about it." Winchell biographer Neal Gabler speculated that the document was a copy of Winchell's divorce decree, the date of which may have shown that Winchell's daughter was illegitimate.

Not long after the Baker affair, whenever Ed and Sylvia went to the Stork Club, Ed requested a table close to Table 50, Winchell's roost. Ed would sit at a nearby table and glare at his foe. According to Broadway lore, one evening he and Sylvia were at the club with a young television production assistant who once worked for Winchell (and who referred to the experience as "the most miserable year of my life"). When Winchell got up to go to the bathroom, Sullivan, as if waiting for the moment, stood up, said, "Excuse me," and walked down the hall after Walter. Sylvia panicked, knowing Ed's volatile temper and knowing, too, that Winchell carried a pistol (he accompanied police on late evening calls). She hurriedly told the production assistant to follow them. The young man walked to the restroom and opened the outer door discreetly. He stood in the anteroom for a moment, listening, then slowly opened the second door. He claimed that he saw Sullivan holding Winchell's head in a toilet bowl and flushing, continuously, with maniacal glee. Winchell, though it was hard to tell above the flushing roar, seemed to be sobbing. The young assistant watched for a moment, then quietly slipped out of the bathroom.

Whether the incident actually took place is unclear. The production assistant's name is unknown and the story's source is unverifiable, although by Sullivan's own account he often took a table at the Stork that allowed him to glare at Winchell. But if the anecdote is invented, or exaggerated, it does contain a kernel of truth, in that it describes the changed relationship of the two men. After years of walking in Walter's shadow, Ed, buoyed by a taste of success on television, was clearly ascendant. Walter, after two decades of supremacy, was faltering, and by the end of the decade would be sinking toward oblivion. Whether this emboldened Ed to the point where he stuck Walter's head in a toilet is certainly possible—his jealous rage had long simmered—yet the story may be merely apocryphal.

The same combative spirit that fueled Ed's feud with Walter Winchell also drove his approach to the 1951–52 television season. Like Winchell, *Comedy Hour* had outshone Sullivan, using its gargantuan budget to top his ratings. The question now was: how to compete against a far larger opponent?

In his first year against the NBC show, Sullivan realized that beating it on its own turf, the variety format, was unlikely. With Colgate-Palmolive's deep-pocketed sponsorship, now grown to $3 million per year, *Comedy Hour* could always field a more compelling variety lineup than *Toast of the Town*. So in the 1951–52 season Ed took a new tack, in certain weeks dispensing with variety altogether. In its place he produced specials—hour-long biographies of entertainment icons, the first of their kind on television. He wrote the scripts for the programs, interviewing their stars and narrating the story line in each episode.

He kicked off the season with a two-part special dedicated to Broadway giant Oscar Hammerstein. Along with Hammerstein himself, Ed presented an ensemble of singers and dancers performing highlights from his work, such as *Show Boat, Ok-*

lahoma, *South Pacific*, and *Carousel*. At the second evening's dramatic high point, Hammerstein stood on a darkened stage in a pin spotlight, reciting the melancholy lyrics to his "The Last Time I Saw Paris," accompanied by a small ensemble and Richard Rodgers on the piano.

Two weeks later, Ed presented a tribute to Helen Hayes. An acclaimed film star, the fifty-year-old actress was best known as the first lady of the American stage (when she died in 1993, the lights on Broadway were dimmed for one minute at eight P.M.). At the evening's conclusion, Sullivan and Hayes chatted about her life, and the actress played the moment for high drama. She told the audience that when the final curtain came down on her, she hoped someone would shout—and here she quoted from *Victoria Regina*, one of her great stage triumphs—"Go it, old girl! You've done it well!" The studio audience members, many in tears knowing that Hayes had lost her daughter to polio not long before, thundered their approval.

The Hammerstein and Hayes specials boosted Sullivan's Nielsen ratings, prompting him to keep interspersing specials with his usual variety format. Later that fall, he presented "The Robert Sherwood Story," producing scenes from the Pulitzer Prize–winning playwright's works; the stage crew built a life-size replica of a train's rear platform as a set for Robert Massey's portrayal of Lincoln in *Abe Lincoln in Illinois*. In early February, "The Bea Lillie Story" celebrated the Broadway comedienne, and later that month Sullivan's version of *George White's Scandals* recreated the lavish Broadway revue. Ed stretched "The Cole Porter Story" over two Sundays, presenting Porter himself and a cast of vocalists (including Roberta Peters, the young Metropolitan Opera star he had just introduced to television) to reprise the tunesmith's musicals. The 1951–52 season ended with a ratings blowout: "The Richard Rodgers Story." Presented on two consecutive Sundays, it featured the composer himself in performances of his hits ranging from the 1920s-era *Garrick Gaieties* to the current *The King and I*, still in its debut run on Broadway.

Still, it wasn't enough. *Comedy Hour* had culled its weak hosts in the previous season, so it now clicked like a well-honed entertainment machine. While Sullivan's two-night version of "The Richard Rodgers Story" topped *Comedy Hour* evenings hosted by Eddie Cantor and Bob Hope, when Cantor or Hope hosted opposite Sullivan's usual mixed bag, Ed saw his Nielsen numbers fall.

Toast of the Town's budget at this point, according to Marlo Lewis, was $25,000 per show; Ed told *The New York Times* it was $15,000. Either Marlo was exaggerating or, more likely, Ed downplayed the number to help him negotiate with talent agents. But even the higher figure was dwarfed by the *Comedy Hour*'s weekly budget, which had levitated to the $100,000 range. The show was now the costliest on television. Due to the budget disparity, there were nights when Ed showcased mid level performers against true heavyweights. When he headlined Joe E. Lewis, a nightclub comic in late career, against audience magnet Bob Hope, his Nielsen rating was far outpaced by *Comedy Hour*'s, 49.3 to 24.3. When Ed presented film star Audrey Hepburn and vaudevillian Pearl Bailey against a Jerry Lewis–Dean Martin *Comedy Hour*, he lost the Nielsen battle by a still more lopsided margin: 56.6 to 24.5. Attempting a creative twist—perhaps inspired by the recent success of *I Love Lucy*—Ed booked Errol Flynn and Paulette Goddard to play a weekly comic sketch about a constantly nattering couple. But the aging screen idols couldn't rise above lifeless scripts, and the effort did little for ratings.

Yet while Sullivan wasn't winning the Nielsen contest, he was surely winning some grudging respect. That he could even stay in the ring with the slugger known as *Comedy Hour*—and sometimes win a round—earned him kudos throughout the TV industry. NBC head Pat Weaver, impressed by Sullivan's specials, decided to start developing some of his own. Television critic Jack Gould lauded Ed for injecting new life into television with his specials, and commended him for the creativity behind the Flynn–Goddard experiment, though he noted it failed dreadfully. (And Gould, for the first time, referred to Sullivan as a producer rather than a host, judging him accordingly.) Ed was himself feeling bullish; *Toast of the Town*'s ratings made it a hit even as it trailed *Comedy Hour*. That winter he told *The New York Times*, "I am the best damned showman on television. . . . I really believe, immodestly, that I am a better showman and have better taste than most and have a better 'feel' as to what the public wants because of my newspaper experience. And I know quicker than anybody else on Sunday nights whether we have done a good performance or not." Ed later tried to backpedal from the "best damn showman" boast, claiming it was taken out of context. But whatever the context, over the years it became clear the quote accurately reflected how he felt about his abilities.

Sullivan went into the 1952–53 season with ever-grander specials planned. For his proposed "The Sam Goldwyn Story" he met with the legendary film mogul and broke new ground. The studios were unequivocally opposed to television; scads of movie theaters across the country had shuttered since television invaded the living room. Consequently, many studios refused to let their movies be shown on the small screen—that would be helping the enemy. Ed, however, talked Goldwyn into the idea of using television to promote his films; TV could be an advertising vehicle for movies, he reasoned, not a competitive force. Goldwyn, impressed, gave him access to a large library of film clips. Not coincidentally, Ed chose clips that featured Bob Hope and Eddie Cantor, provoking protest from NBC—the network was unhappy to see Sullivan present *Comedy Hour*'s hosts on his show. But Ed paid no heed to the complaints. Sullivan as usual wrote and narrated the continuity to "The Sam Goldwyn Story," from the early talkies through Laurence Olivier and Gary Cooper, bringing Goldwyn and his wife Frances onstage for a final bow.

After the success of the Goldwyn tribute, Ed frequently negotiated with the studios to show movie previews on *Toast of the Town*. Some of them Sullivan paid for; others were free promotion. The alliance created an unusual thawing of relations between Hollywood and television, as Ed helped turned television from a threat into a publicity conduit. Not that everything went well with Hollywood. Following the Goldwyn tribute, Ed planned a show dedicated to Cecil B. DeMille. But the legendary filmmaker, ever the egoist, insisted on narrating his tribute show himself, which the actors union wouldn't allow—presumably he wasn't a member—so the program never happened.

The most successful of all Ed's specials was "The Walt Disney Story," for which he flew to California in February and spent five days directing filming in the Disney studio. Ed was so excited about the show that he telegrammed President Eisenhower to ask him to record a testimonial for Disney, which the president declined. During the broadcast, Sullivan talked with the film producer about his career, interspersing their conversation with behind-the-scenes footage of the animator's magic and clips from films like 1950's *Cinderella* and 1937's *Snow White and the*

Seven Dwarfs. Ed talked about traveling through Europe and being amazed at the popularity of Disney films there. "After the war, people were hungry for something to believe in, and they could always find this in a Disney picture," he told the audience. Garnering a whopping 63.4 Trendex rating, the evening was the season's second-highest-rated Sullivan show, topping any of the year's *Comedy Hour* shows, except those hosted by Jerry Lewis and Dean Martin (almost nothing topped Jerry and Dino). Disney, happy with the resulting publicity, hand drew a caricature of Sullivan as a thank-you gift.

The ratings spike produced by the Disney story and Sullivan's other lavishly produced tribute hours was only part of their value. In addition to being television shows they were news events, as the nascent medium expanded before viewers' eyes. Newspapers gave Sullivan reams of free publicity for his tribute programs. And no special generated as many headlines as "The Josh Logan Story."

For Ed's tribute to the famed Broadway director and writer, he took a risk with controversial material. Much of the evening consisted of live performances from plays like *Mr. Roberts* and *Picnic,* with Logan directing an ensemble that included Jimmy Stewart and a still-little-known Paul Newman. During rehearsal, Logan had made a special request: would Ed allow him to talk about his battle with mental illness, how he had suffered from depression and been hospitalized, and how such an ordeal could be conquered? His goal was to break the taboos surrounding mental illness.

Ed discouraged him, fearing the reaction to talk of mental illness, and Logan conceded. But during the broadcast, Sullivan came across Logan backstage looking despondent. The showman asked the director if he still wanted to tell his personal story, and Logan said yes. "Ed was terrified of CBS's reaction," Logan recalled. "But he took a chance with me." Ed abruptly changed the show's running order to allow time for Logan's speech. The director went onstage and described, in very personal terms, the history of his mental breakdown, hospitalization, and subsequent recovery. He urged people to view mental illness as a disease that could be treated, not a moral failing. When he stopped speaking, the studio sat in stunned silence—and then broke into a torrent of applause. CBS received a small mountain of appreciative letters.

Ed himself received a letter from a judge on the Pennsylvania Supreme Court, Justice Michael A. Musmanno (well-known for presiding over the Nuremberg trials), who wrote to say that seeing Josh Logan speak on *Toast of the Town* influenced one of his recent court decisions. A local woman had been briefly confined in a mental institution, after which she experienced a full recovery. But during her stay her husband took permanent custody of their children, which she contested in court. Justice Musmanno ruled, in part based on Logan's story of overcoming mental illness, that confinement in a mental institution does not nullify a parent's rights if that individual can medically certify his or her recovery.

At a later date, Ed recounted the Logan story while speaking to a civic organization in Oklahoma (he accepted countless such invitations). After his talk, the director of a mental health program told Sullivan that the day after Logan's appearance, his state budget director increased his appropriation due to the star's emotional appeal. Such was the power of this new medium. In the late 1960s, Ed pointed to the Logan episode as one of the show's peak moments.

Comedy Hour still led *Toast of the Town* in overall ratings during the 1952–53 season, yet the balance was starting to shift. While in the fall of 1951 the average Trendex rating for *Comedy Hour* topped that of *Toast of the Town* by a comfortable margin, 32.6 to 21.9, by the spring of 1953 that margin had narrowed to 31.3 to 24.7. *Comedy Hour*'s slip was small, yet that slippage revealed a larger trend. Eddie Cantor suffered a heart attack after a 1952 *Comedy Hour* performance, and the following season the sixty-one-year-old declared he would quit. The program's younger hosts were feeling the strain as well. By the 1953–54 season, *Comedy Hour*'s annual budget ballooned to $6 million. In return, Colgate-Palmolive wanted only the biggest names to host. But the top tier, notably Jerry Lewis and Dean Martin—now making $1,000,000 a year from the program—were hard-pressed to keep their routines fresh during months of broadcasts. They weren't alone. A man in Long Island, New York, after yet another Abbot and Costello *Comedy Hour* without new material, shot his television set. (The resultant publicity earned him an appearance on the game show *Strike It Rich*, where he won a new set.) What had once glittered now began to appear lackluster.

The trend was clear as the 1953–54 season concluded. *Comedy Hour*'s elephantine budget no longer guaranteed it Sunday night dominance. Under pressure from Sullivan, and suffering from creative exhaustion, the show's ratings were headed inexorably downward. Although *Comedy Hour* held the lead over *Toast of the Town* in the fall of 1953, by the spring of 1954 the two shows' ratings were running a dead heat. And, as always, *Toast of the Town*'s Nielsens pulled far ahead in the summer, as Ed continued to produce fresh shows while *Comedy Hour* ran reruns. If nothing else, he would outwork his NBC competitor.

One Sullivan maneuver that season was especially revealing of how Ed chipped away at *Comedy Hour*'s ratings. In the fall of 1953, CBS show host Arthur Godfrey was one of the country's most beloved broadcasters. Some forty million people listened to his morning radio program, and two of television's top ten shows were his: *Arthur Godfrey's Talent Scouts* was the third-ranked show, behind only *I Love Lucy* and *Dragnet*; and *Arthur Godfrey and Friends* was the seventh-ranked show, right behind *The Bob Hope Show* and the *The Buick–Berle Show*. With his butterscotch voice and easygoing charm, Godfrey was responsible for twelve percent of CBS's annual revenues. He delivered his own ads in a folksy, intimate style, refusing to stick to the copy, talking to viewers like old friends—when he chatted about Lipton Tea, listeners felt he sipped it every day.

Godfrey used an ensemble format, in which a regular troupe of clean-cut young singers interacted week after week. For the audience, he and his performers became a surrogate family. Godfrey played the genial uncle as his viewers, largely female, bonded with each of the personalities. So on October 19, 1953, when Godfrey summarily fired one of his singers *during a show*, millions of his fans were shocked, even horrified. Dismissed was Julius La Rosa, a cherub-faced ingénue whose vocal talents were modest, but who inspired fierce matronly love in fans. Right after La Rosa finished crooning a song, Godfrey informed viewers, "That was Julius' swan song with us." Afternoon newspapers blared the news in headlines across the country.

With Walt Disney in the early 1950s. Sullivan's tribute show to Disney in 1953 helped him compete with the heavily financed *The Colgate Comedy Hour*, but years later the two men would vie for ratings in the same Sunday night time slot. (Globe Photos)

As the news coverage snowballed, the reason for the firing was clouded in confusion. Godfrey claimed that La Rosa wanted to be released from his contract; rather than announce this in a press conference, he explained, the host decided to tell viewers on the air. La Rosa disputed this, and Godfrey, in a move he soon regretted, explained that the singer had "lost his humility," and so needed to be fired. La Rosa conceded that he had lost his sweet deference; at age twenty-three he was getting six thousand fan letters a week and fielding constant offers from record labels. Nevertheless, fans were dismayed to learn that Godfrey had fired someone because he couldn't stand another star in his stable—was there a controlling egoist under that vanilla charm? The day after Godfrey's remark about "humility," the word appeared in numerous national headlines, and comedians soon began using it for laughs. The incident even generated its own moniker, as commentators dubbed it the La Rosa Affair. To date, this was the biggest news story in television.

For Ed the story offered an obvious opportunity. He immediately called La Rosa and invited him to his Delmonico apartment. Heartbroken over being fired, the singer came with his lawyer and his priest in tow. Ed offered him $5,000 per show for a series of guest appearances on *Toast of the Town*, which La Rosa gladly accepted. Marlo professed amazement at the amount Ed offered the young singer. "He'll be worth it," Ed said, "Just wait and see."

He was right. La Rosa's appearance on October 25, within the week of his firing on Godfrey, was Sullivan's highest-rated show since his 1948 debut, earning a jaw-dropping 76.6 Trendex rating. Its viewership dwarfed that evening's *Comedy Hour* starring Lauren Bacall, and even topped the season's highest rated Jerry Lewis–Dean Martin show. Ed kept exploiting the La Rosa controversy over the next several weeks. The November 29 episode of *Toast of the Town* would undoubtedly have run a distant second to *Comedy Hour* without the publicity sparked by Ed's booking of La Rosa. That night *Comedy Hour* was hosted by Eddie Cantor, with guest stars Frank Sinatra and Eddie Fisher; Fisher had just been offered the unheard of sum of $1 million by Coca Cola to be their national spokesman. Ed's lineup that evening reflected his smaller budget: La Rosa; Dr. Ralph Bunche, a black Harvard professor and civil rights activist, winner of the 1950 Nobel Prize; Sophie Tucker, a popular vaudevillian now in late career; Sam Levenson, a young comic still on his way up; Joe E. Lewis, an aging cabaret comic; the All-American college football players; and The Harmonicats, a mouth-organ trio whose 1947 hit "Peg O' My Heart" sold 1.4 million copies. It was a solid lineup, but it paled by comparison to the Sinatra–Fisher–Cantor triumvirate. Yet that night's *Toast of the Town* earned a 54.8 Trendex rating, clearly besting *Comedy Hour*'s 40.1.

Ed's adept use of the controversy displayed once again how he used his newsman's nose for current events to turn a small budget into a ratings winner. He kept it up by booking a raft of former Godfrey regulars, like Pat Boone and the McGuire Sisters—performers who hadn't reached their later popularity but whose status as Godfrey alumni boosted ratings. CBS was uneasy about Sullivan's continued one-upping of Godfrey; it was a skirmish between two of the network's top-rated shows. But Ed rebuffed suggestions by CBS executive Hubbell Robinson that he stop. With the ratings it produced he saw it as a natural strategy. "There's nothing personal in it," Ed explained. "If Arthur were fired, I'd hire him."

One other incident with Godfrey revealed a side of Ed rarely glimpsed by the public. When Godfrey was hospitalized after hip surgery, Sullivan guest hosted his show. The camera captured a man never before seen on television. He danced and sang a tune with the Little Godfreys, accompanied two singers on the zither, warbled a duet with Frank Parker, then topped it off with a soft-shoe routine. It was all light-hearted fun. A reviewer from *Variety* was aghast: "Why Sullivan can come in strange surroundings and enjoy himself and yet appear so uncomfortable on his very own show is something of an unknown. It's to be hoped that some of the gold dust carries over from that Wednesday night to Sundays."

It didn't. On his own show the effort was too important, too much of a high-stakes struggle, for him to enjoy himself. The self he displayed on the Godfrey show was closer to his Broadway columnist persona, capable of clowning around, comfortable with spontaneity and humor. But that side of Sullivan was stowed backstage when he hosted *Toast of the Town*. He attempted to explain this in the preface to a 1951 book called *The TV Jeebies*, a slender volume that described the new medium's countless pratfalls:

> "People often ask me why I don't smile more when I face the cameras on '*Toast of the Town*.' In television, unlike any other visual medium, a performer gets only one chance. There are no retakes. He either does it right the first time or the sponsor sees to it that the performer forever holds his peace. . . . There are literally thousands of tubes, resistors,

condensers, and other strange devices in the maze of technical equipment that must not fail. Even the performers can bring on a bad attack of the TV Jeebies with their strapless gown slipping their moorings, ad-libbed jokes that are a bit too salty for television, acts that run over their allotted time and a hundred others things that just couldn't happen but sometimes do. . . . In television you get just one chance."

As *Comedy Hour*'s ratings continued to slide, Ed worked behind the scenes to rectify a problem that had long bedeviled *Toast of the Town*. Between 1948 and 1950, network executives learned from the undisputed ratings of Sullivan's show and Berle's *Texaco Theater* that the variety format was a quick path to profitability. In response, a slew of variety hours were launched. Many, like the Dumont network's *Cavalcade of Stars*, had short lives. Yet by the early 1950s a passel of programs were hungry for talent: *Comedy Hour, Toast of the Town, Texaco Theater, The Bob Hope Show, The Jackie Gleason Show, All-Star Revue*—each had variety schedules to fill. In 1948, *Variety* predicted that television would run out of performers to present, and that forecast proved prescient. By the early 1950s the competition for talent pushed prices exponentially higher. Where once a Sullivan column mention and $100 was enough to attract guests, those days were now long gone. The relative scarcity of entertainers turned TV talent agents into major players.

The power that talent agents had over Sullivan enraged him. He had a job to do, and in his view they were preventing him from doing it to the best of his ability. As he saw it, *Toast of the Town* gave early television exposure to many performers, and their agents owed him loyalty. The agents felt differently. To Sullivan's consternation, they employed a well-choreographed set of maneuvers to push up prices, playing one show off another. If Ed called to request a current hot act, the agent explained that the performer was all booked up—until the price went higher. Or agents refused to even respond to his call until Ed made it clear his bid would go higher. Paul Winchell, a ventriloquist whom Ed booked for a small fee in the show's earliest days, now expected $2,500—and demanded multiple bookings to appear for that amount. Another popular ventriloquist, Senor Wences, expected a similar fee. A rising young comic named Dick Shawn succeeded in negotiating a guest shot for $10,000 on the condition he get four more appearances at the same price. But Shawn didn't have enough material and it hurt Sullivan's ratings.

Most agents first attempted to place their acts with *Comedy Hour* because of its august pay scale. Ed, with his singular eye for talent, frequently spotted a rising nightclub act or a singer whose music was inching up the charts; after inquiring about their availability, he often got stonewalled, only to see the act sold to *Comedy Hour*. For this reason, Ed had a fondness for smaller, independent agents, but these representatives didn't handle the most sought-after performers.

As the competition for talent tightened in the early 1950s, Ed constantly railed to Marlo about what he saw as the lowest form of life, the talent agent. He had a special animosity for MCA agent Johnny Greenhut. "That fat-faced bum with the soft-boiled eyes," he said to Marlo. "I just made an offer . . . and Greenhut tells me he has to check to see if David Begelman or Freddie Fields sold them to the *Comedy Hour*. . . . They've even got the little punk agents pulling the same stunt. Everybody's

'checking' to see if an act is available. . . . You know where that bunch of flesh ped-
dlers would have gone over big? Down at the levee at the auction block, raffling off
slaves to the highest bidder!" And then there was George Wood at William Morris.
"It's the old story—George is going with a young broad and he wants to impress her,"
Ed explained to Marlo. "He thinks she'd look great in a shiny new Mercury convertible. He didn't come out and ask for one, but I got the message. . . . I'll call the factory and order one for him. We'll have to pay for it out of our talent budget."

The chief problem was that *Toast of the Town* had no agency dedicated to it. The
William Morris Agency had a tight relationship with *Texaco Theater*, and MCA was
joined at the hip with *Comedy Hour*. But *Toast of the Town*'s smaller budget meant
it was left to fend for itself, working with both agencies and others as a leftover outlet for acts who couldn't be sold to the highest bidder. Ed knew he had to change
this to continue to be competitive. He began cultivating a relationship with Sonny
Werblin, president of MCA's New York office, considered the king of talent agents
and a fearsome dealmaker. The two entered into negotiations, and, after some hag-
gling, came to an agreement. In effect, Sullivan hired Werblin as his own personal
agent, his representative in charge of negotiations with CBS.

As the five-year contract Ed had signed in 1950 approached its expiration date,
Werblin was in place to be Sullivan's advocate with the network. At one level,
Werblin's representation of Ed could have been seen as a conflict of interest. It po-
sitioned MCA as the lead talent representative for two direct competitors, *Comedy
Hour* and *Toast of the Town*. But apparently Werblin, seeing *Comedy Hour*'s ratings
erosion in the 1953–54 season, understood it was time to shift his alliance. Or perhaps he simply saw the value of riding two horses.

Given his reputation as an über-agent, his representation of Sullivan would almost certainly result in a big raise for Ed, as well as a larger talent budget for *Toast
of the Town*. Marlo, however, pointing out that Werblin would take a hefty cut of Ed's
salary for representing him, urged Ed to go directly to CBS head Bill Paley. With no
agent as a middleman, you'll make more money, Marlo told Ed.

But Ed saw a much larger potential in working with Werblin. With the MCA executive as his advocate, he could expect to get choice access to the MCA talent pool.
In essence, the deal would provide Ed with the raw material to produce the best program he was capable of. Short-term, it might mean a smaller salary increase, but
with *Comedy Hour* fading, and Werblin lending MCA's muscle, Sullivan saw a
chance to take his star to an entirely new level.

———

In the early 1950s, a young New York comic named Will Jordan started including a
Sullivan impression in his nightclub act, invariably breaking up the room with his
hunched shoulders, his I've-just-sucked-a-lemon facial contortions, and his version
of Ed's signature arms-crossed gesture.

The audience response landed him gigs on local television shows, notably that of
Steve Allen, an offbeat wit who later hosted a show opposite Sullivan's. Allen took
great delight in Jordan's skewering of the stone-faced host, often inviting the comic
to perform it. Jordan, always looking for a bigger venue, played up his television
success to longtime Sullivan friend Joe Moore, and at Moore's suggestion Ed tuned
in to one of Jordan's local television appearances.

The showman liked what he saw. Despite his vituperative letters to critics who roasted him for his stiffness, he was eager to find some way to counteract the perception of his stilted stage persona. Booking this impressionist who so mercilessly lampooned him would, Ed hoped, deflate reviewers' barbs. He would negate the critics by agreeing with them—you bet, I *am* stiff, and let's all have a good laugh at it.

For Jordan's first appearance in March 1953, Sullivan booked him opposite a Jerry Lewis–Dean Martin *Comedy Hour*, hoping the chatter about a Sullivan impressionist on his own show would draw viewers. But the comic didn't go over too well. "I did Sullivan as he really was—and it bombed," Jordan recalled. Overawed by his first appearance on national TV, "I was afraid to do more." The tepid audience response left Ed unimpressed.

Jordan kept including his Sullivan shtick in his nightclub act, continually riffing on the showman's persona. Over months of club dates his impression grew ever farther away from the original man—and ever more entertaining. Nightclub audiences loved it, and Hy Gardner, a New York *Herald-Tribune* columnist, called Ed to tell him he should book Jordan. Ed was skeptical, but he trusted Gardner, so in June 1954 the comic played the Sullivan show again.

This time Jordan let loose, playing a wildly exaggerated character that took Sullivan's persona to the extreme. "I rolled my eyes up and showed the whites of my eyes, stuck my tongue under my upper lip, and made a monster face," he recalled. As he moved his shoulders with spastic stiffness, he satirized the host's verbal style: "Tonight on our rilly big show we have 702 Polish dentists who will be out here in a few moments doing their marvelous extractions. . . ." The audience roared, and as they laughed the camera periodically cut to Ed, chuckling along—see, the camera shot said, he's a regular guy.

Ironically, while the audience easily recognized Sullivan in Jordan's imitation, the comic himself knew that almost all the impression's details were invented—the knuckle cracks, shoulder shakes, eye rolls, full-body spins; none of these were actual Sullivan mannerisms. "This is the only time I know of where so much of the character is not the real person," he said. Jordan's hyperstretched version of the showman became an audience favorite; Sullivan booked him twelve more times. Over the years, Jordan became typecast as the comic who imitated Ed Sullivan. The impressionist would play him through six decades, including in 1978's *The Buddy Holly Story*, 1991's *The Doors*, and 2003's *Down with Love*.

Most lasting of Jordan's inventions was the phrase "really big show," or, as he played it, "rilly big shew." Not only had Ed himself never said that prior to Jordan, when Ed tried to mimic Jordan's imitation of himself, he goofed the line, voicing it as "truly big show." Only later, after numerous appearances by Jordan and other Sullivan impressionists—all of whom used "really big show"—did the phrase become the showman's own stock setup, the idiom most identified with his onstage persona.

When Ed used the phrase "really big show," he was, in fact, imitating his imitators. It was a kind of comfort for him. Instead of being alone in his natural, awkward onstage self, the parade of Sullivan impressionists he booked—Jack Carter, John Byner, Frank Gorshin, Jackie Mason, Rich Little—gave him a role to play. By turning him into an endearing set of idiosyncrasies, they enabled him to be the stock character known as Ed Sullivan. He could take refuge in playing this one-dimensional caricature, however limited a resemblance this sketch bore to the man himself. Certainly it included no sign of the glad-handing Broadway gossip, or the shrewd producer who aligned with power player Sonny Werblin, or the volcano who stormed the halls of CBS. But no matter. The audience understood and liked this cartoon figure. In time, the caricature became the public image of Ed Sullivan, which he was perfectly happy with. He often tossed off a "really big show," and he kept his trademark arms-crossed gesture long after he learned to avoid other tics.

He took immense pleasure in the fact that these comedians went on other programs and imitated him. It delighted his competitive spirit, knowing that a troupe of impressionists was out there reminding audiences of him and his show. Comics learned that having a good Sullivan impression was a quick way to Ed's heart, and stand-ups across the country began practicing "rilly big shew" to help them land a booking.

Most compellingly for Ed, these impressionists appealed to his long-held hunger for renown. Being mimicked in front of a national audience meant the entire country knew who he was, and presumably, if the audience was laughing, felt some fondness for him. Bogart was imitated, Cagney was imitated, Cary Grant and Jimmy Stewart were imitated. For Ed to be mimicked in comics' routines in 1953 meant he had been inducted into the glorious crowd he had always aspired to join. Will Jordan's first tentative shoulder hunch was, provisionally, the start of Sullivan's iconic status. This was fame. This, as much as anything, was what he had always wanted.

CHAPTER ELEVEN

Stardom

VERY SUNDAY AT THE MAXINE ELLIOT THEATER a furious burst of activity began sometime around 7:00 A.M. With that evening's broadcast looming, Sullivan staffers hustled with intense focus. Handling myriad tasks was a team of young secretaries who worked all day long on Saturday and Sunday. One, having met with that evening's singers to get their exact lyrics—the album version couldn't be trusted—transcribed all the words. She gave the lyrics to director Johnny Wray, who planned camera angles to accent the singer's words; with just three cameras his choices were limited, yet Wray conceived of new shots for each verse. Another secretary, who maintained the show's master script, typed and distributed copies to the production staff; this was revised and redistributed constantly. Throughout the morning, Marlo Lewis worked with set designer Grover Cole to plan the logistics of moving sets on- and offstage quickly; everything had to be assembled during commercial breaks.

When Ed arrived in the early afternoon, carrying that evening's suit over his shoulder, all action began revolving around him. Stowing his suit in his dressing room, he picked up a pencil and an unlined notepad and started preparing for the 4:00 P.M. rehearsal. On his notepad were instructions about virtually every aspect of the show. Some of the notes were for Marlo or the director, but most were for that evening's performers. Comedians new to the show were required to audition in his Delmonico apartment, so his notepad contained edits for their routines. He wrote suggestions for animal or acrobatic acts and ideas for singers, and he frequently issued orders to cover a female guest's cleavage—Ed forbade cleavage, not wanting to offer prurient fare to a family audience. (After viewers wrote to complain, he told the staff to keep yards of tulle for inventive cover-ups.) Additionally, Sullivan used his notepad to write his brief introductions, rewriting them four or five times, then dictating them to a secretary who copied them to the master script.

The heightened energy that the crew buzzed with on Sunday was a kind of happiness, as many recalled. Creating the show carried a very real excitement. Although they worked at least a twelve-hour day there was no complaint—most felt honored to be there. The staffers were always nicely dressed; Ed expected it. None of them were seen on camera, yet in his view the television studio was no place for casual dress.

Ed himself, depending on his mood, might be intense and focused, or moody and sour, or—if the ratings were trending upward—lighthearted enough to indulge a mischievous sense of humor. During one rehearsal he was headed out for a short break and asked a secretary if she wanted anything. Tongue-in-cheek, she requested a scotch and water; Ed brought her back a small container full of scotch.

As Sullivan continued to call out instructions and write notes on his pad, the master script was amended. If he made last-minute changes, as he often did, there wouldn't be enough time to retype it before broadcast. The secretary then resorted to putting small pieces of tape with Ed's comments over the original master, hurriedly copying it on a ditto machine, then rushing around the theater to redistribute it. She sometimes found herself at the ditto machine ten minutes before broadcast.

On certain evenings, Ed even made changes *during* the show. If his instinct told him the program was dragging, he suddenly reshuffled the running order during a commercial break, moving up a musician or a comic to provide extra spark. This prompted panic backstage, as stagehands scrambled to move sets or reposition animal acts, and production assistants told performers their timing needed to be adjusted. Even if Sullivan didn't scramble the running order in mid broadcast, timing shifts during the hour often meant performers were told to shorten or lengthen their routine just minutes before going on live.

This would remain true throughout the life of the show; as many programs shifted to taped broadcasts in the 1960s, the Sullivan show stayed live. Comedian George Carlin, a regular in the 1960s, recalled that playing the show was like performing without a net. "The thing I remember most about *The Ed Sullivan Show* was the great fear I had going over there from the hotel with my garment bag . . . walking over there was ritualistic on a Sunday afternoon before dress rehearsal. I would stop at a little deli store and buy a couple of cans of Rheingold beer. I'd take them up to my dressing room and they took the edge off." The jitters came from two factors: "First of all, it was live, which produces a certain higher nervousness quotient than something that can be done over." Additionally, "The Sullivan staff was notorious for coming to you during the air show and saying, 'the monkey skated too much, and you have to give us back thirty seconds or a minute.' The problem for me was, I didn't do things that were chopped up into segments, I did things that had a thread, so that made it all the more panicky."

At 4 P.M. Ed ran a full dress rehearsal. That evening's show played from beginning to end without stop, including the showman's introductions. Even the commercials were played, with a staffer timing all the segments with a stopwatch. Sullivan brought in a live audience and their applause, in theory, made the timing more accurate. Before rehearsal began, Ed walked onstage and bantered with the crowd, asking people where they were from, cracking a few jokes to warm them up. As the dress rehearsal ran, he stood just offstage, watching on a television monitor, making more notes. Comedian Jack Carter recalled that Ed sometimes stood right onstage, which confused the audience because they also watched Sullivan. Since he was invariably deadpan during a comic's performance, getting a laugh became that much harder.

However reliable the rehearsal audience's response was, Ed read it as he had read the reactions of countless audiences at his Loew's State vaudeville shows, using his sense of the crowd to write still more notes. As the run-through ended he asked the audience for comments and many were shouted out, after which the crowd was ushered out. That evening's show was seen by a fresh audience.

Displaying his sentimental side, Ed invited Johnny Dundee to dress rehearsals. The onetime boxing champion, who had shown Ed around New York when he was a cub reporter, and who had been best man at Sullivan's wedding, was nearly destitute by the 1950s. Ed reserved seats for the boxer and his daughter Lucille, and instructed the staff to treat them as guests of honor. After the afternoon rehearsal, Ed invited Johnny, now a wizened old man who was nearly blind, up onstage. After Lucille helped him up, Ed asked, "What did you think of the show, Johnny?" In his gravelly whiskey voice, Dundee invariably said something like, "I liked it Ed, I *really* liked it." Ed prompted him for suggestions, and after Dundee gave his comments Ed opened his wallet and put cash in Johnny's hand as payment for his advice. Sullivan sent Dundee a weekly check for the remainder of the boxer's life.

After rehearsal, Ed used his notes to take the show apart and put it back together again. First, the bad news: not infrequently, he canceled a performer's appearance. Ed likely booked that entertainer because he or she was a proven crowd pleaser. Yet if he felt the performer wasn't going to delight his viewers on that particular evening, he cut them without hesitation—just hours before showtime. Marlo Lewis had the unenviable task of informing the performer's agent that their client's moment of national television exposure was being nixed.

After Ed's cuts, he reshuffled the running order to provide the balance he had envisioned when he booked the show. The front of the program might need more humor, or, if he had just cut an act, he allowed a singer a second song. Negotiations were begun with comics. If their routines contained material that Ed didn't like or understand, or he felt was too blue or too long, he directed edits. But, the comics would retort, that joke leads to the next; I can't change one joke without changing my whole routine. Back and forth Sullivan and the comic would go, hashing out the act bit by bit. Sometimes Ed gave in and sometimes he demanded changes outright, depending on several variables: his mood, the comic's level of fame—major stars got hands-off treatment—and the show's running time. Many comics complained bitterly about the showman's changes. Comedienne Phyllis Diller, a Sullivan show staple in later years, once quit in disgust after she felt her act had been decimated. "He knew nothing about comedy," Diller said, echoing an opinion voiced by several comics. (On the other hand, Diller, like many performers who were grateful for the career boost, said, "I have Ed Sullivan to thank.")

Altering animal acts presented a special challenge because the chimps, tigers, bears, and horses knew their routine by rote. Nevertheless, Ed demanded edits. On numerous Sundays, Sullivan told an animal trainer to trim his act by two minutes, only to get a response like, "How am I going to explain that to the lion?" In one rehearsal an elephant trainer, after Ed insisted he cut two tricks in the middle, replied, "If you can do it, I'll give you whole damn act," then shoved the elephant prod at the showman. "Take this too, I'm sure you'll know what to do with it."

Singers sometimes offered similar resistance. He had a last-minute showdown with opera star Maria Callas, who decided she wouldn't render her famed aria from *Tosca*—the very aria for which Ed had booked her. With Callas on the eve of a much-anticipated Metropolitan Opera performance, Sullivan sought to garner headlines by presenting her first on *Toast of the Town*. But, she announced in rehearsal, she had decided to save *Tosca* for the Met; this evening she would sing an alternative. The production crew demurred, knowing Sullivan expected *Tosca*, but the diva was firm—the answer was no. Finally Ed issued an ultimatum: either you sing *Tosca* or you're off the show. Callas argued and threatened a legal suit, and then, that evening, delivered her glorious *Tosca*. (The eighteen-minute scene from the Puccini opera proved a ratings disaster, so Ed, committed to a series of four opera performances, edited furiously. The last segment, a lengthy duet from *La Bohème*, was slashed to four minutes.)

By the end of Sunday's rehearsal, a list of acts on paper had been shaped into a show enjoyed by tens of millions of people. Sullivan's formula, he explained, was based on creating a program to appeal to a group he described as the four dominant women in his life: his mother, his older sister Helen, his wife Sylvia, and his daughter Betty. To whatever extent this was his guiding principle, certainly Ed's connection to his viewers was a big part of his success. Although he made plenty of booking mistakes, he rarely needed to guess his audience's response. He wasn't apart from them; he *was* them. If he understood and liked an act, they would; if he didn't, his audience probably wouldn't either. "He sure had his finger on the pulse of the country," recalled comedienne Carol Burnett, who first appeared on Sullivan's show in 1957.

In later years, advertising firms began using focus groups to determine mass taste. Ed would have had no need for these groups, even if they had been available. In the mid 1950s the response of a roomful of average Americans would have been all but identical to his own. Like them, he was square, and that was something to be proud of, not uncomfortable with. He was a square, however, who had lived in the entertainment business for twenty-five years, providing him with an unparalleled education. Most importantly for his current job, his decades spent hobnobbing with New York and Hollywood performers hadn't removed his small-town Port Chester roots. While his success meant he looked at life from an eleventh-floor suite overlooking Park Avenue, he still saw the world with the same eyes as his audience.

Shortly before showtime he again walked onstage to warm up the crowd. Having taken control of every aspect of the program, he would now browbeat even the audience into playing their role properly. One evening in the mid 1950s, a reporter from *Time* magazine recorded the scene:

"Again he leans into a gale of applause. 'How are you all?' he asks. 'How many are here from out of town?' He recoils from the forest of hands, crying, 'Wow! New Yorkers can't even get seats!' He waggles a finger at his people onstage. 'Heads will roll.' The audience loves it. Ed continues: 'Everybody in this audience is duty bound to be happy. So look happy!' They do. 'In thirty seconds Art Hannes is going to introduce me and he will be absolutely astonished that I showed up. They didn't think Old Smiley would do it!'"

In November 1954, Sonny Werblin paid a visit to Bill Paley. It wasn't often that the MCA talent agency's New York president visited the head of CBS. Werblin relegated most of the in-the-trenches negotiations work for individual performers to his underlings. He handled only the agency's biggest clients. But the MCA president knew a lucrative deal when he saw one. Sullivan's five-year contract would expire the following year, and it was time to lay new ink to paper.

A recent development gave Sullivan greater leverage. Raising eyebrows across the industry, NBC had made him an offer, attempting to lure him away from CBS. Just a few years earlier this would have been unthinkable, but something unthinkable had happened. While *Comedy Hour* had topped Sullivan in the overall yearly ratings for the last four seasons, his show won enough weeks to stay near the top, and had steadily gained on its NBC rival. Now in the fall of 1954, Sullivan was besting it week after week—at a fraction of the cost. With his updated vaudeville format and an annual budget of about $2 million, he was embarrassing a show hosted by the biggest names in show business pulling down in excess of $6 million in talent fees. *Comedy Hour*'s sponsor, Colgate-Palmolive, was growing disenchanted. In response, NBC attempted a novel solution: couldn't we just hire Sullivan?

Ed had slain the *Comedy Hour* dragon at just the right time. His contract would expire as his show was overtaking the most expensive program in the industry. Werblin knew it, Sullivan knew it, and Paley was forced to acknowledge it. So Ed, with the help of his lawyer Arnold Grant, and with negotiations led by Werblin, struck a deal.

In contrast to his last contract, this agreement—drafted by Werblin—treated Sullivan like a star. Its language fairly gushed. Stating that Ed had "built and maintained an outstanding reputation" as a "master of ceremonies, performing artist, and producer," it continued, "Whereas, CBS Television is anxious to have Artist's active services for as long a term as possible and to immobilize Artist as a competitor for as long a term as possible. . . ." To secure those long-term services, the contract stretched as far as the eye could see, no less than twenty years. CBS, having considered selling the show to advertisers without him just a few years before, now never wanted to let him go. Ironically, it was the executive who had offered the show to sponsors "with or without" Sullivan, Jack Van Volkenburg, who sent Ed a letter formally accepting the new terms. "I just want you to know how happy we all are at completing arrangements for our long-term marriage," Van Volkenburg enthused.

For the contract's first seven years, his salary would be $176,000 a year; for the following thirteen years, the network guaranteed him $100,000 a year regardless of whether he produced a show, as long as he didn't work for a competing network. He was given an expense account and eight weeks of vacation. Ed also negotiated an increase for Marlo Lewis, up to $1,000 a week.

The following fall, the show's weekly production budget would increase to $50,000. About $24,000 of that was specified as talent budget, which Sullivan could juggle between weeks, spending more on one week and then producing a less-expensive show the following week.

Werblin did particularly well in the deal. Sullivan's contract with MCA stipulated that the agency would receive ten percent of all his earnings from radio and television "for the duration of your life." Additionally, the agency would receive $3,500 from the show's weekly $50,000 production budget.

Ed happily told reporters about his new contract, so its details were soon widely reported, even down to the salary difference between the first seven years and the following thirteen. As industry observers realized that CBS had offered him a twenty-year contract, the news was clear: Sullivan had made it.

Apart from the money, the showman made one major demand: the program had to be renamed *The Ed Sullivan Show*. It would finish the 1954–55 season as *Toast of the Town* and adopt the new name with the start of next fall's season.

The contract was everything he had ever wanted. In contrast to his many failed radio shows, he now had a lock on a major broadcast berth—signed after two networks engaged in a bidding war for his services. Most importantly, at age fifty-three he was set to place his name in lights above a top-rated national television show.

Negotiations completed, and the alliance with Werblin formalized, Ed set out to finish off the *Comedy Hour*. But first he had a score to settle. During Sunday rehearsals, talent agents had always roamed the theater freely, watching their star clients perform, kvetching backstage, and socializing with the crew. But no more. In Ed's view, they had taken advantage of him, so he now forced a petty indignity on them. Henceforth they were denied access to the theater; if they wanted to talk with their clients on Sunday they had to wait in a cramped, uncomfortable area outside the stage door. MCA agent Marty Kummer nicknamed the area "The Wailing Wall," because performers cried or cursed there after hearing of Ed's changes or cancellations.

The agents hated having to wait outside, and many "prayed that Sullivan dropped dead," Marlo Lewis recalled. Years later, Sullivan claimed that he laid down this edict because Sylvia and Betty had once visited the theater and none of the agents offered to give up their seats to allow them to sit. In truth, Sylvia and Betty virtually never visited the theater, preferring to watch the show on television, and at any rate there were hundreds of seats in the Maxine Elliot. But in Ed's mind, talent agents were the kind of men who wouldn't even give a lady a seat.

The minor irritations of talent agents aside, the 1954–55 season was a winning one for Sullivan. The year's Nielsen figures indicated that *Toast of the Town* had climbed to be television's fifth-rated show. On top was *I Love Lucy*, followed by *The Jackie Gleason Show*, *Dragnet*, and *You Bet Your Life*, the humorous game show hosted by Groucho Marx. Incredibly, Sullivan was higher ranked than *The Bob Hope Show*, seventh-rated, and *The Jack Benny Show*, eighth-rated. Milton Berle, who had run just ahead of Sullivan between 1948 and 1950, had fallen to thirteenth. *Comedy Hour* had tumbled out of the Top 20, bested by *Toast of the Town* almost every Sunday.

Lucille Ball and Desi Arnaz, playing off Sullivan's ascendant popularity—and helping promote another CBS property—performed a sketch from *I Love Lucy* on Sullivan's show. Lucy hears remarkable news, which she reports to Ricky: *"Ed Sullivan is going to do the whole show about us!"* The couple, comically, fall all over themselves in an attempt to remain calm in the face of such a portentous development. When Ed himself rings their doorbell, Lucy emits a trademark shriek, and Ricky is so excited he drags Ed through the living room in a manic attempt at hospitality. Lucy shoves him into an easy chair and manhandles him into crossing his legs so he'll be more comfortable. Both try to pretend they hadn't heard the news, waiting to hear it directly from Ed. Finally, amid great fussing by Lucy, he gets out his invitation: he wants to do a show about them. In response, Lucy and Ricky intone in unison: *"About us?"* Ed as straight man played his part with reasonable aplomb, projecting ease with his role as the all-powerful television producer, if not his role as an actor in a comedy skit. At the end he flashed a big smile, yet he managed to look almost completely away from the camera.

Lucy and Desi felt fondly toward Sullivan after he had pitched in to sway public opinion when Ball's career was imperiled. In 1953 she had been called to testify about her alleged communist affiliation before a secret session of the House Un-American Activities Committee (HUAC). Ball admitted that as young woman she had once registered to vote as a communist. But she had done so, she explained, merely to placate her grandfather, a committed socialist. HUAC, satisfied with her explanation, let the matter drop.

However, news of her closed-door testimony leaked to Walter Winchell. In a blind item on his radio broadcast he announced, "The most popular of all television stars was confronted with her membership in the Communist Party." Although he didn't name her, in 1953 that description fit exactly one performer. Suddenly Ball's phone began ringing nonstop for comment. The *Herald Express* printed a copy of her 1936 voter registration card, proving she had planned to vote for the Communist Party. With the story's coverage exploding, and Hearst columnist Westbrook Pegler writing that Ball had to be "tracked down and exposed," the comedienne's career was in serious jeopardy.

But the momentum of her ever-growing popularity, and the helping hand of several columnists, saved her. Ed weighed in firmly with those who felt the issue should be dismissed—no doubt partially driven by his dislike of Winchell. Since Winchell had ignited this controversy, Ed was happy to douse it. As he wrote in his *Daily News* column, "It's a singularly fortunate thing for Lucille Ball that she's been a weekly visitor to millions of American living rooms. . . . TV cameras being as revealing as they are, the Jury of Public Opinion is an informed jury as it renders its verdict on a silly thing she did 17 years ago."

Indeed it was: after the first broadcast of *I Love Lucy* following Winchell's leak, Trendex figures revealed that Ball continued to star in television's top-ranked program.

The trappings of fame arrived quickly now. Ed acquired what every successful Manhattan executive was expected to own, a Connecticut estate. He bought Kettletown Farms, a one-hundred-eighty-acre property in bucolic Southbury, with a ten-room house, swimming pool, two lakes, and an orchard. The family's primary residence continued to be their apartment in the Delmonico, at Park Avenue and 59th Street; the Connecticut estate was a weekend retreat. The problem was finding the time to be there. Ed continued to log miles as a spokesman for Lincoln Mercury, and his *Daily News* column (now syndicated to thirty-five papers) kept calling him to the city.

In his tours for Lincoln Mercury, at every ribbon cutting, store opening, and civic event, the crowds mobbed him like some kind of national folk hero. Benson Ford remarked, "Wherever he goes, women hold up babies for him to kiss, traffic stops, policemen smile. . . . Sullivan is a one-man interfaith council, a chamber of commerce, and an unequaled sales force. The crowds love him." As Ed frequented his many Manhattan haunts—he remained a night owl, making the rounds of clubs like the Copacabana and Lindy's—he was met with squads of autograph hounds. He happily obliged them.

On October 10, 1955, the cover of *Time* featured Richard Nixon, the apple-cheeked vice president projecting a confident smile. On the cover the following week was Ed Sullivan, the showman smiling with a similar sense that all was well with the world. Underneath his portrait was a small cartoon of a television, out of which tumbled a crowd of miniature performers and a flurry of dollar bills. Sullivan, noted *Time*, "is about the longest shot ever to have paid off in show business. It is as if Featherweight Willie Pep knocked out Rocky Marciano with a single punch in the second round."

The cover story detailed Ed's rise, from his Port Chester days to, as *Time* portrayed it, the very top of the television industry. The article quoted TV executives about the medium's potential—its revenues had zoomed to $1 billion annually—then noted Ed's response to their promises of coming attractions: "Everything they're promising to do is something I've already done." *Time* listed the many entertainers whose shows had come and gone during Sullivan's tenure, including Red Buttons, George Jessel, and Bing Crosby. In the section on his background, Ed took the opportunity to jab his perennial rival: "Winchell's all through—and I'm an expert on Winchelliana. I've followed him like a hawk. He's a dead duck. He couldn't be resuscitated by injections at half-hour intervals." (The powerful columnist was indeed beginning to decline. His first attempt at television in 1952, though lauded by critics, had been canceled. Winchell's rat-a-tat-tat insistency didn't translate to the restrained 1950s.)

In the spring of 1955 came the big news: Warner Bros. was planning a film about Ed. As proposed by the studio, *The Ed Sullivan Story* would recount the showman's journey to national stardom. He had been a flop in Hollywood fifteen years earlier, but now Warner Bros. felt his life warranted a major bio-picture. Moreover, they wanted him to produce the film as well as star.

Studio head Jack Warner professed great faith in the film. "Mr. Sullivan's motion picture will be one of the most important forthcoming pictures on our release schedule," he told reporters. He wasn't just posturing: the studio budgeted $1 million for the film, which was higher than the average movie budget in the mid 1950s (though plenty of epics and star vehicles had surpassed this level). As with all his projects, Jack Warner's investment was more than financial: he would oversee the Sullivan film's production, with his usual firm hand. Warner was a man who felt supremely confident in his opinions. Having grown up in vaudeville—he was a boy soprano who sang between acts—and been a film producer since the medium's birth, he had an innate sense of the public's tastes, and in fact had helped mold those tastes. When he barked he expected others to jump, and he was known for his battles with stars like Bogart and Cagney, as well as for steamrolling producers and writers. On the night that *Casablanca* won the Oscar for Best Picture, Warner jumped up onstage to accept it before Hal Wallis, who was the film's producer, which led Al Jolson to quip, "I can't see what J.W. can do with an Oscar. It can't say 'yes.'"

Sullivan's representative in his negotiations with Warner Bros. was his lawyer Arnold Grant, not his talent agent Sonny Werblin. According to Ed's contract with MCA, the agency only got a percentage of his radio and television work—film wasn't mentioned in the contract. Werblin was likely kicking himself for not including film;

it cost him ten percent of Ed's lucrative movie payday. But Werblin's oversight was understandable. That Sullivan would be a highly paid television star was already far-fetched; that he would also be a well-compensated film star almost exceeded the boundaries of imagination. Ed's pay was $100,000, and he retained the television rights to the film.

Ed and Arnold Grant flew out to the coast to sign the paperwork and meet with Warner Bros. executives. While Ed was out there, Sylvia left a phone message for him at Arnold Grant's office: "Mrs. Sullivan called about 6:15 last night and said she had purchased a Renoir and would like you to get a $15,000 advance from Warner in order to pay for same." Ed's agreement with Warner Bros, however, specified that he wouldn't be paid until 1957. The studio, apparently seeking to limit its risk, wasn't going to pay him until after the film was released.

Jack Warner wanted to move quickly on the project. He hoped to get the script written over the summer and begin production on October 1. Warner asked Ed to write a script treatment, and in mid July Ed sent him a six-page synopsis. As he conceived of it, the movie would be a glorified version of his weekly show, a fast-paced array of acts with only a thin narrative about his and the show's history.

Ed's letter to Warner told the real story of why this film was being made. "I believe this will be a tremendous grosser, with a ready-made audience plus the exploitation I can give it on our show." Undoubtedly, Jack Warner saw the potential. Regardless of how unlikely a film star Ed was, with the showman pushing the movie every week to his audience of thirty million, generating box office success wouldn't even require an advertising budget. Ed's earlier alliance with Sam Goldwyn had been based on the then-counterintuitive idea that television and Hollywood could work together; now Sullivan's own bio-picture was about to be the best proof of that.

Warner all but ignored Ed's synopsis. He conceived of the film as a dramatic story, not merely an elaborately produced *Toast of the Town*. In mid August he sent screenwriter Irving Wallace to New York to spend a week with Ed and observe him producing the show. Wallace was a good fit for the project. As a short story writer and novelist, he was adept at crafting stories based on current events; he would write a series of best-selling novels based on contemporary trends. Also an experienced screenwriter, he wrote 1950's *The West Point Story*, starring Jimmy Cagney, as well as a number of TV scripts.

Wallace completed the Sullivan script by late September. Having seen Ed in action, he developed a fictional treatment based on real life. A character named Robbins was inspired by actual CBS executive Hubbell Robinson; Ed's first sponsor was Grimsley, "a large florid, booming man," who owns an appliance firm, much like Ed's real first sponsor, Emerson Radio; his second sponsor was "the chairman of the board of a leading automotive firm." The antagonist was Joyce Jekyll, "a feline slob who dips her pen in arsenic and writes TV tattle for a Manhattan daily."

In Wallace's story, Ed launches the show despite harsh critical barbs. After an initial period of success, his ratings fall as a heavily financed competing program draws viewers away. Things get so bad that Sylvia leaves him. Finally, the show is about to go off the air—but, at the last moment, Sylvia reappears. She hasn't left him; she secretly went to Las Vegas to bring back a singer who will revive ratings. The young singer goes on, the Trendex rating jumps skyward, and everything ends happily ever after.

Ed hated it. Sylvia's disappearance and show-saving last-minute return created dramatic tension, but it embarrassed him. Wasn't the show his creation? (Wallace, despite the odd story twists, was accurate in depicting how supportive Sylvia was of Ed.) Sullivan told Jack Warner the script needed to be rewritten.

Warner agreed, but he was becoming anxious about the film's production schedule. He moved the shooting back to February, but even the delayed date required that the script be rewritten quickly—actors couldn't be hired and acts lined up until the studio had a script. In mid October, Warner dispatched Wallace back to New York to spend a second week with Sullivan, with instructions to turn out a script posthaste. The screenwriter completed his second draft by November 1.

This time Wallace wrote a story line custom-made for Ed's vision of his show. At the plot's critical turning point, with the show imperiled, instead of Sylvia stepping in, Ed's own ingenuity as a producer saves the day. The script shows him breaking precedent by combining jazz and opera in the same program, presenting prerelease Hollywood film clips, producing lavish show business biographies—the first of their kind—and introducing fascinating celebrities in the audience. It portrays him as a driven, competitive showman who assesses the opposition and out-produces it at every turn.

If Wallace's intent was to create a script that so flattered Ed that he had no choice but to approve it, this was a well-aimed arrow: "As these acts go on, we go to a series of flash cuts of Ed's TV audience around the country. We see people phoning neighbors and relatives, excitedly telling them to switch from the opposition to 'Toast of the Town.' . . . Ed winds up in a blaze of glory." At the story's conclusion, CBS is so overjoyed at Sullivan's performance they decide to rename the show in his honor—it will now be called *The Ed Sullivan Show*. They inform him of this in the final scene by changing his cue card text without telling him, so he learns of it only as he announces it to a national audience. As he informs viewers of the show's new name, "Ed looks off into the thunderous ovation. . . ."

Wallace submitted the new script to Jack Warner, who swiftly approved it and rushed it to Ed by airmail. In his cover letter, Warner preempted any concerns Ed might have, in case the script's fawning wasn't enough. "Naturally, this was done in great haste," he wrote. "We will have these incidents slanted so we can get some good heart tug and humor." The studio head closed his letter with a reminder of the pending schedule: "I would like to get your reaction as quickly as possible."

But Ed wasn't feeling the urgency. Moreover, despite all the script's flattery, he didn't like it. He decided he had to toss out Wallace's work and write the script himself. As Jack Warner fumed, Ed sat down to work from scratch.

Two things bothered him about Wallace's script. First, he felt it didn't fully portray the powerful forces that threatened his television survival. Additionally—contradicting his first concern—he did not want to be depicted as so fiercely competing against these forces.

A long month later, he sent his half-finished script treatment to his lawyer Arnold Grant, to pass along to Warner. As Ed noted to Grant in his treatment, "The greatest European pictures, 'The Bicycle Thief,' 'The Baker's Wife,' were built around a deep, fundamental issue. . . . For our picture, Hollywood writers have an equally simple and fundamental premise . . . the powerful and subtle forces that threaten a man's employment." In short, Ed wanted the film to dwell still more on how he had persevered in the face of a critical onslaught—though Wallace's script already included this element.

As Ed wrote in his synopsis: "So this is the story we have: the story of a guy who worked like a bastard in TV and found his employment jeopardized by the critics, some of the network brass, and others." Families across the country would relate to this theme, he wrote, because it mirrored their own breadwinners' struggles in the working world. Ed conceived of two strong characters who were set to undermine him: one was a composite of all the critics who skewered him, and another represented the network brass who didn't believe in him. As he envisioned it, the movie of his life would portray him as surrounded by challengers on every side.

However, in Ed's version his own character's triumph over these obstacles wasn't due to his competitive spirit, as Wallace had portrayed. Instead, his success was a result of how accurately his show reflected what viewers wanted. He even suggested that the film include interviews from typical American living rooms, with families talking about why they liked the show. Ed's script was somewhat contradictory: he wanted to include powerful characters arrayed against him, but he didn't want to be seen as fighting against them. Instead, he portrayed himself as triumphing by transcending them, by going directly to the public.

Wallace's emphasis on his competitive nature made Ed uncomfortable. Although his column readers knew he was no stranger to confrontation, his television audience saw him as reserved and avuncular. As early as 1951, *Time* pointed out, "The TV Sullivan is a strange contrast to the bumptious know-it-all of Sullivan's Broadway column." Onstage, the audience saw an emcee who was nonthreatening and eager to please, bearing a gift bag of acts that offered something for everyone. He was stilted and awkward, yet safe—perhaps even safer because of his stiffness. His lack of slickness led many viewers to believe he was onstage by happenstance, as if whoever was really in charge had picked him at random from the audience. As a fan letter said, "We were discussing your program the other night and all of us agreed that my brother Charlie could do exactly what you do." Families trusted this good-natured uncle enough to invite him into their living rooms every Sunday night. He was one of them. The Warner Bros. script, however, portrayed the *other* man, the one behind the curtain, the competitor, the ambition-driven workaholic. This was a more interesting man, surely a better film subject, but it wasn't the persona that Ed brought into living rooms on Sunday night. And it wasn't the persona he wanted splashed on movie screens across the country.

So Ed's new script included no scenes of him as a competitor, instead emphasizing the show's allures; the script was close to his original concept of the film as a cinematic version of his TV show. Ed's treatment had an open-ended quality, interweaving his theme of triumph over great odds with many stars' performances, from showy Broadway numbers to cameos by sports figures. Rather than finalize his outline, he planned to bring the film together as he produced it, much as he did with his television show.

When Jack Warner realized that Sullivan had completely thrown out Wallace's second version—and that Ed's replacement script was just a work in progress—he was apoplectic. In Warner's view, the production schedule had turned into a series of delays with no end in sight. From his vantage point a troubling specter loomed: with the constant delays, by the time the film was released Sullivan's ratings might have tumbled, or worse, the show might be canceled, making his investment an embarrassment. In early December, Warner wired an angry telegram to Arnold Grant: "We will have to be a magician to put this together. As you know, this is not like putting on a TV show. People expect to see something. . . . If he is going to try and ad-lib this picture as he does his TV show it won't come off, nor will we produce it that way."

Still, notwithstanding Warner's impatience, the studio bent to Ed's conception. Sullivan's script called for a less-fictionalized approach than Wallace's, using more of the showman's actual words. So between late November and mid January, Wallace and two other writers labored to develop a script that included all of Ed's ideas. On January 12 they sent him a draft for his approval. The start of shooting had been pushed back yet again, to March 1, and by this point script approval needed to happen shortly. The studio executive supervising the script wrote to Sullivan: "We will be most anxious for your reaction—by phone, if possible."

Instead of approving it, Ed set to work—yet again—rewriting the script. Four days later, he sent a note to Arnold Grant, noting that he had boiled the first five pages down to three, and complaining, "I don't think that Irving Wallace will ever be able to write the story."

Jack Warner, hearing of Sullivan's plans for still more rewriting, was livid. He canceled the film—that very day. Eight months after the project's start, both parties signed an agreement to mutually void the contract. Warner Bros. would never release *The Ed Sullivan Story*. When reporters asked Ed why the movie was canceled, he claimed that he didn't want to interrupt his show's schedule long enough for filming.

The project had been a train wreck between two controlling men, and one in particular—Sullivan—who could not for a moment relinquish his producer's role. Given a chance to star in a feature film that glorified his life and career—and be paid $100,000 to do so—he was unable to compromise enough to complete the project.

His controlling nature worked well for him in television. It allowed him to pull together, on the fly, week after week, a highly popular one-hour variety show. That same controlling nature doomed *The Ed Sullivan Story*. He had, remarkably, once again proven to be a failure in film, even with a major studio lending every possible support.

Although Sullivan's alliance with Hollywood usually ran much smoother than his attempted project with Warner Bros., in April 1955 it precipitated yet another run-in, this time between the showman and Frank Sinatra.

Ed, continuing to show his viewers a steady diet of film previews, negotiated with Samuel Goldwyn to present excerpts from *Guys and Dolls*, starring Sinatra, Marlon Brando, and Jean Simmons. Ed planned to produce a half hour piece using the excerpts along with interviews of Brando and Simmons. Sullivan paid Goldwyn $32,000 for the excerpts, and he also paid Brando and Simmons for their interviews. He did not, however, ask Sinatra for an interview. Ed explained this by noting that the Simmons interview would be her television debut, and that Brando was the hottest thing in show business, yet Sinatra "is not exactly a TV novelty." In other words, the vocalist had recently appeared opposite Sullivan on an NBC "spectacular," as well as on *Comedy Hour*, and Ed viewed him as a competitor.

As Ed's plans coalesced, the studio let it be known that it expected Sinatra to appear for a Sullivan interview, paid or not, to help promote the film. At this point Sinatra balked. In his view, since Sullivan was paying Brando and Simmons but not him, the showman was attempting to arm-twist him into making an unpaid appearance. That the pressure came from the studio, not Sullivan, wasn't reported in most news articles about Frank's unhappiness. Samuel Goldwyn pointedly told reporters that his actors' contracts required them to make unpaid promotional appearances. But that contractual fine point was lost as the story devolved into a conflict between two egos, Sinatra's and Sullivan's.

The two had once enjoyed a warm friendship. The singer appeared on Sullivan's 1943 radio show and in his war bond rallies. Ed defended Sinatra in his column when the singer came under fire from columnist Westbrook Pegler for not serving in the military. In April 1947, after Sinatra punched Hearst columnist Lee Mortimer, resulting in a spate of bad press—as *Look* magazine archly observed, "The number of things he does besides sing is astounding"—Ed again came to his rescue. "Basically, Sinatra is a decent, warm-hearted person and I think it's about time they stop kicking him around," he wrote. (Ed, for his part, appreciated anyone who slugged Hearst columnists.) Deeply grateful, Frank sent Ed an effusive letter of thanks, along with a gold wristwatch inscribed, "Ed, you can have my last drop of blood. Frankie."

Yet now, upset by the *Guy and Dolls* dispute, Sinatra complained to the Screen Actors Guild (SAG) about unpaid promotional appearances. SAG quickly passed a new regulation prohibiting unpaid appearances on commercial television shows. Not satisfied, the singer went on the attack against Sullivan, decrying "newspaper personalities on TV" who use movie actors "without paying for their services."

Ed counterattacked by taking out full-page ads in *Variety* and the *Hollywood Reporter* to print his open letter to SAG president Walter Pidgeon: "Let us overlook the fact that Sinatra, regularly trounced by us when he becomes part of the rival network's 'spectacular,' hardly qualifies as an impartial or disinterested witness. What I particularly resent is Sinatra's reckless charge that *Toast* does not pay performers." His show had paid over $5,000,000 in performers fees, he claimed, rendering "substantial benefits to motion pictures." Additionally, "If Sam Goldwyn approached Sinatra, that hardly is my concern or problem. Certainly, I never approached Sinatra. My negotiations with Mr. Goldwyn involved an offer by me to pay a substantial sum of money . . . to represent, on film, thirty minutes of *Guys and Dolls* as an exclusive preview. Sincerely, Ed Sullivan.

P.S. Aside to Frankie Boy—never mind that tremulous 1947 offer: 'Ed, you can have my last drop of blood.'"

The letter sent Sinatra into a sputtering rage. He took out full-page ads in the same trade publications, stating, "Dear Ed: You're sick. Frankie. P.S. SICK! SICK! SICK!" To drive the point home, the word "sick" grew larger as it descended the page. The dueling full-page ads gave newspapers the fodder to nurture the story for an additional two weeks. Sinatra did not appear as part of Sullivan's promotion of *Guys and Dolls* (though he was in a film clip that Ed showed), and in the short term their erstwhile friendship foundered.

In the 1955–56 television season, the first year the program was called *The Ed Sullivan Show*, a number of factors combined to make Sullivan's showcase a cultural focal point. In the previous season it had ranked number five among the 122 shows in prime time, and this season's ratings were trending still higher, drawing the attention of not only viewers but entertainers. Performers now practically clawed to get on the show; musicians knew an appearance sent their vinyl sales soaring, and comics knew a Sullivan introduction pushed their nightclub fees skyward. Moreover, MCA president Sonny Werblin provided Sullivan with an open door to his rich hoard of talent, so it was easier to get bigger names, which in turn made the show more attractive to other high-profile performers. Adding momentum was the increased production budget of $50,000 per episode.

With his now-larger budget, Ed often gave Lincoln Mercury automobiles to stars as inducements to appear: Henry Fonda got a black Thunderbird, Robert Mitchum got a black Lincoln Coupe, Bing Crosby got a red station wagon, Gene Kelly got a blue Lincoln convertible, and Gary Cooper got a champagne-colored Premiere.

Many Sundays now included a lavishly produced scene from a current Broadway play, performed by original cast members. In October, for example, actors Tony Randall, Melvyn Douglas, and Ed Begley performed a scene from *Inherit the Wind*, a play about the Scopes Monkey Trial written in response to the hysteria of McCarthyism. That same show saw performances by the Dave Brubeck Jazz Quartet, bejeweled pianist Liberace, vocalist Rosemary Clooney, and animal trainer Robert Lamouret with his talking duck.

In an unorthodox variation on his Broadway presentations, Ed booked film actors to recreate scenes from current movies, in essence performing a live trailer. The season opened with Robert Mitchum and Lillian Gish reprising a scene from *Night of the Hunter*, and later in the year Tony Curtis and Burt Lancaster reenacted a scene from *Trapeze*. These film tableaus were always just one of a half dozen acts on any evening; Curtis and Lancaster, for instance, shared the bill with vaudevillian Benny Fields, Metropolitan Opera singer Lily Pons, and trampoline acrobat Larry Griswold.

Rock 'n' roll was just a squalling infant in November 1955, yet that month the public heard one of its original voices. On the night of November 20, Ed told viewers they were about to hear something novel: "Now ladies and gentlemen, as everyone knows, whenever any new musical trend has evinced itself in the popular trends—the Charleston or the black bottom or any of the rhythm songs—the first area to find out about it in advance is Harlem. A couple of weeks ago I went up to Harlem, I'd seen these shots in the newsreel about thousands of people jamming the streets around the Apollo Theater, all trying to get in to see Dr. Jive's . . ."—and here Ed hesitated, unsure of what the music was called, so he riffed a few variations—"rhythm and roll, rhythm and color, rhythm and blues. So here is Dr. Jive!"

Dr. Jive was the stage name for Tommy Smalls, a tall, handsome, nattily attired black disc jockey, promoter, and band manager, who that evening presented his rhythm and blues revue: Bo Diddley, LaVern Baker, The Five Keys, and Wallis "Gator Tail" Jackson. The electrified beat that the four acts laid down formed the foundation of rock 'n' roll, and that night was the first time that most of Ed's viewers ever heard such a sound.

Most notable among Dr. Jive's acts was Bo Diddley. When the Mississippi-born singer-guitarist moved to Chicago's South Side, he brought a style of polyrhythmic syncopation he learned from black sharecroppers. Called "hambone," it was a chant that was sung over an intensely physical cross-layered beat—its rhythm was the basis for tap dancing. The hambone chant had been handed down from slaves, who brought it with them from Africa. When Diddley recorded his first song with the hambone rhythm in Chess studios in 1955 (just months before his Sullivan appearance) he dubbed it "Bo Diddley." This was the song he wanted to perform tonight.

At rehearsal that afternoon, Ed hadn't liked it. The song was pure rhythm. Instead of a traditional verse and chorus, it was a driving, electrified version of the generations-old hambone chant-song, played over a visceral voodoo beat. Sullivan vetoed the selection. Diddley could remain on the bill, but Ed, casting around for a suitably contemporary alternative, told him to play Tennessee Ernie Ford's "Sixteen Tons." By comparison with "Bo Diddley," Ford's tune was a lumbering dirge, yet it was hot at the moment—it held number one on the charts, having sold more than a million copies in three weeks. Diddley apparently agreed with the song change, otherwise Ed wouldn't have let him on that evening.

Yet during the live broadcast, when the camera cut to Diddley, he jumped into "Bo Diddley" as if he had never considered anything else. He and his three bandmates, dressed in matching light-colored blazers, started with a kick-snare cross-rhythm, then overlaid a percolating maracas; the bass player began thrumming the backbeat, and Bo joined in with rhythm guitar and chant-song vocals. The result was musical combustion, blissful and unapologetic. The tune would reverberate throughout rock 'n' roll for a generation, with musicians from the Rolling Stones to Bruce Springsteen proudly claiming to have been inspired by it. Ed, however, was furious—Diddley never again played the Sullivan show.

Not all the shows that season introduced the audience to such otherworldly sounds. For Ed's program on Christmas Day—he wasn't going to take the day off—actors Gary Cooper and Rod Steiger performed a scene from their film *The Court-Martial of Billy Mitchell*, the Michigan Glee Club sang carols, and Ed presented a taped segment from a holiday ice show featuring Czech skating champion Miroslava Nachodska.

In January's tribute to America's songwriters and composers, famed bandleader Cab Calloway tap-danced in black tie and tails with his daughter Layla. In February, Lucille Ball and Desi Arnaz shared the stage with vocal quartet the Ames Brothers; Desi sang along as Lucy goofed around pretending to be the fifth singer. Later in the hour, Rodgers and Hammerstein chatted with Ed about their music and introduced performances of their favorite songs. Following them was actor Orson Welles rendering a scene from his Broadway production of Shakespeare's *King Lear*, and ventriloquist Rickie Layne riposting with his dummy Velvel.

The following week, Pulitzer Prize–winning poet Carl Sandburg recited his "A Lincoln Portrait" accompanied by the ever-mellow Andre Kostelanetz Orchestra; actor Hal Holbrook monologued as Mark Twain; and Clayton Moore, who played TV's Lone Ranger, demonstrated some swift pistol work, after which acrobatic team the Amandis dazzled with a teeterboard.

As winter turned to spring, the Sullivan show presented actors Jimmy Cagney and Jack Lemmon in a scene from the Broadway play *Mr. Roberts*; Walt Disney gave an award to Fess Parker for his dramatic performance in *Davey Crockett*; French mime Marcel Marceau re-created the story of David and Goliath; and Ed hosted the Mother of the Year Awards, spotlighting actresses Betty Grable, Deborah Kerr, and June Allyson.

For the show's eighth-anniversary program in June, Ed arranged for a crowd of celebrities to pay tribute to the show's longevity. In a group sing-along, Ronald Reagan (host of the popular *General Electric Theater*), Natalie Wood, Robert Walker, Walt Disney, Lucille Ball, and Desi Arnaz all warbled "Happy Anniversary" in a tribute to Ed. Broadway veteran Ethel Merman belted out "Sullivan for Me," longtime friend Louis Armstrong stopped by to sing "Happy Birthday," Harry Belafonte crooned calypso music, and screen star Gregory Peck previewed next week's lineup.

Peck was a natural choice: the following week Ed dedicated the full hour to director John Huston, and Peck gave a dramatic reading from *Moby Dick*, a Huston film currently in production in which he starred. Sullivan presented film clips from the director's work, including *Treasure of the Sierra Madre* and *The Maltese Falcon*, interviewing Huston along with Peter Lorre, Mary Astor, and José Ferrer, who demonstrated getting in and out of makeup for a Hollywood movie. Ed performed mock gangster dialogue with Edward G. Robinson, then Robinson, Ed, and Huston brought on Lauren Bacall, who talked about her husband Humphrey Bogart's work with the director. (Bogart was seriously ill and in the last months of his life.) In the audience for a bow that night was horror maven Vincent Price.

Over the next few weeks, Ed interviewed Bing Crosby, presented Borscht Belt comic Myron Cohen, and introduced the Iowa Highlanders, a Scottish bagpipe squad. In late July—Ed continued to produce new shows almost all summer long— Sullivan showcased the Barnum & Bailey Circus, spotlighting famed clown Emmett Kelly and the full mélange of aerialists, big cats, and trapeze artists.

As the weeks of glittering spectacle and celebrity flew by, *The Ed Sullivan Show*'s ratings edged ever higher. Having been television's fifth-ranked show the previous year, Nielsen ratings for the 1955–56 season indicated that it was now the third-ranked show. It ran behind only *I Love Lucy* and *The 64,000 Question*, and was one spot higher than *Disneyland*. The program had reached its loftiest perch yet. By most accounts the show had been second-ranked in the 1948–50 time period, running behind Milton Berle, yet there was very little competition then. Now, the Sullivan show had regained its earlier leading status in a crowded field, in an industry whose production standards boasted the beginnings of sophistication.

Further sign of the program's ratings dominance was seen in the fate of the show that ran opposite Sullivan's, NBC's *Comedy Hour*, which collapsed that season. As *Time* reported, "Colgate, which was displeased with the failure of its show to equal the drawing power of the Sullivan show, asked to be relieved of its contract." Ed, inarguably, had done it. He had reached the pinnacle of the new medium that was taking over the American living room.

At the tail end of the 1955–56 season, for all the dizzying success Sullivan enjoyed, the showman stumbled. In question was his booking of film star Ingrid Bergman. On his July 18 program, Ed made a titillating announcement about the Swedish-born actress: she was scheduled for a guest appearance in October.

Viewers across the country gave a collective gasp. Known for her luminous portrayals in 1942's *Casablanca* and 1945's *Spellbound*, Bergman had shocked Hollywood and scandalized the public in 1949. Although married, while in Italy filming *Stromboli* she had fallen in love with the film's director, Roberto Rossellini. As news of her pregnancy and her decision to leave her husband made headlines, the public turned away from her.

Yet Bergman proved remarkably resilient. After a career trough in the early 1950s, during which she lived outside the United States, she landed the lead in the 1956 big-budget Hollywood film *Anastasia*. She was in London filming the picture when Ed announced her upcoming appearance. As Sullivan left for London to shoot some footage from the set, reporters deluged him with questions. His announcement of Bergman's return was a national news item—which was why he made it. Between her earlier controversy, her long self-exile, and her current film role, the prospect of the first live Bergman television appearance touched off a publicity firestorm. How, reporters wanted to know, had Sullivan pulled off such a scheduling coup? Responding to their queries the day before he flew to London, Ed explained that the actress's guest shot had been scheduled in conjunction with Twentieth Century Fox.

Sullivan's plans began to backfire on him within the week. His sponsor, Ford, began to grumble about not wanting to be associated with Bergman, and letters from viewers poured in protesting her planned appearance. No small part of his success was his audience's belief in him as their filter; they trusted him as a kind of Minister of Culture. While Ed could pick and choose from almost anything to entertain his viewers, from poet Carl Sandburg to the Barnum & Bailey Circus, his viewers expected him to be a prudent moralist in his choices. Was he now betraying their trust?

A still-thornier problem was posed by Bergman herself. On location in London, she told reporters that she had never agreed to go on Sullivan's program. She acknowledged that a clip of *Anastasia* would be previewed on his show, yet "there was never any question of me going to the States with him." When Ed returned from London and reporters asked him about the discrepancy, he again said that Twentieth Century Fox had been responsible for the announcement. But the studio declined comment.

Ed was now in a public relations conundrum. Some viewers were upset at the proposed appearance, while others were disgruntled at having been promised a glimpse of the controversial actress only to have it withdrawn. And everyone—including the battalion of reporters now following the story—wondered what was going on. He had to find a way to explain, amid escalating negative publicity, why the star would not appear despite his recent and very clear statement that she would.

The solution he chose reflected his anger at Bergman. She could have made an appearance yet instead had publicly embarrassed him. For her part, she likely remembered that he had joined the chorus labeling her a pariah when she announced her intention to have a child with Rossellini. As Ed had then written in his column, "The Ingrid Bergman–Rossellini baby will be baptized because in such a case, the Catholic Church holds that the sins of the parents cannot victimize the child, born out of wedlock. . . ." Despite his column's judgmental excoriation of Bergman, Ed apparently assumed that since he was promoting her film, the studio would strongarm her into an appearance. But the actress was not to be coerced.

When Ed went on the air on the night of July 29, the public awaited an explanation. Instead, he portrayed the situation as an issue to be decided by the viewers themselves. At the very end of the show he addressed the matter: "Now I know that she's a controversial figure, so it's entirely up to you. If you want her on our show, I wish you'd drop me a note and let me know to that effect. And if you don't, if you think it shouldn't be done, you also let me know that, too. Because I say it's your decision and I'd like to get your verdict on it." He told viewers that Bergman had "seven and a half years of time for penance," and it was up to them to decide if that was enough.

Sullivan regretted his comments the moment he made them. He was offstage no more than a few seconds when, spotting talent coordinator Jack Babb, he exclaimed, "Why the hell did I say that?" With his intimate knowledge of his audience he knew that viewer mail would vote against having the actress on; in theory this would relieve him of the need to present her. *Newsweek* reported, presumably based on figures from Sullivan staffers, that mail was running 5,826 for, 6,433 against. But of course the vote meant nothing; Bergman certainly wouldn't appear after Ed asked viewers to vote on the quality of her morality. His attempt to deflect attention from his own mistake was, at best, clumsy, and at worst, pharisaical.

Not since the show's debut were reviewers so united in their attitude toward him—and so vociferous. *New York Post* columnist Leonard Lyons called Sullivan's handling of the issue "tasteless and shocking." *New York Journal-American* critic Jack O'Brian—always Sullivan's toughest critic—printed a long statement by a Catholic priest who had "never seen anything like it," and who noted that an individual's morality could never by judged by public opinion. *The New York Times'* J.P. Shanley pointed out that Sullivan had made no reference to Bergman's morality when he initially announced her appearance, writing, "it would seem the producer's approach to the subject has changed significantly." Los Angeles *Mirror-News* columnist Hal Humphrey, after censuring the showman, snorted, "Incidentally, when is Ed Sullivan up for reelection?"

For once, Ed had no response to the hail of criticism. He knew he had bungled the Bergman affair. In the face of the fusillade of negative publicity he decided to cancel the preview of *Anastasia*.

Contributing to his awkward handling of the incident was his tendency to keep his own counsel in running the show. Director Johnny Wray supervised camera angles, but he had no veto over Ed's on-air comments; likewise Marlo Lewis, like much of the staff, sometimes heard things from Ed for the first time when the showman told the television audience. The Sullivan show was run by exactly one person. And Ed, despite great affability in social situations, maintained a reserve between himself and those around him, handling issues as he saw fit. In this case that led to a serious stumble. "Ingrid never forgave me for what I had done," he told an interviewer in the late 1960s. "And she was right."

In the short term, if Ed wished to divert attention from the Bergman contretemps, he would succeed. Within the week an event happened in his life that effectively erased the incident from the headlines.

CHAPTER TWELVE

Elvis

E D'S DAUGHTER BETTY REMEMBERED HER CHILDHOOD YEARS in Hollywood with great fondness. Her happy memories drew her back to California; in her teenage years she made summer visits, staying with a friend. After graduating from Miss Hewitt's School in New York, she attended the University of California at Los Angeles (UCLA), where she majored in English. It was there, in 1949, that she met Robert Precht, a tall, good-looking classmate majoring in international relations. A romance bloomed, and although Bob transferred to U.C. Berkeley they continued to see each other.

During one of Ed and Sylvia's trips to Los Angeles to visit Betty, she invited her boyfriend to meet her parents, with mixed results. The foursome had dinner at Chasen's, a Beverly Hills restaurant known for its red leather booths and frequent celebrity appearances. At first the dinner went smoothly, the group chatting amiably, but things grew tense when the conversation turned to politics. Bob, an infrequent television viewer who had grown up in California, was only vaguely aware of Ed's background. Thoughtful and articulate, he spoke at length about his antipathy toward the anticommunist fervor engulfing the nation. Specifically, he was upset that teachers were forced to sign loyalty oaths, and he detested what he thought of as the witch hunt of Richard Nixon, then a young senator allied with Joseph Mc-Carthy. "I was a hot-headed college student," Precht remembered. Ed, who was then actively promoting *Red Channels*, cut in with an angry retort: "Well, if you're that upset, why the hell don't you stop talking about it and do something?" An awkward silence fell over the table, with Bob at a loss for words and Betty and Sylvia clearly embarrassed. Recalled Precht: "He put me in place with that line."

From that difficult start, however, the Sullivan family began to accept Bob. When Ed and Sylvia visited Betty during their summer vacations they spent more time with him. Betty temporarily left her sorority house to stay with her parents at the Beverly Hills Hotel, and Bob often met them at the hotel for dinner (though he was careful to park his beat-up 1938 Chevrolet a few blocks away to avoid presenting it to the hotel's valet staff). On the surface, Ed, having come of age in the rough-and-tumble of 1920s-era New York newspapers, came from a world far different from that of Precht, who grew up in middle class surroundings in San Diego. Yet Ed saw something in Precht, perhaps his strength of character or native intelligence, perhaps an ambition not dissimilar to his own. When Betty and Bob got married, shortly after Betty's graduation in 1952, Ed wrote her a note blessing the union: "Betty Dearest: This is the most wonderful day in your lives and the life of your mother and me. You are two fine kids, your love is based on mutual respect for each other's rights, and it will be a happy marriage. . . . Our deep love now reaches out to embrace Bob. . . . God love you both and protect you and grant you just as much happiness as He has granted your mother and daddy. With all my love, Daddy."

Bob, having completed a tour of duty in the Navy during the Korean War, studied Russian and worked in the Navy's security division in Washington, D.C. In the mid 1950s he and Betty made frequent visits up to New York to visit Betty's parents, which created an opportunity for Precht. Ed's connections opened the door to the new field of television, which Bob found glamorous and potentially lucrative. "It was very tempting," he recalled, and all the more so because the couple now had two young children.

In 1956 he made the career change. With his interest in current events, Bob hoped for a position in the news division, but Sullivan's influence opened no doors there. So Ed asked Marlo Lewis to hire him as a production assistant. Since Lewis had branched out, working on other CBS programs as well as the Sullivan show, Bob apprenticed with several shows, including a soap opera, children's programs, and the courtroom drama *The Verdict Is Yours*. Precht also began working on the Sullivan show, sometimes working directly with Ed to help assemble the weekly program. Despite his lack of experience in show business, the son-in-law demonstrated a competency and professionalism that quickly proved his value beyond his family connection. When Ed took the show on one of its many location broadcasts, Bob was usually there as assistant producer.

For the show on August 5, 1956, Bob accompanied Ed to McGuire Air Force Base in Trenton, New Jersey, for a remote broadcast. After the show the Air Force flew them back to the Bridgeport, Connecticut airport, where they were picked up by Ralph Cacace, a handyman-caretaker at Sullivan's estate in Southbury. With a little luck, Bob and Ed hoped to be home not long after eleven o'clock.

Around midnight, Betty and Sylvia began to wonder why they were running so late, Sylvia hoping out loud that nothing was seriously wrong, Betty speculating that the plane was probably late getting in. By the time the clock inched past one in the morning, the two were seriously worried, too concerned to sleep. With little to say, they waited, Betty half resting on the couch. She felt intuitively that this was more than a routine schedule delay. The minutes stretched out in the quiet house, the heavy silence broken only by the solemn ticking of a nautical clock on the fireplace mantle.

When the phone rang shortly after two A.M. Betty felt the breath rush out of her body. Ed and Bob had been in a serious car accident and their condition was unknown, said the police department caller. A squad car was dispatched to rush Sylvia and Betty to the hospital. As the two raced across Connecticut in the back seat of a police car, Sylvia sobbed in great heaves as Betty held onto her. Betty also held onto a reassuring thought: her husband and father must be alive and conscious, otherwise who would have given the police their phone number? The police driver pulled into a hospital emergency entrance, only to realize he had made a terrible mistake: it was the wrong hospital. Betty hurriedly got out and called the correct hospital, holding her breath while the nurse provided details about Ed and Bob's conditions. They were seriously injured—but they were alive. As the car sped to the right hospital, Sylvia had something of a breakdown, nearing total hysteria.

Ed had been driving Bob and Ralph Cacace in his new Lincoln along the narrow twists and turns of Naugatuck Valley Road. They were only about twelve miles from home when the driver of a 1953 Pontiac, heading the opposite direction, fell asleep at the wheel; he was a twenty-two-year-old X-ray technician headed home after a late shift. Swerving suddenly into the oncoming lane, his car collided head-on with Sullivan's. Ed was knocked unconscious and—some of the details remain unclear—apparently thrown from the car.

When he regained a bleary half-awareness he was lying by the side of the road on a piece of tarpaulin, sirens blaring in the distance and a light shining in his eyes. His chest, to the extent he felt it, seemed to be caved in, and he tasted blood in his mouth. A young girl in a party dress held his hand, seemingly unconcerned that Sullivan's blood was staining her outfit; her name was Sue Miles and she lived nearby. A man whom he would never meet held Ed's head in his lap. The light shining in Ed's eyes came from a flashlight held by a doctor's assistant. "Hey, doc, come here quick, this one's Ed Sullivan," he said. "I don't know who he is," the doctor replied. "After a wreck like this they all look alike."

The ambulance crew worked on extricating Bob and Cacace from the car, which was totaled. Sullivan, laboring to breathe, gave the girl his number and told her to phone Sylvia and Betty. "Tell them it's nothing serious," he gasped as she hurried off. The size and heft of the Lincoln had saved them, otherwise they likely would have died in the crash. Sullivan had a fractured rib and a mass of cuts and bruises all over his body. Bob, riding in the front seat, had a broken arm and ankle and deep facial cuts. Cacace suffered chest injuries and a skull fracture. The other driver sustained a fractured hip and jaw. The news was bad, yet considering the nature of the collision it could have been worse. Sylvia and Betty maintained an anxious day-and-night vigil, but were buoyed by the news that Bob and Ed were expected to recover fully. When Marlo Lewis visited, he was horrified by the sight of Ed lying under an oxygen tent looking "frail and concave, like a scarecrow with the stuffing ripped out." Sonny Werblin assigned two of his talent agents to the hospital to ensure that Ed's needs were taken care of.

The crash was a national news item, though there was confusion about how serious it was. Ed made light of it, telling reporters he expected to be home soon and would resume his broadcast the following Sunday; a near-death experience wasn't going to keep him off the air. But his physician quickly vetoed that idea and original press reports were corrected: the show would go on with a substitute host. On Wednesday came the announcement that he would go home after a couple more days; that, too, was soon amended. Due to complications of his bronchial condition—probably exacerbated by his pack-a-day cigarette habit—he required additional hospital time. Ed was released on August 13, seven days after being admitted, and taken to his Southbury home for an expected three- to four-weeks' rest.

But the accident traumatized his system more than he realized. On August 21 he was re-admitted to the hospital for what his doctors referred to as lung congestion; only after a six-day stay did he return to his Southbury estate to convalesce. Resting, however, soon made him tense and unhappy, and he resumed booking the show as guest hosts—Kirk Douglas, Red Skelton, Charles Laughton—took his place. A few years earlier he had undergone minor stomach surgery for his ulcer, and, defying doctor's orders and Sylvia's protests, had missed only one show; when he had resumed hosting ten days later he needed to collapse into a chair between introducing acts. Now he attempted to do the same, lobbying for a return though his condition called for rest.

Through it all the show's regular watchers produced a titanic outpouring of affection. The show normally received box loads of weekly mail, yet now some 36,000 letters arrived voicing concern for the showman. Having inhabited viewers' living rooms for so many Sundays, many audience members saw him as a family member. After the program each week much of the studio audience wouldn't leave, instead approaching the stage and asking a steady stream of questions about Ed's condition. Priests and nuns wrote to say they included him constantly in their prayers. National newspapers kept up a running report on his condition; *The New York Times* ran nearly weekly updates during his five-week absence.

Even Frank Sinatra, his recent feud with Sullivan apparently forgotten, made a get-well phone call to the showman in mid August, telling the *New York Post* "I love Ed and I know he loves me." Eager to make his affection public, within the week Sinatra appeared gratis on the Sullivan show during a program guest hosted by Red Skelton. (He claimed, though, that laryngitis prevented him from singing, so after Skelton read a tribute to him written by Ed, and the singer plugged his new movie, he still had time to dash across town and make an appearance on NBC's 8 P.M. show.)

Ed returned to his show in mid September, though whether he was well enough to do so was arguable. Onscreen he appeared wan and had obviously lost weight. To compare the shows before and after the accident is to see that something vital had been taken from him. Into his early fifties he had retained the glow of his Port Chester athleticism, aided by his love of golf and his many days spent outside at the racetracks. He had been a handsome man, ruddy, projecting a confident masculine glow. If there was a single moment when he most markedly began to lose his youthful vigor, it was with the physical trauma of the head-on collision. The crash was the catalyst that accelerated the aging process.

Not that he acknowledged this in the immediate aftermath. In the months ahead he jumped right back into his old schedule, if anything moving into higher gear as he envisioned broadcasts from ever more exotic locations, requiring more travel and more logistical headaches. His only concession was to stop driving; from then on he took taxis, and his friend Joe Moore picked him up for Sunday's rehearsal. Otherwise he remained in fighting shape, and as always was ready to take on all comers.

The tabloid *Exposed*, which printed gossipy half-invented articles about celebrities, reported on the car crash in a piece entitled "Why Ed Sullivan Needs Bodyguard." According to *Exposed*, Ralph Cacace, Ed's Southbury caretaker who was in the car that night, was actually his full-time bodyguard. (That Cacace never accompanied Sullivan in New York, where he spent most of his time, wasn't reported in

The Sullivan family, mid 1950s. From left: Sylvia, Ed, Betty (holding a very young
Rob Precht), and Bob Precht, who would later become the producer of the Sullivan
show. (Globe Photos)

the article.) The showman needed such a protector, the tabloid claimed, because he
had become so hated by so many:

"Today, living on his 200-acre farm in Southbury, Connecticut, he's a lonely man,
feared, hated, and envied. He's built walls around himself, such as his full-time
bodyguard. Behind the façade, there's a mighty unhappy, afraid man—the victim of
his own consuming egotism.

"Let's face it: Sullivan is a Big Man in the American entertainment business, and
big guys aren't liked. The people who knew him when he was on his way up from
his $10-a-week job as reporter for a hick-town paper are only a few of those who re-
sent the success that has come to him."

As *Exposed* reported it, Ed's ruthless practices—his tendency to push around
others, from Arthur Godfrey to Frank Sinatra to Walter Winchell—made him feared
across the industry. Even his own sponsors were afraid of him, the tabloid claimed:
"They know that behind that frigid smile and glassy eyes there lies a raging blaze
of ambition that keeps driving the ex-small-town kid to the top.

"He's at the top now, but he has bought the Trendex score and the big salary at
the cost of *fear*. His march to the top has left a trail of enemies who would gladly
sink their teeth in his throat—or a knife wherever they can."

NBC faced a challenge in 1956: finding a way to compete with Sullivan. Despite its leviathan budget, *Comedy Hour* had failed, and the network's attempt to hire Ed himself had also come to naught. So now NBC cast around for a fresh challenge to the showman's vise grip on Sunday night. The decision it made was creative and slightly risky. The network maintained the time slot's variety format, but to host it they hired a performer who offered a vivid contrast with Ed, Steve Allen.

Allen was a superb choice as an anti-Sullivan. While Ed played the reserved and stiff guardian of the status quo, Allen was witty and irreverent, and at age thirty-five younger and more forward looking than any previous national television host. His owlish mien and thick black glasses frames belied his gift for unpredictable off-the-cuff comedy. When substituting for Arthur Godfrey on *Talent Scouts* he made a point of forgetting contestants' names, and he poked fun at the sponsor by brewing a cup of Lipton Tea with a package of noodle mix, then dumping the resulting concoction into Godfrey's ukulele. His sharp taste for farce earned him a following as host of the late-evening *Tonight Show*, among other programs. He was also an actor, having starred in 1955's *The Benny Goodman Story*, and an author and prolific songwriter. Allen's cerebral wit and his tendency to tweak the powerful presaged 1960s comics like Mort Sahl and George Carlin. Shortly before launching his show opposite Sullivan's, Allen wired Ed: "Dear Ed. Would you lend me ten Trendex points until payday? Love and kisses, Steve Allen."

Despite the jest, when *The Steve Allen Show* debuted in the summer of 1956, Allen immediately went for the jugular. For his second broadcast on July 1 he booked the one-man rock 'n' roll tornado, the phenomenon who was thrilling teenagers but horrifying adults: Elvis Presley. The singer had only recently burst onto the national scene, having released the moody, noirish—but rhythmic— "Heartbreak Hotel," in January. Its release had been a match thrown in gasoline. The song swiftly scaled the hit chart, fueled by five appearances on Tommy and Jimmy Dorsey's CBS-TV program, *Stage Show*. (The Dorsey brothers, having led top swing orchestras in the war years, were now consigned to a back-of-the-pack television show.) In April, Presley sang "Heartbreak Hotel" on Milton Berle's show; shortly thereafter the tune hit number one—a first for the singer.

Elvis' first guest spot on Berle was sedate, yet when he returned in June his hurricane hips went into action, swiveling in time to the backbeat. His fans swooned, but a good portion of the audience was deeply offended. Rock 'n' roll was seen by many as promoting juvenile delinquency and antisocial behavior, and Presley was the worst of it. He exuded something not completely definable, an unsettling alembic of sex and longing and alienation; whatever it was, it was too primal, too direct, and certainly too rhythmic. And the way he moved as he sang—especially those pelvic gyrations—was lewd and lascivious, many protested. While his records flew off the shelves, letters of protest poured into newspapers and television stations across the country.

Steve Allen, booking Presley for $5,500, downplayed his explosive charisma, instead playing the singer's performance for laughs. Allen's staff dressed Presley in a tuxedo and convinced him to keep his body movements to a minimum. They cast him in a drowsy comedy sketch in which he sang "Hound Dog" to a basset hound. It was closer to sleepwalking than rock 'n' roll, and the singer's fans were horrified. The next day a crowd of teenagers picketed outside the NBC studio in Rockefeller

Plaza, carrying signs with slogans like "Bring Back the Grinds" and "We Don't Like the 'New' Elvis, We Want the 'Old' Presley."

Nonetheless, that evening's Allen show threw down a challenge to Sullivan. When Ed made his weekly call to the Trendex ratings service—he called every Monday morning without fail—he confirmed what he had suspected: Allen's show had soundly beaten his, garnering a 20.2 rating compared with his own show's 14.8. Ed, in an uncharacteristically lighthearted response to a competitor, dashed off a telegram to Allen: "Steven Allen Presley, NBC-TV, New York City. Stinker. Love and kisses, Ed Sullivan."

The kidding aside, Sullivan was smarting from the Presley drubbing. Earlier in the year, he had been alternately dismissive and condemning of the singer. Although he had a chance to book Presley while his price was still reasonable, Ed had scoffed at the thought: "$5,000 for some youngster known only in the south?" After Presley's appearance on Berle ignited protests across the country, Ed told reporters that Elvis was unfit for family viewing. But being outpointed by the upstart Allen led the showman to reconsider his position.

The other programs that had booked Elvis—Berle's, the Dorsey brothers', Steve Allen's—faced less risk in presenting Presley. Berle by 1956 had faded, falling from the Top 20 to never again regain his ratings. The Dorsey show was even lower rated and Steve Allen was brand new. For them, controversy was desirable; they had little to lose. But *The Ed Sullivan Show* was the number three show on television; it wasn't just another variety show, it was *the* variety show. Now in its eighth year, it had earned its coveted spot through Ed's eye for talent and uncanny sense of American tastes. Getting booked on the Sullivan program was the show business equivalent of the *Good Housekeeping* seal of approval. As the unofficial Minister of Culture, he was the guide and the guardian for the American living room. Viewers expected him to disapprove of Elvis.

Or did they? Presley, for the first time, created a division in Sullivan's audience. The singer's recordings were rocketing up the charts, yet authority figures were shaking their heads. Traditional vaudeville producers had never faced this kind of dilemma; they could book something for everyone while offending no one. But this new thing called rock 'n' roll, like nothing before it, was splitting the living room asunder. What was a television producer who wanted an all-inclusive audience to do?

For Ed, that question was answered the moment Allen trounced him in the Trendex matchup. Playing to win meant taking a calculated risk—and fast. Within the week of Allen's ratings victory he called Presley's manager, Colonel Tom Parker. It was time to make a deal. Not only would Elvis, the great corrupter of youth, appear on the Sullivan show—the sacrosanct bastion of American show business—he would be paid handsomely to do so. Colonel Parker, knowing he had Ed where he wanted him, extracted a whopping $50,000 for three appearances, far more than any previous Sullivan guest.

On the day the Presley–Sullivan contract was signed in July 1956, rock 'n' roll took a definitive step toward the mainstream. Ed explained his change of heart to reporters by saying he had been misled by news reports of Presley's outrageous stage behavior, and after reviewing kinescopes from the Dorsey show he found the accounts to be wildly exaggerated. That might have been so, yet he came to that conclusion only after his ratings loss. Steve Allen, poking fun at Ed's about-face, said, "I hereby

A twenty-one-year-old Elvis Presley hours before his debut on the Sullivan show, September 9, 1956. Sullivan resisted booking Presley, yet the singer's volcanic charisma made him a ratings goldmine. (CBS Photo Archive)

offer Ed Sullivan $60,000 for three appearances on my show, and if he accepts, I assure my viewers he will not be allowed to wiggle, bump, grind—or smile."

Sullivan still had to find a way to mitigate the Elvis backlash. Ed's car accident that summer created a problem: he wouldn't return in time for Elvis' debut appearance on September 9, so he wouldn't be there to reassure those viewers whom the singer would upset. Guest hosting that night was Charles Laughton, a classically trained English actor who introduced the evening's performers with an ornate British accent. Ed made an unusual decision in creating the show's running order: the rock 'n' roller would not appear until three other acts had performed. This decision contradicted his longstanding practice of opening with his biggest attraction. Given the fee being paid Elvis and the excitement around his appearance, he was unquestionably the evening's headliner. But Ed was burying him in the lineup, as if to say: I'm booking this kid, but he's not taking over the show.

So that evening's audience first saw an acrobatic team, the Amin Brothers, one of whom spun the other into a virtual blur; Dorothy Sarnoff, a star from Broadway's *The*

Colonel Tom Parker, Elvis, and Sullivan, backstage before Elvis' second Sullivan show appearance. Parker, realizing Sullivan needed an Elvis booking, charged the showman an unprecedented $50,000 for three appearances. (CBS Photo Archive)

King and I, who sang "Something Wonderful"; and the Vagabonds, a four-man comedy-music team who goofed through a mock Hawaiian number.

Elvis' segment was broadcast from a soundstage in Hollywood, where the twenty-one-year-old singer was filming *Love Me Tender*. He stood in a spotlight by himself on a darkened stage, dressed in a checked sport coat, armed with a guitar and a glistening pompadour and extravagant sideburns. He was clearly nervous, as if uncomfortable with all the attention. He mumbled a hello with an aw-shucks humbleness, then launched into the mid tempo "Don't Be Cruel," as his male backup group, the Jordanaires, doo-wopped along. When he introduced his next song, the slow ballad

The hips that shook a nation: Elvis' second appearance on the Sullivan show, October 28, 1956. Adults were horrified, and Elvis was burned in effigy. (CBS Photo Archive)

"Love Me Tender," he stammered, getting the words out on his second try. His two-song set was restrained, even tentative, yet his female fans were enraptured; they voiced their affection with high-pitched screams.

Later in the hour Elvis performed again, this time with his band around him: drums, bass, and rhythm guitar, with the Jordanaires clapping and harmonizing. The tune was "Ready Teddy," not much more than a straight rhythm and blues workout, yet its foot-tapping immediacy seemed to set him free. The camera pulled away as he turned into a dervish, revealing all of him, dancing to the rhythm with his guitar in one arm. To viewers not used to seeing rock 'n' roll dancing he may have appeared possessed, his hips thrumming back and forth with the beat. His fans sounded almost crazed as they screeched with helpless adoration.

When the tune ended he had to pause to catch himself. "Thank you very much— whew!" He was relaxed and warmed up, a dangerous combination. Before continuing, he did a little business: "Mr. Sullivan, we know that somewhere out there, you're looking in, and all the boys here and myself and everybody out here are looking forward to seeing you back on television." With that, he set up his final number: "Friends, as a great philosopher once said. . . . *You ain't nothin' but a hound dog!*" And here he leapt into the song like a man hurling over Niagra Falls, letting go of his guitar to snarl-sing "Hound Dog." The girls erupted and he was in full motion, swiveling, dancing, all the way loose, driving every part of his body to the beat.

In response, the camera pulled up to show only his upper torso—the operator had been readied for this moment, and viewers were not given a direct shot of the volcano. Yet the limited camera angle didn't dampen the effect—if anything, his facial expression, the abandon on his face, was more potent than even his gyrating hips. This was untamed beatific energy, the definition of charisma, a bolt of white-hot energy. The all-girl cheering section sounded like it was on the verge of storming the stage. Never before had so much female sexual desire been broadcast into so many American living rooms.

The evening was a decisive ratings triumph, garnering a 43.7 Trendex rating, translating to some sixty million people, or about a third of the country—the largest television audience to date. Indeed, Elvis' performance of "Hound Dog" that night would be one of a small handful of moments that defined the decade. However, the ratings win was a Pyrrhic victory for Sullivan; the Trendex number masked a deep unhappiness.

Critics, predictably, kept the singer at arm's length. "From his extensive repertoire of assaults on the American ear, Mr. Presley included 'Hound Dog,'" sniffed *The New York Times'* Jack Gould. More worrisome for Ed, viewers were upset. Gould's paper printed a raft of letters about Presley's debut on Sullivan, most of them profoundly outraged. Typical of the responses was that of Howard Spalding, a high school principal in Mount Vernon, New York, who wrote, "If the adverse public reaction that follows an unfortunate performance such as this were directed at the sponsor, would it not cause advertisers to consider more carefully what they wished to present to the public?" Harry Feldman, a high school music teacher, complained, "One shudders to contemplate the cultural level of the next generation."

Mrs. Rhoda Frank attempted something of a defense of Presley: "Adults who forever misunderstand the desires of these teenagers immediately took up the cries of 'suggestive performance,' 'degrading routines,' and 'sexual gyrations.' Believe me, the teenagers were not aware of this interpretation until it was presented to them by the unhealthy few." But Mrs. May Zeoli gave notice: "The few studios that welcome rock 'n' roll and vile characters should be warned that a license to operate a TV station is a privilege that can be taken away by the authorities."

At this point Ed sought to navigate two opposing currents. He wanted to assuage his audience's fears, and he also wanted to keep riding the Presley ratings tidal wave. For the singer's second appearance on October 28, Ed, now recuperated from his car crash, attempted to play both sides. He spaced Elvis' appearances at three points in the program—ensuring that Trendex ratings stayed high throughout the hour—but again did not allow the singer to open. Instead, he began the show with a dose of pure virtue, an Irish children's choir, thirty kids singing a sweet Gaelic folk tune accompanied by piano. Their performance was churchy, with slow tempos and plenty of close-ups of their angelic faces. Clearly, the Sullivan show had not been overtaken by the forces of licentiousness. As Ed led the applause, he made light of the tensions underlying this evening. "Some people have wondered if that little boy in a kilt is Elvis Presley—it's not," he intoned, getting a solid chortle.

When he introduced Elvis, the girls screamed as if they had glimpsed an apparition. Dressed in a light-colored blazer and a skinny tie, the singer seemed to have grown more comfortable with an audience even in the weeks since his first appearance. But the camera didn't share that comfort: it shot his rendition of the finger-snapping "Don't Be Cruel" mainly from the shoulders up. Again, though, the singer couldn't be contained. He projected physical exuberance with a head shot alone, and when he added seductive little vocal twists to his melody line, while sending a knowing smile out to his fans, they deluged him with shrieks.

Before Elvis' second number Sullivan walked on and shook his hand, having to labor to stop the female screaming for a little chitchat. Ed told the audience that Elvis sang this next number, the theme song to the film *Love Me Tender*—his first film, released just seven weeks earlier—in a scene in which "his three brothers come home from the Confederate armies . . . and he sings this song to his mother and his young bride." Certainly, Ed's comments implied, this boy's heart was in the right place; based on Ed's setup the song was almost sanctimonious. The studio audience clearly agreed that Elvis was adorable. As he crooned the moody "Love Me Tender," with minimal movement, it seemed a riot was about to break out, with spontaneous shrieks at melodic pauses. Frantic "shushes" were heard, producing temporary quiet, yet as he finished the final chorus an intense burst of female energy overwhelmed the studio sound system.

As the screams subsided, Ed joined Presley on the set. He tried to talk about the singer's next song—"Now Elvis is going to be back in just a few minutes . . ."—yet the girls cut him off. He and Elvis chatted for a few moments while waiting for the wave to crest, but it wouldn't, so Ed gave up. "All right, *c'mon!*" he shouted, gesturing with his arms to let the screams loose.

To calm the audience, Elvis had to walk offstage, leaving Ed to address the older folks at home. "I can't figure this darn thing out. He just goes like this"—and here Ed did his own little hip shake, earning a few stray female shrieks—"and everybody yells." The showman was placing himself on the side of the reasonable adults in the audience, who couldn't figure it out either.

Before Sullivan went to commercial, he told viewers of Elvis' recent visit to his Delmonico apartment. The singer had startled Sylvia and her friends during an afternoon card game. Ed said that in his conversation with Presley that day, he mentioned to Elvis that he liked the melody to "Love Me Tender," to which the singer replied, that's no wonder, it's based on a Stephen Foster tune. Again, Ed's story attempted to offer a life raft to his older viewers: this wild rock 'n' roller's song was actually based on something as square as a nineteenth-century folk song.

While waiting for Elvis' second appearance that night, the teenagers in the audience had to endure Senor Wences, the Spanish ventriloquist who used his own hand as his dummy, painting it to resemble a face. The audience laughed delightedly as Wences' hand chirped back at him in quirky Spanish-accented phrases. A Sullivan favorite, Wences appeared twenty-three times over the years.

When the camera cut to Elvis, for the first time that evening he had left his guitar backstage, so nothing covered his mid section. He acknowledged Ed's introduction with characteristic politeness: "Thank you very much, Mr. Sullivan." The Jordanaires began harmonizing a slow ballad, and Elvis started singing "Love Me," turning toward Ed offstage during a melodic pause: "It's a new one, Ed," getting a few laughs for his effort. He stumbled on the lyrics but kept going, to the clear joy of his fans. As he gently swayed they shrieked at most every pause.

The moment he finished, Ed came on the set. "I want to thank all you youngsters, you made a promise you wouldn't yell during his songs, and you're very, very good—you haven't," he said. Yet they *had* screamed, in ways that no previous Sullivan audience ever had. Ed appeared almost too eager to congratulate them on their supposed good behavior, as if by praising wayward children he could encourage improvement.

He kept the lid on the teenage energy by allowing Elvis only one song this set, forcing the singer's fans to sit through other acts. Joyce Grenfell, a very proper British comedienne dressed as a grande dame with long white gloves, warbled a novelty tune. Then the full Broadway cast of Frank Loesser's *The Most Happy Fella* kicked and twirled across the stage in a series of visually rich musical dance numbers.

When Elvis came back for his final set, he appeared to be in a lighthearted mood. So too, were his fans. They had behaved, or so they had been told, but they didn't want to anymore. The singer's mere appearance provoked screams that suggested a fire had broken out in the theater. He asked, "Ladies and gentlemen, ah, could I have your attention, please?" and he flashed a beguiling smile, suddenly getting near silence. He started to play with the audience, as if its excitement level could be increased. "I'd like to tell you that we're going to do a sad song for you," he said with a big grin. "This here song is one of the saddest songs you ever heard . . . it really tells a story, friends . . ." He pretended to jumpstart the song several times, teasing the audience with his head fakes, each time eliciting a groan of female anticipation, each time pulling back for a toothy smile, his well-lubricated pompadour glistening in the studio lights.

And then he did it. Presley catapulted into the rapid-fire growl of "Hound Dog"—the song had hardly ever been rendered this fast. For the first time that evening, viewers got all of Elvis, his hips gone mad, the camera pulling back to show full torso, his whole body a quivering, dancing blur. For a moment he caught himself, clearly shaking his head *no*, as if to say, *I shouldn't shake like that*, and he stood ramrod stiff—which lasted all of four beats, after which the dam broke.

As the rock beat kept up a foot-tapping rhythm, he swiveled with untrammeled abandon; not only were his hips gyrating, *everything* about him was gyrating. He was a human zigzag, his lip upturned, his legs akimbo, his head bobbing, unshackled from anything that had come before, dancing and weaving across the stage in immoderate happiness. He wasn't just singing rock 'n' roll, he *was* rock 'n' roll; this was freedom and joy and sex all wrapped up into a moment of spontaneous beatitude. The girls were out of control, their promises of restraint broken and forgotten, their screams erecting a wall of sound over which Elvis was hardly audible. As he concluded his two-and-half-minute revolution, he breathlessly grinned and waved good-bye: "Until we meet again, may God bless you, like he's blessed me." His fans shrieked as if they had been hypnotized. Based on the studio audience's response, this had to be one of the most successful Sullivan shows ever.

But it wasn't. While the evening provided yet another overwhelming ratings victory, far outpacing *The Steve Allen Show*, a segment of the audience felt more deeply upset than ever. Elvis was hanged in effigy in Nashville, and a group of concerned citizens in St. Louis got together and burned him in effigy. That a segment of Sullivan's audience was so unhappy presented him with a dilemma. The singer's contract called for one more appearance. But how was Ed to handle an act that drove ratings into the stratosphere while so profoundly alienating so many of his viewers? He had always produced his show with the belief that there was a single audience, but now, for the first time, there were two very distinct audiences, irreconcilably so. Even for a master showman, rock 'n' roll was proving to be a difficult beast to handle.

Yet Sullivan had a solution. For Elvis' final appearance on January 6, Ed attempted to heal the schism that wouldn't be healed. Pleasing both the Elvis fans and Elvis haters, if such a minefield could be tiptoed through, required him to present the singer with a strict guiding hand.

Ed was in good spirits as he opened the show that night. "Ladies and gentlemen, we have a big show, a real big shew," he said, getting a hearty chuckle with his imitation of Sullivan impressionists, "with Elvis Presley headlining tonight." At the singer's name the female contingent erupted into a full-throated screech. "You promised," Ed said, smiling and pointing up at the offenders, earning him another rippling laugh.

For the first time in his three appearances, Ed presented Elvis first. The singer was dressed in a glittery vest, his moist pompadour letting fly with a few seductively errant strands. Surrounded by the Jordanaires, he opened with a languorous, intimate version of "Love Me Tender," in which the camera, appropriately, focused on a close facial shot. He stopped only to give a short smile—he had, if possible, grown still more charismatic since his last appearance—before launching into an aching "Heartbreak Hotel." His shoulders quaked with the opening guitar twangs, and his entire body shimmied with the descending bass line's plaintive cry. Or rather, it *seemed* as if his entire body was moving, but the camera's eye stayed firmly fixed at chest level, so viewers at home had to surmise what the rest of him was doing based on his flurry of shoulder movements.

As the song whirled to a close, Elvis gave an aw-shucks thanks to his fans for making the next tune his biggest hit of the year—"We really are thankful for all the success you made us have, and everything"—then jumped into a bouncy, midtempo "Don't Be Cruel." He was having fun, flashing his high-wattage smile, though he wasn't moving much. At the song's high point he started working it, spinning into a hip-shaking dance, but again, television viewers couldn't see it. With this restricted camera angle it became clear—*the camera would not show anything beneath his chest.* The spontaneous choreography of his infamous pelvis was only implied, not seen. Ed was censoring Elvis. As the third song ended it was clear, too, that the audience had been browbeaten into its best behavior; they were curiously silent except for right after a song. Elvis, to prompt shrieks during songs, was reduced to periodically cupping his hand to his ear, which coaxed short screeches from his more free-spirited fans. But the wall of squeals came only as the singer danced offstage to end his set.

The show moved on to English ventriloquist Arthur Worsley, whose dummy taunted him. His dummy spoke without moving its lips just as the ventriloquist did, earning hearty audience laughter. Following Worsley was Lonnie Satin, a very stiff black man in a tuxedo who crooned the ballad "I Believe" to polite applause.

Next up was twenty-three-year-old comic Carol Burnett, who pretended to be various girl singers at Broadway auditions, including the Nose Singer, the Jaw Singer, Miss Big Deal, and Miss Old Timer. Burnett simultaneously worked the camera like a close friend and connected with the studio audience, getting continuous waves of laughter with her wildly flexible facial and vocal contortions.

Elvis' second set kicked off with a straight blues romp, "Too Much," featuring a riffing guitarist and a gyrating Presley. But home viewers didn't see much of the singer; the camera cut diplomatically to the guitarist's fingertips. Elvis' swiveling hips fueled a screaming mania in the studio audience, but home viewers were left wondering why, hearing a legion of inflamed studio fans while they got a close-up of guitar picking. For the next tune, the jaunty finger-snapper "When My Blue Moon Turns to Gold Again," the camera was equally chaste, hovering on Elvis' face, venturing no lower than chest level. He spun offstage to end his set, after which Sullivan told the screaming girls "rest your larynx"—the singer was coming back.

Ed brought on boxer Sugar Ray Robinson for a celebrity chat, a common feature on the show. Considered by many experts to be the greatest pugilist in the sport's history, Robinson wore a bandage over his left eye, having just lost the title to Gene Fullmer four days earlier. Ed chastised him, mostly good-naturedly, for what he called the boxer's mistakes in his recent bout. "I was talking to Joe Louis the other day and he said he didn't know what happened to you the other night," Ed said, telling Sugar Ray he needed some lessons—which Ed proceeded to give. First, he taught Ray to clinch, pinning the boxer's arms to his side to prevent him from punching; Robinson accepted the tip with a humble smile. To finish his lesson, Ed demonstrated the effective counterpunch: "Just remember what Sullivan tells you— hit him there!" and he sent a mock left jab to Robinson's mid section.

Following the boxer was ballerina Nancy Crompton, who twirled in a tutu to a frantic cancan beat, rippling across the stage faster than the camera could follow. Then a rotund Brazilian singer, Leny Eversong, growled and belted out "El Cumbanchero" over a bongo-driven Latin beat. She was succeeded by a four-man German acrobatic team, the Gutees, two of whom were dressed as gorillas; their act was a two-minute melee of zoo animals versus zookeepers.

In the audience, Ed introduced two sports stars, Don Budge, the first player to win tennis' Grand Slam, and Jackie Robinson, who had broken baseball's color line in 1947, and who had recently retired. Ed gave a short speech about the greatness of Robinson's career and led a second round of applause for him.

Following this was Bory and Bor, a ballroom dancer in a tuxedo who waltzed with a life-size female mannequin dressed in an elegant evening gown. Accompanied by a wild brassy beat, he flew around the stage with her in his arms, sometimes using the mannequin as support for a leap, sometimes spinning the mannequin as if she was a real woman. His act was brief, no more than ninety seconds, and he whirled so unpredictably the effect was akin to visual chaos. After big applause, Sullivan brought back on Leny Eversong, who belted out "Jezebel" over an orchestral tango. Then Ed introduced two sportswriters in the audience from competing publications, the *Daily News'* Gene Ward and the *New York Post's* Jimmy Cannon; this was diplomacy on Sullivan's part—he worked for the *Daily News* but he wanted good press from the *Post*.

Before Ed brought Elvis back out for the evening's finale, he told viewers how committed the singer was to a charity, Hungarian relief. (Hungarians had attempted to revolt against the Soviet regime in October 1956 and were brutally suppressed.) Elvis was scheduled to perform a benefit for the charity, Ed told the audience, but in the meantime, "because he feels so keenly, he urges us all that immediate relief is needed, so long before his benefit he wants to remind you to send in your checks to your various churches, Red Cross, etc." The audience had never put "Elvis" and "church" in the same sentence, so Ed was revealing a new dimension to the singer. And, if Elvis was such an avid supporter of the forces battling communism, then he couldn't be a bad influence.

The camera cut to Presley and the Jordanaires, looking solemn, who sang an a capella version of the gospel song "Peace in the Valley." It was a lugubrious rendering, with Elvis' voice submerged in the supporting harmonies and the singer standing as motionless as a statue. Still, the camera took no chances, shooting him only from the chest up. His fans likely expected some combustible fireworks from his final performance, yet this sober performance threw a damp blanket over the singer's fire. Never had Elvis been so grave. In the face of such propriety even the singer's screaming section sounded muted, barely screeching louder than the general applause.

To wrap up the evening, Ed came on and chatted with Elvis about the singer's plans. Lest any doubt linger about whether Presley was a subversive force—though after tonight's neutered showing he threatened no one—Ed summed up his experience with Elvis: "I wanted to say to Elvis Presley and the country, that this is a real decent, fine boy. We want to say we've never had a pleasanter experience with a big name on our show, you're thoroughly alright." As he often did, he was speaking in code to his audience, letting them know that he himself, the unstinting watchdog, personally approved of the pompadoured singer. In response, Elvis lit up a winsome smile, the girls screeched, then Ed bid the audience good night.

In the following weeks, Sullivan managed to avoid significant backlash from disgruntled older viewers. His decision to restrict the camera work let these viewers know that their concerns were paramount. He could still be relied upon to safeguard the family living room. It helped, too, that by Elvis' third appearance the singer was virtually omnipresent. His recordings had held the number one chart spot for twenty-five weeks in 1956, and would hold it for another twenty-five weeks in 1957, a feat never since achieved. So any complaints about the singer's corrupting influence now had a diffuse target.

Still, problems loomed. Elvis was only the vanguard. Even a brief glance at the horizon revealed that rock's infectious energy—plus the baby boom that began right after World War II—was spawning a new generation of musicians. Would they all be this difficult?

CHAPTER THIRTEEN

The Globetrotter

T HE *STEVE ALLEN SHOW*, although it had scooped Sullivan on Elvis, rarely provided a serious ratings challenge to Ed. Allen was immeasurably wittier but lacked Sullivan's talent as a producer. Yet since they both put on shows every Sunday night at 8 P.M., at times their head-to-head competition took on a vituperative tone. Newspapers portrayed their competition as a feud, but more accurately it was a straightforward ratings battle with some accompanying grousing. After Elvis, Sullivan vowed never again to let Allen get ahead of him with a new act, and he learned to respect Allen's sense of what was current and compelling.

In October 1956, just weeks before Elvis' second Sullivan appearance, word got out that Allen planned a tribute to James Dean. The screen star's mix of brooding nonconformism and diffident sex appeal had rocketed him to fame after only two major films, *Rebel Without a Cause* and *East of Eden*, both released in 1955. Yet Dean, as if guided by his own legend, died in a high-speed car crash in September of that year, at age twenty-four. His last film, *Giant*, co-starring Elizabeth Taylor and Rock Hudson, was about to be released in the fall of 1956. Allen, hoping to capitalize on the Dean buzz as he had on Elvis, was negotiating to show a preview from *Giant*, and working on booking Dean's aunt and uncle, who had raised the actor.

Sullivan saw an opportunity. With his close relationship with film studios, securing the *Giant* preview was quick work; he also booked Dean's aunt and uncle before Allen could. On October 14, Sullivan presented his Dean tribute. (Sharing the bill were ballerina Nancy Crompton, Japanese aerialist Takeo Usui, and a performing monkey named Jinx.) The ratings grab brought howls of protest from Allen, who told reporters he couldn't believe that it was Ed himself who was "responsible for such tactics"—it must have been a Sullivan staffer. Ed, calling Allen a "crybaby," retorted, "My show is a one-man operation and he knows it." Furthermore, he said, "Most of the variety show things started on our show—not that I'm a genius—they just started there. And now I'm being accused of 'pirating!'" Hence their feud, such as it was, began.

The two showmen had a few more skirmishes. Allen scooped Sullivan in January 1957 by booking Charles Van Doren, the boyishly Brahmin university professor then wowing audiences with his phenomenal success on the quiz show *Twenty One*. (Van Doren was later disgraced in the resulting quiz show scandal.) That summer Allen again cried foul after a stolen booking, this time over Harry Belafonte, the Jamaican-raised actor and singer starring in 1957's *Island in the Sun*. In the late spring, Sullivan announced that Belafonte would appear on his show, confounding the Allen staff, who had offered the performer $25,000 to appear first on their show. In June, Ed presented a clip of Belafonte singing "Lead Man Holler" from *Island in the Sun*—but without the performer himself.

He didn't explain the Belafonte no-show, but he did succeed in disrupting Allen's plans for a ratings win. Allen's producer, Jules Green, claimed that Sullivan was "cheating the public" by claiming he would present Belafonte without actually booking him. When reporters asked Ed for comment, he replied, "I have no comment to make. I have no comment on either of those punks." Ed's feint with the Belafonte booking proved he could out jab the Allen show at will, but in truth Allen's Nielsen victories were few enough that Ed needn't have bothered.

In fact, there was little that offered Sullivan competition in the 1956–57 season. Month after month the show was one of television's top rated. The program had long been a magnet for performers, offering a good payday as well as major exposure. At this point its ratings were so unchallenged that it offered any performer—no matter how renowned—a big bounce. (With one exception: when Ed called Colonel Tom Parker to book more Elvis appearances and he heard the singer's new price—$200,000—he promptly hung up.) With his virtually unlimited access to talent, *The Ed Sullivan Show* became a live canvas that Ed filled however he wanted. Like an artist who starts with a basic knack but grows to enjoy true command over his medium, the showman was now freer and stronger than ever.

In September he booked Edward G. Robinson to perform a scene from Paddy Chayefsky's play *Middle of the Night* on the same show with legendary French vocalist Edith Piaf, who sang "The Poor People of Paris." A few weeks later he interviewed screen stars Rita Hayworth, Jack Lemmon, and Robert Mitchum on the same bill with French comedian Salvador, followed by the Bokaras acrobats, who cavorted with a teeterboard. In November Bing Crosby bantered with comic Phil Silvers before crooning "True Love," after which Julie Andrews sang a Broadway medley and Kate Smith belted out "God Bless America." Later that month Fats Domino—the pioneering rock 'n' roller had five songs in the Top 40 that year—rollicked through "Blueberry Hill" on the same bill with Conn and Mann, a tap dancing duo from New York's Copacabana nightclub.

At the end of November, Maria Callas rendered a selection from Puccini's opera *Tosca* on an evening in which Ed (on film) interviewed Clark Gable on location; later that hour he showed clips of the 1956 All American football squad. In an early December program, Ed opened with vocalist Rosemary Clooney singing "April in Paris," followed by the Princeton Triangle Club (men performing in drag), after which comic Myron Cohen spun his Borscht Belt humor. The show ended with the Modern Screen Awards, featuring appearances by Natalie Wood, Kirk Douglas, Tony Curtis, and Doris Day.

In January 1957 Elvis made his third appearance, with comic Carol Burnett and baseball star Jackie Robinson. Later that month jazz trumpeter Louis Armstrong

A cameo appearance on the Sullivan show by baseball legend Jackie Robinson, who broke the sport's color line in 1947. Sullivan revered Robinson. (Globe Photos)

shared the bill with vocalist Ella Fitzgerald, followed by two Metropolitan Opera stars performing a scene from *Madame Butterfly*, on the same evening ventriloquist Senor Wences earned laughs by chattering with his painted hand. In February Benny Goodman and his big band swung through "Just One of Those Things" on the same bill with young stand-up comedian Johnny Carson, who did impressions of Sullivan and journalist Edward R. Murrow. In March Fred Astaire and Jane Powell dazzled through a tap-dance routine on the same bill with a tap duet by Gene Kelly and Leslie Caron. In April Olympic weightlifter Paul Anderson hoisted twenty people on a show in which ancient vaudeville team Smith and Dale played a sketch about taxes and Henry Fonda introduced a clip from his new movie *Twelve Angry Men*.

Later in the month Bill Haley and the Comets—one of the very first rock 'n' roll bands—romped on "40 Cups of Coffee" and "Rudy's Rock" (with the sax player running through the audience blowing his horn) on a show with Barbara & Her Dog, who performed novelty math tricks. As the weather turned warm, the Corps de Ballet danced a segment of "Czardas" on the same bill with comedian Dewey "Pigmeat" Markham. In mid summer Burt Lancaster performed a comedy sketch with Barbara Nichols, dancer Gene Kelly danced a soft-shoe with Ed—just kidding around—and the Cypress Garden water-skiers showed off their aquatic skills on location. A few weeks later the Everly Brothers harmonized on "Bye, Bye Love" and Ed (on film) appeared at a premiere of the new movie *The Prince and the Showgirl* along with Marilyn Monroe, Arthur Miller, and Robert F. Kennedy.

When the dizzying 1956–57 season concluded and the Nielsen ratings were tallied, Ed found he had succeeded past any reasonable expectation. *The Ed Sullivan Show* was television's number two–ranked program, behind only the perennially top-

With bandleader Benny Goodman during a rehearsal for the Sullivan
show in the 1950s. (Globe Photos)

rated *I Love Lucy*. Close to forty million people a week watched his Sunday showcase. A few years earlier he had used tributes to moguls like Samuel Goldwyn and
Darryl Zanuck to boost ratings. Now, on small screens in living rooms across the
country, he held a comparable stature. Producing a program at its zenith in its ninth
year, he was fully in command: of his show, of his place at the network, and of his
position as a cultural tastemaker.

Not that his eminence as an impresario meant he had grown correspondingly polished as a master of ceremonies. If he was marginally more at ease onstage in 1957
than in 1948, in essence he remained the same monotone show host, continuing to
fumble and sputter despite his overly cautious approach. Sullivan's malapropisms
became show business lore. The talent agents forced to wait outside the stage door
in the "Wailing Wall" area during rehearsal traded stories of Sullivan's missteps,
and they had no lack of material. Comedian Jack Carter was introduced, variously,
as John Crater, Jack Carson, John Kerr, and, once, Carson McCullers. A performing
troupe from New Zealand was called "the fierce Maori tribe from New England."
Famed clarinetist Benny Goodman was lauded as a trumpeter, Roberta Peters became Robert Sherwood, and Ed once introduced Robert Merrill by saying "I'd like
to *prevent* Robert Merrill." Citizens of Miami regularly sent letters correcting his
pronunciation of their city's name—he pronounced it "My-am-ah"—and he always
referred to Baltimore as "Ball-tee-more." He never went through a show without gar-
bling syntax, and polysyllabic words could be mangled to unintelligibility.

Other entertainers took great sport with the showman's stilted stage presence. "Ed Sullivan is the only man who can brighten up a room by leaving it," quipped Joe E. Lewis. Jack Benny asked, "What would happen, Ed, if you weren't here to introduce the acts? As a friend, let me give you some advice. Don't ever stay home to find out." Henny Youngman observed, "In Africa the cannibals adored him. They thought he was some new kind of frozen food." (Eddie Cantor, an almost lone dissenting voice, wrote in his 1957 memoir that Sullivan had "a sense of showmanship second to no one in the business.")

Pop singer Connie Francis remembered dreading being called over to shake Ed's hand after a performance. "You never knew what he was going to say," Francis said. "He was so funny—he didn't mean to be funny. I think the average guy watching television said, 'I could speak better than that.'"

In dress rehearsal, Ed once called over singer Jack Jones to chat, considered a major career boost among performers. "Wasn't your father Allen Jones?" Ed asked the singer. "He still is," Jones replied, getting a big audience chuckle. After rehearsal, Sullivan told Jones that he liked the humorous exchange and wanted to re-create it in that evening's broadcast. During the show Sullivan called over Jones as planned, but Ed goofed up the setup question, asking: "*Isn't* your father Allen Jones?" And all Jones could say was "yes," which fell flat. After the show Ed was furious. Jones tried to explain: "But Mr. Sullivan, you didn't say it the way you said it during rehearsal." "Don't tell me!" Ed retorted. "You should have said '*He still is!*'" Sullivan refused to book Jones for a long time afterward.

"Sometimes you wondered," recalled comedienne Carol Burnett, of the showman's many fumbles. Causing many of these stumbles and stutters was nerves. Even as an established star he battled stage fright, and several Sullivan staffers said that he remained nervous onstage throughout the run of the program. Many veteran performers, of course, suffer stage jitters despite a long career, yet manage to transcend it. With Ed, turning on a camera never stopped prompting a profound dampening. The feisty, opinionated Broadway gossip with a quick left jab became almost funereal, careful to the point of caricature. And he was loath to attempt a change. His sponsor's ad agency, Kenyon & Eckhardt, occasionally suggested he liven up his stage presence, maybe develop an act or tell a few jokes. Ed rejected them summarily. "You don't screw with success," he said.

Paradoxically, his antistyle endeared him with the audience. Being maladroit made him far more likable. Viewers felt they were getting the real thing; clearly this man was anything but a slick salesman. Ed was just Ed. He wasn't part of that alien tribe known as entertainers, or so it seemed, but instead appeared far closer to an audience member. One night he introduced an actress in the audience by saying "she's currently *starving* on Broadway"—perhaps a Freudian slip, given his own hungry struggle as a young Broadway columnist—and then realized his mistake. The audience began to laugh, and he began to laugh with them. Everyone enjoyed a hardy chuckle at Ed's awkwardness. To think, just four hours earlier this man had taken complete dictatorial control over the show, issuing ultimatums, slashing comics' well-honed gags, stepping on toes at will. And here he was on camera, as nonthreatening as the average uncle Charlie.

Sullivan's need to keep his feisty, combative nature off camera was not shared by the man he so envied and admired through the years, Walter Winchell. After some coaxing, Winchell launched his first television show in 1952, pushed into it as radio faltered in the face of TV's bounding growth and Walter's own radio show fell from the top ten. His debut was a telecast of his radio gossip show, with Winchell poised near the typewriter and the set decorated as a busy city newsroom. He projected an intense, on-the-edge energy in his broadcast, just as he always had in his radio show. He even wore his fedora on the air, as if attempting to recreate central casting's idea of a hard-bitten newshound. It was the same persona that he and Ed had projected as they ran up and down Broadway in the 1930s: know-it-all, tough, jazzed up from a second cup of joe. Ed, off the air, was still essentially the same: acerbic and willing to lead with his elbows if necessary; it was only when the camera blinked on that he became the living room's monochromatic supplicant. Yet Walter didn't adapt. Unwilling or unable to fit into the cooler environment of 1950s television, he was a character in the wrong play.

His gossip, always an affront to polite society, now traveled in territory the public wouldn't enter. In his debut television season he announced that President Truman had once belonged to the Ku Klux Klan—a ludicrous charge that Truman angrily dismissed. After suffering abysmal ratings—at one point he was rated 111th—ABC canceled his simulcast television-radio show in 1955. He approached NBC about a television program, offering to host the *Comedy Hour* opposite Sullivan in that show's waning days, but was turned down. He also queried CBS, and as word leaked that he might get a show, Sullivan emitted howls of protest, or so Winchell claimed. Network executive Hubbell Robinson released a statement that CBS had not in fact mentioned Winchell's proposed show to Sullivan. This prompted Walter to shoot an angry note to Robinson: "Dear Hub, This is BULLSH!"

Desperate to get back on television, he organized his own sponsors and re-approached NBC, succeeding in getting *The Walter Winchell Show* signed for thirteen weeks in the fall of 1955. His choice of format revealed a telling irony: it was a variety show that Walter hosted without lengthy introductions—a veritable copy of the Sullivan show. Having so long been ahead of Ed in the public's eye, Walter was reduced to imitating him. Adding ignominy, after a respectable start the show's ratings quickly began to plummet. Oddly, even in his variety show he maintained the storied Winchell edge, wearing his fedora and tossing cigarette butts onstage. The show's director, Alan Handley, noted how out of place Walter seemed. "He couldn't integrate himself into a TV show, and we couldn't feel superior to him the way we could to Sullivan." *The Walter Winchell Show* was canceled within three months of its debut.

The next tidal wave to engulf television was just barely visible at the end of the 1956–57 season. *Gunsmoke*, a radio show since 1952, debuted on CBS-TV in 1955, and by the following year rose to be the eighth-rated show; down at number nineteen that season was *Wyatt Earp*. With the advent of the 1957–58 season the Western began proliferating like well-watered sagebrush: *Tales of Wells Fargo*, *Wagon Train*, and *Have Gun, Will Travel* were all in the top twenty. *Wyatt Earp* climbed to number six and *Gunsmoke* became television's top-rated show.

ABC, enjoying success with *Wyatt Earp* on Tuesday night, made a move to grab Sunday night with still another Western, *Maverick*. Offering a fresh take on the traditional format, the show starred James Garner as the humorous antihero who was better with a wisecrack than with a six-gun. Debuting in September 1957 in the 7:30 time slot, for its first few weeks it was a straight western, but as it found its comedic voice its ratings started climbing. On November 12, 1957, *Maverick*'s Trendex rating bested *The Ed Sullivan Show*'s for the first time.

Sullivan faced an intractable ratings challenge in *Maverick*. Against *Comedy Hour* he could wait for it to present less interesting weeks and then produce specials; against *The Steve Allen Show* he easily out-scooped and out-produced the witty show host. When the quiz show craze began in the mid 1950s, *Time* reported that Ed even stood prepared for that: "He is ready to fight fire with fire if this becomes the year of the big money quiz shows. Says he: 'If what people want are giveaways then we'll add giveaways, too.'" But how could he compete with a Western?

He had a plan. If the Western transported audiences to a distant locale, he would transport them to an even more distant locale, to a world more exotic than the dusty plains. He had long sprinkled acts from other countries into the show, yet they now came in a torrent. Sullivan's talent coordinator Jack Babb booked acts from far and wide: Japanese dancers, Taiwanese acrobats, Italian comedy group The Three Bragazzis, Viennese soprano Rita Streich, Spanish magician Rochiardi, singing group the Kim Sisters from Korea, and others.

But more than bringing international acts to the United States, Ed envisioned transporting the show across the globe. In late 1957 he began planning to produce a program at the Brussels World's Fair. It would cost an extra $50,000 so Ed romanced his sponsor, Eastman Kodak (Ford was now cosponsoring with other advertisers). He convinced Kodak to foot the bill in exchange for a product endorsement during the show; a Sullivan crew filmed the University of Rochester glee club singing in front of Kodak's corporate headquarters, to be shown during the World's Fair broadcast. How this related to the Fair was unclear, but it didn't matter; Ed had his funding.

In March 1958 he and a crew took a chartered flight to Belgium, toting a mass of studio equipment. For the Fair broadcast, Ed walked among the many pavilions, presenting the Ukrainian State Dance Group performing a hyperkinetic spear and sword dance, comic Jacques Tati pantomiming a French fisherman, and the London Symphony Orchestra rendering an excerpt from Wagner's *Lohengrin*. Making cameo appearances were Brigitte Bardot, Sophia Loren, and William Holden. Lest it all seem too far from home, Ed boasted about the American pavilion and included a section honoring the graves of American soldiers in Belgium. In deference to the fact that the United States was deep in the Cold War, and the Fair's theme was "A New Humanism"—the term made some viewers uneasy—Ed gave a short homily at the end making it clear he was against communism and in favor of religion.

The Cold War, however, didn't keep him from the season's biggest ratings triumph. In the spring of 1958 Russia's Moiseyev Ballet was earning hyperbolic reviews as it toured America. Contrary to their name, they were folk dancers, dressed in peasant garb, highly athletic and stylistically muscular. Their Madison Square Garden performance was so anticipated that scalpers sold $8 tickets for $80. Ed haggled for weeks with impresario Sol Hurok for the rights to present the dancers on his show. He dedicated the full hour to the Russian folk performers on the evening of June 29, scoring an artistic and commercial success. (Doubtless part of the appeal was a glimpse of a people that many Americans considered to be their foremost enemy.) Sullivan's Trendex rating was a healthy 40.3, topping *Maverick*'s 33.6 and Steve Allen's 21.4. (Sullivan's Trendex increased in the second half of the hour, as it usually did after *Maverick* ended at 8:30.)

Rock 'n' roll was the other driving force in Sullivan's formula for the 1957–58 season. Having discovered a ratings goldmine with his Elvis bookings, he now presented a bevy of pioneering artists. The Everly Brothers, invited for a string of appearances, sweetly harmonized through "Wake Up Little Susie" and "Be-Bop-a-Lula." The Champs romped through "Tequilla," the Platters doo-wopped "The Great Pretender," and Sam Cooke crooned "You Send Me." Riding the brief rockabilly wave, Gene Vincent and the Blue Caps had fun with "Dance to the Bop" and the Sparkletones rocked on "Black Slacks." Connie Francis wept her romantic teen lament "Who's Sorry Now?" Ed, like many of his viewers, felt that rock 'n' roll needed a tight leash, and he kept a watchful eye on the new arrivals.

Everything went well the night that Ed introduced Buddy Holly and the Crickets for their television debut in December 1957. Holly, in his signature horn-rimmed glasses and armed with a Fender Stratocaster, was backed by drums, rhythm guitar, and plucked upright bass. All the band members were clad in tuxedos as they rocked through their recent number one hit, "That'll Be the Day." The group followed it up with the rambunctious "Peggy Sue," which climbed to number five a month after the show.

When the group came back in January, however, Sullivan and Holly got into a verbal fisticuffs during rehearsal. Ed felt the lyrics to the group's "Oh Boy" were lewd: "All of my life I been a-waitin' / Tonight there'll be no hesitatin'." The verse was quaint by rock 'n' roll standards, yet Irving Berlin would never have penned it. Sullivan told Holly to choose another song. Holly, in a first for a Sullivan guest, issued his own ultimatum: it was that song or nothing. Ed, furious, but unwilling to lose the ratings boost—especially with *Maverick* submerging his Trendex numbers—relented. Still, he cut the Crickets from two songs to one, and placed the band toward the end of the show.

In that evening's broadcast, when Ed listed the Crickets in his opening remarks he pronounced their name correctly, but right before they played he introduced them as "Buddy Hollied and His Crickets!" That might have been merely a Sullivan malapropism, but when the camera cut to the band, both their lighting and sound were low. Holly tried to turn up his guitar, with limited result, then started singing at the top of his voice. As if in retaliation, the band jumped into double time during an instrumental break, allowing them to add a second verse to the song. When the camera cut back to Ed he was clearly livid, and didn't give the Crickets the customary after-song mention before going to the next act.

In addition to rock 'n' roll and many international attractions, Ed continued his all-inclusive Big Tent philosophy in the 1957–58 season. The Glenn Miller Orchestra swung standards, and balladeers Tony Bennett and Nat "King" Cole crooned. George Burns and Gracie Allen earned laughs with their vaudeville-style comedic patter. In January, Ed presented a twenty-two-minute segment of Eugene O'Neill's Pulitzer Prize–winning play *Long Day's Journey into Night*, starring Frederic

March and Florence Eldridge (but Ed insisted that one of the script's epithets be toned down). Actor Douglas Fairbanks recited the Rudyard Kipling poem "If" and famed playwright-actor-singer Noël Coward warbled a medley of his own songs. The cross-dressing men of the Princeton Triangle Club strutted "The Charleston," and eighty-four-year-old W.C. Handy, considered the father of the blues, made a cameo in a wheelchair.

For the kids, diminutive elephant Baby Opal frolicked, puppeteer Joe Castor painted a portrait along with his marionette, and eight-year-old piano player Joey Alfidi dazzled on "The Minute Waltz" as three beauty pageant contestants looked on admiringly. Johnny Carson did a stand-up routine about a children's show host with a hangover, and Carol Burnett sang a comic tune called "I Fell in Love with John Foster Dulles." (Dulles, Eisenhower's secretary of state, was famously dour, but he found Burnett's bit amusing and requested a copy. When reporters asked him why this young woman was singing about falling in love with him, he smiled and said, "I never talk about my private life in public.") The season's political guest was Eleanor Roosevelt, who paid tribute to Israel's tenth anniversary.

But Sullivan's 1957–58 season, despite its global talent show, big names, and fresh rock 'n' roll faces, suffered major ratings erosion in the face of the public's fascination with Westerns. Although *The Ed Sullivan Show* still ran ahead of ABC's *Maverick*, it tumbled from the previous season's number two spot all the way down to number nineteen. Of the eighteen shows that rated higher, seven of them were Westerns. *The Steve Allen Show* also contributed to the ratings fall, though Sullivan still ranked far ahead of Allen, who never entered the top twenty. This season was the first in which Sullivan grappled with more than one serious competitor in his time slot; ABC had always run a distant third. Now, the network's sagebrush and spurs offering was besting Sullivan on certain nights.

Aside from the ratings plunge, June 1958 offered Ed a consolation prize: the show reached its ten-year anniversary. Sullivan was virtually alone in his program's longevity and clearly alone in its success. All the other members of the class of 1948 were either gone or headed that way. *The Milton Berle Show* had been canceled in June 1956, and Arthur Godfrey's *Talent Scouts* would be cut in the summer of 1958 (though Berle would make two one-year comebacks and *Arthur Godfrey and His Friends* limped along to 1959). Sid Caesar's wildly popular *Your Show of Shows* had come and gone. Two other powerhouses of 1950s variety television, Jackie Gleason and Jack Benny, had run behind Sullivan since the 1955–56 season.

Newspapers, whose television critics had so uniformly panned Sullivan's debut, now considered it de rigueur to run an article feting the program's ten-year anniversary. *The New York Times* opined that, "During these ten years Mr. Sullivan has not improved perceptibly as a performer," yet still the show was "remarkably successful." The *Times* reporter, interviewing the showman in his Delmonico apartment, noted that while Ed was jet-lagged (from his trip to Brussels) and had suffered a terrible bout with his ulcer, he answered questions affably—many reporters were surprised at how conversational the showman could be offstage. Most notably, Sullivan claimed that he looked forward to perhaps five more years as a host-producer, after which he hoped to focus exclusively on producing. He was less equivocal in his *New York Journal-American* interview, claiming, "I'm going to quit in five years." As he waxed philosophic about his career, he explained why he booked impressionists to mock his stage persona: "I used to get letters that said I looked as if I took myself too seriously. Unfortunately I have a graver looking kisser than most."

CBS head Bill Paley, to honor the ten-year milestone, hosted a luncheon to which he invited all the network's executives, and he directed CBS vice president Larry Lowman to buy an expensive gift for Sullivan. Lowman called Marlo Lewis, who told him that Ed had been eyeing a Renoir oil painting at a gallery on 57th Street, not far from the Delmonico; Sylvia adored it and stopped to look at it every time she passed.

At the luncheon the guests were full of good spirits, as Paley and other top executives, Frank Stanton and Hubbell Robinson, reminisced with Sullivan, Lewis, bandleader Ray Bloch, and director Johnny Wray about the show's early days. After a couple hours of chatting and eating, Paley presented Sullivan with the gift, wrapped in brown paper. "Ed, here's something I know both you and Sylvia wanted. I am delighted we could find a way to show you how much we think of you and how happy we are that you are part of CBS."

Ed unwrapped the Renoir, and, unable to speak, put it in the middle of the table. Everyone looked at it, thinking Sullivan would soon make a comment. But Ed, speechless, reached into his pocket and took out his handkerchief to cover his eyes. He began to cry, softly, and then slumped in his chair, crying more freely. The Sullivan staff members said nothing, as the executives looked on with small smiles, though network president Frank Stanton seemed surprised. Pulling himself together, Ed gestured toward his production staff. "All of us thank you, Bill." He took a small drink of water, dried his eyes, shook hands with everyone, then took the painting and walked out the door. Afterward, Stanton asked Marlo Lewis, "What was all that about?"

Sullivan's wellspring of emotion, as Lewis recounted it, came from Ed at long last getting something he had so craved from CBS: personal recognition. When he was struggling in the early years they had offered the show to advertisers "with or without" Ed Sullivan; the show had been underfunded during his battle with *Comedy Hour*; and even as he prevailed it was only after an offer from NBC that the show was renamed *The Ed Sullivan Show*. Consequently, he developed a hard defensive shell against what he saw as the network's lack of appreciation.

In interviews in later years he never passed up a chance to hurl a gibe at CBS executives, using pointed language that left no doubt that he detested them. The network's executives were "ungrateful, impolite people," and Frank Stanton was "a hopeless case as a human," he told *Life* magazine in 1967. With the exception of Paley, that is. Ed always drew a distinction between the animus he felt toward the network management and Paley himself, whom Sullivan always respected. Now, Paley's thoughtful personal gift was a sign of something he felt he had seen far too little of, from the one executive whose opinion he held in esteem. He wasn't merely getting paid like a star, he was being treated like one.

Nevertheless, that summer he let it be known—Paley's simpatico notwithstanding—that his decisions about his show would not be guided by network management. Or, remarkably, even by his sponsors. Prompting a deep gasp of consternation from CBS and Ford, he announced that in July he would broadcast two programs from Las Vegas, otherwise known as Sin City.

Some of the show's staff could hardly believe it. Ed . . . in Vegas? It was as if the parish priest had decided to open a strip joint. In 1958 the gambling mecca was completely unredeemed, the closest thing to pure perdition on domestic soil, an id of greed and sex poking through the staid American superego. That Ed, who forbade cleavage on his show and shot Elvis from the waist up—and always had something for the youngsters—would broadcast from Vegas was unthinkable. A reporter from *Variety*, echoing a question wondered by many, asked him if Vegas wasn't a questionable location for *The Ed Sullivan Show*. "The fact that Jack Benny played a Vegas saloon made it okay for me and my sponsors," Ed replied. That was patently untrue; the head of Ford's ad agency, William Lewis, warned that the automaker did not want its name associated with Las Vegas. CBS's Frank Stanton called the Vegas shows highly inadvisable.

But Ed didn't care. After a successful ten-year run he was now in a position to lead rather than follow. And Las Vegas' Desert Inn had offered to put him into a new income bracket in exchange for a Sullivan show. Wilbur Clark, one of the city's most tireless hucksters, opened the $3.5 million Desert Inn in 1950 with the help of Moe Dalitz and other Cleveland organized crime figures; at some point in the late 1950s, Chicago mobster Sam Giancana also acquired an interest. (In 1967 Howard Hughes decided to buy the Desert Inn rather than move out.) Under Dalitz's guidance, and fueled by low-interest loans from the Teamsters' Pension Fund, the Desert Inn became a capstone of Vegas' growth. Clark, as its public relations man, saw great value in Sullivan.

The Desert Inn hired the ritziest nightclub performers—Sinatra made his Vegas debut there in 1951, later joined by Jerry, Dino, and Sammy Davis. But the Rat Pack, although it attracted a fast crowd, couldn't provide the patina of middle-class respectability that Sullivan could. Clark understood that bringing new dollars into Las Vegas meant burnishing its image, making it an acceptable destination for corporate junkets and—the idea was far-fetched in 1958—middle-brow tourists. Ed, with his position as unofficial Minister of Culture, was uniquely qualified to help with this.

The romancing of Ed by Las Vegas business interests had begun the previous fall, when the United Hotel Corporation of Las Vegas purchased his Connecticut estate. After his car crash, Ed lost interest in his country retreat. In truth, semirural Southbury was never a good match for Sullivan, who continued to enjoy rotating between Manhattan nightspots every evening. As he sold the estate, he explained that he was not made for country living. "The noise was terrible," he said. "I mean there'd be a cow mooing at four o'clock in the morning." United Hotel took it off his hands for a handsome sum—$250,000—or more than double what he paid for it in 1954. The deal got sweeter. The Desert Inn agreed to cover all of his living expenses and pay him $25,000 a week for eight weeks, for a contract that stretched over two summers. After Ed broadcast two shows per summer from the hotel, he would stay for additional shows that wouldn't be broadcast, while a guest host emceed his TV show.

As the grumbles of complaint from CBS and Ford grew into a chorus, Ed confided to Marlo Lewis: "I don't give a damn what any of them feel about this deal. I've busted my back . . . running from one city to another. I'm tired of traveling. I'm tired of putting on shows for the CBS affiliates. I'm tired of shaking hands with the Lincoln Mercury dealers, signing autographs, hearing people tell me how surprised they are

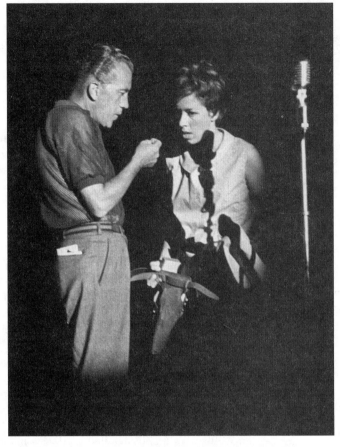

Giving instructions to Carol Burnett in rehearsal, Las Vegas, 1958. Sullivan scandalized CBS by producing a show from Sin City in the 1950s. (Time Life Pictures/Getty Images)

that I can smile—especially when my ulcer is knocking me out and I don't want to smile. A few weeks in that Las Vegas sunshine will do me a world of good and it won't hurt anyone else on the show either. And I'm not about to turn down this pot of gold that Wilbur's throwing at me . . . and nobody's gonna stop me from taking it!"

The family show that Ed presented from the Desert Inn was in marked contrast to the hotel's typical fare. Esther Williams, known as "America's Mermaid" for the string of MGM hits that showcased her aquatic skills and bathing suit pulchritude, introduced "water babies," children diving into swimming pools. Williams gave a little girl a piggyback ride in a pool, introduced the AAU synchronized swimming team, and blew a big kiss at the camera (Ed was furious at her for displaying too much cleavage). "Jumping Joe" Monahan performed a trampoline act, Carol Burnett did a stand-up routine about braces, and the Kirby Stone Four sang "Lazy River" (the appearance led to a Columbia Records contract for the vocal group). The show was a hit in Vegas. "People flocked to see it—we had full houses," recalled Burnett.

The following Sunday's program was a reprise, with an Olympic diving champion, a ventriloquist and a magician for the kids, and the Four Preps singing "Lazy Summer Night." Sullivan asked Wilbur Clark to take a bow from the audience. And, as if living in a parallel universe not connected to America in 1958, Ed touted the gambling mecca's churches and schools as well as its entertainment and casino attractions. Based on his Desert Inn broadcasts, viewers at home might have deduced that Las Vegas was a slightly risqué suburb of Oklahoma City.

As the 1958–59 season began, Ed's traditional variety format seemed to have grown too small for him. Topping his broadcast produced in Brussels, he began the season by planning shows from Alaska, the Hawaiian Islands, and Asia. He turned his trips into travelogues that he presented along with other acts on Sunday evenings. In his Asian travelogue, the black-and-white footage was like his own home movie, as he played baseball with Japanese schoolchildren, talked about the architecture in Hong Kong—"The most exciting place on the globe," he called it—and surveyed Istanbul with Sylvia. The beauty of the Turkish city "will make it one of the great tourist spots in the world," he opined, as the camera panned over ancient minarets, though it's doubtful he changed travel plans in many American living rooms with that claim.

Part of his wanderlust was a competitive desire to go where *Maverick* could not. The Western was regularly trouncing him in the Nielsens, even with the ratings jolt delivered by his increased rock 'n' roll bookings. But his international shows gave him an advantage that *Maverick* couldn't claim: they became news events, covered in newspapers across the country. In particular, his Brussels broadcast had generated an untold fortune in free publicity.

His interest in internationalizing the show, however, was about more than ratings. He began envisioning a time when the show would grow into something larger than entertainment. Ed was, after all, a reporter and columnist, and had worked on newspapers since his teens. He never stopped seeing himself as a newshound. One of his

Live television, circa 1958: the Sullivan show was broadcast live throughout its twenty-three-year run. (Globe Photos)

personal secretaries recalled that even in the 1960s, if he placed a call he identified himself as "Ed Sullivan, of the *News*." (In fact he never gave up his *Daily News* column throughout his television career.) He had always included some element of current events or public service on the show, like the Eleanor Roosevelt tribute to Israel, or his chat with civil rights activist Ralph Bunche, or—a favorite cause of his—a spokesperson from the Association of Christians and Jews.

In the fall of 1958 he began thinking of expanding the role of current events on the show, and of expanding his own role, too. He wanted to build upon his success as an impresario to become a producer who handled both news and entertainment; he imagined that these two forms could be mingled, which in television at that time was unheard of. He hoped to become, as *Journal-American* columnist Atra Baer wrote after talking with him, "the Lowell Thomas of variety show business." Thomas had been an adventurous roving radio journalist who produced stories from Europe in both world wars, as well as from the Middle East and China. Ed's own international shows were a form of this, yet he hoped for much more.

He began lobbying the CBS news department. While he had no desire to be a network newsman, he wanted to have input, to be called upon to comment on issues of the day, much as he did in the *Daily News*. His entreaties to the network news division met with no response. At one point Ed invited legendary CBS newsman Edward R. Murrow on the show in an attempt to form a bridge between himself and the news department. Murrow was flattered by the attention—a bevy of showgirls requested his autograph—and he appreciated Ed's interview. But the door was still shut. Murrow, in fact, in October 1958 gave a speech decrying prime-time television as full of "decadence, escapism, and insulation from the realities of the world in which we live," using *The Ed Sullivan Show* as an example.

As Ed sought to shift his role, it was as if he had outgrown the traditional variety format. At age fifty-seven, he had been producing stage shows for more than twenty-five years. He had clearly mastered the format; indeed he was *the* master of the format. He had accomplished everything he had set out to do. He had hungered to be a nationally famous broadcast star, and, without being able to sing, tell jokes, or be charming, had done so. But fame, apparently, hadn't proven to be a high enough mountain. The inner force that had driven him to success was still there. Now that he had achieved what he had always wanted, he saw a bigger vista to conquer.

In December 1958 he announced that CBS had hired him to produce a program apart from his Sunday show, to be called *Sullivan's Travels*. He would use his annual summer vacations—he certainly didn't want to relax then—to produce four to six ninety-minute travelogue-documentaries. His first would be about India, and he planned pieces from West Germany, Vienna, Rio de Janeiro, and other locations. Yet even the *Sullivan's Travels* series wasn't enough—he was interested in serious journalism, insightful coverage and commentary that spotlighted global events.

The network didn't see him in this role, despite having hired him to produce the travelogues. That CBS never invited him to give his opinion in year-end wrap-ups of national and international news was deeply frustrating for him. "Why the hell not!" he exclaimed to Marlo Lewis. "I've had thirty years' experience as an on-the-line reporter. When it involves the news, they won't call me! But when they hold their drunken station-owner conventions and want to look impressive, they call on me to put on a show!"

However, the fact that CBS had not the slightest whit of interest in his dream didn't deter him. He had always plunged headfirst toward his goals, regardless of what others thought. And now, as he hoped to enlarge the show's concept and his own role, becoming the new Lowell Thomas, he pushed forward with the same headstrong motion.

Ed saw a chance to score the definitive news scoop as the rebel uprising in Cuba came to a head in the late fall of 1958. Led by Fidel Castro and Dr. Ernesto "Che" Guevera, the rebels appeared to be overtaking the Cuban army, edging ever closer to the capital city of Havana. By late December the situation dominated American news, as more than three thousand people died in house-to-house fighting. Rumors circulated that notoriously corrupt Cuban president Fulgencio Batista was preparing to flee.

As Castro took control of Cuba in early January, his political orientation was unclear to U.S. observers. Was he a communist, or merely a fervent nationalist? The son of a wealthy sugarcane farmer, educated in Jesuit schools and the University of Havana law school, he was gifted at public relations. In April 1959, four months after the revolution, the American Society of Newspaper Editors invited him to the United States. During his visit he declared himself in favor of a free press and against dictatorships; he told the Senate Foreign Relations Committee that American property would not be nationalized. In November 1959—almost a year after he took power—the deputy director of the CIA informed a Senate committee, "We believe Castro is not a member of the Communist Party and does not consider himself to be a communist."

In the wake of the revolution, many Cubans viewed Castro as a folk hero. He entered Havana for the first time on January 8, and though the country was still in disorder—and still contained Batista loyalists—he walked the streets unarmed. His enormous popularity was evident as massive crowds lionized him in a spontaneous parade. A carnival atmosphere prevailed, with mobs looting hotels and casinos, and throngs celebrating Batista's overthrow by waving flags and honking horns around the clock.

While it looked like pandemonium to most observers, to Ed it looked like an opportunity. Getting the first television interview with Castro would force CBS to recognize him as a newsman. And since the eyes of the world were on this small nation in turmoil, flying there would thrust him onto the world stage. But if he was going to bag the first Castro TV interview he had to move posthaste. Ed called Jules Dubois, the Latin American correspondent for the Chicago *Tribune*, which was the *Daily News*' parent company. Dubois, a fierce anticommunist who had a good rapport with Castro, agreed to set up an interview. (Some Cuban revolutionaries suspected that Dubois worked for the CIA, a suspicion that was never confirmed.) Sullivan and Dubois made arrangements to rendezvous at the Havana airport.

To gather a crew, Ed certainly wasn't going to call the CBS news department; he was scooping them. Instead, a Sullivan assistant called a young CBS cameraman named Andrew Laszlo, who worked on the situation comedy *The Phil Silvers Show*, and asked him to assemble a crew. (Laszlo's later career as a cinematographer included more than forty feature films, including *Star Trek V* in 1989.) Speed and secrecy were critical to Ed's plan. On Sunday, Laszlo was told to prepare for a Wednesday afternoon departure to the Dominican Republic; he was told he would film an interview with Dominican president Rafael Trujillo. Laszlo hired a soundman and another assistant and, planning for a shoot in Trujillo's presidential palace, packed a heavy-duty movie camera used in making full-length features.

Sullivan and Andy Laszlo had worked together before, and Ed had come to like and trust the young cameraman, inventing an affectionate nickname for him, "Andy-roo." That past summer Laszlo had filmed locations in Ireland and Portugal for Ed's travelogue shows. In Ireland, they were seated together at a restaurant with about twenty crewmembers, many of whom were making petty demands as waiters took their orders. Ed, growing impatient with the crew's self-centered fussing, took Laszlo by the arm. "Andy-roo," he told him, "you and I are getting out of here, we're going to go get a real steak." As Laszlo recalled, the two of them went to a spot Ed knew, a "fantastic little pub, him with his milk, and me with my steak." (Ed's ulcer continued to plague him, hence the milk.) They sat there until closing time, conversing throughout the evening. In Spain, Sullivan and Laszlo were having dinner with a few other people at a nightclub when Ed saw a Hungarian husband and wife dance team he enjoyed. He asked Laszlo, a native Hungarian, to invite the couple on his show. But the dancers had no knowledge of American television and turned him down.

Now, aboard a plane presumably bound for the Dominican Republic, Laszlo wasn't sure what to think when Sullivan sat down next to him with a grave look. Ed sat sipping a glass of milk and, for several moments, said nothing. "Andy-roo, I lied to you," he finally said, explaining that the story about the Dominican Republic had been merely a cover. When Laszlo realized he was headed for Cuba—with the country still embroiled in violence—he told Sullivan he needed to call his wife as soon as he landed. Ed assured him that this was unnecessary because his office was informing the crew's wives. Yet this wasn't true. Ed was telling no one. He couldn't air the interview until Sunday, and he didn't want a news crew to hear about his plan and beat him to the story. Unbeknownst to Sullivan, Ted Ayers, the producer of CBS news program *Face the Nation*, had been working on arranging a Castro interview for weeks. Like Sullivan, Ayers was at that moment heading for Havana, with the understanding that the Cuban leader would grant him an interview in a studio there.

When Sullivan and his crew landed in Havana that evening it wasn't clear that the revolution was over. Castro's soldiers, clad in jungle green and carrying carbines, swarmed the airport. Known as Fidelistas, these revolutionaries were attempting to control the mob who frantically wanted to leave, with limited success. Terrified Cubans pushed and shouted to secure a spot on an outbound plane. Amid the roiling chaos Sullivan rendezvoused with Jules Dubois, who told him that Castro wasn't in Havana. Somehow they needed to travel to Matanzas, a port city sixty miles to the east, a difficult trip in the dark.

The easiest way there was by small plane, and a pilot claiming to be Fidel's official pilot agreed to take them in his Beechcraft six-seater. But as he spoke he kept weaving back and forth, apparently deeply inebriated from days of celebration. Ed, eyeing the man's condition, diplomatically pointed out that his crew's gear was too big for the plane. Dubois conferred with some nearby Fidelistas, who gathered a fleet of six taxicabs. The soldiers accompanied them, so each taxi had its own submachine gun–toting chaperone in the front seat to allow them passage through the many roadblocks. Laszlo recalled the tension as they traveled with the Fidelistas through the Cuban countryside at night: "These people were scary just to look at, and to be next to them was even scarier." Ed, however, played down the danger, and seemed unconcerned.

When they pulled into Matanzas sometime around midnight the city appeared deserted, until they came to the village square. Gathered there were thousands of townspeople listening with rapt attention to Castro, who was holding forth at the tail end of a three-hour speech. As the Cuban leader spoke, Laszlo started setting up his camera in a nearby building, only to encounter a major obstacle: the building didn't have the correct electrical current to power his camera. Having packed for the Dominican Republic's presidential palace, he wasn't equipped for Cuba's rudimentary power grid. He frantically searched the building. After anxious minutes he found an outlet with—he hoped—sufficient current, near where the interview would take place. By the time his gear was set up and Castro was ready it was after 1 A.M.

As the Cuban leader entered the interview room, dozens of his bearded soldiers rushed in with him, bringing a dense cloud of acrid cigar smoke. Dubois scrambled to convince some of them to leave to make space for the interview. Fidel was in an expansive mood and greeted Sullivan and his crew cordially. But suddenly, as they were exchanging greetings, a sharp explosive sound punctured the room—everyone gasped and ducked, and the Fidelistas turned their carbines to the ready. After a tense moment they realized that a soldier had tripped into a camera light, causing it to shatter.

Following some short preliminaries the interview finally began, with Sullivan and Castro sitting on an old wooden desk. Ed, dressed in the same businesslike coat and tie he wore to host his show, seemed to almost lean into Castro, who was clad in combat fatigues with a sidearm. The two were surrounded by soldiers, one of whom kept a Tommy gun trained over Ed's head through part of the interview. Sullivan's demeanor was not that of the stiff and stilted Sunday night show host. Rather, he was closer to the feisty bantamweight that he often was offstage. The interview, at least initially, began as a mano a mano confrontation.

At one point, Ed asked Castro if he was a communist. The Cuban leader "reacted violently," Laszlo recalled. "He almost jumped off the desk. He ripped open his shirt and pulled out this very beautiful crucifix, and bellowed, *'I'm a Roman Catholic, how could I be a communist?'*" At the sound of Castro's pique the Fidelistas shifted their carbines uneasily. Perhaps in response, Ed followed with a softball: "Some refer to you as the liberator, the George Washington, of Cuba. Are you the George Washington of Cuba?" Castro, now smiling and clearly relishing the question, gave a long and windy answer that released the tension in the room. But Ed wasn't through with the tough questions. Jabbing a finger toward Castro for emphasis, he asked, "In Latin America, over and over again, dictators have come along, they've raped the country, they've stolen the money, millions and millions of dollars, tortured and killed people. How do *you* propose to end that in Cuba?"

"[It will] be easy," Castro replied, in broken English. "By not permitting any dictatorships to come to rule our country. You can be sure that Batista is, or will be, the last dictator of Cuba." Moreover, he claimed, the country would improve its democratic institutions. At several points Laszlo needed to stop the interview to reload his camera, which required Sullivan or Castro to repeat their previous statement.

With Fidel Castro, January 1959. Sullivan flew to Cuba just days after the revolution
hoping to land the first TV interview with the new Cuban leader. (CBS Photo Archive)

Laszlo found Castro remarkably adept at resuming his reply mid thought, or repeating his answers verbatim to whatever question Ed asked.

By the end of the nearly hour-long interview the two men warmed to each other. With a disarming smile, Castro said he had never dreamed he would have a chance to address so many English-speaking people, prompting a good-natured chuckle from Ed. Sullivan promised Castro a donation of $10,000 in a gesture of support for the revolution's widows and orphans. A courier delivered a note to Castro from Che Guevera, after which the Cuban leader signaled that the interview had to end. (Castro was headed off to do his interview with *Face the Nation*; in fact, he had kept the CBS-TV news crew waiting while completing his Sullivan interview, though Ed didn't know this.) Before the camera stopped filming, Ed introduced Jules Dubois and thanked him for arranging the interview. The Dubois introduction had an added benefit. Mentioning the reporter's Chicago *Tribune* pedigree—a paper never accused of codling communists—helped establish that Ed hadn't just interviewed an enemy of the United States.

After the interview, Sullivan and his crew bundled back into the taxis for the trek back to Havana, driving through the night to arrive in the city just as dawn was breaking. Finding a street vendor, Ed had him grill as many sausage and cheese sandwiches as he could. Before they got to their hotel, the officer leading the taxi fleet stopped them at the city's sports stadium. While they sat waiting, a long line of trucks filled with people drove into the stadium, after which bursts of automatic gunfire were heard; when the trucks left the stadium they were empty. It was a chilling moment. Laszlo speculated that this was retribution against Batista loyalists.

The Americans got only a few hours sleep before heading to the airport, which had devolved into near chaos. Surging throngs of Cubans screamed and shoved in a desperate effort to flee the country. Only with the help of a phalanx of Fidelistas were Ed and his crew able to force their way into a waiting area. There, to Ed's surprise, he ran into George Raft, an actor known for playing gangsters in a string of Hollywood potboilers. Raft was also known for associating with actual mobsters, like Owney Madden, whom Ed himself had socialized with when he frequented the Silver Slipper speakeasy. Raft was distraught and destitute because the Fidelistas had confiscated his casino and his bank account. Laszlo believed that Ed gave him some money. Around 3 P.M. they boarded the plane, sitting in the crowded cabin until sunset while waiting to take off. As they waited, soldiers boarded the plane to check each passenger's paperwork, in some cases forcefully removing people. Ed arrived back in New York just before dawn on Friday morning, at which point Laszlo rushed to get the film developed.

For Sunday's broadcast, Sullivan edited the interview to about six minutes, with footage of the masses cheering Castro. Since Ed's travelogue pieces were part of the show's typical fare, the audience might have been prepared for a clip from such a foreign locale. The previous August, for instance, he had flown to Jerusalem and filmed an Israeli talent contest (while there he and Sylvia met with David Ben-Gurion, the country's first prime minister). Still, even in a show known for distant locations and high contrast, the Castro segment felt remarkably disconnected to anything else that evening. Sharing the bill was a scene from the current Broadway play *The Disenchanted* performed by Jason Robards and George Grizzard; comedian Alan King did a bit about suburban house parties; a dog trainer presented a poodle fashion show; a comic named Professor Backwards spelled backwards on a blackboard; Tina Louise, who later played Ginger on *Gilligan's Island*, made a cameo; and the Little Gaelic Singers from Ireland sang sweetly. Also squeezed into the hour were a juggler, an impressionist, and a four-man acrobatic team, two of whom wore ape costumes. Castro, incongruously, was presented between Alan King and the couture-clad poodles.

However odd the presentation, the Castro interview was a journalistic coup for Ed. While his interview didn't air first—*Face the Nation*'s Castro segment aired Sunday morning, several hours before his—he had bested the country's top news agencies in getting a TV interview with the Cuban leader. Edward R. Murrow wouldn't interview Castro until early February. Some grumbled that Sullivan had only landed the interview because he had offered to pay $10,000 beforehand, but Marlo Lewis claimed the donation was a postinterview gesture on Ed's part, which is likely.

Yet in either case, despite the journalistic feat the interview proved to be far from the triumph he hoped for. It didn't propel his ratings higher; his Sunday night audience came to the show for the Broadway play and the comic, not breaking news from world hotspots. It did nothing to establish him as a newsman in the eyes of CBS; on the contrary, the network gave him an angry dressing-down, telling him to stick to entertainment and leave the news to them. It's likely the CBS news division was embarrassed, having almost been scooped by the man hired to introduce trained monkeys. The network at that point saw show business and news as mutually exclusive; it wasn't until decades later that television mingled news and entertainment in the way that Sullivan envisioned.

Additionally, Ed soon received a call from New York's Archbishop Spellman, who told him that Castro was not what he seemed, and strongly suggested that Ed stop payment on the $10,000 check. Sullivan agreed, and with time, as Castro began to ally with the Soviets, he realized he had made an embarrassing blunder. By the end of 1959 he was castigating the Cuban leader in his column, with more than a hint of regret: "Castro gets booed by newsreel audiences . . . what a chance he blew, to become another Bolivar!" And soon thereafter, Ed stopped mentioning him altogether, apparently hoping that his impulsive Cuban adventure would be forgotten.

That Ed, at age fifty-seven, wealthy and successful, would fly to a Third World country in the midst of a revolution to get a story showed that he had still had the fire. His competitive streak was as vital now as when he had rushed headlong into skirmishes on the athletic fields of Port Chester. In truth, though, the show itself was beginning to lose its way, at least in terms of its ratings.

Ed wanted to internationalize it, to broaden its vistas as he himself grew. In March he presented a segment he produced in Ireland, in which he interviewed Irish President Eamon de Valera, kissed the Blarney Stone, and presented Myron Cohen telling Irish and Jewish jokes. The following week he showed his travelogue from Portugal, spotlighting flamenco dancer La Chunga. That summer found him at Italy's Spoleto Festival, producing a show featuring Sir John Gielgud delivering Shakespeare, as well as a performance by the Jerome Robbins Ballet troupe, an Italian opera star, and actors rendering scenes from Tennessee Williams's *Night of the Iguana*.

However, Nielsen ratings made it clear that this wasn't what the American public wanted. The one location viewers wanted to travel to during the 1958–59 season was the Old West—the craze had reached a fevered pitch. Of the year's top ten shows, eight of them were Westerns. *Maverick*, running opposite *The Ed Sullivan Show*, had climbed all the way to the number six spot. In the fall of 1958, Sullivan's show was ranked number three out of the 124 programs on the air. But over the course of the season, viewers drifted steadily over to *Maverick*, and by the spring of 1959, Sullivan's Nielsen ranking had tumbled to number thirty.

As he watched the ratings fall, he threw virtually everything and anything onstage in an attempt to dislodge the immovable object known as *Maverick*. His international emphasis, though increased, was just one element among a dazzling array. The 1958–59 season kicked off with the cast from *West Side Story*, celebrating its one-year anniversary on Broadway, performing the number "Cool." The following week Jackie Gleason played his physical comedy for laughs, sharing the bill with genial *General Electric Theater* host Ronald Reagan and actor Steve McQueen, fresh from the huge sci-fi hit *The Blob*. In October, Ed showcased the Milwaukee Braves, then playing in the World Series against the New York Yankees. A few weeks later he built a program around a Friars Club roast of himself, in which CBS newsman Walter Cronkite kept trying to detail Sullivan's history, only to be interrupted by comedians Morey Amsterdam and Jack Carter. In November, actors William Shatner and France Nuyen performed a scene from the musical *The World of Suzie Wong*, one of myriad Broadway scenes that year.

Later that season, Pinky and Perky, a British puppet act, squeaked out the Big Bopper's hit "Chantilly Lace," and Ed, clowning around, croaked a few bars of the Everly Brothers' "Bye Bye Love"; country singer Johnny Cash shared the bill with vocalist Frankie Laine, who recited "the Gettysburg Address"; Samuel Goldwyn and Sullivan presented citations to major film figures, including Indian director Rajaram Vankudre; Ed visited the movie set of *Anatomy of a Murder* and chatted with Jimmy Stewart in an evening in which Henny Youngman told one-liners accompanied by violin; Bobby Darin sang "Mack the Knife" on the same night that Ed presented the Rhesus monkey Able from the U.S. space program—Able had survived a sixteen-minute suborbital flight.

That summer, a pompadoured Frankie Avalon warbled "A Boy Without a Girl" on a bill in which Duke Ellington swung through "Flirty Bird" and Fred Astaire said "hello" from the audience; Fabian sang "Turn Me Loose" and "Tiger" and the Platters doo-wopped through their recent number one hit, "Smoke Gets in Your Eyes"; Ed's Jimmy Cagney tribute presented numerous classic film clips and an interview with the storied actor; to end the season, Sullivan visited Charlton Heston on the set of *Ben-Hur* and took a chariot ride with the actor.

Still, Sunday night viewers could not be lured from *Maverick*. For the first time in his television career, Ed was unable to reach his audience. He had always been one of them, wanting what they wanted, enjoying the things they enjoyed. He may have endeavored to stay a step ahead, but only a step. Now, he wanted to kiss the Blarney Stone, see the cities of Portugal, interview a Cuban revolutionary, and tour Italy. They wanted to be entertained on a Sunday night. His audience was drifting away—the Nielsens indicated that not only was he losing to *Maverick*, but his future on the air might be jeopardized. He had been felled by an upstart trend, and it was unknown how long the Western craze would last. Or, whether the next trend would pull viewers even further from him. His run in television had been unusually long, eleven years. Maybe this was it.

Ed had a choice to make as the curtain fell on the 1950s: would he follow his muse as a globetrotter, or would he be the showman he had always been, eager— hungry—to please his audience? To maintain his stature as a producer, he needed to refocus on his audience, to find some way to bring them back. Given his ratings loss, if he didn't make some changes, and soon, his show was headed the way of those of Milton Berle and Bob Hope and Sid Caesar, and the many other stars whose television debuts he managed to outlast.

However, just before the 1959–60 season began, forcing him to confront these issues, wanderlust once again called him. His annual late-summer vacation had become a period in which he filmed segments from remote locations, like his interview with Brigitte Bardot in Italy, or the previous August's trip to Israel. For this summer's shoot Ed imagined his grandest remote show yet. Gathering his crew, he journeyed to a location that was as far from America as one could get in 1959.

CHAPTER FOURTEEN

The Times
They Are a Changin'

O N A SUNDAY NIGHT IN LATE SEPTEMBER 1959, Americans tuned their televisions to the Sullivan show with a profound sense of curiosity. Was it true? Had Ed Sullivan, the guardian of the family living room, America's unofficial Minister of Culture, really traveled to . . . the Soviet Union?

Not only was the answer yes, but Ed, oddly, was at his most natural in this unlikely location. For the show he produced in the U.S.S.R., he walked the streets of Moscow and Leningrad with a preternatural ease, introducing American viewers to a world they knew only as an evil empire. He addressed the camera like an old friend, a confidant accompanying him on an exotic journey. But despite his uncharacteristic comfort, his three-week trip to Russia that August resembled an exploration of the far side of the moon. Recent developments had pushed America and the Soviet Union into a horrific standoff.

In late 1957 the Soviets had launched Sputnik, a satellite that orbited the earth; they also announced they had successfully launched an intercontinental ballistic missile test. America was caught flat-footed. Not only were the Russians now able to hurl an atomic bomb from half a world away, but the United States had never launched either a satellite or an ICBM. Although by 1958 the United States had caught up—after a hurried rocket launch that burned up on the pad, which the international press dubbed "Kaputnick"—the specter of all-out mutual destruction now loomed as a very real possibility.

Amid the tension there were efforts at rapprochement, however tentative. In the later years of Eisenhower's term he hoped for an accord with the Soviets to limit the arms race. His efforts were bitterly opposed by many who saw any softening of U.S.

stance as a mistake. In July 1959 he sent Vice President Nixon to Moscow to open the Moscow Trade Fair, hoping the resulting goodwill would promote a thaw in relations. Little was accomplished. Nixon, a hard-liner in U.S.–Soviet relations, engaged Soviet premier Khrushchev in the infamous "kitchen debate," a fruitless game of one-upmanship between the two men about which country's lifestyle was superior. It was at this same trade fair a few weeks later that Ed, in a cultural exchange sponsored by the U.S. State Department, produced his Soviet show.

If Eisenhower hoped the cultural exchange would promote the possibility of normalized relations, Sullivan was his man. The showman had begun the 1950s as a bellicose Cold Warrior, trumpeting the blacklist publication *Red Channels*, and using his *Daily News* column to chide President Truman for not providing the Air Force with a ready supply of atomic weapons. But, based on his Soviet show, he was ending the decade as something of a peacenik. As he explained in his Russian broadcast, "Our mission to Moscow was to entertain Russians and to confirm their opinion that Americans are nice people."

In a spirit of détente, Ed arranged the show to spotlight both Soviet and American talent. The program began with a burst of movement, as the Red Army Dancers, peasant-style performers clad in Soviet military uniforms, strutted and kicked in unison, accompanied by a brassy military orchestra. Following them was American accordion wizard Dick Contino rendering popular tunes with bedazzling keyboard technique. Contino was typical of the American performers. Except for Metropolitan Opera star Rise Stevens, the tour's thirty-eight musicians, singers, and dancers were all lesser known—the production was already wildly expensive without bringing celebrity entertainers.

Between acts, Ed presented his tour of Moscow and Leningrad, narrating the sights. "I expected a gloomy city, but it isn't," he said of Moscow. In fact, his observations seemed to suggest, Russians are surprisingly similar to Americans. As the camera panned a city street bustling with apparently middle-class Soviets, he observed, "Now look at these Russians here—fine decent faces of hardworking people." A busy Moscow street, "looks like a boulevard in America crowded with people in their Sunday finery, taking their kids to the ice cream stand." If that didn't prove how normal life could be in the Soviet Union, Ed included a segment in which he and Sylvia enjoyed a riverboat cruise on a sunny day.

One of the show's highlights was tap dancer Conrad "Little Buck" Buckner, whose blazingly fast feet flashed in rhythm with a jazz drummer tapping out double-time. They performed outdoors for a Russian audience who looked on as if spellbound. Ed's show-travelogue moved briskly, from a Russian trained bear to an American plate spinner to Sullivan's tour of the tombs of Lenin and Stalin, with a camera pan of the long line of visitors. Throughout the program, Ed's commentary stressed global harmony: "People are people, regardless of the system that speaks for them," he said.

At one point in the trip, the show's production staff grew frustrated by the morass of bureaucratic roadblocks. Getting permission to film was slow, and events were rescheduled without advance notice. Ed, in a pique, fired off a telegram of protest to Soviet leader Nikita Khrushchev. The next morning he got a call at his hotel from a mid-level functionary who assured him that his way was now cleared. (Ed sent three more telegrams to Khrushchev in the months ahead. Two were demands to be paid, including one complaining that the Russian ministry refused to release $30,000 for the show's funding. Sullivan wrote to Khrushchev: "Unless you intervene sir this can develop into a nasty scandal as Russian artists have never experienced this treatment in the United States." The debt was paid. Having succeeded with this request, Ed cabled the Russian leader again in November, asking him to "release the youngsters who participated in the 1956 [Hungarian] revolution." (This appears to have received no response.)

For the Soviet show's finale, Ed spoke a few sentences in Russian to greet the large Moscow audience, which roared its approval. For the final number he had opera star Rise Stevens sing "Getting to Know You" in Russian, while all thirty-eight American performers waved flags onstage, with half waving American flags and half waving Soviet flags. Of all the shocking sights that Sullivan presented in his twenty-three seasons, from black and white performers onstage together in the early 1950s to the edges of acid rock in the late 1960s, the sight of an American waving a Soviet flag in 1959 was likely the most unusual.

But his intent was more to reassure than to surprise. Unlike his show at the Brussels World Fair earlier that year, Ed didn't take the opportunity at the end to condemn communism; the word wasn't uttered once throughout the program. This show was about similarities, not differences. At the end he signed off: "Long live the United States and the Soviet Union, in peace."

For Ed's Soviet show he had been the grand impresario, straddling two continents while sampling the local vodka and promoting world peace. But as the 1959–60 season began, serious business beckoned: Nielsen ratings. The trip had been a cultural and commercial triumph, generating a big ratings spike and a blizzard of national coverage; Sullivan won a Peabody award for the program. Yet maintaining the show's status as the top-rated talent showcase amid the public's insatiable hunger for Westerns required more than one special evening. The new season's first order of business was to attempt to reverse the prior season's ratings loss to ABC's *Maverick*.

If further impetus was needed to force the showman to focus on the ratings battle, NBC was launching a new variety program opposite the Sullivan show. *The Steve Allen Show*, after losing to Sullivan since its debut, was being moved to Mondays. In its place NBC was putting up *Sunday Showcase*, a revolving-format variety show. Certain weeks would be hosted by Milton Berle, other weeks were to be dramas or musical comedies. Berle was an ingenious choice. Although he had lost his own show, in television's earliest years his ratings had consistently topped Sullivan's. NBC was resurrecting a performer with a proven ability to outdraw the stone-faced show host. It was time for Ed to look homeward.

The previous year had been the show's most internationally diverse, with Ed producing broadcasts from Alaska to Cuba to Ireland to Portugal—France awarded him the rank of "Chevalier" in the French Legion of Honor for segments he produced there. In contrast, this year he would stay home. When push came to shove, he preferred winning to world travel. Indeed, the 1959–60 season was the least adventurous of any he had yet produced. It contained his signature mix of highbrow and low, with the year's brightest stars, but nothing in this season would be exotic or surprising. The showman would take no chances in his bid to get back on top. He had always known how to romance his audience, and this year he would do so by serving them comfort food.

He kept rock 'n' roll to a minimum. That was easy to do: with Elvis in the Army and the British Invasion still years away, the new sound had gone all soft and gooey. Frankie Avalon, armed with a baby face and a number one hit, warbled "Look What One Kiss Can Do." Bobby Darin—Sullivan staffers recalled him as remarkably arrogant—finger-snapped through "Oh, My Darling Clementine," and Paul Anka crooned "Put Your Head on My Shoulders." Theresa Brewer, a prim sex kitten of a vocalist who inspired cartons of fan mail at the Sullivan office before being forgotten, enjoyed numerous guest shots.

Many of the season's musical bookings, however brilliant the talent, were essentially backward looking. The Benny Goodman, Count Basie, and Harry James Orchestras swung through standards. Famed drummer Gene Krupa and actor Sal Mineo appeared with a clip from *The Gene Krupa Story*, starring Mineo. For Easter, gospel queen Mahalia Jackson rendered "Old Rugged Cross." Louis Armstrong, a Sullivan personal friend who appeared eighteen times over the years, jazzed up "When the Saints Go Marching In." (Sullivan later invited Armstrong to play golf with him at an elite country club that was whites-only, and the management tried to keep the jazzman off the course; after a tongue lashing by Sullivan they relented.)

That fall, aging nightclub comic Joe E. Lewis did a routine about Vice President Nixon and Senator Kennedy, who would vie for the presidency a year later. Borscht Belt star Sam Levenson lampooned concerns about the population explosion with jokes like "Somewhere on this globe, every ten seconds, there is a woman giving birth to a child. She must be found and stopped." Jack Carter did his Sullivan imitation and Henny Youngman intoned, as always, "Take my wife . . . *please* take my wife." Also booked were mild-mannered comic Dick Van Dyke, a regular, and the flippant duo Rowan and Martin, who later starred in the late 1960s comedy show *Laugh-In*.

Audiences also saw the choreography of Broadway-ballet legend Jerome Robbins; to accommodate the complexity of Robbins' dance routine the show used seven cameras—far more than normal—and afforded Robbins two extra days of on-set rehearsal, luxurious by the standards of the Sullivan show. In the classical realm, Ed presented performances by opera stars Giulietta Simionato and Eileen Farrell and virtuoso violinist Yehudi Menuhin.

Cast members from two current Broadway hits, *Bye Bye Birdie* and *The Golden Fleecing*, played scenes from their shows, and Jimmy Cagney stopped by with a preview of his new movie *The Gallant Hours*. Ed interviewed director Billy Wilder and showed clips from Wilder's *Some Like It Hot* and *The Apartment*. Charlton Heston appeared to plug *Ben-Hur*, and stayed for a dramatic Bible reading accompanied by full chorus. His stentorian Bible recitation was such a hit that Sullivan invited him back to repeat it later in the year. Not everything went according to plan, as when the horses onstage with vocalist Frankie Laine started to relieve themselves, prompting great merriment in the studio audience.

Ed, oddly, booked the Harlem Globetrotters to play a mock basketball game against the Ames Brothers, a four-man vocal quartet, with baseball star Duke Snyder as referee. The All-American Football squad, fully dressed in helmets and pads, made its perennial appearance. One of the year's biggest shows was an all-circus broadcast in March, featuring tightrope legend the Wallenda family; four of the aerialists rode bikes across a high wire over a parking lot off Eighth Avenue (Ed used his connections to get a permit from the city). The showman flew to Paris—he couldn't stay home completely—to film circus acts in the hundred-year-old Cirque d'Hiver. Almost every week there were acrobats or trained animals, notably the trained chimp dressed as Ed who rode a unicycle.

When the season's ratings were tallied, *The Ed Sullivan Show* was back near the top, at number twelve. Ed's decision to downplay the international had worked. The public's fascination with Westerns hadn't ended—the top three shows were set in the Old West—yet Sullivan's own sagebrush sparring partner, *Maverick*, had fallen to number twenty. And NBC's mixed-format variety show, *Sunday Showcase*, had offered only token resistance. With the show's cancellation after one year, NBC never again tried to compete with Sullivan in the variety format.

Ed received a disconcerting bit of news that season: longtime sponsor Lincoln Mercury, citing the show's high costs, was bowing out. (Ford Motor Company was reeling after losing $250 million from its launch of the Edsel, a car almost no one bought.) While ratings for the Sullivan show meant sponsors were readily found, the new advertiser inflamed Ed's ulcer. Filling Lincoln Mercury's shoes was Colgate-Palmolive, which had sponsored former Sullivan archrival *Comedy Hour*. As one columnist described it, "The Colgate-Palmolive Company has joined a show it couldn't lick."

For Colgate, of course, the shift in shows was simply a business decision. But not for Ed. That Colgate had bankrolled *Comedy Hour* back when the program endangered his survival made the company a mortal enemy in his eyes. For him his show had never been about business; it was personal, intensely so, a reflection of who he was, his tastes, and his attitudes. The showman threw a tantrum at the specter of having Colgate as a sponsor. He lodged a vociferous protest with the CBS management, making it clear he wanted nothing to do with Colgate-Palmolive. In response the network offered him a minor salve that was never disclosed; it may have been an increase in talent budget. Whatever it was, after meetings with network executives Ed pronounced himself reconciled to Colgate's sponsorship.

Colgate or no, Ed's ulcer took a turn for the worse during the season. He was in nearly constant pain (and in fact had been for years) and in January he missed two shows; Jackie Gleason had to substitute host. In June he finally conceded, checking himself in for surgery. While recovering, he put aside any thought of taking it easy. He turned his late-summer retreat to Italy into a working vacation, interviewing Sophia Loren and Clark Gable on the set of *It Started in Naples*.

———

On its face, the 1959–60 season had been such a good one that Sullivan might have decided to stay the course. It had put the showman back near the top in his twelfth year on the air. Nonetheless, Ed felt it was time to make a critical staff change. Or perhaps producer Marlo Lewis left of his own accord, as he claimed, explaining that he needed time off and planned to write a book. If Lewis did leave on his own, there's not a single reference to Ed attempting to convince him to stay. Whatever the case,

Marlo's contract expired in the fall of 1960 and was not renewed. Their parting was by all accounts amicable, though it seemed clear Ed was ready for Marlo to go.

Ed himself, of course, had always been the show's producer, conceiving of its tone and pacing, choosing the balance of acts, exerting control over the material, forging the show to conform to his vision in rehearsal. Although he and Marlo were billed as coproducers, Ed very much ran the show. But Marlo oversaw the logistics, and with such a mélange of performers coming and going every week—from trained chimps to opera divas—that task was hardly secondary.

The decision that Ed made in filling this principal role was to be a central determinant in the show's success in the decade ahead, although the extent to which this was true wasn't clear at the time. The new producer was Bob Precht, Ed's son-in-law. Having worked as a production assistant on the show since the mid 1950s, he had demonstrated an eye for detail and a set of organizational skills that far surpassed Marlo's. Bob had produced many of the remote broadcasts in recent years, working closely with Ed on what were some of his father-in-law's favorite projects. Notably, Precht's supervision of the Soviet show, handling a crew of eighty during a three-week trip in adverse circumstances, proved him to be a meticulous and tireless administrator.

Whether Bob was ready to step into such a vital job was questioned by some. "Bob had a *lot* to learn," recalled Sistie Moffit, an administrative assistant. "And he was coming in with people who had a lot of background and experience. I felt sorry for Bob—we all did." Certain Sullivan staffers whispered about ill-advised nepotism; some of these murmurs were fueled by fear that Bob would clean house of Marlo loyalists. But Ed's decision to hire Bob wasn't nepotism, or at least not purely so. That Precht was his son-in-law had gotten him in the door, but Ed cared too deeply about his show to promote someone to an all-important role merely because he was a relative.

It didn't hurt that Bob was younger. In the fall of 1960 Ed turned fifty-nine; Marlo was forty-five; Bob was twenty-nine. When Ed began producing the show in 1948 he had been immersed in the zeitgeist; he not only wrote about all the day's leading performers in his column, he knew them all personally. But with the passing years he had lost some of that. He had initially missed Elvis, calling him too expensive and unfit for family viewing; only after realizing his mistake did he parlay the rock 'n' roller to a massive ratings win. It was the kind of trend he wouldn't have been late to in 1948. And Marlo hadn't been any more prescient about the Elvis tidal wave. So having a coproducer with a fresh outlook seemed like a good bet—especially when the youthful Jack Kennedy won the presidency that fall, making it feel like the culture had been renewed. Unmistakably, change was in the air.

Ed and Bob formed a partnership far different than that of Ed and Marlo. Or, more accurately, over time they did. Sullivan had no intention of giving up even a small bit of his absolute authority when he promoted his son-in-law. He hired Bob as a sharper and better-organized version of Marlo. But Precht had different ideas. Ed's daughter Betty had married a man not dissimilar to her father. He would not be the minor tyrant that Ed could be, and he was not prone to Ed's competitive rages. Yet he could be headstrong, and he was not content with the essentially secondary role that Marlo had played. "I was aggressive," Precht said. "If I was to do that job, I wanted to really do the job, I didn't want to just take orders and put the cameras out."

That was clear as *The Ed Sullivan Show* began the 1960–61 season, Precht's first as producer. The show looked and moved differently. It was as if with the turning of a decade it was now a new show, or at least looked like one. During the 1950s the stage sets often appeared token, sometimes assembled hurriedly after Ed booked a news-making act the day before. Bob changed that. He hired Bill Bohnert, a young set designer with an MFA from Yale and an architecture degree from Massachusetts Institute of Technology. Bohnert's fondness for clean, geometric designs gave the show a mod look in keeping with the 1960s; alternately, he created big, showy sets for musical numbers, and realistically detailed backdrops for Broadway and opera productions.

Additionally, the show's pacing, previously Ed's exclusive province, was quickened. To help this along, Precht fired Johnny Wray, the show's director throughout the 1950s, and replaced him with Tim Kiley, who at age thirty-four was already an established CBS staff director. The effect was dramatic: intros and outros were smoother, and the entire program seemed to flow better. Ed himself would still walk out of the camera's view unexpectedly, leaving viewers looking at the stage curtain, but most of the other camera angles were better coordinated. In a creative touch, the show sometimes opened with a shot of the evening's performers walking onstage in an eclectic parade, accompanied by contemporary music.

Marlo had sometimes conducted Saturday rehearsals before the Sunday dress rehearsals, especially for elaborate segments. Under Bob's direction these Saturday rehearsals became part of the show's weekly life cycle. His improvements did not come without friction. Some of the longtime staffers resented Precht's changes and the new producer found himself in full-bore arguments. Ed himself, for a period, became more actively involved in the show's technical minutiae, much to Bob's chagrin. But with time the new producer carved out his own turf.

Bob, though willing to be unpopular with the staff when necessary, always used a soft touch with his father-in-law—necessarily, because Ed brooked no rebellion among staffers, related or not. Nonetheless, it's clear from viewing the shows in the early 1960s that Bob diplomatically devised a method to—somewhat—sharpen Ed's stage presence. The showman's introductions could be surprisingly ill-focused; he seemed to know what he wanted to say but could stumble through a handful of sentences getting it out. His comments now tended to be shorter and more to the point, though the old syntax-garbled Ed certainly wasn't gone. (The fact that he wasn't suave still didn't matter to sponsors, who sought to make use of his credibility with viewers. Kodak, as had Lincoln Mercury, had Ed perform the voiceover for dozens of their ads, and he often did an extensive live lead-in before cutting to commercial.)

Bob hoped to make still another change, one that went to the very core of the show: he wanted to have a say in bookings. This, of course, was heresy to Ed. The showman's sense of talent and his intuitive grasp of his audience had always been the heart of *The Ed Sullivan Show*. He had given Marlo the rundown over the phone every week. Sure, Ed accepted tips and suggestions from almost anyone, from cab drivers to family members to those he spoke to during his nightclub prowling. He followed the pop charts, fielded calls from talent agents and show business cronies, read the newspapers, and traveled constantly. But all these sources were funneled down to one producer. It was set in stone: all the artistic decisions of *The Ed Sullivan Show* were made by its namesake.

Yet Bob felt strongly about having input on bookings. He thought about it for weeks before approaching Ed and telling him he wanted to be a producer in the fullest sense of the title. Furthermore, Precht felt the bookings needed some refreshing; using comedian Jack Carter six times in a season was overkill in Bob's view, however good the comic's Sullivan imitation. (Carter, who hosted the variety show *Cavalcade of Stars* in 1949, had for years regularly met Ed for drinks at Danny's Hideaway.) Bob, with his more youthful and liberal worldview, hoped to renew the Sullivan formula.

It's a measure of the respect Ed had for Bob that they came to a reconciliation on this issue. Perhaps the fact that Bob was his son-in-law helped tip the balance; the two of them spent holidays together, and went out for dinner together with their wives after the show every week. Ed, who had always been too driven to develop close friendships, had something of a close friend in Bob. At any rate, it was agreed: Bob and Ed would consult about the bookings. Which is to say, Ed retained final veto power. "Ed was the boss," remembered pop singer Connie Francis, who saw the working relationship between the two men during her twenty-six Sullivan show appearances. "I think Bob Precht had an 'ES' carved out on his ulcers."

If the show's bookings took no major turn in the 1960–61 season—instead continuing as the perfect mirror of current tastes as they always had—one guest reflected the change of decade more than most. Comedian and political satirist Mort Sahl's pointed barbs were a major departure from many comics of the era, who still relied on mother-in-law jokes and vaudeville gags. Sahl had offended enough people to receive violent threats for lampooning the 1950s-era House Un-American Activities Committee, the spearhead of McCarthyism and an entity that Ed wholeheartedly supported. Sahl's left-leaning version of Will Rogers–style populism made him a favorite on the more cerebral *Steve Allen Show*, but Ed had never booked him in the 1950s. His appearance on the Sullivan show, the imprimatur of mainstream acceptance, signaled a change in popular tastes.

In one of his Sullivan show performances, Sahl referred to his army stint during the Korean War, saying that there were "no supplies, no ammunition, no gasoline—but you could buy them." As his morale fell, "One day I said, 'I don't know what we're doing here.' An officer heard me. He was going to send me back." That was considered a terrible punishment, Sahl said, "Although oddly, two officers fought over the right to escort me back." As punishment, the army sent him to a military psychiatric hospital, where they gave him a little ID tag with his photo, which, he quipped, "I could use if I ever wanted to cash a check at a market."

The acerbic comic appeared five times on the Sullivan show, three times that season. Ed took the show on the road that fall, visiting cities across the United States. During a San Francisco broadcast, Sahl skewered presidential candidates Kennedy and Nixon; on the same bill, opera star Dorothy Kirsten sang an aria from *Madame Butterfly* in the city's Japanese Tea Garden and the Dave Brubeck Quartet vamped their jazz classic "Take Five," which made a recent surprise showing on the pop charts. In December pioneering soul singer Jackie Wilson headlined, flashing his choreographed dance moves and dropping to one knee to croon "To Be Loved"; right after Wilson, Sahl performed, sending up American foreign policy and New York

City cops. In June the comic shared the bill with The Limeliters, a folk music group whose ironic wit had been incubated at San Francisco's progressive nightclub The Hungry i, as had Sahl's. (Along the same line, Sullivan presented Odetta, a young black female folksinger who would soon record the protest song "No More Auction Block for Me." Ed booked her for that season's Christmas show to sing "Shout for Joy" and "Poor Little Jesus.")

Most of this season's comics were far from Sahl's territory, though even Jack Carter was now telling jokes about beatniks. In November, Ed booked a show headlined by comic Jerry Lewis, vaudevillian Sophie Tucker, and singer Connie Francis, who had just released a Jewish-themed album and planned to sing a cut from it, "My Yiddishe Mama." However, the singer recalled, "Sophie had a fit, because that was 'her song' and she insisted I not do it." Tucker enlisted Jerry Lewis in her complaint, and Lewis agreed: Connie Francis should not be allowed to sing "My Yiddishe Mama"—it was Sophie Tucker's song. The squabble quickly turned into a minor tempest. "Jerry and Sophie were going to walk off the show, and they were really serious about it," Francis remembered. The singer offered Ed a compromise, telling him she had eleven other songs she could do. But Ed was adamant, siding with Francis: "She'll do whatever she wants." Jerry Lewis and Sophie Tucker gave in, performing as planned, with Lewis doing a routine in which he attempted to teach Ed how to be charismatic, playing the showman's wooden persona for comic hijinks.

In February, Carl Reiner and Mel Brooks performed a lighthearted routine, sharing the bill with Henry Fonda, who read two of Lincoln's speeches, and torch singer Peggy Lee, who smoldered through her 1942 hit "Why Don't You Do Right?" Later that month Lucille Ball saw top billing, reprising the tune "Wildcat" that she had just performed in her Broadway debut. In that same show Rowan and Martin satirized diet doctors.

Ed, true to form, mixed lowbrow with high art this season. In his broadcast from Chicago he toured both the stockyards and the Chicago Art Institute, presenting jazz clarinetist Benny Goodman playing with the city's Fine Arts String Quartet. That same show, Charlton Heston read Carl Sandburg's poem "Chicago" and ventriloquist Edgar Bergen and his dummy conversed about Vikings.

There was virtually no straight theater this year, a change from past seasons, though scenes from Broadway musicals were still staged. For a tribute show to Broadway duo Lerner and Lowe, Richard Burton rendered a scene from their *Camelot*. (Bob Precht had to keep calling Burton's hotel to ensure he was sober enough to go on.) As usual, there were plenty of film clips: John Wayne appeared to promote *The Alamo* and Sal Mineo plugged *Exodus*. Having grown up with vaudeville, Ed booked the genre's aging stars even though the general public had largely forgotten them; this season the show featured Smith and Dale, who had played the Palace in its heyday, now doing one-liners in their seventies.

One of the oddest moments this season was an appearance by Salvador Dalí, the Spanish Surrealist painter. "Tonight, on our stage, Salvador Dalí figures in what we're pleased to call an historic moment in art," Ed said, holding a pistol that shot paint pellets. "Dalí believes that the most unusual patterns in art may be produced by this gun." Dalí, in a dandyish pinstriped suit that complemented his flamboyantly upturned mustache, fired the paint gun at several large canvases, creating original art before an audience of millions, then signed a canvas with a theatrical flourish.

Salvador Dalí on the Sullivan show, 1961. Sullivan touted the painter's appearance as "an historic moment in art," as Dalí shot paint pellets at a canvas for a live television audience. (CBS Photo Archive)

That Ed had begun sharing booking decisions with Bob didn't mean he had gone soft. Sullivan the lion had occasion to roar in January, when Nat "King" Cole, a favorite of Ed's who appeared thirteen times, refused to yield to the showman's song choice. The mellow crooner wanted to perform his new tune, "Illusion." Ed said no—only established material could be performed on his show, he said. The two came to loggerheads, and, in a highly publicized spat, Ed canceled the singer's appearance.

"I feel my integrity as an artist has been questioned," Cole told a reporter after the cancellation. Ed retorted: "We don't intend to have the show used as a vehicle for plugging a record that's not even been released." Having gotten himself into a lather about the issue, Sullivan drove the point home: "We don't think this is a good song; if we're wrong we'll be the first to admit it."

Up until then the two had enjoyed a perfect partnership. Ed, who took pride in championing black performers, found the ideal entertainer in Cole, whose butterscotch-soft persona made this groundbreaking effort comparatively easier. Cole's many Sullivan show appearances helped him land *The Nat King Cole Show* in 1956, the first network variety show hosted by a major black star. (No national sponsor would support the show, reportedly fearing a southern boycott, and several NBC affiliates in the north and south declined to carry it; it was canceled after thirteen months.) After Sullivan and Cole's spat they never repaired their friendship, and the singer never again appeared on the show. However, after Cole's death in 1965, Ed booked his widow Maria Cole as she launched a comeback in her singing career.

———

The Sullivan show's ratings for the 1960–61 season were strong—Nielsen indicated the show dominated its Sunday time slot. Among some one hundred programs in prime time, the Sullivan show ranked fifteenth, one step down from last season, yet clearly holding a coveted spot. The show was withstanding the Western onslaught, which continued apace: five of the top six programs that season were set in the Old West. But the once highly ranked Western running opposite the Sullivan show, *Maverick*, was now homesteading outside the top twenty.

As the season began, and the ratings pointed to the year's success, Ed huddled with his lawyer Arnold Grant and his MCA management team. It was time to renegotiate his compensation package. A few months before, Ed had written a letter to CBS head Bill Paley as a first move in the negotiation process. Pointing out that a recent Sullivan show garnered a remarkable fifty-nine-percent audience share, Ed wrote: "I am looking forward eagerly to the Nielsen report, which should show an even more astounding share of audience." He also sent along a Canadian ratings report, which, Sullivan noted, "shows your oldest show topping the Canadian market." In case all the facts and figures didn't suffice, the showman added a dose of sugar: "I always have held you in affectionate respect and even helped straighten out your golf game!"

Sullivan didn't need to do much sweet-talking. "Paley *loved* Ed Sullivan—he loved hits," recalled Mike Dann, a CBS programming head in the 1960s. The new contract reflected that affection. Its terms stretched over an astonishing thirty-five years, stipulating various pay levels over that period. Given that Ed signed the agreement at age fifty-nine, the network was in essence agreeing to reward him handsomely until the end of his days. While he continued to produce the show, his salary would be $1 million per year, with increases in the years ahead. When he ceased production or when the show was canceled, the network guaranteed him a minimum of $100,000 per year. In the event the show was canceled in the next two years, CBS would make an additional payout to Sullivan. The program's production budget was upped to $73,000 per show.

He was, finally, being paid as a superstar. It had taken a long time, in view of the show's twelve-year run and its dominance during most of those years. It was as if there had been a lingering trace of the original CBS attitude of selling the show "with or without Sullivan." But his new pay level (which he didn't release to re- porters as he had in 1954) put that era well in the past. Still, in the years ahead Sul- livan never stopped intimating that network management didn't appreciate him, though with his new contract those complaints rang hollow.

As Ed emerged from negotiations, there was talk—for the first time—of using re- runs in the summer. It had always been a point of pride for him that the show kept creating fresh programs all year long. He himself took a brief summer vacation, using his "break" to produce on-location segments, but substitute hosts kept the show going. Producing nearly fifty new programs a year had given him a competi- tive edge against the better-financed *Comedy Hour*. In mid season, Ed wasn't will- ing to answer reporters' questions about whether he would create new shows all summer, claiming that nothing had been decided. But in the summer of 1961 *The Ed Sullivan Show* ran six weeks of reruns. Additionally, within a few years Ed began taping a number of shows on Monday nights in front of a studio audience, to allow himself and the staff a rest on certain weeks.

Despite his new generous pay package, the showman was in no danger of mel- lowing. Toward the end of the season, the Federal Communications Commission conducted two weeks of hearings in New York City, investigating the current state of television. The hearings produced substantial hand-wringing. FCC chairman Newton Minnow decried the "wasteland" of TV programming, and many of those testifying pointed to what they saw as the villain: ratings, and the need for pro- grammers to lower their standards in service to them.

Nonsense, said Ed in his testimony. Ratings were "dictated by the people" and "present an accurate picture of what the people prefer." Television is necessarily a wasteland, he said, because the round-the-clock demands of the medium make it impossible to maintain consistent quality. He threw cold water on the comments of David Susskind, a television producer who had launched an erudite public affairs talk show in 1958, and who noted that TV had few such shows. "Nobody in televi- sion has been given so many opportunities by all kinds of networks as David Susskind and nobody has had more flops than David Susskind," Ed said, proving he could lead with his elbows even when he wasn't being attacked.

Moreover, he opined, there was hypocrisy on the part of newspaper commenta- tors. Some who demand opera on television "would be bored to death by it," he claimed. He complained that *The New York Times*, when he presented an opera se- ries, had barely covered it. In truth, the newspaper *had* previewed it, and Ed was forced to concede this. (In fact, after prodding he acknowledged that the paper's cov- erage of his show was "wonderful," which, after the initial barbs by critic Jack Gould, it unquestionably had been. Since the mid 1950s the *Times* had treated Sul- livan's nearly every move as newsworthy.) But Ed's point at the hearings was clear:

he had only disdain for those whom he saw as ivory tower types, expecting television to elevate the masses without regard to market realities. Television, in his view, was as rough-and-tumble as the athletic fields of Port Chester. You either scored or you didn't, and complaining was simply proof that you couldn't make the grade.

Ed's roundhouse at David Susskind was only a warm-up for the bare knuckles spirit he brought to that season's encounter with talk show host Jack Paar. It may have been inevitable that Paar and Sullivan would feud; television was hardly big enough for two such sensitive egos. Paar, who had considerable success in the 1950s as a comic—including numerous Sullivan show appearances—became host of the *Tonight Show* in 1957. His skills as a witty and idiosyncratic conversationalist turned the show into a hit for NBC. Like Sullivan, Paar could be mercurial and at times petulant; in 1960 he staged a twenty-five-day walkout after NBC cut one of his jokes from the tape without his consent. (The joke made reference to a "water closet," or toilet, and so was considered too risque for television.)

On March 5, a little known Canadian singer on her way up named Joan Fairfax appeared on the Sullivan show, earning $1,000—on the low end of the show's pay scale, which went up to $10,000 for headliners. The next night she sang on Paar's show for $320, which was union scale. It was unusual that a performer appeared on another program so soon after Sullivan's. His show's contract usually forbade it; Ed didn't want an act he helped popularize to lift anyone else's ratings. But Fairfax had been bumped from an earlier Sullivan show, and was honoring a Paar commitment made long before the schedule change. A few days later, Ed was leafing through fan mail—he remained highly attuned to viewer comments—and came across a reference to Fairfax performing on both shows.

Livid, he called MCA agent Marty Kummer, who he had worked with to book Fairfax, shouted a stream of profanities in his ear, then fired him. As Ed looked into the issue he realized that a number of his favorites, notably comics Myron Cohen and Sam Levenson, were appearing on both his and Paar's show for very different pay scales. And that, improbably, was what angered him: that Paar could book the likes of Sam Levenson for union scale while the Sullivan show had to pay $2,500. But the pay disparity was unavoidable: the Sullivan show was a ratings powerhouse with huge sponsorship revenue; the Paar show was a distant also-ran in the ratings. Ed himself had taken advantage of similarly disparate pay levels when he booked performers to appear for little after they saw hefty paydays on *Comedy Hour*. Paar's show, while never as underfunded as Sullivan's had been, was not a big-budget affair. It was successful by the then-limited standards of late-evening television, but the *Tonight Show* was far from the franchise it later became.

Yet Ed decided to treat Paar as an arch competitor. He issued a dictum to all talent agents: any performer you book on Paar for $320 will be paid no more than that on my show. It had the effect he knew it would have: many performers and agents suddenly forgot that Paar existed. Within days Myron Cohen canceled his upcoming *Tonight Show* appearance. Paar, whose first resort was usually histrionics—though entertaining histrionics—responded by reading a long open letter to Ed on his program: "Ed, I don't have the money to pay performers. This show is a low-budget freak that caught on because performers want to come on and want time to entertain people without the monkey act and the Japanese jugglers waiting in the wings." After his audience's laughter subsided he challenged Ed to a duel: he would ask NBC for the Sunday time slot opposite Sullivan, so that for one evening they would produce competing variety shows, with the winner decided by the ratings.

Ed, deflecting the challenge, quipped, "I think Paar owes me $320. It's the best show he's had in weeks." Then he proposed his own duel. He would come on Paar's show and debate him, with one stipulation: there could be no studio audience—Sullivan knew that Paar could play to a crowd far more effectively than he could. Over the next few days the NBC host tweaked Ed for requesting to ban the studio audience, yet he countered with generous terms: Sullivan could speak first and last and bring his own moderator. Paar asked only that, "some time be given to the issues that he had raised. I don't want to be given four minutes and then eight acrobats come on in the middle." For Paar, whose ratings were dwarfed by Sullivan's, the mini-farce was a Nielsen booster. The longer he kept it going the better. For Sullivan, for whom this kind of thing wasn't his shtick, it was quickly becoming an embarrassment, especially when the national media started covering the conflict round by round. No real issues existed between the two men, except Ed's irrational insistence on pay parity.

Ed agreed to have a studio audience present for the debate, and after some minor jousting the event was scheduled for the *Tonight Show* broadcast on March 13. That afternoon Ed and Bob Precht met with Paar's producer at the office of publisher Bennett Cerf, whom Ed had chosen as the moderator. In mid meeting Sullivan realized Paar had changed the rules, or at least that's how Ed saw it. The NBC host now wanted a discussion, not a debate—though clearly the agreement had been to debate. To be sure, the difference between a debate and a discussion on a talk show was negligible, but what Ed feared was a freewheeling back and forth. Knowing he was no match for Paar's verbal wit, Ed had agreed to a debate with a plan to read prepared remarks. He wanted no part of a discussion.

He issued a press release at 3:30 P.M., saying it was a debate or nothing. "I am ready to go on tonight and debate. If Paar wants to change his mind before 4 P.M., I will go on. Paar can now put up or shut up and his deadline is 4 P.M. I have no further comment." NBC retorted with its own release claiming that Sullivan had thrown in the towel—provoking an angry response from Ed: "Paar is a welcher. He is a hell of shadow boxer, but I think he chokes up when he realizes that the time has come to stand up and debate." Paar replied in turn, claiming that Sullivan "would not agree to a free and open discussion of the issues, the only condition I made and the only democratic way of clearing up the whole mess." On his show he opined, "Ed Sullivan proved to be as honest as he is talented. . . . Ed Sullivan is a liar. That is libel. He must now sue and he must go to court—not like Winchell and Hoffa [two previous Paar combatants], who sue just to save their face."

The squabble had gone on far too long—many were now calling it ridiculous—and Ed wanted out. He issued a final statement that he was going to Miami to emcee a show for crippled children, asserting, "This controversy, as Paar's behavior proved last night, is clearly a misuse of the airways and has become objectionable to the public. Consequently I will have nothing more to say on the subject." In the aftermath, *Life* magazine's cover showed two puppets, Sullivan and Paar, slugging it out. The accompanying article was composed of photos of the puppets in absurd poses, and the captions quoted the men's actual words, which fit the silly photos all too well.

The irony of the feud was that Ed initiated it just a few months after signing his new contract with CBS. He was the producer of a ratings giant, a star of a major network who had just signed a lucrative contract extending until the very end of his days. But he had picked a fisticuffs with the host of an also-ran show who didn't threaten him in any way.

It was as if Ed, having found the fame he always had hungered for, could not let go of the pugilistic side of himself that helped him achieve it. He needed someone or something to struggle against, even if he had to invent it out of whole cloth. The word that critics most often used to describe him was "wooden," because he showed the public only his stiff emcee persona. Yet his unguarded reactions were almost always uncontrollably visceral. Real woodenness was beyond him.

As Ed took his European vacation that summer the Cold War took a turn toward the frigid. On August 12 East German leader Walter Ulbricht signed the command to close the border between East and West Berlin; the next day construction of the Berlin Wall began. It was exactly the type of event that inspired Ed, who saw the show as a vehicle for reflecting world affairs, regardless of the mixed response this had generated. He immediately flew to Berlin and met with U.S. military authorities. Would they authorize a Sullivan show to entertain the troops stationed in Germany? After getting agreement he began assembling a cast of stars for an October program.

Jack Paar, perhaps inspired by the impending Sullivan show, scrambled to launch his own Berlin Wall show. He succeeded in getting there first, but the Paar program became a minor fiasco. He filmed it literally within the shadow of the wall, commandeering a squad of some fifty American soldiers as a chaperone. The flurry of troop movement not authorized by senior military officials caused grave concern. With White House approval, the Defense Department launched an investigation; the fear was that massing such a force so close to the wall could have sparked an international incident. Two Army officers were censured for cooperating with Paar.

In contrast, the Sullivan show in October was a major public relations victory. Taped in front of an audience of six thousand American troops in West Berlin's Sportspalast, headliner Louis Armstrong blew through—appropriately—"When the Saints Go Marching In." Accompanying the jazz trumpeter was Sullivan's typically eclectic mix: Metropolitan Opera star Roberta Peters; classical pianist Van Cliburn; comic-magician Bob Lewis; pop chart powerhouse Connie Francis singing her hit theme song to MGM's *Where the Boys Are*; comedians Rowan and Martin; and a troupe of French cancan dancers called The Bluebell Girls. Ed asked audience member Lieutenant General Albert Watson to take a bow.

Connie Francis, who had become friends with Ed, suggested that they visit the communist sector of Berlin. "We looked at that wall and I said, 'Ed, we've got to get to the other side,' and he said, 'Yes we do—tomorrow we'll go.'" Ed and Sylvia accompanied Francis on a tour bus that traveled through East Berlin, during which no pictures or questions were allowed. At the sight of the city's gloom, "He was just as distraught as I was," the singer recalled.

On a lighter note, Ed accompanied Louis Armstrong out to West Berlin nightclubs for the trumpeter's local performances. As production assistant John Moffit recalled, one night Ed returned to the hotel giddy from having downed several drinks. The hotel had asked all of its patrons to leave their shoes outside their room doors, to be polished by hotel staff. "Ed was going around and tying all the shoelaces together, laughing and chortling away," Moffit remembered.

The broadcast was such a success that Ed reprised it the following fall, December 1962, taking a show to the Guantanamo Naval Base in Cuba, again booking Louis Armstrong and Connie Francis. Like the Berlin Wall show, this program enabled Ed to thrust *The Ed Sullivan Show* into the international spotlight. The Cuban missile crisis—bringing America and the Soviet Union to an eyeball-to-eyeball nuclear standoff—had unfolded just several weeks earlier. Production assistant Vince Calandra remembered the atmosphere of fear as they flew down; because of the recent tension the Air Force provided an escort of four fighter jets. "It was scary!" he recalled. Armstrong, again choosing a song with great appropriateness, played "Nobody Knows the Trouble I've Seen."

The Louis Armstrong–Connie Francis pairing was typical of Ed's approach to music in the 1961–62 season. The old guard was very much in residence, yet it was increasingly leavened with the new sound. Just a few weeks after the Berlin show Ed booked Duke Ellington for a duet with Armstrong, the two giants interpreting "In a Mellow Mood"; on that same show, sugary pop crooner Paul Anka trilled a jazzy version of "Jingle Bells." (In a similarly unlikely cultural stretch, Anka later shared the bill with poet Carl Sandburg.) In November, the very square Steve Lawrence, a Sullivan favorite, shared the bill with Ray Charles, who laid down a rollicking rhythm and blues sound that had rarely been heard in middle-class households. Two months later, suave Robert Goulet (whom Ed mistakenly introduced as Canadian) glided over the Cole Porter standard "What Is This Thing Called Love?" on the same night that soul singer Jackie Wilson squeezed the emotion out of his Top 40 hit "The Greatest Hurt." That hour also found the Marquis Chimps doing a tumbling act and smoking cigarettes, a booking that may have been a nod to sponsor York Cigarettes.

That winter, pop duo the Everly Brothers—performing in Marine uniforms during their short enlisted stint—harmonized on "Crying in the Rain" in the same hour trumpeter Al Hirt jazzed up Cole Porter's "Night and Day." For every booking of vanguard artists like Fats Domino, Dion, and Chubby Checker there was an equal and opposite booking of Johnny Mathis or the McGuire Sisters. For every appearance by folksingers—now on the increase—such as The Highwaymen, who sang "Michael Row the Boat Ashore" or the fresh-faced The Brothers Four, who harmonized on "This Land Is Your Land," there was a counterweight, like 1940s star Kate Smith belting out "Climb Every Mountain" or balladeer Billy Eckstine getting intimate with "What Kind of Fool Am I?" During these seasons in the early 1960s it was still possible to entertain both teens and their parents without alienating either group.

Broadway continued to star; that spring Ed presented a scene from the long-running hit *West Side Story*, in an hour in which Liberace performed a tribute to vaudeville, dancing a soft-shoe to "Me and My Shadow." And Ed seemed to be on a mission to book every classic jazz act, spotlighting Sarah Vaughn, Lionel Hampton, Dizzy Gillespie, the Woody Herman Orchestra, and their contemporaries.

In June, Ed wrote one of his many letters to *New York Times* critic Jack Gould; a *Times* editor noted that no entertainer wrote as many letters to the paper as Sullivan.

Civil rights was coming to the forefront of national consciousness and Gould had written a piece about the role of black performers on television, noting that it was minimal. But he left out the Sullivan show's contribution. After Ed's letter, Gould issued a correction: "In the past year he has offered thirty-three Negro acts, involving one hundred two individuals and an expenditure of $201,000 in fees. Herewith apologies to Mr. Sullivan for omitting his admirable record."

On a related note, the first Sullivan show of the next season was interrupted by a CBS News bulletin: James Meredith, a black college student, had been admitted to the University of Mississippi, an historic first. An angry mob of two thousand had converged on the campus to block the special Sunday registration. In the ensuing riot, two died, twenty-eight federal marshals were wounded, and one hundred sixty were injured. Ed followed the events closely; his support for the civil rights movement was wholehearted. The following June, at a $100-a-plate dinner in honor of four civil rights leaders, he presented an award to Martin Luther King, Jr.

Ed's lifestyle after his recent pay increase was not perceptibly different than when he had signed his first lucrative contract in the mid 1950s. And this itself had not been markedly higher than when he first moved into the Delmonico in 1944. Ed and Sylvia's apartment was surprisingly modest, given his income. The staffers who visited often remarked that its décor made it hard to believe its inhabitants were affluent, with the exception of a handful of original oil paintings Sylvia had collected.

The furniture was a homey mixture of Italian and French, with antique satin drapes in the living room and sitting room, where Sylvia played games of mah-jongg with her friends when not volunteering for charity concerns, which she did frequently. Ed conducted much of the business of the show from the Delmonico, and his office was littered with show business memorabilia: a copy of *Time* with his face on the cover, photos from the show—Cole Porter, Humphrey Bogart, Ella Fitzgerald—and a picture frame that was a gift from Jerry Lewis. (Lewis had sent his own photo in the frame, which Ed removed and replaced with a photo of himself on the golf course.)

Working quietly amid the clutter, the hundreds of books, and the scattered newspapers, was almost always Ed's man Friday, Carmine Santullo. A quiet, sweet, unassuming man, who virtually worshipped Ed, Carmine handled the incessant stream of phone calls, among countless other duties. After working with Sullivan for decades he could anticipate his response to any request. "Carmine was Ed's Nubian slave," recalled Sullivan show secretary Sistie Moffit. He did most of the legwork for Ed's *Daily News* column (still published twice weekly), and many said he all but wrote it, though Ed made a point of insisting he wrote it himself.

The Delmonico had almost no kitchen, but Ed and Sylvia didn't need one. They continued to dine out almost every evening in fashionable Manhattan restaurants, most often dining by themselves, though fans and friends invariably stopped by to socialize. As many show staffers recalled, Sylvia loved going out and always dressed with great elegance. At dinner, her tastes were gourmet, unlike Ed, who had little sense of smell or taste and so was always complimenting the chef while putting small packets of artificial sugar into his wine. After dinner the couple might see a Broadway show or a nightclub revue, which Ed reviewed in his column (advertisements for

Broadway shows were now in their fourth decade of including one-line blurbs touting his opinion). They often stayed out for late evening drinks at a nightclub, perhaps Danny's Hideaway or the Copacabana, where Ed still scouted for talent; on certain evenings they were out until 3 A.M. Ed almost never watched television, except for *The Tonight Show* with Johnny Carson, which he was quite fond of.

The Sullivans were invited to any number of social galas, but usually declined. Ed didn't like large groups, preferring to socialize with people he knew well. If they were out with a group and Ed didn't know one person it made him uneasy. However, when he granted one of his many interviews, he invited reporters to the Delmonico and chatted volubly, jumping freely from topic to topic. Some interviewers felt they met a completely different man than the one seen on his Sunday show. He also overcame his natural reserve to attend the innumerable events at which he was given an award. In October 1962, for example, he was honored for promoting international goodwill by the People-to-People Sports Committee. City planner Robert Moses, commending Ed's spirit to the six hundred guests, said, "if we can continue that spirit into other international affairs we shall be well on the way to brotherhood and peace."

Ed, out late and usually sleeping late, didn't eat breakfast until around 11 A.M., ordering room service or having Carmine fix it. Either way, the meal rarely varied: a lamb chop, artificially sweetened pears, and a glass of iced tea. Because his breakfast was late morning, his meals were out of sync with the typical schedule; if he had a business lunch in the early afternoon and wasn't hungry, he might drop a chicken leg in his pocket, taking it out after midnight for a snack. When he went to lunch and forgot his wallet, not an uncommon occurrence, the restaurant called the show and put it on his tab. To get around town he hailed his own taxi—he disdained limousines, or anything resembling an entourage. Once inside the cab he invariably quizzed the driver: what did you think of last week's show?

In the 1961–62 season, NBC renewed its attempt to break Sullivan's vise grip on Sunday night, launching *Walt Disney's Wonderful World of Color*, hosted by the beloved Disney himself. Originally debuting on ABC in 1954, the Disney show was one of television's most successful. When the Sullivan show was the fifth-ranked program in 1954–55, *Disney* had run sixth; when *The Ed Sullivan Show* ascended to number three the following year, *Disney* ranked fourth. After that the programs' ratings began to diverge, with *Disney*'s falling further behind. Never before 1961, however, had *Disney* run opposite *The Ed Sullivan Show*, and never had it run on NBC, a far stronger network than ABC at the time. That fall, NBC broadcast *Disney* from 7:30 to 8:30 P.M., opposite the first half hour of *The Ed Sullivan Show*. It was followed by *Car 54, Where Are You?*, a situation comedy that was never a major ratings contender.

The Disney show achieved part of NBC's goal. Although the program trailed Sullivan in the ratings, it pulled his ranking down to number twenty, from the previous season's fourteen. The effect was temporary. In the 1962–63 season, *The Ed Sullivan Show* climbed back to number fourteen, while *Disney*'s ratings remained beneath the top twenty. It wasn't that Sullivan changed his formula; he could do little in response to Disney except include kids' fare as he always had. He merely updated it as the culture updated, as he had since 1948. And he now had the help of his son-in-law Bob Precht, sharpening the show's production values and nudging Ed toward the contemporary.

Central to the 1962–63 season's success was Ed's continuing alembic of the new pop sound with the unquestionably square. The square was as milquetoast as ever—Sammy Davis crooned "What Kind of Fool Am I?"—but the new was heading in unforeseen directions. A notable example was the booking of twenty-one-year-old folksinger Bob Dylan, which ran afoul of network censors that May. At dress rehearsal, Dylan sang his song "Talking John Birch Society Blues," a skewering of the archconservative group's anticommunist fervor ("Well I was looking everywhere for them gol-darned Reds / I got up in the morning and looked under my bed"). Precht had okayed the song beforehand and Ed had approved it in rehearsal. But the CBS Standards and Practices representative who watched all dress rehearsals—this was live TV, so performances were vetted in advance—vetoed the selection, giving no official explanation. Dylan, rather than choose an alternative, decided not to appear on the show. Both Bob and Ed said they wanted to have him back, but he never returned.

That Dylan was booked at all was a sign that Precht was taking a stronger role in the show's choices. Ed knew how to follow the pop charts and had a knack for combining current chart climbers with older artists. But Dylan, though signed with Columbia Records, wasn't on the charts at the time. Not until that summer, when Peter, Paul & Mary turned "Blowin' in the Wind" into a hit, did Dylan start to become widely known. It was Precht's youthful approach that was pushing the show toward performers like Dylan who were ahead of the cultural curve.

That fall Sullivan's comedy bookings took a similarly contemporary turn, when he presented a series of politically pointed segments entitled "What's Going on Here?" Written and performed by the stars of the popular British satirical revues "Beyond the Fringe" and "The Establishment," the segments were presented as mock TV newscasts. Before they were aired, a reporter asked Bob Precht how the notoriously irreverent comics would fit with the Sullivan show. "The actors will be free to prepare whatever they like, but Ed will retain editorial control," Precht said. Ed, in fact, gave them far more latitude than he would have in years past.

In a typical Sullivan mix, the acerbic British comedy team was booked to perform with easygoing comics Bob and Ray, an American duo whose dry wit had been a staple of 1940s radio. But in this case the pairing did nothing to soften the British edge. The English satirists intoned fictional news reports like "Alabama has moved ahead of Mississippi in the race race" and "Fidel Castro is accusing the CIA of launching hurricane Flora. It was last seen heading for Red China." The furthest extreme of the troupe's work was a mock news conference about Vietnam. As performed by actors John Bird and Jeremy Geidt, who portrayed President Kennedy and a reporter, the dialogue disintegrated into meaningless government-speak. Lending extra bite, the segment included a clip of Kennedy himself zigzagging through a near duplicate of the comics' lines. The suggestion that a U.S. president was dissembling on a military effort was unheard of in a major venue at the time.

After the segment ended, Ed attempted to diffuse the effect by telling viewers that the White House had agreed to the use of the Kennedy clip. It was, apparently, all in good fun, but for Ed to watch this material in dress rehearsal and approve it for his national audience meant his approach was changing.

Certainly the politically charged nature of the "What's Going On Here?" segments was the exception in the show's early 1960s comedy bookings, though by now many of the show's comics had evolved past the Henny Youngman–vaudeville school. Their routines tended to involve longer setups and more references to current events, rather than the one-liners and timeless domestic squabbles mined by 1950s comedians. One of Ed's favorites in this period was Stiller and Meara, a husband-and-wife team whose act was developed in Greenwich Village clubs, and whose Jewish–Catholic combination mirrored Sullivan's own marriage; Ed booked them a remarkable thirty-six times. He was also fond of Phyllis Diller, an early female stand-up comedienne known for her lighthearted edge, and Jackie Mason and Alan King, Borscht Belters who could reach Peoria. These comedians' humor was transitional rather than forward looking, contemporary without being edgy.

This same "era between the eras" aesthetic informed the movie that Ed appeared in that year, *Bye Bye Birdie*, based on the Tony Award–winning 1961 Broadway musical. In the film's convoluted plot, Elvis-like singer Conrad Birdie is about to be drafted, but first travels to a small Ohio town to kiss good-bye an adoring teenage fan, an event to be broadcast on *The Ed Sullivan Show*. Dick Van Dyke plays a songwriter who's convinced that if Birdie sings his song on the Sullivan show, fame will automatically follow. Ann-Margret and Bobby Rydell play teenagers in love, with Paul Lynde and Mary LaRoche as the disapproving parents.

Birdie is all about how rock 'n' roll and love-lust drives kids crazy, but in the movie's world these forces are merely catalysts for a lighthearted romp. Protesters converge on Washington carrying signs protesting Birdie's draft, a scene inspired by the real-life protesters now staging the first few placard-carrying parades in the nation's capital. Yet in *Birdie* the protesters are just a bunch of wacky teenagers. The movie was a nod to the emerging youth culture, but its wink at the audience reassured viewers that it was nothing to take seriously.

Ed on film was much smoother than Ed on live television. With a director who had authority over him and with multiple takes, he suffered no fumbled lines and no garbled syntax. A box-office success, the movie paid homage to Ed's now-iconic status—a guest shot on Sullivan, according to *Birdie*, was a guarantee of fame. Ed played himself as completely assured of the movie's main tenet, that is, that Ed Sullivan was a leading promoter of a rock 'n' roll–crazed youth culture. This referenced Ed's real-life booking of Elvis and a long train of other nascent pop-rockers, from Buddy Holly to Sam Cooke. While many adults shook their heads in disbelief, his open invitation to these acts gave the new youth sound the Sullivan imprimatur of approval. And in case viewers were in doubt about the Sullivan show's cultural primacy, the script worked the point hard. Bob Precht, played by the fiftyish Robert Paige, exclaimed, "You know, with a plug like this, this song will sell a million records. Man, what royalties!"

In *Birdie*, the world that Ed helped wrought is in full flower. The teens all seem brainwashed, thinking with one mind, seemingly zombified by adulation of their rock 'n' roll hero. The fresh-faced, clean-cut Birdie, an Elvis clone, wears a gold lamé outfit with gold boots, and his singing causes an entire crowd of teens to actually faint with adoration. The movie's climactic scene, with Birdie-Elvis on *The Ed Sullivan Show* amid wildly enthusiastic teens, is essentially a replay of the real Elvis debut on Sullivan in 1956—but a fully neutered one. Oddly, the movie is a musical about rock 'n' roll but its music isn't Elvis-like. Instead it's a kind of jazzed up full-orchestra sound reminiscent of Bobby Darin. Even Birdie onstage at the Sullivan show plays only lightly strummed folk music. Apparently the filmmakers were attempting a balancing act similar to Ed's: they wanted to attract both a teen and an adult audience, without offending either one.

Birdie opened in theaters the same month, April 1963, that Topo Gigio debuted on the Sullivan show. A diminutive foam rubber hand puppet, Topo was operated by a team of four Italian puppeteers; he gestured, he danced, his giant ears flopped, his little mouth moved, and he voiced sweet endearments with a loopy Italian accent. Ed, breaking his longstanding rule against taking a lead performance role, developed a routine with Topo. When "The Little Italian Mouse" was a guest, the stage went dark except for a spotlight on Sullivan and the marionette, and the two chatted as confidants, the serious-looking showman leaning in to receive the puppet's cute replies. They spoke about nothing in particular, yet their tête-à-têtes went on for several minutes. With the Italian puppeteers' rudimentary English, and Ed's tendency to fumble his lines, the show's staff had to be on its toes as the segment veered off script.

Topo revealed an unseen side of Ed. Onstage he operated at a remove, only in rare moments breaking the self-created wall of formality separating him from his audience. But in the Topo segments this wall dissolved. He seemed to lose himself in conversation with the little mouse, chatting intimately with the character as if he were alive. In their affectionate back-and-forth, Ed displayed a vulnerable side of himself that had never been hinted at in his many years of hosting. On its face the Topo–Ed act was a contradiction. Here was Ed, a man whom his critics (and even

With the Italian puppet Topo Gigio in the mid 1960s. The cute puppet was the prop that Sullivan had always wanted to soften his onstage persona. (CBS Photo Archive)

friends) had called every variation of stiff, who had cursed and elbowed his way to stardom, burning through an ulcer, yet onstage with Topo he was a sentimental ball of sweetness, being childlike for a live audience of forty million viewers.

The little mouse was the prop he had always wanted. This was what he sought when he hired Patsy Flick to heckle him in 1948, or booked Will Jordan to mimic him in 1953. Topo opened him up. With the little mouse Ed was anything but Old Stoneface; he was tender and soft. Their segments invariably ended with Topo imploring "Kees-a-me goodnight, Eddie."

Ed grew to love the little character. He enjoyed the act so much he eventually wore it out; his staff was relieved when he finally quit. He booked Topo an astounding fifty times; only one other act received more bookings (Canadian comedy team Wayne and Schuster, fifty-eight times). Sullivan became so identified with Topo that sometimes as he walked the streets of New York a truck driver would yell out "Kees-a-me goodnight, Eddie!"

It's likely that part of Ed's motivation for developing the Topo character was the competition from Disney. With the animator's show offering the younger set a universe of fantasy and delight, spotlighting the little mouse may have helped parents keep the channel turned to CBS. If Sullivan's plan was to turn Topo into an irresistible character, he succeeded. The foam rubber puppet became a star in his own right, spawning a legion of little Topo figurines and dolls. The United Nations named him their official "spokesmouse." In 1965, United film studios released a movie starring the diminutive puppet (in which Topo attempts a trip to the moon), and acquired the rights to make one Topo film a year for the next four years.

In late May 1963, Ed and Sylvia were invited to Manhattan's Waldorf-Astoria hotel to attend a birthday party for President John Kennedy. The event was a glittering dinner and variety show for six hundred members of the President's Club, each of whom donated at least $1,000 to the Democratic National Committee. Along with the president and his wife, many of the members of his administration were there: Attorney General Robert Kennedy, Vice President Lyndon Johnson, United Nations representative Adlai Stevenson, and Under Secretary of State Averell Harriman.

Ed adored the Kennedys. Other presidents would invite him to the White House; he and Sylvia attended two state dinners hosted by President Johnson, and President Nixon invited the couple to help celebrate Duke Ellington's seventieth birthday. But these occasions never seemed to matter to him as much as a chance to rub shoulders with the Kennedys. He contributed to JFK's presidential campaign, and sent a regular stream of birthday notes and letters of encouragement to members of the Kennedy clan. Sullivan was a friend of patriarch Joe Kennedy, who had been a lion of café society in the 1930s; Ed had lauded him in his column for decades. The two men corresponded, and in one letter Ed suggested that musical theater artists Oscar Hammerstein and Moss Hart write speeches for President Kennedy—an idea that Joe Kennedy liked, though it never happened. The elder Kennedy attended Ed and Sylvia's thirtieth anniversary party in April 1960, and for the event he wrote the couple an affectionate letter that concluded, "All the Kennedys send you and your family our love."

Joe Kennedy also sent Sylvia a note in October of that year as the presidential election neared, making reference to Richard Nixon's problems with makeup in the

Old Blue Eyes and Old Stoneface, at the Eden Roc nightclub, Florida, 1964. The longtime friendship between the two men boiled over into a bitter squabble in the mid 1950s, though Sinatra later made a peace overture. (Time Life Pictures/Getty Images)

recent presidential debates. "Dear Sylvia, I had read that piece about makeup. I agree with you—how many more excuses can they find? Incidentally, things are getting better every day. Sincerely, Joe." In April 1962, Ed sent a letter to Joe Kennedy in which he enthused, "I think that your brilliant young son has wrapped up another term in the White House as a result of his quick and determined handling of Steel. . . . Poor Nixon is in a helluva spot. Now he can write another book and add an additional 'crisis.'"

President Kennedy, in March 1961, sent a short letter to Sullivan agreeing to tape a promotional message Ed had requested, for an event that encouraged international understanding. The letter from Kennedy was typed and addressed "Dear Mr. Sullivan" but the president scratched out "Mr. Sullivan" and wrote in "Ed." "The idea for your International Assembly sounds most interesting and it is certainly a much-needed effort in the field of international communications," Kennedy wrote. "I would be happy to prepare a taped message for your first Assembly."

In later years, Ed contributed to the Kennedy Library, and received letters of thanks from Ted Kennedy, Robert Kennedy, and Jacqueline Kennedy. Ted Kennedy's wife Joan sent Ed a thank-you note in July 1964 with an added postscript: "P.S. Ted and I watch your wonderful show every week and enjoy it so much."

Given his feelings of affection for the Kennedys, it was no surprise that Ed found the birthday party for President Kennedy in late May 1963 to be a magical evening. He called it one of the "unforgettable moments" in his many years of outings with Sylvia. Despite its elegance, there was a touch of informality to the evening—the ballroom contained no dais or head table, and the president circulated through the crowd, reportedly shaking hands with almost all the guests. The Waldorf-Astoria had been transformed for the event. A top Broadway lighting specialist, Abe Feder, designed a display to make the hotel's lobby resemble a palace entryway. The stage was set up as a theater in the round, built around a "Circle of Life" display in the ballroom's floor. In his keynote speech, Kennedy described the Democrats as "the party of hope," and, referencing the many Broadway and Hollywood attendees, said that it was natural that performers "should find themselves at home in the party of hope."

Although Ed was often tapped to emcee high-profile events, for this evening he was invited as a performer. The program's variety show was produced by Alan Jay Lerner, who wrote the book and lyrics to the Broadway shows *My Fair Lady* and *Camelot*; Ed had done a tribute show dedicated to Lerner two year earlier. Ann-Margret, who had appeared with Ed in *Bye Bye Birdie*, sang "Baby Won't You Please Come Home," and Jimmy Durante, who Ed had known since his speakeasy days in the 1920s, donned a Kennedy wig and crooned "Start Off Each Day with a Smile." Bob Newhart, a Sullivan regular, performed a stand-up routine satirizing television and the tobacco industry. For the finale, Mitch Miller entered with an eleven-man chorus singing "Together." Ed was part of the chorus, along with Henry Fonda, Eddie Fisher, Robert Preston, Van Johnson, Peter Lawford, Mel Ferrer, Tony Randall, Donald O'Connor, David Susskind, and Bobby Darin. Henry Fonda surprised everyone by launching into a quick-step tap dance, later confiding to Ed, "I used to be a member of Chorus Equity." Following the chorus onstage was Louis Armstrong, singing "When the Saints Go Marching In," after which Audrey Hepburn sang "Happy Birthday."

However festive, the party at the Waldorf-Astoria was to be the president's last birthday. When the charismatic Kennedy was assassinated while touring Dallas in a motorcade seven months later, it threw the country into a shocked state of mourning. For days, television coverage of the tragedy was nonstop; the Sullivan show on November 24, just two days after the event, was preempted. Earlier that day, Jack Ruby had shot and killed Kennedy's assassin, Lee Harvey Oswald, as he was being transported to a nearby jail.

The following week, Sullivan grappled with how to put on a variety show in a period of national mourning. After extended discussion, he decided to host a show with no comedy. Then, just days later, he reversed himself. He had negotiated with impresario Sol Hurok, who had brought Russia's Obratsov Puppet Theatre to the United States, for the rights to present a full-hour program of the puppets. A show for the kids seemed appropriate.

The Obratsov puppet show was a lighthearted affair, though Ed appeared to take no joy in it. At the beginning of the hour, with his always-grave face now looking almost funereal, he announced that he was presenting the puppet program as a tonic for "the nightmare week we've been through." The look on his face that evening was like a headline: the country had fallen into a deep grief, an innate somberness that it seemed nothing could revive. As the calendar inched toward 1964, the gray national mood felt as if it would stretch into the foreseeable future. Was there nothing that could lift America's spirits?

CHAPTER FIFTEEN

Beatlemania

A S ED WALKED ONSTAGE TO BEGIN HIS BROADCAST on February 9, 1964, little about his demeanor revealed what this night was to be. Yet surely he felt it. In retrospect this evening's show would be a cultural capstone, a black-and-white snapshot that defined the era as much as any of the decade's moments. Its video footage would be replayed endlessly, as if it were some kind of visual mantra that contained the essence of its tumultuous period. Ed's mien, however, was hardly different than during the hundreds of Sunday nights he had walked onstage over the last sixteen years.

As always, he was dressed in his trademark Dunhill suit, with a small white handkerchief jutting from the left breast pocket. His hair was slicked straight back in the same style he had worn it in since his reporter days in the early 1920s, a bit of dark hair dye the only concession to the years. The camera showed his steps to be stiff and measured. As he got to center stage, he managed a momentary smile that did little to brighten his almost cadaverous countenance.

But the studio audience's expectant buzz was palpable. As the applause in CBS Studio 50 went on longer than usual, threatening to run away with itself, he waved his arm in a gesture of, *okay kids, let's quiet down.* That afternoon at dress rehearsal he had warned the audience—largely teenage girls—to behave themselves. Otherwise, he had half-joked, he would "call in a barber." Outside the theater at Broadway and 53rd Street there had been a near riot earlier that day, and an extra contingent of New York's finest had been required to keep order.

He told his viewers he had just received a "very nice" telegram from Elvis and his manager, Colonel Tom Parker, wishing the Beatles—that evening's headliner, making their American debut—"a tremendous success." (Elvis, of course, wished the Beatles no such thing. The Fab Four, having just hit number one on the pop charts three weeks earlier, were pushing Elvis off the rock 'n' roll throne. His resentment and envy of them is well documented; years later, in Elvis' surprise visit to the Nixon White House, woozy with barbiturates, he explained to the president that it was groups like the Beatles who were leading kids toward drugs. But in 1964, sending this telegram was a good way to keep his name in front of the kids.)

The crowd, at the mention of Elvis and the Beatles in the same sentence, once again began bubbling over, and Ed again motioned to quiet them down. Veering from his usual practice, he began listing some of the season's big moments: the singing nun Sister Sourire, the puppet Topo Gigio, the previous week's duet of Sammy Davis, Jr., and Ella Fitzgerald. He was, as he often did, speaking in code: *don't worry, the teenagers don't own this show, there's always something for you older folks, and the little ones, too.* For his studio audience, Sullivan's catalog of the show's allures was a minor agony, something to endure politely while attempting to keep the dam from bursting.

Then he said it. He announced that the Beatles would be out onstage shortly. At that point was heard a single female moan, apparently involuntary, almost sexual in its longing. *The Beatles.* Sullivan ignored it, mimicking himself as he set up the commercial break, after which he would bring on the English group: "If you're a person who needs to be shown, here's a *rilly* big proof from all new Aeroshave shaving cream. . . ."

———

Ed's decision to book the Beatles came about partially by chance—or so the story goes. In truth, he helped invent a fabricated version of the event, a bit of creative storytelling that became accepted as historical fact.

According to Beatles lore, on the previous October 31, Ed and Sylvia were waiting for a flight in London Airport. While in London, they had visited Peter Prichard, an easygoing young Englishman who was Ed's European talent scout, and who also worked for powerhouse British impresarios Lew and Leslie Grade. For Peter, who had performed in English vaudeville as a boy, landing the assignment as Sullivan's eyes and ears in Europe was a dream job. He met Ed when the showman was auditioning talent agents at London's Savoy Hotel; Peter was one of several agents Ed invited to come speak to him about their acts. Ed asked Peter to give his appraisal of the other agents' acts. "I gave him my honest opinion, and I presume he liked it, because he called me in the next day, then he called Lew and said, 'I've got your young man with me, he's very good—he's crafty.'" Over time, Prichard recalled, he and Ed developed something of a father–son relationship.

When Ed made one of his frequent trips to Europe, he always visited Peter in London, where they went to the theater together. If Ed heard of a European performer, he called Peter to investigate; the young agent also flew to Beirut, Russia, and Greece to see acts at Ed's request. When Ed and Sylvia took their annual vacation in France, invariably staying at the Carleton Hotel in Cannes, Ed invited Peter and his wife to join them for a couple weeks. During their annual French vacations the two sat on the beach and talked for hours, Peter telling Ed about current European acts, Ed regaling the younger man with stories of his reporter days. Peter, who addressed Ed as "Mr. Sullivan" in his presence, held the showman in great regard and always listened raptly. Prichard remembered his friend as "a man's man, tough, who wouldn't handle fools easily."

As Ed and Sylvia sat in London Airport in October 1963, an English rock 'n' roll group was returning from a five-day tour of Sweden. The airport was mobbed by frenzied teenagers eager for a glimpse or a word—anything—from these young musicians. By some reports the crowd numbered close to fifteen hundred semicrazed fans. Their manic energy brought the airport to a near standstill—it even delayed Prime Minister Sir Alec Douglas-Home as his limousine was pulling into the airport. Ed knew a phenomenon when he saw one. Soon thereafter he called Peter Prichard; did Peter know who they were? Yes, they were called the Beatles, and they were becoming quite the sensation. Trusting his young friend's opinion, Ed told him to keep track of the band. When they were ready for America he wanted to book them.

The London Airport story makes for a flattering portrait of Ed: in a moment of serendipity, the veteran showman, always looking for the next trend, spots a rock 'n' roll band perched on the cusp of international fame. But it's highly unlikely that Ed was in London Airport on October 31. His twice-weekly *Daily News* column shows him to be in New York on this date. It's possible he could have made a trip to London between columns, but he invariably mentioned his foreign jaunts in the *Daily News*, and this period's columns included no such reference. And nothing in his show's schedule called for a trip to London in October. He *was* in London for a few weeks in September, at the end of his summer vacation, but there was no Beatles airport ruckus then.

By his own account, Ed first learned of the Beatles by reading the newspapers, not in an airport sighting. Ten months after the Beatles debut on his show, he wrote a letter to British showman Leslie Grade: "You have been misinformed—or understandably have forgotten how I came to sign the Beatles. In late September 1963 when we were taping acts in London, I locked up the Beatles, sight unseen, because London papers gave tremendous Page 1 coverage to the fact that both the Queen's flight and the newly elected Prime Minister Douglas-Home's plane to Scotland had been delayed in takeoffs for three hours. The reason: the airport runways had been completely engulfed by thousands of youngsters assembled at the airport to cheer the unknown Beatles!"

The letter contains a misstatement. The only time both the prime minister and the Beatles were at London Airport was October 31, so Ed was incorrect in his reference to late September. But his statement that he read news accounts of the band before seeing them appears true. He said as much in a 1968 interview with the *Saturday Evening Post.* The interviewer, noting that Sullivan told him that he learned of the Beatles in the newspapers, quoted Ed's recollection of seeing the headlines: "'Sylvia,' he said (Mrs. Sullivan recalls it well), 'Sylvia, there must be something here.'"

One other thing the letter doesn't make clear: the news accounts of the Beatles that Ed read were probably the British clippings that Peter Prichard sent him in the fall of 1963. Throughout most of that fall, American newspapers hardly knew the Beatles existed—the band was all but unknown in the United States. And in fact it was a call from the London-based Prichard, along with these clippings, that convinced Ed to give this band a guest shot.

It's not surprising that Sullivan booked the Beatles based on news accounts and a tip from Prichard, given how much he relied on newspapers and his talent scouts. He deserves no less credit for understanding the band's potential. He was agreeing to present a group that, at the time he booked them, had never charted a single U.S. hit—there was an element of risk involved. Moreover, he had long been an adventurous rock promoter. Ever since Elvis he had used his hallowed talent showcase to introduce the latest rock acts to American living rooms, at a time when most adults viewed rock 'n' roll as akin to a social disease. So the story of the London Airport sighting, with its portrait of Ed as a firsthand observer, does capture the spirit with which he stayed current with the new youth sound, if not the actual fact.

Still, Ed enjoyed the London Airport anecdote. It was almost true. He *had* booked the Beatles before any American promoter, he *had* been in London Airport just a few weeks before the band was, and the airport scene had really happened. It's just that Sullivan wasn't there—though at times he claimed he was. (Actually, his version varied based on his mood and what reporter he was talking to.) Just four months after the Beatles debut, he told an interviewer, "We were in London last September. There was a commotion at the airport. We inquired what the cause was and discovered that hundreds of teenagers were at the airport to see the Beatles off." As he repeatedly put himself in London at the time of the first Beatles airport mob scene—complete with the mistaken September date—it became accepted as fact.

Peter Prichard, interviewed decades after the purported London Airport sighting, chuckled, and noted, "Well, as I always said, it's a great press story. What can I say?" The anecdote, he said, sounds like the invention of a public relations expert. "In real life, if it would have happened, he [Sullivan] would have had a photograph of himself there."

However, he hastened to add, "I wouldn't argue with my boss [Sullivan]. After all these many years I wouldn't want to end up being wrong with him. If that's what he said he did, then hey. . . ." In fact, "I would never say aloud that Mr. Sullivan was wrong," remarked Prichard. "I'll be seeing him soon—and watch out! Imagine going through the pearly gates and seeing him coming at me." Prichard laughed, and then imitated the famed Sullivan temper: *"I've got to have a word with you!"*

Regardless of the veracity of the airport story, this much is true: in early November 1963 the Beatles' manager, Brian Epstein, was in America on a twofold mission. He wanted to promote Billy J. Kramer, a young rock singer, and he wanted to replicate the Beatles' European success in the United States. He had major doubts about this latter task. Epstein knew that English bands had never done well in America—and that included the Beatles. The group had released three singles in the United States, with scant success. "She Loves You" had even been played on Dick Clark's popular *American Bandstand* television show in September 1963, yet the tune had cast not even a shadow on the U.S. charts.

Perhaps now was the time. On October 13, the Beatles had performed on *Val Parnell's Sunday Night at the London Palladium*, an English variety program that resembled the Sullivan show. With an audience of more than fifteen million, the band's performance sparked a firestorm of fan interest that London's *Daily Mirror* dubbed "Beatlemania." It was this teenage mania that Epstein hoped to spread to the United States.

Peter Prichard, hearing that the Beatles manager sought an American television audience, placed a quick call to Epstein: "Brian was a friend of mine, and I said, 'Don't do anything until you've met up with Mr. Sullivan.'" Prichard then sent Sullivan a raft of positive reviews of the Beatles' appearance on *Val Parnell*; he also called Ed and said the group was ripe for their American television debut. (These reviews, in fact, were likely the first news reports that Ed read about the Beatles.)

As Prichard recalled, "Ed asked, 'What's the angle?'" meaning, how shall we sell this act to the public? "The angle is that these are the first long-haired boys to play before the Queen," the agent replied. When Ed expressed interest, "I phoned Brian and said, 'You'll be getting a call from Mr. Sullivan.'"

Sullivan met with Epstein at the Delmonico on November 11. They haggled over whether the Beatles would get top billing; Epstein insisted on it, Sullivan refused— the band was virtually unknown in the United States. However, they managed to strike a deal. The Beatles would appear on February 9, and, betting on a ratings bump from the first show, Ed also booked them for the following Sunday's show, to be broadcast from Miami's Deauville Hotel. Additionally, he secured the rights to tape a third performance to be aired at his discretion. The fee was set at $3,500 for each live appearance, plus airfare and hotel, with an additional $3,000 for the taped segment. (The show's budget ledger indicates that each Beatle was paid $875 for the February 9 show, which came to $515 after taxes.) That was about middling for Sullivan guests at the time; the headliners made $10,000 or more, while many acts made in the $2,500 range.

For Bob Precht, who showed up at the meeting only after negotiations were done, the booking was a source of consternation. He had no problem with the Beatles' manager; "Brian was a bright guy—he knew what he wanted," Precht recalled. However, Ed hadn't consulted him, as per their arrangement. And, although Bob knew who the Beatles were, he wasn't sure they warranted a guest shot on *The Ed Sullivan Show.*

Ed himself wasn't too sure. In the second week of December, the *CBS Evening News* ran a report about the Beatles, a short feature produced by one of the network's London correspondents. Shortly after the broadcast, Ed called CBS anchorman Walter Cronkite, who he was friends with. "He was excited about the story we had just run on the long-haired British group," Cronkite said. But Ed didn't remember the band's name. "He said, 'Tell me more about those, what do they call them? Those bugs or whatever they call themselves.'" The newsman himself couldn't remember the group's name, having to glance at his copy sheet to remind himself. Cronkite told Sullivan he knew nothing about the band, but said he would contact the London correspondent to give Ed more details.

Brian Epstein, having secured the Beatles' Sullivan debut, launched his promotional assault in earnest. He had convinced Capitol Records to mount a $50,000 ad campaign, including five million "The Beatles Are Coming" stickers—all of which were reportedly affixed to surfaces across the country—and a mountain of "Be a Beatles Booster" buttons, sent to record stores and radio stations nationwide.

On December 17, a disc jockey in Washington D.C. played an advance copy of "I Want to Hold Your Hand" he had gotten from a stewardess friend; it had begun climbing English pop charts in early December. The effect was like fire in dry grass. Radio stations across the country began airing advance copies in heavy rotation. In an attempt to stay ahead of the escalating demand, Capitol Records moved up the U.S. release date from January 13 to December 26. The single began flying off record store shelves the moment it arrived.

As the mania mounted, Jack Paar attempted to steal the thunder from his rival Sullivan. *The New York Times* reported on December 15 that Sullivan would present the English foursome—"Elvis Presley multiplied by four"—in February. Parr saw his opening. On his January 3 TV broadcast he presented a lengthy clip of the Beatles performing "She Loves You." Paar made light of the hysteria the group engendered, referring to the screaming girls: "I understand science is working on a cure for this." Ed was enraged. In his eyes he had paid for an exclusive debut and the contract had been violated. He immediately called Peter Prichard in London, as the agent recalled: "Ed, as always, had a quick reaction, and said, 'Tell them if that's how they're going to behave, let's cancel them.'" Prichard, however, knew his friend and mentor too well to take immediate action. Instead, he merely waited for what he knew was coming. The very next day, Ed called and said that canceling the Beatles had been "a bit hasty." Prichard assured Ed the issue had been handled.

Sullivan saw that the Paar clip had only fueled interest in the Beatles. Almost immediately, media coverage began building toward blanket saturation. Seemingly every newspaper and magazine, from *The Washington Post* to *Life* (which ran a six-page spread), began covering the band's imminent U.S. debut. Countless publications, so recently filled with grim news of the Kennedy assassination, now had something cheery to focus on. And, of course, every Beatles article pointed to *The Ed Sullivan Show*.

By January 17, "I Want to Hold Your Hand" hit number one on the Cash Box charts, and by February 1st it sat atop the *Billboard* Hot 100. As the Beatles' arrival inched closer—and the excitement spiraled ever higher—radio stations started counting down the days and hours to "B-Day." By the time the band landed at New York's newly renamed Kennedy International Airport on early Friday afternoon, February 7, hysteria ruled. Some three thousand teenagers (chaperoned by one hundred ten police) clamored to greet them. Describing the crowd, one reporter wrote, "There were girls, girls, and more girls." A battalion of two hundred reporters and photographers were on hand, peppering the foursome with queries:

"Will you sing for us?"

"We need some money first," John said.

"Do you hope to get haircuts?"

"We had one yesterday," George explained.

"Are you a part of a social rebellion against the older generation?"

"It's a dirty lie," replied John.

The band's limousines (one for each Beatle) ferried them to the Plaza, one of the city's most recherché hotels, which had to endure days of mania. Girls hired taxicabs to deliver them to the front door, explaining to wary doormen that they had rooms there. The hovering crowd sang Beatles songs, or a tune from *Bye Bye Birdie* with changed lyrics: "We love you Beatles, oh yes we do!"

Ed, overjoyed at all the attention, allowed myriad reporters into Saturday's rehearsal, which he attended, a rarity since Bob Precht normally handled it without him. For one of the band's sets, set designer Bill Bohnert had created an elaborate backdrop spelling out the name *Beatles*. But Ed, examining it while surrounded by reporters, proclaimed: "Everybody already knows who the Beatles are, so we won't use this set." Because it was the only backdrop Ed had ever vetoed, Bohnert was convinced it was Sullivan's way of reminding everyone who was in charge.

Vince Calandra, a production assistant, worked with the Beatles as they set up onstage. George Harrison had stayed back at the hotel suffering a high fever, and Calandra took his place during camera setup, wearing a Beatles wig for authentic-

Pretending to give Paul McCartney a much-needed haircut, February 1964. Sullivan was deliriously happy with the ratings the Beatles generated. (CBS Photo Archive)

ity. Vince began chatting with the musicians, and Paul McCartney told him that he and John Lennon had often dreamed of playing the Sullivan show, long before the actual booking. "McCartney said that he and John were talking on the plane over, and they felt that once they had done *The Ed Sullivan Show*, that was going to be their claim to having made it," Calandra recalled. As they stood talking, John Lennon asked Vince: "Is this the same stage that Buddy Holly performed on?" To Lennon's delight, Calandra confirmed that it was.

Getting a ticket to the rehearsal or broadcast was nearly impossible: the show received over fifty thousand requests, so obtaining one required a personal connection with CBS, Capitol Records, or the show's sponsors. (The night of the performance, a number of girls were caught trying to enter through the air conditioning ducts.) Ed made sure that Jack Paar's daughter Randy got tickets, which helped remind her father that Sullivan had scored the big scoop. On the other hand, Ed denied requests by three CBS vice presidents—his way of snubbing the management. In the moments before rehearsal the seven hundred twenty-eight–seat theater quivered with anticipation. When a crewmember wheeled Ringo's drums onstage, the audience ex-

With the Fab Four, February 1964. Their debut performance on the Sullivan show
signaled a new era in American popular culture. (Getty Images)

perienced its first moment of near hysteria. Ed gave them a stern lecture on the importance of paying attention to *all* the show's performers, and he exacted a promise
of good behavior from the teenagers.

As Ed sat offstage with his unlined pad of paper, preparing his introductory remarks, Brian Epstein approached him. The Beatles' manager, a master of creating
the image of his "boys"—for years they wore matching outfits at his directive—
asked to see Sullivan's remarks about the band. The request was almost comical: a
twenty-nine-year-old rock 'n' roll manager thinking he was going to check Ed's introductions. "I would like for you to get lost," Sullivan said, without looking up.

Almost double *The Ed Sullivan Show*'s usual audience was watching that night as the
black-and-white CBS broadcast returned from its first commercial break. Like most
of the stage shows Ed had produced since the 1930s, this evening's program followed
the columnist's rule: to lead with the top item. So the Beatles' moment had come.

Ed, now apparently feeling the awesome weight of anticipation, shifted back and forth from foot to foot, projecting even more discomfort than in his usual stage unease. As he launched into his introduction, he bobbed forward stiffly, as if he was an old pugilist preparing to throw a late-round knockout punch.

The showman ran pell-mell through his cue card, dropping almost as many syllables as he pronounced:

"Now yesterday and today our theater's been jammed with newspapermen and hundreds of photographers from all over the nation and these veterans agree with me that the city has never witnessed the excitement stirred by these youngsters from Liverpool who call themselves the Beatles"—at this point he refused to pause even for a moment, knowing that if he did the barely constrained volcano might erupt before he finished—"Now tonight, you're going to twice be entertained by them—right now, and again in the second half of our show. Ladies and gentlemen . . . *the Beatles! Let's bring 'em out!*"

Ed let his voice get carried away with the excitement, swooping his right arm in a roundhouse gesture toward stage left—who says this man is wooden?—and the studio audience experienced spontaneous combustion, giving voice to a full-throated primordial shriek expressing some otherworldly frenzy, equal parts romantic longing, lust, and sheer amazement that such creatures as inhabited the stage actually existed.

The camera panned over this female teenage riot, bouffants and pageboys shaking, arms akimbo and mouths agape, then settled on the Beatles, who, after Paul's brisk count off, snapped into the mid-tempo "All My Loving." Dressed in matching Edwardian suits with white shirts and ties, equipped with carefully coiffed mop tops, they appeared closer to terminally cute than revolutionary. The set had a mod look, with oversized white arrows pointing toward a center performance area, bathed in light from above. In the middle of this cleanly geometric stage, bobbing their heads in time to the music, it appeared possible the foursome might be aliens from another planet designed to drive earthlings batty. Paul smiled and sang lead, shaking his bangs with boyish charm, George and John crooned harmonies, and Ringo managed to look cool and goofy at the same time. The music was all but drowned in audience screams through much of the song, but it didn't matter; the foursome's buoyant energy proved able to break through every barrier, social or musical, put before it.

After their first number, they paused only briefly for a bow before beginning the sweet "Till There Was You." In mid song the camera lingered over each member in turn, superimposing his name (during John's section it read "Sorry girls: he's married"). From this ballad the group jumped into "She Loves You" ("she loves you, yeah, yeah, yeah, *yeah!*"). This, finally, was really rock 'n' roll—fast insistent energy, the beat a rapid foot tapper, and they played it like joyful demons, three minutes of exuberant youthfulness, all about love and sex and having a good time. John smiled along with Paul as they belted out the melody. Being young had never seemed so attractive, so unbound by what came before. In the time it took to play three pop songs, America made a tectonic shift toward being a youth-oriented culture. As "She Loves You" ended, the studio audience kept shrieking like the theater was on fire—which, in a sense, it was.

Ed was to bring back the Fab Four for two more numbers, but first the studio audience had to behave itself through the other acts—such a difficult task that Sullivan interrupted his next introduction to demand quiet, papering over his pique with a small smile as he reminded the audience of its pledge of good conduct.

Following the Beatles was tuxedo-clad magician Fred Kaps, who did card tricks and—like magic—poured salt endlessly out of a small salt shaker; the cast from the Broadway musical *Oliver!* (including Davy Jones, who later fronted the pop group the Monkees) reprised two numbers; impressionist Frank Gorshin portrayed the White House staff as if it were peopled with actors (Gorshin went on to play the Riddler in the *Batman* TV series); Tessie O'Shea, an ample-girthed grand dame of English cabaret, wielded a copious fur boa while razzmatazzing show tunes—"This is gonna be sexy!" she warned; the comedy duo McCall and Brill rambled through a routine about casting calls. Then, after a commercial for Kent cigarettes, Ed, visibly relaxed, reintroduced the Beatles with a huge swiveling arm gesture: "Ladies and gentlemen, *once again!*"

Proving that, remarkably, they could top even themselves, the band galloped through "I Saw Her Standing There," Paul and John tossing off sexy yowls while smiling in unison and shaking their matching mop tops. As the Beatles kept jouncing in time to the music, the studio audience's excitement kept escalating in cascading, vibrating waves. Watching from the control room, Bob Precht remarked: "I don't believe this—this is unreal." Then the Beatles destroyed the last remnants of feeble resistance with their current number one hit, "I Want to Hold Your Hand," with Ringo driving the steady backbeat, and John, Paul, and George giving the song a big ending by bobbing their guitars in choreographed rhythm. The boys, after taking their customary bow, walked over and shook Mr. Sullivan's hand, each flashing a big smile as he did so. Speaking would have been impossible amid the hail of screeching, so the emcee sent them offstage with a nod of his head. The British Invasion had just begun, but the American surrender was already unconditional.

As Ed opened the following Sunday's show, broadcast from Miami's Deauville Hotel, he was in obvious high spirits. His introductory remarks explained his ebullience: "Last Sunday, on our show in New York, the Beatles played to the greatest TV audience that's ever been assembled in the history of American TV." Ed's boast was correct. The Sullivan show's Nielsen ratings in the early to mid 1960s hovered in the twenty-three to twenty-five range, meaning its typical audience was close to forty million viewers a week, or somewhat less than a quarter of the country. Surpassing even this gargantuan figure, the Beatles debut was a blowout. Its Nielsen rating of 44.6 translated to 73.9 million viewers—the largest audience in television history at the time.

"Now tonight, here in Miamah Beach"—he never pronounced the city's name correctly despite traveling there annually for decades—"again the Beatles face a record-busting audience." His statement wasn't quite correct; this evening's Nielsens would indicate an audience of seventy million, just a tad down from the prior Sunday's. Still, the skyrocketing ratings were making Ed almost giddy. As the crowd began murmuring at his mention of the Beatles, he held up his hands and bellowed "Wait!" but his high-beam grin appeared so happy the audience responded with a big chuckle. "Ladies and gentlemen, here are four of the nicest young people we've ever had on our stage—*the Beatles, bring 'em on!*"

While Ed was speaking, the band had been struggling to get onstage. Shortly before showtime, they took the elevator down from their hotel rooms, only to see an impenetrable crowd of fans blocking the stage entrance. They tried to get through politely, without making any headway, finally breaking through with the assistance of a phalanx of Miami police. As Sullivan staffer Bill Bohnert remembered, Ed finished his introduction, "Just as Ringo was sitting down and picking up his sticks."

Clad in matching light-colored Edwardian suits, the band vaulted into a foot-tapping "She Loves You." If the week before the group had been charged with energy, now their performance felt freer; apparently having passed the audition allowed them to enjoy playing to its fullest. Paul almost danced along with the backbeat as John happily bobbed in time. After only a moment's pause they slid into the romantic "This Boy." Although the band was at its freest, the Miami audience was more subdued than the previous week's. A camera pan of the audience revealed why: much of the twenty-six-hundred-member crowd was middle-aged. As the *Miami Herald* reported, "The oldsters outdid the kids in mobbing *The Ed Sullivan Show*. A man in a white dinner jacket threw a wicked right at a young usher. A grandmother hammered a head with her high heels in her hand." To end their set, Paul said hello in his charming cockney accent and promoted the band's new album, then sang lead vocal on the up-tempo "All My Loving," with sweet harmonies by John and George.

Outside the theater, some Sullivan crewmembers found themselves in danger. Hundreds of teenagers, unable to get inside, spotted the broadcast control truck parked in back of the theater. As Bill Bohnert remembered, "The door of the truck was open, and I looked out just as I saw a wave of people coming . . . they came roar-

Paul McCartney getting Sullivan's autograph. McCartney and John Lennon had long dreamed of playing the Sullivan show. (Globe Photos)

Rehearsal for the Beatles' second Sullivan show appearance, February 16, 1964.
(CBS Photo Archive)

ing toward the truck, and I slammed the door shut just as this wave literally hit the truck—you could feel the truck shake." The vehicle kept rocking back and forth as the mob attempted to find some way to watch or hear the broadcast.

After the Beatles' first set, Ed introduced two famous boxers in the audience; the switch from rock 'n' roll to boxing felt incongruous, yet it was Sullivan's standard format. Reigning heavyweight champion Sonny Liston stood and waved happily, while 1940s-era champ Joe Louis managed only a dour smile. Then Ed brought on comedy team Marty Allen and Steve Rossi, who bantered in a vaudeville-style routine in which a reporter interviews a boxer:

Rossi: Would you say you're the best fighter in the country?
Allen: Yeah, but in the city they murder me.
Rossi: Who taught you to fight?
Allen: Rocky Marciano, Joe Louis, Sugar Ray, and Elizabeth Taylor.

Following the comics was a singer who would have been this evening's headliner if the Beatles had bombed the prior week, leggy Hollywood chanteuse Mitzi Gaynor. In a blond bouffant and accompanied by four tuxedoed dancers, Gaynor shimmied through "Too Darn Hot," changing up the mood with a sultry cocktail ballad, finishing with a brassy blues medley that ended with "When the Saints Go Marching In."

Ed came on and told the audience an impressive bit of fiction: "The greatest thrill for the Beatles—and we got a big kick out of it—is the fact that they were actually going to meet Mitzi Gaynor tonight on our show." If his intent was to make the Beatles appear as typical starstruck youth, he succeeded with at least part of the studio audience, who sighed appreciatively. But the idea that the foursome was eager to meet the milquetoast star of light musicals was patently absurd. Still feeling chipper, Ed interrupted himself to check his microphone. "Is this off, too?" he asked, glancing up at the microphone above him. Getting no answer, he muttered "Communists!" which prompted a reflexive laugh from the audience.

The showman presented a taped segment from Miami's Hialeah Race Track in which a four-person acrobatic troupe named the Nerveless Nocks swayed on one-hundred-foot poles while performing tricks—"One of them almost lost their life doing that," Ed reported. The live broadcast resumed as Sullivan brought on comic Myron Cohen, whose routine was pure Borscht Belt. ("A priest, a minister, and a rabbi are playing cards . . .")

When Ed reintroduced the Beatles for their final set, he attempted a joke based on their song titles. In two weeks, boxer Sonny Liston would face Cassius Clay (soon to change his name to Muhammad Ali). "Sonny Liston, some of these songs could fit you in your fight—one song is 'From Me to You.' And another one could fit Cassius, because that song is 'I Want to Hold Your Hand.'" The attempt at humor fell like a dull thud, though the audience offered a polite chuckle. Then: "Ladies and gentlemen, *here are the Beatles!*"

The energized quartet launched into an exuberant "I Saw Her Standing There," in which John had to stoop to reach his too-low mike stand, but it didn't seem to matter—the band was in rollicking good spirits, bouncing up and down as they strummed. John and Paul howled in unison at the verse's end to set up a guitar solo by George. They stopped just long enough for Paul to count off—"One! Two! Three!"—before jumping into a fast take of "From Me to You." To introduce their last number, Paul made his own attempt at humor: "This is one that was recorded by our favorite American group, Sophie Tucker." The audience didn't get the cheeky humor; was an eighty-year-old vaudevillian really this rock 'n' roller's favorite band? (The joke went over well in England, where audiences understood that Paul meant that the large-sized Tucker was big enough to be called a group.) The crowd's silent response was interrupted by a single man laughing, very loud, continuing to guffaw through the first guitar strums; it sounded like Sullivan, who doubtless found the notion amusing. Then the band delivered "I Want to Hold Your Hand" as a dose of fun-loving sunshine, galloping through verse and chorus like the tune was happiness itself.

As the audience wailed and cheered, the Beatles walked over to Ed, who told them—and here Ed was addressing older viewers at home: "Richard Rodgers, one of America's greatest composers, wanted to congratulate you, and tell the four of you that he is one of your most rabid fans. And that goes for me, too. Let's have a fine hand for these fellows!"

A few days later, Ed and Bob Precht hosted a dinner for the Beatles and the staff, partially as a perk for the staff; their reward for working hard was an opportunity to mingle with the band. The musicians split up to sit at different tables, so all of the fifteen or so staff members had a chance to say hello. Over the course of the evening the crew found the foursome thoroughly charming. One of the secretaries remarked

The Beatles on the Sullivan show, February 1964. Sullivan attempted to quiet the crowd, which was hardly possible. (CBS Photo Archive)

that Ringo felt a touch of melancholy because, having enjoyed himself so profoundly on his first American trip, he observed, "This was the best it was ever going to be— it could never get better than this."

Ed had bestowed the Sullivan seal of approval on the new rock 'n' roll sensation, and that, initially at least, appeared to be a safe bet. Within sixty days the Beatles held the top five spots on the *Billboard* Hot 100, with fourteen of their hits in the top one hundred chart positions, two feats that have never been topped. The band's third Sullivan appearance on February 23 provided still another ratings jolt, though not as dramatic as the first two evenings. This third Beatles performance was taped the afternoon of their debut, and edited together with a show taped in front of a live audience to present the illusion of a live performance. Ed even recorded introductions suggesting the Beatles were live: "You know, we discussed it today, we're all gonna miss them. They're a nice bunch of kids." (Additionally, in the spring of 1964, Ed flew to London to interview the Beatles on the set of *A Hard Day's Night*, and presented this segment during a May broadcast.) The publicity value of the Beatles appearances was incalculable, as legions of reporters and television crews trailed the band's every move during their first American trip, with all the reports mentioning the Sullivan show. The Beatles broadcasts and the attendant tidal wave of publicity boosted *The Ed Sullivan Show*'s ratings enough to make it the 1963–64 television season's eighth-ranked show.

The meeting of these two major entities, the life force of the Beatles with the national institution that was *The Ed Sullivan Show*, produced some kind of cultural fission, an inestimable spark of change, a sense that the season had turned irrevocably. It was all anybody was talking about. If Ed had always dreamed of fame, in these weeks he entered a stratosphere of cultural primacy that even he had never imagined. The showman basked in his glory.

Dissenters, however, sat unhappily in living rooms across America. Their apprehension was only partially voiced by the critics, who reviewed the Beatles' Sullivan debut as if it were slightly rotten fruit. The *New York Times* reviewer, who compared the Beatles' haircuts to that of children's show host Captain Kangaroo, and who referred to Ed as "the chaperone of the year," observed that, "In their sophisticated understanding that the life of a fad depends on the performance of the audience, and not on the stage, the Beatles were decidedly effective." Joining the chorus, *The Washington Post*'s critic opined that the musicians were "imported hillbillies who look like sheepdogs and sound like alley cats in agony." Critics, however, were a group that Ed had always succeeded in spite of; it was the home audience he worried about, and he understood that a deep sense of unease hid beneath the mostly bemused reviewers' barbs.

For some, the Beatles were a novelty; for others, of course, the group was as thrilling as anything they had ever seen. For another segment, however, the fast music, the long hair, the out-of-control teens—it all made them distinctly uncomfortable. "I was offended by the long hair," recalled Walter Cronkite, who represented the voice of mainstream America as much as anyone. "Their music did not appeal to me either." Part of Ed's nearly flawless sense of the public's taste was his deep reverence for—even wariness toward—conservative values. He was, after all, helping to create the status quo. He decided which artists and entertainers performed live for his massive national audience, which performers received the hallowed Sullivan imprimatur of acceptability. This was a delicate balancing act since survival meant entertaining everyone while offending no one.

Sullivan's cautious, stolid nature worked in his favor in this regard. He had never wanted to be a leader, never wanted to take the public where it wasn't ready to go. To keep the show in a dominant position he had to walk in lockstep, or just a step ahead, with a fickle public. Any move toward change had to be made carefully. His most precious talent was his ability to sense audience desire and to gratify that desire. The Beatles booking demonstrated that Sullivan the producer—the global talent scout—continued to have an unerring nose for ratings gold. But was his audience the unified entity it always had been?

Elvis, seven years earlier, had prompted a major backlash, with angry letter writers decrying what they saw as the singer's corrupting influence on youth. Yet while Presley turned the pop song into a vehicle for rambunctious sexuality, ultimately he was a nice boy with an "aw shucks" quality, who used his royalties to buy a new house for his parents. The Beatles were something else. All those teens in near riot—they actually required police to contain them—whatever this was about, it wasn't about deep reverence for conservative values. When the New York press corps greeting the Beatles at the airport had asked, "Are you part of a social rebellion against the older generation?" it had been a serious question. And social rebellion was not part of what had allowed Sullivan to outlast the competition since 1948.

The Reverend Billy Graham, who had violated his rule against television on the Sabbath to watch the Beatles, seemed to speak for some of Sullivan's audience. The band was a symptom of "the uncertainty of the times and the confusion about us," he said. The problem for those viewers who felt as Graham did was that the show would soon take on a new tone. Spurred by the Beatles ratings spike, by the spring of 1964 Sullivan was booking a plethora of rock acts, changing the program in ways that many found disturbing. "Frequent appearances of rock 'n' roll groups on *The Ed Sullivan Show* have turned the show into a teenage attraction that creates problems for the producers and the Columbia Broadcasting System," reported *The New York Times*. The problem was the teenagers themselves. Something had changed; the teens visiting the Sullivan show "set up an hour-long din that distracts other performers and mars the audio portion of the show." In response, the show stopped admitting anyone under age 16 unless accompanied by a parent. That was one solution, but a reporter—surely echoing what many parents hoped—suggested another: couldn't the show just stop booking rock 'n' roll?

"That's a possibility," Bob Precht said, "but we feel strongly that rock 'n' roll is part of the entertainment scene. Such groups are selling records like mad. We can't ignore an important trend in our business. We don't want to be a rock 'n' roll show, but there is value in having youngsters watch our show." In other words, *The Ed Sullivan Show* was trying to have it both ways, to satisfy two audiences—teens and their parents—who now wanted very different things. The "Big Tent" was being stretched further than ever before.

CHAPTER SIXTEEN

The Generation Gap

HAVING OPENED PANDORA'S BOX WITH THE BEATLES, Ed launched the 1964–65 season with the full fury of twanging guitars and pounding drums. He had featured the new sound in his mix since Elvis' debut in 1956, but now it was pushed center stage. Almost every show featured a new rock band. Headlining the season opener were The Beach Boys singing "I Get Around" in a set decorated with vintage roadsters. In October, Ed presented a very fresh-faced version of the Rolling Stones who, eyeing the titanic success of the Beatles' Sullivan debut, were eager to follow. "We got it into our heads that Ed Sullivan was the thing to do—the only thing worth doing," said Stones pianist Ian Stewart. The group's performance of "Time Is on My Side" and "Around and Around" served a dual purpose: it lifted Sullivan's ratings, and it helped the band sell more than $1 million in concert tickets that fall. Ed, however, was horrified by them. In contrast to the Beatles, who were cheery and had worn matching outfits, the Stones were sulky bad boys and, in Ed's view, thoroughly unkempt. He declared he would never book them again.

Three months later, Stones manager Eric Easton attempted to change Sullivan's mind. Requesting another booking, Easton wrote: "I know that these men are controversial entertainers, but it would seem that they have established quite a following in America and indications are that their popularity will increase." Ed wasn't going to make Easton's job easy. "We were deluged with mail protesting the untidy appearance—clothes, and hair of your Rolling Stones," he replied to Easton. "Before even discussing the possibility of a contract, I would like to learn from you, Eric, whether your young men have reformed in matter of dress and shampoo." Whatever Easton said must have convinced Sullivan, and at any rate the potential Nielsen boost from the group made it tough for him to stand on principle. Several months later Ed introduced a Stones set that featured "The Last Time" and "Little Red Rooster."

Along with the Rolling Stones that season were the other leading troupes in the British Invasion, including The Animals performing "House of the Rising Sun," the

In rehearsal with Mick Jagger, September 1966. Sullivan tried to rein in the Stones on a number of occasions, with limited success. (CBS Photo Archive)

clean-cut Dave Clark Five (who insisted on lip-synching, which Ed frowned on), singing "Anyway You Want It," and Herman's Hermits warbling "Mrs. Brown You've Got a Lovely Daughter." Making her first of eleven appearances was Petula Clark, equipped with go-go boots, performing her number one hit "Downtown." Motown was starting to take hold of the pop charts, and the Supremes—a Sullivan favorite—made their first of fifteen appearances. Before one of their sets, Ed introduced them with a windy laud, at the end of which he forgot their name, so he just bellowed, *"Here's the girls!"*

As prevalent as younger musicians were, they still shared the stage with Ed's something-for-everyone mix. The same night Petula Clark sang "I Know a Place," Alan King did a stand-up routine about how parents bother kids, the West Point Glee Club harmonized, and the Elwardos acrobats defied gravity. The Animals shared billing with Las Vegas crooner Wayne Newton; the Dave Clark Five shared billing with big band leader Cab Calloway. Duke Ellington and Ella Fitzgerald performed a medley of Duke's 1940s hits the same evening Ed introduced a clip from 1965's The *Sound of Music*, after which Julie Andrews sang "My Favorite Things." Football star Jim Brown chatted with Ed on a program in which a troupe of contortionists called the Morilodors, consisting of a man in a black mask with two female assistants, bent the human body into unlikely poses.

With Richard Pryor, in the mid 1960s. Sullivan fought CBS censors to allow the comic to perform material as he pleased. (CBS Photo Archive)

International dance stars Rudolf Nureyev and Margot Fonteyn, of Britain's Royal Ballet, performed an except from Tchaikovsky's classic *Swan Lake* on the same show that juggler Ugo Garrido kept an odd assortment of objects in motion. Making his first of thirteen appearances was twenty-four-year-old comedian Richard Pryor, sharing the bill with the Three Stooges. Ed did a routine with the puppet Topo Gigio in which Topo was homesick and gets a call from his mama.

The eclectic mix was popular with the public, a fact that CBS sought to take advantage of. In 1964 the network asked Ed to expand *The Ed Sullivan Show* to ninety minutes. The program had long dominated its time slot; from the network's perspective adding an extra thirty minutes was the easiest way to increase ratings. Ed agreed to the ninety-minute format, yet just a few weeks later, before actually adopting it, he demurred. The greater workload looked daunting, and worse, the longer format might not have been popular.

His change of heart did nothing to hamper negotiations for the new contract he signed that year. Ed decided he deserved a substantial raise and the network put up no argument. "We will be presenting Ed every Sunday night just as long as he wants," announced CBS-TV president James Aubrey after the signing. The showman's paycheck jumped to $32,000 a week, with increases over the next seven years, scheduled to reach $47,000 a week by 1971. When reporters questioned him,

he revealed no contract details, noting only that CBS had been "very, very generous." (It might have punctured his image as Uncle Ed to admit he earned more every
week than most families earned all year.) The show's weekly production budget was
pegged at $124,500; with graduated increases it was scheduled to reach $170,000
by 1971.

More important, the showman now owned *The Ed Sullivan Show*, previously
owned by the network. Since the deal was retroactive, Sullivan Productions owned
the copyright to all the shows back to 1948, and to all shows produced henceforth.
Ed owned fifty-one percent of Sullivan Productions, with forty-nine percent held by
Bob Precht and Betty Sullivan Precht. By most accounts it was Bob's idea to take
show ownership from the network. Ed's son-in-law, who had been a novice assistant
producer in the late 1950s, was now not just coproducer but also part owner of one
of television's highest rated programs.

In October, Ed booked one of his comic mainstays, Jackie Mason, in an evening that
sparked a major conflict and generated a bevy of headlines. The young Borscht Belter benefited enormously from being a Sullivan favorite. Nothing had boosted his career more than his many *Ed Sullivan Show* appearances since Ed discovered him at
the Copacabana in the early 1960s. Mason was part of a transitional school of
comics who had taken a step past their 1950s forebears; he could poke fun at political figures yet offend no one, combining tried-and-true mother-in-law jokes with a
lighthearted take on current events. His Sullivan impression made Ed laugh.

Mason remembered working with Ed as a process of negotiation. After the comic
ran through his routine in Sunday's dress rehearsal, Ed began editing. "He was totally in charge of every move on the show, and he enjoyed running it," Mason recalled. "But he was always generous to me because he seemed to like me a lot.
Sometimes he tried to cut a minute, and I would say, 'But that minute is the main
transition to the next joke,' and he would say, 'Maybe you could make it half minute,
because I really don't have the time.'"

Back and forth they would go, with Sullivan attempting to shape his act at every
turn. "So I would kibitz with him, to try to soften it, because he would seem very
nervous about how it was going to work out." Sullivan often acquiesced if Mason insisted. Over the course of his twenty Sullivan show appearances the comic saw Ed
negotiate with many performers. "He treated different people differently in terms of
how much he felt he needed them or how good he thought they were." A compara-
tive unknown might have no recourse in the face of Sullivan's directives, but he usually treated the biggest stars with deference, Mason recalled.

Ed "was always an unpredictable commodity, because you couldn't tell what
mood he would be in, and who he would be attacking and who he would be settling
for. . . . It was a sporadic, totally indefinable system," the comic remembered. "He
was insecure and uncertain about almost everything. He tried to be firm, but he
wasn't sure about how firm to be. He was very authoritative, but at the same time,
he was malleable, because he wasn't so sure of himself, so he would second-guess
himself. To some people he came across as arrogant and obnoxious, but I don't believe that. He was just somewhat insecure and he was trying to do the show as best
he could. He was intensely preoccupied, but he wasn't in any way arrogant."

With Jackie Mason. Sullivan became enraged at Mason after a controversial appearance by the Borsht Belt comic. (CBS Photo Archive)

For Mason's October 1964 appearance, with the presidential race between Lyndon Johnson and Barry Goldwater nearing Election Day, the comic was told to drop his political material. As innocuous as it was, Sullivan felt it was too sensitive given the imminent election. That evening's broadcast was partially preempted by President Johnson, who began an address to the nation at 8:30 P.M. The show continued while the president spoke, resuming its broadcast around 8:52, with Mason in the middle of his routine. The preemption threw the schedule off-kilter, and Ed was anxious about running out of time. He began urgently gesturing to Mason to cut his act short, holding up two fingers for two minutes, then one finger as time elapsed. Mason's jokes were met with silence as Ed's frantic gesturing distracted the studio audience. Mason, afraid that home viewers would interpret the studio audience's silence as a sign that he was bombing, began ad-libbing based on Ed's hand gestures. "I thought I'd generate some laughs by making fun of him," Mason said.

"What are you, showing me fingers? You got fingers for me, I've got fingers for you," he said, as he comically mirrored Ed's finger signs. The comedian's gesticulations grew more exaggerated as the studio audience's laughter fueled his improvising. "Who talks with fingers in the middle of a performance, you think they came here to watch your fingers?. . . If your fingers are such a hit, why do you need me, why don't you come here and show your fingers?"

Mason concluded his act feeling like his performance was a hit, that he had rescued himself from a career disaster. But Ed felt differently. Visibly upset onscreen after Mason's exit, he was livid after the program. As he saw it, the comic's finger improvisations included the profane middle finger gesture. Mason had just insulted him in the most profound manner, on live television, or so Ed thought. There *had* been a slight ambiguity to what Mason had done; he made so many gestures so rapidly that, if one were predisposed to view them as obscene, a viewer might have interpreted them as such. And Mason had treated Ed irreverently on the air, which alone was enough to anger him. But it was clear to most observers on the set—like Vince Calandra, who later became the show's talent coordinator—that even at close range, Mason's gestures were not profane.

After the show, "Ed came over to me and blew his top," Mason recalled. "He said, 'Who the fuck are you to use these filthy gestures, you son of a bitch—on national TV!'" The showman called him "a variety of four-, ten-, and eleven-letter words of Anglo-Saxon origin having to do with the subject of sex and perversion." At first Mason didn't know what Ed was mad about. The comic had been a rabbi and continued to serve part-time as one until about six months beforehand; by his account, he wasn't even familiar with the gesture Ed referred to. "A guy who uses that kind of terminology and vulgarity as a way of life on the streets of New York is from a different world than I come from," he said. Mason tried to explain to the enraged showman that he meant no insult, that Sullivan misinterpreted the gestures, but Ed wouldn't hear it. "He was too wound up and furious," the comic recalled. The damage was done. According to Mason, at the end of their encounter Ed bellowed "I'll destroy you in show business!" Ed denied having said this.

The headlines began blaring almost immediately. Ed canceled the comedian's $45,000 contract for six appearances, charging "insubordination and gross deviation from the material agreed upon." The thirty-three-year-old comic, once eagerly sought by nightclubs, saw his bookings evaporate. After four months of skimpy bookings, in February he filed a $3 million libel suit against Sullivan and Bob Precht, charging that his professional reputation had been injured.

In January 1966, Sullivan lost the first round of the court case. State Supreme Court judge Harry Frank reviewed the tape in court, finding that there was nothing offensive or obscene in Mason's performance. (The judge also noted that he was a fan of the Sullivan show, "although I don't know why I watch it," he said.) Soon afterward, the two parties decided to settle; Mason dropped his suit and Sullivan agreed to have him back on the show. During the following September 12 show— two years after the original broadcast—Ed told his audience: "Highlighting the show will be an old friend of mine and yours, Jackie Mason." The comic, as if to say bygones could be bygones, performed his Sullivan imitation.

Prior to that evening, the two men ran into each other in an airport. By Mason's account, he pretended he didn't see the showman, but Sullivan came up to him and apologized profusely. "He said he never forgave himself for doing that to me . . . and he felt terrible that he had done it," Mason said. "Then he gave me the example of a man who had a fight with his wife, and both people felt that they'd like to make up, but nobody bent enough to say it."

There may have been an extra factor contributing to the Sullivan–Mason fracas. Ed was getting tired. It was clearly visible onscreen as 1964 turned into 1965. The sixty-four-year-old showman had not aged gracefully; the years had taken their toll. The previous August (two months before Mason's disputed appearance) he was hospitalized briefly for an intestinal disorder, and at moments onstage it seemed as if he hadn't fully recovered. The once-virile newsman was now baggy-eyed and sunken-cheeked. His onstage persona had always been famously stiff and reserved, but now, toward the end of a broadcast he could be almost listless. Late in the hour when the camera cut back to him after a commercial break he sometimes had a momentarily vacant look in his eyes.

And it was more than that. There was a forgetfulness, a mental confusion that was starting to become frequent. His associates had seen it, an inability to remember names or even a directive he had just given. One Sunday night he told a stagehand to lay a golf mat onstage in preparation for the following act; a few minutes later, having forgotten his request, he became enraged at the crewmember for setting up too early, and fired him on the spot. He ignored staff members' explanations that he himself gave the order. This same tendency toward mental confusion, coupled with his general cantankerousness, may have led him to misinterpret Jackie Mason's gestures.

In any case, these lapses were passing and Ed could summon the old energy when need be. Over the last few years he had developed a technique of introducing an act by running through a couple of sentences in a low-level monotone, then exploding into a shout at the end. The effect was disjointed but it helped create the sense that something thrilling was coming. And, after all these years, he found a somewhat better relationship with the camera. Ed had always treated the camera's eye like an interloper to be avoided; he addressed the studio audience and let the television lens follow him if it could—ignoring the camera was a symptom of his stage nerves. "He always had stage fright," said John Moffit, the show's director. "He just wasn't comfortable in front of the audience." Yet in the mid 1960s he began looking straight into the camera at times, usually turning away to address the studio after a few moments. After some sixteen seasons on the air it was a modest improvement.

If the showman was feeling his years, the show pulsed with more youthful energy than ever before. Opening the 1965–66 season was the Beatles, in their last "live" *Ed Sullivan Show* appearance. (Although the band performed on the Sullivan stage for a live audience, their performance had been taped a month earlier as they arrived in New York to launch an American tour. Over the next few years they sent in five more taped guest shots, but they never again performed live on the Sullivan show.)

To introduce the foursome, still looking cherubic in their matching dark suits and skinny ties—though their hair was getting shaggy—Ed brought over each Beatle in turn for a handshake, with each band member hailed by an unbroken wall of screeches. They rocked through "I Feel Fine," which had topped the charts the previous December; "I'm Down," a blues romp that was one of their least memorable songs; and "Act Naturally," featuring a self-described "nervous and out-of-tune" Ringo on lead vocal. After the first song Paul tried his own Ed impression: "We'd like to carry on . . . *the shew*," he intoned, dropping into Sullivanese.

Later in the hour they performed a rollicking "Ticket to Ride," which had hit number one the previous May; "Yesterday," with an intimate solo vocal by Paul— the song hit number one three weeks later; and the hard-charging "Help," which held the current number one chart spot. Afterward Ed brought the band over and tried to chat with them, but the screams submerged his and the Beatles' voices; the kids were out of control. (That hysteria had been in full fury when the Beatles performed at New York's Shea Stadium four weeks earlier for fifty-five thousand crazed teenagers. Ed introduced them onstage, and Brian Epstein hired Sullivan Productions to film the concert, with Bob Precht as director.)

In the weeks ahead, the show (broadcasting in color for the first time) presented Sonny and Cher crooning their number one hit "I Got You Babe"; later in the hour Cher sang solo—she didn't always need Sonny. That fall saw appearances by British Invasion bands like Herman's Hermits, who played "Just a Little Bit Better," and rising American groups like blue-eyed soul duo the Righteous Brothers, who sang "Turn on Your Love Light." Also upping the energy level were Motown acts like Marvin Gaye, singing the rambunctious soul ballad "Take This Heart of Mine," and Martha and the Vandellas, harmonizing on "Dancin' in the Streets."

In October, Barry McGuire growled his number one hit "Eve of Destruction," which was banned by some radio stations after a deluge of complaints about the lyrics: "And think of all the hate there is in Red China / Then take a look around to Selma, Alabama." As much as any performance that season, "Eve of Destruction" foreshadowed the changes inherent in 1960s youth culture. The song was a leap forward from just a few years back, when the Sullivan show's newest music was the sugary confections of pop kitten Connie Francis and dreamboat Frankie Avalon.

The comedy, too, was changing. That same month, Ed booked Woody Allen, a twenty-nine-year-old stand-up comic whose material was decidedly forward looking. Instead of mother-in-law jokes he mined sex and psychology for laughs, with his trademark cerebral style. In Sunday's dress rehearsal, Allen performed without censoring himself, planning a safer routine for that evening's broadcast—but he hadn't told Ed that. His afternoon performance included a reference to "orgasmic insurance." As soon as he finished, Sullivan gave him a severe tongue lashing, calling Allen lewd and all but blaming him for what Ed saw as the country's moral decay. "Attitudes like yours are why kids are burning their draft cards," he shouted at the comedian.

Caught off guard, Allen briefly considered responding in kind, but instead spontaneously apologized. Ed was mollified, and the comic delivered his less adventurous material in that evening's broadcast. "When the storm abated, from that day on I had no better ally in show business," Allen said. Ed plugged him in his column and booked the comic for three additional appearances.

For rock bands, playing the Sullivan show became an important rite of passage, as well as an exponential boost to record sales. The new groups came fast and furious now. To fit them all in, Ed sometimes booked two to an evening, clearly bending his sacrosanct rule about balance. In December, the Byrds sang "Mr. Tambourine Man" and "Turn, Turn, Turn" the same night the Dave Clark Five trilled "Catch Us If You Can." In February, The Animals performed "We Gotta Get Out of This Place" on a show in which Simon and Garfunkel harmonized on "Sounds of Silence." In May, James Brown funked it up with "(I Got You) I Feel Good" after the Supremes sang "Love Is Like an Itching in My Heart."

In the winter and spring of 1966, the Sullivan show's combination of young and old became almost surrealistic. The program had always been a Big Tent, offering an act for every taste, but now the contrast between performers almost strained credulity. In February, the Rolling Stones rocked on "(I Can't Get No) Satisfaction"

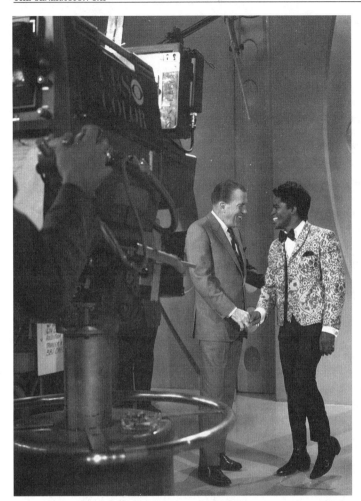

With James Brown, the Godfather of Soul, October 1966. (CBS Photo Archive)

the same night that Ethel Merman, who debuted in film shortly after the invention of talkies, belted out "There's No Business Like Show Business." In April, Petula Clark miniskirted through "A Sign of the Times" the same evening that Jimmy Durante—whom Ed had met in the Silver Slipper speakeasy in 1923—crooned "Inka Dinka Doo." On that same broadcast, acrobat Jose Cole balanced on top of a cane, which itself was on top of a bottle, while twirling five rings. His balancing act was no less impressive than that of Sullivan and Precht: in June, a taped Beatles performance of "Paperback Writer" shared the bill with the very middle-aged Robert Goulet drowsing through "Two Sleepy People." In May, James Brown quick-stepped to "Papa's Got a Brand New Bag" the same night that Tin Pan Alley legend Harold Arlen played an excerpt from his classic "Over the Rainbow."

This same unlikely mix occurred in the realm of comedy, with one broadcast combining Richard Pryor, the Smothers Brothers, and Myron Cohen—a young black comic who embraced his racial identity; a duo whose lighthearted goofiness softened their irreverent edge; and a traditional Borscht Belter, respectively. Pryor's routine invoked the name of a public figure Ed had banned from the show, Muhammad Ali, as the stand-up mock reenacted the title bout between Sonny Liston and Ali. Ed had playfully bantered with Ali back when the boxer was called Cassius Clay, but declared he would have nothing to do with Ali as long as he remained connected with the Nation of Islam. (Like many of Ed's statements foreswearing a performer, this too was reversed.)

It got confusing at times, finding the cultural boundaries. For viewers who looked to Ed not just for entertainment but for cultural guidance, as the source of a show business seal of approval, the program's current offering must have been perplexing. In earlier years, Sullivan's stage presented an eclectic lot, yet its underlying worldview had been unified. Now the show's performers purveyed messages that seemed markedly at odds with one another, and furthermore, the music and comedy grew more strident and questioning with every passing month.

Even Ed's censorship, that ever-reliable watchful eye, seemed to be navigating with a changing lodestar. In June, he presented an unknown rock 'n' roll group called the Thomas Band, whom he booked as a favor to well-known entertainer Danny Thomas, whose son fronted the group. The band was a nonentity, a well-scrubbed bunch with crew cuts and preppie clothes who sang a generic, neutered rock number. The group's lyrics, however, would never have gotten past Ed in years past: "You don't know what she does to me / when she's making love to me." Sullivan had threatened to cancel Buddy Holly in 1958 for far less.

Clearly, the showman was less mentally present. As he wrapped up that evening's broadcast he began to extemporize: "We're delighted that you're here tonight, specifically, have a nice time, those of you who are visiting our city. And right down the street here is the river, the Hudson River. You should go and take a look—I don't want you to jump in—and have a nice time while you're here with us. Good night!"

It was odd: promoting the Hudson River? Warning the audience not to jump in? On the surface it was a standard Sullivan goof, perhaps an awkward attempt at humor. But, based on his semidazed on-screen appearance, the sign-off revealed that his mind was wandering further afield than a mere goof. The mental fatigue, or whatever it was, seemed to be catching up with him. Several months later, he was standing onstage after the broadcast returned from a deodorant ad. The girl in the ad had explained to the boy—who did not use Ban deodorant—that she liked him "not much." As the camera cut to Ed, he editorialized on the ad: "That's a fine crack—'not much.'" It was, again, perhaps a funny bit of irreverence. But it didn't appear as such. It seemed as if he had momentarily gotten lost in the ad's little scenario, forgetting where he was before he commented. Strangely, his tone of voice suggested he was truly annoyed at the girl's comment.

———

Few Sullivan critics had been as harsh as *The New York Times*' Jack Gould. In the early 1950s he provided a running lambaste of Sullivan's foibles. Gould's attitude had softened in the late 1950s as Ed's focus grew international. Now, in 1965–66 season, the *Times* critic reversed himself altogether. Sullivan "is unquestionably one of the medium's great intuitive showmen," he wrote. And while Sullivan on camera "may be about as animated as an untipped cab driver," his success had allowed him "the enviable position of being a world unto himself amid the competitive scramble." The critic, however, bemoaned the show's greater emphasis on rock 'n' roll, referring to it as a "compromise" that sacrificed the program's well-rounded quality for ratings. "Mr. Sullivan shouldn't go unsung; with all due deference to the noisy disc jockeys of radio, he's really one of the fathers of rock 'n' roll."

Indeed, "If the lay sociologist wants firm evidence that the younger generation has taken command of the home dial, Mr. Sullivan is their case in point," Gould wrote. The critic voiced an opinion held by many: "Mr. Sullivan undoubtedly has an obligation to keep the teenagers in mind when he plans his show, but perhaps he will also see the wisdom of not disenfranchising other members of the family too regularly, if only because they are the ones who have somewhat larger allowances to spend with advertisers."

Behind the scenes, Ed was not solely responsible for many of these bookings. More and more, his son-in-law Bob Precht was handling not just production chores but actually choosing the acts. The move toward rock was certainly made with Ed's blessing—Bob never made a move without conferring with Ed. As many staffers recalled, Bob always handled his father-in-law with great deference. But where their partnership had once been master to mentor, it was now far closer to equal. Ed no longer decided, or much less frequently decided, to cancel an act during dress rehearsal. If he opted to change the running order after rehearsal it was not a complete scrambling. And the 1950s-era Sullivan practice of changing the running order during the broadcast was now nearly impossible; his son-in-law put together too complex a production for such a maneuver. Precht, in fact, was becoming the man behind the curtain, keeping the Sullivan formula spinning like one of the show's many plate spinners.

The gradual shift in power between the two men was resisted by many of the talent agents who dealt with the show. "Because Ed had gone so many years of doing it on his own, many of the agents and managers continued to go directly to him, to try to get him to okay something," Precht said. Some performers, too, grumbled about Precht, as they realized that a second gatekeeper stood between them and the lucrative exposure of a Sullivan booking.

Agents and performers weren't alone in resisting this power shift. Surrendering control didn't come naturally to Ed, and he sparred with Bob on a regular basis, chiefly over the direction of the show's bookings. At one point they argued over a puppet act from Italy, which Ed enjoyed and wanted to dedicate an entire hour to. Bob felt the act was mediocre. "I did everything I could to persuade Ed not to do this. . . . But this was another example of his will, persevering and dominating, so we shot the hour." When Ed introduced it, he told the audience that if they liked it, they should write in to say so. "Now, of course, *tons* of mail came in," Precht recalled, with a laugh. "People loved Ed and loved the show, it was like he could do no wrong, so he had a lot of people saying how wonderful these puppets were, and how wonderful this hour was. So now I'm gritting my teeth." The evening, however, wasn't a ratings success—yet Ed still wanted to prove his point to Bob. "Finally, after all this mail had accumulated, bags and bags and bags, he had all the mail put on the stage floor, in a big pile. And he said to the audience, '*Bob Precht* and I want to thank you for this great response.' Talk about having your nose rubbed in it—he really did it."

Among the bookings Precht and Sullivan argued about were those of older performers. Ed was a soft touch for old vaudevillians and aging athletes. His sentimental fondness for both meant that he booked boxers or baseball players far past their prime, or ancient Palace veterans, regardless of their audience appeal. He had done this since the show's inception and would continue to do so. As talent coordinator Vince Calandra recalled, Ed booked old vaudevillians because he wanted to ensure they got the minimum yearly salary required by the actors union to maintain their retirement benefits. (Not that his patience with vaudevillians was limitless. After he cut Sophie Tucker from two numbers to one and she started to get upset, he said, "Shut your mouth and get back up onstage and do one number, or you're off the show.")

As late as 1970, Ed introduced Jack Dempsey from the audience, and Dempsey had lost the heavyweight title in 1927. (Ed often went to the boxer's Broadway restaurant for lunch, talking with Jack for hours about old times.) But as the show increased its emphasis on acts aimed at younger viewers, and set designer Bill Bohnert's sleek, geometric sets started sporting the bright paisley flowers that typified the 1960s, these 1930s-era guests felt increasingly out of place. It was Precht who kept this urge of his father-in-law's in check, always pushing the show toward the contemporary.

In 1966 Ed appeared in a movie with Sister Luc-Gabrielle, a musical performer whose Sullivan show appearance helped vault her to stardom. Starring Debbie Reynolds and Ricardo Montalban, *The Singing Nun* told the story of the Belgian nun's rise to fame, fueled by her real-life 1963 number one hit "Dominique," a lilting folk song which earned her a Grammy and a 1964 booking on the Sullivan show. As in *Bye Bye Birdie*, this Warner Bros. release used a Sullivan show appearance to signify the pinnacle of success.

The film's theme is the struggle between the sanctity of a religious life and the temptations of the secular world. Sister Luc-Gabrielle, called Sister Ann in the film, experiences budding fame as a singer—a record pressing is an unintentional hit—after which she faces the new challenges of worldly success. As her burgeoning celebrity calls into question her commitment to her religious vocation, she wonders which path she'll take: will she remain committed to her spiritual calling? At one point, looking out at the secular life, Sister Ann visits a local rock 'n' roll club, a trip she finds distressing—the fast music and the dancing teens are deeply unpleasant for her. Still, her direction in life remains unclear.

Ed, playing himself, portrays a character whose meaning is twofold. No one could be more respectful toward the nuns, yet he still represents worldly success. He travels to Belgium to request that Sister Ann perform on his show, but first he must face the stern Mother Superior, who disdains the secular life. Although Ed's assistant assures her his program is a "very clean, family-type show," she denies his request. Ed, wallowing in piousness, requests just one thing: could he at least meet Sister Ann before he goes home?

Upon meeting the young nun, who's still scrubbing floors while her record climbs the charts, Ed repeats his offer directly to her: would she come to New York to perform?

Sister Ann: New York . . . ?
Mother Superior: Of course I told him no.

Ed: I regret that Mother, because our Cardinal in New York has proposed perhaps we'd get something for your order that is badly needed.

Priest: We could have used a jeep, Mr. Sullivan, particularly when we reopen in Africa.

Ed: I was thinking of several jeeps, Father.

Priest: Several jeeps!

Mother Superior: One is all we will need, Mr. Sullivan.

And with that, Ed, having used material goods to prompt change at the nunnery, presents Sister Ann to America. (In real life, the Mother Superior requested two jeeps after hearing of the size of Sullivan's audience.) Sister Ann's performance on the Sullivan show becomes the movie's fulcrum point. She has now bitten the apple, and is thrown into a period of extreme moral doubt. In the end, however, she is seen in Africa ministering to the needy, having reaffirmed her commitment to her religious choice.

While critics panned the film as cloying and saccharine it did well at the box office, and also inspired the TV sitcom *The Flying Nun*, which ran for three years. (Ironically, the real singing nun faced similar choices. She decided to leave the convent after the film's release, yet despite a sustained publicity blitz never had another hit. In 1985, after years of battling Belgian authorities over back taxes, she committed suicide with her lesbian companion.)

Ed didn't invite the Singing Nun back on the show to promote the film, as he had Dick Van Dyke after the 1963 release of *Bye Bye Birdie*. Sullivan and Precht had other priorities as they launched the 1966–67 season: namely, keeping the show fresh while continuing to appeal to older viewers. Opening the season was the Rolling Stones performing "Paint It Black," on a bill in which Louis Armstrong blew through "Cabaret" and Joan Rivers did stand-up. For Rivers, the Sullivan show was a major opportunity, though the thirty-three-year-old comic was booked only after a Sullivan gaff.

The week before, as the showman was listing the following week's lineup, he had meant to say *Johnny* Rivers, the pop singer, yet he slipped and said *Joanie* Rivers. Once Ed had announced that she would appear he felt obligated. "I was booked for the next Sunday," Rivers remembered. Ed so enjoyed her performance that over the next few years he invited her nineteen more times, a series of appearances that Rivers relished. She particularly enjoyed Sullivan's ritual around wardrobe. "They always took you and got you your clothes at Bergdorf's or Bonwit Teller, and they were always fitted to you. After the performance—it was like a little ritual—either Bob Precht would come in, or the wardrobe lady, and say 'Mr. Sullivan would like you to have your dress.' Then you would send a thank-you note. It was one way that you knew he liked you."

On the day of her debut appearance, Ed made a special demand on that evening's rock 'n' roll headliner. "I was in the dressing room next to the Rolling Stones, and I remember he insisted they get their hair washed—and he was right. And they got their hair washed."

Additional shampoo was the least of what confronted the Stones for their Sullivan guest shots, recalled production assistant Jim Russek. For one of their appearances, simply getting the group into the theater proved dangerous. The band had been warned not to leave the theater between dress rehearsal and showtime, but they disregarded this advice. As they returned, such a huge crowd of fans awaited them at the stage door that the band's limousine hurriedly drove around the block toward an alternate entrance—which unfortunately had a glass door. The band jumped out to try to make it into the theater, "but the fans figured it out, so they got there at the same time," Russek said. "There was such a crush that the window broke and they squeezed themselves through. Three of the guys got in pretty quickly, but [guitarist] Brian Jones was last, and I had to help pull him through."

The Stones, undaunted by hair washing requests or crazed fans, returned in January for a set that included both sides of their new single, "Let's Spend the Night Together" and "Ruby Tuesday." Many radio stations were refusing to play what they saw as the overtly sexual "Let's Spend the Night Together," so they aired only the B side, making "Ruby Tuesday" a number one hit by March. Ed, wanting the ratings boost from both new songs, demanded that the Stones alter the lyric to the controversial song to "Let's spend *some time* together."

The band balked, but Ed issued his standard ultimatum: "Either the song goes, or you go." The Stones reluctantly acceded. By the time the group played the song for dress rehearsal, the directive had been stressed to lead singer Mick Jagger repeatedly, to the point where he was getting angry. When the CBS Standards and Practices representative arrived, he needed to witness Jagger being told to change the lyric, but he didn't want to approach the band himself. So the task was given to talent coordinator Vince Calandra, who dutifully walked up onstage and told the singer, once again, that he needed to change the lyric. "Fuck off, mate," Jagger said, as Calandra recalled. During the broadcast, the Stones singer performed as requested but briefly rolled his eyes upward to theatrically mime his protest.

As was now expected, Sullivan again this season presented all the latest bands in the suddenly exploding pop-rock scene. The Mamas and the Papas harmonized on "California Dreamin'" and the Lovin' Spoonful, performing in front of a spinning kaleidoscope backdrop, sang "Do You Believe in Magic." Paul Revere and the Raiders romped through "Kicks," the Turtles rendered their number one hit "Happy Together," and the Young Rascals performed "Lonely Too Long." Many of the groups from the last few years returned, most notably the Beatles, who offered a taped performance of "Penny Lane" and the psychedelic "Strawberry Fields Forever."

Although rock 'n' roll was now a central element in the show, it had reached a saturation point. Sullivan and Precht would not allow the new sound to take up yet more program time. If anything, the two producers retreated somewhat from rock in 1966–67, usually booking no more than one band in an evening. This left ample time for traditional acts. Over the course of the season, Jack Benny did stand-up, Henny Youngman tossed out one-liners, and sketch comedy team Wayne and Schuster made three of their fifty-eight appearances. The Woody Herman Orchestra accompanied velvety vocalist Mel Tormé on "I Left My Heart in San Francisco." Bandleader Xavier Cugat, who was a strolling violinist at the Casa Lopez nightclub the night that Ed met Sylvia there, jumped through "Tequila." The U.S. Marine Silent Drill Team displayed their precision maneuvers, as did the show's never-ending stream of jugglers, contortionists, and acrobats. The Sullivan show, or so it seemed, could balance its offering for all audiences just as it always had.

The program's emphasis on high art had lessened greatly—it was not a ratings winner. With rock 'n' roll now taking up a hefty percentage of airtime, something had to be cut, and the stage plays and classical musicians so frequent in the 1950s fell victim. Still, there continued to be at least a token nod to fine art. In December, the Berlin Mozart Choir performed, and a month later dancers Edward Villella and Patricia McBride of the New York City Ballet performed a pas de deux from Asafieff's *Flames of Paris*. Ballerina Sandra Balesti floated through a solo, though her accompaniment was a Rodgers and Hammerstein medley.

From a ratings standpoint, the updated Sullivan show remained a hardy perennial. As the 1966–67 season ended—Sullivan's nineteenth year on the air—*The Ed Sullivan Show* was television's thirteenth-ranked program, and continued to win its time slot. It was the longest-running prime-time show, and its ratings verified it was as much an institution as a television show.

Mellow. That was a word that had never been used to describe Ed Sullivan. In the reams of newsprint that the New York press had churned out about the showman since the late 1940s, never once had that descriptive been employed. However, as the mid 1960s turned toward the late 1960s, Ed demonstrated that even Irish whiskey could lose its edge.

"I remember once I came in to talk with him and he was taking a nap—and I thought, that's crazy," recalled comic Joan Rivers, a regular in this period. The naps between dress rehearsal and broadcast—which never happened in earlier years—

Chatting with Joan Rivers, 1966. "If he put his arm around you, you knew you had made it," recalled Rivers. "The power he had was enormous." (CBS Photo Archive)

had become a weekly occurrence. The personal secretaries who worked with him in these years all remembered him as a kind, gentle man who rarely raised his voice, though they had heard tales of the Sullivan temper. "He was always very nice to me," recalled Barbara Gallagher, a production assistant who worked closely with Ed in the mid to late 1960s. "He would tease me—'Hey legs, how you doing?'" She knew he ran a "tight ship" in previous years, yet now "he became more docile, more introspective." The show seemed to bustle around him, as the veteran crew went about its work like a well-tuned machine, guided by Bob Precht.

Vinna Foote, a production assistant in the late 1960s, remembered Ed calling her to join him at the neighborhood restaurant he ate at before airtime, ostensibly to make last-minute changes. But he had no changes to make. "A couple times he had me come over, he just wanted me to have a drink with him." She declined the drink, but sat and talked with him as he had his customary preshow Dubonnet liquor with Sweet 'n Low. "He never chased me around or anything—he was lonely, he was a lonely person."

Ed's forgetfulness and mental confusion were becoming more pronounced. "You knew there was a really sharp guy at home somewhere, but he wasn't showing it as much," recalled production assistant Jim Russek. "Because he wasn't as in the loop as much as he was in earlier years, that was frustrating to him, and he was capable of lashing out at people when he felt out of control." One Sunday evening, Ed came down from his nap about an hour before showtime, mistakenly thinking it was just minutes before broadcast. "He started screaming, 'Where the hell is everybody?—We've got a show to do!—Why am I the only one standing here?'" After a few moments of yelling, Russek explained to him, "Sir, it's quarter to seven." After the show Ed and the staff had a laugh about it.

In June 1967, he considered plastic surgery; his baggy eyes were beginning to give him a haggard look. He set up an appointment and went to the doctor's office, sitting in the waiting room. After a while he got up and took a walk, then decided to skip surgery. Ed would be Ed, unvarnished as always.

That same June, in an interview with *Ladies Home Journal*, he had kind words for, of all people, Walter Winchell. Walter "invented the Broadway column and wrote it better than anybody else," Ed said. He conceded something that had long bedeviled him in earlier decades: "Any columnist had to run in his shadow. Me included. . . . No matter which way I turned, there was Winchell in my way." Ed even offered an olive branch: "Winchell and I haven't spoken to each other in years. But I wish we'd continue to be friends." His assessment of Winchell's earlier power was accurate, yet the younger Ed Sullivan had been loathe to acknowledge it. Never in his many years of snarling at Walter had he admitted he was envious of the hugely famous columnist.

Several weeks later the former archrivals both happened to be having dinner at Dinty Moore's restaurant. Ed was dining with Sylvia; Winchell was dining with Dorothy Moore, the executive secretary of the Runyon Fund, a cancer research fund he founded after the death of writer Damon Runyon. Walter, by 1967, had hit bottom. His influential radio show was long gone and his column's distribution had dwindled to the vanishing point. (In desperation, he began visiting the El Morocco nightclub and handing out mimeographed copies of his column.) Perhaps due to his lessened circumstances, Ed's kind comments in *Ladies Home Journal* meant all the

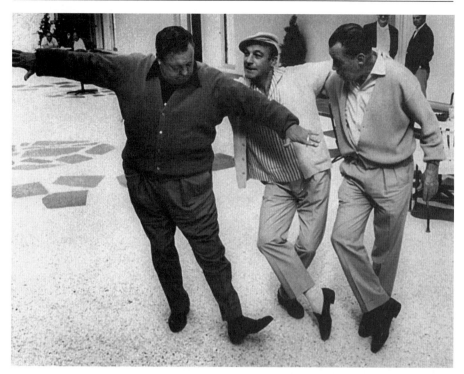

From left, Jackie Gleason, Gene Kelly, Sullivan. When Sullivan visited the set of Jackie Gleason's TV show in January 1967, the three men goofed through an impromptu tap dance. In the late 1940s, Sullivan introduced Jackie Gleason to the television audience. (Time Life Pictures/Getty Images)

more to him. Seeing Ed across the room, Walter got up and said hello. He greeted Sullivan warmly and Ed reciprocated. Suddenly, they were chums. The decades spent cursing at each other, glaring at one another at the Stork, faded away. Walter invited Ed to join the board of the Runyon Fund, which Ed accepted. The two made a date to meet later that week for cocktails at El Morocco. Either by coincidence or invitation, onetime *Graphic* columnist Louis Sobol also showed up at the nightclub. The trio had a photo snapped: three smiling newspapermen, three old friends.

In Sullivan's September 10 broadcast, he introduced Winchell from the audience. Ed, momentarily confused, referred to Walter as a sports star, an introduction meant for football hero Frank Gifford, also in the audience. He then found his place in the cue cards and touted Walter as the "daddy of the Broadway columnists." (In that same show, featuring the rock group the Young Rascals, the girls in the audience screamed so much that Ed yelled, with a smile, "Quiet or I'll thrash you!" proving he hadn't turned into complete butterscotch.)

A year later the Friars honored Sullivan for his twentieth year on the air; at the ceremony Walter sat up on the dais with Ed. In his speech, Winchell spoke glowingly of his former rival: "As we both grew older, we found that we were citizens of a kingdom more beautiful than Camelot. Not a never-never land, but a very real and magic place called Broadway. Ed Sullivan is as much a part of Broadway as Times

Square, Dinty Moore's, Toots Shor's, Lindy's, Max's Stage Deli, *Variety*. . . ." As the evening concluded, Ed shook Walter's hand and said, "Walter, don't ever let thirty-five years separate us again."

The 1967–68 season opened with a scream. Headlining the September 17 show were The Doors, who in July had hit the charts for the first time—at number one—with "Light My Fire." If ever a group was guaranteed to draw extra scrutiny from the CBS Standards and Practices department, it was this pioneering psychedelic rock band fronted by Jim Morrison, who wore skintight leather pants and performed as if gripped by a hallucinatory frenzy. He earned the nickname the Lizard King, a phrase from one of his rambling, incantatory poems, for his grand and otherworldly approach to life.

Doors keyboard player Ray Manzarek recalled the unusual way he found out the band was about to play the Sullivan show. All through the Summer of Love, as the summer of 1967 was known, Manzarek made of point of turning the channel to CBS on Sunday night. "You watched *The Ed Sullivan Show*, if you could, because there was always going to be a rock act on, and there were very few ways to see rock 'n' roll on television." As he watched on September 10, he gasped with amazement as he heard Sullivan announce that The Doors would be on—the following week. The band's manager had neglected to tell them. "We were very excited—it was fabulous," Manzarek said.

The band showed up at rehearsal, recalled Sullivan staffer Jim Russek, with "a smugness in their attitude, kind of 'We're going to do what we're going to do.'" But the group ran through two numbers, their current hit and "People Are Strange," without incident. After dress rehearsal Ed briefly visited the band's dressing room. As he walked in, the band members were goofing around, laughing at guitarist Robbie Krieger's imitation of the Three Stooges. Ed, taking in the scene, commented, "Hello boys, you know, you're very good—but you'd look a lot better if you'd smile more." As soon as he left, the band began imitating his famous stiffness, to general hilarity. Ed Sullivan, telling them to smile more?

A few minutes later, Bob Precht walked in to deliver a message from the CBS Standards and Practices department. "Boys, we've got a problem," he said, explaining that the lyrics to the song "Light My Fire" needed to be changed. The phrase "Girl we couldn't get much higher" had caught the attention of censors. "You can't say the word 'higher' on national television," Precht said, because it would be perceived as a drug reference.

The band members were shocked: change the lyric? "To what?" Morrison spat out, quickly growing angry. "I don't know, you're the poet," Precht replied, throwing out a few possibilities. Morrison, who wrote many of the band's lyrics—including some to this song—was furious at the idea. "Jim had clenched his fist and was about to move on the guy," Manzarek recalled. But the keyboard player stepped in to assure Precht: "Okay, don't worry, we'll come up with something."

As soon as Precht left the room, Morrison turned to Manzarek: "Ray, what are you talking about?" The other band members all expressed dismay at the thought of changing the lyric. "Wait a minute," Manzarek said. "This is national television, this is our shot. Tell them anything you have to tell them—then you do what you want. This is live TV." The musicians all high-fived one another in anticipation of their moment of anarchy.

During the live broadcast, Morrison, clad in his signature leather pants, Byronic white shirt, and black leather jacket—and appearing in a trancelike state, likely enhanced by his preshow marijuana—sang the original lyric. He performed with an orgiastic fury, ending the song with a piercing, primal scream, followed by an abstracted downward stare. The Sullivan technical crew, over years of dealing with rock 'n' rollers, had developed a technique of boosting the guitar volume enough to bury the singer's voice as a censored lyric approached; this had been used with Mick Jagger, among others. But The Doors had brought their own engineer to control the sound board so their performance was uncensored. After their set, Ed clapped with barely veiled disgust, his body language projecting awesome distaste. Just a couple of years ago he would have stormed at them backstage and cursed a sailor's streak. But those days were behind him. The task of bawling them out was left to Bob Precht.

As Manzarek recalled, "We came back to our dressing room afterward, opened a can of beer, and toasted each other: 'Yeah! that was good!'" In came Precht: "You said it!—You said you weren't going to say it!" Manzarek tried to backpedal: "You have to understand, sir, we're just boys, and we've done the song this way so many times, and there we were, on national television, and we just got so nervous—it just came out."

"He knew I was jiving him," Manzarek remembered. "He said, 'Mr. Sullivan liked you boys. He wanted you on for six more shows. You know what that would have done for your career? But you know what? You'll *never* work *The Ed Sullivan Show* again!'"

Morrison looked at him, dismissively, and retorted, "Hey man, so what? We just *did The Ed Sullivan Show*."

Whatever headaches they caused, bookings of rock bands proceeded apace, though many of the acts that season had a softer sound. In late September, Ed interviewed The Mamas and the Papas, who performed in a set decorated in bright paisley splendor, asking them about breakup rumors and their upcoming European tour. In October, Nancy Sinatra, armed with a pink miniskirt and white go-go boots, growled "These Boots Are Made for Walking"; later in the program, Ed introduced the Ladies Auxiliary of the Polish Legion, in the audience. In November, The Turtles sang "Happy Together" on the same program that Joan Rivers, now in late-term pregnancy, did a stand-up routine about her condition (though Ed forbade her to use the word "pregnant"). Later in the month the Beatles, on film, performed "Hello, Goodbye," sharing the bill with middle-of-the-road pop star Connie Francis, who sang "Going Out of My Head." In early December, Ray Charles and Billy Preston rollicked on the rhythm and blues "Double-O-Soul," after which Japanese rock band The Blue Comets (inspired by the Beatles) raced through "Blue Chateau." On that same show, Ed introduced All-American Football team members O.J. Simpson and Larry Czonka.

The December 10 broadcast featured a film clip of the ceremony in which CBS renamed Studio 50, the Sullivan show's theater, as the Ed Sullivan Theater. In Ed's eyes this was the ultimate honor, one that touched him profoundly. Ratings could come and go, programs could be canceled, but now he was enshrined in the heart of

Manhattan's theater district, in the neighborhood that he had worked in his entire adult life. (The Ed Sullivan Theater, at Broadway and 53rd Street, later became home to the *Late Show with David Letterman*.) Hosting the well-attended event was New York mayor John Lindsay. Ed's friend Peter Prichard, the talent agent, was with him that evening, and he recalled the showman walking among the crowd: "The moment he walked out onto Broadway to walk to the rostrum, Ed knew everybody, every street guy in New York. He was wandering over to say 'Hi, how are you, nice to see you,' and we were trying to get him onstage because time was running short."

There was no small irony to the evening. Ed had been all but booed off the air in the show's early years because of his maladroit fumbling as an emcee, while his talents in his more significant role—producer—were little understood. It had been his skill as a producer, not his wooden stage persona, that kept the show highly rated for two decades. Yet as he received this most august honor as a showman, he was in fact little more than the program's emcee. Bob Precht was now the producer. Ed's son-in-law, of course, was using Sullivan's formula. But Ed himself was doing little but okaying the choices Bob made in fulfilling that formula. Sullivan certainly retained final veto power; throughout the show's run, "There was never a doubt that whatever it was he wanted, he got," Precht recalled. But with Ed's slipping mental acuity he was letting go of the reins. And, as the show's pace moved ever faster, his onstage time, never long in the first place, was cut to a bare minimum. Oddly, Ed was becoming a figurehead on his own show.

As the calendar flipped to 1968, the show's balancing act between young and old continued, although social commentators, referring to something called the Generation Gap, suggested this was getting harder. According to the new theory, the differences between parents and teenagers had grown so great as to be irreconcilable. But *The Ed Sullivan Show* had always gathered the whole family, and the program remained firmly in denial of the Generation Gap.

In January, Duke Ellington shared the bill with Vanilla Fudge, who played their current hit "You Keep Me Hanging On." In February, Motown crew Gladys Knight & The Pips performed on the same broadcast as singer Dinah Shore, who had entertained the troops during World War II. In March, new pop sensation the Bee Gees harmonized on "Words" right before Lucille Ball talked with Ed about her newest film, *Yours, Mine, and Ours*. In April, Ella Fitzgerald sang a swing version of the Beatles' "Can't Buy Me Love" shortly before George Carlin did a vaguely subversive routine about a politician on a fictional "Meet the Candidate" program.

The Sullivan show expanded to ninety minutes for one night in April for an eightieth birthday tribute to Irving Berlin, whom Ed had interviewed on radio in 1943. Bob Hope contributed a stand-up routine ("I always thought the Ed Sullivan Theater would be a wax museum," he cracked), Bing Crosby crooned, and President Johnson sent a taped birthday message. As if to prove that even Irving Berlin could be modernized, Diana Ross and the Supremes accompanied Ethel Merman in a Berlin medley, which veered briefly into the Motown hit "Heat Wave."

For all the show's intergenerational offerings, denying the Generation Gap and the other conflagrations now burning right outside the Ed Sullivan Theater was getting harder. Television was evolving, dragged reluctantly into the current day by a changing world. In January 1968, NBC launched *Rowan and Martin's Laugh-In*, a fresh

Ed attempts to interrupt Sylvia's game of Solitaire, February 1967.
(Time Life Pictures/Getty Images)

take on the comedy-variety format. Network executives didn't know if viewers were ready for the program's fast pace and non sequiturs, but the show quickly began climbing toward number one. Over on *Dragnet '67*, detective Joe Friday chased a demented LSD pusher, who died of an overdose at the episode's end. And a new rule was instituted for *The Smothers Brothers Comedy Hour*, which ran on CBS right after *The Ed Sullivan Show*. Now a tape had to be sent to affiliate stations before broadcast, due to complaints about the show's controversial nature—particularly how the comics handled the antiwar struggle at that summer's Democratic convention in Chicago.

Undeniable semaphores signaling these changes appeared on the Sullivan stage by the end of the 1967–68 season. Certainly The Doors' primal scream and the Rolling Stones' mockery of the show's sexual prudery signaled changing times, but still more direct signs were seen as well. In November, Ed presented Victor Lundberg, a surprise spoken-word one hit wonder. He performed his "Open Letter to My Teenage Son," a bitter condemnation of the antiwar movement ("If you burn your draft card, you're no son of mine"). In May, Ed gave an audience bow to a newly visible group, a coterie of wounded Vietnam veterans. Comedian Jack Carter, who once included one-liners about beatniks, now told jokes about hippies. Comedy duo Wayne and Schuster did a routine about TV violence. Charlton Heston had given dramatic Bible readings in the 1950s, but now he promoted his new film *Planet of the Apes*, whose last scene suggested mankind would destroy itself.

And in the greatest signifier of change, the show's twentieth-anniversary program was rescheduled; presidential candidate Robert F. Kennedy had been assassinated, dying on June 6 (just two months after Martin Luther King, Jr.,'s assassination), so the June anniversary was curtailed. Planned as a two-parter, Ed turned the second week into a memorial tribute to Kennedy. Dionne Warwick sang "The Battle Hymn of the Republic," Duke Ellington performed "David Danced Before the Lord," and actor Richard Harris reprised a scene from *Camelot*.

The Sullivan show, which had always been a perfect mirror of American culture—combining corn pone and high art, the Polish Ladies Auxiliary, Borscht Belters, sports heroes, rock 'n' roll, and Irving Berlin into an hour of diversion and entertainment—was now forced to reflect some unpleasant images.

Still, amid the roiling turmoil, *The Ed Sullivan Show* appeared to be some sort of eternal verity. As the year's Nielsens were tallied, they revealed that the Sullivan show had held its ground. The live broadcast continued to own its time slot, and of the eighty-some shows in prime time, it was ranked thirteenth, with a weekly audience of around thirty million viewers. The Sullivan show, it seemed, might just last forever.

CHAPTER SEVENTEEN

Ripped Asunder

OMETHING FUNDAMENTAL WAS CHANGING, or so it appeared by watching *The Ed Sullivan Show*'s 1968–69 season. Until this season, the show had felt like an updated version of its circa-1950s offering, despite the increased volume and tempo since the Beatles' 1964 debut. But now, as the tumultuous changes happening outside the theater door began playing center stage, the show felt markedly different. Typifying the season was an act Ed presented in January 1969, the Peter Gennaro Dancers. An acclaimed Broadway performer-choreographer, Gennaro led his troupe that evening in a routine inspired by the headlines. Ed, with speech more garbled than ever before, brought them out with a flourish.

Dressed in a bulky astronaut outfit, Genarro danced as if he were gamboling on a moonscape. Six female dancers rotated around him, dressed in skintight silver polyester, with bare midriffs and tall silver headdresses. Their musical accompaniment was "Strangers in the Night," but the arrangement was far from the familiar orchestral strains. Instead, the romantic ballad was rendered as if by a computer, the melody burbling forth in a disjointed bleep-blip style, twanged by filtered, syncopated guitars. The astronaut and his silver-clad space nymphs moved likewise, floating or moving herky-jerky like moon explorers buffeted by random lunar winds. As they concluded, Ed led the applause and mentioned that New York governor Nelson Rockefeller had invited him to the Waldorf-Astoria to meet the astronauts, who would attempt the first moon landing that summer.

Gennaro's routine was enchanting. The problem was that, for Ed's older viewers, there were now just too many dancing astronauts, strange rock bands, and comedians with a pointed sense of humor. It wasn't that the show's approach had changed—though it was making something of a shift—it was that the world outside had changed. In many ways, *The Ed Sullivan Show* was doing what it had always done: mirroring the culture as it evolved with the times. When Milton Berle's vaudeville one-liners made him the leading comic in the early 1950s, Ed booked him; when Elvis burst on the scene in the mid 1950s, Ed (reluctantly) presented him; when shifting tastes in the early 1960s made Mort Sahl's socially conscious humor palatable to mainstream audiences, Ed invited him on. Sullivan's coup in booking the Beatles, for all its headlines, was simply his latest step in staying culturally current. But in the 1968–69 season, as the national mood heated to a boiling point, mirroring the culture meant presenting a mix the show's older viewers had little interest in watching.

In truth, this shift didn't happen in just one season; it was a continuum. Surely, Doors lead singer Jim Morrison's frenzied vocal performance in September 1967 lead plenty of viewers to switch channels in disgust. Even the wave of relatively well-scrubbed rockers in the mid 1960s, like Herman's Hermits and The Turtles, had tried the patience of many older viewers. But if there was a single tipping point when the elements aimed at older and younger audiences grew so oppositional they began to tear the show apart, it was in its 1968–69 season. This was, not coincidentally, about the same moment that the culture itself erupted into a generational divisiveness never before seen in American history.

In addition to mirroring social changes that made older viewers uncomfortable, the show's format was shifting. While still hewing faithfully to its something-for-everyone approach, the program's booking choices now reflected a desire to reach a younger, hipper audience. America was making the shift toward being a youth-oriented culture, and the Sullivan show was as well, or at least was attempting to.

Opening its 1968–69 season was psychedelic rock band Jefferson Airplane, who had personified San Francisco's Summer of Love hippiefest the year before. Following them that fall was Tiny Tim, the gender-bending ukulele player popularized by *Laugh-In*, and the Beach Boys performing their homage to psychedelia, "Good Vibrations." In September the Supremes used the Sullivan show to introduce a new song, "Love Child," which represented a left turn in the trio's direction. Unlike their previous hits, this tune was socially conscious, reflecting ghetto life and the legacy of poverty. That evening the Supremes abandoned their sequined glamour to perform in sweatshirts and bare feet. Ed's introduction may have been the most jarring change. Hearing the sixty-seven-year-old showman enthusiastically shout a song title that referred to an illegitimate child—"and now, here's 'Love Child!'"—only reinforced the idea that something profound was changing.

Clearly, the musical beat was picking up a different vibe, with appearances by Sly and The Family Stone, Blood, Sweat & Tears, and Steppenwolf, who performed their hallucinatory ode "Magic Carpet Ride." Janis Joplin let loose with a shout-singing rendering of "Raise Your Hand" and "Maybe." (In rehearsal Ed introduced the singer as "from Joplin, Missouri," and although she corrected him, he still introduced her that evening as "from Joplin. . . .") The cast of the Broadway tribal rock musical *Hair*—the show was charged with desecration of the American flag, and its use of nudity and profanity sparked a lawsuit that went to the U.S. Supreme Court—sang "Aquarius/Let the Sun Shine In."

There was, as always, plenty of material aimed at squarer sensibilities. Ed interviewed retired boxer Sugar Ray Robinson about his picks for the ring's best fighters, and World Series winning pitcher Bob Gibson strummed guitar. An ensemble called Your Father's Mustache harmonized on "Take Me Out to the Ballgame," and vanilla balladeer John Davidson intoned "Didn't We." Jim Henson presented his Muppets for the kids. In a nod to former years when the show presented more high

With the Supremes, December 1969. Sullivan was particularly fond of the Motown
group, booking them fifteen times. (CBS Photo Archive)

art, ballet stars Allegra Kent and Jacques d'Amboise danced a pas de deux, and
British actor David Hemmings recited a Dylan Thomas poem.

But it felt like the balance had tipped. For every time Rodney Dangerfield played
the regular guy ("I don't get no respect"), Richard Pryor did one of his offbeat routines, like a bit about what it means to be "cool." Norm Crosby played his working-
class fractured English for laughs, to be followed not long after by Flip Wilson, a
black comic who sometimes dressed as a woman. During dress rehearsal in the fall
of 1968, comedian George Carlin was asked to eliminate one of two particularly
trenchant segments; delivering both would have been too abrasive, Bob Precht and
Sullivan felt. One of Carlin's segments skewered archconservative politician George
Wallace for decrying "pointy-headed intellectuals"—Carlin's routine turned the
phrase around to refer to the Ku Klux Klan; his other segment referred to Muhammad Ali, who had been stripped of his boxing license for refusing military induction: "Muhammad Ali, whose job is beating people up, didn't want to go overseas
and kill people. And the government said, 'If you're not going to kill them, we're not
going to let you beat them up.'" Of the two segments, Carlin chose to perform the
Ali material for that evening's broadcast, because "it had more resonance in what
was wrong with the society than the Governor Wallace pointy-head line."

In response to the Sullivan show's more challenging material, many of Ed's viewers turned the channel. *The FBI*, a crime drama on ABC that had played opposite *The Ed Sullivan Show* since 1965, had always run far behind. But during the 1968–69 season, a large portion of Sullivan's audience preferred the square-jawed certitude of its weekly triumph of good over evil. That season *The FBI* was ranked eighteenth, while the Sullivan show tumbled to number twenty-three, its first time outside the top twenty since the Western craze of the late 1950s.

If the show was on the ropes, its host seemed all but down for the count. Ed's forgetfulness had progressed far past the typical absentmindedness of an elderly man. He was clearly in the early stages of what his colleagues referred to as Alzheimer's, although it was never diagnosed as such. Whatever it was, it didn't prevent him from functioning effectively much of the time, yet by this point he was only a shadow of the shrewd producer he had been. At times he seemed shaky and almost feeble. While early in the broadcast he might appear to be his former self, stiff but sure, later in the hour he would seem noticeably vacant. After he delivered his introduction his face might go slack and detached before the camera cut to the act he was introducing. He came to rely heavily on Bob Precht. His son-in-law continued to confer closely with him but was now very much in charge of keeping the Sullivan formula spinning. It was an odd truth of Ed's life: though no one could have planned it, his daughter had delivered to him a man who extended his career long past when it otherwise would have ended.

Not that the showman was resigned to becoming a fossil. After maintaining his 1920s hairstyle for decades, he now incongruously sported long sideburns, much like the young rock 'n' rollers who played the show. He would, of course, never wear his hair long, but it was no longer strictly slicked back. Instead it was allowed to follow its natural wave, and with the color and improved video clarity of the show's later years, his hair appeared distinctly auburn, not the black it had always seemed to be. Those cosmetic enhancements, however, didn't distract from his timeworn, hollowed-out look.

Sullivan and his show were moving in opposite directions. As the program's 1969–70 season kicked off, its production values were ever more contemporary as Ed appeared ever more antique. The program's theme music was a bold orchestral rock number, and its sets were increasingly elaborate and realistic, some with brilliant electric colors; the weekly budget for sets had grown to a hefty $10,000. Amid it all, with his haggard face and sometimes unsteady manner, Ed seemed as if he had wandered onto the wrong set. That is, until the old energy came back—his odd alembic of reserve and moxie—and he bantered with a guest or played a cameo in a comedy skit.

The show's 1969–70 season presented the most culturally discordant combinations ever seen on the Sullivan stage. That past August, the youth counterculture's leading rock bands had held forth in a three-day bacchanal known as the Woodstock Music and Art Festival. Now the Sullivan show combined the festival's shaggy iconoclasm with the butterscotch gentility of the musical establishment, as Woodstock alumni shared billing with far older performers. Santana reprised his Woodstock performance of "Persuasion" shortly before film composer Henry Mancini led an orchestra in the theme from *Romeo and Juliet*. The next week The Band romped through "Up on Cripple Creek," to be followed by aging vaudevillian Pearl Bailey singing "You're Nobody Till Somebody Loves You" (Ed clowned around with her that evening, pretending to sing and then dancing a few steps). Douglas Fairbanks Jr.—who had appeared in silent movies—performed an excerpt from a stage revival of *My Fair Lady* on the same show that Creedence Clearwater Revival sang their antiwar anthem "Fortunate Son."

That fall, the Rolling Stones were in California for the notorious tour that culminated in the death of a fan at the Altamont Raceway. Eager to showcase the band, Ed, Bob, and a production crew flew to Los Angeles to film the Stones at a CBS studio. The three tunes they filmed, "Gimme Shelter," "Love in Vain," and "Honky Tonk Woman," were shown on a November broadcast featuring jazz legend Ella Fitzgerald interpreting "You Better Love Me" and "Open Your Window."

In January 1970, Muhammad Ali—a vilified figure in some quarters after refusing military induction on religious grounds—bantered with Ed onstage, then sang the spiritual "We Came in Chains." He was an engaging performer, but the controversial boxer didn't appeal to Ed's more traditional audience. Nor were they likely entertained by that February's appearance by comic Richard Pryor. The CBS censors were eager to tone down Pryor, but Bob and Ed insisted he be allowed to perform as he wanted. "Ed *adored* Richard," recalled staffer Russ Petranto. That evening the comic played the character of a black poet reciting his newest poems, one of which was Pryor screaming the word *"BLACK!"* as loud as possible. "That's what we got to do, brothers and sisters, we got to organize ourselves against whitey!"

Shaking the hand of a bearded Muhammad Ali, January 1970. At the time, Ali was a highly controversial figure after refusing military induction. (CBS Photo Archive)

Introducing the Jackson 5, December 1969. One Sullivan crew member recalled watching over Michael Jackson backstage: "He was such a cute little guy." (CBS Photo Archive)

proclaimed Pryor as poet. The joke was that every time he came to the word "white," he had to struggle to pronounce it, because the term made him so anxious. Clearly, this was a generational leap past the always-smiling deference of Nat "King" Cole.

Attempting to bolster ratings, Bob Precht produced some traditional specials, like that season's *Holiday on Ice*. But it wasn't enough to reverse the slide. Over the last several years, Sullivan's audience had trended steadily older, despite the cornucopia of rock acts and increasingly edgy comedians. Tens of millions of viewers had bonded with the show in earlier years, and many stayed loyal as the program updated itself. Or rather, they had until now. The 1969–70 Nielsen rankings revealed that many viewers were uninterested in watching the program's all-too-accurate reflection of current trends; *The Ed Sullivan Show* slid to number twenty-seven. In January 1970, a woman named Beatrice Rapp wrote a letter to the *Philadelphia Sunday Bulletin* that spoke for many of Sullivan's viewers: "Whatever happened to *The Ed Sullivan Show*? It was a good family show until recently. Now with the suggestive dancers that he puts on and the disgusting display of that character Tiny Tim—what is happening?"

That spring, Ed received troubling news: CBS was canceling a handful of still successful shows, including *The Jackie Gleason Show* and *The Red Skelton Hour*. The Skelton show had been that season's seventh-ranked program, so its cancellation raised numerous eyebrows. A major shift was underway in the television industry. Networks faced pressure from advertisers, who were adopting a new approach based on demographics. Having a sizable audience was no longer enough to make a show attractive; advertisers now wanted an audience with a desirable composition, which in their view meant younger viewers, ideally living in urban areas. Advertisers were most eager to reach the eighteen- to thirty-four-year-old age group. As Irwin Segelstein, then CBS's New York head of programming, recalled, "The changeover in audience composition [requirements] meant we were losing shows that had good ratings, like *Skelton* . . . we were getting big ratings, but not the right audience composition . . . it was a disaster for the programming department."

Bob Precht understood the changes taking place in television: "We made every effort to appeal to a younger audience," he said, hence the season's highly contemporary feel. While Ed's formula had *always* targeted a younger audience, it also catered to an older audience, as well as urban, suburban, and rural audiences. Its Big Tent philosophy ran counter to the notion of focusing exclusively on one group. (That many of Sullivan's viewers were rural was a related problem, in the network's eyes; over the next year, CBS would cancel mainstay *Petticoat Junction* and the highly rated *Beverly Hillbillies* to counteract the perception that its audience was older and rural.)

With its plethora of rock acts, the Sullivan show should have been able to offer advertisers the younger audience they desired. But by 1970 the younger set no longer wanted to sit through ancient vaudevillians and oldsters like Henry Mancini, and Ed himself was the very definition of square. The show had never been hip, though it had hip elements; instead, getting booked by Ed was the imprimatur of establishment success—precisely what younger viewers found so off-putting. (In January 1969 the rock group The Rascals announced they would stop appearing on the Sullivan show because they didn't want to perform on "establishment shows.") Worse, watching *The Ed Sullivan Show* meant enduring an hour with one's parents. As for the older audience, they still revered Ed but they couldn't stomach the show's current youth-oriented fare. Getting the entire family to sit down together was increasingly difficult. The culture was coming apart at the seams; the big tent was being ripped asunder. In February 1969, ABC debuted *The Generation Gap*, a humorous game show pitting teens against adults. It was canceled after ninety days; for most, the widening gap was no laughing matter.

Mike Dann, then CBS's programming head, recalled being in a network meeting that included discussion of the Sullivan show's falling ratings. "We didn't know what to do . . . we had to be very careful, he had built [a major following]." Compounding the network's indecision was the fact that it had no ready replacement. As a result, despite the changes roiling the television industry, Sullivan escaped the fate of canceled performers like Red Skelton and Jackie Gleason.

But if Ed harbored any optimism it was dashed by the first few Nielsen reports of the 1970–71 season. Indicating a steady slippage, they revealed that the declining Nielsens of the past two years were part of a continuing trend. Perhaps if Ed had been fully mentally present he might have found a way to turn this around, to renew his format as he had always shifted it to boost ratings. Battling the heavily financed *Comedy Hour*, his decision to veer from a variety format to produce tributes to Broadway and Hollywood stars kept the program alive. Through the 1950s he maintained the show's appeal by looking far and wide for the best talent, internationalizing it as he himself traveled. He hadn't wanted to book Elvis, but the ratings potential prompted him to phone Colonel Parker; he then rode the rock 'n' roll wave hard for years, and his wanderlust allowed him to present the Beatles before any American promoter. Now, with the younger set's aversion to the show's square façade, and older viewers' dislike of twanging guitars, Sullivan's rock offering no longer kept his Nielsens aloft. As the calendar said good-bye to the 1960s, the show's direction needed to be shifted once again. But how was an inventive producer to recreate *The Ed Sullivan Show* in 1970?

The program faced its most organic problem: the format itself was exhausted. The concept of appealing to everyone was exhausted. And in truth, Ed himself was exhausted. The sixty-nine-year-old showman could no longer bob and weave with the culture as he had for so many years. CBS sent a questionnaire to the show each year, requesting details about its direction for the upcoming season. Ed, who never lost his disdain for management, responded: "Fuck 'em, we'll do the same thing we did last year." (Bob Precht then very conscientiously filled it in.) The erosion of his memory continued, and the attendant mental fog grew thicker. On one occasion, a reporter in the theater asked Sullivan his age, and he blanked on the question, having to turn to a staff member for help. Mary Lynn Shapiro, one of his personal secretaries, recalled him asking on a Sunday afternoon, "Who's on the show tonight?" The same producer who once controlled every detail, from who was booked to what material they performed, now simply showed up to read his cue cards as best he could.

The Sullivan show launched its 1970–71 season with a format as diverse—if not more so—as ever. In October, Engelbert Humperdinck sang the Sinatra warhorse "My Way" on a broadcast with Tiny Tim, who trilled a medley of children's songs that included "On the Good Ship Lollipop." A few weeks later, legendary bluesman B.B. King performed "The Thrill Is Gone" on the same evening saccharine pop sensation Karen Carpenter sang her number one hit "(They Long to Be) Close to You." A broadcast that fall seemed to sum up the season. Billed as a United Nations twenty-fifth-anniversary tribute, it ran the gamut from sitar master Ravi Shankar, known to rock fans for his influence on the Beatles, to Brazilian songstress Astrud Gilberto performing "Girl from Ipanema," to the Ballet Africains, a percussion outfit jamming on an Afro-Caribbean groove. In a world heading toward niche programming, the Sullivan show's focus was growing ever broader. The Big Tent was as big as it ever had been.

The audience kept slipping away. Attempting to satisfy older viewers, Bob Precht produced a special dedicated to Richard Rodgers. That kind of program had saved Sullivan in the early 1950s, but now it wasn't enough. On Sunday night at 8 P.M., many of Ed's traditional viewers were tuned to ABC's *The FBI*, which had surged into television's top ten. The youngest set was entranced by NBC's *The Wonderful World of Disney*, television's fourteenth-ranked show, which ran opposite the Sullivan show's first half hour. In the second half hour, NBC presented *Bill Cosby*, starring a forward-looking young comic whom Ed himself had booked in the last few years.

The Sullivan show normally topped *Bill Cosby* yet was now running far behind its other time slot competitors. By the winter of 1971 *The Ed Sullivan Show*'s ranking had slid to forty-third. Of the eighty or so shows in prime time, it was middle of the pack, which it had never been in more than two decades. The show's production staff assumed the end was near. Ed, however, had his mind set on a goal. With its debut in 1948, the show was in its twenty-third season. He desperately hoped to make it to the twenty-fifth-season mark.

In March 1971, Precht received a call from CBS-TV president Bob Wood. Some changes were being made, Wood explained. Long the leading network, CBS had now fallen even with NBC. A major schedule revamp was needed to pull ahead. In the management's view, too many of its shows, while still successful, catered to an older or rural audience. After seeing success with its two new contemporary situation comedies, *The Mary Tyler Moore Show* and *All in the Family*, the network wanted to continue to refresh its programming. CBS sought to more actively target a younger, urban audience. Eight shows were being canceled, including three that were highly rated in the previous season. Wood informed Precht that *The Ed Sullivan Show* was one of those being canceled.

Bob called Ed at the Delmonico. In Ed's eyes, the cancellation was one more example of the network management's lack of respect for him. "Well I'll be a son of a bitch," he said. "After all I've done for the network over the years." A letter was written to CBS head Bill Paley to appeal the decision, but the cancellation was final. However, the network wanted to soften the blow—and hedge its bet, in case cancellation proved to be a mistake—so it offered a consolation. In honor of what Wood called the show's "grand tradition," the network asked Sullivan to do eight ninety-minute *Ed Sullivan Show* specials.

To Ed, this was no consolation. He had been canceled and the specials didn't change that. There was discussion about how to end the show; a big good-bye broadcast was suggested, but Ed didn't like the idea. He couldn't face going on to say farewell; it was like announcing he had lost his show. He decided to play reruns for the remainder of the season, so the last new show aired on March 28. The reruns ran until the official cancellation date of June 6, 1971, after which the network was deluged with letters protesting the decision.

Ironically, one of the many letters Ed received was from FBI director J. Edgar Hoover, who was indirectly involved with *The FBI*, the very show that had drawn viewers away from the Sullivan show. The two men had corresponded over the years, and now the Bureau director offered his condolences. "I was indeed sorry to learn that your show will no longer be seen on television," Hoover wrote. "Your presentations have always been most interesting and entertaining. Your outstanding contributions over the years will be long remembered. . . . Sincerely, Edgar."

The show was over. For many of the staff, working on it had come to seem like working for a well-established family business. Television shows might have runs of three to five years, with staff on the lookout for a new job the entire time; unemployment loomed just one bad Nielsen report away. In contrast, the Sullivan show had appeared virtually permanent. The staff felt as if they had familial ties with one another (and some three decades after cancellation many continued to stay in touch). After every Sunday's broadcast, when Ed and Sylvia went to Danny's Hideaway, the production crew gathered at the China Song restaurant next to the theater to compare notes, laugh, and kibitz long into the night.

Most of the staff recalled working on the show as one of the high points of their life. The job was consuming; some worked six days a week, usually all day long on Saturday and Sunday. But the visceral excitement of a live broadcast and the glittering parade of stars more than made up for it. Staff member Susan Abramson remembered Irving Berlin coming into the office and noticing a painting of a bright blue sky above her desk. Berlin, whose song "Blue Skies" had been a huge hit, looked at the painting with a twinkle in his eye and said to her: "You know, I could write a song about that." On another occasion, Duke Ellington told her he was going to compose a tune about her blue eyes. Sistie Moffit, an administrative assistant, recalled that Michael Jackson, then a boy star of Motown, tended to wander off before rehearsal. Assigned the task of watching him, she tied a short rope between her waist and his; many years later she still chuckled about babysitting the singer. "I dragged him around with me all day. . . . Michael was such a cute little guy."

In the immediate aftermath of cancellation, the staff's disappointment was tempered by knowledge that it had been coming. When the final call came, there was a certain shrug of the shoulders. No one was surprised. (And for several of the crew the show launched them to further success in television.) Still, set designer Bill Bohnert had a lump in his throat as he cleared out his warehouse of props, to be picked up by garbage trucks.

Ed, while not surprised, was absolutely heartbroken. Soon afterward he met his friend, singer Jerry Vale, at Toots Shor's restaurant. Tears were in his eyes, Vale remembered. "How about that? I've been canceled," Ed said. "After all these years, they canceled me. I wanted to do twenty-five seasons, but they wouldn't let me do it." Vale tried to console his friend, but Ed was inconsolable. That the showman had achieved everything he set out to do, walking into millions of living rooms every Sunday for decades, and having the Ed Sullivan Theater named in his honor, didn't matter. The show had been his identity, and now he had nothing else to look forward to.

That summer a reporter from *Show* magazine interviewed him at his apartment in the Delmonico. As they sat in Ed's memento-strewn office, the showman seemed "in a period of deep reminiscence," the reporter wrote. "His manner appeared nostalgic, full of pauses and prolonged glances, and with a wee touch of sadness."

"I feel empty now that the show's over. Very empty," Ed said. "It was the excitement, the fun of it, that I miss . . . meeting celebrities, going out after the show with stars [which in fact Ed rarely did]. It was the thrill of going out onstage in front of a live audience every Sunday at 8 P.M. All of a sudden, that was over and there was nothing."

"Even after CBS's decision, I went on thinking, in myself, that I was still doing the show. You see I had put a big part of my life into it, and I don't think it was just conceit. No, it was a terrific letdown, the news . . . like getting a slap in your face from your teacher. I brood about it, do a lot of walking. If I'm out and a cab driver stops me and says, 'Hey Ed, what have you got on Sunday night,' what can I do but just laugh?

"The people were just getting tired of that old routine. In the course of twenty-three years, I've shown everything that vaudeville had ever produced. I think they just felt 'For Christ's sake, not again!' At any rate, the ratings collapsed."

He expressed regret that he didn't do more to shake up the show's format as the ratings slid, like producing more specials. "Like a horse's ass I didn't say to myself 'What the hell am I worrying about? This is what we should do! Specials!' I just got into the habit of the old routine, I guess."

The reporter asked Sullivan how his show had lasted so long. "I know a hell of a lot about show business and I know a hell of a lot about performers. On our show my opening act was just like my newspaper leads—the grabber that held people's interest. This act would be a good one, and then we'd go to commercials. You grab them instantly. It was just like the makeup of a newspaper—when I was on the *Mail* I used to do the makeup. You know, by putting in your one-column boxes, cuts in here and there, you could make the page interesting to look at. My shows were just like a newspaper—it had sports, drama, movies, celebrities."

His thoughts often turned to the past. "I think more about the old days than I did before. My wife, Sylvia, tells me I think too much about it. It was an exciting past, especially those early newspaper days when I was running around and meeting all kinds of new people."

Did Ed mind the ratings game, which so many said turned television into a sea of mediocrity? No, he said, the public will make its tastes known. "It always has and it always will. The ratings game is legitimate. Saying that TV shouldn't cater to public taste is like saying let's give up the presidential election because public taste has picked so-and-so."

Would he retire? "Every time I think of leaving New York and going off to the country . . . well, I just couldn't do it." His plans at this point were unclear. He noted that Sylvia, after many years of marriage, knew to say nothing to him in the days right after cancellation. But after a week, she asked, "Ed, what are we going to do on Sundays now?"

In fact, Ed hadn't given up the idea of returning to his weekly show. He told the *Show* reporter that if ratings for his fall specials were high enough, the network might be convinced to reinstate the weekly program. He looked over at the reporter with a smile described as sly but charming, and said: "Maybe I can prove to CBS that they're wrong." It was classic Ed. Just as after his many canceled radio programs, once again, losing a show simply meant it was time to start planning to get back on the air.

But he wasn't the hustling thirty-five-year-old newspaperman he had been. Ed's daily life now bumped along without much sound and fury. As always, he had his habitual 11 A.M. breakfast of a lamp chop and a glass of iced tea with artificial sweetener. He went out for a shave, same place, same time. He attended a benefit for the Dance Collection at the New York Public Library. He accepted the Brotherhood Award from Temple Ohabei Shalom, one of dozens of awards from Jewish groups he received over the decades. In August he and Sylvia took their perennial sojourn to Cannes, France, along with a few other couples. He had never stopped penning his *Daily News* column, though in reality it had long been shepherded by his faithful assistant, Carmine Santullo. With his show gone, Ed turned back to *Little Old New York* and began putting more energy into his twice-weekly column.

In September, he appeared on NBC's *The Flip Wilson Show.* Debuting in 1970, Wilson's program was the first successful network variety show hosted by a black performer; in its first two seasons it zoomed to television's number two ranking. Every week, Wilson portrayed comic characters who skewered contemporary life, like Reverend LeRoy, pastor of the Church of What's Happenin' Now, and Geraldine, the sassy, liberated black girl who cried, "The devil made me do it!" He was one of the next-generation comics whom *The Ed Sullivan Show* helped launch; Ed had booked him twelve times.

On the Wilson show, Sullivan performed two skits with Wilson and Lucille Ball. In the first, Wilson played Charlie Brown to Ed's Snoopy (dressed as a WWI fighter ace) and Ball's Lucy, as the trio philosophized about life. In the second, Ed played an aging hipster who finds himself in the middle of a catfight between Wilson, cross-dressed as Geraldine in a hot pink miniskirt, and a modishly attired Lucille Ball. This latter skit seemed to reflect Ed's changed circumstances. The last time he had played a comedy sketch with Lucille Ball was in 1954, and it revolved around Lucy and Ricky's breathless excitement at getting on Ed's show. Now, dressed in garish purple pants and a hippie-style fringe jacket, he was a player who was past his prime.

Since Sullivan was such a universally known celebrity, he was in demand by advertisers for television commercials. Although he certainly didn't need the money, he appeared in TV ads for an antacid—an unlikely role, given how his ulcer plagued him and how little antacid had helped. "I got the feeling he was trying to hold on, to hang onto fame," recalled his grandson Rob Precht, then in his late teens, who often spent time with his grandfather. "I remember thinking at the time that it was pathetic—I was sad to see him do it."

An oddity about Ed's life in this period was that cultural commentators used references to his famously stiff persona in articles about current president Richard Nixon. Typical of the commentary was an Op-Ed piece in *The New York Times* by playwright Arthur Miller: "For my own taste, Nixon is a god-awful actor; for one thing, his gestures are always at odds with what he's saying. . . . It's a lot like Ed Sullivan, a performer who was so at odds with his own arms that he finally took to clasping his chest." As remote as these two men were from one another, they did have similarities. Both first became major public figures in the 1950s, and both were largely incapable of projecting warmth or intimacy in their public selves. And, coincidentally, both had their careers canceled at about the same time. Yet the showman, unlike the politician, inspired a reservoir of affection in his audience, despite his wooden stage presence. At no time was this more evident than in the aftermath of the cancellation.

As countless newspaper and magazine homages poured forth in the months after the show's end, he was bathed in the glow of a newly beloved status. Everything about him that had been lampooned, often with great seriousness—his jerky gestures, the stilted vocal style—was now described endearingly. *Los Angeles Times* TV critic Cecil Smith called Ed's performance of Snoopy on *The Flip Wilson Show* "a classic of comedy by anyone's standards." The United Press International's Dick West bemoaned the loss of the show, calling Sullivan "a powerful stabilizing influence amid the vicissitudes of life. An anchor, so to speak, in a transmutable sea." Bill Barrett in *The Cleveland Press*, pondering the cancellation, asked, "What goes next? The Bill of Rights? The gold standard?" It was as if TV columnists' perception of his stiffness had magically reversed itself and they suddenly decided he was a loveable character. Someone that wooden must be genuine, the consensus seemed to be. Ed had somehow bonded with the audience—now even winning the critics— despite only rarely breaking his distant reserve.

Indeed, the response to his first special seemed to verify that absence made the heart grow fonder. Aired in October 1971 (four months after the last regular show), *The Sullivan Years: A Kaleidoscope* featured Ed presenting a library of highlights from the show back to the 1950s. The public flocked to it; the program dominated its Sunday night time slot and scored a jaw-dropping Nielsen rating. The one-night special, however, was what the show itself had not been. *The Ed Sullivan Show*, to the detriment of its ratings at the end, had never been backward looking. Or rather, it had been backward looking, fully contemporary, and forward-looking, simultaneously. The *Kaleidoscope* special presented Sullivan's signature compendium of rock bands, saloon crooners, comics, athletes, and trained animals. But its retrospective approach put it all into soft focus, carefully exorcising the socially charged elements the show itself had presented of late.

Ed became a kind of celebrity on call. In January he flew to Las Vegas to host CBS's *Entertainers of the Year Awards*, where he was roundly mock-insulted by comic Don Rickles: "I spoke to the wax museum. They're accepting you Friday." This broadcast's ratings ran just behind those of television's current number one show, *All in the Family*. A month later he was an award presenter at the Grammy Awards, broadcast on ABC. The Friars Club, a show business fraternal society, elected him as their Abbot, succeeding in a line that went back to George M. Cohan. And that September he appeared on ABC's *25 Years of Television*, receiving a special achievement award along with Lucille Ball, Bob Hope, and Milton Berle.

He also attended a number of funerals, including that of baseball legend Jackie Robinson, whom he had long lauded for breaking the sport's color line. In February 1972, Walter Winchell died. (Critic John Crosby eulogized Winchell by observing, "He was truly a fourteen-carat son-of-bitch.") After Winchell's death, Ed, having accepted Walter's invitation to sit on the board of the Damon Runyon Cancer Fund, was elected its president. It was fitting: Runyon had been the archetypical chronicler of 1930s New York café society, and now Ed, one of the era's few survivors, was custodian of his namesake fund.

The Ed Sullivan Show remained on peoples' minds. A year after cancellation, a man in Nebraska named Werner Hensley wrote a letter to *The New York Times* mourning the program's end, chiefly because he had been training a frog for eleven years in anticipation of a guest shot. "We would have made it if the cheek puffing hadn't taken an extra year of work," Hensley claimed.

The network hadn't forgotten it either; CBS commissioned Sullivan to produce an all-comedy special culled from previous shows. Broadcast in February 1973, *Ed Sullivan Presents the TV Comedy Years* ran opposite *Marcus Welby, MD*, a Tuesday night hit aimed at older viewers. The *Comedy Years* special, even more than the previous *Kaleidoscope*, was in contrast to what Ed had always produced. Instead of his all-inclusive approach, *Comedy Years* was an example of what was later called narrowcasting, the practice of focusing on a niche audience. The special gave short shrift to younger stand-ups like George Carlin and Richard Pryor, instead presenting comics from the show's earliest days, including Jack Benny, Jackie Gleason, Lucille Ball, Red Buttons, and Jimmy Durante. By focusing on a single audience, older viewers, the program handily won its time slot and ranked fifth for the week.

CBS realized it had found a formula. The library of Sullivan shows contained an ocean of material—one thousand eighty-seven episodes spanning twenty-three seasons—presenting performers of every stripe. If a show was edited together from elements that appealed to a specific audience, without the contrasting elements, a ratings win was likely. Making it still more appealing, Sullivan Productions owned all the programs; producing such a broadcast was simply a matter of calling Bob Precht.

Eager to repeat the success of the *Comedy Years* special, a month later CBS commissioned another special, *Ed Sullivan's Broadway*. For this tribute to the Great White Way, the showman strolled through the streets of New York, dispensing Broadway anecdotes as he introduced Sullivan show excerpts from theater classics. He also read blurbs from his column, which were original reviews from the period. Like the prior month's special, the Broadway retrospective garnered impressive ratings. It was now established: by choosing one audience among the several the program had reached, the Sullivan show could once again be a ratings powerhouse.

But suddenly, Ed didn't care. The day of the broadcast, March 16, he suffered a shock from which he never recovered. Sylvia had checked into Mount Sinai hospital for a routine procedure a few days earlier. At age sixty-nine, she appeared hale and healthy, and looked far younger than her years. She enjoyed traveling as they always had; just the week before she and Ed had returned from a jaunt to Miami Beach. In a recent society column spotlighting the two of them at dinner, the columnist commented on how attractive she continued to be. Since she was in the hospital the day that *Ed Sullivan's Broadway* was broadcast, she ordered a television set into her room to watch Ed. But, unexpectedly, she died that morning of a ruptured aorta. CBS News broadcast the announcement of her death shortly before that evening's Sullivan special. Sylvia's sudden death was a devastating blow to her family.

Ed fell into a bottomless grief. The show had been his identity, and it was gone, and now Sylvia, his lifelong companion, was also gone. Compounding the loss, she had become his protector and caretaker, handling many of the details of his daily life as his mental faculties lessened. Several people helped Ed as his Alzheimer's progressed, but none more so than Sylvia, recalled Joan Rivers, who knew Ed personally and professionally (Sullivan was the godfather of Rivers' daughter Melissa). "She took care of him like a hawk," Rivers said. "She was his Nancy Reagan." In the weeks after her memorial service, led by Rabbi Arthur Buch and with a eulogy by Bob Precht, Ed drifted into an emotional no-man's zone. With little to look forward to, his sadness and sense of emptiness became overwhelming. "My grandfather just disintegrated," remembered Rob Precht.

Jack Benny, hearing of Ed's bereavement, offered to fly in from California to spend some time with him. But Ed waved him off. He had heard, he claimed, that Benny himself "was not feeling too well, so why knock yourself out." When a reporter from *Variety* called, Ed explained that he would be "just keeping himself very busy with the column."

He did in fact keep plugging away at *Little Old New York*, reporting and commenting on show business and current events, with a good deal of help from Carmine Santullo. With Betty and Bob Precht living in Scarsdale, New York, Carmine became his sole daily companion. Ed also became closer with his older sister Helen, who still lived in Port Chester, and with whom he had stayed in touch through the years.

He had always been a loner, despite a vast network of contacts and long professional relationships. Now he seemed to retreat still further into himself. He continued his nightly rounds of Manhattan's nightclubs, but refused to let anyone go with him. His friend Jerry Vale remembered checking with Ed about a social outing, being rebuffed, and growing worried. "He went to Danny's Hideaway once, and I decided I was going to follow him," Vale recalled. "I followed him to the restaurant, I waited for him to get through, and he came out, and he walked from 48th Street up to his apartment on 59th. I followed him in my car. He was walking and I followed him very slowly, to make sure he got home okay. I was a very good friend of his and I wanted to see him do well." Vale described the depth of Ed's depression in this period: "When Sylvia died and the show went off, he was a beaten man."

In December, his experience at a charity event was painfully coincident with his current fortunes. The Loyal League Philanthropies asked him to emcee an awards banquet at the Waldorf-Astoria, attended by about eight hundred people. Ed presented an award to the owner of a clothing store chain, Mortimer Janis, for his efforts on behalf of underprivileged children. Shortly after Ed handed him the award, Janis, sitting at the dais, collapsed. A nurse tried to revive him but to no avail. He died of an apparent heart attack. In the numberless such events that Ed had hosted over the decades, such a mortal calamity had never happened. It appeared to be some form of omen.

Bill Gallo, a *Daily News* cartoonist who had sometimes met Ed for lunch in earlier decades, ran into him on the street. "I saw him on Broadway, very forlorn—believe it or not, no one recognized him, he just looked so goddamned sad and puffy." To cheer him up, Gallo organized a luncheon in his honor hosted by the Boxing Writers Association. Ed got up and gave a speech, and then began to relate anecdotes, traveling back through the decades. "It was nonstop stories," Gallo recalled, "about the Dempsey–Tunney fight, the Firpo fight, golfing with Joe Louis . . . ."

Notwithstanding his shaky mental state, the entertainment industry kept calling him. In January 1974, the seventy-two-year-old showman was invited to be master of ceremonies for CBS's *Entertainers of the Year Awards*, taped in Las Vegas with guests Carol Burnett, Sammy Davis, Jr., and Sonny and Cher. Producing the show were Bob Precht and John Moffit, the Sullivan show's director, who decided to videotape Ed's lead-ins for fear he couldn't handle the live audience. But the night before, as they taped Ed reading his cues from a TelePrompTer, he kept fumbling his lines. He spoke in a small, weak voice, often stopping to ask, "Bob, who's this? I can't read it." As Moffit recalled, "Bob finally threw up his hands and said, 'John, we're not going to get it, he's tired, we'll do the best we can tomorrow.'" The evening of the show, a huge audience—including a very concerned Precht and Moffit—filled the Caesar's Palace ballroom. The show's brassy music began pumping, and as the announcer gave Ed a rousing introduction, the audience began to cheer and scream with wild enthusiasm.

"Ed came out onstage," Moffit remembered, "straightened himself up, walked across the stage, and said,"—in a big bold voice—"'*Good evening ladies and gentlemen! Tonight, from Caesar's Palace . . .*' and it was the old Ed, the old warhorse, he got it together, the crowd brought him up, and all of a sudden this weak old man was the old Ed Sullivan for one hour."

During his Las Vegas trip, Ed had dinner with comedian Shecky Greene, whom he had gotten to know over the course of booking him six times. After Sylvia's death the two became good friends. Greene remembered Sullivan as a cantankerous host who not infrequently found reason to curse at him. Before one broadcast, Greene requested that Sullivan introduce him as a German comic (though Greene wasn't), and Ed complied. Shecky, in a fake German accent, did a routine in which he explained Ed had been on the air so long "because he has no talent—he doesn't sing, he doesn't dance, he doesn't do anything." As soon as he walked offstage, Ed accosted him, storming, "You son of a bitch—I've got more talent in my little finger than anyone I've ever had on this stage!"

Despite their rows, Greene was enormously fond of Sullivan, especially as they grew closer after Sylvia died. "I loved him," Greene said. "I thought he was some kind of guy." The comedian recalled how mentally confused Ed was in this period. Although Sylvia had died several months before, when he and Sullivan spoke, Ed invariably told him, "Sylvia and I were talking about you the other night."

The night of their dinner together in Las Vegas, Shecky told Ed the story of his decision to skip an airplane flight after one of his comedy performances—a decision that saved his life when the plane crashed. Ed so liked the anecdote that he asked Greene to repeat it; he wanted to use it in his *Little Old New York* column. But even transcribing an anecdote was difficult in Ed's current state. "He got cocktail napkins, a lot of them, and he was writing one line at a time, and [the ink] kept spreading," Greene recalled. As written in Ed's column the story lacked coherence. "When he put it in the paper, people called me and asked, 'What was that about?' He never put in the punch line." (By one account, the *Daily News* was growing restive with Ed's tenure and wanted to ease him out, but Carmine begged them to let him stay a little longer.)

Those close to him saw a surprising change. Ed had always enjoyed being out in public, delighting in the attention. John Moffit once gave him a ride across town during which Ed leaned out the window and directed traffic the entire time, playfully bossing the other drivers. He had always been famously accessible to fans, signing autographs with great care, asking a fan's name then writing a sentence dedicated to him or her. Now he turned away from the public. One night as he was finishing dinner at an Italian restaurant in midtown with his grandson Rob Precht, then in his late teens, Ed noticed a group of fans waiting outside the door. "My grandfather very abruptly turned to me and said, 'I'm not going to deal with them.'"

Still, despite his deepening depression, Sullivan might surprise his grandson with flashes of his former spirit. On one occasion during these months, Rob was walking Ed home late in the evening, going up Park Avenue toward the Delmonico, when he spotted two figures walking toward them who were obviously prostitutes, dressed in tight miniskirts and high heels. Rob felt a twinge of anxiety as they approached, thinking, "I hope they don't recognize him and start to engage him in conversation—he's frail, and sad, and I want to spare him any inconvenience." But as the ladies neared, it was Ed himself who decided to say hello, bellowing out *"Hello, girls, how are you?"* The women were momentarily startled, then seemed to realize who he was, at which point Rob guided his grandfather by the elbow toward home.

In May 1974, Sullivan was hospitalized for a problem related to his long-standing ulcer condition. He was released at the end of the month with instructions to come back for daily visits. However, he began skipping visits, making it in perhaps once a week. That summer, having spent very little time in churches throughout his life, Ed was seen praying at St. Malachy's Church in midtown.

On September 6, an X-ray revealed bad news. Sullivan's doctor checked him into Lenox Hill hospital and called his family, who decided not to tell him the full nature of his illness. Ed had inoperable cancer of the esophagus, and his doctor told his family that he wasn't expected to live much longer. "We had consulted with his doctors and it was felt that if he were told the truth, it would severely dampen his spirits and make him totally depressed," Bob Precht said. "It was best he didn't know. Right up until the day he died, his spirits were fine and he believed he was going to get well."

He spent five weeks in the hospital. Bob and Betty visited regularly, and Carmine Santullo was there constantly. On September 28, his seventy-third birthday, he was given two parties: one by the nurses, relishing their celebrity guest; the other by his family, at which he ate cake and ice cream and talked about looking forward to getting back to work. In fact he hadn't left work. He continued to write his column from his hospital bed, piecing together *Little Old New York* from press releases delivered by Carmine.

On the afternoon of October 13 his doctor called the Prechts; Ed's condition had worsened dramatically. They immediately drove to the hospital, sitting at his bedside while he lay unconscious. At 7:30 P.M., when Carmine arrived, they left. Carmine sat with him through the evening as Ed remained unconscious.

It was a Sunday night. Since 1948 he had lived for Sunday nights, and now he was dying on one. But not until the show was over. Shortly after 10 P.M., as the evening's program would have been finished, and Sylvia would have been picking him up for dinner at Danny's Hideaway, he stopped breathing.

The funeral, on October 16, was a celebrity affair. Held on a rainy autumnal day, with some three thousand people crowded into and right outside of St. Patrick's Cathedral, the event drew both mourners and those seeking a glimpse of the famous. The crowd outside, most carrying black umbrellas, watched a long line of limousines deliver entertainment, sports, and political figures to the front door. Cardinal Cooke led the service, and the attendees included Mayor Abe Beame, former Mayor John Lindsay, Attorney General Louis Lefkowitz, restaurateur Toots Shor, boxer Jack Dempsey, vaudevillian Peg Leg Bates, comedian Rodney Dangerfield, and Metropolitan Opera star Rise Stevens. Classical pianist Van Cliburn praised Sullivan for his "faithfulness to the serious arts." CBS head Bill Paley called the showman "an American landmark." Walter Cronkite, who first met Sullivan before World War II, said, "Ed had a remarkable quality of toughness in pursuing what he saw as right. He was an Irish grabber and I think that's admirable."

Ed had updated his will in March 1973. He left virtually all of his estate to Betty, with $10,000 going to Carmine, and a smaller amount left to his siblings. He noted in his will that he made no bequest to charity because he had done so much for charitable concerns during his life. He was buried next to Sylvia in Ferncliff Cemetery in Hartsdale, New York.

The day after he died, the *Daily News* printed Ed's last column, which he had written in his final days at Lenox Hill hospital. He composed that edition's *Little Old New York* much as he had written the column for the last forty-two years, using a series of ellipses to connect disparate items, one bit flowing into another, a stylistic invention he borrowed from Walter Winchell in the early 1930s. Because he believed he would soon leave the hospital, the column was its usual all-inclusive mix, spotlighting events across myriad fields:

> "Bennett Cerf's widow, Phyllis, partied [*sic*] Sinatra after Garden blockbuster . . . Mia Farrow okay after appendectomy . . . Richard Zanuck and Linda Harrison derailed . . . French President Giscard d'Estaing holds press conference on 24th to outline France's policy in foreign affairs . . . Dionne Warwick packing Chicago's Mill Run theater . . .
>
> President Ford's ex-press sec'y, J.F. TerHorst, guest speaker at Nat'l Academy of TV luncheon at Plaza on Thursday . . . Hal ("Candide") Prince's backers got another $217,500 from his three hits: "Fiddler," "Cabaret," and "Night Music" . . . David Frost and Lady Jane Wellesley a London duet . . . Nirvana Discotheque, a $250,000 shipwreck, to reopen as Nirvana East restaurant . . . The Jimmy (Stage Deli) Richters' fifth ann'y . . . Cardinal Cooke presents special awards to couples married 50 years, at St. Patrick's Cathedral on Jan. 12 . . ."

The tidbits flowed continuously, seemingly without end, providing something for everyone in a rapidly moving one-column parade. Ed was gone, but *Little Old New York*, as it always had, kept bustling on.

At Yonkers Raceway, 1967. (Time Life Pictures/Getty Images)

Epilogue

AME IS WHAT EDWARD VINCENT SULLIVAN DESIRED, and fame is what he achieved. In his lifetime, there were few public figures who spent as many hours in as many American living rooms as Ed Sullivan. He was known, and in many cases revered, by the tens of millions of almost ritualistic viewers who gathered each Sunday to watch his weekly circus. He is forever memorialized as the monochromatic purveyor of a wildly polychromatic mélange, a graven-faced emcee who turned hosting a lively showcase of high and low art into a remarkably sober task. That this compressed icon of Ed Sullivan bore only nominal resemblance to the flesh-and-blood Ed Sullivan is of little import. Certainly, the vituperative, epithet-hurling Stork Club habitué, the Fidel Castro interviewer and earnest blacklister, the rock 'n' roll patron saint and strict moralist, the producer who was tyrannical and sentimental, shrewd and irrational, petty and generous, was only glimpsed at moments on screen. But no matter. He is stored for the millennia with his name atop the marquee, as he so hungered for.

Reruns and retrospectives of *The Ed Sullivan Show*—his beloved creation that he placed at the center of his life—have continued to fuel that fame. The show has never fully gone off the air. After cancellation of its original run in 1971, it became a bottomless source of clips, the ultimate trove for television and documentary producers. Throughout the 1970s and 1980s, Ed was seen swinging his right arm and pointing to any number of acts. In 1980, a "Best of Sullivan" series appeared in syndication, broadcasting edited thirty-minute versions of the one-hour show periodically throughout the decade.

The showman's return to major network success came on February 17, 1991, in a broadcast, appropriately, on CBS on Sunday night. The program was produced by Andrew Solt, a television and film producer who had often mined the Sullivan show for clips, and who bought the complete library from the Sullivan family in 1990. Called *The Very Best of Ed Sullivan*, the two-hour show was a decisive ratings victory for the network. It was the second-highest-rated program for the week, and helped CBS win the February sweeps for the first time since 1985. The network commissioned three more retrospectives, each of which was a Nielsen booster.

Solt also produced a series of one hundred thirty half-hour Sullivan shows, which went into syndication in various outlets, including *Ed Sullivan's Rock 'n' Roll Classics*, played on the cable channel VH1, and a "Best of" program shown on the TV Land cable channel. PBS stations began airing Sullivan shows in 2001, typically on Saturday nights, broadcasting them regularly until 2004. Additionally, Solt produced a series of DVDs, including *The Best of Broadway Musicals*, *Unforgettable Performances*, and *Rock 'n' Roll Forever*. Bootleg copies of the show do a healthy trade: Sullivania is sold continuously on eBay, further distributing not just show tapes but also photos of Ed with performers, ticket stubs, and, occasionally, odd items like a plaque awarded to the showman in the late 1960s.

He was heartbroken that CBS wouldn't allow him to extend the program into its twenty-fifth year. But as the clips and specials and DVDs keep getting viewed, the show finds its way into living rooms decades beyond cancellation, much less two more seasons. It appears *The Ed Sullivan Show* will have a longer life than the showman himself did.

For someone who felt so long frustrated in his desire for national renown, launching short-lived radio shows again and again, trying abortively to break into film, and finding a rough early road in television, he succeeded surprisingly well. He pushed and shoved and cursed and worried, and he managed to propel the name Ed Sullivan on a continuous course through the decades. He achieved the fame he hungered for, and then some.

———

Yet his fame, whether it lasts or recedes to the vanishing point, is incidental to his greatest accomplishment. His legacy for posterity, stored in the Library of Congress as befitting the archive it is, is the complete collection of Ed Sullivan shows. Taken in their entirety, the one thousand eighty-seven episodes, spanning twenty-three seasons, are an incomparable cultural document.

For someone of a later age to ask: What was it like? What was the nature of American culture between 1948 and 1971? Their answer lies on those videotapes. The twenty-three seasons of live performances fully capture American tastes and views at a defining moment, both in the history of broadcast and in national history. They reveal the very birth of television, from its technical infancy to its first maturity, from a period when commercials were performed live onstage to the era when demographics began to rule the medium. They also reflect the American zeitgeist, from the dawn of the country's status as a world power to the era when the Baby Boom generation first exerted its influence. That the library of shows offers such a telling panoramic record of both these arcs makes it more than worth the considerable shelf space it occupies in the national archives.

Many television shows, of course, can be said to reflect American tastes or reveal something of their time period. But *The Ed Sullivan Show* transcends its compatriots because of the catholicity of Ed's vision. The Sullivan show was everything. His formula was vaudeville expanded to its furthermost edge, then beyond. It was opera and rock 'n' roll, boxing and ballet, slapstick and social consciousness, the Vienna Boys Choir and the Woody Herman Orchestra, dramatic Bible readings and psychedelia, blacks and whites, Jews and gentiles, Fred Astaire, Tiny Tim, Richard Burton, Duke Ellington, John Lennon, Ronald Reagan, and Eleanor Roosevelt, Carl

Sandburg and Karl Wallenda, Eugene O'Neill, and Rodney Dangerfield, Jason Robards and Jessica Tandy, Mort Sahl and Janis Joplin and Michael Jackson, Cole Porter and Walt Disney and Bill "Bojangles" Robinson, Salvador Dalí and Elvis Presley and Margaret Truman and Van Cliburn and Frankie Avalon, and—the list exhausts itself, the list breaks the very definition of a list because all the items on it could not appear on a single list. Yet they did. Some ten thousand performers graced the Sullivan stage.

The Ed Sullivan Show stands alone, too, because its impresario was such an inveterate newshound, with one eye cocked toward the latest headline and one moist finger hoisted in the air, always ready to proceed with cautious boldness wherever his audience was ready to go, and sometimes where they weren't. He was a man of the moment, *that* week, wanting the show to be as newsworthy, and as news making, as the best of his Broadway columns. This made his program, unlike most other popular long-running shows, an immediate sonar ping reflection of its season. Each episode was a curio snapshot of its moment.

Cementing the show's status as an archive of its time was Sullivan's intuitive knack for reaching, some might say pandering to, the mass audience. He called to get the evening's ratings every Monday morning, like a penitent bowing down to his deity, and he lived by those numbers. Because he reached so many viewers for so long, he created a show that influenced the tastes of the mainstream audience for decades. Magnifying his influence was the then-limited nature of the media universe. There was very little competition in his day: no cable television, no Internet, no movie rental. He was routinely watched by some thirty-five million people a week, year after year—a staggering number by comparison to later eras, when changes in media distribution fractured audiences into small slivers focusing on mutually exclusive material. His audience size during the ratings "slump" at the show's end would have made the program a resounding success in later decades. Sullivan was one of the only games in town, which greatly amplified his role as a cultural tastemaker, and correspondingly amplifies the show's position as a cultural archive.

It was an archive of his own life as well. For most of the show's years there was some kind of circulatory system between him and his audience, allowing him to see as they saw, feel as they felt. If he had a genius, it was his ability to understand his viewers. He walked among his audience as an equal, and they saw that. He was at their service, his goal was to please them, yet he wasn't separate from them; as he shaped the program in rehearsal each week his tastes were all but identical to theirs. So while the show was a reflection of his time, it also reflected Sullivan himself, how he saw the world, what he believed in. *The Ed Sullivan Show* was a self-portrait. Now, his body of work sits quietly on the shelf, finally freed from the constraints of ratings or sponsors, ready to provide an inimitable portrait of its time, and, if you know his story, the man himself.

To view his life in another way, his greatest achievement was temporal, completely of the moment. In this alternate view, likely the one he took himself, his life's most significant moments took place every Sunday night between 1948 and 1971, and then they were gone. The Sullivan show had a unique quality, one that stood in marked contrast to the many shows it competed with. Because he structured it to offer something for every member of the family, the show brought the entire family together. It was a shared experience. This communal, ritualistic togetherness gave the program, and Sullivan's life, its greatest meaning.

Few television viewers in later decades, used to programs geared for their specific interests and armed with a remote control, would sit through *The Ed Sullivan Show*. Fully half the hour or more every week was not intended for them. Yet during most of the years the program ran, entire families sat together and watched it, each member bored in turn, each member aware of and influenced by the others' reactions. The glow of the cathode-ray tube fell upon a group sitting together, laughing, sighing, or gawking together, not on one or two viewers nurturing an already-established niche interest.

As Ed garbled his syntax and glanced nervously at the cue cards, bonding went on. Sister saw brother take an interest in the Cassius Clay interview, and brother saw sister's eyes light up while watching Elvis. The older folks enjoyed seeing ancient vaudevillians like Sophie Tucker. Everybody endured opera, because Ed had access to the biggest opera stars, and he was determined to showcase the best of every field, whether it be ballet or football or acrobatics or film.

Sullivan's grandson Rob Precht, who as a teen often spent time with his grandfather, sometimes wondered how Ed wanted to be remembered. Rob very clearly saw his grandfather's desire for renown, but he also saw something else. It was almost a sense of "ministering" to his audience, Precht recalled. "I definitely think he had a sense that he was talking to Americans, he was watching out for them, he was giving them entertainment, he was showing them diversity. If you pressed him, in his more lucid days, I would not be surprised that if he were asked, What do you want to be remembered for? He would say, yes, fame, but also, bringing people together."

It was clearly the central paradox of his life. He was a confirmed loner, distant from the countless people he knew, even removed in family gatherings, yet he was the producer of a program that brought the entire clan together like few others. *The Ed Sullivan Show* was the ultimate family show, produced by a man who had little patience for the rituals of familial togetherness. "He found family life entirely overrated," Precht recalled. "He did not, on a personal level, enjoy family life . . . but, the way he connected to people was to be this family man on TV."

Somehow, the calculus worked. The master showman, gifted at manufacturing the pixie dust of entertainment, created a convincing fictional image of himself as the ultimate Uncle Ed. He wasn't a family man, but he played one on television. Yet on those Sunday evenings between 1948 and 1971, the result wasn't an illusion; the television family man brought people together in real life. The entire family sat and shared, while he connected to them, as much as he was able, through the camera's eye. It was television, but it was real.

Sources

One of the CBS executives I interviewed for this book, Irwin Segelstein, pointed out the difficulty of re-creating the past by talking to its participants. "One of the problems with what you do for a living," he said, referring to writing a biography, "is that everyone gives you a version of what took place from their narrow, self-congratulatory point of view."

That may be true, and certainly the passage of time changes memory, but the fact remains that I owe a heartfelt thanks to everyone who shared their recollections for this book. The scores of people—family members, performers, Sullivan staffers, and others who knew him personally—who shared their memories for this book added immeasurably.

First and foremost, I am deeply indebted to Betty Sullivan Precht, who generously spent hours on the telephone with me, and whose candor so greatly enriched this portrait of her father; and to her husband, Bob Precht, the Sullivan show's producer, who not only shared his invaluable recollections, but also provided me with a list of phone numbers, and, finally, reviewed the manuscript and made suggestions; also, to Rob Precht, Sullivan's grandson, for his nuanced and insightful sense of his grandfather.

I owe a special thanks to those Sullivan staff members who shared their thoughts; their behind-the-scenes insight on the show and Sullivan helped immeasurably: Susan Abramson, Bill Bohnert, Vince Calandra, Emily Cole, Vinna Foote, Barbara Gallagher, Verna Grafeld, Bernie Illson, Kathy Kuehl, John Moffit, Sistie Moffit, Russ Petranto, Peter Prichard, Jim Russek, and Mary Lynn Shapiro.

Equally important were the memories of performers and others who knew Sullivan or his times intimately, including Carl Ballantine, Carol Burnett, George Carlin, Jack Carter, Mike Dann, Larry Epstein, Phyllis Diller, Eric Fettmann, Connie Francis, Bill Gallo, Shecky Greene, Sherry Hackett, Will Jordan, Jane Kean, Andrew Lazlo, Preston Levi, Ray Manzarek, Jackie Mason, Jean Moore, Paul Winchell, Walter Podrazik, Joan Rivers, Irwin Segelstein, Andrew Solt, and Bruce Spizer.

Adding particular insight was Ed Sullivan's collection of personal papers, some eighteen boxes of correspondence, contracts, and miscellaneous Sullivania stored at the Wisconsin Center for Film and Theater Research, in Madison, Wisconsin. The days I spent at Madison proved invaluable. Also essential was the time I spent catacombed at the Library of Congress, reviewing the library's collection of *The Ed Sullivan Show*.

Additionally, the New York Public Library's microfilm collection enabled me to read Sullivan's newspaper writings back to 1919, from his teenage reporting for the *Port Chester Daily Item* to his last days at the New York *Daily News*.

Ed Sullivan's life was written about voluminously in periodicals after his television show's debut, and I was able to review countless periodicals with the help of two sources: the New York Public Library, which keeps a file of clippings going back to the 1950s, containing everything from *Time* and *Newsweek* to *Life* and *Editor and Publisher*, as well as many regional newspapers; and the Center for American History, in San Antonio, Texas, which mailed me a thick file of Sullivan-related news clippings.

Among the many books I consulted, a few deserve special mention. Of particular aid were three earlier books about Sullivan and his show: *Always on Sunday, Ed Sullivan: An Inside View*, written in 1968 by CBS press agent Michael David Harris; *A Thousand Sundays: the Story of The Ed Sullivan Show*, written in 1980 by Jerry Bowles; and *Prime Time*, a memoir written in 1979 by Marlo Lewis, who worked with Sullivan to launch his television show. Also helpful was Neal Gabler's superb *Winchell: Gossip, Power, and the Culture of Celebrity*. Few books have so captured the culture of New York in the 1930s and 1940s.

Of the myriad books on television history I used, none were as helpful and as complete—and as entertainingly written—as *Watching TV: Six Decades of American Television*, by Walter Podrazik and Harry Castleman.

Selected Bibliography

Books

Allen, Mearl L. *Welcome to the Stork Club*. New York: A.S. Barnes & Company, 1980.

Amburn, Ellis. *Buddy Holly: A Biography*. New York: St. Martin's Press, 1995.

Anderson, John Lee. *Che Guevara: A Revolutionary Life*. New York: Grove Press, 1997.

Baker, Jean-Claude. *Josephine: The Hungry Heart*. New York: Random House, 1993.

Baker, Josephine and Jo Bouillon. *Josephine*. New York: Marlowe & Company, 1977.

Bakish, David. *Jimmy Durante: His Show Business Career*. London: McFarland & Company, 1994.

Barnouw, Erik. *The Golden Web: A History of Broadcasting in the United States, 1933–1953*. New York: Oxford University Press, 1968.

Barnouw, Erik. *The Image Empire: A History of Broadcasting in the United States from 1953*. New York: Oxford University Press, 1970.

Barnouw, Erik. *Tube of Plenty: The Evolution of American Television*. London: Oxford University Press, 1975.

Barzman, Norma. *The Red and the Blacklist: The Intimate Memoir of a Hollywood Expatriate*. New York: Thunder's Mouth Press, 2003.

Bauer, Douglas, editor. *Prime Times: Writers on Their Favorite TV Shows*. New York: Crown Publishers, 2004.

Bedell, Sally. *Up the Tube: Prime Time TV in the Silverman Years*. New York: Viking Press, 1981.

Behr, Edward. *The Good Frenchman: The True Story of the Life and Times of Maurice Chevalier*. New York: Villard Books, 1993.

Bell, Christopher. *East Harlem*. Portsmouth, NH: Arcadia, 2003.

Benny, Joan, with Jack Benny. *Sunday Nights at Seven: The Jack Benny Story*. New York: Warner Books, 1990.

Berg, A. Scott. *Goldwyn: A Biography*. New York: Alfred A. Knopf, 1989.

Berle, Milton. *Milton Berle*. New York: Dell, 1974.

Berliner, Louise. *Texas Guinan: Queen of the Nightclubs*. Austin: University of Texas Press, 1993.

Booth, Stanley. *The True Adventures of the Rolling Stones*. Chicago: A Capella Books, 2000.

Bowles, Jerry. *A Thousand Sundays: The Story of the Ed Sullivan Show*. New York: G.P. Putnam's Sons, 1980.

Brady, Kathleen. *Lucille: The Life of Lucille Ball*. New York: Hyperion, 1994.

Breslin, Jimmy. *Damon Runyon: A Life*. New York: Ticknor & Fields, 1991.

Bronson, Fred. *The Billboard Book of Number One Hits*. New York: Billboard Books, 2003.

Brooks, Tim, and Earle Marsh. *The Complete Directory to Prime Time Network TV Shows*, 1946–Present. New York: Ballantine, 1979.

Bruck, Connie. *When Hollywood Had a King: The Reign of Lew Wasserman, Who Leveraged Talent into Power and Influence*. New York: Random House, 2003.

Buskin, Richard. *Phyllis Diller: Like a Lampshade In a Whorehouse, My Life In Comedy*. New York: Penguin Group, 2005.

Cantor, Eddie. *Take My Life*. Garden City: Doubleday & Company, 1957.

Castleman, Harry, and Walter Podrazik. *Watching TV: Six Decades of American Television*. Syracuse: Syracuse University Press, 2003.

Chernow, Ron. *Titan: The Life of John D. Rockefeller*. New York: Vintage Books, 1998.

Clarke, Donald. *All Or Nothing At All: A Life of Sinatra*. New York: Fromm International, 1997.

Coffey, Michael, editor. *The Irish in America*. New York: Hyperion, 1997.

Coleman, Ray. *The Man Who Made the Beatles: An Intimate Biography of Brian Epstein*. New York: McGraw-Hill, 1989.

Davies, Hunter. *The Beatles: The Authorized Biography*. New York: McGraw-Hill, 1968.

Davis, Stephen. *Jim Morrison: Life, Death, Legend*. New York: Gotham Books, 2004.

DeMille, Cecil B. *The Autobiography of Cecil B. DeMille*. New York: Garland Publishing, 1959.

Densmore, John. *Riders on the Storm: My Life with Jim Morrison and the Doors*. New York: Delacorte Press, 1990.

Dewey, Donald. *James Stewart: A Biography*. Atlanta: Turner Publishing, 1996.

Edwards, Anne. *Katharine Hepburn*. New York: St. Martin's Griffin, 2000.

Edwards, Anne. *Shirley Temple: An American Princess*. New York: William Morrow and Company, 1988.

Eells, George. *Hedda and Louella: A Dual Biography of Hedda Hopper and Louella Parsons*. New York: G.P. Putnam's and Sons, 1972.

Eliot, Marc. *Cary Grant: A Biography*. New York: Harmony Books, 2004.

Eliot, Marc. *Walt Disney: Hollywood's Dark Prince*. New York: Carol Publishing Group, 1993.

Ellis, Edward Robb. *The Epic of New York City*. New York: Old Town Books, 1966.

Epstein, Daniel Mark. *Nat King Cole*. New York: Farrar, Straus, and Giroux, 1999.

Erdman, Andrew L. *Blue Vaudeville: Sex, Morals, and the Mass Marketing of Amusements, 1895–1915*. London: McFarland and Company, 1965.

Fields, Armond, and Marc Fields. *From the Bowery to Broadway: Lew Fields and the Roots of American Popular Theater*. New York: Oxford University Press, 1993.

Fisher, Charles. *The Columnists*. New York: Howell, Soskin, 1944.

Fisher, Eddie. *Been There, Done That*. New York: St. Martin's Press, 1999.

Fisher, James. *Eddie Cantor: A Bio-Bibliography*. Westport: Greenwood Press, 1997.

Gabler, Neal. *Winchell: Gossip, Power and the Culture of Celebrity*. New York: Random House, 1994.

Gauvreau, Emile. *My Last Million Readers*. New York: E.P. Dutton & Co., 1941.

Gehring, Wes D. *W.C. Fields: A Bio Bibliography*. Westport: Greenwood Press, 1984.

Geller, Debbie. *In My Life: The Brian Epstein Story*. New York: St. Martin's Press, 2000.

Gentry, Curt. *J. Edgar Hoover: The Man and the Secrets*. New York: W.W. Norton & Company, 1991.

Goldman, Albert. *The Lives of John Lennon*. New York: William Morrow and Company, 1988.

Goldman, Herbert G. *Banjo Eyes: Eddie Cantor and the Birth of Modern Stardom*. Oxford: Oxford University Press, 1997.

Goldsmith, Martin. *The Beatles Come to America*. Hoboken, NJ: John Wiley & Sons, 2004.

Gray, Barry. *My Night People: 10,001 Nights in Broadcasting*. New York: Simon & Schuster, 1975.

Guaralnick, Peter. *Last Train to Memphis: The Rise of Elvis Presley*. Boston: Little, Brown, and Company, 1994.

Hack, Richard. *Puppetmaster: The Secret Life of J. Edgar Hoover*. Beverly Hills: New Millennium Press, 2004.

Halberstam, David. *The Fifties*. New York: Fawcett Columbine, 1993.

Halberstam, David. *The Powers That Be*. Chicago: University of Illinois Press, 2000.

Harris, Michael David. *Always on Sunday, Ed Sullivan: An Inside View*. New York: Signet Books, 1968.

Haskins, Jim, and N.R. Mitgang. *Mr. Bojangles: The Biography of Bill Robinson*. New York: William Morrow and Company, 1988.

Havig, Alan. *Fred Allen's Radio Comedy*. Philadelphia: Temple University Press, 1990.

Haygood, Wil. *In Black and White: The Life of Sammy Davis, Jr*. New York: Alfred A. Knopf, 2003.

Hopper, Hedda. *The Whole Truth and Nothing But*. Garden City: Doubleday & Company, 1963.

Josefberg, Milt. *The Jack Benny Show: The Life and Times of America's Best-Loved Entertainer*. New Rochelle, NY: Arlington House, 1977.

Jowitt, Deborah. *Jerome Robbins: His Life, His Theater, His Dance*. New York: Simon & Schuster, 2004.

Kammen, Michael. *The Lively Arts: Gilbert Sedes and the Transformation of Cultural Criticism in the United States*. New York: Oxford University Press, 1996.

Kanfer, Stefan. *Ball of Fire: The Tumultous Life and Comic Art of Lucille Ball*. New York: Random House, 2003.

Kanfer, Stefan. *Groucho: The Life and Times of Julius Henry Marx*. New York: Random House, 2000.

Kean, Jane, as told to Kris Paradis. *A Funny Thing Happened on the Way to the Honeymooners . . . I Had a Life*. Boalsburg, PA: BearManor Media, 2003.

Kelley, Kitty. *His Way: The Unauthorized Biography of Frank Sinatra*. New York: Bantam Books, 1987.

King, Alan. *Name-Dropping: The Life and Lies of Alan King*. New York: Scribner, 1996.

Kissel, Howard. *David Merrick: The Abominable Showman*. New York: Applause, 1993.

Kisseloff, Jeff. *The Box: An Oral History of Television, 1920–1961*. New York: Penguin, 1995.

Klingaman, William K. *1929, The Year of the Great Crash*. New York: Harper and Row, 1989.

Klurfeld, Herman. *Winchell: His Life and Times*. New York: Praeger, 1976.

Koskoff, David E. *Joseph P. Kennedy: A Life and Times.* Englewood Cliffs, NJ: Prentice Hall, 1974.

Kriegel, Mark. *Namath, A Biography.* New York: Penguin Group, 2004.

Kunhardt, Philip B. *P.T. Barnum: America's Greatest Showman.* New York: Alfred A. Knopf. 1995.

Kuntz, Tom, and Phil Kuntz, editors. *The Sinatra Files.* New York: Three Rivers Press, 2000.

Lackmann, Roon, editor. *The Encyclopedia of American Radio.* New York: Checkmark Books, 1996.

Laszlo, Andrew, ASC. *It's a Wrap!* Hollywood: ASC Press, 2004.

Lax, Eric. *Woody Allen: A Biography.* New York: Alfred A. Knopf, 1991.

Laurie, Joe, Jr. *Vaudeville: From the Honky Tonks to the Palace.* New York: Henry Holt and Company. 1953.

Lawrence, A. H. *Duke Ellington and His World.* New York: Routledge, 2001.

Leamer, Laurence. *King of the Night: The Life of Johnny Carson.* New York: William Morrow and Company, Inc., 1989.

Leaming, Barbara. *Katharine Hepburn.* New York: Crown Publishers, 1995.

Leonard, John. *A Really Big Show: A Visual History of the Ed Sullivan Show.* New York: Penguin Group, 1992.

Leonard, John. *Smoke and Mirrors: Violence, Television, and Other American Cultures.* New York: The New Press, 1997.

Levy, Shawn. *King of Comedy: The Life and Art of Jerry Lewis.* New York: St. Martin's Press, 1996.

Lewis, Frederic Allen. *Only Yesterday, An Informal History of the 1920's.* New York: Harper and Row, 1931.

Lewis, Frederic Allen. *Since Yesterday, The 1930's in America.* New York: Harper and Row, 1939.

Lewis, Jerry, with Herb Gluck. *Jerry Lewis in Person.* New York: Atheneum, 1982.

Lewis, Marlo, with Mina Bess Lewis. *Prime Time.* Los Angles: J.P. Tarcher. 1979.

Logan, Josh. *My Up and Down, In and Out Life.* New York: Delacorte Press, 1976.

Louvish, Simon. *Man on the Flying Trapeze, The Life and Time of W.C. Fields.* New York: W.W. Norton and Company, 1997.

Mallen, Frank. *Sauce for the Gander.* White Plains, NY: Baldwin Books, 1954.

Manchester, William. *The Glory and the Dream: A Narrative History of America. 1932–1972.* Boston: Little, Brown & Company, 1973.

Martin, Ralph G. *Cissy: The Extraordinary Life of Eleanor Medill Patterson.* New York: Simon & Schuster, 1979.

Marx, Arthur. *The Secret Life of Bob Hope.* New York: Barricade Books, 1993.

McCabe, John. *Cagney.* New York: Alfred A. Knopf, 1997.

McDougal, Dennis. *The Lost Mogul: Lew Wasserman, MCA, and the Hidden History of Hollywood.* New York: Da Capo Press, 2001.

McIntyre, O.O. *The Big Town: New York Day by Day.* New York: Dodd, Mead & Company, 1935.

McNeil, Alex. *Total Television: A Comprehensive Guide to Programming from 1948 to the Present.* New York: Penguin, 1980.

McPherson, Edward. *Buster Keaton: Tempest in a Flat Hat.* New York: Newmarket Press, 2004.

Meade, Marion. *Dorothy Parker: A Biography*. New York: Villard Books, 1988.

Miles, Barry. *Hippie*. New York: Sterling Publishing Company, 2003.

Miller, Jim, editor. *The Rolling Stone Illustrated History of Rock & Roll*. New York: Rolling Stone Press, 1980.

Mosedale, John. *The Men Who Invented Broadway: Damon Runyon, Walter Winchell, and Their World*. New York: Richard Marek, 1981.

Mott, Robert L. *Radio Live! Television Live!* London: McFarland and Company, 1993.

Mustazza, Leonard. *Ol' Blue Eyes: A Frank Sinatra Encyclopedia*. London: Greenwood Press, 1998.

Nasaw, David. *The Chief: The Life of William Randolph Hearst*. Boston: Houghton-Mifflin Company, 2000.

Nash, Alanna. *Elvis Aaron Presley*. New York: Harper Collins, 1995.

Paar, Jack. *P.S. Jack Paar*. Garden City, NY: Doubleday & Company, 1983.

Paley, William S. *As It Happened: A Memoir by William S. Paley*. Garden City, NY: Doubleday & Company, 1979.

Paper, Lewis J. *Empire: William S. Paley and the Making of CBS*. New York: St. Martin's Press. 1987.

Parrish, Robert. *Hollywood Doesn't Live Here Anymore*. Boston: Little, Brown, and Company, 1988.

Parsons, Louella. *Tell It to Louella*. New York: Lancer Books, 1963.

Parsons, Louella. *The Gay Illiterate*. Garden City: Doubleday, Doran, and Co., 1944.

Pierce, Patricia Jobe. *The Ultimate Elvis: Elvis Presley Day by Day*. New York: Simon & Schuster, 1994.

Quirk, Robert E. *Fidel Castro*. New York: W.W. Norton & Company, 1993.

Rampersad, Arnold. *Jackie Robinson: A Biography*. New York: Alfred A. Knopf, 1997.

Ritts, Paul. *The TV Jeebies*. Philadelphia: The John C. Winston Company, 1951.

Rivers, Joan. *Bouncing Back: I've Survived Everything . . . and I Mean Everything . . . and You Can Too!* New York: Harper Collins, 1997.

Samuels, Louise and Charles. *Once Upon a Stage: The Merry World of Vaudeville*. New York: Dodd, Mead & Company, 1974.

Sandford, Christopher. *Mick Jagger: Rebel Knight*. London: Omnibus Press, 2003.

Savo, Jimmy. *Hello Little World!* New York: Simon & Schuster, 1947.

Schieffer, Bob. *Face the Nation: My Favorite Stories from the First 50 Years of the Award-Winning News Broadcast*. New York: Simon & Schuster, 2004.

Schoell, William. *Martini Man: The Life of Dean Martin*. Dallas: Taylor Publishing, 1999.

Singer, Arthur J. *Arthur Godfrey: The Adventures of an American Broadcaster*. Jefferson, NC: McFarland and Company, 2000.

Skinner, Kiron K., et al., editors. *Reagan: A Life in Letters*. New York: Simon & Schuster, 2003.

Skolsky, Sidney. *Don't Get Me Wrong, I Love Hollywood*. New York: G.P. Putnam's Sons, 1975.

Slide, Anthony, editor. *Selected Vaudeville Criticism*. London: The Scarecrow Press, Inc., 1988.

Slide, Anthony, editor. *The Encyclopedia of Vaudeville*. London: Greenwood Press, 1994.

Slide, Anthony. *The Vaudevillians: A Dictionary of Vaudeville Performers*. Westport: Arlington House, 1981.

Smith, Sally Bedell. *In All His Glory. The Life of William S. Paley*. New York: Simon & Schuster, 1990.

Sobol, Louis. *Some Days Were Happy*. New York: Random House, 1947.

Sobol, Louis. *The Longest Street*. New York: Crown, 1968.

Sperber, A.M. *Murrow: His Life and Times*. New York: Freundlich Books, 1986.

Sperling, Cass Warner, and Cork Millner, with Jack Warner, Jr. *Hollywood by Thy Name: The Warner Brothers Story*. New York: Prima Publishing, 1994.

Spizer, Bruce. *The Beatles Are Coming! The Birth of Beatlemania In America*. New Orleans, LA: 498 Productions, 2003.

Spitzer, Marian. *The Palace*. Kingsport, TN: Kingsport Press, Inc., 1969.

Stark, Steven D. *Glued to the Set: The 60 Television Shows and Events That Made Us Who We Are Today*. New York: The Free Press, 1997.

Starr, Michael Seth. *Bobby Darin: A Life*. Dallas: Taylor Trade Publishing, 2004.

Stein, Charles W., editor. *American Vaudeville As Seen by Its Contemporaries*. New York: Alfred A. Knopf, 1984.

Stiller, Jerry. *Married to Laughter: A Love Story Featuring Anne Meara*. New York: Simon & Schuster, 2000.

Stuart, Lyle. *The Secret Life of Walter Winchell*. [Location unknown]: Boar's Head Books, 1953.

Sturcken, Frank. *Live Television: The Golden Age of 1946–1958 in New York*. Jefferson, NC: McFarland & Company, 1990.

Sullivan, Ed, editor. *Christmas with Ed Sullivan*. New York: McGraw-Hill Company, 1959.

Summer, Harrison B., editor. *A Thirty-Year History of Radio Programs, 1926–1956*. Salem: Ayer Company, 1993.

Synder, Robert W. *The Voice of the City: Vaudeville and Popular Culture in New York*. Chicago: Oxford University Press, 1989.

Rosenblum, Constance. *Gold Digger: The Outrageous Life and Times of Peggy Hopkins Joyce*. New York: Henry Holt and Company, 2000.

Terrace, Vincent. *The Complete Encyclopedia of Television Programs, 1947–1976*. Cranberry: A. S. Barnes and Co., 1976.

Thomas, Bob. *Clown Prince of Hollywood: The Antic Life of Jack L. Warner*. New York: McGraw-Hill Publishing, 1990.

Thompson, David. *Showman: The Life of David O. Selznick*. New York: Alfred A. Knopf. 1992.

Tosches, Nick. *Dino: Living High in the Dirty Business of Dreams*. New York: Doubleday, 1992.

Truman, Margaret. *Bess W. Truman*. New York: Arbor House, 1986.

Von Schilling, James. *The Magic Window: American Television, 1939–1953*. New York: The Haworth Press, 2003.

Walls, Jeanette. *Dish: The Inside Story on the World of Gossip*. New York: Avon Books, 2000.

Wilson, Earl. *Hot Times: True Tales of Hollywood and Broadway*. Chicago: Contemporary Books, 1984.

Winchell, Walter. *Winchell Exclusive: "Things That Happened to Me—And Me to Them."* Englewood Cliffs, NJ: Prentice-Hall, 1975.

Yagoda, Ben. *Will Rogers: A Biography*. New York: Harper Collins West, 1993.

Zeidman, Irving. *The American Burlesque Show*. New York: Hawthorn Books, 1967.

Zhito, Lee. *American Entertainment: A Unique History of Show Business*. New York: Billboard Books, 1978.

Zollo, Paul. *Hollywood Remembered: An Oral History of Its Golden Age*. New York: Cooper Square Press, 2002.

Articles

Astor, David. "Ed Sullivan Was Also a Syndicated Writer." *Editor and Publisher*, December 7, 1991.

Baer, Atra. "Sullivan Goes On and On . . ." *New York Journal-American*, June 24, 1963.

Barthel, Joan. "Sullivan Survives." *New York Times Magazine*, April, 1967.

Beck, Marilyn. "Rascals Cuts Ties with Establishment." *Milwaukee Journal*, January 13, 1969.

Bender, Harold. "Ed Sullivan Recalls His Most Memorable TV Moment." *Pictorial Tview*, February 18, 1962.

Bishop, Jim. "The Inside Story of Ed Sullivan." *New York Journal-American*, March 17, 1957 (three-part series).

Crist, Judith. "His Ratings Sinking, Godfrey Drops 6 Singers, 3 Writers." New York *Herald-Tribune*, April 16, 1955.

Crosby, John. "Last Big Laugh on Television May Be Sooner Than You Think." New York *Herald-Tribune*. January 15, 1951.

Crosby, John. "Why? Why? Why?" New York *Herald-Tribune*. December 31, 1948.

Davis, Alvin. "The Ed Sullivan Story." *New York Post*, March 26, 1956 (six-part series).

"Dawn Patrol Revue Heads Loew's Bill." *New York Journal-American*, November 2, 1935.

"DeMille is Off Sullivan Show." *The New York Times*, March 8, 1953.

"Ed Sullivan and His Dawn Club Patrol Revue." *The Brooklyn Citizen* [advertisement], May 3, 1934.

"Ed Sullivan Is Offering Revue at Loew's State." New York *Herald-Tribune*, July 7, 1934.

"Ed Sullivan M.C. at State." *New York Journal-American*. August 24, 1942.

"Ed Sullivan [profile]" *Saturday Evening Post*, April 20, 1968.

"Ed Sullivan Revue at State." *New York Journal-American*, October 31, 1936.

"Fearless Ed Sullivan." *TV Guide*, June 19, 1953.

"Feud's Fire Nips Barry Gray." *New York Post*, March 12, 1952.

"Fiance Is with Her As Death Summons." *Chicago American*, January 31, 1927.

Fricke, David. "It Was 40 Years Ago Today." *Rolling Stone*, February 19, 2004.

Gardella, Kay. "CBS-TV Fighting Irishman Still in There Punching." The *Daily News*, July 21, 1959.

"Girl Swimmer Dies, Planning to Marry." *New York Telegram*, January 31, 1927.

"Goodbye, Ed Sullivan" *Los Angeles Times*, June 13, 1971.

"'Graphic' Just Blows, Makes No Statement." *Variety*, July 12, 1932.

Grove, Gene. "A Sunday with Ed Sullivan." *Tuesday Magazine*, March, 1966.

Harris, Eleanor. "That 'No Talent' Ed Sullivan." *Look*, April 5, 1955.

Higgins, Robert. "The Bumbling Barnum of Sunday Night." *TV Guide*, June 17, 1967.

Humphrey, Hal. "Second Generation Performs for Sullivan." *The Courier-Journal & Times*, March 17, 1968.

Kilgallen, Dorothy. "Gossip in Gotham." *New York Journal-American*, March 9, 1961.

Knickerbocker, Cholly. "Ed Sullivan Assailed for Permitting Paul Draper to Appear." *New York Journal-American*, January 24, 1950.

Kempton, Murray. "The Reason Why." *New York Post*, October 31, 1962.

Knox, C.M. "Why Ed Sullivan Needs Bodyguard." *Exposed*, March, 1957.

Laguardia, Robert. "Ed Sullivan: Where, Why, and How Has He Gone." *Show*, Summer, 1971.

Lardner, John. "A Happy Sullivan Day." *New Yorker* [Exact date unknown; the mid 1960s].

MacKenzie, Bob. "The Really Big Shew." *Oakland Tribune*, March 17, 1971.

Martin, Pete. "I Call on Ed Sullivan." *Saturday Evening Post*, February 15, 1958.

"Mason Says He Will Sue Sullivan for $10 Million." *New York Journal-American*, October 20, 1964.

"Mines of Music." *Radio Guide*, May 12, 1934.

Mosby, Aline. "Ed Sullivanov Mumbles in Russian." United Press International, August 4, 1959.

O'Brian, Jack. "*Comedy Hour* Anything But!" *New York Journal-American*, January 9, 1956.

O'Brian, Jack. "So What's Ed Scowling About?" *New York Journal-American*, June 19, 1963.

"Opera Can't Compete with Elvis, So Ed Sullivan Parts with the Met." *New York Post*, February 28, 1957.

"Paar vs. Sullivan." *Life*, March 24, 1961.

Pascal, John. "Ed 'Laughs Off' Paar, Stills Wants to Debate." *New York Journal-American*, March 14, 1961.

Pegler, Westbrook. "About 'Celebrities' Who Laud Themselves." *New York Journal-American*, July 16, 1947.

Plummer, Evans. "Plums and Prunes." *Radio Guide*, May 5, 1934.

"Radio Reports." *Variety*, February 2, 1932.

Rosen, George. "'Vaudeo' Comes of Age in Texaco Show." *Variety*, June 16, 1948.

Schaap, Dick. "How to Be a TV Immortal for Seventeen Years." New York *Herald-Tribune*, June 20, 1965.

"Skolsky Didn't Know Radio Is That Tough." *Variety*, July 5, 1932.

Sobol, Louis. "A Bit of This and That About People and Things." *New York Journal-American*, January 24, 1941.

Stewart, Sam. "TV Drops old favorites." *Copley News Service*, April 5, 1971.

"Sullivan Apologizes on Draper As Public Indignation Grows." *New York Journal-American*, January 25, 1950.

"Sullivan at 25G for Vegas Unit." *Variety*, [Exact date unknown], 1958.

"Sullivan Begins 2nd Week at State." *New York Journal-American*, September 3, 1942.

Sullivan, Betty. "My Daddy, Ed Sullivan." *Family Circle*, May, 1957.

"Sullivan Directs Show at Loew's State." New York *Herald-Tribune*, September 2, 1938.

Sullivan, Ed. "B'Way Column Writing As Exposed by Ed Sullivan, Who's One of 'em." *Variety*, January 16, 1932.

Sullivan, Ed. "Don't Make Me Laugh: Ed Sullivan Tells His Colorful Life Story." *Ladies Home Journal*, June, 1967.

Sullivan, Ed. "I'm the Luckiest." *This Week*, August 16, 1969.

Sullivan, Ed. "My Story." *Colliers*, September 14, 1956 (three-part series).

Sullivan, Ed. "The Ed Sullivan Story." *New York Post*, March 21, 1956.

Sullivan, Ed. "The Greatest Acts I've Ever Presented." *TV Guide*, January 16, 1953.

"Sullivan Gives Air Guests Paid Notice." *Variety*, January 12, 1932.

"Sullivan Narrator at Chanukah Fete." *New York Journal-American*, November 14, 1958.

Sullivan, Sylvia. "I'm Married to the Great Stone Face." *Colliers*, June 21, 1952.

Sylvester, Robert. "Wrong Way, Right Way, and Ed's Way." The *Daily News*, October 15, 1974.

"That Winchell–Sullivan Feud Growing Hotter." *New York Post*, October 16, 1956.

"Tempest in a TV Pot." *Newsweek*, March 20, 1961.

"The *Toast of the Town*." *Time*, June 26, 1951.

"*Toast of the Town*." *Variety*, July 23, 1948.

Torre, Marie. "Ed Sullivan's Opinions of TV and His Career." New York *Herald-Tribune*, June 16, 1960.

Tosches, Nick. "Mr. Sunday Night." *Vanity Fair*, July, 1997.

"Tremendous Empathy." *Newsweek*, June 25, 1962.

"TV's Amazing Ed Sullivan." *Time*, Oct. 17, 1955.

Weiler, A.H. "Toast of Town in Pact with Fox." *The New York Times*, March 4, 1953.

Wetzig, Mina. "Are You Jittery in Front of an Audience?" *TV Notes*, February 23, 1958.

Williams, Bob. "Sullivan Defends TV 'Wasteland.'" *New York Post*, June 23, 1961.

Williams, Robert. "Sullivan Does About Face, Signs Elvis for 50G." *New York Post*, July 13, 1956.

"Winchell vs. Sullivan." *TV Guide*, October 14, 1952.

Endnotes

Prologue

1   "Oh . . . you mean Ed Sullivan.": Harris, Michael David. *Always on Sunday, Ed Sullivan: An Inside View*. New York: Signet Books, 1968, p. 74.

2   "Dear Miss Van Horne . . .": Harris, p. 108.
    "about the longest shot ever to have paid off in show business.": *Time*, October 17, 1955.
    "Public opinion . . .": *The New York Times*, April 30, 1967.

3   "If he put his arm around you . . .": Joan Rivers, interview with author.

4   "one of the fathers of rock 'n' roll.": *The New York Times*, September 13, 1965.

5   "One of the small but vexing questions . . .": The New York *Herald-Tribune*, December 31, 1948.
    "is unquestionably one . . .": *The New York Times*, September 13, 1965.
    "Ed literally came close to slapping me . . .": *Vanity Fair*, July, 1997.
    "He was a whole different man offstage . . .": Jack Carter, interview with author.

6   "like it was built-in,": Bill Gallo, interview with author.

Chapter One

11 "My father was . . .": Sullivan, Ed, editor. *Christmas with Ed Sullivan*. New York: McGraw-Hill Company, 1959, p. 10.

12 "if only Danny were here.": *Time*, October 17, 1955.
    "That's where my brother Danny . . .": Ed Sullivan, *The Ed Sullivan Show*, author interview with viewer.

14 "Oh children!": Sullivan, p. 5.
    "marveling at the people . . .": The *New York Journal-American*, interview with Sullivan, March 19, 1957.

15 "He could be very kind . . .": Bowles, Jerry. *A Thousand Sundays: The Story of The Ed Sullivan Show*. New York: G.P. Putnam's Sons, 1980, p. 81.
    "As an athlete Ed . . .": Harris, p. 50.
    "real stinker.": The *New York Post*, "The Ed Sullivan Story" by Ed Sullivan, March 19, 1956.
    "You'll find that all through your life,": *Ibid.*
    "When we went up into Connecticut . . .": The *New York Post*, "The Ed Sullivan Story," by Ed Sullivan, March 20, 1956.

16 "Luckily, he sat near Bill Cigliano . . ."; Colliers, September 14, 1956.
    "the farther I got from home . . .": Sullivan, p. 7.

17 "beat the hell out of me" and "It was the first time . . .": *Ladies Home Journal*, by Ed Sullivan, June, 1967.

18 "He didn't think of Port Chester fondly . . .": Betty Sullivan Precht, interview with author.
    "It is not yet decided . . .": *Port Chester Daily Item*, 1919, exact date unknown.

19 "To maintain a position . . .": *Port Chester Daily Item*, May 20, 1919.

20 "Port Chester High sure came back . . .": *Port Chester Daily Item*, May 24, 1919.
    "Port Chester displayed . . .": *Port Chester Daily Item*, May 28, 1919.
    "Sullivan drove in . . .": *Ibid.*
    "The slugging of Walker . . .": *Port Chester Daily Item*, June 16, 1919.

Chapter Two

21 "He delivered his address . . .": *Port Chester Daily Item*, June 26, 1919.

22 All headlines from *Port Chester Daily Item*, 1919.
    "I never worked so hard . . .": Harris, p. 53.
    "'Slim' Kelly played a fine . . .": *Port Chester Daily Item*, July 6, 1919.
    "a laughingstock": The *New York Post*, March 20, 1956.

"Oh, you Irish!": *Ibid.*

"Good for him . . .": *Ibid.*

"Even to a young Democrat . . .": *Ibid.*

23 "built up its sports page . . .": *Port Chester Daily Item*, October 2, 1920.

"I read about the Hartford . . .": Sullivan, p. 10.

24 All headlines from The New York *Evening Mail*, January–February, 1921.

"The Columbia *Spectator* . . .": The New York *Evening Mail*, January 13, 1921.

"How do they wash . . .": Harris, 57.

"The truth of the matter . . .": The New York *Evening Mail*, February 12, 1921.

25 "The former class . . .": *Ibid.*

"I became more and more . . .": Harris, p. 57.

"The challenge was met . . .": The New York *Evening Mail*, May 14, 1921.

"Miss Wainwright ordered . . .": The New York *Evening Mail*, 1922, exact date unknown.

26 "died a thousand deaths . . .": The *Daily News*, September 10, 1937.

"hottest of the 'hot' spots . . .": *Ibid.*

27 "soft shoe man, tough guy, gambler . . .": Bakish, David. *Jimmy Durante: His Show Business Career.*
        London: McFarland & Company, 1994.

"Moore, who is reported to be a Klu [*sic*] Klux . . .": The New York *Evening Mail*, March 7, 1923.

"Slipping the gentle razzberry . . .": *Ibid.*

"Down and out a hundred Times, . . .": The New York *Evening Mail*, July 25, 1923.

28 "At the club, we used to sit . . .": The *New York Post*, March 28, 1956.

"Fay had just bought the Rendezvous . . .": *Ibid.*

"brought some sunshine . . .": Bakish, p. 27.

29 "There are winsome girlies . . .": *Ibid.*

"When I knocked at Dempsey's door . . .": Harris, p. 58.

"more than a propaganda organ . . .": The *New York Leader*, October 1, 1923.

30 "Printers Win . . .": The *New York Leader*, October 5, 1923.

"Eugene V. Debs, former political prisoner . . .": The *New York Leader*, October 1, 1923.

"Russian Workmen . . .": The *New York Leader*, October 3, 1923.

"Instead of acknowledging . . .": The *New York Leader*, October 1, 1923.

"Battling Siki, the Senegalese dark horse . . .": The *New York Leader*, October 5, 1923.

31 "Army never got over . . .": The *New York Leader*, October 26, 1923.

"It seemed in every way right . . .": *The New York Times*, November 13, 1923.

32 "When you are broke . . .": The *New York Post*, March 21, 1956.

"a very human note,": Harris, p. 62.

"a barney refuge . . .": McIntyre, O.O. *The Big Town: New York Day by Day.* New York: Dodd, Mead
        & Company, 1935, p. 116.

34 "very stunning brunette youngster.": Harris, p. 72.

"Of course I said I loved it . . .": The *New York Post*, March 30, 1956.

36 "From what I understand . . .": Betty Sullivan Precht, interview with author.

"her life had contradicted . . .": International Swimming Hall of Fame, undated document.

"Sybil, a girl from Chicago . . .": Bowles, p. 91.

"I can't stand it . . .": and "Afterward we would . . .": The *New York Post*, March 30, 1956.

"I guess Ed was the first Christian boy . . .": Sylvia Sullivan, *Ladies Home Journal*, June, 1967.

"Oh, you mean Ed . . .": Harris, p. 74.

37 "regular Marjorie Morningstar,": The *New York Post*, March 30, 1956.

"I can honestly say . . .": *Ibid.*

"Her family was thrilled . . .": Rob Precht, interview with author.

Chapter Three

38 All headlines, The *New York Evening Graphic*, 1928–1931.

"Does your boyfriend's . . .": The *New York Evening Graphic*, May 23, 1931.

39 "after peering . . .": The *New York Evening Graphic*, February 24, 1928.

"Why does Tex shy . . .": *Ibid.*

40 "For the next week . . .": The *New York Post*, March 23, 1956.

"erased any immediate . . .": The *New York Evening Graphic*, February 29, 1928.

"While his associates . . .": Mallen, Frank. *Sauce for the Gander*. White Plains, NY: Baldwin Books, 1954, p.159.

"Those who mistook his . . .": *Ibid.*

42 "This is a family . . .": Winchell, Walter. *Winchell Exclusive: "Things That Happened to Me—And Me to Them"* Englewood Cliffs, NJ: Prentice Hall, 1975, p. 42.

"Walter, what can . . .": The *New York Post*, March 12, 1952.

43 "Along Broadway they are selling extras . . .": The *New York Evening Graphic*, June, 1929, exact day unknown.

"I really thought a lot of Carnera . . .": The *New York Post*, March 28, 1956.

"Speaking for the Duffy interests . . .": The *Daily Mirror*, April 25, 1930.

"Eddie picked the argument . . .": The *Daily Mirror*, October 15, 1930.

44 "facetious twitting . . .": Supreme Court, State of New York, Docket 36151, quoted in The *New York Post*, March 28, 1956.

"I settled with the Hearst lawyers . . .": The *New York Post*, March 28, 1956.

"I was will to call the whole thing off . . .": *Ibid.*

45 "Ed had no intention of getting married . . .": Harris, p. 73.

46 "At that point . . .": The *New York Post*, March 30, 1956.

"all devout Catholics . . .": Harris, p. 73.

"I didn't want the job . . .": Harris, p. 64.

"He takes my ringside . . .": Winchell, p. 79.

47 "Ellmaker . . . called him to his office . . .": Mallen, p. 163.

"on [the] condition . . .": *Ibid.*

"not a newcomer . . .": The *New York Evening Graphic*, May 29, 1931.

48 "He's a curiosity . . .": *Ibid.*

Chapter Four

49 "So many have asked . . .": The *New York Evening Graphic*, July 1, 1931.

"The uppermost stratum . . .": *Ibid.*

50 "Divorces will not be propagated . . .": *Ibid.*

"Sullivan is well known . . .": *Variety*, July 9, 1931.

"Did you mean . . . in the toilet bowl.": The *New York Post*, March 12, 1952.

"Empty vessels . . .": Gabler, Neal. *Winchell: Gossip, Power, and the Culture of Celebrity*. New York: Random House, 1994, p. 131.

"I'll rip your . . .": Bowles, p. 86.

"To my former . . .": The *New York Evening Graphic*, June 8, 1931.

51 "velvet hammer . . . *Variety* box score.": The *New York Evening Graphic*, June 3, 1931.

"desperate need for . . .": *Ibid.*

"ALWAYS CONSIDERED YOU A FRIEND . . .": The *New York Evening Graphic*, March 29, 1932.

"A First-night . . .": The *New York Evening Graphic*, June 5, 1931.

52 "Grover Cleveland Alexander . . .": The *New York Evening Graphic*, June 17, 1931.

"Everyone who played . . .": The *New York Evening Graphic*, July 19, 1931.

"Jean Malin belted . . .": The *New York Evening Graphic*, August 1, 1931.

"Eddie,": I cooed . . .": Winchell, p. 81.

"those cocktails at Alice Brady's . . .": The *New York Evening Graphic*, January, 1932

"6,000 Hunger Marchers . . .": The *New York Evening Graphic*, January 5, 1932.

"Mid-West Farmer . . .": The *New York Evening Graphic*, January 16, 1932.

53 "If you find . . .": The *New York Evening Graphic*, September 1, 1931.

"Before Larry Hart . . .": The *New York Evening Graphic*, November 28, 1931.

"In a speakeasy . . .": *Ibid.*

"Jack Benny felt . . .": The *New York Evening Graphic*, September 14, 1931.

"I said he would . . .": The *New York Evening Graphic*, March 30, 1932.

"Every time one . . . Paramount Building clock.": The *New York Evening Graphic*, September 2, 1931.

54 "So many have . . .": The *New York Evening Graphic*, September 1, 1931.

"They say that Broadway . . .": The *New York Evening Graphic*, January, 1932, exact date unknown.

"I remember my mother saying . . .": Betty Sullivan Precht, interview with author.

"one of the unhappiest days . . .": Sylvia Sullivan, The *New York Post*, March 30, 1956.

"He didn't have national prominence . . .": *Ibid.*

55   "I linked Thelma Todd . . .": The *New York Evening Graphic*, September 2, 1931.

"Claire Windsor . . .": The *New York Evening Graphic*, January, 1932, exact date unknown.

"The Ginger Rogers–Mervyn Le Roy . . .": The *New York Evening Graphic*, September 28, 1931.

"conspicuous on the . . .": The *New York Evening Graphic*, January 4, 1932.

"Mrs. Violet Swanstrom . . .": The *New York Evening Graphic*, September 17, 1931.

"Al Jolson . . .": The *New York Evening Graphic*, July 7, 1931.

"wound up by blowing . . .": September 2, 1931.

"The idea is that we go along . . .": *Variety*, January 16, 1932.

56   "It puts them in the same . . .": The *New York Evening Graphic*, January 15, 1932.

"a he-man . . .": The *New York Evening Graphic*, May 29, 1931.

"Bert Savoy . . .": The *New York Evening Graphic*, July 1, 1931.

"the late spots . . .": The *New York Evening Graphic*, January 4, 1932.

"Not long ago . . .": The *New York Evening Graphic*, July 1, 1931.

"I watched Maurice Chevalier . . .": *Ibid.*

"In case you don't know . . .": The *New York Evening Graphic*, March 26, 1932.

57   "I wouldn't be . . .": Winchell, p 80.

58   "The greatest thrill . . .": The *New York Evening Graphic*, February 4, 1932.

"The mail from St. Louis . . .": March 18, 1932.

"Good evening, folks . . .": The *New York Evening Graphic*, April 16, 1932. Ed slightly misquoted Benny's words; I've used the popularly accepted version of the quote. In his column, Ed quoted Benny as opening with "This is Jack Benny. There will be a second's pause, just long enough for you who are listening to say 'what of it'?"

"In announcing Sullivan doesn't . . .": *Variety*, February 2, 1932.

59   "My operatives . . .": The *New York Evening Graphic*, January 19, 1932.

"At the premiere of *Jewelry Robbery* . . .": The *New York Evening Graphic*, January 19, 1932.

"The rubbing out . . .": The *New York Evening Graphic*, February 10, 1932.

60   "Like Broadway . . .": The *New York Evening Graphic*, February 20, 1932.

"Success on Broadway . . .": The *New York Evening Graphic*, June 16, 1932.

Chapter Five

61   "uncomplimentary ballyhoo.": *Variety*, July 12, 1932.

62   "no private scandal . . .": Stevens, John D. *Sensationalism and the New York Press.* New York: Columbia University Press, 1991, p. 127.

63   "'You can't do . . .'": The *Daily News*, August 2, 1932.

"nationally-known comic . . .": The *Daily News*, date unknown, 1932.

"his refusal . . .": The *Daily News*, date unknown, 1932.

"Overhead the L trains rattled . . .": The *Daily News*. December 1, 1934.

64   "He seldom . . .": As quoted by Nick Toshe, *Vanity Fair*, July, 1997, p.126.

"Take, for instance . . .": The *Daily News*, March 10, 1933.

65   "Phil Baker . . .": The *Daily News*, July 23, 1923.

"Maurice Chevalier . . .": *Ibid.*

"Romances fizzle . . .": *Ibid.*

"Funny, the reactions . . .": *Ibid.*

"By far the smartest . . .": The *Daily News*, January 26, 1933.

66   "Jack Benny . . .": The *Daily News*, July 23, 1932.

"secretly registered": The *Daily News*, July 28, 1932.

"On the way . . .": *Ibid.*

"Months before Wild Bill . . .": The *Daily News*, October 12, 1932.

Walker would be cleared: Ed wrote "After Walker is cleared . . .": on July 12, 1932.

"The information I got . . .": The *Daily News*, October 12, 1932.

"Hugest individual hit . . .": The *Daily News*, April 17, 1933.

67   "I left them at 5 A.M. . .": The *Daily News*, January 26, 1933.

"My parents never ate at home . . .": Betty Sullivan Precht, interview with author.

"When I was about two years old . . .": *Ibid.*

"wasn't in his nature,": Ibid

69   "didn't like it all . . .": Bowles, p. 94.

"There is nothing . . .": *The New York Times*, September 14, 1933.

"As entertainment, it fails to measure up . . .": *Variety*, September 26, 1933.

"I can't give Cantor . . .": The *Daily News*, January 24, 1933.

1:04 A.M.—"Hello . . .": The *Daily News*, January 25, 1933.

70   "I suggest Cantor . . .": *Ibid.*

"How about establishing . . .": The *Daily News*, December 13, 1934.

"We think the time . . .": *The New Yorker*, as quoted by Winchell, p. 102.

71   "We endorse . . .": The New York *Daily Mirror*, December 18, 1934.

"There's one letter . . .": The *Daily News*, December 19, 1934.

"Your Monday column . . .": Sullivan to Winchell, July 20, 1931, from Sullivan file, Walter Winchell personal papers, Gabler, p. 132.

"fit to be with decent people": Grady, Billy. *The Irish Peacock*. New Rochelle, New York: Arlington House, 1972, Gabler, p. 142.

"If you let me know . . .": Sullivan to Winchell, February 1, 1932. *Ibid.*, Gabler, p. 143.

72   "you are the only . . .": Sullivan to Winchell, December 16, 1932, *Ibid.*, Gabler, p. 161.

"The other night . . .": The *Daily News*, October 12, 1932.

"Picking the first . . .": The *Daily News*, November 1, 1932.

73   "You must be crazy.": Harris, p. 85.

74   "No longer does . . .": The *New York Evening Graphic*, July 6, 1932.

75   "knows when to strike . . .": *The New York Times*, November 27, 1933.

76   "Though at war . . .": *Time*, October 17, 1955. The *Time* article does not verify the date of the show.

"During a single evening twenty . . .": *Radio Guide*, May 12, 1934.

"has been renewed . . .": *Radio Guide*, April 7, 1934.

"Ed Sullivan, who writes a mean column . . .": *Radio Guide*, May 5, 1934.

78   "sat in complete silence . . .": The *Daily News*, October 22, 1937.

79   "a variety of singers": The New York *Herald-Tribune*, July 7, 1934.

"In customary fashion . . .": The *New York Journal-American*, August 27, 1937.

"in the true Harlem manner": The *New York Journal-American*, November 2, 1935.

"in the accepted . . .": Bowles, p. 95.

80   "a one-legged Negro tap . . .": *Ibid.*

"swift, funny . . .": The *New York Journal-American*, October 31, 1936.

"Some weeks ago . . .": The *New York Evening Journal*, 1936, exact date unknown.

"Ed Sullivan's *Dawn Patrol* revue . . .": The *New York Journal-American*, September 1, 1937.

"In his third appearance . . .": Bowles, p. 95.

"Harry Rose with . . .": *Variety*, exact date unknown.

81   "In Person—Ed Sullivan . . .": *Brooklyn Citizen*, April 26, 1935, advertisement.

"Booking agents . . .": The *Daily News*, Harvest Moon promotional article, July 16, 1937.

"Oh, just like . . .": Harris, p. 87.

83   "Notice how . . .": The *Daily News*, July 12, 1932.

"This is the new . . .": The *Daily News*, June 11, 1936.

"When Gary Cooper . . .": The *Daily News*, July 13, 1936.

"When I arrived . . .": The *Daily News*, May 30, 1936.

84   "I pleaded with . . .": Frank Hause personal letter to Walter Winchell, Rose Bigman collection of private papers, quoted by Gabler, p. 252.

"Broadway columns . . .": *Variety*, September 15, 1937.

"the Cole Porters . . .": The *Daily News*, July 16, 1937.

"Then a boy . . .": *Ibid.*

"You get a funny . . .": The *Daily News*, September 9, 1937.

"There is a letter . . .": *Ibid.*

85   "Patronize the standard clubs . . .": The *Daily News*, September 9, 1937.

Chapter Six

86   "As I devoured them . . .": The *Daily News*, September 13, 1937.

87   "curly-haired youngster": The *Daily News*, September 15, 1937.

"'I am not envious . . .": The *Daily News*, November 8, 1938.

"Fred Astaire and your correspondent . . .": The *Daily News*, February 19, 1939.

"One wonders how Joan . . .": Bowles, p. 93.

"cheap, tawdry . . .": *Ibid.*

"'The night we had . . .": The *Daily News*, September 15, 1937.

89   "Are you sure she didn't say columnist . . .": Skolsky, Sidney. *Don't Get Me Wrong, I Love Hollywood.* New York: G.P. Putnam's Sons, 1975, p. 43.

"Dr. Harry Martin . . .": The *Daily News*, November 7, 1938.

"I know of no performer . . .": The *Daily News*, October 25, 1937.

"There are certain things . . .": The *Daily News*, November 5, 1938.

90   "Midnight—the guests have departed . . .": The *Daily News*, November 7, 1938.

91   "I wish you could . . .": The *Daily News*, November 6, 1938.

"Cornelius Vanderbilt, Jr. . . .": The *Daily News*, August 15, 1938.

"Don't be startled . . .": The *Daily News*, February 19, 1939.

92   "Greta Garbo . . .": The *Daily News*, October 24, 1937.

"Howard Hughes . . .": The *Daily News*, November 7, 1938.

"Tyrone Power . . .": The *Daily News*, October 24, 1937.

"The Ross girl . . .": *Ibid.*

"A Filipino . . .": The *Daily News*, October 9, 1937.

"Hollywood dance director . . .": The *Daily News*, November 7, 1938.

"I asked Joan Crawford . . .": The *Daily News*, August 14, 1938.

93   "Business perked up . . .": The *Daily News*, August 15, 1938.

"[Jack] Haley . . .": The *Daily News*, November 17, 1938.

"four midgets . . .": The *Daily News* November 19, 1938.

"I spoke with blonde . . .": The *Daily News*, September 15, 1937.

"Carole Lombard . . .": The *Daily News*, December 12, 1938.

"1,000 to 1": The *Daily News*, January 9, 1939.

"Dear Ed . . .": The *Daily News*, January 10, 1939.

94   "Answer this question . . .": The *Daily News*, September 13, 1938.

"hammy.": : The *Daily News*, June 4, 1938.

"hardly qualified . . .": The *Daily News*, January 11, 1939.

"Edward G. Robinson's . . .": *Ibid.*

"Reel for reel . . .": The *Daily News*, June 5, 1938.

"When this reporter . . .": The *Daily News*, August 15, 1938.

95   "Listen Ed . . .": The *Daily News*, September 11, 1938.

"the house comes down": The *Daily News*, September 15, 1938.

"Alice Faye . . .": The *Daily News*, January 11, 1939.

96   "a hilarious and dexterous . . .": The *Daily News*, October 14, 1938.

"virtually a play-by-play . . .": *The New York Times*, October 16, 1938.

97   "Now watch all the film writers . . .": The *New York Journal-American*, February 13, 1939.

"Story has many weak moments . . .": *Variety*, April 26, 1939.

"A bustling little melodrama . . .": *The New York Times*, May 4, 1939.

98   "We went down Wilshire . . .": Betty Sullivan Precht, interview with author.

99   "spoiled brat,": The *Daily News*, October 20, 1937.

"Let this be entered . . .": *Ibid.*

"We ate out on the porch . . .": The *Daily News*, October 18, 1938.

100 "Mr. Fields would prefer . . .": Peter Prichard, interview with author.

"After the Louis Massacre . . .": The *Daily News*, 1938, exact date unknown.

"An Indianapolis poison-penner . . ." and other critics' comments: The *Daily News*, September 18, 1939.

101 "This is the season for fashion shows . . .": *The New York Times*, April 26, 1940.

"picture that's deficient . . .": *Variety*, May 1, 1940.

"swims upstream": The *Daily News*, November 17, 1938.

102 "Having come to Hollywood . . .": The *Daily News*, February 28, 1940.

"I pointed out . . .": Frank Hause letter to Walter Winchell, May 5, 1953, Gabler, p. 253.

"I acted hastilly [sic] . . .": Frank Hause letter to Walter Winchell, May 5, 1953, Gabler, p. 253.

"I was heartbroken . . .": Betty Sullivan Precht, interview with author.

Chapter Seven

104 "When I asked the boss . . .": The *Daily News*, July 22, 1940.

105 "Instead of sitting . . .": The *Daily News*, August 18, 1940.

"It was a terrible place . . .": Betty Sullivan Precht, interview with author.

106 "If you can better yourself . . .": Harris, p. 68.

"because of his high regard . . .": *Editor and Publisher*, December, 1940.

"We are taking the constructive . . .": *The New York Times*, January 19, 1941.

107 "By day a columnist surveys . . .": The *Daily News*, March 9, 1941.

108 "At any continental dinner party . . .": The *Daily News*, February 27, 1940.

"Chinese, Italians, Germans . . .": *The New York Times*, June 21, 1941.

"Nightclubs did a terrific business . . .": The *Daily News*, January 12, 1942.

109 "*Harlem Cavalcade* . . .": *The New York Times*, May 2, 1942.

"Triumphantly at the end . . .": *The New York Times*, July 29, 1942.

110 "Then I noticed the tears . . .": Sullivan, p. 17.

"Editorialists throughout the land . . .": The *Daily News*, September 14, 1942.

111 "Erasers on pencils . . .": The *Daily News*, December 14, 1942.

"The wolves no longer . . .": The *Daily News*, September 17, 1942.

"The Lieut. Douglas Fairbanks . . .": The *Daily News*, September, 14, 1942.

"Dear Ed: From us fellows . . .": The *Daily News*, September 12, 1943.

"Dear Ed: Over here in England . . .": *Ibid.*

"'Would you like to meet Jack Benny? . . .": The *Daily News*, September 1, 1943.

112 "Your CBS radio program . . .": The *Daily News*, September 11, 1943.

113 "Although Sullivan's voice . . .": *Variety*, exact date unknown.

"a bright quarter hour . . .": *Variety*, quoted in Bowles, p. 107.

"*Wheeler*: Well, Frank, it seems to me . . .": Radio script from *Ed Sullivan Entertains*, November 8, 1943.

114 "didn't think it was appropriate . . .": Betty Sullivan Precht, interview with author.

"I couldn't believe . . .": *Ibid.*

"overdoing it,": Harris, p. 76.

"an intimate stranger.": Rob Precht, interview with author.

115 "I go swimming with Harry . . .": *The New York Times*, March 3, 1946.

"The town is chuckling at Winchell's . . .": The *Daily News*, September 17, 1942.

"Tip to Washington, D.C. . . .": The *Daily News*, September 14, 1942.

116 "the most cynical grafting . . .": *The New York Times*, June 4, 1946.

"When 666 came up on Friday . . .": The *Daily News*, February 1, 1943.

"pleaded with the Mayor . . .": *The New York Times*, June 4, 1946.

"I always respect . . .": *Ibid.*

"Dogs have the capacity for grief . . .": The *Daily News*, May 1946; quoted here from a reprint in *Cosmopolitan*, February, 1950.

"I couldn't refrain from writing . . .": J. Edgar Hoover letter to Sullivan, dated May 23, 1946, from Sullivan personal papers.

"It does warm one's heart . . .": J. Edgar Hoover letter to Sullivan, dated January 7, 1947, from Sullivan personal papers.

117 "New York—Vindication has finally come . . .": From script for *Ed Sullivan's Pipeline*, April, 16, 1946.

"He was very attractive to women . . .": Jane Kean, interview with author.

118 "an acrobatic dancer with a great body . . .": Jack Carter, interview with author.

"egocentric—very much so": Mike Dann, a CBS programming executive. From interview with author.

Chapter Eight

120 "as far back on the shelf . . .": The *Saturday Evening Post*, February 21, 1942.

"When somebody got a TV set . . .": Paul Winchell, interview with author.

121 "If I had dreamed . . .": Harris, p. 97.

"likeable and relaxed": *Ibid.*

122 "Ed Sullivan was hired as a temporary master . . .": Paley, William S. *As It Happened: A Memoir by William S. Paley*. Garden City, NY: Doubleday & Co., 1979, pp. 238–239.

123 "Screw 'em! . . .": Lewis, Marlo, with Mina Bess Lewis. *Prime Time*. Los Angeles: J.P. Tarcher, 1979, p. 66.

125 "could come in . . .": Lewis, p. 70.

"I'm sorry that I've been moody . . .": Betty Sullivan Precht, interview with author.

"This is the most fascinating thing . . .": The *Daily News*, June 17, 1948.

Chapter Nine
126   "Marlo, you're going . . .": Lewis, p. 79.
      "a roof garden with the Manhattan skyline . . .": Harris, p. 99.
127   "I've done plenty of benefits . . .": Lewis, p. 82.
      "blockbuster of a show.": Lewis, p. 83.
128   "It's nothing . . .": Lewis, p. 84.
      "*Ladies and gentlemen, the Columbia Broadcast System* . . .": Lewis, p. 84.
129   "When somebody asked . . .": Mike Dann, interview with author.
      "brought to his emcee role . . .": *Variety*, June 16, 1948.
      "With a top talent array . . .": *Variety*, June 23, 1948.
130   "I panicked . . .": Paul Winchell, interview with author.
      "Register Mr. B. . . .": *The New York Times*, July 4, 1948.
      "Your review of my . . .": *The New York Times*, July 11, 1948.
131   "paid a flat fee to Mr. Sullivan . . .": *Ibid.*
      "Apparently we're being made . . .": *The New York Times*, July 23, 1948.
      "no pressure, direct, indirect . . .": *Ibid.*
      "a later date": *The New York Times*, July 28, 1948.
132   "Ventriloquist Paul Winchell . . .": The *Daily News*, July 12, 1948.
      "kept the event moving smoothly . . .": *Variety*, July 1948.
133   "neo-modern jazz vocalistics,": *Ibid.*
137   "One of the small but vexing questions . . .": The New York *Herald-Tribune*, December 31, 1948.
      "Public opinion, I'm certain . . .": Harris, pp. 102–103.
138   "I'd like to meet this fella . . .": From Sullivan personal papers.
      "Come on, Solomon . . .": Bowles, p. 71.
      "He got where he is not by . . .": New York *World Telegram & Sun*, exact date unknown.
      "Dear Miss Horne . . .": Bowles, p. 104.
      "Don't get swellheaded . . .": The *Daily News*, July 17, 1948.
139   "Frankly Marlo . . .": Lewis, p. 7.
      "You can't imagine how sick . . .": Harris, p. 105.
      "We were out having dinner . . .": *Ibid.*
      "making him more of a fighter,": Betty Sullivan Precht, interview with author.
140   "As a result of this session with the doctor . . .": Sullivan letter to Lincoln Mercury executive, dated
          February 1, 1952, from Sullivan personal papers.
      "My problem . . .": Lewis, p. 93.
      "Ed, you were in that little box there . . .": Quote from Barbara Gallagher, a Sullivan show production
          assistant, interview with author. Sullivan told her this story late in his own life.
141   "one long blast . . .": The *Daily News*, July 8, 1948.
      "Tip to mobs . . .": The *Daily News*, July 17, 1948.
      "the Humphrey Bogart stork . . .": The *Daily News*, July 5, 1948.
      "Before she filed . . .": The *Daily News*, June 30, 1948.
      "ice cream and gambling.": *The New York Times*, November 29, 1949.
      "grayer and plumper,": The *Daily News*, June 20, 1948.
      "pretty grim over the coldblooded . . .": The *Daily News*, July 5, 1948.
      "Can you imagine the cleanup job . . .": The *Daily News*, June 28, 1948.
      "The Russian conflict . . .": The *Daily News*, July 3, 1948.
142   "GOP leaders . . .": The *Daily News*, July 19, 1948.
      "Commies in this area bolder . . .": The *Daily News*, July 15, 1948.
      "Commies in this area have labored overtime . . .": The *Daily News*, July 1, 1948.
143   "I am deeply distressed . . .": Barnouw, Erik. *Tube of Plenty: The Evolution of American Television.*
          London: Oxford University Press, 1975, p. 121.
      "Kirkpatrick has sat in my living room . . .": The *Daily News*, June 21, 1950.
144   "If he put the word out on you . . .": Mike Dann, interview with author.
145   "Long before Senator McCarthy . . .": The *New York Post*, March 12, 1952.
      "fearing McCarthy's retaliation . . .": Halberstam, David. *The Fifties.* New York: Fawcett Columbine,
          1993, p. 251.

Chapter Ten

146   "It was toward the end of the evening . . .": *The New York Times*, August 21, 1949.

147   "I don't want you to misunderstand . . .": Lewis, p. 99.

     "What Ed is getting at . . .": *Ibid.*

     "that won't change . . .": *Ibid.*

     "I'll see you Sunday . . .": *Ibid.*

148   "Any successor to Mr. Lewis . . .": Contract between CBS and Ed Sullivan, dated August 31, 1950, from Sullivan personal papers.

     "They will work as a team . . .": *The New York Times*, April 17, 1950.

149   "For the most part . . .": Lewis, p. 105.

150   "I've never met you, but if I do . . .": *The New York Times*, December 9, 1950.

152   "I'll never forget when . . .": Mike Dann, interview with author.

153   "What does Sullivan do . . .": Harris, p. 112.

     "Maybe Fred should rub . . .": *Ibid.*

154   "looked right through me.": Baker, Josephine and Jo Bouillon. *Josephine.* New York: Marlowe & Co., 1977, p. 179.

     "a pathetic little steak . . .": *Ibid.*

155   "I thought a shameful thing had been done . . .": Gray, Barry. *My Night People: 10,001 Nights in Broadcasting.* New York: Simon & Schuster, 1975, pp. 170–188.

     "I don't think that Winchell . . .": *Ibid.*

     "I didn't hear what Sullivan said . . .": *Time*, January 7, 1952.

     They rarely ever knock a guy . . .": From a poem by Grantland Rice, used by Walter Winchell in his *Daily Mirror* column, December 26, 1951, quoted in Gabler, p. 422.

     "so devastating that Winchell . . .": Lewis, p. 23.

156   "I've got it—and Walter knows . . .": Lewis, p. 24.

     "the most miserable year . . .": Bowles, p. 113.

     "Excuse me,": *Ibid.* Stork confrontation anecdote from Bowles.

158   "I am the best damned showman . . .": *The New York Times*, March 23, 1952.

159   "Ed was terrified of CBS's reaction . . .": Logan, Josh. *My Up and Down, In and Out Life.* New York: Delacorte Press, 1976, p. 309.

160   "That was Julius' swan song . . .": Arthur Godfrey. Quoted in Singer, Arthur J. *Arthur Godfrey: The Adventures of an American Broadcaster.* Jefferson, NC: McFarland & Co., 2000.

161   "He'll be worth it . . .": Lewis, p. 152.

162   "There's nothing personal . . .": *Time*, October 17, 1955.

     "Why Sullivan can come in strange surroundings . . .": *Variety*, May 27, 1953.

     "People often ask me why I don't smile more . . .": Ed Sullivan, from the Foreward to Ritts, Paul. *The TV Jeebies.* Philadelphia: The John C. Winston Company, 1951.

163   "That fat-faced bum . . .": Lewis, p. 121.

164   "It's the old story . . .": Lewis, p. 122.

165   "I did Sullivan as he really was . . .": Will Jordan, interview with author.

Chapter Eleven

168   "The thing I remember most . . .": George Carlin, interview with author.

169   "What did you think of the show . . .": Vince Calandra, interview with author.

     "He knew nothing about comedy,": Phyllis Diller, interview with author.

     "How am I going to explain . . .": Harris, p. 137.

     "If you can do it . . .": Lewis, p. 126.

170   "He sure had his finger . . .": Carol Burnett, interview with author.

     "Again he leans into a gale . . .": *Time*, October 17, 1955.

171   "built and maintained an outstanding reputation . . .": Contract between CBS and Ed Sullivan, dated November 23, 1954, from Sullivan personal papers.

     "I just want you to know how happy . . .": Letter from Jack Van Volkenburg to Sullivan, dated November 23, 1954, from Sullivan personal papers.

     "for the duration of your life.": Contract between MCA and Ed Sullivan, dated March 19, 1955, from Sullivan personal papers.

172   "prayed that Sullivan dropped dead,": Lewis, p. 125.

"*Ed Sullivan is going to do . . .*": Dialogue from *Toast of the Town*, 1954.

173 "The most popular of all . . .": Gabler, p. 468.

"tracked down and exposed,": Quote from the column of Westbrook Pegler, *New York Journal-American*, 1953, as quoted in Kanfer, Stefan. *Ball of Fire: The Tumultuous Life and Comic Art of Lucille Ball*. New York: Vintage Books, 2003, p. 172.

"It's a singularly fortunate thing . . .": The *Daily News*, 1953, exact date unknown.

"Wherever he goes . . .": Lewis, p. 96.

174 "is about the longest shot . . .": *Time*, October 17, 1955.

"Everything they're promising . . .": *Ibid.*

"Mr. Sullivan's motion picture . . .": Associated Press, date unknown, most likely from June 1955.

175 "Mrs. Sullivan called about 6:15 . . .": Note to Arnold Grant, May 24, 1955, from Sullivan personal papers.

"I believe this will be a tremendous grosser . . .": Sullivan letter to Jack Warner, dated July 15, 1955, from Sullivan personal papers.

"a large florid, booming man,": From original script for *The Ed Sullivan Story*, 1955, Sullivan personal papers.

176 "As these acts go on . . .": From revised script to *The Ed Sullivan Story*, 1955, from Sullivan personal papers.

"Naturally, this was done in great haste . . .": Jack Warner letter to Ed Sullivan, dated November 1, 1955, from Sullivan personal papers.

"The greatest European pictures . . .": Sullivan script revision of *The Ed Sullivan Story*, from Sullivan personal papers.

177 "The TV Sullivan is a strange contrast . . .": *Time*, June 25, 1951.

"We were discussing your program . . .": Fan letter, quoted in the *New York Journal-American*, June 19, 1963.

178 "We will have to be a magician . . .": Jack Warner letter to Arnold Grant, dated November 25, 1955, from Sullivan personal papers.

"We will be most anxious . . .": Warner Bros. executive letter to Sullivan, dated January 12, 1956, from Sullivan personal papers.

"I don't think that Irving Wallace . . .": Sullivan letter to Arnold Grant, dated January 16, 1956, from Sullivan personal papers.

"is not exactly a TV novelty.": The *New York Post*, April 30, 1955.

179 "The number of things he does . . .": *Look*, August 5, 1947.

"Basically, Sinatra is decent . . .": The *Daily News*, 1947, quoted in Kelley, Kitty. *His Way: The Unauthorized Biography of Frank Sinatra*. New York: Bantam, 1987, p. 583.

"newspaper personalities . . . 'without paying for their services.'": *Ibid.*

"Let us overlook . . .": *Variety*, April 1955.

182 "Colgate, which was displeased . . .": *Time*, June 2, 1959.

183 "there was never any question . . .": *The New York Times*, August 5, 1956.

"The Ingrid Bergman–Rossellini baby . . .": The *Daily News*, February 9, 1950.

184 "Why the hell did I say that?" Bowles, p. 125.

"tasteless and shocking.": The *New York Post*, August 4, 1956.

"never seen anything like it,": *New York Journal-American*, July 30, 1956.

"it would seem the producer's approach . . .": *The New York Times*, August 5, 1956.

"Incidentally, when is Ed Sullivan . . .": Harris, p. 210.

"Ingrid never forgave me . . .": Harris, p. 210.

Chapter Twelve

185 "I was a hot-headed college student,": Bob Precht, interview with author.

"Well, if you're that upset . . .": Bowles, p. 61.

"He put me in place . . .": Bob Precht, interview with author.

186 "Betty Dearest: This is the most wonderful . . .": The *New York Post*, exact date unknown.

"It was very tempting,": Bob Precht, interview with author.

187 "Hey, doc, come here quick . . .": Bowles, p. 130.

"Tell them it's nothing serious,": *Ibid.*

"frail and concave . . .": Lewis, p. 183.

188 "I love Ed . . .": Kelley, p. 585.

189 "Today, living on his 200-acre farm in Southbury . . .": *Exposed*, March, 1957.

190 "Dear Ed. Would you lend me . . .": Quoted by Sullivan in *Colliers*, September 14, 1956.

191 "Bring Back the Grinds . . .": Quoted in the New York *Herald-Tribune*, July 3, 1956.

"Steven Allen Presley . . .": Bowles, p. 121.

"$5,000 for some youngster . . .": Leonard, John. *A Really Big Show: A Visual History of* The Ed Sullivan Show. New York: Penguin Group, 1992, p. 181. This quote likely comes from The *New York Post*, spring, 1956.

"I hereby offer Ed Sullivan $60,000 . . .": The *New York Post*, July 13, 1956.

195 "From his extensive repertoire . . .": *The New York Times*, September 10, 1956.

"If the adverse public reaction . . .": First three letters quoted from *The New York Times*, September 23, 1956.

"The few studios that welcome rock 'n' roll . . .": Letter printed in *The New York Times*, September 30, 1956.

Chapter Thirteen

201 "responsible for such tactics" and Sullivan's response: The *New York Post*, October 3, 1956.

"crybaby,": The *New York Post*, October 4, 1956.

202 "I have no comment to make . . .": *Variety*, date unknown.

205 "Ed Sullivan is the only man . . .": Harris, p. 109.

"a sense of showmanship . . .": Cantor, Eddie. *Take My Life*. New York: Doubleday and Company, 1957, p. 246.

"You never knew what he was going to say . . .": Connie Francis, interview with author.

"Wasn't your father Allen Jones?": Jack Jones anecdote, as told by Carol Burnett, interview with author.

"Sometimes you wondered,": *Ibid.*

"You don't screw . . .": Lewis, p. 97.

206 "Dear Hub . . .": Gabler, p. 487.

"He couldn't integrate himself . . .": Gabler, p. 497.

207 "He is ready to fight fire . . .": *Time*, October 17, 1955.

209 "I never talk about . . .": As quoted by Carol Burnett, from interview with author.

"During these ten years . . .": *The New York Times*, June 22, 1958.

"I'm going to quit . . .": *New York Journal-American*, June 21, 1958.

210 "I used to get letters . . .": *The New York Times*, June 22, 1958.

"Ed, here's something I know . . .": Lewis, p. 166.

"All of us thank you . . .": *Ibid.*

"What was all that about?": *Ibid.*

"ungrateful, impolite people . . .": *Life*, October 20, 1967.

211 "The noise was terrible . . .": *London Evening Standard*, July 10, 1971.

"I don't give a damn . . .": Lewis, p. 168.

212 "People flocked to see it . . .": Carol Burnett, interview with author.

214 "Ed Sullivan, of the *News*.": Barbara Gallagher, interview with author.

"the Lowell Thomas . . .": *New York Journal-American*, June 21, 1958.

"decadence, escapism, and insulation . . .": Text of a speech given by Murrow on October, 15, 1958 in Chicago at the Radio and Television News Directors Association.

"Why the hell not . . .": Lewis, p. 154.

215 "We believe Castro is not a . . .": Halberstam, p. 721.

216 "Andy-roo, you and I are getting out of here . . .": Andrew Laszlo, from interview with author.

"Andy-roo, I lied to you,": Laszlo, interview with author. All Laszlo and Sullivan quotes from Castro story are from Laszlo interview with author. Information also comes from Laszlo, Andrew, ASC. *It's a Wrap*. Hollywood: ASC Press, 2004.

217 "reacted violently . . .": Laszlo, p. 22.

"[It will] be easy . . .": Sullivan's question and Castro's answer from the broadcast interview, as seen on *The Ed Sullivan Show*.

220 "Castro gets booed by newsreel audiences . . .": The *Daily News*, November 2, 1959.

Chapter Fourteen

223 "Our mission to Moscow . . .": *The Ed Sullivan Show*, August, 1959.

"I expected a gloomy city . . .": *Ibid.*

224 "Unless you intervene sir . . .": Sullivan telegram to Nikita Khrushchev, dated September 5, 1959, from Sullivan personal papers.

"release the youngsters who participated . . .": Sullivan telegram to Nikita Khrushchev, dated November 4, 1959, from Sullivan personal papers.

225 "Somewhere on this globe . . .": *The Ed Sullivan Show,* 1959–60.

226 "The Colgate-Palmolive Company . . .": *The New York Times,* June 2, 1959.

227 "Bob had a *lot* to learn . . .": Sistie Moffit, interview with author.

"I was aggressive . . .": Bob Precht, interview with author.

229 "Ed was the boss . . .": Connie Francis, interview with author.

230 "Sophie had a fit . . .": *Ibid.*

232 "I feel my integrity as an artist . . ." and Sullivan's reply: *The New York Times,* January 28, 1961.

"I am looking forward eagerly . . .": Sullivan letter to Bill Paley, dated March 22, 1960, from Sullivan personal papers.

"Paley *loved* Ed Sullivan . . .": Mike Dann, interview with author.

233 "dictated by the people . . .": *The New York Times,* June 24, 1961. All FCC quotes in this section are *Ibid.*

234 "Ed, I don't have the money . . .": Quotes for the account of Paar vs. Sullivan come from a variety of news and trade publications, including *Variety, Life,* the *New York Post,* and *Newsweek.*

236 "We looked at that wall . . .": Connie Francis, interview with author.

237 "Ed was going around . . .": John Moffit, interview with author.

"It was scary!": Vince Calandra, interview with author.

238 "In the past year . . .": *The New York Times,* June 17, 1962.

"Carmine was Ed's Nubian slave,": Sistie Moffit, interview with author.

239 "if we can continue that spirit . . .": *The New York Times,* October 17, 1962.

240 "The actors will be free . . .": *The New York Times,* September 3, 1963.

"Alabama has moved ahead of Mississippi . . .": "What's Going On Here": quotes from *The Ed Sullivan Show,* 1963–64.

243 "All the Kennedys send you . . .": Joseph Kennedy letter to Sullivan, dated April 28, 1960, from Sullivan personal papers.

244 "Dear Sylvia, I had read that piece . . .": Letter from Joe Kennedy to Sylvia Sullivan, dated October 4, 1960, from Sullivan personal papers.

"I think that your brilliant young son . . .": Sullivan letter to Joseph Kennedy, dated April 20, 1962, from Sullivan personal papers.

"The idea for your International Assembly . . .": President John Kennedy letter to Sullivan, dated March 15, 1961, from Sullivan personal papers.

245 "P.S. Ted and I watch your wonderful show . . .": Joan Kennedy letter to Sullivan, dated July 17, 1964, from Sullivan personal papers.

"unforgettable moments": The *Daily News,* March 23, 1973.

"the party of hope . . .": *The New York Times,* May 24, 1963.

"I used to be a member . . .": The *Daily News,* May 24, 1963.

246 "the nightmare week . . .": *The Ed Sullivan Show,* 1963.

Chapter Fifteen

247 "call in a barber.": Bowles, p. 184.

248 "I gave him my honest opinion . . .": Peter Prichard, interview with author.

249 "You have been misinformed . . .": Sullivan letter to Leslie Grade, dated November 13, 1964, from Sullivan personal papers.

"'Sylvia,' he said (Mrs. Sullivan recalls it well) . . .": *Saturday Evening Post,* April 20, 1968.

250 "We were in London last September . . .": *Press-Enterprise,* Riverside, California, June 14, 1964.

"Well, as I always said . . .": Peter Prichard, interview with author.

"Brian was a friend of mine . . .": Peter Prichard, interview with author.

251 "Brian was a bright guy . . .": Bob Precht, interview with author.

"He was excited about the story . . .": Spizer, Bruce. *The Beatles Are Coming! The Birth of Beatlemania in America.* New Orleans, LA: 498 Productions, 2003.

252 "Ed, as always, had a quick reaction . . .": Peter Prichard, interview with author.

"There were girls . . .": *The New York Times,* February 8, 1964.

"Will you sing for us? . . .": *Ibid.*

"Do you hope to get haircuts . . .": Davies, Hunter. *The Beatles: The Authorized Biography.* New York: McGraw-Hill, 1968, p. 195.

"Everybody already knows who the Beatles are . . .": Ed Sullivan as quoted by Bill Bohnert, from interview with author.

253   "McCartney said that he and John . . .": Beatles comments, as quoted by Vince Calandra, interview with author.

254   "I would like for you . . .": Sullivan, quoted by Vince Calandra, interview with author.

256   "I don't believe this . . .": Bob Precht, quoted by Vince Calandra, interview with author.

257   "just as Ringo was sitting down . . .": Bill Bohnert, interview with author.

"The oldsters outdid the kids . . .": Goldsmith, Martin. *The Beatles Come to America.* Hoboken, NJ: John Wiley & Sons, 2004, p. 161.

"The door of the truck was open . . .": Bill Bohnert, interview with author.

260   "This was the best it was ever going to be . . .": Ringo Starr, as quoted by a Sullivan secretary, retold by Bill Bohnert, interview with author.

261   "In their sophisticated understanding . . .": *The New York Times,* February 10, 1964.

"imported hillbillies who look like sheepdogs . . .": Goldsmith, p. 147.

"I was offended by the long hair,": Spizer, p. iv.

262   "the uncertainty of the times . . .": Davies, p. 196.

"set up an hour-long din . . .": *The New York Times,* November 4, 1964.

"That's a possibility . . .": *Ibid.*

Chapter Sixteen

263   "We got it into our heads . . .": Booth, Stanley. *The True Adventures of the Rolling Stones.* Chicago: A Capella Books, 2000.

"I know that these men are controversial entertainers . . .": Letter from Eric Easton to Sullivan, dated January 25, 1965, from Sullivan personal papers.

"We were deluged with mail . . .": Letter from Sullivan to Rolling Stones manager, dated February 8, 1965, from Sullivan personal papers.

265   "We will be presenting Ed . . .": New York *Herald-Tribune,* March 20, 1964.

266   "very, very generous.": *Ibid.*

"He was totally in charge . . .": Jackie Mason; all quotes from Mason anecdote, from interview with author unless otherwise noted.

268   "a variety of four-, ten-, and eleven-letter words . . .": *The New York Times,* February 24, 1965.

"I'll destroy you . . .": *Ibid.*

"insubordination and gross deviation . . .": *The New York Times,* October 20, 1964.

"although I don't know why . . .": *The New York Times,* January 29, 1966.

269   "He always had stage fright . . .": John Moffit, interview with author.

270   "orgasmic insurance.": Lax, Eric. *Woody Allen: A Biography.* New York: Alfred A. Knopf, 1991, p. 189.

"When the storm abated . . .": *Ibid.*

272   "is unquestionably one of the . . .": *The New York Times,* September 13, 1965.

273   "I did everything I could . . .": Bob Precht, interview with author.

274   "Shut your mouth . . .": Sullivan, quoted by Russ Petranto, production assistant, interview with author.

275   "I was booked for the next Sunday . . .": Joan Rivers, interview with author.

276   "but the fans figured it out . . .": Jim Russek, interview with author.

"Either the song goes, or you go.": Sandford, Christopher. *Mick Jagger: Rebel Knight.* London: Omnibus Press, 2003, p. 104.

"Fuck off, mate": Mick Jagger, quoted by Vince Calandra, interview with author.

277   "I remember once I came in . . .": Joan Rivers, interview with author.

278   "He was always very nice to me . . .": Barbara Gallagher, interview with author.

"A couple times he had me come over . . .": Vinna Foote, interview with author.

"You know there was . . .": Jim Russek, interview with author.

"invented the Broadway column . . .": *Ladies Home Journal,* June, 1967.

279   "As we both grew older . . .": Winchell, p. 320.

280   "Walter, don't ever let . . .": *Ibid.*

"You watched *The Ed Sullivan Show* . . .": All quotes from Doors anecdote, Ray Manzarek, interview with author, unless otherwise noted.

"a smugness in their attitude . . .": Jim Russek, interview with author.

282 "There was never a doubt . . .": Bob Precht, interview with author.

Chapter Seventeen

286 "from Joplin, Missouri,": Sullivan, quoted by Bill Bohnert, interview with author.

287 "it had more resonance . . .": George Carlin, interview with author.

289 "Ed *adored* Richard,": Russ Petranto, interview with author.

290 "Whatever happened to *The Ed Sullivan Show?* . . .": *Philadelphia Sunday Bulletin*, January 25, 1970.

291 "The changeover in audience composition . . .": Irwin Segelstein, interview with author.

"We made every effort . . .": Bob Precht, interview with author.

"establishment shows.": The Milwaukee Journal, January 13, 1969.

"We didn't know what to do . . .": Mike Dann, interview with author.

292 "Fuck 'em, we'll do . . .": Bowles, p. 196.

"Who's on the show tonight?": Mary Lynn Shapiro, interview with author.

293 "Well I'll be a . . .": Bowles, p. 203.

"grand tradition,": *Ibid.*

"I was indeed sorry . . .": J. Edgar Hoover letter to Sullivan, dated April 7, 1971, from Sullivan personal papers.

294 "You know, I could write a song . . .": Susan Abramson, interview with author.

"I dragged him around . . .": Sistie Moffit, interview with author.

"How about that? . . .": Sullivan, quoted by Jerry Vale, interview with author.

"in a period of deep reminiscence . . .": All quotes from Delmonico interview, *Show* magazine, summer, 1971.

296 "I got the feeling . . .": Rob Precht, interview with author.

"For my own taste, Nixon . . .": *The New York Times*, November 4, 1972.

"a classic of comedy . . .": *Los Angeles Times*, September 20, 1971.

"a powerful stabilizing influence . . .": United Press International, March 23, 1971.

"What goes next? The Bill of Rights? . . .": The *Cleveland Press*, March 23, 1971.

297 "I spoke to the wax museum . . .": The *Daily News*, January 15, 1972.

"He was truly a fourteen-carat . . .": Gabler, p. xiv.

"We would have made it . . .": *The New York Times*, April 9, 1972.

298 "She took care of him like a hawk . . .": Joan Rivers, interview with author.

"was not feeling too well . . .": *Variety*, March 28, 1973.

"just keeping himself very busy . . .": *Ibid.*

299 "He went to Danny's Hideaway . . .": Jerry Vale, interview with author.

"When Sylvia died . . .": *Ibid.*

"I saw him on Broadway, very forlorn . . .": Bill Gallo, interview with author.

300 "You son of a bitch . . .": all Shecky Greene quotes, interview with author.

"My grandfather very abruptly . . .": Rob Precht, interview with author.

301 "We had consulted with his doctors . . .": *National Enquirer*, November, 1974.

"faithfulness to the serious arts.": Bowles, p. 212.

"an American landmark.": *The New York Times*, October 17, 1974.

"Ed had a remarkable quality . . .": *Ibid.*

302 "Bennett Cerf's widow . . .": The *Daily News*, October 14, 1974.

Epilogue

306 "I definitely think he had a sense . . .": Rob Precht, interview with author.

Index